Achieving Access to Justice in a Business and Human Rights Context

OBserving Law – IALS Open Book Service for Law

Achieving Access to Justice in a Business and Human Rights Context

An Assessment of Litigation and Regulatory Responses in European Civil-Law Countries

Virginie Rouas

First published by the Institute of Advanced Legal Studies for the SAS Humanities Digital Library, School of Advanced Study, University of London, 2022

ISBN (print): 978-1-911507-18-5
ISBN (epub): 978-1-911507-27-7
ISBN (web PDF): 978-1-911507-19-2

Institute of Advanced Legal Studies
University of London
Charles Clore House
17 Russell Square
London WC1B 5DR
http://ials.sas.ac.uk

For my husband Joshua and our children Raphael, Orson and Gaël.
For my mother Charline.

Contents

Preface and acknowledgements

In March 2019, I had the great honour of receiving the first IALS PhD Thesis Book prize. This allowed me to publish my doctoral thesis, which I completed at SOAS between 2010 and 2015, as a monograph. While the process of converting my thesis into a monograph was supposed to be relatively quick, it nonetheless took several years for a variety of reasons. The business and human rights field is a dynamic one, with laws and jurisprudence evolving at breakneck speed over the last decade, owing in large part to the efforts of corporate accountability activists and the momentum created by the UN Guiding Principles on Business and Human Rights. As a result, my thesis, which I had finished at the end of 2015, needed to be thoroughly revised. Furthermore, the significant advances that occurred while I was writing this manuscript, particularly in corporate group liability and human rights due diligence, could not be ignored, even after the final version of my manuscript was completed. This resulted in numerous revisions, which pushed back the publication date. The publication of this manuscript was also delayed for personal reasons. My twins, Orson and Gaël, were born in the late summer of 2018 and required my undivided attention as a mother. In addition, the global Covid-19 pandemic that began in 2019 and the subsequent juggling of work and family life slowed the writing of this manuscript. The last few years have made me painfully aware of the challenges that many academics, especially women, face in balancing academic career and family life. Despite these challenges, it is a great pleasure for me to see this project come to fruition.

This book could not have been published without the support and assistance of others. I am greatly indebted to the wonderful people who made this journey possible.

First and foremost, I would like to express my heartfelt gratitude to Professor Peter Muchlinski, my PhD research supervisor, for reading parts of the manuscript and providing moral support throughout the PhD and the writing of this monograph. I am privileged to have received his insights and intellectual guidance, as well as his mentoring.

I would like to thank my PhD examiners, Professors Nadia Bernaz and Bill Bowring, who encouraged me and gave me the confidence to pursue publication of my doctoral thesis.

I would also like to thank the SOAS School of Law for allowing me to complete my PhD and write this monograph as a Research Associate, as well as everyone who helped and encouraged me during and after the PhD, especially Professors Nicholas Foster, Philippe Cullet, Lutz Oette, and Lynn Welchman. Thanks are also due to Milieu, my employer, for providing the flexibility I needed to work on this personal project. Further thanks are due to my colleagues at Milieu, especially Chloé Fages, Lise Oulès and Cindy Schoumacher, for their support over the years.

I would also like to extend my thanks to the lawyers and campaigners I met during my research who took the time to provide invaluable information and to facilitate my research journey. Their fight for corporate accountability and access to justice is an inspiration for me, and I hope to have captured it in this book. Thanks are also due to the many academics who contribute to business and human rights scholarship and provide stimulating ideas to improve corporate accountability and access to justice. I am especially grateful to Professor Nadia Bernaz, who I have already acknowledged, and Dr Rachel Chambers for kindly reviewing my publication proposals and papers.

This book would not have been possible without the IALS, especially the IALS Open Book Service for Law editorial board and judging panel, which bestowed the first IALS PhD Thesis Book prize on me and believed in the academic strength of my writing project. I am honoured to have received this award and to be able to publish my book in open access. Thanks are also due to Sandy Dutczak and Steven Whittle for their support throughout the writing and publication of this monograph, and Fiona Cownie for her helpful comments on the manuscript. At University London Press I would like to thank Robert Davies for managing the manuscript's publication with patience and professionalism, Lauren De'Ath for marketing, and the copy-editors for their excellent and thorough work.

I would like to thank all of my family and friends for their encouragement and support throughout my PhD journey and the writing of this monograph. My heartfelt gratitude goes to my SOAS colleagues, particularly Dr Demetra Loizou, Dr Jonathan Bashi Rudahindwa, Dr Laïla Fathi, Dr Hany Rashwan and Dr Qing-Chao Wang, with whom I shared the joys and lows of the PhD.

I am grateful to my mother Charline Décaudin, as well as my husband Joshua Roberts, whose unconditional love and support have enabled me to embark upon the path to this monograph. I owe a special thanks to Joshua Roberts, who spent countless hours reviewing my chapters and assisting me in reflecting on my research to produce what I hope is a valuable study. Finally, I would like to thank my three sons Raphael, Orson and Gaël for their patience in waiting for their mother to complete her writing project.

I have made every effort to accurately state the law as of 1 May 2021. Where possible, later updates have been included.

Virginie Rouas, 8 December 2021

Table of cases

Decisions of national courts and tribunals

Australia

- Dagi v Broken Hill Proprietary Co Ltd (No 2) [1997] 1 VR 428

- Kamasaee v Commonwealth of Australia & Ors S CI 2014 6770, [2017] VSC 537

- Sanda v PTTEP Australasia (Ashmore Cartier) Pty Ltd (No 3) [2017] FCA 1272; (No 5) [2019] FCA 932 (17 June 2019)

Canada

- Anvil Mining Ltd v Association Canadienne Contre L'Impunité, 2012 QCCA 117

- Araya v Nevsun Resources Ltd, 2016 BCSC 1856; 2017 BCCA 401; 2020 SCC 5

- Choc v Hudbay Minerals Inc, 2013 ONSC 1414

- Das v George Weston Limited, 2017 ONSC 4129; 2018 ONCA 1053

- Garcia v Tahoe Resources Inc, 2015 BCSC 2045; 2017 BCCA 39

- Piedra v Copper Mesa Mining Corporation, 2011 ONCA 191

- Recherches Internationales Quebec v Cambior Inc, 1998 QJ 2554 (SCJ)

England

- AAA v Unilever Plc [2018] EWCA Civ 1532 [36]

- Arroyo v BP Exploration Company (Colombia) Ltd [2010] EWHC 1643 (QB)

- Arroyo v Equion Energia Ltd [2013] EWHC 3150 (TCC)

- Bodo Community v Shell Petroleum Development Company of Nigeria Ltd [2014] EWHC 1973 (TCC)

- Chandler v Cape Plc [2011] EWHC 951 (QB), [2012] EWCA Civ 525

- Connelly v RTZ Corporation Plc [1996] QB 361 (CA), [1997] UKHL 30, [1998] AC 854, [1999] CLC 533

- Guerrero v Monterrico Metals Plc [2009] EWHC 2475 (QB), [2010] EWHC 160 (QB), [2010] EWHC 3228 (QB)

- Kalma v African Minerals Ltd [2018] EWHC 3506 (QB), [2020] EWCA Civ 144

- Lubbe v Cape Plc [1998] EWCA Civ 1351, [2000] UKHL 41

- McDonald's Corporation v Steel and Morris [1997] EWHC QB 366

- Motto v Trafigura Ltd [2006] Claim BV HQ06X03370, [2009] EWHC 1246 (QB), [2011] EWCA Civ 1150

- Ngcobo v Thor Chemicals Holdings Ltd The Times (10 November 1995)

- Okpabi v Royal Dutch Shell Plc [2017] EWHC 89 (TCC), [2018] EWCA Civ 191, [2021] UKSC 3

- Sithole v Thor Chemicals Holdings [1999] EWCA Civ 706, [2000] WL 1421183

- Vava v Anglo American South Africa Ltd [2011] Claim No HQ11X03245, [2012] EWHC 1969 (QB)

- Vedanta Resources Plc v Lungowe [2019] UKSC 20

France

- Chambre de l'Instruction, CA Paris 13 February 2004

- Cons Conc, Décision n°05-D-49 du 28 juillet 2005 relative à des pratiques mises en œuvre dans le secteur de la location entretien des machines d'affranchissement ostal

- Cons Conc, Décision n° 07-D-12 du 28 mars 2007 relative à des pratiques mises en œuvre dans le secteur du chèque-cinéma

- Cons const 23 March 2017, Décision n° 2017-750

- Conseil des Prud'Hommes Paris 26 January 2011, nº F 08/06791

- CA Nîmes 8 July 2002 (Ould Dah)

- CA Paris 20 March 1986 (1987) Rev Soc 98 (comments Y Guyon)

- CA Paris 12 May 1987 (1989) Somm D 5f (comments F Derrida)

- CA Paris, 31 May 1989 D 1989 IR 227

- CA Paris 15 January 1999, n° 1998/04408

- CA Paris 30 March 2010, n° 08/02278

- CA Paris 20 June 2013, nº 08/07365

- CA Paris 24 October 2013, n° 12/05650, 12/05777, 12/05651

- CA Paris, 28 March 2019, n°17/21751

- CA Paris 17 September 2020, n° 19/20669

Netherlands

- Central Appeal Council 11 November 1980, WW 1980/79 (Centrale Raad Van Beroep)

- CA Amsterdam 21 June 1979, NJ 1980, 217 (BATCO)

- CA Arnhem 10 May 1994, TMA 94-6, 155 et seq (Roco BV v De Staat der Nederlanden)

- CA The Hague 9 May 2007, Case No 2200050906 – 2 (Public Prosecutor v Van Anraat)

- CA The Hague 10 March 2008, Case No 220043306 (Public Prosecutor v Kouwenhoven)

- CA The Hague 12 April 2011, NJFS 2011, 137

- CA The Hague 18 December 2015, C/09/337058/HAZA09-1581 + C/09/365482/HAZA10-1665

- CA The Hague 29 January 2021, C/09/365498/HAZA10-1677 (case a) + C/09/330891/HAZA09-0579 (case b) (Oguru); C/09/337058/HAZA09-1581 (case c) + C/09/365482/HAZA10-1665 (case d) (Dooh); C/09/337050/HAZA09-1580 (cases e + f) (Akpan)

- DC The Hague 23 December 2005, Case No 09/751003-04 (Public Prosecutor v Van Anraat)

- DC The Hague 7 June 2006, Case No AX7098 (Public Prosecutor v Kouwenhoven)

- DC The Hague 30 December 2009, Judgement in Motion Contesting Jurisdiction, 330891/HAZA09-579

- DC The Hague 14 September 2011, Judgment in the Ancillary Actions Concerning the Production of Exhibits and in the Main Actions, 337050/HAZA09-1580 (Akpan v Royal Dutch Shell Plc); 330891/HAZA09-0579 (Oguru v Royal Dutch Shell Plc); 337058/HAZA09-1581 (Dooh v Royal Dutch Shell Plc)

- DC The Hague 30 January 2013, C/09/337050/HAZA09-1580 (Akpan v Royal Dutch Shell Plc); C/09/330891/HAZA09-0579 (Oguru v Royal Dutch Shell Plc); C/09/337058/HAZA09-1581 (Dooh v Royal Dutch Shell Plc)

- DC The Hague 1 May 2019, C/09/540872/HAZA17-1048 (Kiobel v Royal Dutch Shell Plc)

- DC The Hague 26 May 2021, C/09/571932/HAZA19-379

- DC Zutphen 1 August 1991, Vermande D-8-85 (Roco BV v De Staat der Nederlanden)

United States

Decisions of international and regional courts

Court of Justice of the European Union

European Court and Commission of Human Rights

International Court of Justice

Others

Table of legislation

National legislation

England

- Legal Aid, Sentencing and Punishment of Offenders Act 2012 (LASPO)
- Modern Slavery Act 2015 (MSA)

France

- Code civil
- Code de l'environnement
- Code de la consommation
- Code de la sécurité sociale
- Code de procédure civile
- Code de procédure pénale
- Code du commerce
- Code du travail
- Code monétaire et financier
- Code pénal
- Loi du 1er juillet 1901 relative au contrat d'association
- Loi n° 71-1130 du 31 décembre 1971 portant réforme de certaines professions judiciaires (Loi sur les professions judiciaires)
- Loi n° 78-17 du 6 janvier 1978 relative à l'informatique, aux fichiers et aux libertés
- Loi n° 91-647 du 10 juillet 1991 relative à l'aide juridique (Loi sur l'aide juridique)
- Loi n° 2004-204 du 9 mars 2004 portant adaptation de la justice aux évolutions de la criminalité
- Loi n° 2009-967 du 3 août 2009 de programmation relative à la mise en œuvre du Grenelle de l'environnement (Loi Grenelle I)
- Loi n° 2010-788 du 12 juillet 2010 portant engagement national pour l'environnement (Loi Grenelle II)

- Loi n° 2014-344 du 17 mars 2014 relative à la consommation (Loi Hamon)

- Loi n° 2013-711 du 5 août 2013 portant diverses dispositions d'adaptation dans le domaine de la justice en application du droit de l'Union européenne et des engagements internationaux de la France

- Loi n° 2013-1117 du 6 décembre 2013 relative à la lutte contre la fraude fiscale et la grande délinquance économique et financière

- Loi n° 2016-41 du 26 janvier 2016 de modernisation de notre système de santé

- Loi n° 2016-1087 du 8 août 2016 pour la reconquête de la biodiversité, de la nature et des paysages

- Loi n° 2016-1547 du 18 novembre 2016 de modernisation de la justice du XXIe siècle

- Loi n° 2016-1691 du 9 décembre 2016 relative à la transparence, à la lutte contre la corruption et à la modernisation de la vie économique

- Loi n° 2017-399 relative au devoir de vigilance des sociétés mères et entreprises donneuses d'ordre

- Proposition de loi n°1524 du 6 novembre 2013 relative au devoir de vigilance des sociétés mères et des entreprises donneuses d'ordre

- Proposition de loi n°1519 du 6 novembre 2013 relative au devoir de vigilance des sociétés mères et des entreprises donneuses d'ordre

- Proposition de loi n° 2578 du 11 février 2015 relative au devoir de vigilance des sociétés mères et des entreprises donneuses d'ordre

Germany

Gesetz über die unternehmerischen Sorgfaltspflichten zur Vermeidung von Menschenrechtsverletzungen in Lieferketten vom 16. Juli 2021

The Netherlands

- Burgerlijk Wetboek

- Legal Aid Act 1994

- The Constitution of the Kingdom of the Netherlands 2008

- Wet Collectieve Afhandeling Massaschade 2005 (WCAM)

- Wet Conflictenrecht Onrechtmatige Daad 2001 (WCOD)

- Wet Internationale Misdrijven 2003

- Wet van 20 maart 2019 tot wijziging van het Burgerlijk Wetboek en het Wetboek van Burgerlijke Rechtsvordering teneinde de afwikkeling van massaschade in een collectieve actie mogelijk te maken (Wet afwikkeling massaschade in collectieve actie)

- Wet van 22 juni 1950, houdende vaststelling van regelen voor de opsporing, de vervolging en de berechting van economische delicten

- Wet van 24 oktober 2019 houdende de invoering van een zorgplicht ter voorkoming van de levering van goederen en diensten die met behulp van kinderarbeid tot stand zijn gekomen (Wet zorgplicht kinderarbeid)

- Wetboek van Burgerlijke Rechtsvordering

- Wetboek van Strafrecht

United States

- Alien Tort Statute 28 USC § 1350 (1789) Alien's Action for Tort

International and regional legislation

European Union

- Charter of Fundamental Rights of the EU [2012] OJ C326/392 (EU Charter)

- Commission Recommendation of 11 June 2013 on common principles for injunctive and compensatory collective redress mechanisms in the Member States concerning violations of rights granted under Union Law [2013] OJ L201/60 (Recommendation on collective redress)

- Consolidated Version of the Treaty on the Functioning of the European Union [2012] OJ C326/ 47

- Council Directive 2002/8/EC of 27 January 2003 to improve access to justice in cross-border disputes by establishing minimum common rules relating to legal aid for such disputes [2003] OJ L26/41 (Directive on legal aid)

- Council Regulation (EC) No 44/2001 on jurisdiction and the recognition and enforcement of judgments in civil and commercial matters [2001] OJ L12/1 (Brussels I Regulation)

- Directive 2003/35/EC of the European Parliament and of the Council of 26 May 2003 providing for public participation in respect of the drawing up of certain plans and programmes relating to the environment and amending with

- Regulation (EU) No 1215/2012 of the European Parliament and of the Council of 12 December 2012 on jurisdiction and the recognition and enforcement of judgements in civil and commercial matters [2012] OJ L351/1 (recast Brussels I Regulation)

- Regulation (EU) No 995/2010 of the European Parliament and of the Council of 20 October 2010 laying down the obligations of operators who place timber and timber products on the market [2010] OJ L295/23 (EU Timber Regulation)

- Treaty of Lisbon Amending the Treaty on European Union and the Treaty Establishing the European Community [2007] OJ C306/1 (Treaty of Lisbon)

International

- Basel Convention on the Control of Transboundary Movements of Hazardous Wastes and their Disposal (adopted 22 March 1989, entered into force 5 May 1992) 1673 UNTS 57

- Convention against Torture and other Cruel, Inhuman or Degrading Treatment or Punishment (adopted 10 December 1984, entered into force 26 June 1987) 1465 UNTS 85 (Convention against Torture)

- Convention for the Protection of Human Rights and Fundamental Freedoms (European Convention on Human Rights, as amended)

- Convention on Access to Information, Public Participation in Decision-Making and Access to Justice in Environmental Matters (adopted 25 June 1998, entered into force 30 October 2001) 2161 UNTS 447 (Aarhus Convention)

- Convention on Biological Diversity (adopted 5 June 1992, entered into force 29 December 1993) 1760 UNTS 79

- Convention on Jurisdiction and the Enforcement of Judgements in Civil and Commercial Matters (adopted 27 September 1968, entered into force 1 February 1973) 1262 UNTS 153

- Convention on the Protection of the Environment through Criminal Law (adopted 4 November 1998) CETS No 172

- Convention on the Rights of Persons with Disabilities (adopted 13 December 2006, entered into force 3 May 2008) 2515 UNTS 3

- Declaration of the UN Conference on the Human Environment (adopted on 16 June 1972) UN Doc A/CONF.48/14/Rev.1

- International Convention for the Protection of All Persons from Enforced Disappearance (adopted 20 December 2006, entered into force 23 December 2010) 2716 UNTS 3

- International Convention on Civil Liability for Oil Pollution Damage (adopted 29 November 1969, entered into force 19 June 1975) 973 UNTS 3

- International Convention on the Elimination of All Forms of Racial Discrimination (adopted 7 March 1966, entered into force 4 January 1969) 660 UNTS 195

- International Convention on the Protection of the Rights of All Migrant Workers and Members of their Families (adopted 18 December 1990, entered into force 1 July 2003) 2220 UNTS 3

- International Covenant on Civil and Political Rights (adopted 19 December 1966, entered into force 23 March 1976) 999 UNTS 171

- International Covenant on Economic, Social and Cultural Rights (adopted 16 December 1966, entered into force 3 January 1976) 993 UNTS 3

- Optional Protocol to the Convention on the Rights of the Child on the sale of children, child prostitution and child pornography (adopted 25 May 2000, entered into force 18 January 2002) 2171 UNTS 227

- Rio Declaration on Environment and Development (adopted on 13 June 1992) UN Doc A/CONF.151/26 (vol I)

- Rome Statute of the International Criminal Court (adopted 17 July 1998, entered into force 1 July 2002) 2187 UNTS 3

- Universal Declaration of Human Rights (adopted 10 December 1948) UNGA Res 217 A(III) (UDHR)

List of abbreviations

AFPS	Association France Palestine Solidarité
ATS	Alien Tort Statute
BHR	Business and human rights
BHRRC	Business and Human Rights Resource Centre
BV	Besloten vennootschappen
CEDAW	Convention on the Elimination of all Forms of Discrimination Against Women
CJEU	Court of Justice of the European Union
CoE	Council of Europe
CORE Coalition	Corporate Responsibility Coalition
CPED	International Convention for the Protection of All Persons from Enforced Disappearance
CRPD	Convention on the Rights of Persons with Disabilities
CSO	Civil society organization
CSR	Corporate social responsibility
DRC	Democratic Republic of Congo
EC	European Commission
ECCHR	European Center for Constitutional and Human Rights
ECCJ	European Coalition for Corporate Justice
ECHR	European Convention on Human Rights
ECtHR	European Court of Human Rights
EESC	European Economic and Social Committee
eg	For example
EOA	Economic Offences Act
EP	European Parliament
EU	European Union
FDL	Foreign direct liability
FGTI	Fonds de Garantie des Victimes des Actes de Terrorisme et d'Autres Infractions
HRDD	Human rights due diligence
ICA	International Crimes Act
ICC	International Criminal Court
ICCPR	International Covenant on Civil and Political Rights

ICERD	International Convention on the Elimination of All Forms of Racial Discrimination
ICESCR	International Covenant on Economic, Social and Cultural Rights
ICJ	International Court of Justice
ICMW	International Convention on the Protection of the Rights of All Migrant Workers and Members of their Families
ie	That is
KCM	Konkola Copper Mines
LASPO	Legal Aid, Sentencing and Punishment of Offenders Act
LDH	Ligue des Droits de l'Homme
MEA	Multilateral environmental agreement
MLA	Mutual legal assistance
MNE	Multinational enterprise
NAP	National Action Plan
NFRD	Non-financial reporting Directive
NGO	Non-governmental organization
NV	Naamloze vennootschappen
OECD	Organisation for Economic Co-operation and Development
OEIGWG	Open-ended intergovernmental working group on transnational corporations and other business enterprises with respect to human rights
OHCHR	Office of the High Commissioner for Human Rights
PIL	Public Interest Litigation
PLO	Palestinian Liberation Organisation
Puma	Puma Energy International BV
RDS	Royal Dutch Shell Plc
SARVI	Service d'Aide au Recouvrement des Victimes d'Infractions
SPDC	Shell Petroleum Development Company of Nigeria Ltd
SRSG	Special Representative of the Secretary-General on the issue of human rights and transnational corporations and other business enterprises
TASS	Tribunal des affaires de la sécurité sociale
TFEU	Treaty on the Functioning of the European Union
TGI	Tribunal de grande instance
Trafigura BV	Trafigura Beheer BV
UCC	Union Carbide Corporation

UK	United Kingdom
UN	United Nations
UNCCPR	UN Human Rights Committee
UNCERD	UN Commission on the Elimination of Racial Discrimination
UNCESR	UN Committee on Economic, Social and Cultural Rights
UNCHR	UN Commission on Human Rights
UNECE	UN Economic Commission for Europe
UNFCCC	UN Framework Convention on Climate Change
UNGPs	UN Guiding Principles on Business and Human Rights
UNHRC	UN Human Rights Council
UNWG	UN Working Group on the issue of human rights and transnational corporations and other business enterprises
US	United States
WACAM	Wet Afwikkeling Massaschade in Collectieve Actie
WCAM	Wet Collectieve Afhandeling Massaschade
WCOD	Wet Conflictenrecht Onrechtmatige Daad

Part I
Setting the scene: access to justice and corporate accountability in Europe

Chapter 1
Introduction

The belief that corporate benevolence and social responsibility can and should be achieved through market forces, to the point where government regulation becomes unnecessary, is premised on a dangerous diminishment of the importance of democracy.

Joel Bakan, *The Corporation: The Pathological Pursuit of Profit and Power* (Constable 2004) 151

1 In search of justice and corporate accountability in Europe

Following World War II, multinational enterprises (MNEs) emerged as the main actors of economic globalization.[1] The rapid growth of foreign investments, and the adoption of international legal rules that encourage international trade, allowed MNEs, based mainly in Western countries, to develop their activities throughout the rest of the world. As a result, they now dominate economic activity across the world and operate in all sectors.[2] MNEs can contribute to economic prosperity and social development in the countries where they operate. However, their activities may also directly or indirectly cause, or benefit from, harm to humans and the environment.[3] Following a number of widely publicized corporate scandals over the past years, MNEs have faced growing criticism from international organizations, civil society

---

1   Luzius Wildhaber, 'Asser Institute Lectures on International Law: Some Aspects of the Transnational Corporation in International Law' (1980) 27 Netherlands International Law Review 79, 80.

2   Boaventura de Sousa Santos, *Toward a New Legal Common Sense: Law, Globalization, and Emancipation* (2nd edn, CUP 2002) 183; Michael Kerr and Marie-Claire Cordonier Segger, 'Corporate Social Responsibility: International Strategies and Regimes' in Marie-Claire Cordonier Segger and Christopher Weeramantry (eds), *Sustainable Justice: Reconciling Economic, Social and Environmental Law* (Martinus Nijhoff Publishers 2005) 135.

3   For an overview of corporate-related human rights abuse, see SRSG, 'Corporations and Human Rights: A Survey of the Scope and Patterns of Alleged Corporate-Related Human Rights Abuse' (23 May 2008) UN Doc A/HRC/8/5/Add.2. See also Beth Stephens, 'The Amorality of Profit: Transnational Corporations and Human Rights' (2002) 20 Berkeley Journal of International Law 45; Karen Erica Bravo, Jena Martin and Tara Van Ho (eds), *When Business Harms Human Rights: Affected Communities that Are Dying to Be Heard* (Anthem Press 2020).

organizations (CSOs),[4] and academics over their involvement in human rights abuses and environmental damage, especially in developing countries.[5]

The case of the oil industry in Nigeria provides a clear example of poor environmental practices by MNEs resulting in severe environmental destruction and human rights abuses.[6] For example, intensive use of gas flaring has resulted in severe air pollution and acid rain. Continuous oil spills have also contaminated land and water, destroying important natural resources and the livelihoods of local communities. In turn, the impact of oil pollution on local communities in the Niger Delta has been severe and has resulted in health problems, polluted drinking water, and unproductive soils and ponds.[7] In addition to violations of the right to a clean environment, constant abuses of other human rights, such as the rights to property and to life, have been reported.[8] In general, the worst cases of corporate-related human rights abuses occur in countries where governance challenges are greatest. According to the United Nations (UN), the risk of business-related harm is especially high in low-income countries, in conflict-affected or post-conflict countries, and in countries where the rule of law is weak and the level of corruption is high.[9]

In various cases, victims of business-related harm have sought to obtain redress in the country where the abuse took place. However, they have faced various legal, procedural, and political obstacles, such as inadequate regimes of liability or procedural rules. In poor countries, MNEs may provide the State with its

4   In this book, the expression CSOs includes various actors such as non-governmental organizations (NGOs), trade unions, and faith-based organizations. However, it excludes business actors.

5   Brandon Prosansky, 'Mining Gold in a Conflict Zone: The Context, Ramifications, and Lessons of AngloGold Ashanti's Activities in the Democratic Republic of the Congo' (2007) 5 Northwestern Journal of International Human Rights 236; Priscilla Schwartz, 'Corporate Activities and Environmental Justice: Perspectives on Sierra Leone's Mining' in Jonas Ebbesson and Phoebe Okowa (eds), *Environmental Law and Justice in Context* (CUP 2009); 'The True Cost of Chevron: An Alternative Annual Report' (The True Cost of Chevron 2009, 2010, 2011). The Business and Human Rights Resource Centre (BHRRC) also publishes daily information on reported cases of corporate abuse. See the Home page of the BHRRC website: <http://business-humanrights.org/en> accessed 1 May 2021.

6   Joshua Eaton, 'The Nigerian Tragedy of Environmental Regulation of Transnational Corporations, and the Human Right to a Healthy Environment' (1997) 15 Boston University International Law Journal 261; Jedrzej Frynas, *Oil in Nigeria: Conflict and Litigation between Oil Companies and Village Communities* (LIT 2000); *Environmental Assessment of Ogoniland* (UNEP 2011).

7   Alison Shinsato, 'Increasing the Accountability of Transnational Corporations for Environmental Harms: The Petroleum Industry in Nigeria' (2005) 4 Northwestern Journal of International Human Rights 186, 192.

8   *Gas Flaring in Nigeria: A Human Rights, Environmental and Economic Monstrosity* (Friends of the Earth Nigeria and Climate Justice Programme 2005).

9   UNHRC, 'Protect, Respect and Remedy: A Framework for Business and Human Rights' (UN Framework) (7 April 2008) UN Doc A/HRC/8/5, para 16.

main source of income, thus creating a situation where States are reluctant to regulate corporate activities. Furthermore, judicial institutions may be unreliable, as a result of severe delays in legal proceedings or corruption. MNE subsidiaries may also become financially insolvent, preventing victims from obtaining financial compensation.[10] Moreover, the political situation of the host country may be unstable, thereby creating a risk of State abuse of human rights and a lack of real legal protection.[11]

During the 1990s, new types of claims emerged that challenged MNEs' activities in developing countries. In order to have access to remedy, and to hold MNEs liable for the abuse of human rights and environmental damage occurring in the context of their global business activities, victims and non-governmental organizations (NGOs) started bringing liability claims against MNEs directly in their home countries. An increasing number of claims have been brought for human rights abuse or environmental damage occurring in foreign countries (host countries) against MNEs in the country where they are headquartered or have their main business activity (home country).[12] In this book, this legal phenomenon will be referred to as 'transnational litigation against MNEs'. The character of the claims falling under this type of litigation varies considerably, ranging from tort suits for environmental pollution caused by oil spills to criminal proceedings alleging forced labour, or contractual liability claims for violations of international law. In addition, these cases raise complex legal questions and require overcoming important procedural obstacles. To date, these claims have rarely resulted in a court ruling in favour of the plaintiffs. Nonetheless, the number of transnational claims against MNEs is increasing and expanding to more countries.

Until recently, transnational litigation against MNEs was mainly concentrated in common law jurisdictions in the global North, most notably in the United States (US) and England.[13] In the 1990s in the US, foreign victims brought the first tort claims against MNEs under the Alien Tort Statute (ATS)[14] for violations of international customary law or international treaties to which the US was a contracting State. At the same time in England, the first tort claims against MNEs were based in common law. In these proceedings, plaintiffs raised the

10   Kerr and Cordonier Segger, 'Corporate Social Responsibility', 141.

11   Hari Osofsky, 'Learning from Environmental Justice: A New Model for International Environmental Rights' (2005) 24 Stanford Environmental Law Journal 71, 75.

12   Kerr and Cordonier Segger, 'Corporate Social Responsibility', 140.

13   See Saman Zia-Zarifi, 'Suing Multinational Corporations in the US for Violating International Law' (1999) 4 UCLA Journal of International Law and Foreign Affairs 81; Peter Muchlinski, 'Corporations in International Litigation: Problems of Jurisdiction and the United Kingdom Asbestos Cases' (2001) 50 International and Comparative Law Quarterly 1; Sarah Joseph, *Corporations and Transnational Human Rights Litigation* (Hart Publishing 2004).

14   28 USC § 1350 (1789) Alien's Action for Tort.

tort liability of the parent company for damage arising out of its subsidiary's activities in foreign countries, often under the law of negligence.

Nonetheless, since the beginning of the 21st century transnational litigation against MNEs has developed significantly in European countries of civil law tradition. If cases against MNEs in common law and civil law countries hold in common the search for remedy and corporate accountability, they are different in their form. While the use of tort claims has been the favoured approach in common law countries, plaintiffs have used both civil and criminal litigation against MNEs in European civil law countries. For instance, Total, a French oil and gas MNE, faced various criminal lawsuits in France and Belgium for gross human rights abuses which had taken place in Myanmar in the 1990s.[15] In 2013, an NGO filed a tort claim in Sweden against Boliden Mineral AB, a Swedish company, for dumping 20,000 tonnes of toxic mining waste in Chile in the 1980s.[16] In Germany, a senior manager of Danzer, a timber trading company, was accused of failing to prevent its Congolese subsidiary from participating in State-sponsored violence against civilians in the Democratic Republic of Congo (DRC).[17] In Switzerland, Nestlé, a food MNE, faced a criminal lawsuit for its involvement in the murder of a trade unionist in Colombia.[18]

Overall, there is an increasing trend for MNEs to face liability claims in the national courts of European countries over human rights abuses and environmental damage taking place in developing countries.[19] Despite the difference in the nature of these claims, they share a common aim, which is to hold parent companies of MNEs liable for the negative impacts of their global activities. These claims represent 'the flip side of foreign direct investment',[20] as they target the parent company 'as the apparent "orchestrator" of company-wide investment standards and policies'.[21]

In parallel to the emergence of transnational litigation against MNEs, the debate on access to justice and corporate accountability has gained momentum

---

15   Benoît Frydman and Ludovic Hennebel, 'Translating Unocal: The Liability of Transnational Corporations for Human Rights Violations' in Manoj Kumar Sinha (ed), *Business and Human Rights* (SAGE 2013).

16   Rasmus Kløcker Larsen, 'Foreign Direct Liability Claims in Sweden: Learning from *Arica Victims KB v. Boliden Mineral AB*?' (2014) 83 Nordic Journal of International Law 404; Sebastián Ureta, Patricio Flores and Linda Soneryd, 'Victimization Devices: Exploring Challenges Facing Litigation-Based Transnational Environmental Justice' (2019) 29 Social and Legal Studies 161.

17   'Human Rights Violations Committed Overseas: European Companies Liable for Subsidiaries. The KiK, Lahmeyer, Danzer and Nestlé Cases' (ECCHR 2015).

18   'Case Report: Luciano Romero and the Nestlé Case' (ECCHR 2014).

19   Halina Ward, 'Securing Transnational Corporate Accountability through National Courts: Implications and Policy Options' (2001) 24 Hastings International and Comparative Law Review 451, 454.

20   Ibid.

21   Jennifer Zerk, *Multinationals and Corporate Social Responsibility: Limitations and Opportunities in International Law* (CUP 2006) 198.

with the development of the business and human rights (BHR) field. At the international level, States, NGOs, businesses, and international organizations have discussed the need to regulate MNEs to hold them responsible for the human rights abuses and environmental pollution they cause. In 2008, the UN Human Rights Council (UNHRC) adopted the UN 'Protect, Respect and Remedy' Framework (UN Framework). This policy document aims at 'adapting the human rights regime to provide more effective protection to individuals and communities against corporate-related human rights harm'. In 2011, the UN Framework was completed by the UN Guiding Principles on Business and Human Rights (UNGPs),[22] which aim at providing recommendations for the implementation of the UN Framework. Both the UN Framework and the UNGPs recognize three complementary and interdependent principles, or 'pillars': (1) the State duty to protect against human rights abuses by third parties, including businesses; (2) the corporate responsibility to respect human rights; and (3) the need for effective access to remedy.

Under the third pillar, or the 'remedy pillar', the UN Framework acknowledges that victims of corporate abuse have sought remedy outside the State where the harm occurred, particularly through home State courts, but have faced extensive obstacles. These challenges may deter claims and prevent victims from gaining effective access to remedy. In order to avoid such a situation, the UNGPs provide that States, as part of their duty to protect against business-related human rights abuse, must take appropriate steps, through judicial, administrative, legislative, or other means, to ensure that victims have access to effective remedy and to guarantee the effectiveness of domestic judicial mechanisms.

Also of importance is the inclusion, under the second pillar on corporate responsibility to respect human rights, of 'human rights due diligence' (HRDD), which is seen as 'a process whereby companies not only ensure compliance with national laws but also manage the risk of human rights harm with a view to avoiding it'.[23] It is also described as 'the steps a company must take to become aware of, prevent and address adverse human rights impacts'.[24]

Following the adoption of the UN Framework and the UNGPs, some States have enacted legislation, or have adopted policy instruments, to impose due diligence upon corporate actors and improve effective access to remedy. In Europe in 2017, France enacted groundbreaking legislation imposing a general 'duty of vigilance' on parent and controlling companies in respect of the impact

---

22   UNHRC, 'Guiding Principles on Business and Human Rights: Implementing the United Nations "Protect, Respect and Remedy" Framework' (UNGPs) (21 March 2011) UN Doc A/HRC/17/31.

23   UN Framework, para 25.

24   Ibid, para 56.

of their global activities on human rights and the environment.[25] Any damage resulting from the failure to respect this duty may lead to liability in tort for these companies. HRDD legislation has also been enacted in the Netherlands[26] and Germany,[27] while some countries such as Finland,[28] as well as the European Union (EU),[29] are discussing the adoption of such legislation. In most of these States, the growing influence of the corporate accountability movement has been a key trigger in the adoption of these legislative and policy instruments, and the inclusion of access to justice as a topic of major importance.

Regional supranational actors in Europe have also increasingly paid attention to the debate on corporate accountability and access to justice, especially since the adoption of the UN Framework and the UNGPs. First of all, the EU recognized the UNGPs as an 'authoritative policy framework' and stated the importance of working towards their implementation in the EU, as 'better implementation of the UNGPs would contribute to EU objectives – some of them enshrined in the Treaties – in relation to specific human rights issues'.[30] This is an important statement, as the EU is a major economic player. It is home to a large number of MNEs and has competence in fields touching upon the economic life of the Union. As a result, any policies and/or standards it adopts on BHR issues are likely to have a significant impact in the EU and beyond. However, until recently the EU has shied away from imposing legal obligations on companies, preferring a voluntary approach based on corporate social responsibility (CSR).[31] Moreover, the EU's contribution to the implementation

25   Loi n° 2017-399 du 27 mars 2017 relative au devoir de vigilance des sociétés mères et des entreprises donneuses d'ordre.

26   Wet van 24 oktober 2019 houdende de invoering van een zorgplicht ter voorkoming van de levering van goederen en diensten die met behulp van kinderarbeid tot stand zijn gekomen (Wet zorgplicht kinderarbeid).

27   Gesetz über die unternehmerischen Sorgfaltspflichten zur Vermeidung von Menschenrechtsverletzungen in Lieferketten vom 16. Juli 2021.

28   Ministry of Economic Affairs and Employment of Finland, 'Judicial Analysis Specifies the Planned Corporate Social Responsibility Act in Finland' (Ministry of Economic Affairs and Employment of Finland, 30 June 2020) <https://tem.fi/en/-/judicial-analysis-specifies-the-planned-corporate-social-responsibility-act-in-finland> accessed 1 May 2021.

29   RBC, 'European Commission Promises Mandatory Due Diligence Legislation in 2021' (RBC, 30 April 2020) <https://responsiblebusinessconduct.eu/wp/2020/04/30/european-commission-promises-mandatory-due-diligence-legislation-in-2021/> accessed 1 May 2021.

30   European Commission, 'Commission Staff Working Document on Implementing the UN Guiding Principles on Business and Human Rights – State of Play' SWD(2015) 144 final, 2.

31   European Commission, 'A Renewed EU Strategy 2011–2014 for Corporate Social Responsibility' COM(2011) 681 final. See also Olivier de Schutter, 'Corporate Social Responsibility European Style' (2008) 14 European Law Journal 203.

of the UNGPs has been insufficient so far. It has lacked a general vision on BHR and has adopted a piecemeal approach to the implementation of the UNGPs.

In relation to the effective access to remedy pillar, the Treaty of Lisbon has, over the years, strengthened the role and powers of the EU institutions in the field of civil and criminal justice, imposing a general requirement on the EU to facilitate access to justice.[32] Article 47 of the Charter of Fundamental Rights of the EU (EU Charter),[33] which has the same legal binding force as EU treaties, also guarantees the right to an effective remedy and to a fair trial. Despite this increase in power in the justice field, the EU has, however, neglected to offer a targeted and comprehensive response to the need for effective access to remedy in the context of corporate abuse, especially when such abuse takes place extraterritorially. To date, the 2017 opinion of the EU Agency for Fundamental Rights (EU FRA) on improving access to remedy in the area of BHR at the EU level[34] is the only policy document providing a general approach for further work on the third pillar.

Another important regional actor is the Council of Europe (CoE), which offers one of the most developed legal regimes protecting the right to an effective remedy through the European Convention on Human Rights (ECHR)[35] and the case law of the European Court of Human Rights (ECtHR). Following the adoption of the UN Framework and the UNGPs, the CoE initiated a reflection on the feasibility of setting new standards in the field of CSR. It stressed the central place of the UNGPs as an authoritative reference point for its work on this topic.[36] Notably, there were discussions on the elaboration of a complementary legal instrument, such as a convention or an additional protocol to the ECHR, on human rights and business. However, the CoE ultimately refrained from adopting binding standards for companies to respect human rights. Furthermore, while the CoE has recognized the importance of effective access to remedy in the context of corporate abuse, it has neglected to spell out a coordinated and effective approach to guarantee the adequate implementation of the third pillar.[37]

Finally, under the auspices of the United Nations Economic Commission for Europe (UNECE), the Aarhus Convention on Access to Information, Public

---

32   Treaty of Lisbon Amending the Treaty on European Union and the Treaty Establishing the European Community [2007] OJ C306/1.

33   Charter of Fundamental Rights of the European Union [2012] OJ C326/392.

34   EU FRA, 'Improving Access to Remedy in the Area of Business and Human Rights at the EU Level' FRA Opinion – 1/2017 [B&HR].

35   Convention for the Protection of Human Rights and Fundamental Freedoms as amended by Protocols 11 and 14 (adopted 4 November 1950, entered into force 3 September 1953), ETS 5.

36   Declaration of the Committee of Ministers on the UN Guiding Principles on Business and Human Rights (16 April 2014).

37   Recommendation CM/Rec(2016)3 of the Committee of Ministers to Member States on human rights and business (2 March 2016).

Participation in Decision-making and Access to Justice in Environmental Matters (Aarhus Convention)[38] guarantees the right of access to justice to members of the public in specific situations, including when private persons contravene national environmental law. However, the interplay between the Aarhus Convention and the third pillar of the UN Framework and the UNGPs has not been explored yet, and it remains to be seen whether the Aarhus Convention can play an effective role in improving access to remedy in the context of business-related environmental pollution. Overall, European supranational organizations have lacked an ambitious approach to imposing corporate accountability and improving access to justice for victims of business-related harm, despite their economic power (EU) or their role in guaranteeing human rights (CoE) and the protection of the environment (UNECE) in Europe.

2 Aim of the book

This book aims to explore the interplay between access to justice and corporate accountability through the study of transnational litigation against MNEs, especially in European civil law countries, and ongoing legal and policy reforms at the international, European, and national level. Using national litigation experiences as a starting point, and focusing on the European region, this book asks the following questions: how effective has litigation against MNEs been in achieving access to justice and corporate accountability in Europe? Furthermore, how will ongoing regulatory developments, both legal and policy, achieve access to justice and corporate accountability in the future?

To answer these questions, this book follows an analysis in three stages. It first describes the wider legal and social context in which demands for access to justice and corporate accountability have emerged. It then compares civil and criminal litigation against MNEs for their involvement in human rights abuse and environmental damage in two European civil law countries, namely France and the Netherlands. This second part assesses how the substantive and procedural laws applying to transnational litigation against MNEs create opportunities and/or challenges for foreign victims of business-related harm when they seek to obtain remedy and hold MNEs accountable before domestic courts. Finally, this book questions how recent international, European, and national regulatory developments may contribute to the realization of access to justice and corporate accountability in the future.

---

38   Aarhus Convention (adopted 25 June 1998, entered into force 30 October 2001) 2161 UNTS 447.

3 Scope

This book focuses on European civil law countries for a number of reasons. Until recently, transnational litigation against MNEs had been predominantly practised in common law countries,[39] and most of the existing scholarship had, therefore, largely focused on litigation under the ATS in the US[40] and tort-based claims in England[41] and other common law countries (eg the US, Canada, and Australia).[42] For some time, scholars generally assumed that transnational litigation against MNEs was a legal phenomenon limited to, or mainly possible in, common law countries.[43] However, the significant development of transnational litigation against MNEs in European civil law countries since the beginning of the 21st century has provided material to reflect on the adequacy of the legal systems of these States to deal with such claims and the feasibility of seeking justice through their courts. Importantly, the progressive decline of the ATS as an instrument to hold corporations accountable in the US[44] and the threat of the potential reintroduction of the doctrine of *forum non conveniens* in

---

39   Ward, 'Securing Transnational Corporate Accountability through National Courts', 455. In 2001 Ward predicted that, although most of the claims against MNEs had been brought in common law countries where, she argued, legal cultural links between Anglo-Saxon lawyers and procedural rules probably facilitated FDL claims, in the longer term these cases would more likely emerge in European countries of civil law tradition, particularly the Netherlands and France.

40   For a discussion of the ATS, see Hari Osofsky, 'Environmental Human Rights under the Alien Tort Statute: Redress for Indigenous Victims of Multinational Corporations' (1996) 20 Suffolk Transnational Law Review 335; Michael Koebele, *Corporate Responsibility under the Alien Tort Statute: Enforcement of International Law through US Torts Law* (Martinus Nijhoff Publishers 2009); Beth Stephens, 'The Curious History of the Alien Tort Statute' (2014) 89 Notre Dame Law Review 1467.

41   Peter Muchlinski, 'Holding Multinationals to Account: Recent Developments in English Litigation and the Company Law Review' (2002) 23 The Company Lawyer 168; Richard Meeran, 'Tort Litigation against Multinational Corporations for Violation of Human Rights: An Overview of the Position outside the United States' (2011) 3 City University of Hong Kong Law Review 1.

42   Barnali Choudhury, 'Beyond the Alien Tort Claims Act: Alternative Approaches to Attributing Liability to Corporations for Extraterritorial Abuses' (2005) 26 Northwestern Journal of International Law & Business 43; Simon Baughen, *Human Rights and Corporate Wrongs: Closing the Governance Gap. Corporations, Globalisation and the Law* (Edward Elgar 2015).

43   On the prospects of non-ATS claims, see Liesbeth Enneking, *Foreign Direct Liability and Beyond: Exploring the Role of Tort Law in Promoting International Corporate Social Responsibility and Accountability* (Eleven International Publishing 2012) 271–275.

44   On the decline of the ATS, see Paul Hoffman, 'The Implications of Kiobel for Corporate Accountability Litigation under the Alien Tort Statute' in Lara *Blecher*, Nancy Kaymar Stafford and Gretchen Bellamy (eds), *Corporate Responsibility for Human Rights Impacts: New Expectations and Paradigms* (ABA 2014); Jonathan Kolieb, 'Jesner v Arab Bank: The US Supreme Court Forecloses on Accountability for Corporate Human Rights Abuses' (2018) 24 Australian International Law Journal 209.

the United Kingdom (UK) following Brexit[45] are likely to push litigators to look at other jurisdictions for litigation opportunities. In this respect, European civil law countries may look attractive, in particular in a context where an increasing number of these States and the EU are adopting mandatory HRDD statutes likely to open the door to a new type of litigation against corporations for their impact on human rights and the environment. As a result, research on the contemporary challenges of access to justice in European civil law countries is timely due to the likelihood of its growing importance.

This book focuses on France and the Netherlands for two main reasons. First, the recent increase in the number of claims brought against MNEs in these countries, especially in France, provides sufficient material from which to draw conclusions on the accessibility of their legal systems for victims of corporate abuse and the transformative potential they hold for corporate accountability. Second, France and the Netherlands are European countries of civil law tradition. They share a common legal history, which has, to some extent, influenced the shaping of their current legal systems.[46] Therefore, it is instructive from a comparative law perspective to assess the similarities and differences in the way these countries treat transnational claims against MNEs. It also allows for a better understanding of the influence of legal culture on transnational claims against MNEs and whether this type of litigation has developed its own characteristics in civil law countries. Furthermore, their legal and procedural frameworks are, to a certain extent, influenced by the existence of common institutions and rules in Europe. Since the end of World War II, various regional organizations, such as the EU, CoE, and the UNECE, have contributed to the development of a common legal and policy framework, which is now shared by a majority of countries in Europe.

It should be said that the above-mentioned developments and the growing popularity of access to justice as a research and advocacy topic within the BHR sphere have already led to an increasing interest by scholars and CSOs in the study of claims brought against MNEs in countries outside the common law tradition.[47] As a result, a number of academic and non-academic studies were published on claims against MNEs in Europe during the time of the research for

---

45   Axel Marx and others, 'Access to Legal Remedies for Victims of Corporate Human Rights Abuses in Third Countries' (European Parliament 2019) 16.

46   Jeroen Chorus and E. Chris Coppens, 'History' in Jeroen Chorus, Piet-Hein Gerver and Ewoud Hondius (eds), *Introduction to Dutch Law* (4th edn, Kluwer Law 2006) 8.

47   Enneking, *Foreign Direct Liability and Beyond*; Gwynne Skinner and others, 'The Third Pillar: Access to Judicial Remedies for Human Rights Violations by Transnational Business' (ICAR, ECCJ and CORE 2013).

this book.[48] However, this book remains relevant as it provides a comparative study of both civil and criminal claims against MNEs in civil law countries. Until recently, the existing scholarship mainly focused on the study of tort claims and, as a result, the study of the role of criminal proceedings as a means to achieve MNE accountability remains largely unexplored.[49] Furthermore, this book analyses how the most recent BHR developments – that is the increasing adoption of mandatory HRDD legislation and the negotiations for a legally binding instrument on BHR[50] – will contribute to the achievement of access to justice and corporate accountability.

4 Key concepts

This book adopts a number of frequently used terms that need to be defined and understood from the outset.

Multinational enterprises

There is a multitude of types of business entities operating across borders and, consequently, various terms are used to describe them (multinational corporations, transnational corporations, etc).[51] Different definitions may focus on the type of foreign investment (direct/portfolio), the nature of operations (transnational/multinational), or the extent of managerial control.[52] In its 2011 Guidelines for Multinational Enterprises (OECD Guidelines), the Organisation

---

48   Juan José Álvarez Rubio and Katerina Yiannibas (eds), *Human Rights in Business: Removal of Barriers to Access to Justice in the European Union* (Routledge 2017); Marx and others, 'Access to Legal Remedies for Victims of Corporate Human Rights Abuses in Third Countries'.

49   For a discussion of access to remedy in the context of criminal proceedings in Europe, see Adriana Espinosa González and Marta Sosa Navarro, 'Corporate Liability and Human Rights: Access to Criminal Judicial Remedies in Europe' in Angelica Bonfanti (ed), *Business and Human Rights in Europe: International Law Challenges* (Routledge 2018).

50   In June 2014 the UNHRC decided to establish an open-ended intergovernmental working group with the mandate to elaborate an international legally binding instrument to regulate, in international human rights law, the activities of transnational corporations and other business enterprises. UNHRC, Res 26/9 (2014) UN doc A/HRC/26/L.22/Rev.1

51   Ebbesson argues, 'There is no general agreement on how to label the various forms of transboundary economic organization, and neither does the given distinction reveal the diversity of corporate structures. Rather, the difficulty in terming and defining them reflects the multitude of structures and relationships.' Jonas Ebbesson, 'Transboundary Corporate Responsibility in Environmental Matters: Fragments and Foundations for a Future Framework' in Gerd Winter (ed), *Multilevel Governance of Global Environmental Change: Perspective from Science, Sociology and the Law* (CUP 2011) 200–201.

52   For a discussion of these definitions, see Peter Muchlinski, *Multinational Enterprises and the Law* (2nd edn, OUP 2007) 5–9.

for Economic Co-operation and Development (OECD) provides for a flexible definition of MNEs:

> These enterprises operate in all sectors of the economy. They usually comprise companies or other entities established in more than one country and so linked that they may coordinate their operations in various ways. While one or more of these entities may be able to exercise a significant influence over the activities of others, their degree of autonomy within the enterprise may vary widely from one multinational enterprise to another. Ownership may be private, State or mixed.[53]

The OECD's definition of MNEs is the one used in this book. This definition insists on 'the ability to coordinate activities between enterprises in more than one country'.[54] It is broad enough to encompass various legal forms of undertaking while emphasizing the notion of direct investment.[55] As this book will show, MNEs' structure, organization, and management are significant obstacles to holding parent companies and other entities of MNEs accountable.

Corporate accountability

This book explores the use of legal mobilization as a strategy to achieve corporate accountability. It is not concerned with the search for corporate responsibility through private regulation and other types of soft law instruments.[56] As a result of linguistic constraints imposed by the English language, and to represent various legal realities, this book distinguishes between the concepts of corporate responsibility, liability, and accountability.[57]

Responsibility refers to 'a moral obligation to behave correctly towards or in respect of' something or someone. Thus, corporate responsibility imposes

---

53   OECD Guidelines for Multinational Enterprises: 2011 Edition (OECD 2011) 17.

54   Muchlinski, *Multinational Enterprises and the Law*, 7.

55   Ibid.

56   There is already an extensive scholarship on the merits and challenges of private law regulation and corporate responsibility instruments. See Ilias Bantekas, 'Corporate Social Responsibility in International Law' (2004) 22 Boston University International Law Journal 309; Larry Backer, 'Economic Globalization and the Rise of Efficient Systems of Global Private Law Making: Wal-Mart as Global Legislator' (2007) 39 Connecticut Law Review 1739; Olufemi Amao, *Corporate Social Responsibility, Human Rights and the Law* (Routledge 2011); Jedrzej Frynas, 'Corporate Social Responsibility or Government Regulation? Evidence on Oil Spill Prevention' (2012) 17 Ecology and Society 4; Lara Blecher, 'Code of Conduct: The Trojan Horse of International Human Rights Law' (2016) 38 Comparative Labor Law and Policy Journal 437.

57   It should be noted that other languages may use the same word to represent various legal realities (eg French uses the word *responsabilité* for accountability, liability, and responsibility). Furthermore, various legal fields may use similar words in different ways (eg the word 'responsibility' as used in public international law compared with its use in other legal fields).

a moral, not a legal obligation upon companies.[58] Liability evokes 'the state of being legally responsible for something'.[59] As a result, corporate liability implies a legal obligation upon companies. Accountability refers to the fact or condition of being 'required or expected to justify actions or decisions'.[60] Therefore, corporate accountability is a wider concept than corporate liability. It encompasses 'the idea that those accountable should be answerable for the consequences of their actions' and refers to both legal and non-legal risks.[61]

Transnational litigation against MNEs

In the existing scholarship on transnational litigation against MNEs, authors use various expressions to talk about claims alleging the liability of corporate actors in the context of foreign investment, including 'foreign direct liability litigation' and 'transnational human rights litigation'.

Ward was the first author to use the expression 'foreign direct liability' (FDL). She described it as follows:

> The parent companies of an increasing number of multinational corporate groups in the extractive and chemical industries have found themselves in their home courts defending against 'foreign direct liability' – legal actions in which foreign citizens (mostly from developing countries) have claimed damages for the negative environmental or health impacts of the group's foreign direct investment.[62]

Ward distinguishes between domestic liability claims raising 'the direct responsibilities of corporations under international law' (eg the ATS in the US) and other domestic claims raising the liability of parent companies in home country courts.[63] However, she suggests that both types of litigation question the contribution and the adequacy of existing international or national legal

---

58 OUP, 'Responsibility' (*Lexico* 2021) <https://www.lexico.com/definition/responsibility> accessed 1 May 2021. Nonetheless, 'responsibility' may also evoke 'the state or fact of having a duty to deal with something or of having control over someone'. This word may be used to refer to State obligations under public international law.

59 OUP, 'Liability' (*Lexico* 2021) <https://www.lexico.com/definition/liability> accessed 1 May 2021.

60 OUP, 'Accountable' (*Lexico* 2021) <https://www.lexico.com/definition/accountable> accessed 1 May 2021.

61 Nadia Bernaz, 'Enhancing Corporate Accountability for Human Rights Violations: Is Extraterritoriality the Magic Potion?' (2013) 117 Journal of Business Ethics 493, 494.

62 Halina Ward, *Foreign Direct Liability: A New Weapon in the Performance Armoury* (The Royal Institute of International Affairs 2000) 1.

63 Ward, 'Securing Transnational Corporate Accountability through National Courts' 451.

frameworks to solve issues of transnational corporate accountability.[64] Following Ward, other authors have used the same expression, most notably referring to tort claims brought directly against the parent company of an MNE before its home country courts for its involvement in activities occurring in foreign countries. For instance, Enneking, who has written extensively on this topic, has used the term 'foreign direct liability cases' to refer to:

> tort-based civil liability claims brought against parent companies of multinational corporations before courts in their Western society home countries for harm caused to the people- and planet-related interests of third parties (local employees, neighbours, local communities, etc.) in developing host countries as a result of the local activities of the multinational corporations involved.[65]

As a result, other types of claims, such as criminal complaints, have rarely been regarded as FDL litigation. Other authors have used the expression 'transnational human rights litigation', especially in the context of tort claims for violations of international human rights law under the ATS in the US.

In this book, the use of both expressions is excluded. The expression 'transnational litigation against MNEs' is favoured in order to emphasize the cross-border dimension and, as a result, challenges of this type of litigation. Furthermore, the transnational nature of legal claims against MNEs echoes that of the economic activities of the same actors across borders. It also highlights the contemporary challenges created by economic globalization, particularly foreign investment, to classical theories of the domesticity of law, State sovereignty, and international law. The expression 'transnational litigation against MNEs' is also broader, as it includes not only tort proceedings, but also criminal proceedings, as well as liability claims against not only parent companies but also their subsidiaries, partners, or other companies under control. It also covers litigation not only for human rights abuse but also for environmental damage. Ultimately, the expression 'transnational litigation against MNEs' is broad enough to encompass the variety of legal strategies used by litigators to hold MNEs to account and obtain remedies.

5 Background to the book

Transnational litigation against MNEs is the indirect result of the imbalance between the economic and political power accumulated by MNEs following an increase in foreign investment and trade over the last decades, and the

---

64 Ibid.

65 Enneking, *Foreign Direct Liability and Beyond*, 92.

absence of legal responsibility for the harm they may cause in the context of their worldwide activities. This situation demonstrates a two-speed globalization: while companies have benefited from the considerable development of economic globalization, victims of corporate wrongdoing have been left behind as a result of unachieved legal globalization. This asymmetrical situation has led to counter-hegemonic globalization, or 'insurgent cosmopolitanism', where 'oppressed groups' organize their resistance on the same scale and through the same type of coalitions used by their 'oppressors' to victimize them.[66] The corporate accountability movement is the visible face of this insurgent cosmopolitanism and has organized in the same way as MNEs through transnational networks. Access to justice is a significant aspect of the identity of the corporate accountability movement. In this context, access to justice goes beyond simply access to a court or to a remedy. It also means holding businesses to account and claiming a paradigm shift in the way the law envisages business actors.

Globalization

Transnational litigation against MNEs is directly linked to the debate on corporate accountability in the context of globalization.[67] Generally, authors disagree on the nature and the novelty of globalization, as well as its normative values and processes.[68] De Sousa Santos insists on the fact that globalization comprises a very broad set of phenomena and dimensions and, as a result, there is no 'one sole entity called globalization, instead there are globalizations'.[69] The existing legal scholarship offers various definitions of the concept of 'globalization'. Twining defines it as economic, political, social, and cultural processes that 'tend to create and consolidate a unified world economy, a single ecological system, and a complex network of communications that covers the whole globe, even if it does not penetrate to every part of it'.[70] Other authors insist on the fact that national frontiers are becoming irrelevant in the context of globalization.[71] For Garcia, globalization is 'the sum total of political, social, economic, legal and symbolic processes rendering the division of the globe into national boundaries increasingly less important for the purpose of individual

---

66 Boaventura de Sousa Santos, 'Globalizations' (2006) 23 Theory, Culture & Society 393, 398.

67 Ward, 'Securing Transnational Corporate Accountability through National Courts', 452.

68 Frédéric Mégret, 'Globalization' (MPEPIL 2009) <http://opil.ouplaw.com/> accessed 1 May 2021.

69 De Sousa Santos, *Toward a New Legal Common Sense*, 187.

70 William Twining, *Globalization and Legal Theory* (CUP 2000) 4.

71 On the relation between norms and space in the context of globalization, see Paul Berman, 'From International Law to Law and Globalization' (2005) 43 Columbia Journal of Transnational Law 485, 511–518.

meaning and social decision'.[72] Ultimately, globalization is an economic, political, social, and legal phenomenon where the relevance of national borders and sovereignty to individual and societal decision-making processes is challenged.

In the more recent phase of economic globalization, MNEs have gained in power and influence.[73] However, the law has been slow to respond to this evolution and inadequate in controlling MNEs' behaviour.[74] Although the modern MNE emerged in the second half of the 19th century, MNEs started to acquire unprecedented importance in international production following World War II.[75] The period from the 1990s until the time of writing has seen the influence of MNEs grow as a result of various factors, including growth in foreign direct investment (FDI), the adoption of truly global production chains by MNEs, a marked shift from raw materials and manufacturing towards services-based FDI, and the development of major regional trade and investment liberalization regimes, alongside the establishment of the World Trade Organization (WTO). As a result, MNEs can potentially bring economic and social benefits to the countries where they operate. At the same time, they may also pose a threat to the enjoyment of human rights and a clean environment.[76]

If international law has allowed MNEs to increasingly gain rights in the fields of foreign investment and international trade, thus facilitating their global expansion, it has also been unable to ensure that MNEs respect human rights or the environment, especially in States where regulation provides little protection to individuals or the environment. MNEs may use their 'transboundary *subjectivity* and *structure*' to escape from liability when they cause harm to people or the environment in other countries.[77] Moreover, international law is fragmented into a myriad of treaties and institutions with different objectives, sets of values, and decision-making processes. The excessive specialization in

72   Frank Garcia, 'Global Market and Human Rights: Trading Away the Human Rights Principle' (1999) 25 Brooklyn Journal of International Law 51, 56.

73   Upendra Baxi, *The Future of Human Rights* (2nd edn, OUP 2006) 236. For a discussion of corporate power, see Jean-Philippe Robé, 'Multinational Enterprises: The Constitution of a Pluralistic Legal Order' in Gerd Teubner (ed), *Global Law without a State* (Ashgate 1997); Nicholas Connolly and Manette Kaisershot, 'Corporate Power and Human Rights' (2015) 19 International Journal of Human Rights 663.

74   Michael Addo, 'Human Rights and Transnational Corporations: An Introduction' in Michael Addo (ed), *Human Rights Standards and the Responsibility of Transnational Corporations* (Kluwer Law International 1999) 9.

75   Muchlinski, Multinational Enterprises and the Law, 15.

76   Jeffrey Dunoff, 'Does Globalization Advance Human Rights?' (1999) 25 Brooklyn Journal of International Law 125; Ward, 'Securing Transnational Corporate Accountability through National Courts', 452–453.

77   Ebbesson, 'Transboundary Corporate Responsibility in Environmental Matters', 201 (emphasis in original).

each field of international law, and the lack of coordination and dialogue among those various fields, contribute to the creation of conflicts, especially between international economic law and international human rights law. Garcia suggests that these conflicts raise a problem of justice, as 'the inquiry into the effects of market globalization on human rights law becomes an inquiry into how the economic facts and regulatory infrastructure of globalization enhance, or interfere with, the contributions which international human rights law seeks to make towards the attainment of justice'.[78] National law also appears ill-adapted, as its predominant focus on domestic issues and its devotion to the *economic persona* have impeded its effectiveness in regulating and controlling MNEs.[79]

At the same time, globalization has given rise to new demands on corporations to exercise their power responsibly and to account for it. It can exert a transformative effect on corporate accountability, turning it from a choice into an imperative.[80] Transnational litigation against MNEs is the visible face of these demands. Several aspects of the interplay between globalization and transnational litigation against MNEs must be considered here.

First, the processes of globalization are fundamentally changing the significance of national and societal boundaries, generally making them less important.[81] In the same way, transnational claims against MNEs challenge territorial conceptions of State jurisdiction firmly embedded in international and domestic legal systems. In particular, they point out 'the mismatch between the territorial scope of State regulatory jurisdiction and the globally integrated organisation of the MNE'.[82]

Second, globalization has renewed the debate on legal personality.[83] While businesses have insisted on keeping a traditional interpretation, advocates for greater corporate accountability have supported new definitions of legal personality under international law.[84] Similarly, plaintiffs in transnational

---

78 Garcia, 'Global Market and Human Rights', 57.

79 Addo, 'Human Rights and Transnational Corporations', 11–19.

80 Ward, 'Securing Transnational Corporate Accountability through National Courts', 453.

81 Twining, *Globalization and Legal Theory*, 7.

82 Peter Muchlinski, 'Limited Liability and Multinational Enterprises: A Case for Reform?' (2010) 34 Cambridge Journal of Economics 915, 920.

83 Twining, *Globalization and Legal Theory*, 10.

84 For an overview of the debate, see Dimitra Kokkini-Iatridou and Paul J I M de Waart, 'Foreign Investment in Developing Countries: Legal Personality of Multinationals in International Law' (1983) 14 Netherlands Yearbook of International Law 87; Karsten Nowrot, 'New Approaches to the International Legal Personality of Multinational Corporations: Towards a Rebuttable Presumption of Normative Responsibilities' (ESIL Research Forum on International Law: Contemporary Problems, Geneva, 2005).

claims against MNEs have challenged the application of separate legal personality and limited liability to MNEs.

Third, a variety of significant actors who are relevant to the analysis of patterns of legal and law-related relations in the modern world are emerging in the context of globalization.[85] While MNEs are increasing their economic and political importance on the world stage, transnational activist movements advocating for new forms of corporate accountability are becoming influential in shaping international and domestic policies and laws through various strategies, including legal mobilization. Ultimately, transnational claims against MNEs represent one aspect of the globalization of the international legal system.[86] Paul holds that they 'represent both a frustration with the limits of traditional international institutions and cooperative regimes and a positive step toward building a new international legal order'.[87]

Another fundamental characteristic of the litigation discussed in this book, which is reinforced by globalization, is its transnational legal nature. Jessup defines the term 'transnational law' to include 'all law which regulates actions or events that transcend national frontiers. Both public and private international law are included, as are other rules which do not wholly fit into such standard categories'.[88] Importantly, transnational law may not be formally enacted by States, as it may be concerned with legal activity involving various actors, including States but also individuals, corporations, CSOs, and other groups.[89] Transnational litigation against MNEs reflects the intertwining of both public and private international law, as these claims raise not only questions of private international law (eg the choice of jurisdiction or applicable law) but also issues of public international law (eg the application of international human rights and environmental law to non-State actors in cross-border situations). It also involves a variety of actors, such as lawyers and CSOs, who seek to influence regulatory behaviour by challenging the application of legal norms and practice beyond borders.

Transnational claims against MNEs also provide an example of the concept of 'interlegality', described by De Sousa Santos as the phenomenological

---

85   Twining, *Globalization and Legal Theory*, 9.

86   Joey Paul, 'Holding Multinational Corporations Responsible under International Law' (2001) 24 Hastings International & Comparative Law Review 285, 290.

87   Ibid, 289.

88   Philip Jessup, *Transnational Law* (Yale University Press 1956) 136. For a discussion of transnational law, see also Harold Koh, 'Transnational Legal Process' (1996) 75 Nebraska Law Review 181; Paul Schiff Berman, 'A Pluralist Approach to International Law' (2007) 32 Yale Journal of International Law 301.

89   Carrie Menkel-Meadow, 'Why and How to Study "Transnational" Law' (2011) 1 UC Irvine Law Review 97, 103.

dimension of legal plurality in which 'everyday life crosses or is interpenetrated by different and contrasting legal orders and legal cultures'.[90] Interlegality is:

> the conception of different legal spaces surimposed, interpenetrated and mixed in our minds, as much as in our actions, either on occasions of qualitative leaps or sweeping crises in our life trajectories, or in the dull routine of eventless everyday life. We live in a time of porous legality or of legal porosity, multiple networks of legal orders forcing us to constant transition and trespassing.[91]

In Europe, transnational claims against MNEs reveal the interactions between various legal orders, namely EU/Member States, host/home countries, international/national. Furthermore, litigators have developed creative legal strategies, mixing aspects of different legal orders, to challenge the perceived increase in corporate power and force a debate on corporate accountability for human rights and environmental abuse.

Social movements and cause-lawyering

Since the 1990s, CSOs and lawyers have played an important role in ensuring that global companies are held accountable for human rights and environmental abuse.[92] Therefore, the concepts of social movements and cause-lawyering are useful for understanding how the development of transnational litigation against MNEs is closely associated with the existence and the demands of the corporate accountability movement.[93]

---

90   De Sousa Santos, *Toward a New Legal Common Sense*, 97.

91   Ibid.

92   On the role of CSOs in holding companies to account, see Robin Broad and John Cavanagh, 'The Corporate Accountability Movement: Lessons & Opportunities' (1999) 23 Fletcher Forum of World Affairs 151; Rory Sullivan, 'The Influence of NGOs on the Normative Framework for Business and Human Rights' in Stephen Tully (ed), *Research Handbook on Corporate Legal Responsibility* (Edward Elgar Publishing 2005); Jonathan Doh and Terrence Guay, 'Corporate Social Responsibility, Public Policy, and NGO Activism in Europe and the United States: An Institutional-Stakeholder Perspective' (2006) 43 Journal of Management Studies 47; Jem Bendell, *The Corporate Responsibility Movement* (Greenleaf Publishing 2009).

93   For a history of the corporate accountability movement, see Jem Bendell, 'Barricades and Boardrooms: A Contemporary History of the Corporate Accountability Movement' (2004) UNRISD Technology, Business and Society Programme Paper No 13 <http://www.unrisd.org/unrisd/website/document.nsf/(httpPublications)/504AF359BB33967FC1256EA9003CE20A?OpenDocument> accessed 1 May 2021.

Scholars from various fields of social sciences have written extensively on the concept of 'social movements'.[94] Therefore, there is no unique definition of what a social movement is. Diani provides a basic definition of social movements as 'networks of informal interactions between a plurality of individuals, groups and/or organisations, engaged in political or cultural conflicts, on the basis of shared collective identities'.[95] In general, social movements are different from interest groups, political parties, protest events, and coalitions.[96] According to Della Porta, four elements are common in social science definitions of social movements: a network structure, the use of unconventional means, shared beliefs and solidarity, and the pursuit of some conflictual aims.[97] Della Porta and Diani argue that the beginning of the 21st century saw the emergence of a wave of mobilizations for a 'globalization from below'.[98] They also call this new wave the 'global justice movement'. Della Porta and Diani suggest that the initiatives of the global justice movement are very heterogeneous and not necessarily connected to each other. Actors address a range of issues, from child labour and corporate human rights abuses to deforestation. Their initiatives take a myriad of forms and different points of view.[99]

Keck and Sikkink have also provided a landmark analysis of transnational advocacy networks.[100] They argue that activist networks, both transnational and national, share similar central values or principled ideas, make creative use of information, and employ sophisticated political strategies in targeting their campaigns.[101] In particular, Keck and Sikkink suggest that:

> [They] mobilize information strategically to help create new issues and categories and to persuade, pressure, and gain leverage over much more powerful organizations and governments. Activists in networks try not only to influence policy outcomes,

94   Donatella della Porta and Mario Diani, *Social Movements: An Introduction* (2nd edn, Blackwell 2006) 1. On social movements, see David Snow, Sarah Soule and Hanspeter Kriesi (eds), *The Blackwell Companion to Social Movements* (Blackwell 2004); Daniel Cefaï, *Pourquoi se Mobilise-t-on? Les Théories de l'Action Collective* (La Découverte 2007); Suzanne Staggenborg, *Social Movements* (OUP 2011).

95   Mario Diani, 'The Concept of Social Movement' (1992) 40 The Sociological Review 1, 1.

96   Ibid.

97   Donatella della Porta, 'Social Movement' (*Oxford Bibliographies* 2011) <http://www.oxfordbibliographies.com/view/document/obo-9780199756384/obo-9780199756384-0050.xml> accessed 1 May 2021.

98   Della Porta and Diani, *Social Movements*, 2.

99   Ibid.

100 Margaret Keck and Kathryn Sikkink, *Activists Beyond Borders: Advocacy Networks in International Politics* (Cornell University Press 1998).

101 Keck and Sikkink define 'principled ideas' as '[i]deas that specify criteria for determining whether actions are right and wrong and whether outcomes are just or unjust': ibid, 1.

but also to transform the terms and nature of the debate. They are not always successful in their efforts, but they are increasingly relevant players in policy debates.[102]

It was pointed out earlier that De Sousa Santos describes different globalizations.[103] In this context, he distinguishes between hegemonic and counter-hegemonic globalizations. One mode of production of counter-hegemonic globalization is 'insurgent cosmopolitanism'.[104] De Sousa Santos describes this as follows:

> It consists of the transnationally organized resistance ... through local/global linkages between social organizations and movements representing those classes and social groups victimized by hegemonic globalization and united in concrete struggles against exclusion, subordinate inclusion, destruction of livelihoods and ecological destruction, political oppression, or cultural suppression, etc. They take advantage of the possibilities of transnational interaction created by the world system in transition.[105]

An important feature of insurgent cosmopolitanism, as defined by De Sousa Santos, is 'the aspiration by oppressed groups to organize their resistance on the same scale and through the same type of coalitions used by the oppressors to victimize them, that is, the global scale and local/global conditions'.[106]

Insurgent cosmopolitanism lies at the heart of the mobilization and construction of the corporate accountability movement. At the beginning of the 21st century, CSOs, lawyers, and victims started grouping together to challenge corporate impunity and demand accountability for business-related human rights abuse and environmental damage resulting from the various processes of economic globalization. They have organized their resistance through transnational activist networks, thus operating on the same scale as MNEs.[107] They have also mobilized financial and modern communication resources to build campaigns and other activities, such as transnational litigation against

---

102 Ibid, 2.

103 De Sousa Santos, *Toward a New Legal Common Sense*, 187.

104 De Sousa Santos, 'Globalizations', 397.

105 Ibid.

106 Ibid, 398.

107 Similarly, Yaziji and Doh observe that, in the context of changes in the economic and political systems of Western industrialized societies, we have seen the parallel development of the societal importance of corporations on the one hand and NGOs on the other. Michael Yaziji and Jonathan Doh, *NGOs and Corporations: Conflict and Collaboration* (CUP 2009) 27.

MNEs, which help them strategically to achieve their aims. In particular, the corporate accountability movement focuses on the role of States and national courts in imposing human rights and environmental obligations on companies. Ultimately, the corporate accountability movement is a major actor in counter-hegemonic globalization.

The interactions of the corporate accountability movement with cause-lawyers have contributed to the development of transnational litigation against MNEs as a strategic form of legal mobilization.[108] The concept of cause-lawyering poses a number of definitional challenges, as a result of the range of possible settings and styles of cause-lawyering.[109] Generally, cause-lawyers are activist lawyers who seek to use the courts as a vehicle to achieve social change or social justice beyond the individual claim at stake.[110] Menkel-Meadow defines cause-lawyering as 'any activity that seeks to use law-related means or to change laws or regulations to achieve great social justice – both for particular individuals (drawing on individualistic "helping" orientations) and for disadvantaged groups'.[111]

Cause-lawyering contrasts with conventional lawyering in the sense that cause-lawyers participate in parallel advocacy and legal reform activities for the benefit of the cause they fight for. Furthermore, scholars suggest that cause-lawyers have the propensity to transgress conventional or generally accepted professional ethical standards of legal practice, such as neutrality, client selection, or partisanship.[112] Another important aspect of cause-lawyering is that it is often said to be characteristic of common law countries, especially the US, where strategic litigation and public interest litigation are widely accepted.[113]

Various types of cause-lawyers have been involved in transnational claims against MNEs. While plaintiffs have been represented by lawyers practising in activist law firms in the UK, the Netherlands, and Belgium, claims against MNEs have been led by NGOs created by lawyers in France and Germany. One

---

108 On the relationship between cause-lawyering and social movements, see Austin Sarat and Stuart Scheingold (eds), *Cause Lawyers and Social Movements* (Stanford University Press 2006).

109 Andrew Boon, 'Cause Lawyers and the Alternative Ethical Paradigm: Ideology and Transgression' (2004) 7 Legal Ethics 250, 252.

110 Thelton Henderson, 'Social Change, Judicial Activism and the Public Interest Lawyer' (2003) 33 Washington University Journal of Law and Policy 33, 37.

111 Carrie Menkel-Meadow, 'The Causes of Cause Lawyering: Toward an Understanding of the Motivation and Commitment of Social Justice Lawyers' in Austin Sarat and Stuart Scheingold (eds), *Cause Lawyering: Political Commitments and Professional Responsibilities* (OUP 1998) 37.

112 Boon, 'Cause Lawyers and the Alternative Ethical Paradigm', 254–257. However, such an allegation is difficult to establish due to the absence of empirical evidence.

113 Ibid, 251.

commonality between these lawyers is that they are specialized in human rights, environmental, and, in particular, corporate accountability litigation. These cause-lawyers demonstrate a particular legal entrepreneurship, as they make 'creative use of existing laws and procedures' to seek redress and challenge corporate impunity in the home country of MNEs.[114] Furthermore, they have been involved in advocacy and legal reform activities in parallel to litigation.

Access to justice

Access to justice is a central concept of this book. However, defining access to justice is a difficult task, as there is a lack of clarity or consensus about what it means.[115] In the context of this book, the multidimensional nature of access to justice raises several questions pertaining to the dichotomy between the procedural and the substantive nature of access to justice, the difference between access to justice and access to remedy, and the meaning of 'effective access to justice'.

Procedural versus substantive access to justice

Access to justice is often conceived from a procedural perspective.[116] However, its substantive nature is equally important. Discussing the problem of access to justice in the US context, Rhode rightly asks the following question: 'To what should Americans have access? Is it justice in a procedural sense: access to legal assistance and legal processes that can address law-related concerns? Or is it justice in a substantive sense: access to a just resolution of legal disputes and social problems?'[117] This question has been debated beyond the US legal

---

114 Peter Muchlinski, 'The Provision of Private Law Remedies against Multinational Enterprises: A Comparative Law Perspective' (2009) 4 Journal of Comparative Law 148, 167.

115 On access to justice, see Mauro Cappelletti and Bryant Garth, 'Access to Justice: The Newest Wave in the Worldwide Movement to Make Rights Effective' (1978) 27 Buffalo Review 181; Deborah Rhode, *Access to Justice* (OUP 2004); Francesco Francioni (ed), *Access to Justice as a Human Right* (OUP 2007).

116 However, the extent of the procedural nature of access to justice is also subject to discussion. According to an OECD and Open Society's Workshop Background Paper on access to justice, 'One of the important recent developments is a shift to a broader understanding of access to justice needs and a more encompassing definition of legal assistance services in the public sector. While at one time access to justice was seen as synonymous with access to a lawyer and a court, today the legal and justice services are increasingly understood to encompass a continuum including access to legal information, advice, and representation, access to judicial and non-judicial proceedings, as well as access to alternative mechanisms, access to premises that provide possibilities for a fair resolution of a dispute, access to pre- and post-resolution support, and so on.' See 'Understanding Effective Access to Justice' (OECD and Open Society 2016) 14.

117 Deborah L Rhode, 'Access to Justice: An Agenda for Legal Education and Research' (2013) Journal of Legal Education 531, 532.

sphere for a long time now. In the 1970s, access to justice received particular attention in the work of Cappelletti and Garth.[118] According to these authors, the words 'access to justice' serve to focus on two basic purposes of the 'legal system'.[119] Access to justice means that the legal system must be 'equally accessible to all' and lead to results that are 'individually and socially just'.[120] Their basic premise is that 'social justice, as sought by our modern societies, *presupposes* effective access'.[121] The effectiveness of justice is undermined when litigants must overcome barriers resulting not only from procedural rules but also from the social realities and practicalities shaping the legal system, such as litigation costs, party capability (including financial resources and competence to recognize and pursue a claim or defence), and the existence of diffuse interests.[122] Cappelletti and Garth observe that 'the obstacles created by our legal systems are most pronounced for small claims and for isolated individuals, especially the poor; at the same time, the advantages belong to the "haves", especially to organizational litigants adept at using the legal system to advance their own interests'.[123] However, any reform to improve effective access to justice must take into account that barriers to access, as a result of their interrelationship, cannot simply be eliminated one by one.[124]

Access to justice is a central aspect of the rule of law and, as a result, the procedural and substantive aspects of access to justice take on a different meaning. Ghai and Cottrell argue that a critical feature of the rule of law is the equality of all before the law and, as a result, that all persons are entitled to the protection of their rights by State organs concerned with the enforcement of law, particularly the judiciary.[125] Nonetheless, in such a context, there is a narrow and broad meaning of the concept of access to justice. The narrow approach focuses on the courts and other institutions administering justice, and with the process whereby a person presents a case for adjudication.

118 Cappelletti and Garth, 'Access to Justice'.

119 Cappelletti and Garth have defined the legal system as 'the system by which people may vindicate their rights and/or resolve their disputes under the general auspices of the State.' Ibid, 182.

120 Ibid.

121 Ibid, emphasis in original.

122 Cappelletti and Garth have provided that diffuse interests 'are collective or fragmented interests such as those in clean air or consumer protection. The basic problem they present – the reason for their diffuseness – is that either no one has a right to remedy the infringement of a collective interest or the stake of any one individual in remedying the infringement is too small to induce him or her to seek enforcement action'. Ibid, 194.

123 Ibid, 195.

124 Ibid, 196.

125 Yash Ghai and Jill Cottrell, 'The Rule of Law and Access to Justice' in Yash Ghai and Jill Cottrell (eds), *Marginalized Communities and Access to Justice* (Routledge 2010) 3.

The broader approach, however, addresses the process of lawmaking, the contents of the law, the legitimacy of the courts, alternative modes of legal representation, and dispute settlement.[126] Ghai and Cottrell also suggest that access to justice means more than being able to raise one's case in a court or other judicial institution:

> Justice is defined as fairness; in the legal and political sphere; it usually means 'exercise of authority in maintenance of rights'. Fairness covers both the procedures of access and the substantive rules that determine the exercise of authority. Access to justice therefore means the ability to approach and influence decisions of those organs which exercise the authority of the State to make laws and to adjudicate on rights and obligations.[127]

Therefore, as a broad concept, access to justice goes beyond the processes of getting to the courts. It can be understood as covering 'the entire machinery of law making, law interpretation and application, and law enforcement'. It also covers 'the ways in which the law and its machinery are mobilized, and by whom or on whose behalf'.[128]

The way we understand the nature of access to justice may need to be extended for disadvantaged and marginalized groups in order to respond to the specific needs of these groups. Discussing access to justice by people with disabilities, Flynn adopts a definition 'which goes beyond the formal legal system and questions of "access" to this, to a more holistic understanding of what justice means for people with disabilities'.[129] To fully understand the various barriers experienced by people with disabilities in accessing justice, Flynn sets an intersectional frame for analysis in which she notably considers the work of Bahdi – who defines access to justice as comprising three distinct but interlinking components, namely substantive, procedural, and symbolic — with reference to the lived experience of people with disabilities.[130]

First, *substantive access to justice* 'concerns itself with an assessment of the rights claims that are available to those who seek a remedy'.[131] It focuses on

---

126 Ibid.

127 Ibid.

128 Ibid.

129 Eilionóir Flynn, *Disabled Justice? Access to Justice and the UN Convention on the Rights of Persons with Disabilities* (Routledge 2015) 11.

130 Bahdi developed that definition of access to justice in the context of women's access to justice in the Middle East and North Africa Region. See Reem Bahdi, 'Background Paper on Women's Access to Justice in the MENA Region' (31 October 2007).

131 Flynn, *Disabled Justice?*, 13.

the content of the legal rules and principles which shape the decisions made about those who make a 'justice' claim. Flynn argues that substantive access to justice 'extends beyond individual tribunal or court rulings into the realms of constitutional and statutory law reform processes and demands the adoption of laws promoting substantive equality which are sensitive to social context'.[132] The substantive element of access to justice requires the development of laws and policies that promote substantive equality. However, this cannot be achieved without the involvement of the disadvantaged group. Flynn notes that the negotiation of the Convention on the Rights of Persons with Disabilities (CRPD) is often acknowledged to be the most inclusive human rights treaty-drafting process with an overwhelming number of CSO participants. One result is that this 'involvement can be directly linked to the innovative articulation of equality of opportunity which appears in the CRPD'.[133]

Second, *procedural access to justice* 'is closer to the traditional, or narrow, interpretation of "access to justice" as the process by which claims are adjudicated, generally in legal or administrative systems'. However, a wider approach to the procedural component of access to justice should include 'the type of institutions where one might bring a claim, the rules that govern the complaint and conduct of the parties once the complaint is brought within a particular institution, the particular mandate of a given institution and the factors – outside of the substantive law itself – which influence the nature and quality of the encounter for [individuals] within a particular legal institution'. In order to achieve procedural justice, one should examine the opportunities and barriers to getting one's claim into court or another dispute resolution forum.[134]

Third, *symbolic access to justice* steps outside doctrinal law and asks to what extent a particular legal regime promotes citizens' belonging and empowerment. This requires a society in which individuals from marginalized communities are fully included and empowered to participate as equal citizens, thanks in part to that society's laws and justice system. Symbolic access to justice is closely linked to the 'precursor access to justice question', meaning 'the extent to which law can be harnessed to achieve progressive social change'.[135] Flynn argues that a participatory component of access to justice should be added to this definition, which reflects the importance of participation of disabled people in all aspects of the life of their communities.[136]

132 Ibid.
133 Ibid, 14.
134 Ibid, 15.
135 Ibid, 17.
136 Ibid.

Access to justice or to remedy?

When unpacking the concept of access to justice, the question of the relationship between access to *justice* and access to *remedy* arises. Is access to remedy comparable to access to justice? While both concepts are intertwined, access to remedy does not imply access to justice. From a lexical perspective, the words *remedy* and *justice* have different meanings. While the Oxford Dictionary defines *remedy* as 'a means of legal reparation',[137] it defines *justice* as 'just behaviour or treatment' or 'the quality of being fair and reasonable'.[138] While access to remedy entails obtaining 'reparation' or compensation for the loss suffered, access to justice appears to have a broader meaning than access to remedy, as it presupposes obtaining just or fair and reasonable treatment.

The distinction between access to remedy and access to justice is particularly relevant in the BHR context; both terms can be found in the BHR literature. However, there is no clear conceptual distinction between the two terms. The UNGPs, which have shaped the debate about BHR over the last decade, focus solely on access to remedy. They do not mention access to justice once. The UNGPs state that access to effective remedy has both procedural and substantive aspects. In particular, 'the remedies provided by the grievance mechanisms … may take a range of substantive forms the aim of which, generally speaking, will be to counteract or make good any human rights harms that have occurred'.[139] The UN Working Group on the issue of human rights and transnational corporations and other business enterprises (UNWG) has clarified the difference between access to remedy and access to justice.[140] The concept of access to effective remedies is derived from, and dependent on, the right to an effective remedy. However, simply providing access to remedial mechanisms will not suffice. At the end of the process, there should be an effective remedy in practice. This is why access to an effective remedy as having both procedural and substantive aspects is recognized in the UNGPs.[141] Access to justice, on the other hand, is a more elastic concept than the notions of the right to an effective remedy and access to an effective remedy. The UNWG explains:

> In a narrow sense, access to justice can be equated with the right of access to effective judicial remedies, and in this sense effective remedies should often result in justice being provided to rights

137 OUP, 'Remedy' (*Lexico* 2021) <https://www.lexico.com/definition/remedy> accessed 1 May 2021.

138 OUP, 'Justice' (*Lexico* 2021) <https://www.lexico.com/definition/justice> accessed 1 May 2021.

139 UNGPs, Commentary, 25.

140 UNWG, 'Report of the Working Group on the issue of human rights and transnational corporations and other business enterprises' (18 July 2017) UN Doc A/72/162, para 16.

141 Ibid, paras 14–15.

holders. Nevertheless, access to justice can also be used in a broader sense to deal with larger issues of injustice that may not be addressed through individualized remedies offered for a given set of human rights abuses, but would require more fundamental changes in social, political or economic structures.[142]

As a result, the meaning of access to justice varies depending on whether it is understood from an individual perspective (where it can be equated with access to remedy) or a societal perspective (where it requires more than access to remedy to benefit others and society as a whole). Both meanings, however, produce different expectations and outcomes, which may lead to tension. This tension has been visible in the context of out-of-court settlements between plaintiffs and MNEs, as will be seen later in this book.

Effective access to justice

Even when there is access to justice, one can question whether this is effective. What does effectiveness mean in the context of access to justice? According to the Oxford Dictionary, *effectiveness* means 'the degree to which something is successful in producing a desired result' or success.[143] Therefore, based on the aforementioned understandings of access to justice, 'effective access to justice' can mean several things. From a procedural perspective, it means the successful opportunity to bring a legal complaint to the legal system, meaning the courts or other bodies with the authority to adjudicate, in order to solve a dispute. However, from a substantive perspective, it means the successful opportunity to see one's claim be treated in a fair manner or lead to just outcomes. Although interrelated, both visions of 'effective access to justice' differ.

The question of what effectiveness means in relation to access to justice has gained renewed interest over recent years.[144] Looking at civil legal services, Albiston and Sandefur claim that an explicit theory of 'effectiveness' is still lacking.[145] Nonetheless, the current socio-legal literature offers a broad base for conceptualizing effectiveness on the individual, institutional, and societal levels. Based on this literature, Albiston and Sandefur suggest defining effectiveness more broadly in order to shift the 'focus from individualistic measures limited to legal remedies to consider how legal problems affect the well-being of

142 Ibid, para 16.

143 OUP, 'Effectiveness' (*Lexico* 2021) <https://www.lexico.com/definition/effectiveness> accessed 1 May 2021.

144 See Catherine Albiston and Rebecca Sandefur, 'Expanding the Empirical Study of Access to Justice' (2013) Wisconsin Law Review 101, 111–114; OECD and Open Society, 'Understanding Effective Access to Justice'.

145 Albiston and Sandefur, 'Expanding the Empirical Study of Access to Justice', 111–114.

claimants, their families, and society in multiple, interconnected ways'.[146] They explain the need for such a theoretical move based on several arguments that resonate with the approach taken in this book. First, when looking at legal representation, effectiveness encompasses more than case outcomes, so any definition of effectiveness should therefore consider the broader, systemic effects of representation on individuals and those around them. Second, not all outcomes relevant to effectiveness are material; some operate at the level of social meaning, such as empowerment (or disempowerment) of individuals who claim their legal rights. Third, effective legal representation may help clients overcome subjective barriers to accessing legal rights that address, for instance, poverty and inequality. Importantly, legal representation may provide important benefits beyond an individual case. It can improve perceptions of fairness.

Access to justice and corporate accountability

The aforementioned conversations about the meaning of access to justice are relevant and, at times, resonate with ongoing debates on access to justice and corporate accountability in the context of transnational litigation against MNEs.

Transnational litigation against MNEs raises access to justice issues of both a *procedural* and *substantive* nature. Complainants have faced various procedural barriers when seeking to hold MNEs to account and obtain remedy for the harm they have suffered. One of these obstacles has been the victims' difficulty in accessing a court that will hear their claim, especially when legal doctrines such as *forum non conveniens* apply.[147] The inability for victims to bring group claims has also been a major hurdle. On a substantive level, existing international and domestic liability regimes have failed to take into account the reality of corporate groups' impacts on humans and the environment. In transnational claims against MNEs, current standards of corporate liability make it almost impossible for plaintiffs to hold the parent company of an MNE liable for the harm occurring in the context of its group activities.[148]

Transnational litigation against MNEs also raises access to justice issues of a *symbolic* nature. Plaintiffs, lawyers, and NGOs have challenged not only the perceived impunity of businesses towards human rights and the environment in the context of foreign investment, but also international, regional, and

---

146 Ibid, 113.

147 For an analysis of the impact of the application of the *forum non conveniens* doctrine on business-related victims, see Daysheelyn Anne P Brillo, 'The Global Pursuit for Justice for DBCP-Exposed Banana Farmers' in Karen Erica Bravo, Jena Martin and Tara Van Ho (eds), *When Business Harms Human Rights: Affected Communities that Are Dying to Be Heard* (Anthem Press 2020).

148 For a discussion of the implications of separate legal personality and limited liability for litigation against MNEs, see Muchlinski, 'Limited Liability and Multinational Enterprises'.

national lawmaking processes, the contents of corporate liability regimes, and the role of national and regional courts in protecting the interests of the most vulnerable. As such, transnational litigation against MNEs questions the extent to which the legal system can lead to fair and just outcomes regarding corporate accountability. Moreover, it has shed light on the inability of legal and justice systems to include, take into account the specific needs of, and empower victims of harm caused by MNEs, especially when they are poor and from developing countries. More broadly, this reflects the exclusion of citizens from economic, legal, and political decisions in both host and home States.

Ultimately, transnational litigation against MNEs is a search for justice for both the direct victims of corporate abuse and society at large. It aims to restore the balance between the interests of corporations and those of the most exposed elements in society by influencing policy-makers and courts.

6 Structure of the book

This book is divided into nine chapters grouped under three parts.

Part I aims to describe the legal and social backdrop against which demands for access to justice and corporate accountability have emerged in home countries, especially in Europe. **Chapter 1**, which is the present chapter, introduced the setting, aim, scope, key concepts, and background of this book. **Chapter 2** discusses how international and European legal systems regulate the activities of business actors and guarantee access to justice, and presents existing normative gaps. **Chapter 3** provides a historical, legal, and social account of the general development of transnational litigation against MNEs. It describes the main characteristics of the various cases brought in common law and European civil law jurisdictions. Finally, Chapter 3 sheds light on the relationship between social movements and transnational litigation against MNEs.

Part II aims to understand whether transnational litigation against MNEs in European home countries of civil law tradition has been an effective strategy to achieve justice for victims of business-related harm abroad. **Chapter 4** and **Chapter 5** compare the relevant legal and procedural aspects of civil and criminal litigation in France and the Netherlands respectively. They use case law to illustrate the opportunities and barriers faced by plaintiffs while seeking to hold corporations accountable, and highlight similarities and differences in the legal strategies used by plaintiffs. **Chapter 6** deals with the study of civil and criminal corporate liability regimes in the context of MNEs in France and the Netherlands.

Part III offers a comprehensive analysis of the most recent regulatory responses towards achieving access to justice in the field of BHR at international, European, and national levels. **Chapter 7** discusses the development of mandatory HRDD legislation at national and European levels, and its potential impacts on access to justice. **Chapter 8** then examines the current negotiations on a potential legally binding instrument on BHR, as well as the potential options and impacts on access to justice. Finally, **Chapter 9** evaluates the achievements of transnational litigation against MNEs in Europe and discusses the potential future of access to justice in the context of BHR.

Chapter 2

Corporate accountability and access to justice in international and European legal frameworks

1 Introduction

By nature, MNEs operate across borders of sovereign States. Therefore, an internationally coordinated approach appears to be an appropriate way to provide an effective normative framework for regulating MNE activity and offering redress in situations of corporate human rights abuse and environmental damage.[1] However, until now the international community has been unable to establish an effective international legal framework for holding MNEs accountable. While MNEs have benefited from increased protection under investment and trade law in recent decades, this has not been matched by a necessary counterbalance in legal responsibility for the harm MNEs may cause in the course of their global operations. Furthermore, despite the various frameworks on access to justice and remedy under international law, victims of abuse involving MNEs may frequently find themselves with limited or no recourse to proceedings to secure redress for the harm they have suffered. Under international human rights law, access to justice is important for the injured individual whose human rights have been violated. In particular, the availability of effective judicial remedies under both international and national law is critical to guarantee the respect and the protection of human rights.[2] Similarly, in order for international and national regimes of environmental law to be effectively protective, victims of environmental damage and NGOs must be able to bring a claim before a court and have access to various remedies, such as damages and restoration. However, the adoption and implementation of the UN Framework[3] and the UNGPs[4] have attempted to close the gaps.

---

1   Halina Ward, 'Securing Transnational Corporate Accountability through National Courts: Implications and Policy Options' (2001) 24 Hastings International and Comparative Law Review 451, 470.

2   Francesco Francioni, 'The Right of Access to Justice under Customary International Law' in Francesco Francioni (ed), *Access to Justice as a Human Right* (OUP 2007) 1.

3   UNHRC, 'Protect, Respect and Remedy: A Framework for Business and Human Rights' (7 April 2008) UN Doc A/HRC/8/5 (UN Framework).

4   UNHRC, 'Guiding Principles on Business and Human Rights: Implementing the United Nations "Protect, Respect and Remedy" Framework' (21 March 2011) UN Doc A/HRC/17/31 (UNGPs).

2 The corporate accountability gap

To date, a number of international instruments have been designed to address the human rights and environmental impacts of MNEs. However, voluntary and soft law instruments, such as the UN Global Compact and the OECD Guidelines, have been the favoured form of international regulation.[5] Although a few international treaties require States to hold corporate actors liable for a limited number of crimes,[6] no international instruments have imposed human rights or environmental obligations on corporations in general. This is due, in part, to the lack of consensus on the international legal personality of corporate actors and whether MNEs have rights and obligations under international law.[7]

The international legal personality of non-State actors

Under international law, 'entities only owe responsibilities to the international community when they are considered to be subjects of law, in other words, the bearers of international legal personality'.[8] As such, the question of whether individual persons equate to 'subjects of international law' is an important one.

According to a basic definition, a subject of international law is an entity capable of possessing international rights and duties.[9] A more elaborate definition would describe a subject of international law as 'an entity possessing international rights and obligations and having the capacity (a) to maintain its rights by bringing international claims; and (b) to be responsible for its breaches of obligation by being subjected to such claims'.[10] One peculiarity

---

5   UN Global Compact <https://www.unglobalcompact.org/about> accessed 1 May 2021; *OECD Guidelines for Multinational Enterprises: 2011 Edition* (OECD 2011).

6   Convention on Combating Bribery of Foreign Public Officials in International Business Transactions (adopted 21 November 2007, entered into force 15 February 1999). Article 2 on the responsibility of legal persons provides that each Party must take measures to establish the liability of legal persons for the bribery of a foreign public official.

7   See Jennifer Zerk, *Multinationals and Corporate Social Responsibility: Limitations and Opportunities in International Law* (CUP 2006); Larry Backer, 'Multinational Corporations as Objects and Sources of Transnational Regulation' (2008) 14 ILSA Journal of International and Comparative Law 499; Alexandra Gatto, *Multinational Enterprises and Human Rights. Obligations under EU Law and International Law* (Edward Elgar 2011).

8   Nicola Jägers, 'The Legal Status of the Multinational Corporation under International Law' in Michael Addo (ed), *Human Rights Standards and the Responsibility of Transnational Corporations* (Kluwer Law International 1999) 261.

9   Christian Walter notes that '[t]he terms international legal personality and international legal capacity describe the same characteristic, namely the fact that an entity is capable of possessing international rights and/or duties'. See Christian Walter, 'Subjects of International Law', MPEPIL (2007), para 21 <http://opil.ouplaw.com/> accessed 1 May 2021.

10   James Crawford, *Brownlie's Principles of Public International Law* (8th edn, OUP 2012) 115.

of international legal personality is that '[it] not only denotes the quality of having rights and duties as well as certain capacities under the law, but ... it also includes the *competence to create the law*'.[11] However, the existing literature disagrees on the various aspects of international legal personality, such as the modalities to acquire it or the precise consequences attached to it.[12]

Traditionally, States are considered to be the main subjects of international law.[13] However, international courts have progressively accepted that other actors could be subjects of international law and, therefore, have international rights and obligations. In 1949, the International Court of Justice (ICJ) accepted that the UN had the capacity to bring an international claim, thus recognizing that actors other than States could possess international legal personality.[14] Nonetheless, the ICJ was cautious to specify that 'the subjects of law in any legal system are not necessarily identical in their nature or in the extent of their rights, and their nature depends upon the needs of the community'.[15] Following World War II, the Nuremberg International Military Tribunal also accepted that 'international law imposes duties and liabilities upon individuals as upon States'.[16] The subsequent development of international criminal law and international human rights law has led to the acceptance that 'the individual today has acquired a legally relevant position in international law. It has internationally been granted rights and is made subject to obligations.'[17] Furthermore, international humanitarian law places duties on rebel groups to respect certain human rights of persons under their control.[18]

Since the period after 1945, scholars and lawyers have debated the question whether MNEs may be subjects of international law.[19] Under the State-centric

11   Roland Portmann, *Legal Personality in International Law* (CUP 2010) 8 (emphasis in original).

12   Jäger, 'The Legal Status of the Multinational Corporation under International Law' 262; Portmann, *Legal Personality in International Law*, 7–12.

13   Walter, 'Subjects of International Law', para 2.

14   *Reparation for Injuries Suffered in the Service of the United Nations* (Advisory Opinion) [1949] ICJ Rep 174 [184]–[185].

15   Ibid, [178].

16   *Judgement of the Nuremberg International Military Tribunal 1946* (1947) 41 AJIL 172, 220.

17   Walter, 'Subjects of International Law', para 18.

18   Steven Ratner, 'Corporations and Human Rights: A Theory of Legal Responsibility' (2001) 111 Yale Law Journal 443, 466.

19   Walter, 'Subjects of International Law', para 19. On the subject, see Arghyrios Fatouros, 'Problèmes et méthodes d'une réglementation des entreprises multinationales' (1974) 101 Journal du Droit International 495; Theo Vogelaar, 'Asser Institute Lectures on International Law: Multinational Corporations and International Law' (1980) 27 Netherlands International Law Review 69; Dimitra Kokkini-Iatridou and Paul JIM de Waart, 'Foreign Investment in Developing Countries: Legal Personality of Multinationals in International Law' (1983) 14 Netherlands Yearbook of International Law 87; Robin Hansen, 'The International Legal Personality of Multinational Enterprises: Treaty, Custom and the Governance Gap' (2010) 10 Global Jurist.

paradigm of public international law, MNEs are not considered to be subjects of international law. As such, they have no rights or obligations, or only some limited ones. Each member of an MNE has legal personality only under the jurisdiction of the country in which it has its statutory seat.[20] However, the intensification of MNE activities, as a result of the liberalization of international trade and the multiplication of foreign direct investments, has shaped new legal interactions at the international level. For example, under foreign investment law, MNEs have been granted significant rights in international investment agreements in order to protect foreign investments against interference by the host State.[21] Furthermore, international arbitration tribunals and scholars have occasionally accepted that MNEs could be subjects of international law when they enter into investment agreements with States.[22] This is the case when such agreements contain specific arbitration clauses to avoid litigation before the domestic courts of the contracting State in order to create a situation of equality between the contracting parties.[23] Such a view may lead to MNEs acquiring at least 'partial' or 'qualified' international legal personality.[24] At the same time, such contractual clauses do not change the nature of the contractual relationship or the legal capacity of the contracting parties.[25]

Ultimately, the intensification of MNE activities and the transnational nature of such business activities challenge the idea that MNEs cannot have rights and obligations under public international law. Furthermore, the State-centric paradigm of public international law appears inadequate, or limited in its ability, to regulate MNEs' activities or deal with the intricate interactions between MNEs, States, and human rights and the environment.[26]

Scholars, lawyers, and NGOs have criticized the classical approach of public international law regarding MNEs. They have suggested that MNEs benefit from their international non-status, which 'immunizes them from direct

20 Vogelaar, 'Multinational Corporations and International Law', 76.

21 Luzius Wildhaber, 'Asser Institute Lectures on International Law: Some Aspects of the Transnational Corporation in International Law' (1980) 27 Netherlands International Law Review 79, 84; David Kinley and Junko Tadaki, 'From Talk to Walk: The Emergence of Human Rights Responsibilities for Corporations at International Law' (2004) 44 Virginia Journal of International Law 931, 946; Peter Muchlinski, *Multinational Enterprises and the Law* (2nd edn, OUP 2007) 577.

22 Irmgard Marboe and August Reinish, 'Contracts between States and Foreign Private Law Persons', MPEPIL (2011), para 14 <http://opil.ouplaw.com/> accessed 1 May 2021; Peter Muchlinski, 'Corporations in International Law', MPEPIL (2014), para 7 <http://opil.ouplaw.com/> accessed 1 May 2021.

23 Marboe and Reinish, 'Contracts between States and Foreign Private Law Persons', para 13.

24 Walter, 'Subjects of International Law', para 20; Muchlinski, 'Corporations in International Law', para 7.

25 Marboe and Reinish, 'Contracts between States and Foreign Private Law Persons', para 15.

26 Kinley and Tadaki, 'From Talk to Walk', 945; Gatto, *Multinational Enterprises and Human Rights*, 9.

accountability to international legal norms and permits them to use sympathetic
national governments to parry outside efforts to mould their behaviour'.[27]
They have also formulated new theories on the rights and obligations of MNEs
under international human rights and environmental law.[28] Such theories aim
to provide solutions that allow groups to be held accountable for their negative
impacts on human rights and the environment.

Corporate accountability in international and European human rights law

To this day, there is no international regime of binding norms governing the
interactions between MNEs and human rights.[29] As a result, corporations do
not have any duties towards human rights under international law. In the past,
there have been several ambitious initiatives to impose some sort of legally
binding obligations on MNEs, such as the UN Norms on the Responsibilities
of Transnational Corporations and Other Business Enterprises with regard to
Human Rights (UN Norms).[30] However, in 2005 the international community
rejected the UN Norms, partly as a result of the absence of international
consensus on the question of binding regulation of corporate accountability.[31]

The UN treaty bodies, which are responsible for monitoring the implementation
of the core international human rights treaties, have touched upon the
question whether private actors have obligations under international human
rights law. However, they have cautiously avoided formulating legally binding

27   Jonathan Charney, 'Transnational Corporations and Developing Public International Law'
[1983] Duke Law Journal 748, 767.

28   Ibid, 753; Kinley and Tadaki, 'From Talk to Walk', 1021; Olivier de Schutter, 'The Challenge
of Imposing Human Rights Norms on Corporate Actors' in Olivier de Schutter (ed), *Transnational
Corporations and Human Rights* (Hart Publishing 2006) 33. Kinley and Tadaki suggest that 'there
is an urgent need to reassess the traditional concepts and structures of international human rights
law, so that the focus is on the *effective protection* of human rights, rather than on the entities from
which human rights have to be protected' (emphasis in original).

29   Kinley and Tadaki, 'From Talk to Walk', 935.

30   UNCHR, 'Norms on the Responsibilities of Transnational Corporations and Other Business
Enterprises with regard to Human Rights' (UN Norms) (26 August 2003) UN Doc E/CN.4/Sub.2/
2003/12/Rev.2.

31   For a discussion of the UN Norms, see David Weissbrodt and Muria Kruger, 'Norms on the
Responsibilities of Transnational Corporations and Other Business Enterprises with Regard to
Human Rights' (2003) 97 The American Journal of International Law 901; Carolin Hillemanns,
'UN Norms on the Responsibilities of Transnational Corporations and Other Business Enterprises
with Regard to Human Rights' (2003) 4 German Law Journal 1065; Larry Backer, 'Multinational
Corporations, Transnational Law: The United Nations' Norms on the Responsibilities of
Transnational Corporations as a Harbinger of Corporate Social Responsibility in International
Law' (2006) 37 Columbia Human Rights Law 287; John Ruggie, 'Business and Human Rights: The
Evolving International Agenda' (2007) 101 The American Journal of International Law 819.

obligations on corporate actors with regard to human rights treaties. The UN Human Rights Committee (UNCCPR)[32] clearly stated that, under Article 2(1) of the International Covenant on Civil and Political Rights (ICCPR),[33] obligations are binding only on States Parties and do not have direct horizontal effect as a matter of international law.[34] Therefore, the ICCPR produces no direct effect for private third parties. Likewise, private actors, such as MNEs, do not have obligations under the ICCPR.[35]

The UN Committee on Economic, Social and Cultural Rights (UNCESCR) has taken a different stance on the question of MNEs' obligations regarding economic, social, and cultural rights. On several occasions, the UNCESCR has faced 'the growing impact of business activities on the enjoyment of specific Covenant rights relating to health, housing, food, water, social security, the right to work, the right to just and favourable conditions of work and the right to form and join trade unions'.[36] In general, it has acknowledged that corporate actors have a non-binding responsibility to respect the rights protected by the ICCPR. For example, the UNCESCR stated that violations of the right to adequate food could occur through the direct action of States or other entities insufficiently regulated by States.[37] In particular, while only States are parties to the International Covenant on Economic, Social and Cultural Rights (ICESCR),[38] and are thus ultimately accountable for compliance, all members of society, including the private business sector, have responsibilities in the realization of the right to adequate food.[39] Specifically, the private business sector, either national or transnational, 'should pursue its activities within the framework of a code of conduct conducive to respect of the right to adequate food, agreed upon jointly with the Government and civil society'.[40] More recently, the UNCESCR affirmed that, 'under international standards, business entities are expected to respect Covenant rights regardless of whether domestic laws exist or are fully enforced in practice'.[41] This position is based on the UN Framework and the UNGPs, which formulate a non-binding corporate responsibility to respect

---

32 In order to avoid any confusion with the UN Human Rights Council, the acronym used throughout this book for the UN Human Rights Committee is UNCCPR.

33 ICCPR (adopted 16 December 1966, entered into force 23 March 1976) 999 UNTS 171.

34 UNCCPR, 'General Comment 31' (26 May 2004) UN Doc CCPR/C/21/Rev.1/Add.13, para 8.

35 Christian Tomuschat, 'International Covenant on Civil and Political Rights (1966)', MPEPIL (2010), para 21 <http://opil.ouplaw.com/> accessed 1 May 2021.

36 UNCESCR, 'General Comment 24' (10 August 2017) UN Doc E/C.12/GC/24, para 2.

37 UNCESCR, 'General Comment 12' (12 May 1999) UN Doc E/C.12/1999/5, para 19.

38 ICESCR (adopted 16 December 1966, entered into force 3 January 1976) 993 UNTS 3.

39 UNCESCR, 'General Comment 12', para 20.

40 Ibid.

41 UNCESCR, 'General Comment 24', para 5.

human rights whose scope is defined by social expectations (or the company's social licence to operate), as will be seen later in this book.

In Europe, private companies cannot be held responsible for human rights violations under the ECHR.[42] This convention covers violations of rights by States and does not impose direct obligations on corporate actors. Since the ECHR does not recognize the principle of direct third-party effect, ECHR rights do not have any horizontal effect.[43] This situation has direct consequences on the ability of victims to bring claims raising violations by business actors before the ECtHR. An individual alleging a violation of their rights by a private company cannot raise their claim before the ECtHR.[44] Any application brought against a company is inadmissible as being incompatible *ratione personae* with the ECHR's provisions.[45] Applications may be brought only against contracting States.[46] So far, the existing case law of the ECtHR in relation to private companies has been limited to cases where such actors invoke their own rights under the ECHR. Besides the lack of a direct approach for holding companies accountable for human rights abuse under the ECHR, the conservatism of the ECtHR is likely to be an obstacle to protecting human rights against private actors in Europe. Khoury suggests that judges of the ECtHR lack the awareness and/or commitment to creatively hold companies accountable for human rights abuse under the ECHR.[47]

The ECtHR has nonetheless recognized that contracting States must take measures to enable the full enjoyment of ECHR rights in private relations.[48] In certain circumstances, a State may be responsible for failing to protect a right, or for tolerating the violation of that right by a private person. The ECtHR has already found that States have failed to protect ECHR rights

---

42   For a discussion of corporations' obligations under European human rights law, see Olivier de Schutter, 'The Accountability of Multinationals for Human Rights Violations in European Law' in Philip Alston (ed), *Non-State Actors and Human Rights* (OUP 2005).

43   CoE (Steering Committee for Human Rights), 'Draft Preliminary Study on Corporate Social Responsibility in the Field of Human Rights: Existing Standards and Outstanding Issues' (4 June 2012) CDDH(2012)012, para 26.

44   Ibid, paras 25–29.

45   Ibid, paras 25–26.

46   Convention for the Protection of Human Rights and Fundamental Freedoms as amended by Protocols 11 and 14 (adopted 4 November 1950, entered into force 3 September 1953), ETS 5 (European Convention on Human Rights), Articles 33 and 34.

47   See Stéphanie Khoury, 'Transnational Corporations and the European Court of Human Rights: Reflections on the Indirect and Direct Approaches to Accountability' (2010) 4 Sortuz Oñati Journal of Emergent Socio-Legal Studies 68.

48   For a discussion of States' positive obligations under the ECHR, see Alastair Mowbray, *The Development of Positive Obligations under the European Convention on Human Rights by the European Court of Human Rights* (Hart Publishing 2004); Richard Kay, 'The European Convention on Human Rights and the Control of Private Law' (2005) 5 European Human Rights Law Review 466.

from harmful business activities.[49] In *López Ostra v Spain*,[50] the ECtHR found that the nuisance and health problems caused by a private waste treatment plant had disproportionately interfered with the applicant's right to privacy and family life. While the Spanish authorities were not directly responsible for the pollution in question, they allowed the plant to be built on public land and subsidized the plant's construction. The ECtHR found that Spain 'did not succeed in striking a fair balance between the interest of the town's economic well-being – that of having a waste-treatment plant – and the applicant's effective enjoyment of her right to respect for her home and her private and family life'.[51]

While States have a positive obligation to ensure the full enjoyment of ECHR rights in private relations, it is unclear whether this obligation has an extraterritorial dimension. Article 1 ECHR provides that the contracting States 'shall secure to everyone within their jurisdiction the rights and freedoms' of the convention. However, States have been held responsible in only a few situations for failing to protect ECHR rights in an extraterritorial context.[52] In most cases, State responsibility was found for extraterritorial violations involving acts or omissions by State organs, not acts by private persons. Thus, it remains unclear whether a State could be held responsible for tolerating or failing to prevent the extraterritorial violation of an ECHR right abroad by a company which is under its jurisdiction.[53] However, scholars have argued that 'the ECHR, as interpreted by the [ECtHR], does not in general provide a basis for State liability for failure to exercise control over the conduct abroad of business enterprises incorporated under states parties' laws or having their headquarters in their territories, even when such conduct leads to human rights abuses'.[54]

Over the past decades, there has been an extensive debate regarding whether corporate actors should have obligations under international human rights law. Scholars, lawyers, and NGOs have widely criticized the absence of human rights obligations on MNEs. For instance, Kinley and Tadaki talk of the 'invisibility' of

49 For cases involving corporate human rights abuse, see *Young, James and Webster v UK* (1981) 4 EHRR 38; *Sibson v UK* (1993) 17 EHRR 193; *Fadeyeva v Russia* (2007) 45 EHRR 10.

50 *López Ostra v Spain* (1995) 20 EHRR 277.

51 Ibid, para 58.

52 *Al-Skeini v UK* (2011) 53 EHRR 18, para 131; *Issa v Turkey* (2004) 41 EHRR 567, paras 68 and 71; *Ilaşcu and v Moldova and Russia* (2005) 40 EHRR 1030, paras 314 and 318.

53 CoE (Steering Committee for Human Rights), 'Feasibility Study on Corporate Social Responsibility in the Field of Human Rights' (30 November 2012) CDDH(2012)R76 Addendum VII, para 33.

54 Claire Methven O'Brien, *Business and Human Rights: A Handbook for Legal Practitioners* (Council of Europe 2019) 63.

MNEs' accountability under international human rights law.[55] This situation is explained by the influence of the State-centric paradigm of public international law on the development of international human rights law. Since MNEs are not usually recognized as traditional subjects of international law, they cannot be direct bearers of legal obligations under international human rights law.[56] Furthermore, human rights were originally devised to protect individuals against the arbitrary exercise of power by the authorities of the territorial State, not non-State actors.[57] However, this traditionalist approach has been challenged by the fact that MNEs can interfere with the enjoyment of human rights as a result of the 'enormous power' they have acquired.[58] At the same time, States have been unable or unwilling to regulate MNEs, while MNEs have used the 'innocent bystander rhetoric' to avoid accountability with regard to human rights abuse.[59]

Some scholars have suggested that to avoid a situation of impunity, MNEs' increase in power should be accompanied by an increase in accountability under international human rights law.[60] It is not necessary for MNEs to possess full international legal personality, such as the one possessed by States, to be subject to human rights obligations.[61] Transplanting notions of State responsibility to businesses would prove too difficult.[62] Instead, MNEs could have 'limited rights and responsibilities, such as the right to sue and be sued, the ability to assert a right, and the acceptance of legal responsibility in judicial forums, but not have the status as a party to intergovernmental forums or international instruments'.[63] This solution would constitute 'a sound base upon which to build a regime of direct human rights responsibilities at international law, but it would also preserve the primacy of States on the international plane'.[64]

55   Kinley and Tadaki, 'From Talk to Walk', 937.

56   See Sarah Joseph, *Corporations and Transnational Human Rights Litigation* (Hart Publishing 2004) 9; Zerk, *Multinationals and Corporate Social Responsibility*, 104; Peter Muchlinski, 'Multinational Enterprises as Actors in International Law: Creating "Soft law" Obligations and "Hard Law" Rights' in Math Noortmann and Cedric Ryngaert, *Non-State Actor Dynamics in International Law: From Law-Takers to Law-Makers* (Ashgate 2010) 11.

57   Kinley and Tadaki, 'From Talk to Walk', 937.

58   Andrew Clapham, *Human Rights in the Private Sphere* (Oxford University Press 1996) 137; Ratner, 'Corporations and Human Rights', 462–465.

59   Jena Martin Amerson, 'What's in a Name? Transnational Corporations as Bystanders under International Law' (2011) 85 St John's Law Review 1.

60   Weissbrodt and Kruger, 'Norms on the Responsibilities of Transnational Corporations, 901–922; Kinley and Tadaki, 'From Talk to Walk' 933.

61   Kinley and Tadaki, 'From Talk to Walk' 945.

62   Ratner, 'Corporations and Human Rights', 496–523.

63   Kinley and Tadaki, 'From Talk to Walk', 946.

64   Ibid.

Furthermore, corporate actors should not carry the same responsibilities as States, as some of these are simply impossible for companies to carry out.[65]

Where there is agreement that MNEs can have duties under international human rights law, opinions diverge on the scope of obligations MNEs should be subject to. In particular, authors have various views on the normative nature (ie binding/non-binding), the type (ie respect, protect, fulfil), and the range (ie all human rights or a limited number) of human rights obligations MNEs should be subject to.

First, there are various views on the normative nature of human rights standards that could apply to MNEs. Three types of approaches are generally relevant here: (1) legally binding human rights norms imposed directly on corporate actors; (2) voluntary standards adopted through soft law instruments and private regulation initiatives; and (3) a mix of mandatory and voluntary standards. To date, most international human rights norms directly applicable to MNEs have been formulated in soft law and private regulation instruments. For some observers, soft law and private regulation have filled a normative gap when governments were unable or unwilling to assume their duty to protect human rights.[66] Furthermore, the adoption of soft law and private standards is more politically and technically feasible.[67] As a result, soft law and private instruments would have a normative impact on MNEs by calling them to respect certain conduct vis-à-vis human rights.[68]

One major obstacle with soft law and private norms is that they are generally legally unenforceable, which limits, in practice, corporate compliance and the possibility for victims of corporate harm to access remedy. However, there is an emerging debate as to whether soft law norms may produce some legal effects.[69] For instance, Blecher argues that codes of conduct are not remaining voluntary or unenforceable, and are moving into legally binding, legally enforceable terrain.[70] Regarding the adoption of legally binding human rights norms on MNEs, proponents argue that such norms are more likely to produce corporate compliance as they are legally enforceable. Furthermore, some authors postulate that the international legal framework on human rights already provides the basis for 'drawing out strong legally-binding obligations

---

65   Muchlinski, 'Corporations in International Law', para 34.

66   Justin Nolan, 'Refining the Rules of the Game: The Corporate Responsibility to Respect Human Rights' (2014) 30 Utrecht Journal of International and European Law 7, 8–12.

67   Vogelaar, 'Multinational Corporations and International Law', 76.

68   Kinley and Tadaki, 'From Talk to Walk', 958.

69   Halina Ward, *Legal Issues in Corporate Citizenship* (IIED 2003) 5.

70   Lara Blecher, 'Code of Conduct: The Trojan Horse of International Human Rights Law' (2016) 38 Comparative Labor Law and Policy Journal 437.

for corporations'.[71] For instance, the Universal Declaration of Human Rights (UDHR)[72] has often been quoted as 'a potential legal source of corporate human rights responsibilities'.[73] However, there is disagreement on the question of whether an international instrument could impose mandatory obligations on corporate actors.[74]

Second, the debate focuses on the extent of MNEs' responsibility under international human rights law, as well as the type of human rights obligations that MNEs should bear (ie obligations to respect, protect, and fulfil). This question demonstrates at least the perception of competition between imposing obligations on either State or non-State actors under international human rights law. In general, experts agree that MNE responsibility should not exclude State responsibility. Furthermore, it is frequently held that MNEs should not simply have the same human rights obligations as States because such an approach would 'ignore the differences between the nature and functions of States and corporations'.[75] Corporate obligations under international human rights law should therefore be modelled in the light of the characteristics of corporate activity.[76] However, there is disagreement as to the types of human rights obligation that MNEs should bear. While some authors argue that MNEs should have only an obligation to respect human rights,[77] others suggest that in certain circumstances corporate groups should also have an obligation to protect, even to fulfil, human rights.[78] For example, a company should ensure that its business partners do not abuse human rights in their own activities. Previous normative efforts to impose human rights obligations on MNEs considered the possibility that MNEs may bear other types of obligation. For instance, the UN Norms provided that, within their respective spheres of activity and influence, MNEs had the obligation 'to promote, secure the fulfilment of, respect, ensure respect of and protect human rights recognized in international as well as

71   David Bilchitz, 'A Chasm between "Is" and "Ought"? A Critique of the Normative Foundations of the SRSG's Framework and the Guiding Principles' in Surya Deva and David Bilchitz, *Human Rights Obligations of Business: Beyond the Corporate Responsibility to Respect?* (CUP 2013) 136.

72   UDHR (adopted 10 December 1948) UNGA Res 217 A(III).

73   Kinley and Tadaki, 'From Talk to Walk', 948.

74   This question is discussed in detail in Chapter 8, which examines the current negotiations on a potentially legally binding instrument on business and human rights.

75   Kinley and Tadaki, 'From Talk to Walk', 961. See also Daniel Aguirre, 'Corporate Liability for Economic, Social and Cultural Rights Revisited: The Failure of International Cooperation' (2011) 42 California Western International Law Journal 123.

76   Ratner, 'Corporations and Human Rights', 496–523.

77   This is the view adopted in the UNGPs.

78   Kinley and Tadaki, 'From Talk to Walk', 962–966; David Bilchitz, 'The Ruggie Framework: An Adequate Rubric for Corporate Human Rights Obligations?' (2010) 12 SUR – International Journal on Human Rights 199, 207.

national law'.[79] However, this view was rejected during the elaboration of the UN Framework, partly because of the difficulties associated with the concepts of spheres of activity and influence.[80]

Third, there are various views on the question of whether the entire body of human rights law should apply directly to MNEs, and to corporations more generally. One approach accepts that MNEs should have specific international obligations only with regard to gross human rights abuses, such as the crime of genocide or crimes against humanity.[81] In theory, international criminal law seems to admit that MNEs must refrain from participating in the commission of genocide.[82] Other authors differentiate between human rights that corporations can directly infringe, and human rights that only States can directly violate. Ratner argues that the duties of the corporation with regard to the latter can only be complicity-based, and that links between the corporation and the State are a necessary factor for the derivation of corporate duties.[83]

Corporate accountability in international environmental law

While MNEs contribute considerably to worldwide stress on the environment, their transnational nature poses a significant challenge to global environmental governance.[84] International environmental law is said to focus on the 'transboundary *effects* on health and the environment, and transboundary *fluxes* of harmful substances'.[85] However, it appears unable to apprehend and govern harm arising from MNE transnational activities.[86] Furthermore, it fails to

---

79   UN Norms, para 1.

80   Ruggie, 'Business and Human Rights', 825–826.

81   This is the approach suggested by the Office of the High Commissioner for Human Rights (OHCHR). See Jennifer Zerk, *Corporate Liability for Gross Human Rights Abuses: Towards a Fairer and More Effective System of Domestic Law Remedies* (Report prepared for the OHCHR, 2014).

82   Michael Kelly, 'Prosecuting Corporations for Genocide under International Law' (2012) 6 Harvard Law & Policy Review 339. Kelly suggests that international law does not prevent the prosecution of corporations for complicity in genocide *per se*. However, to date, corporate involvement in genocide has been dealt with through individual criminal liability for corporate officers or civil liability for the corporate entity.

83   Ratner, 'Corporations and Human Rights', 489–496.

84   André Nollkaemper, 'Responsibility of Transnational Corporations in International Environmental Law: Three Perspectives' in Gerd Winter (ed), *Multilevel Governance of Global Environmental Change: Perspectives from Science, Sociology and the Law* (CUP 2006) 180.

85   Jonas Ebbesson, 'Transboundary Corporate Responsibility in Environmental Matters: Fragments and Foundations for a Future Framework' in Gerd Winter (ed), *Multilevel Governance of Global Environmental Change: Perspectives from Science, Sociology and the Law* (CUP 2006) 201 (emphasis in original).

86   Sara Seck, 'Transnational Business and Environmental Harm: A TWAIL Analysis of Home State Obligations' (2011) 3 Trade, Law and Development 164, 173–174.

acknowledge MNEs' abuse of their 'transboundary subjectivity and structure' to escape environmental liability.[87] As a result, international environmental law offers little assistance in solving environmental challenges created by the activities of MNEs.[88]

Generally, multilateral environmental agreements (MEAs) lack a comprehensive approach to the regulation of corporate actors.[89] They mainly create State obligations and, as a result, do not directly bind companies. Provisions imposing obligations on corporate actors are usually indirect, as their implementation rests primarily on States and national courts.[90] Furthermore, other constraints, such as the restricted territorial or substantive scope of MEAs, the lack of ratification by some States, or the failure of many MEAs to enter into force, limit the ability of these agreements to impose obligations on corporate actors.[91]

Nevertheless, MEAs have the potential to influence corporate environmental behaviour in various ways.[92] First, a number of MEAs create civil liability regimes in which corporate actors, where they qualify as operators in the context of specified activities, may be held liable for environmental pollution.[93] This is the case for a number of harmful activities, such as dumping of waste at sea, transboundary shipment of hazardous wastes, oil pollution at sea, hunting and trading in endangered species, and the use of various hazardous and ozone-depleting substances.[94] Second, some MEAs require the adoption of criminal penalties to regulate certain business conduct,[95] such as the Convention on

---

87   Ebbesson, 'Transboundary Corporate Responsibility', 201.

88   Elisa Morgera, *Corporate Accountability in International Environmental Law* (OUP 2009) 39.

89   Ebbesson, 'Transboundary Corporate Responsibility', 202. See also Morgera, *Corporate Accountability in International Environmental Law*.

90   Muchlinski, 'Corporations in International Law', para 42. Some authors argue that, as a result, MNEs have 'indirect responsibility under national law and direct responsibility under international law': Nollkaemper, 'Responsibility of Transnational Corporations in International Environmental Law', 188; Stavros-Evdokimos Pantazopoulos, 'Towards a Coherent Framework of Transnational Corporations' Responsibility in International Environmental Law' (2014) 24 Yearbook of International Environmental Law 131, 147–148.

91   Pantazopoulos, 'Towards a Coherent Framework of Transnational Corporations' Responsibility in International Environmental Law', 164.

92   Linda Siegele and Halina Ward, 'Corporate Social Responsibility: A Step Towards Stronger Involvement of Business in MEA Implementation?' (2007) 16 RECIEL 135, 136.

93   Nollkaemper, 'Responsibility of Transnational Corporations in International Environmental Law', 188; Pantazopoulos, 'Towards a Coherent Framework of Transnational Corporations' Responsibility in International Environmental Law', 144–148.

94   Ebbesson, 'Transboundary Corporate Responsibility', 207.

95   Patricia Birnie, Alan Boyle and Catherine Redgwell, *International Law and the Environment* (3rd edn, OUP 2009) 330.

the Protection of the Environment through Criminal Law of the CoE.[96] Other MEAs explicitly create other types of State obligations regarding corporate actors. For example, Article 10(e) of the Convention on Biological Diversity[97] requires each State to 'encourage cooperation between its governmental authorities and its private sector in developing methods for sustainable use of biological resources'. Third, some MEAs contain provisions that may directly and indirectly affect free trade rules, or conflict with the measures contained in agreements concluded under the World Trade Organization.[98] Fourth, international environmental law has seen the development of general concepts and principles (eg the precautionary and the polluter pays principles, environmental impact assessment, transparency, etc), and policies which are directly relevant to the regulation of corporate actors.[99] However, MEAs ultimately offer only a fragmented and indirect response to the regulation of corporations and their impact on the environment.

In parallel, self-regulation of corporate actors through soft law instruments has gained in importance in international environmental law over the last decades. Some scholars argue that such an approach has contributed to the emergence of a number of standards on corporate conduct which are now rooted in international environmental law. The soft law nature of these instruments and the participation of companies in these processes have generally facilitated the development of such standards.[100] Although these standards are non-binding, they constitute criteria against which business activities may be measured with respect to environmental protection.[101] In addition, the participation of corporate actors in international environmental standard-setting processes may increase the chances that companies will follow environmentally sound behaviour.[102] Some authors argue that these environmental standards are now converging to a considerable extent and may be directly applicable to MNEs.[103] Furthermore, when developed in the context of international

96   Convention on the Protection of the Environment through Criminal Law (adopted 4 November 1998) CETS No 172. However, this instrument has not yet come into force as a result of a lack of ratifications.

97   Convention on Biological Diversity (adopted 5 June 1992, entered into force 29 December 1993) 1760 UNTS 79.

98   Siegele and Ward, 'Corporate Social Responsibility', 141.

99   Ebbesson, 'Transboundary Corporate Responsibility', 208.

100 Pantazopoulos, 'Towards a Coherent Framework of Transnational Corporations' Responsibility in International Environmental Law', 148.

101 Ibid, 160.

102 Ibid, 155.

103 Morgera, *Corporate Accountability in International Environmental Law*, 172; Jorge Viñuales, *Foreign Investment and the Environment in International Law* (CUP 2012) 60; Pantazopoulos, 'Towards a Coherent Framework of Transnational Corporations' Responsibility in International Environmental Law', 148.

initiatives, the levels to which corporate actors respect these standards may be monitored by international mechanisms, which 'contribute to the establishment of a coherent corporate responsibility framework'.[104] For some authors, international environmental law has found innovative and pragmatic normative ways to address environmental challenges arising from corporate behaviour.[105] However, it is also unclear whether self-regulation through soft law instruments is an effective way to prevent the occurrence of environmental damage by companies. Looking at oil spill prevention, Frynas found that there was a lack of clear evidence demonstrating causality between CSR and oil spill reduction. At the same time, causality between mandatory government regulation and oil spill reduction was much more clearly established.[106] Furthermore, self-regulation of corporate actors through soft law instruments does not create any obligations on corporations to conform to the voluntary norm or provide victims with a remedy.

3 Legal frameworks on access to justice

According to Francioni, '[i]n international law, as in any domestic legal system, respect and protection of human rights can be guaranteed only by the availability of effective judicial remedies. When a right is violated, access to justice is of fundamental importance for the injured individual and it is an essential component of the system of protection and enforcement of human rights.'[107] This section evaluates how various international and European legal frameworks consider and guarantee access to justice in the context of human rights abuse and environmental damage caused by corporations.

Access to justice in international law

In the context of this book, the question whether international law protects an individual right of access to justice is relevant. In customary international law, there is currently no right of access to justice in international proceedings.[108] Nonetheless, a number of international instruments in the human rights and environmental fields guarantee access to justice in the context of domestic law. They recognize that States are under an obligation to make available a system of

---

104 Pantazopoulos, 'Towards a Coherent Framework of Transnational Corporations' Responsibility in International Environmental Law', 161.

105 Ibid, 165.

106 Jedrzej Frynas, 'Corporate Social Responsibility or Government Regulation? Evidence on Oil Spill Prevention' (2012) 17 Ecology and Society 4.

107 Francioni, 'The Right of Access to Justice under Customary International Law', 1.

108 Ibid, 41.

effective remedies to all persons subject to their jurisdiction.[109] Furthermore, a number of human rights instruments, such as the ECHR, have established their own review mechanism to which individuals have direct access.[110] However, the recognition of this type of mechanism and the provision of remedies rely on their ratification by States and the provision of suitable legal and procedural systems that ensure access to remedies.

Access to justice in international human rights law

The main international human rights instruments do not generally protect a right of access to justice per se.[111] An exception is the CRPD, which explicitly recognizes that States shall ensure effective access to justice for persons with disabilities on an equal basis with others.[112] Nonetheless, the core international human rights instruments generally recognize the right to an effective remedy by courts for acts violating human rights and/or the protection of procedural rights and guarantees to ensure the conduct of a fair trial in criminal and civil matters.

A number of international human rights instruments protect the right to an effective remedy by a competent national court or authority for acts violating the human rights they enshrine.[113] Article 8 UDHR provides that '[e]veryone has the right to an effective remedy by the competent national tribunals for acts violating the fundamental rights granted him by the constitution or by law'. Moreover, Article 2(3)(a) ICCPR provides that each State Party undertakes to

109 Ibid.

110 Ibid, 20.

111 International human rights instruments use different expressions in different provisions, such as effective remedy, the right to a fair and public hearing, etc. Francioni suggests that 'it is not always clear whether reference is made to the right to bring a claim before a competent court, or rather to the right to have a measure or remedy provided in connection with an injury suffered by the claimant'. Notably, he asks 'whether in the context of human rights law access to justice is a self-standing individual right or, rather, a procedural guarantee that exists only to the extent that there is a substantive right to enforce': ibid, 24–30.

112 Convention on the Rights of Persons with Disabilities (CRPD) (adopted 13 December 2006, entered into force 3 May 2008) 2515 UNTS 3, Article 13.

113 UDHR, Article 8; ICCPR, Article 2(3); International Convention on the Elimination of All Forms of Racial Discrimination (ICERD) (adopted 7 March 1966, entered into force 4 January 1969) 660 UNTS 195, Article 6; Convention against Torture and Other Cruel, Inhuman or Degrading Treatment or Punishment (CAT) (adopted 10 December 1984, entered into force 26 June 1987) 1465 UNTS 85, Article 14; International Convention on the Protection of the Rights of All Migrant Workers and Members of their Families (ICMW) (adopted 18 December 1990, entered into force 1 July 2003) 2220 UNTS 3, Article 83; International Convention for the Protection of All Persons from Enforced Disappearance (CPED) (adopted 20 December 2006, entered into force 23 December 2010) 2716 UNTS 3, Article 8(2); Optional Protocol to the Convention on the Rights of the Child on the sale of children, child prostitution and child pornography OP-CRC-SC) (adopted 25 May 2000, entered into force 18 January 2002) 2171 UNTS 227, Article 9(4)(.

ensure that any person whose rights or freedoms recognized by the ICCPR are violated must have an effective remedy. Similarly, the International Convention on the Protection of the Rights of All Migrant Workers and Members of their Families (ICMW) and the International Convention for the Protection of All Persons from Enforced Disappearance (CPED) oblige States to ensure that any person enjoying rights protected by those conventions have an effective remedy if their rights are violated. The ICCPR and the ICMW go further by specifying that States must 'ensure that the competent authorities shall enforce such remedies when granted'.[114] Under the International Convention on the Elimination of All Forms of Racial Discrimination (ICERD), victims of racial discrimination have 'the right to seek from such tribunals just and adequate reparation or satisfaction for any damage suffered as a result of such discrimination'.[115]

One exception is the ICESCR, which remains silent on the provision of remedy in the context of economic, social, and cultural rights violations. Given that MNEs have been found on many occasions to interfere with economic and social rights,[116] this lack of recognition could limit the protective opportunities of the ICESCR in the context of business-related human rights abuse. In its General Comment No. 9, the UNCESCR acknowledged that, contrary to the ICCPR, the Covenant does not obligate 'States parties to, inter alia, develop the possibilities of judicial remedy'.[117] Nevertheless, a State party seeking to justify its failure to provide any domestic legal remedies for violations of economic, social, and cultural rights would need to show either that such remedies are not 'appropriate means' within the terms of Article 2(1) ICESCR or that, in view of other means used, they are unnecessary. As the UNCESCR pointed out, it would be difficult to show this and, in many cases, the other 'means' used could be rendered ineffective if they are not reinforced or complemented by judicial remedies.[118]

The texts of international human rights instruments show that access to justice is not perceived as a self-standing individual right. According to Francioni, it 'is rather construed as a procedural guarantee dependant [sic] on other substantive rights and freedoms, which are protected by the same treaty and sometimes by renvoi to the constitution and the law of state parties'.[119] Furthermore, 'the

---

114 ICCPR, Article 2(3)(c); ICMW, Article 83(c).

115 Article 6.

116 See for instance UNCESCR, 'General Comment 24'; Aguirre, 'Corporate Liability for Economic, Social and Cultural Rights Revisited'; Jernej Letnar Černič, *Corporate Accountability under Socio-Economic Rights* (Routledge 2018).

117 UNCESCR, 'General Comment 9' (3 December 1998) UN Doc E/C.12/1998/24, para 3.

118 Ibid.

119 Francioni, 'The Right of Access to Justice under Customary International Law', 32.

distinction between the cause of action, which must necessarily derive from the substantive legal interest invoked by the claimant, and the right of access to justice often becomes blurred.'[120]

In general, there is no indication that the acts violating the protected rights should have been committed by the State alone in order to trigger the application of the right to an effective remedy. For instance, the ICCPR provides for an effective remedy 'notwithstanding that the violation has been committed by persons acting in an official capacity'. Therefore, victims of human rights violations committed by non-State actors, such as businesses, are, in theory, entitled to an effective remedy. According to the UNCESCR, victims may be able to sue the business either directly on the basis of the human rights instrument in jurisdictions which consider that the instrument imposes self-executing obligations on private actors, or on the basis of domestic legislation incorporating the instrument in the national legal order.[121]

Recently, the UNCESCR addressed the question of the State obligation to provide remedies in the context of business-related human rights abuse. It clearly provided that 'State parties must provide means of redress to aggrieved individuals or groups and ensure corporate accountability', and this should preferably take the form of ensuring access to independent and impartial judicial bodies.[122] In addition, States have the duty to take the necessary steps to address the specific obstacles that victims of transnational corporate abuse face in accessing effective remedies in order to prevent a denial of justice and to ensure the right to effective remedy and reparation.[123]

International human rights law also provides that court proceedings in criminal and civil matters must respect a number of procedural guarantees in order to ensure a fair trial. Article 14(1) ICCPR provides that, in the determination of any criminal charge against them, or of their rights and obligations in a suit at law, everyone is entitled to a fair and public hearing by a competent, independent, and impartial tribunal established by law. Among the core international human rights instruments, there is generally a strong emphasis on the protection of procedural guarantees and the rights of the defence in criminal proceedings, including the presumption of innocence,[124] the principle of the legality of criminal offences and penalties,[125] the right to remain silent and not incriminate

---

120 Ibid.

121 UNCESCR, 'General Comment 24', para 51.

122 Ibid, para 39.

123 Ibid, paras 43 and 44.

124 UDHR, Article 11(1); ICCPR, Article 14(2); Convention on the Rights of the Child (CRC) (adopted 20 November 1989, entered into force 2 September 1990) 1577 UNTS 3, Article 40(2)(b) (i); ICMW, Article 18(2).

125 UDHR, Article 11(2); ICCPR, Article 15; CRC, Article 40(2)(a); ICMW, Article 18(7).

oneself,[126] and the right to appeal,[127] to name a few. Some of these instruments also refer, albeit to a lesser extent, to procedural guarantees in the context of civil proceedings.[128]

Equality before courts and tribunals is a common feature of international human rights instruments. Article 14(1) ICCPR states explicitly that all persons shall be equal before courts and tribunals. Similarly, Article 5(a) ICERD provides that States must guarantee the right of everyone to equality before the law, notably the enjoyment of the right to equal treatment before the tribunals and all other organs administering justice. In addition, some instruments call for equality for specific groups of individuals. For instance, Article 15(1) of the Convention on the Elimination of all Forms of Discrimination Against Women (CEDAW) provides that States shall accord to women equality with men before the law. Article 13(1) CRPD also requires States to ensure effective access to justice for persons with disabilities on an equal basis with others. The CRPD is innovative in this regard, as it requires States to provide procedural and age-appropriate accommodations, 'in order to facilitate their effective role as direct and indirect participants, including as witnesses, in all legal proceedings, including at investigative and other preliminary stages'. The right to equality before courts and tribunals is therefore a key element of human rights protection and serves as a procedural means to safeguard the rule of law.[129] It usually imposes a positive obligation on States to provide equal access to courts and procedural rights in their legal systems.[130]

Another important feature of the right to equality before courts and tribunals, which is relevant in the context of human rights litigation against MNEs, is equality of arms. According to the UNCCPR, this means that the same procedural rights must be provided to all the parties, unless distinctions are based on law and can be justified on objective and reasonable grounds.[131] In the context of civil proceedings, the principle of equality between parties demands, inter alia, that each side be given the opportunity to contest all the arguments and evidence adduced by the other party.[132]

Next to the core international human rights instruments, the Basic Principles and Guidelines on the Right to a Remedy and Reparation for Victims of Gross Violations of International Human Rights Law and Serious Violations of

---

126 ICCPR, Article 14(3)(g); CRC, Article 40(2)(b)(iv); ICMW, Article 18(3)(g).

127 ICCPR, Article 14(5); CRC, Article 40(2)(b)(v); ICMW, Article 18(5).

128 UDHR, Article 10; ICCPR, Article 14(1); ICMW, Article 18(1); CRPD, Article 13(1).

129 UNCCPR, 'General Comment 32' (23 August 2007) UN Doc CCPR/C/GC/32, para 2.

130 Ilias Bantekas and Lutz Oette, *International Human Rights Law and Practice* (CUP 2013) 348.

131 UNCCPR, 'General Comment 32', para 13.

132 Ibid.

International Humanitarian Law (Basic Principles on Remedy),[133] adopted by the UN General Assembly in 2005, articulate, in one document, the rights of victims to have access to justice and the right to reparation for their injuries. Under their obligation to respect, ensure respect for and implement international human rights and international humanitarian law, States must take appropriate measures to prevent violations; investigate violations effectively, promptly, and impartially and, where appropriate, take action against those allegedly responsible; provide victims with equal and effective access to justice irrespective of who may ultimately be the bearer of responsibility for the violation; and provide victims with effective remedies, including reparation. The victims' right to remedies include equal and effective access to justice; adequate, effective, and prompt reparation for harm suffered; and access to relevant information concerning violations and reparation mechanisms. Ultimately, the Basic Principles on Remedy provide valuable guidance for framing access to justice in the context of corporate human rights abuse.

Access to justice in international environmental law

Access to justice has gained momentum in the field of international environmental law with the proclamation of the 1992 Rio Declaration on Environment and Development (Rio Declaration). Principle 10 Rio Declaration specifically provides that:

> Environmental issues are best handled with the participation of all concerned citizens, at the relevant level. At the national level, each individual shall have appropriate access to information concerning the environment that is held by public authorities, including information on hazardous materials and activities in their communities, and the opportunity to participate in decision-making processes. States shall facilitate and encourage public awareness and participation by making information widely available. Effective access to judicial and administrative proceedings, including redress and remedy, shall be provided.

In the Rio Declaration, access to justice is therefore perceived as being closely related to access to information and public participation in environmental governance.[134]

---

133 UNGA, Res 60/147 (2006) UN Doc A/Res/60/147.

134 Jonas Ebbesson, 'Access to Justice in Environmental Matters', MPEPIL (2009) <http:// opil.ouplaw.com/> accessed 1 May 2021, para 5.

In 1998, the UNECE adopted the Aarhus Convention,[135] which advances the notions reflected in Principle 10 Rio Declaration.[136] The Aarhus Convention generally aims to guarantee the rights of access to information, public participation in decision-making, and access to justice in environmental matters in order to protect the right to live in an environment adequate to human health and well-being. It has been hailed as a 'reflection of the procedural dimension to the intersection between environmental and human rights'.[137] It should be noted that despite the fact it is a regional instrument, this convention is seen as having global significance.[138]

The Aarhus Convention sees access to justice as a procedural right in the domestic context. Its provisions provide standards and criteria on access to justice to be implemented by the States Parties in their domestic jurisdiction, and which are to be made applicable for members of the public. Article 9 Aarhus Convention is the most relevant provision regarding access to justice in environmental matters. It provides access to justice in two main situations. First, Article 9(1) and (2) ensures access to justice in the context of requests for environmental information and public participation in environmental decision-making, thus strengthening the two other rights protected by the Aarhus Convention. Second, Article 9(3) guarantees access to justice for general breaches of environmental law in both horizontal and vertical relationships. Accordingly, each State Party 'shall ensure that, where they meet the criteria, if any, laid down in its national law, members of the public have access to administrative or judicial procedures to challenge acts and omissions by private persons and public authorities which contravene provisions of its national law relating to the environment'. In addition, Articles 9(4) and 9(5) set out requirements applicable to all the procedures under Articles 9(1) to 9(3). For instance, administrative and judicial procedures must provide adequate and effective remedies, including injunctive relief, and must be fair, equitable, timely, and not prohibitively expensive.[139] State officials and authorities must also consider the establishment of appropriate assistance mechanisms to remove or reduce financial and other barriers to access to justice.[140] Finally, they must provide guidance to the public in seeking access to justice in

---

135 Aarhus Convention (adopted 25 June 1998, entered into force 30 October 2001) 2161 UNTS 447.

136 Ebbesson, 'Access to Justice in Environmental Matters', para 5.

137 Catherine Redgwell, 'Access to Environmental Justice' in Francesco Francioni (ed), *Access to Justice as a Human Right* (OUP 2007) 153.

138 Morgera, *Corporate Accountability in International Environmental Law*, 189.

139 Aarhus Convention, Article 9(4).

140 Ibid, Article 9(5).

environmental matters,[141] most notably by informing the public of available administrative and judicial review procedures.[142]

In the context of this book, it is relevant to question whether the Aarhus Convention, and its Article 9(3) in particular, could be an appropriate instrument to guarantee access to justice when corporate actors cause environmental damage, especially in a transnational context. At first glance, the scope of Article 9(3) Aarhus Convention makes it a suitable instrument for various reasons. First, this provision targets breaches of the law committed by private persons, which include corporate actors. Second, it applies to all acts and omissions contravening national law relating to the environment in a broad sense.[143] Third, its scope is not limited to environmental law per se, and the Aarhus Convention Compliance Committee (Aarhus Committee) has interpreted the term 'relating to the environment' in an expansive manner.[144] Finally, the term 'members of the public' is interpreted broadly enough to encompass both individuals and NGOs. Furthermore, the Aarhus Convention guarantees that the public have access to justice in environmental matters 'without discrimination as to citizenship, nationality or domicile and, in the case of a legal person, without discrimination as to where it has its registered seat or an effective centre of its activities'.[145]

At the same time, the relevance of Article 9(3) to access to justice for business-related environmental damage occurring extraterritorially is likely to be limited for two main reasons. First of all, access to justice must be ensured to members of the public 'where they meet the criteria, if any laid down in [States'] national law'. Therefore, States Parties have a wide discretion in defining the meaning of standing, in other words who can initiate legal proceedings. Conditions of standing have been a recurrent issue over the years, especially for environmental NGOs.[146] Restrictive conditions on standing may limit their ability to seek remedies for acts and omissions harmful to public environmental interests. The Aarhus Committee has repeatedly held that States Parties can decide that members of the public must meet some criteria to challenge a decision, such as being affected by it or having an interest in it.[147] However, they should not introduce or maintain overly strict criteria that effectively bar members of

---

141 Ibid, Article 3(2).

142 Ibid, Article 9(5).

143 Ebbesson, 'Access to Justice in Environmental Matters', para 22.

144 Anaïs Berthier and others, 'Access to Justice in European Union Law: A Legal Guide on Access to Justice in Environmental Matters' (ClientEarth 2019), 32.

145 Aarhus Convention, Article 3(9).

146 For an overview of the legal standing of environmental NGOs, see Elena Fasoli, 'Legal Standing of NGOs in Environmental Disputes in Europe' in Nerina Boschiero and others (eds), *International Courts and the Development of International Law* (Springer 2013).

147 ACCC/C/2005/11 (Belgium), ECE/MP.PP/C.1/2006/4/Add.2, para 36.

the public, environmental NGOs in particular, from having access to effective remedies.[148] Second, it is unlikely that Article 9(3) would be applicable to claims raising the extraterritorial breach of a State's national law relating to the environment. Article 9(3) specifically refers to breaches of the law of the State where the proceedings are taking place. On their face, claims raising breaches of international environmental standards or of the national environmental law of third States would seem to be outside the scope of Article 9(3). However, in past transnational environmental claims against MNEs, plaintiffs have usually raised the violation of international environmental standards and/or of the domestic environmental law of host States.

Article 9(3) could nonetheless be relevant to claims raising violations of environmental laws presenting an element of extraterritoriality, such as national law applying MEAs that provide extraterritorial reach or solving transnational issues (for example, the Basel Convention on the Control of Transboundary Movements of Hazardous Wastes and their Disposal).[149] Ultimately, it is necessary to clarify the meaning of 'national law relating to the environment' to understand which legal breaches by business actors in an extraterritorial context could fall under the scope of Article 9(3).

To date, litigators have not relied on or invoked the Aarhus Convention, or national implementing legislation, in the context of transnational claims against MNEs concerning environmental damage. There is also little research on the interplay between this convention and access to justice when businesses cause environmental pollution. It is unclear why the Aarhus Convention has not been considered in this regard. The public interest nature of this convention seems appropriate in the context of strategic litigation seeking to hold businesses accountable for their impacts on the environment. One suggestion is that the Aarhus Convention is perceived as a tool to challenge, first and foremost, public authorities' own violations of environmental legislation in the context of administrative procedures. This perception may limit the potential of this convention to challenge, in the context of judicial procedures, acts and omissions by private actors, such as companies, that are detrimental to the environment. Another possible reason is the above-mentioned lack of certainty regarding the territorial meaning of 'national law relating to the environment'. Finally, the absence of EU provisions implementing the private dimension of Article 9(3) may also explain the lack of interest in the role of this convention. The Aarhus Convention is widely ratified in Europe – including by all EU Member States – and the EU itself has approved it. The EU has adopted

---

148 Ibid, para 37. See also ACCC/C/2006/18 (Denmark), ECE/MP.PP/2008/5/Add.4 paras 29–30; ACCC/C/2010/48 (Austria), ECE/MP.PP/C.1/2012/4 paras 68–70.

149 Basel Convention on the Control of Transboundary Movements of Hazardous Wastes and their Disposal (adopted 22 March 1989, entered into force 5 May 1992) 1673 UNTS 57.

two directives to harmonize its Member States' laws with regard to access to environmental information and public participation.[150] These directives contain provisions on access to justice that allow members of the public to have access to review procedures when their request for information is ignored or refused, or to challenge decisions regarding public participation. However, they do not implement Article 9(3) Aarhus Convention as such. Furthermore, the EU has adopted Regulation 1367/2006 (Aarhus Regulation), which requires EU institutions and bodies to implement the obligations contained in the Aarhus Convention.[151] The Aarhus Regulation implements Article 9(3) by granting access to justice in environmental matters at Community level. However, it addresses only acts and omissions by public authorities.

The influence of the Aarhus Convention on transnational claims against MNEs should, nonetheless, not be underestimated. Until now, this convention has exerted an important influence on the development of national environmental law and practice in European countries, making it a major asset for gaining access to justice in Europe.[152] Recently, in the European Green Deal Communication,[153] the European Commission (EC) committed to revise, or to consider the revision of, EU instruments pertaining to the Aarhus Convention in order to improve access to justice at both EU and national levels for citizens and NGOs. If such a revision were to take place and effectively strengthened the procedural rights of members of the public in the context of Article 9(3), it could potentially enhance the ability of victims and NGOs to gain access to justice when companies damage the environment in the future.

Access to justice in European law

In Europe, the CoE and the EU have adopted a number of standards on ensuring effective access to justice which are directly relevant in the context of transnational litigation against MNEs.

---

150 Directive 2003/4/EC of the European Parliament and of the Council of 28 January 2003 on public access to environmental information and repealing Council Directive 90/313/EEC [2003] OJ L41/26; Directive 2003/35/EC of the European Parliament and of the Council of 26 May 2003 providing for public participation in respect of the drawing up of certain plans and programmes relating to the environment and amending with regard to public participation and access to justice Council Directives 85/337/EEC and 96/61/EC [2003] OJ L156/17.

151 Regulation (EC) No 1367/2006 of the European Parliament and of the Council of 6 September 2006 on the application of the provisions of the Aarhus Convention on Access to Information, Public Participation in Decision-making and Access to Justice in Environmental Matters to Community institutions and bodies [2006] OJ L264/13.

152 Birnie, Boyle and Redgwell, 294. See also Myanna F Dellinger, 'Ten Years of the Aarhus Convention: How Procedural Democracy Is Paving the Way for Substantive Change in National and International Environmental Law' (2012) 23 Colorado Journal of International Environmental Law & Policy 309.

153 European Commission, 'The European Green Deal' (Communication) COM(2019) 640 final.

Access to justice under the European Convention on Human Rights

The ECHR does not protect a right to access to justice per se. However, it protects the right to a fair trial (Article 6) and the right to an effective remedy (Article 13).

Article 6 ECHR protects the right to a fair trial in both civil and criminal proceedings. Article 6(1) provides that, '[i]n the determination of his civil rights and obligations or of any criminal charge against him, everyone is entitled to a fair and public hearing within a reasonable time by an independent and impartial tribunal established by law'. In general, judgments should be pronounced publicly. Article 6(2) and (3) also require contracting States to respect a number of procedural guarantees in the context of criminal proceedings, such as the presumption of innocence and the rights to be informed promptly of the accusation and to receive legal assistance.

The ECtHR has developed a rich body of case law in relation to Article 6 ECHR, which has helped to strengthen access to justice in contracting States over the years. In relation to civil proceedings, the ECtHR held that the right of access to a court[154] was an inherent aspect of the safeguards enshrined in Article 6,[155] and that it must be 'practical and effective'.[156] If States Parties are not obliged to provide free legal aid in all civil disputes, they should nonetheless provide for the assistance of a lawyer when such assistance proves indispensable for effective access to a court.[157] Furthermore, the ECtHR has ruled that the right to a fair trial requires that litigants should have an effective judicial remedy enabling them to assert their civil rights.[158] It has also ruled on the principle of equality of arms, which, as will be seen later in Chapter 4 of this book, has been a source of tension in the context of transnational litigation against MNEs. Equality of arms, in the sense of a fair balance between the parties, is inherent to the right to a fair trial and the adversarial principle, and applies to both civil and criminal cases.[159] It implies that each party must be afforded a reasonable opportunity to present their case, including evidence, under conditions that do not place that party at a substantial disadvantage compared to the other party.[160] Failure to observe the equality of arms principle was found when the

---

154 *Golder v UK* (1975) Series A no 18, paras 28–36.

155 *Zubac v Croatia* App no 40160/12 (ECtHR, 5 April 2018), para 76.

156 *Bellet v France* (1995) 29 EHRR 591, para 38; *Zubac v Croatia*, paras 76–79.

157 *Airey v Ireland* (1980) 2 EHRR 305, para § 26.

158 *Běleš v Czech Republic* App no 47273/99 (ECtHR, 12 November 2002), para 49; *Naït-Liman v Switzerland* App no 51357/07 (ECtHR, 15 March 2018), para 112.

159 *Regner v Czech Republic* App no 35289/11 (ECtHR, 19 September 2017), para 146; *Feldbrugge v Netherlands* (1986) 8 EHRR 425, para 44.

160 *Regner v Czech Republic*, para 146; *Dombo Beheer BV v Netherlands* (1994) 18 EHRR 213, para 33.

opposing party enjoyed significant advantages regarding access to relevant information and occupied a dominant position in the proceedings,[161] or when the denial of legal aid deprived the parties of the opportunity to present their case effectively before the court in the face of a far wealthier opponent (in this case, an MNE).[162] In relation to criminal proceedings, the ECtHR has held that Article 6(1) applies to civil-party complaints in criminal proceedings, meaning when an individual, often the victim of a criminal offence, is allowed to join the criminal proceedings as a civil party.[163] It applies from the moment the individual joins as a civil party, including during the preliminary investigation stage.[164] Article 6(1)'s applicability does not depend on the recognition of the formal status of a 'party' in domestic law.[165] However, the ECHR does not confer any right, as such, to have third parties prosecuted or sentenced for a criminal offence.[166]

Article 13 ECHR also protects the right to an effective remedy. Everyone whose rights under the ECHR are violated must have an effective remedy before a national authority notwithstanding that the violation has been committed by persons acting in an official capacity. In general, States Parties have a positive obligation to secure this right to everyone within their jurisdiction. The interpretation of Article 13 ECHR has, however, been complex, since the right guaranteed by this provision is not a freestanding right. It only arises for consideration if the applicant raises a complaint involving another substantive right under the ECHR.[167] Nevertheless, the ECtHR has clarified on many occasions that Article 13 guarantees the availability of a remedy at national level to enforce the substance of rights and freedoms under the ECHR in whatever form they may happen to be secured in the domestic legal order.[168] Article 13 requires that States provide a domestic remedy to deal with the substance of an 'arguable complaint'[169] under the ECHR and grant appropriate relief. However, Article 13 does not require any particular form of remedy and States have a margin of discretion in how to comply with this obligation. Nonetheless, the remedy 'must be "effective" in practice as well as in law',[170] the

---

161 *Yvon v France* (2005) 40 EHRR 41, para 37.

162 *Steel and Morris v UK* (2005) 41 EHRR 22, para 72.

163 *Tomasi v France* (1992) Series A no 24-1A; *Perez v France* (2005) 40 EHRR 39, paras 66–71.

164 *Tănase v Romania* App no 41720/13 (ECtHR, 25 June 2019), para 207.

165 *Arnoldi v Italy* App no 35637/04 (ECtHR, 7 December 2017), para 29.

166 *Tunç v Turkey* App no 24014/05 (ECtHR, 25 June 2019), para 218.

167 For a discussion of Article 13 ECHR, see Annabel Lee, 'Focus on Article 13 ECHR' (2015) 20 Judicial Review 33.

168 *Aksoy v Turkey* (1996) 23 EHRR 553, para 95; *Kudla v Poland* (2002) 35 EHRR 198, para 157.

169 *Çakıcı v Turkey* (2001) 31 EHRR 5, para 112.

170 *İlhan v Turkey* (2002) 34 EHRR 36, para 97.

term 'effective' meaning that the remedy must be adequate and accessible.[171] The effectiveness of a remedy does not, however, depend on the certainty of a favourable outcome for the applicant.[172]

Access to justice in the European Union

Despite the lack of clarity around access to justice as a concept in EU law,[173] some observers have pointed out the 'constitutionalization'[174] of access to justice in the EU over the past years.

Until recently, the EU had little competence in the justice field. However, progressive changes in EU primary law have strengthened the role and the powers of the EU institutions to legislate in civil and criminal justice.[175] Pursuant to Article 4(2)(j) of the Treaty on the Functioning of the European Union (TFEU),[176] the EU and its Member States share competence in the areas of freedom, security, and justice. Article 67(1) TFEU specifies that the EU shall constitute an area of freedom, security, and justice with respect for fundamental rights and the different legal systems and traditions of the Member States. Furthermore, Article 67(4) imposes a general requirement on the EU to facilitate access to justice, in particular through the principle of mutual recognition of judicial and extrajudicial decisions in civil matters.

The TFEU contains provisions pertaining to access to justice in the context of its chapters describing the EU competences on 'judicial cooperation' in civil and criminal matters. In civil matters, the EU is competent to develop judicial cooperation with cross-border implications, based on the principle of mutual recognition of judgments and decisions in extrajudicial cases.[177] It must adopt measures which aim to ensure various aspects of such cooperation, including the compatibility of the rules applicable in the Member States concerning conflict of laws and of jurisdiction, effective access to justice, or the elimination of obstacles to the proper functioning of civil proceedings.[178] The EU should adopt these measures particularly when necessary for the proper functioning of the internal market. In criminal matters, judicial cooperation must be based

---

171 *Paulino Tomás v Portugal* App no 58698/00 (ECtHR, 27 March 2003).

172 *Kudla v Poland*, para 157.

173 Elvira Méndez Pinedo, 'Access to Justice as Hope in the Dark: In Search for A New Concept in European Law' (2011) 1 International Journal of Humanities and Social Sciences 9, 9.

174 For a discussion of 'constitutionalization', see Martin Loughlin, 'What Is Constitutionalisation?' in Petra Dobner and Martin Loughlin (eds), *The Twilight of Constitutionalism?* (OUP 2010).

175 Pinedo, 'Access to Justice as Hope in the Dark', 18.

176 Consolidated Version of the Treaty on the Functioning of the European Union [2012] OJ C326/47.

177 TFEU, Article 81(1).

178 Ibid, Article 81(2).

on the principle of mutual recognition of judgments and judicial decisions.[179] The TFEU recognizes that the EU has different types of competences in criminal matters. Of relevance here is the EU competence to establish minimum rules, by means of directives, concerning the rights of victims of crime.[180] The EU can also establish minimum rules concerning 'the definition of criminal offences and sanctions in the areas of particularly serious crime with a cross-border dimension resulting from the nature or impact of such offences or from a special need to combat them on a common basis'.[181] These areas of crime include terrorism, trafficking in human beings and sexual exploitation of women and children, illicit drug trafficking, illicit arms trafficking, money laundering, corruption, counterfeiting of means of payment, computer crime, and organized crime. Other areas of crime may potentially be identified. The EU has already used its new powers to improve specific rights related to access to justice. For instance, it enacted Directive 2012/29/EU (Victims' Rights Directive),[182] which establishes minimum standards on the rights, support, and protection of victims of crime.

Furthermore, the Treaty of Lisbon[183] gave the EU Charter[184] the same legal binding force as EU treaties.[185] As a result, the EU Charter is primary EU law. Therefore, it 'is not a text setting out abstract values, it is an instrument to enable people to enjoy the rights enshrined within it when they are in a situation governed by Union law'.[186] However, the provisions of the EU Charter are addressed to the EU institutions, bodies, offices, and agencies without restriction, and to Member States only when they are implementing EU law.[187] For instance, this covers situations where Member States implement EU regulations and directives.[188]

---

179 Ibid, Article 82(1).

180 Ibid, Article 82(2)(c).

181 Ibid, Article 83(3).

182 Directive 2012/29/EU of the European Parliament and of the Council of 25 October 2012 establishing minimum standards on the rights, support and protection of victims of crime, and replacing Council Framework Decision 2001/220/JHA [2012] OJ L315/57.

183 Treaty of Lisbon Amending the Treaty on European Union and the Treaty Establishing the European Community [2007] OJ C306/1.

184 EU Charter [2012] OJ C326/392.

185 For a discussion of the new status of the EU Charter, see Koen Lenaerts, 'Exploring the Limits of the EU Charter of Fundamental Rights' (2012) 8 European Constitutional Law Review 375.

186 European Commission, 'Strategy for the Effective Implementation of the Charter of Fundamental Rights by the European Union' (Communication) COM(2010) 573 final, 3.

187 EU Charter, Article 51.

188 C-617/10 Åklagaren v Fransson [2013] CMLR 36, paras 17–21.

Article 47 of the EU Charter provides for the right to an effective remedy and to a fair trial, echoing Articles 6 and 13 ECHR.[189] Article 47 provides that everyone whose rights and freedoms guaranteed by EU law are violated has the right to an effective remedy before a tribunal. In addition, everyone is entitled to a fair and public hearing within a reasonable time by an independent and impartial tribunal previously established by law. Article 47 also provides for the right to legal advice and representation, and to legal aid when it is necessary to ensure effective access to justice. Given the status of the EU Charter, the rights protected under Article 47 have become primary law that the EU and its Member States must respect when implementing EU law. Therefore, Article 47 could play a decisive role in improving the effectiveness of rights granted under European law.[190] In this regard, the Court of Justice of the EU (CJEU) plays an increasing role in protecting the rights and guarantees enshrined in Article 47 and, therefore, in promoting effective access to justice in the EU.[191] The CJEU has already guaranteed effective judicial protection and access to legal aid on the grounds of Article 47.[192] However, much uncertainty remains regarding the direct horizontal effect of the EU Charter and its exact scope of applicability in EU Member States.[193] Furthermore, restrictive standing requirements before the CJEU for natural and legal persons limit the role of the court in protecting effective access to justice in the EU.[194]

189 Nonetheless, the scope of application of Article 47 is broader. See Chantal Mak, 'Rights and Remedies – Article 47 EUCFR and Effective Judicial Protection in European Private Law Matters' (2012) Amsterdam Law School Research No 2012-88, 4 <http://ssrn.com/abstract=2126551> accessed 1 May 2021.

190 Ibid. For a discussion of the effects of the EU Charter on the domestic plane, see Richard Layton and Cian Murphy, 'The Emergence of the EU Charter of Fundamental Rights in United Kingdom Law' [2014] European Human Rights Law Review 469.

191 Derrick Wyatt and others, *European Union Law* (5th edn, Hart Publishing 2006) 310. Article 47 is one of the EU Charter's provisions that have generated the most considerable amount of litigation in the CJEU. See Sara Iglesias Sánchez, 'The Court and the Charter: The Impact of the Entry into Force of the Lisbon Treaty on ECJ's Approach to Fundamental Rights' (2012) 49 Common Market Law Review 1565, 1572.

192 Case C-279/09 *DEB Deutsche Energiehandels- und Beratungsgesellschaft mbH v Bundesrepublik Deutschland* [2010] ECR I-13849. See also Sánchez, 'The Court and the Charter', 1579.

193 European Commission, 'Strategy for the Effective Implementation of the Charter of Fundamental Rights by the European Union', 3. See also Eleni Frantziou, 'The Horizontal Effect of the Charter of Fundamental Rights of the EU: Rediscovering the Reasons for Horizontality' (2015) 21 European Law Journal 657; Thomas von Danwitz and Katherina Paraschas, 'A Fresh Start for the Charter: Fundamental Questions on the Application of the European Charter of Fundamental Rights' (2017) 35 Fordham International Law Journal 1396, 1425.

194 Mariolina Eliantonio and others, 'Standing up for your right(s) in Europe: Locus Standi' (European Parliament 2012).

4 The UN Framework and Guiding Principles on Business and Human Rights

In 2005, John Ruggie was appointed as the Special Representative of the Secretary-General on the issue of human rights and transnational corporations and other business enterprises (SRSG).[195] Ruggie's mission was to move beyond the impasse created by the rejection of the UN Norms and to clarify the respective roles and responsibilities of States and businesses under public international law.

In 2008, the SRSG submitted a report to the UNHRC, in which he presented the UN Framework, meaning 'a conceptual and policy framework to anchor the business and human rights debate, and to help guide all relevant actors'. The UN Framework aims at 'adapting the human rights regime to provide more effective protection to individuals and communities against corporate-related human rights harm'.[196] It comprises three core pillars, also called principles:

- Pillar I: The State duty to protect against human rights abuses by third parties, including businesses;
- Pillar II: The corporate responsibility to respect human rights; and
- Pillar III: The need for more effective access to remedies.

The SRSG described the UN Framework as follows:

> Each principle is an essential component of the framework: the State duty to protect because it lies at the very core of the international human rights regime; the corporate responsibility to respect because it is the basic expectation society has of business; and access to remedy, because even the most concerted efforts cannot prevent all abuse, while access to judicial redress is often problematic, and non-judicial means are limited in number, scope and effectiveness. The three principles form a complementary whole in that each supports the others in achieving sustainable progress.[197]

In 2011, the UN Framework was completed by the UNGPs, which provide recommendations for the implementation of the three core principles of the UN Framework. The UNGPs aim at enhancing standards and practices with regard to BHR and contributing to a socially sustainable globalization.[198]

195 UNCHR, Resolution 69 (2005) UN Doc E/CN.4/RES/2005/69.
196 UN Framework, para 1.
197 Ibid, para 9.
198 UNGPs, General Principles.

Nonetheless, neither the UN Framework nor the UNGPs create new international legal obligations upon States or businesses, and they are not legally binding.[199] Furthermore, they do not address environmental issues in the context of business activities.[200]

The UNHRC adopted the UN Framework and the UNGPs by consensus, and States and businesses gave them a positive reception. At the same time, both documents, especially the UNGPs, have generated dissatisfaction, particularly among CSOs and academics.[201] Despite the diverging views on the UN Framework and the UNGPs, these instruments have become a common reference point in the BHR field and are regularly invoked by most stakeholders, including States, businesses, CSOs, academics, and international organizations.[202] As such, they provide the most important policy response to the issue of corporate accountability and access to justice in recent years. It is therefore necessary to understand their added-value in the context of this book.

Pillar I: The State duty to protect human rights

According to Guiding Principle (GP) 1, 'States must protect against human rights abuse within their territory and/or jurisdiction by third parties, including business enterprises. This requires taking appropriate steps to prevent, investigate, punish and redress such abuse through effective policies, legislation, regulations and adjudication.' The Commentary to GP 1 clarifies that *the State duty to protect* is a standard of conduct and that States are not per se responsible for human rights abuse by private actors. However, States may breach their international human rights obligations in various circumstances, including when they fail to take appropriate steps to prevent, investigate, punish, and redress abuse by private actors. States also have the duty to protect

---

199 Ibid.

200 For a discussion of the interplay between the UN Framework, the UNGPs, and the environment, see Katinka Jesse and Erik Koppe, 'Business Enterprises and the Environment: Corporate Environmental Responsibility' (2013) 4 The Dovenschmidt Quarterly 176.

201 For a critical evaluation of the UNGPs, see Surya Deva and David Bilchitz (eds), *Human Rights Obligations of Business: Beyond the Corporate Responsibility to Respect?* (CUP 2013). For an overview of the position on the UNGPs of major human rights organizations, see 'Joint Civil Society Statement on Business and Human Rights to the 17th Session of the UN Human Rights Council' (FIDH, ICJ, HRW, ESCR-Net, RAID, 15 June 2011) <https://www.escr-net.org/docs/i/1605781> accessed 1 May 2021. More CSO statements can be found on the website of the BHRRC. See 'Statements to Human Rights Council by NGOs and Business Organisations' (BHRRC) <https://old.business-humanrights.org/en/un-secretary-generals-special-representative-on-business-human-rights/reports-to-un-human-rights-council/2011> accessed 1 May 2021.

202 David Bilchitz and Surya Deva, 'The Human Rights Obligations of Business: A Critical Framework for the Future' in Surya Deva and David Bilchitz (eds), *Human Rights Obligations of Business: Beyond the Corporate Responsibility to Respect?* (CUP 2013) 2.

and promote the rule of law, including by providing for adequate accountability, legal certainty, and procedural and legal transparency. As the Commentary to GP 1 specifies, Pillar III on access to remedy outlines remedial measures.

Moreover, pursuant to GP 2, 'States should set out clearly the expectation that all business enterprises domiciled in their territory and/or jurisdiction respect human rights throughout their operations.' Specifically, the Commentary to GP 2 provides that States are not generally required under international human rights law to regulate the extraterritorial activities of businesses domiciled in their territory and/or jurisdiction. At the same time, they are not prohibited from doing so where a recognized basis for jurisdiction exists. For instance, States have adopted a range of approaches in this regard, such as direct extraterritorial legislation and enforcement through criminal regimes that allow for prosecution based on the nationality of the perpetrator regardless of where the offence occurs. In general, there is 'increasing encouragement at the international level, including from the treaty bodies, for home States to take regulatory action to prevent abuse by their companies overseas'.[203]

Pillar I on the State duty to protect human rights has produced mixed feelings from scholars. Bernaz argues that the SRSG 'settled for a middle-of-the-road position' regarding the extraterritorial nature of State obligations under international human rights law.[204] In the opinion of a number of scholars, the UNGPs fail to reflect recognition by various international bodies of the legal obligation for States to take action to prevent abuses by their companies overseas.[205] For De Schutter, the UNGPs set the bar below the current state of international human rights law when it comes to the extraterritorial human rights obligations of States.[206] Furthermore, the SRSG missed the opportunity to recognize an extraterritorial State obligation to protect, which would have bridged the protection gap that currently exists in some host countries and would have prevented 'relocations of convenience', meaning the situation where companies decide to register in countries which do not subject them to regulations that protect human rights.[207] Another weakness of the UNGPs is that

---

203 UN Framework, para 19; Bilchitz and Deva, 'The Human Rights Obligations of Business'.

204 Nadia Bernaz, 'Enhancing Corporate Accountability for Human Rights Violations: Is Extraterritoriality the Magic Potion?' (2013) 117 Journal of Business Ethics 493, 493. See also Daniel Augenstein and David Kinley, 'When Human Rights "Responsibilities" Become "Duties": The Extraterritorial Obligations of States that Bind Corporations' in Surya Deva and David Bilchitz (eds), Human Rights Obligations of Business: Beyond the Corporate Responsibility to Respect? (CUP 2013).

205 Bernaz, 'Enhancing Corporate Accountability for Human Rights Violations', 494; Olivier de Schutter, 'Towards a New Treaty on Business and Human Rights' (2016) 1 Business and Human Rights Journal 41; Augenstein and Kinley, 'When Human Rights "Responsibilities" Become "Duties"'.

206 De Schutter, 'Towards a New Treaty on Business and Human Rights', 45.

207 Bernaz, 'Enhancing Corporate Accountability for Human Rights Violations', 494.

they provide little indication of the nature and scope of potential extraterritorial measures (eg domestic measures with extraterritorial implications or direct extraterritorial legislation and enforcement). At the same time, other authors have challenged the notion that States have an extraterritorial obligation to protect against human rights abuse by corporate actors. Methven O'Brien argues that the current state of international human rights treaties cannot lead to the conclusion that States have a positive obligation to prevent abuses by MNEs beyond national borders. As a result, 'the position articulated by the UNGPs, that states may be entitled, but are not obliged as a matter of human rights law, or indeed public international law, generally to regulate their companies' extraterritorial activities or human rights impacts, remains a correct one.'[208]

Pillar II: The corporate responsibility to respect human rights

The SRSG rejected the view that companies, where they have influence, should have the same range of responsibilities as States.[209] Companies are economic actors and, as such, their responsibilities 'cannot and should not simply mirror the duties of States'.[210] Furthermore, the SRSG rejected that idea that companies should have responsibilities for a limited list of human rights. Since businesses can have an impact on the entire spectrum of internationally recognized rights,[211] limiting the rights for which they may be responsible would have negative consequences in particular instances.[212] Businesses should, at least, respect internationally recognized human rights.[213] As a result, the UN Framework and the UNGPs rest on 'differentiated but complementary responsibilities' in relation to all human rights.[214]

The UN Framework and the UNGPs recognize *the corporate responsibility to respect human rights*, which exists independently of States' duties.[215] According

---

208 Claire Methven O'Brien, 'The Home State Duty to Regulate the Human Rights Impacts of TNCs Abroad: A Rebuttal' (2018) 3 Business and Human Rights Journal 47, 72.

209 UN Framework, para 6.

210 Ibid, para 53.

211 UNHRC, 'Corporations and Human Rights: A Survey of the Scope and Patterns of Alleged Corporate-Related Human Rights Abuse' (23 May 2008) UN Doc A/HRC/8/5/Add.2, para 16.

212 UN Framework, para 6.

213 UNGPs, Commentary to GP 12. They are understood, at a minimum, as those expressed in the International Bill of Human Rights and the International Labour Organization's Declaration on Fundamental Principles and Rights at Work. However, businesses may need to consider additional standards, including the UN instruments protecting the human rights of specific groups or individuals.

214 UN Framework, para 9.

215 Ibid, para 55; UNGPs, GP 11.

to GP 11, business enterprises should respect human rights. They should avoid infringing the human rights of others and should address adverse human rights impacts with which they are involved. The term 'responsibility' was preferred to 'duty' to indicate that respecting human rights is not currently an obligation that international human rights law generally imposes directly on companies. The Commentary to GP 11 explains that the responsibility to respect human rights is a global standard of expected conduct for all business enterprises wherever they operate. It 'exists over and above compliance with national laws and regulations protecting human rights'.[216] Companies should respect human rights 'because it is the basic expectation society has of business'.[217] As a result, the UN Framework and the UNGPs define corporate responsibility on the basis of social expectations (the social licence of companies to operate) and not legal standards.[218]

Importantly, GP 15 provides that, in order to meet their responsibility to respect human rights, business enterprises should have an HRDD process in place to identify, prevent, mitigate, and account for how they address their impacts on human rights. The HRDD process 'should include assessing actual and potential human rights impacts, integrating and acting upon the findings, tracking responses, and communicating how impacts are addressed'.[219] Therefore, HRDD refers to the steps a company must take to become aware of, prevent, and address adverse human rights impacts. The UNGPs develop the parameters and components for HRDD in more detail.[220] It is important to note the potential impact of the HRDD process in the context of liability claims. The SRSG noted that, to discharge its responsibility to respect, a company should carry out due diligence.[221] 'Conducting appropriate human rights due diligence should help business enterprises address the risk of legal claims against them by showing that they took every reasonable step to avoid involvement with an alleged human rights abuse.' At the same time, 'business enterprises conducting such due diligence should not assume that, by itself, this will automatically and fully absolve them from liability for causing or contributing to human rights abuses.'[222]

216 UNGPs, GP 11.

217 UN Framework, para 9.

218 Nicola Jägers, 'Will Transnational Private Regulation Close the Governance Gap?' in Surya Deva and David Bilchitz (eds), *Human Rights Obligations of Business: Beyond the Corporate Responsibility to Respect?* (CUP 2013) 298. For a discussion of the social licence to operate under the UNGPs, see Sally Wheeler, 'Global Production, CSR and Human Rights: The Court of Public Opinion and the Social Licence to Operate' (2015) 19 International Journal of Human Rights 757.

219 UNGPs, GP 17.

220 UNGPs, GPs 18–21.

221 UN Framework, para 56.

222 UNGPs, Commentary to GP 17.

If the UN Framework and the UNGPs have been acknowledged as representing an important step in setting out corporate responsibility for human rights, they have not closed the long-running debate about corporations and the demands for international legal obligations and corporate accountability.[223] In particular, scholars and CSOs have criticized the voluntary nature of corporate responsibility to respect human rights.[224] Both instruments emphatically emphasize the role of the State as the sole duty-bearer of human rights obligations while avoiding the establishment of clear international standards and/or obligations for companies. As a result, the 'rather minimalist take' on corporate responsibility leads to missed opportunities and weaknesses, especially since companies are already legally obliged not to perpetrate, aid, or abet international crimes.[225] Scholars have also pointed out that 'it is difficult to see how, without the complement of international legal obligations, this privatized voluntary process will be significantly more effective than other voluntary self-regulation regimes in regulating and enforcing the compliance of corporations with human rights norms'.[226]

Furthermore, they have criticized the scope of the corporate responsibility to respect, arguing that 'corporate obligations should not only involve "negative" obligations to avoid harm but also include a "duty to fulfil": obligations to contribute actively to the realisation of fundamental rights'.[227] Scholars have also pointed out that the SRSG failed to acknowledge that corporations may have an obligation to realize human rights based on their social function.[228] At the same time, the SRSG's views of the ambit of the corporate responsibility to respect, especially the HRDD process, is sometimes ambiguous. At times, the SRSG seems to imply that corporations may have a positive duty to protect human rights against abuse by third parties, which is similar to the State obligation to protect under international human rights law.[229] Commentators

---

223 Carlos López, 'The "Ruggie Process": From Legal Obligations to Corporate Social Responsibility' in Surya Deva and David Bilchitz (eds), *Human Rights Obligations of Business: Beyond the Corporate Responsibility to Respect?* (CUP 2013) 77.

224 See 'Problematic Pragmatism – The Ruggie Report 2008: Background, Analysis and Perspectives' (Misereor and Global Policy Forum Europe 2008) 13; Penelope Simons, 'International Law's Invisible Hand and the Future of Corporate Accountability for Violations of Human Rights' (2012) 3 Journal of Human Rights and the Environment 5; John Knox, 'The Ruggie Rules: Applying Human Rights Law to Corporations' in Radu Mares (ed), *The UN Guiding Principles on Business and Human Rights: Foundations and Implementation* (Martinus Nijhoff Publishers 2012).

225 Nicola Jägers, 'UN Guiding Principles on Business and Human Rights: Making Headway Towards Real Corporate Accountability' (2011) 29 Netherlands Quarterly of Human Rights 159, 160.

226 Simons, 'International Law's Invisible Hand', 38.

227 Bilchitz, 'The Ruggie Framework', 200.

228 Ibid, 208–211.

229 Ibid, 206.

have also criticized the practical approach to corporate HRDD.[230] For instance, the absence of any template or indicative methodology for the production of accurate HRDD makes it difficult for outsiders to evaluate whether a company respects human rights, or for companies to learn and share best practice with each other.[231]

At the same time, other authors have argued that the corporate responsibility to respect is an important improvement in comparison with what existed previously. Despite its soft law nature, it may nonetheless produce 'real legal consequences'.[232] Some authors have posited that, in general, the UNGPs are gaining legal effect through law, regulation, contracts, and dispute resolution processes as a result of their increasing inclusion in instruments that produce legal effects, such as bilateral investment treaties, project finance agreements, and so on.[233] To date, the corporate responsibility to respect has been welcomed by various actors with competing interests and, in the long term, it may be universally accepted as an international standard.[234]

Moreover, HRDD may create a direct duty of care upon businesses either where they have voluntarily accepted to carry it out,[235] or where States have enacted statutes governing the HRDD of companies. As will be seen in Chapter 7, the HRDD process under the UNGPs has influenced the adoption of statutory norms imposing mandatory due diligence upon businesses. In 2017, France enacted the first legislation forcing certain companies to establish an HRDD process within their group activities. Furthermore, when properly conducted, HRDD can help companies to demonstrate that they took every reasonable step to avoid involvement in a human rights violation, and can provide protection against mismanagement claims by shareholders.[236] The implementation of HRDD also encourages companies to depart from an exclusive shareholder-based corporate governance model towards a more stakeholder-based model, which allows the interests of victims of business-related human rights abuse to be represented in the decision-making processes of companies.[237]

---

230 For a discussion of the efficacy of the HRDD process, see James Harrison, 'Establishing a Meaningful Human Rights Due Diligence Process for Corporations: Learning from Experience of Human Rights Impact Assessment' (2013) 31 Impact Assessment and Project Appraisal 107.

231 Wheeler, 'Global Production, CSR and Human Rights', 768.

232 Peter Muchlinski, 'Implementing the New UN Corporate Human Rights Framework' (2012) 22 Business Ethics Quarterly 145, 146.

233 Blecher, 'Code of Conduct', 474.

234 Simons, 'International Law's Invisible Hand', 38.

235 Muchlinski, 'Implementing the New UN Corporate Human Rights Framework', 146.

236 Ibid, 149.

237 Ibid, 165–167.

Pillar III: Effective access to remedy

The UN Framework recognizes that '[e]ven where institutions operate optimally, disputes over the human rights impact of companies are likely to occur'.[238] In such a context, it is crucial that victims have effective access to remedy. However, despite the existence of a 'patchwork' of judicial and non-judicial mechanisms, a considerable number of individuals whose human rights are impacted by corporations still lack effective access to remedy. The UN Framework acknowledges two main issues in this regard: access to formal judicial systems is often difficult, especially in places where the need is greatest; and non-judicial mechanisms are seriously underdeveloped at various levels (corporate, national, and international).[239] It therefore suggests improving both judicial and non-judicial mechanisms.

Pillar III of the UN Framework is operationalized in Guiding Principles 25 to 31 of the UNGPs. GP 25 is the 'foundational principle' of Pillar III while the other GPs are 'operational principles'. They are divided as follows:

- GP 25 asserts the State duty to ensure access to effective remedy;
- GP 26 deals with State-based judicial mechanisms;
- GP 27 focuses on State-based non-judicial grievance mechanisms;
- GPs 28 to 30 deal with non-State-based grievance mechanisms; and
- GP 31 provides effectiveness criteria for non-judicial grievance mechanisms.

From the outset, GP 25 provides that:

> As part of their duty to protect against business-related human rights abuse, States must take appropriate steps to ensure, through judicial, administrative, legislative or other appropriate means, that when such abuses occur within their territory and/or jurisdiction those affected have access to effective remedy.

The SRSG linked the concept of 'access to effective remedy' (Pillar III) to the State duty to protect against business-related human rights abuse (Pillar I). GP 25 recognizes that States must adopt measures to ensure victims have access to remedy when human rights abuses occur within their territory and/or jurisdiction. Remedy may include apologies, restitution, rehabilitation, financial or non-financial compensation, and punitive criminal or administrative sanctions. Remedy could also include the prevention of harm through injunctions or guarantees of non-repetition. According to the Commentary

238 UN Framework, para 26.
239 Ibid.

to GP 25, State-based judicial and non-judicial grievance mechanisms should form the foundation of a wider system of remedy. The GPs use the term 'grievance mechanism' to indicate 'any routinized, State-based or non-State-based, judicial or non-judicial process through which grievances concerning business-related human rights abuse can be raised and remedy can be sought'.

At first glance, Pillar III on access to remedy is characterized by the predominant role of States in ensuring that victims have access to effective remedy and a strong emphasis of the UN Framework and the UNGPs on non-judicial grievance mechanisms. Several factors influenced the SRSG's vision of Pillar III. First, the SRSG accepted from the beginning that remedy must be part of the BHR discussion, as 'human rights without meaningful remedies are effectively nullities'.[240] Second, States and businesses have different functions and should, therefore, have different responsibilities. Third, the SRSG saw importance in non-judicial grievance mechanisms, and corporate-level grievance mechanisms in particular.[241] However, as will be seen below, aspects of this vision, such as the strong emphasis on non-judicial grievance mechanisms, have received a cold reception from many CSOs and academics.

Framing effective access to remedy in the BHR context

Both the UN Framework and the UNGPs recognize that judicial mechanisms are often under-equipped to provide effective remedies for victims of corporate abuse. Importantly, they acknowledge obstacles specific to transnational litigation against MNEs.

The UN Framework states that victims of corporate abuse have sought remedy outside the State where the harm occurred, particularly through home State courts, but have faced obstacles (eg prohibitive costs, absence of legal aid, lack of legal standing for non-citizens, etc). Matters are further complicated when they seek redress from a parent corporation for actions by a foreign subsidiary. As a result, these obstacles may deter claims and prevent victims from gaining access to remedy.[242] Therefore, the UN Framework calls States to 'strengthen judicial capacity to hear complaints and enforce remedies against all corporations operating or based in their territory, while also protecting against frivolous claims'.[243] Furthermore, 'States should address obstacles to access to

---

240 Jonathan Drimmer and Lisa J Laplante, 'The Third Pillar: Remedies, Reparations, and the Ruggie Principles' in Jena Martin and Karen E Bravo (eds), *The Business and Human Rights Landscape: Moving Forward, Looking Back* (CUP 2015) 318.

241 Ibid.

242 UN Framework, para 89.

243 Ibid, para 91.

justice, including for foreign plaintiffs – especially where alleged abuses reach the level of widespread and systematic human rights violations.'[244]

GP 26 aims to operationalize access to remedy in the context of State-based judicial mechanisms. It provides that:

> States should take appropriate steps to ensure the effectiveness of domestic judicial mechanisms when addressing business-related human rights abuses, including considering ways to reduce legal, practical and other relevant barriers that could lead to a denial of access to remedy.

The Commentary to GP 26 emphasizes that States should ensure that they do not erect barriers to prevent legitimate cases from being brought before the courts in situations where judicial recourse is an essential part of accessing remedy, or where alternative sources of effective remedy are unavailable. Barriers may be of a legal nature. For instance, the distribution of liability within a corporate group may lead to 'avoidance of appropriate accountability', or plaintiffs may not be able to access home State courts and thereby face a denial of justice in a host State. Certain vulnerable groups, such as indigenous peoples and migrants, may not receive the same level of legal protection for human rights as applies to the wider population. The Commentary to GP 26 also recognizes that practical and procedural barriers may arise, such as the high costs of litigation, difficulty accessing legal representation, unavailability of group actions, or inadequate resources of prosecution services. Importantly, it acknowledges the asymmetry between victims and businesses in legal proceedings. It provides that '[m]any of the barriers victims face are the result of, or compounded by, the frequent imbalances between the parties to business-related human rights claims, such as in their financial resources, access to information and expertise'. Furthermore, vulnerable and/or marginalized groups are more likely to face additional obstacles impeding their ability to access remedy.

The UN Framework clearly states that non-judicial mechanisms play an important role alongside judicial processes.[245] They are essential both in countries where courts are unable to provide adequate and effective access to remedy and in countries with well-functioning rule-of-law institutions but where non-judicial mechanisms may provide a more immediate, accessible, affordable, and adaptable recourse.[246] Non-judicial mechanisms may be set up by States,[247] companies,[248] industry associations, multi-stakeholder

244 Ibid.
245 Ibid, para 84.
246 Ibid.
247 UNGPs, GP 27.
248 Ibid, GP 29.

organizations, or international and regional human rights bodies.[249] The considerable recognition gained by non-judicial mechanisms is visible in the UNGPs in which five GPs are fully dedicated to the development of these procedures. Importantly, the UN Framework and the UNGPs list a number of principles, or criteria, that non-judicial mechanisms must meet in order to be credible and effective. In particular, they must be legitimate; accessible; predictable; equitable; rights-compatible; transparent; a source of continuous learning; and, in the context of operational-level mechanisms, based on engagement and dialogue.[250] It is important to note that the SRSG did not include a similar list in relation to judicial mechanisms, which appears to be a significant oversight.

Added-value of Pillar III

The insertion of a pillar solely dedicated to access to remedy should be welcomed. The UNGPs stress the need to employ multiple grievance mechanisms to make companies accountable and list a number of options that should be available to victims (State/non-State; judicial/non-judicial).[251] The UNGPs also recognize the various types of barriers that victims may face, including those that will have a greater impact on vulnerable individuals and groups. Acknowledgement of the asymmetry of resources and, ultimately, power between victims and businesses is a crucial step forward from an access to justice perspective.

Nonetheless, despite these qualities, the formulation of Pillar III has disappointed a significant number of CSOs and academics. The access to remedy pillar has often been labelled as the weakest of the three pillars, and the SRSG has been criticized for having particularly neglected the formulation of access to judicial remedy.[252] As Deva pointed out, the vision of access to remedy as flowing from the State duty to protect instead of being a self-standing human right obligation contributes to diminishing the added-value of Pillar III.[253]

From an access to justice perspective, some criticisms can be made of the formulation of Pillar III. First, the language used by the SRSG is, on several

---

249 Ibid, GP 30.

250 UN Framework, para 92; GP 31 added two principles: they must be a source of continuous learning and based on engagement and dialogue.

251 Surya Deva, 'Treating Human Rights Lightly: A Critique of the Consensus Rhetoric and the Language Employed by the Guiding Principles' in Surya Deva and David Bilchitz (eds), *Human Rights Obligations of Business: Beyond the Corporate Responsibility to Respect?* (CUP 2013) 102.

252 See *Needs and Options for a New International Instrument in the Field of Business and Human Rights* (International Commission of Jurists 2014) 9; Tebello Thabane, 'Weak Extraterritorial Remedies: The Achilles Heel of Ruggie's "Protect, Respect and Remedy" Framework and Guiding Principles' (2014) 14 African Human Rights Law Journal 43.

253 Deva, 'Treating Human Rights Lightly', 102–103.

occasions, problematic.[254] In general, the SRSG has carefully chosen the words used in the UN Framework and UNGPs, employing a seemingly depoliticized vocabulary and avoiding words with perceived strong legal meaning. If the UNGPs' vocabulary at times presents 'transformative potential' (eg the expression 'human rights impacts'),[255] it can also weaken the normative strength of the UNGPs' assertions. This is particularly visible with Pillar III. For instance, the UNGPs define the concept of 'grievance' when discussing the various 'grievance mechanisms' that should be available to victims. A grievance should be understood as 'a perceived injustice evoking an individual's or a group's sense of entitlement, which may be based on law, contract, explicit or implicit promises, customary practice, or general notions of fairness of aggrieved communities'. One strength of this definition is that its scope is broad enough to cover a wide range of situations where individuals and groups have suffered loss from business activities. At the same time, it is unclear how the concept of grievance can translate into a valid cause for action when victims bring a claim against companies. Furthermore, the use of words such as 'perceived injustice' and 'sense of entitlement' risks watering down the reality of the harm suffered by victims of gross human rights abuse.[256] In the context of transnational claims against MNEs, plaintiffs have alleged the direct and indirect involvement of businesses in some of the worst human rights violations, including forced labour, torture, murder, rape, and child labour. In such a context, the fact that the system of remedy under the UN Framework and the UNGPs appears to be built on the availability of mechanisms that solve disputes on 'a perceived injustice evoking an individual's or a group's sense of entitlement' is questionable. Such a vision ignores the social justice dimension of most claims brought against businesses as well as the discourse of a large number of CSOs advocating for stronger corporate accountability and access to justice norms.

The language of the UNGPs is also problematic in other circumstances. The concept of 'access to justice' is practically absent from the text of the UN Framework and the UNGPs. There is one reference to 'access to justice' in the UN Framework in relation to judicial mechanisms. Accordingly, States should address obstacles to access to justice, especially where alleged abuses

---

254 For an overview of the various views on the language used by the UNGPs, see ibid; David Birchall, 'Any Act, Any Harm, to Anyone: The Transformative Potential of "Human Rights Impacts" Under the UN Guiding Principles on Business and Human Rights' (2019) 1 University of Oxford Human Rights Hub Journal 120.

255 Birchall, 'Any Act, Any Harm, to Anyone'.

256 The concept of 'grievance' is far from the concept of harm that can be found under some international human rights instruments. For instance, under the Basic Principles on Remedy, harm includes 'physical or mental injury, emotional suffering, economic loss or substantial impairment of their fundamental rights, through acts or omissions that constitute gross violations of international human rights law, or serious violations of international humanitarian law'.

reach the level of widespread and systematic human rights violations.[257] However, the UNGPs do not follow up on this aspect. Furthermore, while GP 25 provides that States 'must' take judicial, administrative, legislative, or other appropriate steps to ensure access to an effective remedy, GP 26 merely recommends that States 'should' consider ways to reduce legal, practical, and other relevant barriers that could lead to a denial of access to remedy. Referring to GP 26, Deva rightly asks why States should not be obliged to remove some of the well-known obstacles that have hampered victims of human rights abuses by businesses in seeking redress.[258] Ultimately, this choice of words limits the 'transformative potential' of the UNGPs when it comes to access to remedy.

Beyond the language issue, other criticisms can be addressed to the content of Pillar III. For instance, several aspects of the UNGPs relevant to access to remedy are unclear. GP 25 states that access to effective remedy has both procedural and substantive aspects. However, the UNGPs do not detail what these aspects specifically entail. Furthermore, the UN Framework and the UNGPs do not provide clear solutions to addressing obstacles preventing effective access to remedy, which is possibly one of their most important weaknesses.[259] With regard to judicial mechanisms, the UNGPs, which are supposed to operationalize the UN Framework, keep repeating a list of obstacles already identified in the UN Framework without suggesting a way to actually deal with them. This is particularly visible when looking at the content of GPs 25 and 26. Moreover, in relation to transnational litigation against MNEs, the UNGPs do not offer guidance to victims on the ways in which to gain access to courts in home States.[260]

As will be seen later in this book, the shortcomings in the way access to remedy was framed in the UN Framework and the UNGPs, and the lack of practical guidance on how to carry out Pillar III, have led to an insufficient implementation of this pillar to date. Such shortcomings have strengthened calls for a legally binding instrument on BHR.

Reception of the UNGPs in Europe

The EU and the CoE welcomed the adoption of the UNGPs and pledged to support their implementation in Europe. The EU has stated that it is a 'strong supporter' of the UNGPs, which it regards as 'the authoritative policy framework' in the BHR field.[261] However, while it has stated its commitment

257 UN Framework, para 91.

258 Deva, 'Treating Human Rights Lightly', 102–103.

259 *Needs and Options for a New International Instrument*, 10.

260 Thabane, 'Weak Extraterritorial Remedies', 57.

261 EU Permanent Delegation to the UN Office and Other International Organisations in Geneva, 'Contribution of the EU before the first session of the UN Working Group on Human Rights and Transnational Corporations and Other Business Enterprises' D(2012)703034.

to implementing the UNGPs, the EU has never adopted a formal BHR strategy to do so. It has instead included a limited number of specific actions on BHR and the UNGPs in its EU Action Plans on Human Rights and Democracy.[262] In response to the lack of a general EU strategy on the UNGPs, the Responsible Business Conduct Working Group (RBC WG), an informal and cross-party group of Members of the European Parliament (EP), adopted the 'Shadow EU Action Plan on the Implementation of the UNGPs within the EU'.[263]

Nonetheless, the EU institutions have adopted separate policy documents on BHR and the implementation of the UNGPs. Shortly after the UNGPs were adopted in 2011, the EC adopted a new CSR policy called *Renewed EU Strategy 2011–2014 for Corporate Social Responsibility* (2011 CSR Strategy).[264] In this document, the EC revised its CSR policy to reflect various aspects of the UNGPs, such as the corporate responsibility to respect and the concept of due diligence. In general, the EC has used a voluntary approach to encourage companies to respect human rights. The EC has also released two Staff Working Documents detailing previous and ongoing efforts to implement and streamline the UNGPs in EU activities.[265] In parallel, the Council of the EU adopted its *Conclusions on Business and Human Rights* in 2016, which provided guidance on how the UNGPs should be implemented.[266] Furthermore, while the EP has not passed a resolution on the UNGPs specifically, it has passed a number of resolutions on BHR-related issues.[267] The EU has also considered, to some extent, the implementation of Pillar III of the UNGPs on access to remedy. Following a request from the Council of the EU, in 2017, the EU FRA issued an opinion on improving access to remedy in the area of BHR at the EU level.[268] The EU FRA

262 European Commission, 'Joint Communication to the European Parliament and the Council – EU Action Plan on Human Rights and Democracy 2020–2024' JOIN(2020) 5 final; Council of the European Union, 'Council Conclusions on the Action Plan on Human Rights and Democracy 2015–2019' 10897/15.

263 RBC, 'Shadow EU Action Plan on the Implementation of the UN Guiding Principles on Business and Human Rights within the EU' (19 March 2019).

264 European Commission, 'A Renewed EU Strategy 2011–14 for Corporate Social Responsibility' COM(2011) 681 final.

265 European Commission, 'Commission Staff Working Document on Implementing the UN Guiding Principles on Business and Human Rights – State of Play' SWD(2015) 144 final; European Commission, 'Commission Staff Working Document – Corporate Social Responsibility, Responsible Business Conduct, and Business & Human Rights: Overview of Progress' SWD(2019) 143 final.

266 Council of the European Union, 'Council Conclusions on Business and Human Rights' 10254/16.

267 See European Parliament resolution of 25 October 2016 on corporate liability for serious human rights abuses in third countries (2015/2315(INI)).

268 EU FRA, 'Improving access to remedy in the area of business and human rights at the EU level' FRA Opinion – 1/2017 [B&HR].

concluded that 'more could be done to ensure effective access to remedy for business-related human rights abuse within the EU'.

In general, the EU has supported the implementation of the UNGPs through several legal and policy initiatives addressing BHR issues both directly and indirectly. For example, as early as 2011 the EC was encouraging its Member States to develop National Action Plans (NAPs) on BHR.[269] Furthermore, the EU has addressed BHR-related issues in sectoral policy and legal instruments (eg adoption of Directive 2014/95/EU on corporate disclosure of non-financial information).[270] The EU has also promoted adherence to the UNGPs in its internal and external policies and programmes.[271]

The EU has been active in implementing the UNGPs. However, as a result of a lack of a general strategy on BHR, it has taken a piecemeal approach, which raises the risk of incoherence. Furthermore, despite the EU's competence in company law and the primary legal value of fundamental rights, it has primarily used a voluntary approach to encourage companies to respect human rights. It has also failed to include Pillar III on access to remedy into its legal and policy initiatives in the justice sector.

Following the adoption of the UNGPs, the CoE began to consider how its activities could address business-related human rights abuse. An important step in this process was the CoE Steering Committee for Human Rights' recognition that the ECHR posed serious limitations in preventing human rights violations by private companies and ensuring victims of corporate abuse access to remedies.[272] Furthermore, in 2014 the Committee of Ministers of the CoE adopted the Declaration on the UNGPs,[273] in which it recognized the UNGPs 'as the current globally agreed baseline for its own work in the field of business and human rights'. It also emphasized that effective implementation of the UNGPs, both by States and business enterprises, is essential to ensure respect for human rights in the business context, and expressed 'its willingness

---

269 European Commission, 'A Renewed EU Strategy 2011–14 for Corporate Social Responsibility'.

270 Directive 2014/95/EU of the European Parliament and of the Council of 22 October 2014 amending Directive 2013/34/EU as regards disclosure of non-financial and diversity information by certain large undertakings and groups [2014] OJ L330/1.

271 European Commission, 'Commission Staff Working Document on Implementing the UN Guiding Principles on Business and Human Rights – State of Play'; European Commission, 'Commission, 'Commission Staff Working Document – Corporate Social Responsibility, Responsible Business Conduct, and Business & Human Rights: Overview of Progress'.

272 See CoE (Steering Committee for Human Rights), 'Draft Preliminary Study on Corporate Social Responsibility in the Field of Human Rights: Existing Standards and Outstanding Issues' (4 June 2012) CDDH(2012)012.

273 Declaration of the Committee of Ministers on the UN Guiding Principles on business and human rights (16 April 2014).

to contribute to their effective implementation at the European level, by identifying and analysing specific gaps and proposing appropriate solutions'.

While a specific legally binding instrument on BHR was initially considered, the Committee of Ministers ultimately adopted a non-binding document on the subject, namely the Recommendation on human rights and business (2016 Recommendation).[274] In general, this Recommendation calls for Member States to effectively implement the UNGPs, including through the adoption of NAPs. It also recommends a number of actions for Member States to take in order to implement each of the UNGPs' pillars. For example, 'Member States should apply additional measures to require business enterprises to respect human rights, including, where appropriate, by carrying out HRDD.'[275] In relation to access to remedy, the 2016 Recommendation suggests that Member States ensure the effective implementation of their obligations under Articles 6 and 13 ECHR to grant everyone access to a court in the determination of their civil rights, and to everyone whose rights have been violated an effective remedy before a national authority, including where such violation arises from business activity. It also recommends the adoption of measures to ensure civil and criminal liability for business-related human rights abuses.[276] Efforts to implement the UNGPs have so far focused on Member States implementing the 2016 Recommendation. There have been no specific initiatives launched to develop a new regional legal framework on BHR or to address the ECHR's limitations in the context of access to justice for business-related human rights violations.

5 Conclusions

This chapter has discussed the relevant legal frameworks on corporate accountability and access to justice at international and European levels.

Generally speaking, there is a normative gap in ensuring corporate accountability. Under the traditional State-centric approach to international law, only States have international rights and obligations. Non-State actors,

---

274 Recommendation CM/Rec(2016)3 of the Committee of Ministers to Member States on human rights and business (2 March 2016).

275 Ibid, para 22 of Annex.

276 The Conference of INGOs and the Parliamentary Assembly have generally called for the promotion of the 2016 Recommendation. See Conference of INGOs of the CoE, 'Recommendation: Business and Human Rights' (CONF/PLE(2017)REC2); Parliamentary Assembly of the CoE, 'Human Rights and Business – What Follow-up to Committee of Ministers Recommendation CM/Rec(2016)3?' Resolution 2311 (2019); Parliamentary Assembly of the CoE, 'Human Rights and Business – What Follow-up to Committee of Ministers Recommendation CM/Rec(2016)3?' Recommendation 2166 (2019).

such as MNEs, lack international legal personality, which means they have neither rights nor obligations and cannot be held accountable for violations of international law obligations, such as human rights or environmental ones. This view limits the effectiveness of public international law to protect human rights and the environment against interference from businesses in their transnational commercial activities.[277] Furthermore, it ignores the fact that MNEs have some rights and may be subject to certain obligations under various areas of international law, such as international investment law. To date, no international instruments impose international human rights and environmental obligations on MNEs.

If the core international human rights instruments do not recognize a right to access to justice per se, they provide, for the most part, for the right to an effective remedy for the violation of the human rights they enshrine. They also articulate procedural safeguards crucial to ensuring the right to a fair trial. In Europe, the ECHR and the EU Charter create a solid legal framework on access to justice, which ensures the rights to a fair trial and to an effective remedy to victims of human rights abuse. Moreover, progressive changes in EU primary law have strengthened the role and the powers of the EU institutions to legislate in civil and criminal justice in recent years. However, the direct applicability of international and European standards on access to justice in domestic law is not necessarily guaranteed. Furthermore, until the adoption of the UN Framework and the UNGPs, international and European instruments on access to justice had failed to consider the specificity of access to justice in the BHR context.

The UN Framework and the UNGPs have been a major breakthrough in the BHR sphere. They recognize the corporate responsibility to respect human rights and the need for access to remedy in the context of corporate-related human rights abuse. However, they espouse a vision far removed from that of access to justice centred on the realization of corporate accountability standards and effective access to remedy, as advocated by a number of CSOs and academics. On the contrary, Pillar III focuses overwhelmingly on concepts that risk watering down the experience of victims and on non-judicial grievance mechanisms led by companies, and provides little guidance as to what to do to effectively address barriers to access to justice, particularly when it comes to judicial mechanisms.

More generally, the content, implementation, and added-value of the UNGPs have dominated scholarly and policy discussions since 2010. For a number of scholars and CSOs, the UNGPs do not fully reflect the state of international human rights law in many respects, and the SRSG sacrificed 'principle for the purposes of achieving agreements'.[278] As a result, the UNGPs did not put an end

---

277 Ratner, 'Corporations and Human Rights', 461.

278 Bilchitz, 'The Ruggie Framework', 200.

to the doctrinal debates of the extraterritoriality dimension of the State duty to protect or the obligations of business actors under international human rights law. Furthermore, the normative added-value of the UNGPs has generally been called into question. They do not create new international legal obligations for States or businesses. Instead they are a series of practical recommendations that elaborate on the implications of existing international obligations.[279] The vague details provided by the UNGPs for the implementation of the three pillars have led to legitimate questions as to how best to proceed with them. At the same time, the UNGPs have become 'the reference' in the BHR sphere and beyond, and have influenced policies and discourses at international, regional, and national level. They are also gaining legal effect through their inclusion in legally binding instruments. An example of this influence is the growing adoption of mandatory HRDD standards in various countries. Moreover, NGOs, which have criticized both the drafting process and the content of the UNGPs, are nonetheless using this instrument to call out States and corporations to protect and respect human rights respectively.

Chapter 3 gives an account of the emergence of transnational litigation against MNEs in common law countries and its development in European civil law countries, with an emphasis on cases in France and the Netherlands.

---

279 López, 'The "Ruggie Process"'.

Chapter 3

The rise of transnational litigation against multinational enterprises

1 Introduction

Transnational litigation against MNEs originated in common law jurisdictions – mainly the US and England – in the 1980s and 1990s. However, the nature of this litigation has been different in both countries. While in England victims of business-related human rights abuse and environmental damage brought general tort claims against parent companies of MNEs, in the US they mainly took advantage of the particularities of the ATS[1] to challenge wrongful corporate conduct in foreign countries. In both countries, plaintiffs have nevertheless hoped to gain faster and easier access to financial compensation and to obtain the recognition of the harm they have suffered. By contrast, the practice of transnational litigation against MNEs in European civil law countries appeared more recently. It has developed under various forms of law, including criminal, tort, and specialized law, as a result of litigators using various legal strategies.

In both common law and civil law jurisdictions, the existence of cause-lawyers and CSOs linked to the corporate accountability movement has been crucial in triggering the emergence of transnational litigation against MNEs. This type of litigation has direct links to the broader civil society agenda on globalization and corporate accountability.[2] It supports the aim of improved regulation of business activities at both international and national levels. In general, cause-lawyers and CSOs behind transnational claims seek not only effective remedy for victims but also MNE accountability for their involvement in human rights abuse and environmental damage. Litigation is therefore a strategic tool for attracting visibility, revealing MNE impunity towards human rights and the environment, and demanding legal and policy reform for improved corporate accountability.

---

1   28 USC § 1350 (1789) Alien's Action for Tort.

2   Halina Ward, 'Securing Transnational Corporate Accountability through National Courts: Implications and Policy Options' (2001) 24 Hastings International and Comparative Law Review 451, 465.

2 Origins of transnational litigation against MNEs in common law jurisdictions

Transnational litigation against MNEs emerged in common law jurisdictions around two sets of cases that started in the 1990s. First, plaintiffs brought civil actions based on the ATS before the US federal courts against foreign companies for their involvement in alleged violations of human rights in their foreign operations. Second, a series of tort actions were brought before the domestic courts of various common law jurisdictions – including the US, England, Canada, and Australia – to hold MNEs accountable for wrongs committed abroad. In this second set of cases, plaintiffs have typically targeted the parent company for a tort committed in the context of its subsidiaries' activities.[3] These cases will be briefly considered in this section.

The rise and fall of Alien Tort Statute litigation in the United States

The ATS is a US federal statute that was enacted in 1789.[4] It provides: 'The district courts shall have original jurisdiction of any civil action by an alien for a tort only, committed in violation of the law of nations or a treaty of the United States.' Although there is little information about the origins of the ATS, it is assumed that the statute was enacted to ensure that the US, then a new nation, had an obligation to comply with international law. More practically, the US Congress feared that international law violations could trigger retaliation against the US by a more powerful State.[5]

For almost 200 years the ATS was rarely used.[6] It remained more or less dormant until the 1980s when the first claim in relation to gross human rights violations was brought under it. In the landmark *Filártiga v Peña-Irala* case,[7] the plaintiffs argued that the US courts had jurisdiction under the ATS to hear their civil action against a former Paraguayan police official for the alleged torture and killing of a member of their family. The US Court of Appeals for the

---

3   Peter Muchlinski and Virginie Rouas, 'Foreign Direct-Liability Litigation: Toward the Transnationalization of Corporate Legal Responsibility' in Lara Blecher, Nancy Kaymar Stafford and Gretchen Bellamy (eds), *Corporate Responsibility for Human Rights Impacts: New Expectations and Paradigms* (American Bar Association 2014) 360.

4   The ATS is now a section of the US Code.

5   Beth Stephens, 'Human Rights Litigation in U.S. Courts: From 1789 to the Present' in Lara Blecher, Nancy Kaymar Stafford and Gretchen Bellamy (eds), *Corporate Responsibility for Human Rights Impacts: New Expectations and Paradigms* (American Bar Association 2014) 181.

6   Ibid. For an overview of the history of the ATS, see Beth Stephens, 'The Curious History of the Alien Tort Statute' (2014) 89 Notre Dame Law Review 1467.

7   630 F.2d 876 (2d Cir 1980).

Second Circuit eventually ruled in favour of the plaintiffs. It found that it had jurisdiction under the ATS based on the universal acknowledgement that acts of official torture are contrary to the law of nations. It held the former police official liable for the torture and killing of the plaintiffs' family member. The plaintiffs were also awarded around US$ 10 million in damages. This ruling was a decisive moment for the adjudication of human rights claims based on the ATS. As Enneking notes, 'the statute fast became famous for providing a legal basis upon which those who had suffered egregious breaches of their human rights could bring civil lawsuits against their wrongdoers before US federal courts.'[8]

Following *Filártiga*, more ATS-based claims were filed against many different perpetrators of human rights violations. At first, claims were mainly aimed at States and foreign high officials.[9] However, they progressively targeted private actors, such as private individuals alleged to have perpetrated genocide or forced labour[10] and, eventually, corporate actors. In *Doe v Unocal*,[11] a group of Burmese villagers alleged that they were subjected to gross human rights violations, including forced labour, murder, rape, and torture, by the Burmese military regime in the context of the construction of the Yadana gas pipeline. They accused the US-based oil MNE Unocal, as well as other corporate actors, of complicity for the violations they had suffered. According to the plaintiffs, Unocal was liable because it hired the Burmese military to provide security knowing that the military would violate human rights while doing so. In 1997, the US District Court for the Central District of California ruled that it had jurisdiction to hear the plaintiffs' claim against Unocal under the ATS. The case never reached a verdict, as the parties eventually settled. Nevertheless, *Unocal* became a milestone in providing precedent for the use of ATS-based claims to hold companies accountable for human rights violations.[12]

Since *Unocal*, companies have regularly found themselves defendants for their direct and indirect involvement in human rights violations. In most claims, plaintiffs relied on secondary, or vicarious, liability to hold corporate defendants liable for their assistance in, or other formal connection to, human rights violations committed by the government with which they do business.[13] For example, in *Wiwa v Royal Dutch Petroleum Co.*,[14] the plaintiffs alleged that

8   Liesbeth Enneking, *Foreign Direct Liability and Beyond: Exploring the Role of Tort Law in Promoting International Corporate Social Responsibility and Accountability* (Eleven International Publishing 2012) 178.

9   *Hilao v Estate of Marcos* 103 F.3d 767 (9th Cir. 1996).

10   *Kadić v Karadžić* 70 F 3d 232 (2d Cir 1995).

11   *Doe v Unocal Corp* 963 F Supp 880 (CD Cal 1997); 395 F 3d 932 (9th Cir 2002); 395 F 3d 978 (9th Cir 2003).

12   Muchlinski and Rouas, 'Foreign Direct-Liability Litigation', 360.

13   Stephens, 'Human Rights Litigation in U.S. Courts', 189.

14   226 F.3d 88 (2d Cir 2000); 2002 WL 319887 (SDNY 2002).

the oil MNE Royal Dutch Shell conspired with, or aided and abetted, Nigeria's military in the commission of human rights violations, including the conviction of the Ogoni Nine.[15] However, cases against corporations have raised the issue of how to distinguish 'actionable corporate complicity in egregious human rights abuses from non-tortious doing business in foreign countries'.[16] This is an issue that has divided US federal courts.

Until 2010, there was a strong consensus among US federal courts that corporations could be subject to suit under the ATS to the same extent as natural persons. However, this consensus started to crumble in *Kiobel v Royal Dutch Petroleum Co*. In 2010, the divided panel of the US Court of Appeals for the Second Circuit ruled that the ATS does not provide jurisdiction over claims against corporate defendants.[17] The two-judge majority held that international law governs the scope of the violations actionable under the statute, including who can be held liable for those violations, and that international law does not recognize corporate liability for human rights violations.[18] The US Supreme Court reviewed the case in 2013.[19] However, it did not address the question whether corporations could be sued under the ATS. It focused instead on the separate question of the extraterritorial application of the ATS. The US Supreme Court ruled that 'the presumption against extraterritoriality applies to claims under the ATS, and that nothing in the statute rebuts that presumption'. In this case, all the relevant conduct took place outside the US. Therefore, the petitioners' case was barred from seeking relief for violations of the law of nations occurring outside the US. The Supreme Court added that:

> even where the claims touch and concern the territory of the United States, they must do so with sufficient force to displace the presumption against extraterritorial application. ... Corporations are often present in many countries, and it would reach too far to say that mere corporate presence suffices. If Congress were to determine otherwise, a statute more specific than the ATS would be required.

This ruling struck a blow against the use of the ATS to hold foreign companies accountable for human rights violations committed abroad. In 2018, the US Supreme Court definitively closed the doors of the ATS to claims targeting foreign companies. In *Jesner v Arab Bank*,[20] the Supreme Court held that foreign corporations cannot be sued, and therefore are excluded from liability,

---

15   Stephens, 'Human Rights Litigation in U.S. Courts', 189.

16   Ibid.

17   621 F.3d 111 (2nd Circ 2010).

18   Stephens, 'Human Rights Litigation in U.S. Courts', 191.

19   133 S Ct 1659 (2013).

20   138 S Ct 1386 (2018).

under the ATS. For some observers, this ruling completed the exclusion of transnational human rights litigation from US federal courts started by *Kiobel*.[21]

At the present time, ATS-based claims remain possible against domestic corporations. However, a number of substantial barriers may limit the possibility of bringing these claims.[22] First, US corporations often do business abroad through subsidiaries incorporated under foreign law. When human rights violations take place in the context of a foreign subsidiary's activities, plaintiffs will have to either convince the court to attribute the tortious conduct of the subsidiary to the parent company or find tortious conduct on the part of the parent itself. However, US courts have been reluctant to pierce the corporate veil in ATS cases.[23] Second, most ATS claims against corporations allege that the company aided and abetted violations by foreign governments. To date, US courts have nonetheless been divided on the required criminal intent (*mens rea*) standard applicable to corporations to hold them liable for aiding and abetting.[24] Third, ATS-based claims must satisfy *Kiobel*'s requirement that they touch and concern US territory. Again, US courts have disagreed on the meaning of this requirement. While some have held that the US nationality of the defendant is not sufficient by itself, others have ruled that only the location of the conduct matters.[25] In *Nestle USA Inc. v Doe*,[26] a case alleging US companies' involvement in child slavery on Ivory Coast cocoa farms, the Supreme Court dismissed the plaintiffs' claim on the grounds that they improperly sought extraterritorial application of the ATS. Furthermore, because the statute did not apply extraterritorially, the plaintiffs should have established that the relevant conduct to the ATS' focus occurred in the US, even if other conduct occurred abroad. However, pleading general corporate activity, like 'mere corporate presence', did not draw a sufficient connection between the cause of action sought by the respondents and domestic conduct. The Supreme Court's decision suggests that few ATS-based claims against corporations will be allowed to proceed in the future. Furthermore, the likely difficulty in showing the involvement of the US parent company in the human rights violations complicates the task further. As Dodge ironically points out, 'So, while corporations continue to be subject to customary international law norms of human rights law, the prospects of holding them liable for violating those norms in US courts have faded nearly to vanishing point.'[27]

---

21   Rebecca J Hamilton, 'Jesner v. Arab Bank' (2018) 112 American Journal of International Law 720. See also Jonathan Kolieb, 'Jesner v Arab Bank: The US Supreme Court Forecloses on Accountability for Corporate Human Rights Abuses' (2018) 24 Australian International Law Journal 209.

22   William S Dodge, 'Corporate Liability Under the US Alien Tort Statute: A Comment on Jesner v Arab Bank' (2019) 4 Business and Human Rights Journal 131, 135.

23   Ibid.

24   Ibid, 136.

25   Ibid, 136.

26   141 S Ct 1931 (2021).

27   Ibid, 137.

Transnational tort claims against MNEs

Civil actions based on general tort law have also been brought before domestic courts of various common law jurisdictions in order to hold MNEs accountable for wrongs committed abroad. Flexible rules on access to evidence, class or group actions, and the possibility of obtaining a high amount of damages, including punitive damages, have contributed to the appeal of common law countries, especially the US and England, as forums for transnational claims against MNEs. At the same time, plaintiffs have faced a number of obstacles in accessing courts in these countries. In most cases, plaintiffs have struggled with the application of the *forum non conveniens* doctrine and other jurisdictional issues, which have prevented their claims from reaching the merits phase. Moreover, the high costs of bringing these lawsuits remain problematic. Furthermore, reforms in England regarding legal aid and cost recovery have reduced accessibility to the domestic courts by victims of business-related abuse from host countries. The following overview of claims in the US, Canada, Australia, and England therefore shows the main opportunities and challenges for holding MNEs accountable in common law jurisdictions.

United States

In the US, the first transnational tort claim was brought against the US chemical company Union Carbide following the infamous industrial disaster that took place in Bhopal, India, in 1984. However, the case was dismissed on grounds of *forum non conveniens*, as India was seen as the appropriate forum for the claims against Union Carbide. The doctrine of *forum non conveniens* 'deals with the discretionary power of a court to decline to exercise a possessed jurisdiction whenever it appears that the case before it may be more appropriately tried elsewhere'.[28] It was originally invoked to protect the defendant from being harassed by a plaintiff choosing a genuinely inconvenient or inappropriate forum. However, 'it has become in many instances a device for parent companies to escape liability for tortious acts committed abroad.'[29] Critics of *forum non conveniens* point out that this doctrine is simply inadequate to treat claims that arise in modern transnational business patterns and that it limits access to justice by victims.[30]

In general, tort claims relating to human rights violations against foreign corporations are unlikely to succeed,[31] most notably as a result of the Supreme

---

28   Paxton Blair, 'The Doctrine of Forum Non Conveniens in Anglo-American Law' (1929) 29 Columbia Law Review 1, 1. On the doctrine of *forum non conveniens*, see also Ronald Brand and Scott Jablonski, *Forum Non Conveniens: History, Global Practice, and Future Under the Hague Convention on Choice of Court Agreements* (OUP 2007).

29   Michael Anderson, 'Transnational Corporations and Environmental Damage: Is Tort Law the Answer?' (2002) 41 Washburn Law Journal 399, 412.

30   Ibid, 413.

31   Beth Stephens, 'Remarks by Beth Stephens' (2019) 113 Proceedings of the ASIL Annual Meeting 166, 167.

Court's recent decisions strictly limiting the assertion of general personal jurisdiction over corporations.[32] In particular, in *Daimler AG v Bauman* the Supreme Court rejected the idea that courts in California could have jurisdiction to hear a suit against German car-maker Daimler for the actions of its subsidiary in Argentina.[33] In this case, the plaintiffs had filed a suit in the California Federal District Court alleging that MB Argentina, a subsidiary of Daimler, had collaborated with state security forces during Argentina's 1976–1983 dictatorship to kidnap, detain, torture, and kill workers of the subsidiary. The Supreme Court held that Daimler was not amenable to suit in California for injuries allegedly caused by the conduct of MB Argentina that took place entirely outside the US. It rejected the idea that general jurisdiction can be exercised 'in every State in which a corporation engages in a substantial, continuous, and systematic course of business'. Continuous and systematic activities alone are not sufficient for jurisdiction over claims unrelated to those activities. A corporation's affiliations with a State must be so continuous and systematic as to render it essentially at home in the forum State.[34] The Supreme Court also concluded that California's exercise of general jurisdiction over Daimler would violate the Due Process Clause of the Fourteenth Amendment. For most observers, *Daimler* put an end to an era of general jurisdiction jurisprudence in the US.[35]

Canada

In Canada, around seven transnational claims have so far been brought against MNEs.[36] In particular, most of these claims have concerned Canadian extractive companies operating abroad.[37] This is not surprising since Canada is alleged to be home to half of the world's mining companies.[38] In these cases, plaintiffs have accused extractive companies of having directly and indirectly contributed to

---

32 *Goodyear Dunlop Tires Operations SA v Brown* 131 S Ct 2846 (2011); *Daimler Ag v Bauman* 134 S Ct 746 (2014).

33 For a discussion of this case, see Judy M Cornett and Michael H Hoffheimer, 'Good-Bye Significant Contacts: General Personal Jurisdiction after Daimler AG v. Bauman' (2015) 76 Ohio State Law Journal 101, 105.

34 Linda J Silberman, 'The End of Another Era: Reflections on Daimler and its Implications for Judicial Jurisdiction in the United States' (2015) 19 Lewis and Clark Law Review 675.

35 Ibid.

36 Most of these claims are displayed on the BHRRC's website.

37 See Sara L Seck, 'Environmental Harm in Developing Countries Caused by Subsidiaries of Canadian Mining Corporations: The Interface of Public and Private International Law' (2000) 37 Canadian Yearbook of International Law 139; Penelope Simons, 'Canada's Enhanced CSR Strategy: Human Rights Due Diligence and Access to Justice for Victims of Extraterritorial Corporate Human Rights Abuses' (2015) 56 Canadian Business Law Journal 167; Miriam Cohen, 'Doing Business Abroad: A Review of Selected Recent Canadian Case-Studies on Corporate Accountability for Foreign Human Rights Violations' (2020) The International Journal of Human Rights DOI: 10.1080/13642987.2020.1729134.

38 Cohen, 'Doing Business Abroad', 1.

human rights violations and environmental damage, including environmental pollution following a tailings dam failure in Guyana,[39] war crimes and gross violations of human rights in the DRC,[40] bodily injuries, death threats, and intimidation by private security forces against demonstrators in Ecuador[41] and in Guatemala,[42] rape and murder by security personnel in Guatemala,[43] and use of forced labour and inhuman and degrading treatment in Eritrea.[44] Recently, a tort claim targeted a retail company for its liability in the collapse of the Rana Plaza building in Bangladesh.[45]

Plaintiffs have generally struggled to establish jurisdiction in Canada. One early case was a claim brought against Cambior, a mining MNE based in Quebec, for pollution originating from its gold mine in Guyana.[46] In 1998, the Quebec Superior Court[47] dismissed the case on grounds of *forum non conveniens*, finding that Guyana was the appropriate forum given the location of the evidence and witnesses, and the interests of justice.[48] Furthermore, the plaintiffs did not have a right to a forum in Quebec.[49] In *Anvil Mining*, the Court of Appeal for Quebec dismissed a collective redress action for lack of jurisdiction. In this case, plaintiffs alleged that Anvil Mining, an extractive company based in Australia but with activities in Quebec, had provided logistical assistance to the DRC military, which then committed war crimes and crimes against

---

39   *Recherches Internationales Quebec v Cambior Inc*, 1998 QJ 2554 (SCJ).

40   *Anvil Mining Ltd v Association Canadienne Contre L'Impunité*, 2012 QCCA 117.

41   *Piedra v Copper Mesa Mining Corporation*, 2011 ONCA 191.

42   *Garcia v Tahoe Resources Inc*, 2015 BCSC 2045; 2017 BCCA 39. For an analysis of this case, see Cohen, 'Doing Business Abroad'.

43   *Choc v Hudbay Minerals Inc*, 2013 ONSC 1414. For an analysis of this case, see Cohen, 'Doing Business Abroad'; Philip Woram, 'Are Their Chickens Coming Home to Roost in Ontario: Why Hudbay and Yaiguaje May Signal a New Era of Heightened Liability for the International Extractive Industry' (2015) 49 The International Lawyer 243.

44   *Araya v Nevsun Resources Ltd*, 2016 BCSC 1856; 2017 BCCA 401; 2020 SCC 5. For an analysis of this case, see Jolane T Lauzon, 'Araya V. Nevsun Resources: Remedies for Victims of Human Rights Violations Committed by Canadian Mining Companies Abroad' (2018) 31 Revue Québécoise de Droit International 143.

45   *Das v George Weston Limited*, 2017 ONSC 4129; 2018 ONCA 1053.

46   *Recherches Internationales Quebec v Cambior Inc*.

47   It should be mentioned that while Canada is a common law country, Quebec, a predominantly French-speaking province of Canada, is a mixed jurisdiction. As a result of the French heritage of this province, Quebec derives its civil law from both the civil law and the common law traditions. On this topic, see William Tetley, 'Mixed Jurisdictions: Common Law v Civil Law (Codified and Uncodified)' (2000) 60 Louisiana Law Review 677.

48   Muchlinski and Rouas, 'Foreign Direct-Liability Litigation', 363.

49   Gwynne Skinner and others, 'The Third Pillar: Access to Judicial Remedies for Human Rights Violations by Transnational Business' (ICAR, ECCJ & CORE 2013) 27.

humanity in Katanga, DRC. The Court of Appeal found that the dispute had no connection with Anvil Mining's activities in Quebec. In *Copper Mesa*, the Court of Appeal for Ontario dismissed the claims for failing to disclose a reasonable cause of action. The plaintiffs were Ecuadorian residents who alleged that two directors of Copper Mesa, a British Colombian company that controlled a mining project in Ecuador, were negligent in failing to prevent acts of violence and threats committed against them by security forces hired by the operating subsidiary. According to the plaintiffs' claim, the directors were liable for what happened because the facts gave rise to an affirmative duty on their part to prevent the harm that materialized. However, the Court of Appeal rejected that the directors could be held liable in negligence for failing to prevent harm. It also held that a 'corporate director had no established duty in law to be mindful of the interests of strangers to the corporation when discharging their duties as a director'.[50]

In recent years, however, plaintiffs have been more successful in establishing jurisdiction in Canada. In *Tahoe Resources*, the British Columbia Court of Appeal allowed an action against Tahoe Resources to be heard in Canada. It held that there was substantial risk of an unfair trial should the case be heard in the Guatemalan courts due to, among other things, procedural obstacles, the limitation period, and evidence pointing to a high risk of injustice because of widespread corruption in the Guatemalan court system.[51] In *Hudbay Minerals*, the defendant originally contested that the claims should be heard in Canada. However, it withdrew its opposition and the Superior Court of Ontario ruled in July 2013 that the claims could proceed to trial in Canada. Finally, the Supreme Court of Canada addressed the issue of jurisdiction in a landmark ruling in *Nevsun*.[52] In this case, the plaintiffs filed a lawsuit against Nevsun Resources Ltd (Nevsun), a Canadian mining company, for its complicity in the use of forced labour at a mine it owns in Eritrea. The plaintiffs claimed they had been conscripted into forced labour and subjected to violent, cruel, inhuman, and degrading treatment by Nevsun's subcontractor. In February 2020, the Supreme Court allowed the case to go forward. Importantly, it held that the breaches of customary international law, or *jus cogens*, relied on by the Eritrean plaintiffs could apply to Nevsun. It added, 'Since the customary international law norms raised by the Eritrean workers form part of the Canadian common law, and since Nevsun is a company bound by Canadian law, the claims of the Eritrean workers for breaches of customary international law should be

---

50 *Piedra v Copper Mesa Mining Corporation*, para 85. See also Michael Marin, 'Third-Party Liability of Directors and Officers: Reconciling Corporate Personality and Personal Responsibility in Tort' (2019) 42 Dalhousie Law Journal, 335, 347–348.

51 Cohen, 'Doing Business Abroad', 6.

52 *Araya v Nevsun Resources Ltd.*

allowed to proceed.' For some observers, the Supreme Court opened the door for international human rights tort claims in Canada.[53]

Despite the plaintiffs' success in establishing the jurisdiction of courts in Canada, in the coming years courts will decide on the merits in *Hudbay Minerals* alone, as in *Tahoe Resources* and *Nevsun* the parties reached an out-of-court settlement.[54] Such settlements are welcome as a way to provide for speedy dispute resolution and effective redress to victims for the damage they have suffered. However, at the same time they prevent the formulation of judgments that could outline the contours of corporate liability in human rights cases involving MNEs. Unless a settlement is also reached in *Hudbay Minerals*, the outcomes of this case will show whether Canada could become a valid jurisdiction for victims in search of corporate accountability.

Australia

Although transnational litigation against MNEs started in Australia in the 1990s, less than a handful of claims have been brought before Australian courts to date. These claims have produced limited results from a corporate accountability perspective; two cases ended up in out-of-court settlements, and another case is still ongoing. The first claim was brought as early as 1994 by landowners from Papua New Guinea against BHP, an Anglo-Australian mining company.[55] In this case, the plaintiffs alleged that BHP dumped mine tailings waste into local rivers, which led to environmental damage and destruction of their traditional lifestyle. Their claim was admissible on jurisdictional grounds because of Australia's generally pro-plaintiff approach to the issue of choice of jurisdiction.[56] The parties eventually reached an out-of-court settlement. For almost 20 years afterwards no transnational claims were brought against MNEs. However, in 2014 an Iranian national became the lead plaintiff in a class action lawsuit brought before the Supreme Court of Victoria against Australia and two corporate contractors who operated an immigration detention centre on Manus Island in Papua New Guinea. The plaintiff alleged that the defendants breached a duty of care they owed to asylum seekers detained in the centre.[57]

---

53   Miranda Lam, Meghan S Bridges and Edmond Chan, 'Supreme Court of Canada Cracks open the Door for International Human Rights Tort Claims in Nevsun Resources Ltd. v. Araya' (McCarthy Tetrauld, 4 March 2020) <https://www.mccarthy.ca/en/insights/blogs/mining-prospects/supreme-court-canada-cracks-open-door-international-human-rights-tort-claims-nevsun-resources-ltd-v-araya> accessed 1 May 2021.

54   Elizabeth Steyn, 'Slavery Charges Against Canadian Mining Company Settled on the Sly' (The Conversation, 26 October 2020) <https://theconversation.com/slavery-charges-against-canadian-mining-company-settled-on-the-sly-148605> accessed 1 May 2021.

55   *Dagi v Broken Hill Proprietary Co Ltd (No 2)* [1997] 1 VR 428.

56   Muchlinski and Rouas, 'Foreign Direct-Liability Litigation', 363.

57   *Kamasaee v Commonwealth of Australia & Ors* S CI 2014 6770.

In 2017 the parties agreed to settle.[58] Finally, in 2016 approximately 15,000 Indonesian seaweed farmers filed a class action lawsuit before the Federal Court of Australia against PTTEP Australasia, a subsidiary of a Thai state-owned oil and gas company, following the Montara oil spill in the Timor Sea in 2009.[59] The plaintiffs alleged that the oil spill caused damage to seaweed farming activities in Indonesia. Hearings started in June 2019 and the case was ongoing at the time of writing.

As a result of settlements between plaintiffs and defendants, transnational litigation against MNEs has barely developed in Australia. It is therefore difficult to assess the potential of Australia as a reliable forum for future claims. Some scholars have nonetheless argued that Australia remains a viable forum for various reasons.[60] First, its pro-plaintiff approach departs from that in common law jurisdictions with respect to the application of the doctrine of *forum non conveniens*, which has plagued litigation in other countries. In general, cases will only be stayed on *forum non conveniens* grounds if Australia is a 'clearly inappropriate forum'.[61] Second, Australian courts may be more inclined to hear tort claims involving damage suffered partly within the jurisdiction, since foreign corporations are susceptible to the exercise of personal jurisdiction where they conduct business in Australia. Courts have taken a particularly permissive approach to establishing presence in the jurisdiction, and in practice it is not a significantly high threshold to overcome.[62] Third, when determining the applicable law, although courts will apply the *lex loci delicti* principle strictly, there is a deal of flexibility around the test for determining where the relevant wrong has occurred. Finally, Australia allows class action suits, which is an advantage for plaintiffs.[63] At the same time, issues such as funding and costs remain significant barriers for plaintiffs.[64]

England

In Europe, transnational litigation against MNEs started in England where the first tort claims were brought against parent companies of MNEs for harm resulting from their subsidiaries' activities in developing countries. These claims have alleged a variety of harms, such as asbestos-related occupational

---

58   *Kamasaee* [2017] VSC 537.

59   *Sanda v PTTEP Australasia (Ashmore Cartier) Pty Ltd (No 3)* [2017] FCA 1272; *(No 5)* [2019] FCA 932 (17 June 2019).

60   Gabrielle Holly, 'Transnational Tort and Access to Remedy under the UN Guiding Principles on Business and Human Rights: Kamasaee v Commonwealth' (2018) 19 Melbourne Journal of International Law 52, 74.

61   Ibid, 74–75.

62   Ibid, 76.

63   Ibid.

64   Ibid.

disease,[65] oil spills and environmental pollution,[66] toxic waste dumping,[67] and torture and ill treatment.[68] According to Richard Meeran, a British lawyer from Leigh Day, the London-based law firm that pioneered this type of litigation, the fundamental objectives of tort litigation against MNEs are twofold: to 'provide a level of compensation to a victim which as much as possible reinstates the victim in the position that he or she would have been in if the negligence had not occurred', and to 'act as a deterrent against future wrongdoing by the perpetrator and others generally'.[69]

England has been a favoured home country forum for victims of business-related abuse as a result of its flexible rules on evidence and group actions. At the same time, plaintiffs have faced various procedural hurdles, in particular to establish the jurisdiction of the English courts, as well as practical obstacles, such as the costs of proceedings. Courts have also often been reluctant to hold parent companies liable for human rights abuse taking place in the context of their overseas activities. However, recent Supreme Court decisions suggesting that a parent company may incur a duty of care in respect of the activities of a subsidiary indicate a potential shift in the legal landscape governing corporate accountability.

Jurisdiction

The first plaintiffs who brought tort litigation against MNEs for conduct committed abroad in the English courts had to deal with the doctrine of *forum non conveniens*.[70] The significance of this obstacle was particularly visible in two cases concerning personal injuries or death caused by exposure to

---

65   Peter Muchlinski, 'Corporations in International Litigation: Problems of Jurisdiction and the United Kingdom Asbestos Cases' (2001) 50 International and Comparative Law Quarterly 1; Richard Meeran, 'Cape Plc: South African Mineworkers' Quest for Justice' (2003) 9 International Journal of Occupational and Environmental Health 218.

66   *Arroyo v BP Exploration Company (Colombia) Ltd* [2010] EWHC 1643 (QB); *Arroyo v Equion Energia Ltd* [2013] EWHC 3150 (TCC). See also Diane Taylor, 'BP Oil Spill: Colombian Farmers Sue for Negligence' *The Guardian* (London, 11 January 2011) <http://www.theguardian.com/environment/2011/jan/11/bp-oil-spill-colombian-farmers> accessed 1 May 2021.

67   *Motto v Trafigura Ltd* [2009] EWHC 1246 (QB), [2011] EWCA Civ 1150.

68   *Guerrero v Monterrico Metals Plc* [2009] EWHC 2475 (QB), [2010] EWHC 160 (QB). See also Ian Cobain, 'Abuse Claims against Peru Police Guarding British Firm Monterrico' *The Guardian* (London, 18 October 2009) <http://www.theguardian.com/environment/2009/oct/18/british-mining-firm-peru-controversy> accessed 1 May 2021.

69   Richard Meeran, 'Tort Litigation against Multinational Corporations for Violation of Human Rights: An Overview of the Position Outside the United States' (2011) 3 City University of Hong Kong Law Review 1, 3.

70   Ibid, 11.

uranium and asbestos respectively: *Connelly v RTZ Corporation Plc*[71] and *Lubbe v Cape Plc.*[72] In both cases, the parent company applied for a stay of proceedings on the grounds that the host State (Namibia and South Africa respectively) was the more appropriate forum to hear the claim. The High Court of Justice (High Court) originally accepted the defendants' argument, granting a stay of proceedings. However, in both cases the House of Lords ultimately rejected the decision to decline jurisdiction in favour of either Namibia or South Africa. It found that a stay would lead to a denial of justice where the plaintiffs could demonstrate, through evidence such as the absence of adequate funding or legal representation in the host State, that they would be unable to obtain justice in the foreign forum.

Things changed after the 2005 *Owusu v Jackson* case,[73] in which the CJEU foreclosed the use of the *forum non conveniens* doctrine in the English courts.[74] The CJEU reasserted that Article 2(1) of Regulation 44/2001[75] was directly applicable to all EU Member States, who could not derogate from this rule. In particular, the doctrine of *forum non conveniens* was deemed incompatible with the 1968 Brussels Convention on Jurisdiction and the Enforcement of Judgments in Civil and Commercial Matters,[76] as it would undermine the principle of legal certainty and the uniform application of European rules of jurisdiction. Consequently, since *Owusu, forum non conveniens* is no longer an issue in transnational cases against MNEs in England, thus opening the way for subsequent litigation.[77] However, following the UK's withdrawal from the EU, observers have validly questioned whether English courts will resume the application of the *forum non conveniens* doctrine.[78]

Despite the progress made with regard to *forum non conveniens*, the jurisdiction of the English courts has remained problematic for plaintiffs and continues to consume the majority of their resources during litigation. In particular, plaintiffs face the question of whether they have a sufficiently substantial case on the merits to justify the court's exercise of jurisdiction. This question, which

---

71   [1996] QB 361 (CA), [1997] UKHL 30, [1998] AC 854, [1999] CLC 533.

72   [1998] EWCA Civ 1351, [2000] UKHL 41.

73   Case C-281/02 *Owusu v Jackson* [2005] ECR I-1383.

74   John Burke, 'Foreclosure of the Doctrine of Forum Non Conveniens under the Brussels I Regulation: Advantages and Disadvantages' (2008) 3 The European Legal Forum I-121.

75   Council Regulation (EC) No 44/2001 on jurisdiction and the recognition and enforcement of judgments in civil and commercial matters [2001] OJ L12/1.

76   Convention on Jurisdiction and the Enforcement of Judgements in Civil and Commercial Matters (adopted 27 September 1968, entered into force 1 February 1973) 1262 UNTS 153.

77   Meeran, 'Tort Litigation', 14.

78   Axel Marx and others, 'Access to Legal Remedies for Victims of Corporate Human Rights Abuses in Third Countries' (European Parliament 2019) 16.

demonstrates how closely jurisdictional and liability issues are intertwined, was exemplified in the *Okpabi v Royal Dutch Shell Plc* case. In this ongoing case, two Nigerian communities have sought redress against Royal Dutch Shell Plc (RDS), an Anglo-Dutch oil company,[79] and Shell Petroleum Development Company of Nigeria Ltd (SPDC), its Nigerian subsidiary, for environmental damage caused by several oil spills that occurred from SPDC's pipelines. The claimants argue that the oil spills were caused by SPDC's negligence. They also contend that RDS owed them a common law duty of care because it exercised significant control over material aspects of SPDC's operations and/or assumed responsibility for SPDC's operations, and that RDS allegedly failed to protect the claimants against the risk of foreseeable harm arising from SPDC's operations. Both the High Court[80] and the Court of Appeal[81] rejected the suggestion that the English courts should exercise jurisdiction over the claims. Both courts concluded that although they had jurisdiction to try the claims against RDS, the claimants were unable to demonstrate a properly arguable case that RDS owed them a duty of care. Since the claims against RDS, the anchor defendant, did not have a real prospect of success, the conditions for granting permission to serve the claim on SPDC as a 'necessary or proper party' to the claims against RDS were not met. Both rulings raised concerns about the risk of seeing the interlocutory stage transformed into a 'mini-trial', which would place 'an unreasonably high burden on the claimants to establish an arguable case on the duty of care at the jurisdictional stage of proceedings'.[82] Victims may face significant barriers as a result of this approach, as they would have to present a substantial case before disclosure proceedings could start.[83]

However, in a landmark judgment given in February 2021,[84] the UK Supreme Court rejected the lower courts' approach. It clarified that courts should not conduct a mini-trial when deciding on jurisdictional issues. It is not the task of the courts to assess the weight of the evidence and to exercise judgement based on that evidence at the interlocutory stage. The factual assertions made in support of the claim should be accepted unless, exceptionally, they are demonstrably untrue or unsupportable.[85] This was not the case in this instance. Furthermore, the UK Supreme Court rejected the contention that a

---

79   RDS is incorporated in England and Wales but has its headquarters in The Hague.

80   [2017] EWHC 89 (TCC).

81   [2018] EWCA Civ 191.

82   Ekaterina Aristova, 'Tort Litigation against Transnational Corporations in the English Courts: The Challenge of Jurisdiction' (2018) 14(2) Utrecht Law Review <http://doi.org/10.18352/ulr.444> accessed 1 May 2021.

83   Lucas Roorda, 'Jurisdiction in Foreign Direct Liability Cases in Europe' (2019) 113 Proceedings of the ASIL Annual Meeting 161, 165.

84   *Okpabi and others v Royal Dutch Shell plc and another* [2021] UKSC 3.

85   Ibid, [101]–[119].

parent company could never incur a duty of care in respect of the activities of a subsidiary by maintaining group-wide policies and guidelines. It found that the Shell group's vertical corporate structure involved significant delegation of authority, including in relation to operational safety and environmental responsibility. How this organizational structure worked in practice and the extent to which authority was delegated clearly raised triable issues.[86]

The Supreme Court's decision in *Okpabi* is significant for a number of reasons, one of which being that it removes some of the barriers that plaintiffs have recently faced in establishing the jurisdiction of the English courts, including the risk of a mini-trial at the interlocutory stage and the assumption that claims based on the parent company's duty of care for its subsidiary activities do not raise a triable issue.[87] In particular, this judgment helps to improve access to justice and reparation by clarifying 'the application of the jurisdictional test in such a way as to expedite claimants' access to a proper fair trial'.[88]

Corporate group liability

In the majority of claims against MNEs, plaintiffs have raised the tort liability of the parent company for its negligence arising from a breach of a duty of care.[89] They have used this legal basis in order to circumvent the corporate veil theory. As Chambers and Tyler suggest, 'By targeting the parent company, claimants have avoided having to argue that the corporate veil should be pierced to trace liability for the actions of the local subsidiary back to the parent company or other branch of the business in the [UK].'[90]

The English courts have, at times, shown receptiveness to such arguments raised by plaintiffs. In claims against MNEs, judges have accepted the need 'to be more creative and influential in solving the legal problems before them, which enhances the chances of success for plaintiffs who are bringing novel legal arguments'.[91] This was particularly visible in *Chandler v Cape Plc*, which

---

86   Ibid, [155]–[158].

87   Aspects of the decision pertaining to liability are discussed later in this chapter.

88   Ekaterina Aristova and Carlos López, 'UK Okpabi et al v Shell: UK Supreme Court Reaffirms Parent Companies May Owe a Duty of Care Towards Communities Impacted by Their Subsidiaries in Third Countries' (*OpinioJuris*, 16 February 2021) <http://opiniojuris.org/2021/02/16/uk-okpabi-et-al-v-shell-uk-supreme-court-reaffirms-parent-companies-may-owe-a-duty-of-care-towards-communities-impacted-by-their-subsidiaries-in-third-countries/> accessed 1 May 2021.

89   Meeran, 'Tort Litigation', 14.

90   Rachel Chambers and Katherine Tyler, 'The UK Context for Business and Human Rights' in Lara Blecher, Nancy Kaymar Stafford and Gretchen Bellamy (eds), *Corporate Responsibility for Human Rights Impacts: New Expectations and Paradigms* (American Bar Association 2014) 325.

91   Sarah Joseph, *Corporations and Transnational Human Rights Litigation* (Hart Publishing 2004) 16.

opened the door to liability of parent companies when they breach their duty of care towards their subsidiaries' employees. Chandler was employed by Cape Building Products Ltd (Cape Products) in England between 1959 and 1962. Cape Products was a wholly-owned subsidiary of Cape Plc that manufactured asbestos products. In 2007, Chandler discovered that he had contracted asbestosis as a result of exposure to asbestos during his employment with Cape Products. However, by that time Cape Products no longer existed and its remaining insurance policies excluded asbestosis. Therefore, Chandler brought a claim for damages against Cape Plc, the parent company, for breach of its duty of care towards Chandler.

In 2011, the High Court ruled that Cape Plc was liable to Chandler on the basis of the common law concept of assumption of responsibility.[92] Applying the three-stage test in *Caparo Industries Plc v Dickman* (1990) for determining whether the situation gives rise to a duty of care, the High Court found that Cape Plc owed, and had breached, a duty of care to Chandler. First, the defendant should have foreseen the risk of injury to the claimant. Second, there was sufficient proximity between Chandler and Cape Plc. Third, it was fair, just, and reasonable for a duty of care to exist. Cape Plc appealed against that decision. In 2012, the Court of Appeal upheld the High Court's decision and found that Cape Plc owed a direct duty of care to the employees of Cape Products.[93] Given Cape Plc's superior knowledge about the nature and management of risks from asbestos, it was appropriate to find that Cape Plc assumed a duty of care either to advise Cape Products on what steps it had to take in light of the knowledge then available to provide those employees with a safe system of work, or to ensure that those steps were taken. In this case, Cape Plc failed to advise on precautionary measures.[94] Importantly, the Court of Appeal provided guidance on the conditions under which a parent company could be held liable for harm suffered by its subsidiaries' employees:

> In summary, this case demonstrates that in appropriate circumstances the law may impose on a parent company responsibility for the health and safety of its subsidiary's employees. Those circumstances include a situation where, as in the present case, (1) the businesses of the parent and subsidiary are in a relevant respect the same; (2) the parent has, or ought to have, superior knowledge on some relevant aspect of health and safety in the particular industry; (3) the subsidiary's system of work is unsafe as the parent company knew, or ought to have known; and (4) the parent knew or ought to have foreseen that the

92   [2011] EWHC 951 (QB).
93   [2012] EWCA Civ 525.
94   Ibid, [78]–[79].

subsidiary or its employees would rely on its using that superior knowledge for the employees' protection. For the purposes of (4) it is not necessary to show that the parent is in the practice of intervening in the health and safety policies of the subsidiary. The court will look at the relationship between the companies more widely. The court may find that element (4) is established where the evidence shows that the parent has a practice of intervening in the trading operations of the subsidiary, for example production and funding issues.[95]

Chandler was a landmark case in the development of parent company liability for the harm caused by subsidiaries in the context of corporate group activities. However, in this case both the parent company and the subsidiary were registered in England and the subsidiary's activities took place in England.

Following *Chandler*, in several cases the English courts had to answer the question whether parent companies owe a duty of care to third parties affected by the operations of their foreign subsidiaries. In *AAA v Unilever Plc*, the Court of Appeal held that the law of tort does not recognize that the parent company has a legal responsibility vis-à-vis persons affected by the activities of its subsidiary. However, a parent company may have a duty of care in relation to its subsidiary's activity if ordinary, general principles of the law of tort regarding the imposition of a duty of care on the parent are satisfied in the particular case.[96] A parent company may have a duty of care in relation to its subsidiary's activities in two situations: (1) where the parent has in substance taken over the management of the relevant activity of the subsidiary in place of, or jointly with, the subsidiary's own management; or (2) where the parent has given relevant advice to the subsidiary about how it should manage a particular risk.[97] However, none of the claims in *Unilever* fell within one of these two situations. The Court of Appeal also rejected the claim that *Chandler* laid down a separate test, distinct from general principles, for the imposition of a duty of care on the parent.

Shortly after *Unilever*, the Supreme Court clarified the contours of the parent company's duty of care for the activities of its subsidiary in its landmark judgment in *Vedanta Resources Plc v Lungowe*.[98] In this case, the plaintiffs were farmers from Zambia who alleged that their health and farming activities had been damaged by the discharge of toxic matter from the Nchanga Copper Mine owned by Konkola Copper Mines Plc (KCM), a Zambian company. They brought

95   Ibid, [80].
96   *AAA v Unilever Plc* [2018] EWCA Civ 1532 [36].
97   Ibid, [37].
98   [2019] UKSC 20.

a group claim against KCM and Vedanta Resources Plc (Vedanta), its parent company, for negligence and breach of statutory duty. In 2019, the Supreme Court considered a procedural appeal regarding jurisdiction of the English courts for the group tort claim and had to answer, among other questions, whether there was an arguable case against Vedanta. It clarified that 'the liability of parent companies in relation to the activities of their subsidiaries is not, of itself, a distinct category of liability in common law negligence'.[99] It held as follows:

> Direct or indirect ownership by one company of all or a majority of the shares of another company (which is the irreducible essence of a parent/subsidiary relationship) may enable the parent to take control of the management of the operations of the business or of land owned by the subsidiary, but it does not impose any duty upon the parent to do so, whether owed to the subsidiary or, a fortiori, to anyone else. Everything depends on the extent to which, and the way in which, the parent availed itself of the opportunity to take over, intervene in, control, supervise or advise the management of the relevant operations (including land use) of the subsidiary.[100]

Furthermore, the Supreme Court rejected that all cases of the parent's liability could be shoehorned into the specific categories developed in *Unilever*, as '[t]here is no limit to the models of management and control which may be put in place within a multinational group of companies'.[101] It also dismissed the claim that 'a parent could never incur a duty of care in respect of the activities of a particular subsidiary merely by laying down group-wide policies and guidelines, and expecting the management of each subsidiary to comply with them' as '[g]roup guidelines about minimising the environmental impact of inherently dangerous activities, such as mining, may be shown to contain systemic errors which, when implemented as of course [sic] by a particular subsidiary, then cause harm to third parties'.[102] Group-wide policies may give rise to a duty of care to third parties if the parent takes active steps, by training, supervision, and enforcement, to see that they are implemented by relevant subsidiaries. Moreover, 'the parent may incur the relevant responsibility to third parties if, in published materials, it holds itself out as exercising that degree of supervision and control of its subsidiaries, even if it does not in fact do so. In such circumstances its very omission may constitute the abdication

---

99   Ibid, [49].
100 Ibid, [39].
101 Ibid, [51]
102 Ibid, [52].

of a responsibility which it has publicly undertaken.'[103] Ultimately, the Supreme Court found that Vedanta's published materials in which it asserted its own assumption of responsibility for the maintenance of proper standards of environmental control over the activities of its subsidiaries, and the implementation of those standards by training, monitoring, and enforcement, were sufficient on their own to show that a substantial level of intervention by Vedanta in the conduct of operations at the mine may be demonstrable at trial. Therefore, the Supreme Court recognized that a parent company may owe a duty of care to third parties affected by its foreign subsidiary's activities in specific circumstances.

Two years after *Vedanta*, the Supreme Court reaffirmed its position and clarified various points pertaining to the parent company's duty of care in *Okpabi*.[104] First, it clarified the factors and circumstances that may give rise to a duty of care of the parent company. It held that the Court of Appeal's conclusion that a parent company could never incur a duty of care in respect of the activities of a subsidiary by adopting group-wide policies and standards was inconsistent with *Vedanta*.[105] Moreover, the Supreme Court found that the Court of Appeal had focused inappropriately on the issue of control. While control is a starting point in considering the extent to which the parent did take over or share with the subsidiary the management of the relevant activity, it may not demonstrate the de facto management of the activity. As the Supreme Court pointed out, a 'subsidiary may maintain de jure control of its activities, but nonetheless delegate de facto management of part of them to emissaries of its parent'.[106] Second, the Supreme Court clarified the analytical framework to determine whether a duty of care of the parent company exists. It reasserted that 'there is "no special doctrine in the law of tort of legal responsibility on the part of a parent company in relation to the activities of its subsidiary, vis-à-vis persons affected by those activities"'.[107] This approach results from the fact that MNEs may put in place various models of management and control.[108] Furthermore, 'the liability of parent companies in relation to the activities of their subsidiaries is not, of itself, a distinct category of liability in common law negligence. ... The general principles which determine such liability "are not novel at all" ... 'It "require[s] no added level of rigorous analysis beyond that appropriate to any summary judgment application in a relatively complex case."'[109]

---

103 Ibid, [53].

104 *Okpabi and others v Royal Dutch Shell plc and another* [2021] UKSC 3.

105 Ibid, [143]–[145].

106 Ibid, [146]–[148].

107 Ibid, [149].

108 Ibid, [150].

109 Ibid, [151].

Plaintiffs have also tried to hold parent companies liable for the acts of third parties under the theory of accessory liability for assisting torts.[110] However, this strategy has been unsuccessful so far. In *Kalma v African Minerals Ltd*, plaintiffs from Sierra Leone brought a tort claim against African Minerals Ltd (AML), a minerals company listed on the Alternative Investment Market (AIM) of the London Stock Exchange and headquartered in London.[111] In this case, AML had provided various types of support (accommodation, vehicles, and money) to the police in exchange for protection of its mining operations in the Tonkoli district in Sierra Leone. However, when local unrest broke out as a result of the impact of the mine on inhabitants, the police responded to the unrest with excessive force, 'during the course of which many villagers were variously beaten, shot, gassed, robbed, sexually assaulted, squalidly incarcerated and, in one case, killed'.[112] The plaintiffs sought to hold AML liable for the wrongful acts of the police on different legal grounds, including accessory liability in furtherance of a common tortious design with the police and breach of the defendants' direct duty in failing to take adequate steps to prevent the police from committing torts. However, both the High Court and the Court of Appeal rejected the plaintiffs' claims.[113]

The courts found that AML could not be held liable based on accessory liability by reason of common design for the police's violence. In providing resources to the police, AML may have foreseen that the police might use excessive violence to suppress the disturbance. However, foreseeability does not justify the imposition of accessory liability. 'In order to establish tortious liability for common design, there needs to be something more than the foreseeability that, in certain circumstances, a tort might be committed by a third party.'[114] In this case, the courts did not find that AML had intended for the police to use violence. In particular, the fact that AML sought protection and assistance from the police could not lead to an inference that AML intended that the police 'should quash protest, if need be by violent means'.[115]

The courts also rejected the contention that AML owed a duty of care to the plaintiffs. The Court of Appeal adopted the position that this was a pure omissions case.[116] In this context, AML did not have a duty of care because it

---

110 For a discussion of accessory liability for assisting torts, see Paul S Davies, 'Accessory Liability for Assisting Torts' (2011) 70 Cambridge Law Journal 353.

111 *Kalma v African Minerals Ltd* [2018] EWHC 3506 (QB), [2020] EWCA Civ 144.

112 [2020] EWCA Civ 144, [2].

113 Permission to appeal to the UK Supreme Court was refused in August 2020 because the application did not raise an arguable point of law.

114 *Kalma v African Minerals Ltd* [2020] EWCA Civ 144, [86].

115 Ibid, [102].

116 Ibid, [135].

had not carried out any relevant activity, and the damage was not caused by anything which AML had done. Furthermore, the provision of money, vehicles, and accommodation was not a breach of any duty, as such assistance was common in Sierra Leone.[117] The Court of Appeal also dismissed the claim that AML could have had a freestanding duty of care according to the three-stage criteria from *Caparo*.[118] A relationship of proximity between the plaintiffs and AML was not established, and it would not have been fair, just, or reasonable to impose the alleged duty of care in this case. Another important point here is that the Court of Appeal rejected the idea that companies' voluntary commitment could create a duty of care. It held that:

> there is nothing in the Voluntary Principles [on Security and Human Rights] which make companies operating abroad generally liable for the unlawful acts of the police forces of the host countries in which they are operating: on the contrary, the Voluntary Principles are drafted on the basis that, whilst companies operating abroad may properly help to facilitate the law and order expected to be provided by host countries, it is the governments of those countries (and not the companies) who have 'the primary responsibility to promote and protect human rights'.[119]

This review of cases in England has revealed that, for a long time, uncertainty around the contours of corporate group liability posed a significant barrier to victims seeking justice for corporate human rights abuses. Courts have, in particular, been reluctant to hold parent companies liable for the damage caused by their group activities. However, recent Supreme Court decisions have clarified the circumstances under which parent companies may have a duty of care for the activities of their subsidiaries. In the future, how lower courts will interpret the Supreme Court's guidance in *Vedanta* and *Okpabi*, particularly how the intervention of the parent company in the management of its subsidiary's activities can give rise to a duty of care, will be critical in determining whether parent companies can be held liable for the harm caused by their subsidiaries.

Access to evidence

In England, plaintiffs must be able to prove that the parent company had a role in causing the harm to have a cause of action for liability against the parent company. However, MNEs are often in possession of documents containing

---

117 Ibid, [124].
118 Ibid, [138]–[151].
119 Ibid, [149].

important supporting evidence. Therefore, it is crucial for plaintiffs to be able to gain access to such material.

Despite the existence of a number of restrictions, the disclosure process has been favourable to plaintiffs in transnational litigation against MNEs.[120] Courts have generally been inclined to order disclosure of documents needed by claimants. For instance, in *Vava v Anglo American South Africa Ltd*[121] the High Court held that, if no orders were to be made requiring the MNE to produce documents, 'there [was] a very great risk that the claimants [would] be contesting the jurisdiction issue at an unfair disadvantage and that must be addressed'.[122] As a result, the disclosure system has allowed plaintiffs to demonstrate the parent company's role in the cause of the harm. Importantly, it has reduced the inequality of arms between the parties by improving the opportunities of plaintiffs to put pressure on MNEs to reach a fast resolution of the dispute, and their capacity to negotiate strategically.

In some cases, the English disclosure process has also benefited plaintiffs in similar cases in other European countries. In the *Bodo Community v Shell Petroleum Development Company of Nigeria Ltd* case,[123] a Nigerian fishing and farming community known as the Bodo City community (Bodo community) filed a tort claim against SPDC, a Nigerian oil company, for the harm suffered following two successive oil spills. During the proceedings before the High Court, SPDC was required to disclose a number of internal documents. Information from these documents was later used as evidence in the context of similar proceedings against SPDC and its parent company in the Netherlands.[124]

In recent years, a number of cases have raised concerns that the lack of access to evidence at the early stages of proceedings may affect the ability of plaintiffs to establish jurisdiction in England. In *Okpabi*, the Court of Appeal rejected the plaintiffs' group claim on the grounds that the plaintiffs had not demonstrated a properly arguable case that RDS owed a duty of care to third parties affected by the operations of its Nigerian subsidiary. However, it reached this conclusion even though there had been no opportunity for cross-examination and minimal disclosure from RDS.[125] Ultimately, the Supreme Court found that such an approach was inappropriate at the interlocutory stage and concluded that the Court of Appeal had erred in its approach as to the prospect of the disclosure

---

120 Skinner and others, 'The Third Pillar', 53.

121 [2012] EWHC 1969 (QB).

122 Ibid, [69].

123 [2014] EWHC 1973 (TCC).

124 'Statement of Appeal Regarding the Dismissal of the Motion to Produce Documents by Virtue of Section 834A DCCP (Interlocutory Judgement District Court of The Hague 14-09-2011)' (Prakken d'Oliveira 2014), para 8.

125 *Okpabi v Royal Dutch Shell plc* [2018] EWCA Civ 191.

of internal corporate documents material to the claims made.[126] Significantly, it emphasized the importance of internal corporate documents 'in the context of cases concerning the negligence liability of a parent company for the acts of its subsidiary'.[127]

Litigation costs

The transnational nature of claims against MNEs and the complexity of the legal issues at stake render this type of litigation particularly costly for plaintiffs. In particular, evidence-gathering and representation for large groups of claimants exacerbate litigation costs and lawyers' fees. Excessive litigation costs raise a number of issues regarding accessibility of English courts by foreign victims with few financial resources. For instance, they generally deter law firms from engaging in transnational claims against MNEs.

The availability of collective redress in England has allowed large numbers of victims of corporate abuse to seek justice. For instance, in *Motto v Trafigura Ltd* the British law firm Leigh Day filed a tort claim in the High Court on behalf of 30,000 Ivorians against Trafigura Ltd and Trafigura Beheer BV[128] for damages relating to personal injury and economic loss caused by illegal dumping of toxic waste in Abidjan, Ivory Coast.[129] However, group actions mean higher procedural costs. In this case, Leigh Day undertook to represent the claimants on a conditional fee basis, also known as 'no win no fee'. This means that, in general, if the plaintiff loses, the lawyer will recover no fees, and if the plaintiff wins, the lawyer will claim fees, but they will almost always be paid by the defendants. When acting on such a basis, lawyers can charge a 'success fee', which is capped at a maximum of 100 per cent of the lawyer's ordinary fee, and the success fee is treated as part of the recoverable costs if the defendants have to pay the claimant's costs. Moreover, Leigh Day also took on the full costs of evidence-gathering in Ivory Coast.[130] Ultimately, the group action took a huge amount of logistical organization and required a large sum of financial resources.[131]

In *Motto*, in 2009 the parties reached a confidential out-of-court settlement in which Trafigura agreed to pay approximately £30 million to the claimants,

126 *Okpabi v Royal Dutch Shell plc* [2021] UKSC 3, [120]–[140].

127 Ibid, [129].

128 Both companies will be referred to as 'Trafigura'.

129 [2006] Claim BV HQ06X03370. For more information on the facts, see the description of the *Trafigura* case in France later in this chapter.

130 'The Toxic Truth about a Company Called Trafigura, a Ship Called the Probo Koala, and the Dumping of Toxic Waste in Côte d'Ivoire' (Amnesty International & Greenpeace Netherlands 2012) 161.

131 Afua Hirsch and Rob Evans, 'Lawyers for Claimants in Trafigura Case Seek £105m in Costs'

which amounted to roughly £1,000 per claimant.[132] Trafigura also agreed to pay the costs of the claimants.[133] Nonetheless, a new judicial battle took place when Leigh Day presented a £105 million bill to Trafigura for the entirety of its costs and sought a 100 per cent success fee.[134] Trafigura contested the bill, which it found 'staggeringly high'.[135] The costs claim also stirred controversy among lawyers and litigation experts.[136] Leigh Day came under attack for these unusually high costs, for seeking what was perceived as a huge success fee, and for its lack of costs management.[137] In October 2011, the Court of Appeal upheld an earlier ruling which had reduced Leigh Day's success fee from 100 to 58 per cent.[138] However, the parties reached a confidential agreement in December 2011.[139]

Since 2010, changes to domestic legislation governing legal aid in England have affected the financing of transnational claims against MNEs. Following its entry into force in 2013, the Legal Aid, Sentencing and Punishment of Offenders Act 2012 (LASPO) has fundamentally reformed the civil costs system and the provision of civil legal aid.[140] Before LASPO, law firms litigating against MNEs, such as Leigh Day, were able to fund their cases based on their ability to recover the full legal costs, success fees, and litigation insurance premiums from

The Guardian (London, 10 May 2010) <http://www.theguardian.com/world/2010/may/10/trafigura-claimants-lawyers-costs-bill> accessed 1 May 2021.

132 'Agreed Final Joint Statement (Issued on Behalf of All Parties to the Trafigura Personal Injury Group Litigation)' (Trafigura and Leigh Day 2009).

133 *Motto v Trafigura Ltd* [2011] EWCA Civ 1150 [22].

134 Katy Dowell, 'CoA Agrees that Leigh Day Must Reduce Trafigura Success Fee' (*The Lawyer*, 12 October 2011) <http://www.thelawyer.com/coa-agrees-that-leigh-day-must-reduce-trafigura-success-fee/1009750.article> accessed 1 May 2021.

135 Hirsch and Evans, 'Lawyers for Claimants in Trafigura Case'.

136 Ibid.

137 Since cause-lawyers tend to attract hostility from other lawyers and cause-lawyering is often associated with a pure quest for justice, any attempts by lawyers to obtain more remunerative cases may be perceived as ambiguous, even contradictory, with the aims of cause-lawyering. Therefore, it is not surprising to see that litigation costs are used by other lawyers and businesses to delegitimize the motives and activities of cause-lawyers in transnational litigation against MNEs. See Andrew Boon, 'Cause Lawyers and the Alternative Ethical Paradigm: Ideology and Transgression' (2004) 7 Legal Ethics 250.

138 *Motto v Trafigura Ltd* [2011] EWCA Civ 1150.

139 '£105m Trafigura Costs Dispute Settles, Leaving Lawyers Seeking Clarity on Interest' (*Legal Futures*, 18 January 2012) <http://www.legalfutures.co.uk/latest-news/105m-trafigura-costs-dispute-settles-leaving-lawyers-seeking-clarity-on-interest> accessed 1 May 2021.

140 Richard Meeran, 'Access to Remedy: The United Kingdom Experience of MNC Tort Litigation for Human Rights Violations' in Surya Deva and David Bilchitz (eds), *Human Rights Obligations of Business: Beyond the Corporate Responsibility to Respect?* (CUP 2013) 396. For a general overview of the impact of LASPO, see James Organ and Jennifer Sigafoos, *The Impact of LASPO on Routes to Justice* (Equality and Human Rights Commission 2018).

corporate defendants. However, LASPO has generally eliminated the ability to recover success fees and insurance premiums.[141] Furthermore, legal fees for a successful claimant now have to be paid out of the claimant's damages and they cannot exceed 25 per cent of the damages.[142] Finally, LASPO introduced a new test of proportionality in costs assessment.

Lawyers and NGOs have contended that LASPO restricts funding in transnational claims against MNEs, making these claims even less attractive for law firms.[143] In 2011, Ruggie, in his capacity as SRSG, also wrote to the UK Minister of Justice to express his concerns that the proposed reforms would 'constitute a significant barrier to legitimate business-related human rights claims being brought before UK courts in situations where alternative sources of remedy are unavailable'.[144]

3 Progressive development of transnational litigation against MNEs in European civil law jurisdictions

Since the beginning of the 21st century, transnational claims against MNEs have gained in importance in European civil law jurisdictions. A recent study commissioned by the EP shows that, in the EU, cases have been concentrated in only a few Member States.[145] France is the country where most cases have been brought. Other countries where cases have been heard include Germany, Italy, the Netherlands, Sweden, and Switzerland. The uneven distribution of cases across Member States is likely the result of the fact that the MNEs targeted by legal proceedings – usually large companies or companies with operations or controlled suppliers in third countries – are concentrated in a few Member States. Another potential explanation is the lack of social movement structure or interest to support these claims. CSOs in other EU Member States might use legal mobilization less often or focus on other more pressing domestic issues.[146]

In general, claims have targeted large MNEs with brand recognition from various economic sectors, such as textiles, natural resource extraction, banks, information technology (IT), or construction. However, there is a slight

---

141 Michael Goldhaber, 'Corporate Human Rights Litigation in Non-US Courts: A Comparative Scorecard' (2013) 3 UC Irvine Law Review 127, 133.

142 Skinner and others, 'The Third Pillar', 59.

143 Ibid, 134; Meeran, 'Access to Remedy', 396.

144 Letter from John Ruggie to Jonathan Djanogly (16 May 2011), 2.

145 Marx and others, *Access to Legal Remedies*.

146 Ibid, 18.

over-representation of companies in natural resources extraction.[147] MNEs have been sued for a wide range of human rights abuses taking place in third countries, including forced labour and slavery; State-sponsored violence against civilians; killing of trade unionists; genocide, crimes against humanity, and war crimes; labour rights violations; torture; and violation of privacy. They have also been sued for environmental damage occurring in host States,[148] such as oil pollution, dumping of toxic waste, illegal deforestation, and land-grabbing.

An important aspect of litigation against MNEs in European civil law countries is that plaintiffs have initiated both civil and criminal proceedings. In most countries, criminal litigation has been the favoured way to hold MNEs liable. For instance, in France most claims have been of a criminal nature (12 out of 16 claims since 2002). In Germany, the first tort claim was filed in March 2015 against a German textile retailer for its involvement in a factory fire in Pakistan. Litigators point out that despite Germany's influence in international trade and foreign direct investment, and the fact that it hosts a high number of companies accused of human rights abuse, 'Germany has not been at the centre of tort-based business and human rights litigation thus far'.[149] The focus on criminal litigation is surprising in a country where corporate criminal liability does not exist. Nonetheless, tort litigation against MNEs is slowly expanding among European civil law jurisdictions.

To date, transnational claims against MNEs have rarely led to a successful outcome for the plaintiffs. Most criminal claims have been dismissed for lack of evidence or as a result of the reluctance of prosecutors to pursue complex and sensitive cases involving MNEs. Furthermore, while courts have generally agreed to hear civil claims against MNEs, procedural rules regarding time limitation or access to evidence, and the absence of clear standards to hold corporate groups liable, have proved to be major obstacles for plaintiffs.

This section provides a short summary of cases in France and the Netherlands, on which Part II of this book focuses.

France

Criminal litigation

The first criminal claim in France was brought in 2002 against Rougier, a French timber company, SFID, its Cameroonian subsidiary, and their executive directors by a group of Cameroonian villagers and les Amis de la Terre, the

147 Ibid.

148 Climate-related litigation has been excluded from the scope of this book.

149 Philipp Wesche and Miriam Saage-Maaß, 'Holding Companies Liable for Human Rights Abuses Related to Foreign Subsidiaries and Suppliers before German Civil Courts: Lessons from Jabir and Others v KiK' (2016) 16 Human Rights Law Review 370, 371–372.

French branch of Friends of the Earth. In *Rougier*, the plaintiffs alleged that they suffered harm from the destruction of their agricultural resources and source of livelihoods after SFID had illegally cut down trees and built roads on their plantations. They accused the defendants of various criminal offences, including criminal destruction of property, forgery and use of forgery (*faux et usage de faux*), fraud, receiving (*recel*), and corruption of governmental officials. In particular, they alleged that Rougier and its directors were guilty of receiving[150] by accepting dividends from SFID which resulted from the commission of the illegal acts. The criminal complaint was eventually dismissed by the Court of Cassation (Cour de cassation) in 2005 on the grounds that the prosecution of misdemeanours could only be instigated at the behest of the prosecutor in this case and that there had not been any final judicial decision in Cameroon.[151]

One of the most emblematic cases against an MNE in France was the *Total* case. In 2002, a group of Burmese villagers initiated criminal proceedings against three executive directors of Total, a French oil and gas MNE, by bringing a civil action before the examining magistrate (*juge d'instruction*) for Nanterre. The claim concerned the construction of the Yadana gas pipeline in Myanmar, which was operated by various foreign and national companies including Total. The project was plagued by various human rights abuses, including forced labour, land confiscation, forced relocation, rape, torture, and murder.[152] Because the French Criminal Code (*Code pénal*) did not criminalize forced labour at the time of the facts, the plaintiffs alleged the defendants were criminally liable for abduction and illegal confinement (*séquestration*). In 2004, the prosecutor requested the dismissal of the complaint on the grounds that the facts did not qualify as criminal offences under French law. Nonetheless, the examining magistrate rejected the prosecutor's request and continued the judicial enquiry. The prosecutor appealed this decision before the Versailles Court of Appeal, which dismissed the appeal and ordered the continuation of the judicial enquiry. However, in 2005 the plaintiffs and Total settled out of court. The examining magistrate subsequently dismissed the complaint in 2006.[153]

---

150 Article 321-1 French Criminal Code provides that receiving 'is the concealment, retention or transfer of a thing, or acting as an intermediary in its transfer, knowing that that thing was obtained by a felony or misdemeanour. Receiving is also the act of knowingly benefitting in any manner from the product of a felony or misdemeanour.'

151 Cass crim 12 April 2005, n° 04-82318.

152 See 'Total Impact: The Human Rights, Environmental, and Financial Impacts of Total and Chevron's Yadana Gas Project in Military-Ruled Burma (Myanmar)' (EarthRights International 2009).

153 Benoît Frydman and Ludovic Hennebel, 'Translating Unocal: The Liability of Transnational Corporations for Human Rights Violations' in Manoj Kumar Sinha (ed), *Business and Human Rights* (SAGE 2013).

Trafigura is another famous case that was heard in France. In late 2005, Trafigura, an MNE trading international commodities, refined a large amount of petroleum through an industrial process called caustic washing on board the ship *Probo Koala*. After several unsuccessful attempts to dispose of the waste produced during the caustic washing, in August 2006 the *Probo Koala* illegally unloaded the shipment of toxic waste in the city of Abidjan, Ivory Coast. During the following days, more than 100,000 individuals experienced various physical symptoms, including headaches, skin irritations, breathing difficulties, and nosebleeds. The Ivorian authorities attributed at least 15 deaths to exposure to the waste.[154] The *Probo Koala* incident resulted in one of the worst sanitary crises in the history of the Ivory Coast. In 2007, FIDH, a French NGO, filed a criminal complaint with the prosecutor for Paris on behalf of a group of Ivorian citizens against Claude Dauphin and Jean-Pierre Valentini, two French executives of Trafigura.[155] The complaint alleged administration of noxious substances, manslaughter, corruption, and criminal offences related to transboundary movements of hazardous waste.[156] In 2008, following a preliminary enquiry, the prosecutor declined to investigate further.[157] Although FIDH appealed this decision, no further progress was made on this case.[158] It should be mentioned that the events in Abidjan led to litigation in the Ivory Coast, England, France, and the Netherlands.

In *DLH*[159] in 2009, a Liberian national and various French and British NGOs (Sherpa, Greenpeace France, les Amis de la Terre, and Global Witness) filed a criminal complaint with the prosecutor for Nantes against DLH Nordisk A/S, a Danish timber company, and DLH France, its subsidiary.[160] The plaintiffs argued that, between 2001 and 2003, the companies purchased, imported into France, and distributed across Europe timber from Liberian companies that were

---

154 'The Toxic Truth', 23.

155 'L' Affaire du "Probo Koala" ou la Catastrophe du Déversement des Déchets Toxiques en Côte d'Ivoire' (FIDH, LIDHO and MIDH 2011) 43.

156 Ibid.

157 Ibid; 'The Toxic Truth', 168.

158 'L' Affaire du PROBO KOALA relancée: Le Président de TRAFIGURA passible de poursuites aux Pays-Bas – Quid de la procédure en France?' (*FIDH*, 3 February 2012) <https://www.fidh.org/fr/themes/actions-judiciaires/actions-judiciaires-contre-des-etats/Affaire-Cote-d-Ivoire-dechets/L-affaire-du-PROBO-KOALA-relancee> accessed 1 May 2021.

159 'International Timber Company DLH Accused of Funding Liberian War' (*Global Witness*, 18 November 2009) https://www.globalwitness.org/en/archive/international-timber-company-dlh-accused-funding-liberian-war/.

160 'L'entreprise forestière internationale DLH accusée d'avoir financé la guerre au Libéria' (*Global Witness*, 18 November 2009) <https://www.globalwitness.org/en/archive/7641/> accessed 1 May 2021.

directly involved in human rights abuse and war crimes under Charles Taylor's regime. The complaint alleged concealment of bribery (*recel de corruption*), influence-peddling, and destruction of property. After the complaint was transferred to the prosecutor for Montpellier, it was eventually dismissed for lack of evidence in 2013. In 2014, the plaintiffs initiated new criminal proceedings by bringing a civil action before the examining magistrate for Montpellier.[161] In December 2017, the examining magistrate discontinued the criminal proceedings on the grounds that the facts were time-barred, as it could not be proven that DLH still benefited from the trade of illegal timber. However, in March 2018 the Investigating Chamber (*chambre de l'instruction*) overruled this decision and ordered the continuation of the investigation.[162] The case was pending at the time of writing.

NGOs have initiated several criminal proceedings against IT companies for alleged complicity in the commission of torture and gross human rights abuse in third countries. In the *Amesys* cases, FIDH and Ligue des Droits de l'Homme (LDH) filed a criminal complaint against Amesys, a French IT company, with the prosecutor for Paris in 2011. They alleged that Amesys was complicit in acts of torture committed by the Gaddafi regime in Libya before the Arab Spring. The NGOs accused Amesys of providing the Libyan government with software, equipment, and assistance, which subsequently led to the arrest and torture of several individuals.[163] Amesys was eventually placed under the status of assisted witness (*témoin assisté*).[164] In addition, in 2017 FIDH and LDH filed a new criminal complaint against Amesys (now renamed Nexa Technologies) with the specialized unit responsible for prosecuting crimes against humanity and war crimes in France (Crimes against Humanity Unit) for complicity in torture and enforced disappearances in Egypt. The NGOs alleged that Amesys sold the Egyptian government surveillance technology similar to

---

161 'Complaint Accuses International Timber Company DLH of Trading Illegal Timber and Funding Liberian War' (*Global Witness*, 12 March 2014) <https://www.globalwitness.org/en/archive/complaint-accuses-international-timber-company-dlh-trading-illegal-timber-and-funding-0/> accessed 1 May 2021.

162 'Investigation Resumes in the Case of concealment of Liberian Blood Timber v. DLH: An Important Step Forward in the Defense of Human Rights' (*Sherpa*, 29 March 2018) <https://www.asso-sherpa.org/investigation-resumes-in-the-case-of-concealment-of-liberian-blood-timber-v-dlh-an-important-step-forward-in-the-defense-of-human-rights> accessed 1 May 2021.

163 Skinner and others, 'The Third Pillar', 81; 'The Amesys Case' (FIDH 2015).

164 In France, an assisted witness is a person accused of certain facts during a judicial inquiry, which is an investigation conducted by an examining magistrate.

that it had sold to Libya.[165] The prosecutor for Paris opened a formal judicial investigation.[166] Both cases were pending at the time of writing.

In *Qosmos*,[167] FIDH and LDH filed a criminal complaint against French IT company Qosmos with the prosecutor for Paris in 2012. They alleged that Qosmos was complicit in serious human rights violations committed by the Bashar al-Assad regime in Syria. The NGOs claimed that the al-Assad regime used a large-scale electronic communication surveillance system installed by Qosmos in order to track, torture, and execute al-Assad's opponents in Syria. In 2014, the case was transferred to the Crimes against Humanity Unit, and a judicial investigation into the alleged role of Qosmos in aiding and abetting acts of torture in Syria was opened. In 2018, the examining magistrate in charge of the case expressed their intention to close the investigation. Shortly after, FIDH and LDH filed an application to hear a new witness, which was accepted by the examining magistrate.[168] The case was pending at the time of writing.

CSOs have also initiated criminal proceedings against MNEs for misleading advertising. In these cases, the plaintiffs alleged that the companies had deceived French consumers by providing false information about the working conditions in their factories. They also accused the companies of violating their voluntary CSR commitments.

In *Samsung*, a group of CSOs, including Sherpa, filed a criminal complaint against Samsung France, the French subsidiary of the South Korean MNE Samsung, with the prosecutor for Bobigny in 2013. Based on a report by China Labor Watch describing labour rights abuse in Samsung's factories in China,[169] the complaint alleged that Samsung France had breached its ethical commitments. The prosecutor opened a preliminary enquiry, but eventually dismissed the complaint in 2014. Nonetheless, in 2018 Sherpa and ActionAid France filed two new criminal complaints against Samsung France and its Korean parent company, the first one with the prosecutor for Paris, who eventually

---

165 'Sale of Surveillance Technology to Egypt: Paris Prosecutor Asked to Open a Criminal Investigation' (*FIDH*, 9 November 2017) <https://www.fidh.org/en/region/north-africa-middle-east/egypt/sale-of-surveillance-technology-to-egypt-paris-prosecutor-asked-to> accessed 1 May 2021.

166 'Sale of Surveillance Equipment to Egypt: Paris Prosecutor Opens a Judicial Investigation' (*FIDH*, 22 December 2017) <https://www.fidh.org/en/region/north-africa-middle-east/egypt/sale-of-surveillance-equipment-to-egypt-paris-prosecutor-opens-a> accessed 1 May 2021.

167 'Questions/réponses sur l'affaire Qosmos' (FIDH, 27 July 2012) https://www.globalwitness.org/en/archive/international-timber-company-dlh-accused-funding-liberian-war/.

168 'Qosmos' (*Trial International*, 12 August 2019) <https://trialinternational.org/latest-post/qosmos/> accessed 1 May 2021.

169 'Exploitation d'enfants et conditions de travail indignes: Samsung accusée de bafouer ses engagements éthiques en Chine' (*Sherpa*, 26 February 2013) <http://www.asso-sherpa.org/conditions-de-travail-indignes-sherpa-et-ses-partenaires-portent-plainte-contre-samsung-pour-publicite-trompeuse#.VldFZLv81Og> accessed 1 May 2021.

dismissed it, and the second one with an examining magistrate, who indicted Samsung France on the charge of deceptive marketing practices.[170] However, in April 2021 a French judge ruled that the complaint was inadmissible after Samsung argued that the NGOs did not have standing to file a complaint about deceptive marketing practices. The indictment was eventually dismissed. Both NGOs filed an appeal with the Court of Cassation.[171] The case was still pending at the time of writing.

In *Auchan* in 2014, a group of NGOs, including Sherpa, filed a criminal complaint against Auchan, a French retailing MNE, with the prosecutor for Lille.[172] This complaint was brought following the collapse of the Rana Plaza factory in Bangladesh in April 2013.[173] The prosecutor opened a preliminary enquiry, but eventually dismissed the complaint in 2015. The plaintiffs initiated new criminal proceedings by bringing a civil action directly before the examining magistrate for Lille.[174] The case was still pending at the time of writing.

In *Vinci*, Sherpa filed a criminal complaint against Vinci, a French construction company, and the French executive directors of its Qatari subsidiary with the prosecutor for Nanterre in 2015.[175] Sherpa claimed that Vinci was involved in human rights abuses committed during the construction of arenas for the 2022 FIFA World Cup in Qatar. The complaint alleged forced labour, slavery, and receiving stolen property. The prosecutor opened a preliminary enquiry,[176] but decided to close the case in 2018. Following this dismissal, Sherpa and other NGOs filed a new criminal complaint and an examining magistrate opened

170 'Violations of Workers' Rights: Landmark Indictment of SAMSUNG France for Misleading Advertising' (*Sherpa*, 3 July 2019) <https://www.asso-sherpa.org/violations-of-workers-rights-landmark-indictment-of-samsung-france-for-misleading-advertising> accessed 1 May 2021.

171 'Violation des droits chez Samsung: notre plainte jugée irrecevable' (*ActionAid*, 9 April 2021) <https://www.actionaid.fr/publications/responsabilite-sociale-des-entreprises/violation-des-droits-chez-samsung-notre-plainte-jugee-irrecevable> accessed 1 May 2021.

172 'Le groupe Auchan visé par une plainte pour pratique commerciale trompeuse dans le cadre de l'effondrement du Rana Plaza' (*Sherpa*, 24 April 2014) <http://www.asso-sherpa.org/le-groupe-auchan-vise-par-plainte-pour-pratique-commerciale-trompeuse-dans-le-cadre-de-leffondrement-du-rana-plaza#.Vlg4Lbv81Og> accessed 1 May 2021.

173 'Bangladesh Factory Collapse Toll Passes 1,000' *BBC News* (London, 10 May 2013) <http://www.bbc.com/news/world-asia-22476774> accessed 1 May 2021.

174 'Rana Plaza 2 ans déjà – Plainte contre Auchan pour pratiques commerciales trompeuses: les associations se constituent partie civile' (*Sherpa*, 8 June 2015) <http://www.asso-sherpa.org/rana-plaza-2-ans-deja-plainte-contre-auchan-pour-pratiques-commerciales-trompeuses-les-associations-se-constituent-partie-civile#.VbkrMflVhBc> accessed 1 May 2021.

175 'Mondial 2022 au Qatar: Sherpa porte plainte contre Vinci Construction et les dirigeants de sa filiale au Qatar QDVC' (*Sherpa*, 23 March 2015) <http://www.asso-sherpa.org/mondial-2022-au-qatar-sherpa-porte-plainte-contre-vinci-construction-et-les-dirigeants-de-sa-filiale-au-qatar-qdvc#.VRGd0eH9miw> accessed 1 May 2021.

176 'Accusations de travail forcé au Qatar: enquête sur Vinci ouverte à Nanterre' *Le Point* (Paris, 25 April 2015) <https://www.lepoint.fr/sport/accusations-de-travail-force-au-qatar-enquete-sur-vinci-ouverte-a-nanterre-25-04-2015-1924185_26.php> accessed 1 May 2021.

a judicial inquiry in 2019.[177] The case was pending at the time of writing. In parallel, Vinci brought various libel actions against Sherpa and its staff members, which were eventually dismissed.[178]

In *Lafarge* in 2016, a group of Syrian employees, together with Sherpa and the European Center for Constitutional and Human Rights (ECCHR) (two NGOs), filed a criminal complaint against Lafarge, a cement company, for alleged abuses committed by its subsidiary in Syria. They argued that Lafarge had been complicit in war crimes, crimes against humanity, financing a terrorist enterprise, deliberate endangerment of people's lives, and forced labour. Between 2011 and 2014, Lafarge decided to maintain its business activities in Syria in the midst of the Syrian Civil War. In order to do so, the company allegedly bought raw material from diverse jihadist groups, including the Islamic State of Iraq and the Levant (ISIS), and allegedly negotiated safe passage for its workers and products in exchange for compensation. In June 2017, a judicial investigation (*information judiciaire*) was opened, and Lafarge was charged in June 2018 with complicity in crimes against humanity, financing a terrorist enterprise, and endangering the lives of others. In December 2018, Lafarge referred the case to the Investigating Chamber, seeking a ruling on the nullity of its indictment.[179] In October 2019, the Investigation Chamber of the Paris Court of Appeal lifted Lafarge's charge of complicity in crimes against humanity while upholding the charges of financing terrorism and endangering people's lives. It also declared that Sherpa's and ECCHR's civil party claims were inadmissible.[180] However, in September 2021, the Court of Cassation issued an important decision in the *Lafarge* case.[181] It overturned the Investigating Chamber's decision to annul Lafarge's indictment for complicity in crimes against humanity. It also confirmed the company's indictment for financing terrorism. Furthermore, the Court of Cassation decided that only the NGO ECCHR could bring a civil action, and only in relation to the offence of complicity in crimes against humanity for which Lafarge was charged. Finally, it overturned the Investigating Chamber's decision to uphold Lafarge's indictment for endangering the lives of Syrian employees. The Court of Cassation's decision is significant because it clarifies the contours of complicity in crimes against humanity, how NGOs can participate in criminal proceedings,

177 'VINCI-QATAR: ouverture d'une information judiciaire' (*Sherpa*, 25 February 2020) <https://www.asso-sherpa.org/vinci-qatar-ouverture-dune-information-judiciaire> accessed 1 May 2021.

178 'Vinci échoue à faire condamner Sherpa pour atteinte à la présomption d'innocence' *Le Moniteur* (Paris, 30 June 2015) <http://www.lemoniteur.fr/article/vinci-echoue-a-faire-condamner-sherpa-pour-atteinte-a-la-presomption-d-innocence-28983008> accessed 1 May 2021.

179 Simon Carraud, 'France's Lafarge Has Charge of Crimes against Humanity Lifted' Reuters (Paris, 7 November 2019) <https://www.reuters.com/article/us-lafargeholcim-syria-appeal/frances-lafarge-has-charge-of-crimes-against-humanity-lifted-lawyers-idUSKBN1XH14X> accessed 1 May 2021.

180 Investigating Chamber of the CA Paris (2) 7 November 2019.

181 Cass crim 7 September 2021, n° 19-87.031, 19-87.036, 19-87.040, 19-87.367, 19-87.376 and 19-87.662.

and the impact of the parent company's interference in its foreign subsidiary. The case was pending at the time of writing.

Banks have also been targeted by criminal complaints for complicity in genocide, crimes against humanity, and war crimes in third countries. In the *BNP Paribas* cases, the French bank BNP Paribas has been accused of complicity in genocide, crimes against humanity, and war crimes for the events that took place in Rwanda in 1994,[182] and in Sudan in the 2000s.[183] In the case pertaining to the events that took place in Rwanda, following a complaint from a group of French NGOs, including Sherpa, in 2017, an examining magistrate from the Crimes against Humanity Unit subsequently opened a judicial inquiry.[184] Both cases were ongoing at the time of writing.

Civil litigation

In *Alstom*, in 2007, Association France Palestine Solidarité (AFPS), an NGO, and the Palestinian Liberation Organization (PLO) brought a civil claim against Alstom and Veolia, two French energy and transportation MNEs, before the Nanterre Regional Court (*Tribunal de grande instance*[185] or TGI).[186] The plaintiffs sought the annulment of various concession contracts concluded between Israel and Citypass, a joint venture in which Alstom and Veolia participated, to build a light rail system in the occupied West Bank. They also requested an injunction prohibiting the defendants from performing the contract, and claimed damages. The plaintiffs argued that the contracts were illicit because they related to a project which violated international law, including international humanitarian law conventions and customary international law.[187] However, the French courts successively dismissed their claim on the merits.[188] Finally, the plaintiffs lodged an application with the ECtHR, which

182 'BNP Paribas Faces Accusations over the Rwandan Genocide' *The Economist* (London, 8 July 2017) <https://www.economist.com/finance-and-economics/2017/07/08/bnp-paribas-faces-accusations-over-the-rwandan-genocide> accessed 1 May 2021.

183 'Sudanese Victims ask French Judges to Investigate BNP Paribas' Role in Atrocities' (*FIDH*, 26 September 2019) <https://www.fidh.org/en/region/Africa/sudan/sudanese-victims-ask-french-judges-to-investigate-bnp-paribas-role-in> accessed 1 May 2021.

184 'Implication de BNP Paribas dans le génocide des Tutsi au Rwanda: Ouverture d'une information judiciaire et désignation d'un juge d'instruction' (*Sherpa*, 26 September 2017) <https://www.asso-sherpa.org/implication-de-bnp-paribas-genocide-tutsi-rwanda-ouverture-dune-information-judiciaire-designation-dun-juge-dinstruction> accessed 1 May 2021.

185 The *Tribunal de grande instance* was a former general jurisdiction court that handled disputes that were not specifically assigned to another court. As of 1 January 2020, it was replaced by the *Tribunal judiciaire* (Judicial Court).

186 'Communiqué sur l'état de la procédure engagée par l'AFPS et l'OLP relative à la construction et à l'exploitation d'un tramway à Jérusalem' (*AFPS*, 2 October 2008) <http://www.france-palestine.org/Communique-sur-l-etat-de-la> accessed 1 May 2021.

187 Noah Rubins and Gisèle Stephens-Chu, 'Introductory Note to AFPS and PLO v Alstom and Veolia (Versailles Ct App)' (2013) 52 International Legal Materials 1157, 1157.

188 TGI Nanterre 30 May 2011, n° 10/02629. CA Versailles 22 March 2013, n° 11/05331.

was rejected in April 2015. In parallel to these civil proceedings, AFPS initiated proceedings before the administrative courts, which were also rejected.[189]

In *COMILOG*, in 2007, a group of more than 800 former Congolese employees of COMILOG, a Gabonese mining company, filed civil claims with the Paris Labour Court against COMILOG, ERAMET (COMILOG's parent company based in France), COMILOG International, and COMILOG France.[190] The plaintiffs alleged that, in 1991, COMILOG dismissed them without just and sufficient cause and without providing any compensation. Following their dismissal, they sought to obtain their severance pay before the courts of the Republic of Congo, but were never able to obtain a final decision on their case. In 2011, the Labour Court ruled it was incompetent to hear the claims and rejected the suggestion that the plaintiffs had faced a denial of justice in their own country.[191] However, in 2013 the Paris Court of Appeal overturned this judgment.[192] In 2015, in a landmark ruling, the Court ruled that COMILOG had to pay financial compensation to around 600 plaintiffs who could prove that they had been unable to obtain justice in the Republic of Congo.[193] However, in 2017 the Court of Cassation overturned this ruling.[194] It held that the foreign court was already seised of the dispute, which showed that it was therefore possible for the employees to have access to a judge responsible for ruling on their claim. Furthermore, the mere acquisition by a French company of a shareholding in the capital of COMILOG was not a connecting factor by virtue of the denial of justice doctrine. In 2019, the Court of Appeal rejected the claims in order to align with the Court of Cassation's ruling.[195]

In *AREVA*, in 2010, the family of Serge Venel brought a civil claim for damages against AREVA, a French nuclear power company, and AREVA NC, its subsidiary,

---

189 Ibid.

190 Since the 1990s, COMILOG has been the subject of numerous capital operations. See *Rapport d'activité 2007: Rendre concrète la notion de responsabilité sociale et environnementale des acteurs économiques publics et privés* (Sherpa 2008) 13.

191 Conseil des Prud'Hommes Paris 26 January 2011, n° F 08/06791.

192 CA Paris 20 June 2013, n° 08/07365. The Court of Appeal postponed its decision regarding the French courts' jurisdiction over COMILOG because the communication of a piece of evidence was necessary to decide the matters regarding COMILOG. Confirmed in cassation Cass soc 28 January 2015, n° 13-22.994 to 13-23.006.

193 CA Paris 10 September 2015, n° 11/05955. Concepcion Alvarez, 'Devoir de vigilance: une filiale gabonaise d'Eramet condamnée par la justice française à indemniser ses ex-salariés' (*Novethic*, 14 September 2015) <http://www.novethic.fr/empreinte-sociale/sous-traitance/isr-rse/26-ans-apres-la-justice-francaise-donne-raison-aux-salaries-congolais-de-la-comilog-143600.html> accessed 1 May 2021.

194 Cass soc 14 September 2017, n° 15-26.737, 16-26.738.

195 CA Paris, 28 March 2019, n° 17/21751. However, there are more rulings of the Paris Court of Appeal in this case, since the group of plaintiffs had to file individual complaints as a result of the absence of collective action mechanisms in France.

before the Melun Social Security Tribunal (Tribunal des affaires de la sécurité sociale or TASS).[196] The plaintiffs alleged that Venel died of lung cancer as a result of his exposure to dangerous levels of radioactive substances while working at the Nigerien uranium mine of COMINAK, a joint venture between AREVA NC and the State of Niger, between 1978 and 1984. In 2012, the TASS held that AREVA NC was Venel's co-employer and was liable for gross negligence (*faute inexcusable*).[197] However, in 2013 the Paris Court of Appeal overturned the judgment.[198] The Court of Appeal's ruling was upheld by the Court of Cassation in 2015.[199]

In *Bolloré*,[200] in 2015, a group of Cambodians brought a civil claim against Bolloré, a French MNE, and Compagnie du Cambodia, a subsidiary of Bolloré, before the Nanterre Regional Court.[201] The plaintiffs claimed damages for land-grabbing, environmental destruction, and human rights abuse in Cambodia. The case was pending at the time of writing.

Netherlands

Criminal litigation

Litigation was also brought in the Netherlands against Trafigura following the dumping of toxic waste in Abidjan, Ivory Coast. A first set of criminal proceedings focused on events that occurred in the Netherlands. Before the *Probo Koala* illegally unloaded the toxic waste in Abidjan, it had tried to dispose of the waste on several occasions. Most notably, in June 2006 Trafigura arranged to deliver the waste to the Amsterdam Port Services (APS) in the Netherlands. However, while unloading the waste, APS discovered that the waste was far more contaminated than it had thought and raised the price for treatment. Trafigura rejected the new quote and asked for the waste to be reloaded onto the *Probo Koala*. A few weeks later, the waste was illegally dumped in the Ivory Coast.[202]

In 2008, the prosecutor brought charges against Trafigura Beheer BV (Trafigura BV) and one executive of Trafigura Ltd for illegal export of hazardous waste to Ivory Coast and other criminal offences.[203] The Dutch courts found

196 The TASS rules on disputes between the French insurance fund and its users.

197 TASS Melun 11 May 2012, n° 10-00924/MN.

198 CA Paris 24 October 2013, n° 12/05650, 12/05777, 12/05651.

199 Cass civ 22 January 2015, No 13-28.414.

200 TGI Nanterre 10 February 2017 No. 15/10981.

201 Dan Israel, 'Bolloré attaqué en France pour ses plantations au Cambodge' *Mediapart* (Paris, 28 July 2015) <https://www.mediapart.fr/journal/economie/280715/bollore-attaque-en-france-pour-ses-plantations-au-cambodge?onglet=full> accessed 1 May 2021.

202 See 'The Toxic Truth'.

203 Ibid, 156.

that the defendants were guilty of delivering and concealing hazardous goods, and ordered Trafigura BV to pay a €1 million fine.[204] Trafigura BV and the prosecutor appealed this ruling to the Dutch Supreme Court (Hoge Raad).[205] In parallel, in 2008 Claude Dauphin, Trafigura's chairman, was initially charged with various criminal offences, including the illegal export of waste from the Netherlands. No progress was made until January 2012, when the Amsterdam Court of Appeal decided that Dauphin could be prosecuted. Dauphin challenged the jurisdiction of the Dutch Court and the absence of evidence, but the Court of Appeal dismissed his claim. Ultimately, in 2012 the prosecutor and Trafigura BV reached an out-of-court settlement, after which the criminal proceedings against Trafigura BV and Dauphin were withdrawn. Neither the MNE nor its chairman faced any conviction or admitted liability.[206]

A second set of criminal proceedings focused on the events that occurred in Ivory Coast. In 2008, the Dutch prosecutor decided not to investigate potential criminal offences in Ivory Coast. However, in 2009 Greenpeace appealed this decision. In 2011, the Court of Appeal of The Hague held that the Dutch courts did not have jurisdiction for events in Ivory Coast and rejected Greenpeace's complaint.[207]

In *Riwal*, in 2010 Al-Haq, a Palestinian NGO, submitted a criminal complaint to the prosecutor for Rotterdam against Lima Holding BV and other companies of the Riwal group, as well as a number of executive directors.[208] Al-Haq alleged that, since 2004, the companies had contributed to the commission of war crimes and crimes against humanity in the Netherlands and/or the Occupied Palestinian Territory (OPT). The complaint referred directly to contributions of the Riwal companies to the construction of the wall and illegal settlements by Israel in the West Bank.[209] Following the complaint, the prosecutor opened an investigation into the Riwal group's activities in Israel and the OPT. However, in 2013 he decided not to initiate criminal proceedings against the Riwal group.[210]

---

204 However, in July 2011 the Court of Appeal annulled the verdict against Trafigura Ltd's executive.

205 See 'The Toxic Truth', 156.

206 'Trafigura's Punishment Final, Top Executive Settles' (*Openbaar Ministerie*, 16 November 2012) <https://www.business-humanrights.org/fr/derni%C3%A8res-actualit%C3%A9s/pdf-trafiguras-punishment-final-top-executive-settles/> accessed 1 May 2021.

207 CA The Hague 12 April 2011, NJFS 2011, 137. See also 'The Toxic Truth', 160.

208 Corporate Complicity, Access to Justice and the International Legal Framework for Corporate Accountability (International Commission of Jurists 2013) 4.

209 'Al Haq/Report of War Crimes and Crimes against Humanity by Riwal (Complaint to National Public Prosecutor's Office)' (Böhler Advocaten 15 March 2010).

210 Letter of Dismissal from National Public Prosecutor's Office to Mr Van Eijck (14 May 2013).

Civil litigation

Oil MNE Shell has been targeted by several civil claims for its activities in Nigeria. In *Shell* in 2008, several victims of oil spills in Nigeria and Milieudefensie, the Dutch branch of Friends of the Earth, brought a tort claim against RDS[211] and its Nigerian subsidiary SPDC before the Dutch courts. The plaintiffs claimed that both companies were liable for the environmental and economic damages they had suffered. In 2009, the District Court of The Hague held that it had jurisdiction to hear the claims.[212] However, it later rejected their request to access evidence in the defendants' possession.[213] In January 2013, the District Court sentenced SPDC to pay damages in one of the claims while dismissing the other claims.[214] Regarding the liability of RDS, the District Court dismissed all the claims. Both the claimants and the corporate defendants appealed this ruling. In September 2013, the claimants filed a motion to request that the defendants produce specific documents.[215] In 2015, the Court of Appeal of The Hague reversed the District Court's judgment. It also confirmed the jurisdiction of the Dutch courts to hear the claims against RDS and SPDC and ordered disclosure of a number of internal documents.[216] In January 2021, in several landmark rulings,[217] the Court of Appeal of The Hague found SPDC liable for the damage caused by two of the oil spills in question. Although it did not find RDS liable for those oil spills, it held that the parent company owed the plaintiffs a duty of care. The Court of Appeal imposed an obligation on both SPDC and RDS to build a better warning system in the pipelines to detect future leaks. At the time of writing, the amount of compensation had yet to be determined in a follow-up procedure. Furthermore, in *Kiobel* in 2017 a group of Nigerian plaintiffs brought a civil claim against RDS and SPDC before the Dutch courts. They alleged that the companies were liable for complicity in the unlawful arrest, detention, and execution of their husbands in Nigeria in the

---

211 RDS is incorporated in England and Wales but has its headquarters in The Hague.

212 DC The Hague 30 December 2009 Judgement in Motion Contesting Jurisdiction, 330891/HAZA09-579.

213 DC The Hague 14 September 2011, Judgement in the Ancillary Actions Concerning the Production of Exhibits and in the Main Actions, 337050/HAZA09-1580 (*Akpan v Royal Dutch Shell Plc*); 330891/HAZA09-0579 (*Oguru v Royal Dutch Shell Plc*); 337058/HAZA09-1581 (*Dooh v Royal Dutch Shell Plc*).

214 DC The Hague 30 January 2013, C/09/337050/HAZA09-1580 (*Akpan*).

215 'Motion to Produce Documents' (Prakken d'Oliveira 10 September 2013) 200.126.843 (*Dooh*); 200.126.849 (*Milieudefensie v Royal Dutch Shell Plc*); 200.126.834 (*Oguru*).

216 CA The Hague 18 December 2015, C/09/337058/HAZA09-1581 + C/09/365482/HAZA10-1665.

217 CA The Hague 29 January 2021, C/09/365498/HAZA10-1677 (case a) + C/09/330891/HAZA09-0579 (case b) (*Oguru*); C/09/337058/HAZA09-1581 (case c) + C/09/365482/HAZA10-1665 (case d) (*Dooh*); C/09/337050/HAZA09-1580 (cases e + f) (*Akpan*).

1990s.[218] In 2019, the District Court of The Hague ruled that it had jurisdiction to hear the case,[219] which was pending at the time of writing.

In the context of the various proceedings brought against Trafigura for the illegal dumping of toxic waste in Ivory Coast, in 2015 more than 110,000 Ivorian victims brought a tort claim against Trafigura before the Dutch courts.[220] They alleged that the MNE caused bodily, moral, and economic injury to the plaintiffs, and they requested that Trafigura pay each plaintiff €2,500 in damages and clean up the pollution. The case was pending at the time of writing.

4 The role of the corporate accountability movement

The corporate accountability movement has played an instrumental role in the emergence of transnational claims against MNEs. While cause-lawyers have represented victims in courts, NGOs have provided important evidentiary support and have helped to make these cases visible in the public sphere. Furthermore, the procedural and substantive obstacles that victims face in the context of transnational litigation against MNEs are blatant examples of the need for the legal and policy reform advocated by the corporate accountability movement. This section will provide an overview of the corporate accountability movement and describe the benefits of using strategic litigation as a way to achieve reform.

Understanding the corporate accountability movement

The corporate accountability movement at issue in this book is historically recent. Influenced by previous social movements concerned with human rights and environmental protection, and the global justice movement, it emerged at the beginning of the 21st century.[221] It is characterized by a discourse that advocates corporate obligations and the importance of the right of victims to seek redress. The corporate accountability movement has been particularly

---

218 'Writ of Summons' (Prakken d'Oliveira 2017).

219 DC The Hague 1 May 2019, C/09/540872/HAZA17-1048 (*Kiobel v Royal Dutch Shell Plc*).

220 '100,000 Victims of Ivory Coast Toxic Spill Launch Dutch Suit' *AFP* (The Hague, 20 February 2015) <http://news.yahoo.com/100-000-victims-ivory-coast-toxic-spill-launch-164550722.html> accessed 1 May 2021.

221 Jem Bendell, 'Barricades and Boardrooms: A Contemporary History of the Corporate Accountability Movement' (2004) UNRISD Technology, Business and Society Programme Paper 13, 16 <http://www.unrisd.org/unrisd/website/document.nsf/(httpPublications)/504AF359BB33967FC1256EA9003CE20A?OpenDocument> accessed 1 May 2021; Peter Utting, 'The Struggle for Corporate Accountability' (2008) 39 Development and Change 959, 960.

active in Europe, where NGOs and lawyers regularly cooperate to hold businesses to account.

Emergence

Traditionally, human rights and environmental CSOs were concerned with State violations of human rights abuse, and State territorial and extraterritorial environmental pollution. However, with the liberalization of the global economy and the increase in the number of MNEs operating across borders, they started to observe the negative impacts of corporate activities on humans and the environment, especially in developing countries.[222] In particular, disasters caused by corporate activities, such as the 1984 Bhopal tragedy or the 1989 *Exxon Valdez* oil spill, triggered CSO campaigns against corporations.[223]

Since its emergence, activism regarding corporate impacts on humans and the environment has evolved considerably.[224] These changes are directly linked to the evolution of the relationship between CSOs and businesses. In the 1980s, CSOs focused their activities on governmental commitments to regulate companies. However, they started to be critical of what they perceived as failed attempts by governments and international organizations, such as the UN or the OECD, to regulate MNEs.[225] This led CSOs to direct their attention to private regulation by businesses themselves. During the 1990s, there was an evolution of the CSO strategy from 'barricades' to 'boardrooms'.[226] CSOs increased engagement with companies to solve social, human rights, and environmental issues. As a result, the concepts of CSR and private, or voluntary, regulation became prevalent in CSO discourse. However, towards the end of the 1990s, some CSOs and other activists began to question the effectiveness of CSR initiatives and private regulation. In particular, these actors were concerned about corporate control over the way the CSR agenda was framed, how some crucial issues related to global injustice remained largely out of bounds, and the general failure of CSR initiatives to restrict the growth of corporate power.[227] As

---

222 Bendell, 'Barricades and Boardrooms', 14. See also Robin Broad and John Cavanagh, 'The Corporate Accountability Movement: Lessons and Opportunities' (1999) 23 The Fletcher Forum of World Affairs 151; Oliver Balch, 'Activist NGOs Briefing Part 1: History of Campaigning – Manning the Barricades' (Ethical Corporation, 7 March 2013) <https://www.reutersevents.com/sustainability/stakeholder-engagement/activist-ngos-briefing-part-1-history-campaigning-manning-barricades> accessed 1 May 2021.

223 Utting, 'The Struggle for Corporate Accountability', 960.

224 Ibid, 959.

225 Peter Utting, 'Corporate Responsibility and the Movement of Business' (2005) 15 Development in Practice 375, 376.

226 Bendell, 'Barricades and Boardrooms', 14.

227 Ibid, 16–18. On the trend for businesses to lead the discourse on CSR, and business and human rights, see Christian Scheper, 'From Naming and Shaming to Knowing and Showing: Human Rights and the Power of Corporate Practice' (2015) 19 International Journal of Human Rights 737.

a result, some CSOs shifted to a new type of activism and started to mobilize around the banner of 'corporate accountability'.[228]

Characteristics

The agenda of the corporate accountability movement is based on a distinction between corporate responsibility and corporate accountability.[229] While corporate responsibility refers to any attempts to encourage companies to behave responsibly towards humans and the environment on a voluntary basis, corporate accountability refers to requiring companies to comply with legal norms or face consequences.[230] Utting suggests that the corporate accountability movement seeks to redirect 'attention to the question of corporate obligations, the role of public policy and law, the imposition of penalties in cases of non-compliance, the right of victims to seek redress, and imbalances in power relations'.[231]

The tactics of the corporate accountability movement have focused on social contestation, critical research, and campaigns pushing for legal reforms.[232] Among its portfolio of actions, the corporate accountability movement has organized public campaigns, lobbied for legal and policy reforms, and tested and used soft and hard law to seek redress.[233] As a result, it has contributed to several regulatory developments.[234] The corporate accountability movement also emphasizes the role of traditional regulatory organizations and institutions, including policy-makers, courts, and State enforcement bodies, in improving corporate behaviour.[235] Importantly, it pays strong attention to the role of courts in punishing companies when they do not comply with legally binding obligations and in providing victims with remedies.

The corporate accountability movement does not adhere to the view that voluntary initiatives should be a preferred substitute for legally binding

---

228 Jennifer Clapp, 'Global Environmental Governance for Corporate Responsibility and Accountability' (2005) 5 Global Environmental Politics 23, 25; Utting, 'The Struggle for Corporate Accountability', 965.

229 Craig Bennett and Helen Burley, 'Corporate Accountability: An NGO Perspective' in Stephen Tully (ed), *Research Handbook on Corporate Legal Responsibility* (Edward Elgar Publishing 2005) 372; Linda Siegele and Halina Ward, 'Corporate Social Responsibility: A Step Towards Stronger Involvement of Business in MEA Implementation?' (2007) 16 RECIEL 135, 136.

230 Andrew Clapham, *Human Rights Obligations of Non-State Actors* (OUP 2006) 195.

231 Utting, 'The Struggle for Corporate Accountability', 965. See also Anita Ramasastry, 'Corporate Social Responsibility Versus Business and Human Rights: Bridging the Gap between Responsibility and Accountability' (2015) 14 Journal of Human Rights 237.

232 Utting, 'The Struggle for Corporate Accountability', 966.

233 Ibid, 968.

234 Ibid, 969.

235 Ibid.

regulation. Instead, it reasserts the role of the law in social, human rights, and environmental domains. It also expands the terrain for hybrid regulation where voluntary and mandatory regulations merge.[236] Moreover, the corporate accountability movement has drawn attention to the need for an expanding body of hard and soft law that targets companies, especially in international law.[237]

Ultimately, Utting suggests that 'the corporate accountability agenda attempts to strengthen an arena of law that is sometimes referred to as "subaltern legality" or "counter-hegemonic legality"'.[238] He explains this as follows:

> This involves efforts on the part of social groups, individuals and communities whose livelihoods, identity, rights and quality of life are negatively affected by states and corporations, to use the existing legal apparatus to seek redress for injustice and participate in struggles and processes associated with accountability. A key feature of such struggles is transnational activism that connects actors at local, national, regional and global levels. Prominent examples of subaltern legality include public interest litigation in India and the approximately thirty cases that have been brought against corporations under the [ATS] in the [US].[239]

The corporate accountability movement involves a more representative cross-section of civil society actors and international, regional, and national coalitions, connecting actors and organizations that were previously disconnected or wary of each other's agendas. Utting argues that the coalitions of the modern corporate accountability movement are overcoming the fragmentation and tensions that have divided CSOs concerned with MNEs.[240] In particular, the movement has brought together CSOs from Northern and Southern countries in national, regional, and international networks. Such relations are visible in transnational campaigns and legal actions, such as transnational litigation against MNEs.[241] Furthermore, the corporate accountability movement has used networking to enhance resource mobilization, political opportunities, and collective identity formation.

However, a number of issues exist with regard to the potential of networks, including significant imbalances in power relations favouring CSOs from

236 Ibid.
237 Ibid.
238 Ibid, 970.
239 Ibid.
240 Ibid, 971.
241 Ibid.

the North.[242] Scholars have argued that CSOs from developed countries can marginalize the interests and the role of local CSOs from developing countries.[243] Moreover, campaigns for corporate accountability have been criticized for the marginalization of victims of business-related abuse from developing countries. Transnational solidarity is often produced through socially thin relations and raises questions about the durability and potential of its agency for social change, and the practices of human rights and democracy that are locally routinizing within civil society.[244]

The European corporate accountability movement

Since its creation, the corporate accountability movement has grown across Europe. It is composed of a broad range of CSOs, including NGOs traditionally concerned with environmental and human rights (eg Friends of the Earth, Amnesty International), trade unions (eg the Trades Union Congress (TUC)), scholars and universities (eg the Essex Business and Human Rights Project at the University of Essex), and lawyers and law firms (eg William Bourdon, Leigh Day). While some organizations focus on specific business sectors (eg extractive or garment industries), others target companies in general. The European corporate accountability movement is characterized by the existence of networks operating at national[245] and regional[246] levels. There are close links between these various networks, which regularly collaborate on common issues, initiatives, and campaigns (eg global supply chains or oil activity in Nigeria). They take advantage of opportunities offered by transnational interactions, through the Internet, social media, and regional and international institutions, to achieve common aims. For instance, the annual UN Forum on Business and Human Rights in Geneva gives CSOs the opportunity to work together in order to raise awareness about specific issues and influence policy-makers.[247]

Importantly, the presence of regional institutions contributes to the elaboration of common strategies around the topic of corporate accountability in Europe. In

---

242 Ibid.

243 Jem Bendell, 'In Whose Name? The Accountability of Corporate Social Responsibility' (2005) 15 Development in Practice 362, 363; John Dale, *Free Burma: Transnational Legal Action and Corporate Accountability* (University of Minnesota Press 2011) 207.

244 Dale, *Free Burma*, 207. See also Linda Waldman, 'When Social Movements Bypass the Poor: Asbestos Pollution, International Litigation and Griqua Cultural Identity' (2007) 33 Journal of Southern African Studies 577.

245 For instance, the Corporate Responsibility Coalition (CORE Coalition) in the UK, CorA – Network for Corporate Accountability in Germany, the Forum citoyen pour la responsabilité sociale des entreprises in France, and the MVO Platform in the Netherlands.

246 For instance, the European Coalition for Corporate Justice (ECCJ).

247 'UN Forum on Business and Human Rights' (OHCHR) <http://www.ohchr.org/EN/Issues/Business/Forum/Pages/ForumonBusinessandHumanRights.aspx> accessed 1 May 2021.

particular, the EU institutions have been the object of intense campaigning, as they have a major influence on the drafting of national policies and legislation governing business activities and access to justice. Furthermore, the excessive focus of the EU on CSR policies has contributed to renewed demands for corporate accountability from CSOs since 2000.[248] Finally, the EU is generally a major source of funding for NGOs in the region. As such, it may contribute resources to corporate accountability NGOs, helping to fund, directly or indirectly, campaigns or projects related to corporate accountability and access to justice.

Within the European corporate accountability movement, lawyers, law firms, and legal NGOs have provided the main impetus towards transnational litigation against MNEs. For instance, the British law firm Leigh Day was one of the first law firms to bring human rights claims against MNEs in England at the end of the 1990s. Leigh Day is generally identified with the British corporate accountability movement as a result of its litigation work against companies and its involvement in the Corporate Responsibility Coalition (CORE Coalition).[249] In France, the legal NGO Sherpa was created in 2001 by William Bourdon, a French lawyer involved in human rights NGOs,[250] to prevent and fight 'economic crimes'.[251] Sherpa campaigns actively for the adoption of binding norms to govern MNE activities, and has been involved in most of the claims brought against MNEs before the French courts. In Germany, a group of human rights lawyers created the legal NGO ECCHR in 2007. Since its creation, the ECCHR has been involved in most cases against MNEs in Germany and Switzerland.[252] In the Netherlands, Prakken d'Oliveira (formerly Böhler Advocaten) is a law firm specializing in international law and human rights.[253] This law firm's name has been associated with a number of famous human rights and international criminal law cases.

---

248 See Jonathan Doh and Terrence Guay, 'Corporate Social Responsibility, Public Policy, and NGO Activism in Europe and the United States: An Institutional-Stakeholder Perspective' (2006) 43 Journal of Management Studies 47; Olivier De Schutter, 'Corporate Social Responsibility European Style' (2008) 14 European Law Journal 203.

249 John Vidal, 'Lawyers Leigh Day: Troublemakers Who Are a Thorn in the Side of Multinationals' *The Guardian* (London, 2 August 2015) <http://www.theguardian.com/global-development/2015/aug/02/leigh-day-troublemaker-fight-dispossessed-lawyers> accessed 1 May 2021.

250 Bourdon was the Secretary General of FIDH from 1995 to 2000. See Olivier Petitjean, 'Comment mettre les entreprises multinationales face à leurs responsabilités? L'action de Sherpa' (Observatoire des Multinationales, 24 March 2014) <http://multinationales.org/Comment-mettre-les-entreprises> accessed 1 May 2021.

251 'Association Sherpa Statuts' (Sherpa 20 May 2009) Article 3.

252 'Human Rights Violations Committed Overseas: European Companies Liable for Subsidiaries. The KiK, Lahmeyer, Danzer and Nestlé Cases' (ECCHR 2015).

253 'Who Are We?' (Prakken d'Oliveira) <https://www.prakkendoliveira.nl/en/who-are-we/our-history> accessed 1 May 2021.

These actors are cause-lawyers, meaning activist lawyers who seek to use the courts as a vehicle to achieve social change or social justice beyond the individual claim at stake.[254] They usually specialize in human rights and environmental law issues, and they regularly work with disadvantaged groups. They are often the only litigators to offer legal assistance or representation to foreign victims of corporate abuse. In general, law firms and lawyers are reluctant to take on transnational cases against MNEs, not only because of the costs and complexity of this type of litigation but also to avoid potential conflicts with other corporate clients.[255]

Ward distinguishes between two main categories of cause-lawyers involved in transnational litigation against MNEs.[256] The first category is composed of legal NGOs that work on strengthening MNE accountability. They receive support for their work from major foundations and see litigation as part of their broader work. In France, Sherpa was created to hold parent companies of corporate groups legally and financially liable for the activities of their foreign companies, and to support foreign victims in accessing courts.[257] It engages in litigation as well as awareness-raising and lobbying. The second category is composed of profit-making law firms which take on cases that have strong public interest elements either on the basis of 'no win no fee' or legal aid. They work to obtain remedies for victims who would otherwise not be compensated for their injuries.[258] In the Netherlands, Prakken d'Oliveira represents individuals and groups which are oppressed or experience difficulties gaining access to law.[259] Its lawyers are currently representing the plaintiffs in the *Shell* case on the basis of legal aid.

One can observe a constructive tactical alliance between CSOs and cause-lawyers relative to the challenges and opportunities confronted at various stages of transnational litigation against MNEs.[260] In general, the existence of networks facilitates collaboration between CSOs and cause-lawyers in building, pursuing, and raising the visibility of claims. Cause-lawyers benefit from their collaboration with CSOs regarding access to evidence, funding, and visibility.

254 Thelton Henderson, 'Social Change, Judicial Activism, and the Public Interest Lawyer' (2003) 33 Washington University Journal of Law and Policy 33, 37.

255 For a discussion of conflicts of interests for law firms in general, see Stephen Daniels and Joanne Martin, 'Legal Services for the Poor: Access, Self-Interest, and Pro Bono' in Rebecca Sandefur (ed), *Access to Justice* (Emerald Jai Press 2009).

256 Ward, 'Securing Transnational Corporate Accountability', 464.

257 'Une interview de William Bourdon: l'arrogance des multinationales devient leur pire ennemi' *Le Nouvel Observateur* (Paris, 14 March 2013).

258 Ward, 'Securing Transnational Corporate Accountability', 464.

259 Prakken D'Oliveira, 'Who Are We?'.

260 Cheryl Holzmeyer, 'Human Rights in an Era of Neoliberal Globalization: The Alien Tort Claims Act and Grassroots Mobilization in Doe v. Unocal' (2009) 43 Law & Society Review 271, 300.

For example, Leigh Day built its legal case against Monterrico, a mining MNE, thanks to information provided by various American and Peruvian NGOs.[261] Similarly, Prakken d'Oliveira used various documents produced by other NGOs, such as Amnesty International and Platform London, to build its claims against Shell in the Netherlands.[262] Milieudefensie has also played a decisive role in funding, collecting evidence, and raising the visibility of the case. In France, Sherpa strategically mobilizes a network of various actors, including lawyers, law professors, and NGOs, to work on specific cases, or to develop legal arguments on corporate liability or access to justice. Furthermore, the presence of international NGOs, such as Friends of the Earth, within the European corporate accountability movement is advantageous for lawyers, as these NGOs usually have a presence in host countries that allows them easier access to information and to victims of human rights and environmental abuse. For instance, Milieudefensie collaborated with the Nigerian section of Friends of the Earth to collect evidence for *Shell*. CSOs also benefit from collaboration with cause-lawyers, as they may lack the legal expertise to put together a legal strategy or bring a claim directly before a court. Therefore, cause-lawyers are precious collaborators, as they are more willing to work on complex claims raising human rights abuse and environmental damage.

At the same time, collaboration between CSOs and cause-lawyers presents some challenges. Lawyers may perceive that such collaboration interferes with their relationship with their clients. Furthermore, lawyers are bound by confidentiality vis-à-vis their clients, which complicates the possibility of disclosing certain information to CSOs, and by their clients' decisions during the proceedings. In this regard, settlement agreements may create tensions between CSOs and cause-lawyers when their interests diverge.

Legal mobilization for corporate accountability in Europe

Transnational litigation against MNEs is an indissociable component of the corporate accountability movement. Legal mobilization is one of the strategies used by activist organizations and lawyers to achieve political and legal reform regarding MNE conduct in host countries.

Strategic litigation

The nature of transnational litigation against MNEs is twofold. First, it is a traditional form of litigation in the sense that it seeks to hold specific companies

261 'Peruvian Torture Claimants Compensated by UK Mining Company' (Leigh Day, 20 July 2011) <http://www.leighday.co.uk/News/2011/July-2011/Peruvian-torture-claimants-compensated-by-UK-minin> accessed 1 May 2021.

262 See the list of productions in 'Writ of Summons: Oguru, Efanga & Milieudefensie vs Shell plc and Shell Nigeria' (Böhler Advocaten 7 November 2008).

liable for the harm they cause, while providing an opportunity for victims to obtain a judicial remedy for the damage they suffer. At the same time, it is a strategic form of litigation, as it also seeks to achieve broader goals beyond the success of a specific case. Scholars have argued that transnational litigation against MNEs is similar to public law litigation.[263] Often, plaintiffs are not simply acting on their own behalf, but also serve as representatives of the larger community affected by the company.[264] More importantly, litigators use transnational claims against MNEs to encourage legal reform to strengthen corporate accountability and improve access to justice. On multiple occasions, European litigators have asserted the twofold nature of these claims. For instance, Sherpa insists that 'the law can be a tool for rights advocacy, at the same time fighting against the impunity of economic (public and private) actors and providing a remedy for the damage suffered by the victims'.[265] In Germany, the ECCHR claims to use strategic litigation to hold non-State actors accountable for human rights violations in selected 'pilot cases' which highlight structural problems, raise legal questions that have until now gone unanswered, and hopefully provide a precedent for enforcing human rights in the future.[266] A goal of such litigation is 'to effect change above and beyond the individual case at hand'.[267]

As a strategic form of litigation, transnational claims against MNEs aim to achieve various goals. First, they invite home country courts to clarify specific legal concepts, such as the boundaries of corporate liability.[268] For instance, the ECCHR has used litigation to ensure that clear guidelines exist on the extent of the parent company's liability.[269] Second, transnational claims against MNEs raise the visibility of existing regulatory gaps and encourage legal and policy reforms at both national and European levels. This approach is particularly observable in France where Sherpa has brought transnational claims against MNEs to 'concretely show decision-makers and legislators the difficulties which exist to hold companies liable for the harm they commit'.[270] After several years of litigation and lobbying, in 2013 Sherpa and other corporate accountability activists achieved enough support in the French Parliament

263 Benjamin Fishman, 'Binding Corporations to Human Rights Norms through Public Law Settlement' (2006) 81 New York University Law Review 1433, 1436.

264 Ibid, 1431.

265 Petitjean, 'Comment mettre les entreprises multinationales' (author's translation).

266 'Criminal Complaint against Senior Manager of Danzer: Accountability for Human Rights Violations in the Democratic Republic of Congo' (ECCHR 25 April 2013) 12.

267 Ibid. See also Michael Bader, Miriam Saage-Maaß, and Carolijn Terwindt, 'Strategic Litigation against the Misconduct of Multinational Enterprises: An anatomy of Jabir and Others v KiK' (2019) 52 VRÜ Verfassung und Recht in Übersee 156.

268 Ward, 'Securing Transnational Corporate Accountability', 468.

269 'Human Rights Violations Committed Overseas'.

270 Petitjean, 'Comment mettre les entreprises multinationales' (author's translation).

for the introduction of a legislative bill creating a duty of care of parent and controlling companies.[271] This initiative eventually led to the adoption of the groundbreaking Act on the duty of vigilance of parent companies and controlling companies.[272] In Germany, the ECCHR has used litigation to point out loopholes in national criminal law and encourage the German legislator to introduce a regime of corporate criminal liability.[273] Litigation against MNEs is also a tool to assess the extent of the legal and policy reform needed. Third, transnational litigation against MNEs breathes new life into, or raises the visibility of, campaigns deemed unsuccessful. In the Netherlands, the *Shell* case was partly the result of a strategic decision by corporate accountability activists to improve the effectiveness of a public campaign seeking Shell's accountability for its activities in Nigeria. Ultimately, the rise of transnational claims against MNEs is linked to the absence of effective global mechanisms to hold corporations accountable. Until political leaders address the imbalance between corporate rights and obligations, NGOs and local communities will continue to call for further litigation against MNEs.[274]

The existence of a hostile legal opportunity structure[275] and the strategic nature of transnational litigation affect the number of claims that successfully end up in home country courts. To date, plaintiffs have faced a number of obstacles (eg high litigation costs, complex regimes of corporate liability, limited substantive legal victories, etc). To improve their chances of success, litigators carefully select the claims they bring against MNEs.[276] The claim must also 'make sense' in the context of the litigator's aims and activities. In France, Sherpa brought the claim against Vinci at a time when it strategically coincided with the debate on the duty of care of parent and controlling companies in the French Parliament. Sherpa claimed that the human rights violations alleged in the claim demonstrated the need to enact a law which would regulate MNE

---

271 Proposition de loi n° 1524 & Proposition de loi n° 1519 du 6 novembre 2013 relatives au devoir de vigilance des sociétés mères et des entreprises donneuses d'ordre.

272 Loi n° 2017-399 du 27 mars 2017 relative au devoir de vigilance des sociétés mères et des entreprises donneuses d'ordre.

273 'Criminal Complaint against Senior Manager of Danzer', 10.

274 Jedrzej Frynas, 'Social and Environmental Litigation against Transnational Firms in Africa' (2004) 42 Journal of Modern African Studies 363, 385.

275 For a discussion of legal opportunity structures, see Lisa Vanhala, 'Legal Opportunity Structures and the Paradox of Legal Mobilization by the Environmental Movement in the UK' (2012) 46 Law & Society Review 523.

276 Scholars hold that cause-lawyers have the propensity to transgress conventional or generally accepted professional ethical standards of legal practice. A first area of possible transgression is client selection, which offends the principle of neutrality dictating that lawyers accept all clients. However, such a principle appears to be more predominant in some countries, such as the US, than others. See Boon, 'Cause Lawyers and the Alternative Ethical Paradigm', 254–257.

activities abroad.[277] Ability to collaborate with victims and CSOs in host States is also an important criterion for litigators. They will evaluate victims' profiles and motivations as potential claimants, as well as the reliability of potential partners in host countries. Some litigators have developed specific procedures to select potential cases. In 2013, Sherpa created a formal procedure to select situations of alleged abuse that could potentially become claims based on their strategic importance and the amount of resources required.[278] The case must comply with the mandate of Sherpa and it must give rise to judicial or non-judicial proceedings.[279] Ultimately, an important criterion for launching proceedings is the strategic benefit that the claim may bring.[280]

The strategic nature of transnational litigation against MNEs is visible in the way lawyers and CSOs cultivate links with the media. William Bourdon, the founder of Sherpa, stated that 'the media are an instrument for lawyers'.[281] They are 'a tool to spark public debates, to create power relations, and, sometimes, to use as a strategy of intimidation of the opponent'.[282] Media attention reinforces public pressure on MNEs and adversely impacts their reputation. Lawyers and CSOs strategically use the media to raise the profile of claims. In England, the *Monterrico* case became highly publicized after newspaper *The Guardian* published pictures of police and army officers brutalizing local demonstrators in Peru.[283] Transnational cases against MNEs targeting companies with highly visible brands are more likely to receive media attention.[284] For instance, litigation against Shell in England, the Netherlands, and the US has received extensive media coverage, most notably due to campaigns running in parallel. Ultimately, the relationship between the media on the one hand and CSOs and lawyers on the other is mutually enriching, as litigators may benefit from broad public coverage while the media may have access to sellable stories.

277 'Mondial 2022 au Qatar: Sherpa Porte Plainte Contre Vinci Construction et les Dirigeants de sa Filiale au Qatar QDVC' (Sherpa, 23 March 2015) <http://www.asso-sherpa.org/mondial-2022-au-qatar-sherpa-porte-plainte-contre-vinci-construction-et-les-dirigeants-de-sa-filiale-au-qatar-qdvc#.VkY3i7v81Og> accessed 1 May 2021.

278 'Règlement du COPIL' (Sherpa 5 April 2013), Preamble.

279 Petitjean, 'Comment mettre les entreprises multinationales' (author's translation).

280 Boon suggests that most lawyers build practices on the best business opportunities rather than out of commitment to a cause. See Boon, 'Cause Lawyers and the Alternative Ethical Paradigm', 253.

281 Les nouveaux métiers de l'avocat podcast, *L'avocat militant* (25 February 2014) comments by William Bourdon, Centre Perelman de Philosophie du Droit in Brussels <http://www.philodroit.be/L-avocat-militant?lang=fr> accessed 1 May 2021 (author's translation).

282 Ibid.

283 Ian Cobain, 'Abuse Claims against Peru Police Guarding British firm Monterrico' *The Guardian* (London, 18 October 2009) <http://www.theguardian.com/environment/2009/oct/18/british-mining-firm-peru-controversy> accessed 1 May 2021.

284 Ward, 'Securing Transnational Corporate Accountability', 465.

Measuring the success of transnational litigation against MNEs

As mentioned above, transnational litigation against MNEs aims to achieve various goals: victims seek to gain access to remedies, lawyers want to hold corporate actors liable, and CSOs seek to shed light on corporate human rights abuse and the need for legal and policy reform. Legal mobilization may successfully achieve one or several of these aims while failing to attain others.

Legal and non-legal benefits

Legal mobilization theory shows that there are multiple ways of assessing the 'success' or the 'failure' of litigation for law reform.[285] In transnational litigation against MNEs, success may be interpreted in terms of legal and non-legal benefits.

Looking at legal benefits, litigators have won on some legal and procedural issues, such as jurisdiction or NGO standing. In the Netherlands, the Dutch courts' decisions to hear the claims against the parent company of Shell was seen as a victory. At the same time, few cases have, to date, reached the merits stage and, when they did so, home State courts have rarely found MNEs liable for human rights or environmental abuse taking place in host countries (only recently in the *Shell* case before the Dutch courts). As a result, one could suggest that legal mobilization has contributed little towards achieving corporate liability. Furthermore, plaintiffs have rarely been awarded financial compensation for the harm suffered or other remedies, such as clean-up of environmental pollution.

The most important benefits of transnational litigation against MNEs may be its non-legal benefits or indirect effects. Legal mobilization has contributed to improving the visibility of the corporate accountability movement, especially in the context of campaigns against specific MNEs or for legal and policy reform. In some instances, plaintiffs and litigators pursue litigation for reasons other than winning legal arguments or obtaining financial compensation.[286] Victims may get the mental satisfaction of obtaining 'justice' by having an official acknowledgement of the corporate wrongs or crimes.[287] Litigation may also buy time to mobilize resistance around a project.[288] In one case, the ECCHR stated that:

> [T]he acts of investigating the circumstances of what happened and drafting a legal complaint can in themselves represent important steps for victims in voicing their complaints,

285 Vanhala, 'Legal Opportunity Structures', 526–527.

286 Frynas, 'Social and Environmental Litigation', 378.

287 Ibid, 379; Peter Newell, 'Access to Environmental Justice? Litigating against TNCs in the South' (2001) 32 IDS Bulletin 83, 85.

288 Newell, 'Access to Environmental Justice?', 85.

overcoming their trauma, and fighting for their rights. Irrespective
of whether an action succeeds before a judge, legal proceedings
can play a significant role when it comes to the political debate on
responsibility for human rights abuses.[289]

The impact of bringing or threatening to bring cases may also be more important
than the legal outcomes.[290] Litigation may affect corporate behaviour in host
countries by incentivizing companies to pay attention to the impacts of their
activities on local communities, employees, and the environment. However, it
is difficult to evaluate exactly how litigation changes corporate behaviour.[291]
Since litigation may play a key part in larger activist campaigns against a
specific company, 'it is often impossible to disaggregate the impact of litigation
from the impact of other forms of activist campaigning on the firm's public
perception or its share price'.[292]

Holzmeyer explains that legal mobilization in *Doe v Unocal* had four principle
indirect effects on the corporate accountability movement: organizational
growth and capacity-building; growth of transnational advocacy networks and
potential for boomerang effects; broadening tactical repertoires of activists
and litigators, including possibilities for synergy among different tactics and
movements; and cultivation of symbolic and communicative resources for
movement-building and mobilization.[293] Therefore, transnational claims
against MNEs can bolster the organizational strength, tactical repertoires, and
discursive resources of activists.[294]

Transnational litigation against MNEs can also be an efficient public education
and reform tool.[295] It may demonstrate inequities in existing laws and highlight
the need for legal and policy change, such as in the case against Vinci in France.
Therefore, the success of legal mobilization against MNEs is linked to the
capacity of its participants to create an alternative discursive space where
hegemonic discourse on neoliberal globalization and legal norms sustaining
inequality and corporate impunity are challenged.[296]

289 'Criminal Complaint against Senior Manager of Danzer', 3.

290 Newell, 'Access to Environmental Justice?', 85.

291 Ward, 'Securing Transnational Corporate Accountability', 466.

292 Frynas, 'Social and Environmental Litigation', 377.

293 Cheryl Holzmeyer, 'Human Rights in an Era of Neoliberal Globalization: The Alien Tort Claims
Act and Grassroots Mobilization in Doe v. Unocal' (2009) 43 Law & Society Review 271, 286–287.

294 Ibid, 287.

295 Ibid, 292.

296 Dale, *Free Burma*, 200–201.

Out-of-court settlements

In a number of cases, especially in common law countries, plaintiffs and business defendants have reached out-of-court settlements. In general, MNEs agree to compensate the claimants or to create a fund to develop local projects to help host country communities. For instance, in France in 2005, Total and the plaintiffs reached a confidential out-of-court settlement.[297] Total agreed to pay €10,000 to each plaintiff in exchange for the withdrawal of the complaint. In addition, the company pledged to create a fund of €5.2 million to implement humanitarian and development projects.[298] In England, a significant number of transnational claims against MNEs have resulted in out-of-court settlements between claimants and MNEs.[299]

Settlements offer advantages to both claimants and corporate defendants. Transnational litigation against MNEs is expensive and time-consuming, and its outcome is uncertain for both parties, especially plaintiffs. Therefore, settlements offer victims a negotiated resolution of the conflict and improve their opportunities to obtain remediation in a much faster way than through litigation.[300] Litigation can also damage the MNE's reputation and negatively impact business opportunities. Settlements limit such risks by ending the legal proceedings, since plaintiffs generally agree to withdraw their claim. Furthermore, settlements can influence the dismissal of criminal complaints, such as in the case against Total in France.[301] In this case, the settlement between the victims and Total allowed the company 'to buy a certain peace of mind by ending the embarrassing proceedings and limiting the subsequent publicity'.[302]

---

297 'Myanmar: Total et l'association Sherpa concluent un accord prévoyant la création d'un fonds de solidarité pour des actions humanitaires' *Nextnews* (Paris, 29 November 2005) <http://www.nextnews.fr/if_communique.asp?id_communique=5124&lg=fr&type_com=html&type_source=d> accessed 1 May 2021.

298 *Annual Report 2006* (Sherpa 2 May 2007) 2.

299 For instance, this was the case in *Motto, Bodo, Guerrero,* and *Vedanta.* In 2021, Leigh Day settled several claims filed against the Camellia group for allegations of serious human rights violations on its estates in Malawi and Kenya. See 'Leigh Day Settles Claims against the Camellia Group Arising out of Rape and Other Forms of Gender-Based Violence on Malawian Tea Estates' (Leigh Day, 14 February 2021) <https://www.leighday.co.uk/latest-updates/news/2021-news/leigh-day-settles-claims-against-the-camellia-group-arising-out-of-rape-and-other-forms-of-gender-based-violence-on-malawian-tea-estates/> accessed 1 May 2021; 'Settlement of Claims against Camellia Plc of Allegations of Serious Human Rights Abuses in Kenya' (Leigh Day, 14 February 2021) <https://www.leighday.co.uk/latest-updates/news/2021-news/settlement-of-claims-against-camellia-plc-of-allegations-of-serious-human-rights-abuses-in-kenya/> accessed 1 May 2021.

300 Frydman and Hennebel, 'Translating Unocal'.

301 Ibid, 31.

302 Ibid, 32.

Litigators usually present out-of-court settlements as great successes. Following the settlement with Total, William Bourdon, the founder of Sherpa, stated:

> The agreement reached is an innovative, pragmatic, and generous solution that solves problems related to the conditions that an industrial group sometimes faces when operating in certain developing countries. ... [B]eyond the financial compensation for the damage alleged by the complainants, for acts which the Total Group has always said it had not been informed of, the agreement brings concrete remedies for some citizens of the concerned States who face difficult situations. ... [T]his exemplary agreement heralds, for the future, what could be the resolution of this type of situation.[303]

In the future, settlements may be the favoured way to solve disputes, as part of 'the contemporary trend to "privatize" justice'.[304] In particular, they may provide a 'pragmatic'[305] approach to achieving the ideals behind transnational litigation against MNEs in comparison with judicial proceedings, especially since courts are reluctant to remedy corporate human rights and environmental abuse.[306] Future settlements could include 'the creation of pre-emptive codes, the aggressive monitoring of those codes, the involvement of communities and local NGOs, and efforts to persuade consumers, NGOs, and judges to give force to the norms expressed in those codes'.[307]

At the same time, settlements raise a number of issues. First, claimants and MNEs may struggle to reach an out-of-court settlement. In *Bodo v Shell*, even though the corporate defendant formally admitted liability for the oil spills in 2011,[308] the plaintiffs and the company were originally unable to reach an agreement regarding various aspects of a potential settlement (eg the quantity of spilled oil, the extent of the damage to the Bodo community and the ecosystems of the Bodo region, and the amount of financial compensation

303 'Myanmar' (author's translation).

304 Francesco Francioni, 'The Right of Access to Justice under Customary International Law' in Francesco Francioni (ed), *Access to Justice as a Human Right* (OUP 2007) 5.

305 William Bourdon used that word. See 'Myanmar' (author's translation).

306 Fishman, 'Binding Corporations to Human Rights Norms', 1466.

307 Ibid, 1467.

308 'Shell-Bodo' (Leigh Day) <https://www.leighday.co.uk/latest-updates/cases-and-testimonials/cases/shell-bodo/> accessed 1 May 2021.

owed by SPDC).[309] After four years of intermittent talks, SPDC and Leigh Day eventually agreed to a £55 million settlement.[310]

Second, settlements are usually confidential. Apart from the parties' press releases, it is very difficult to know how those agreements are negotiated and what they contain. Furthermore, the confidentiality of these agreements may have a negative impact on other victims of corporate abuse. Following the settlement between Leigh Day and Trafigura in *Motto*, medical expert evidence could not be seen by other victims or used to aid effective health interventions.[311] NGOs and scholars have suggested that the lack of transparency prevents the rights of victims' access to justice, truth, and remedy.[312]

Third, in most cases MNEs refuse to recognize their involvement, or liability, in the human rights abuse or environmental pollution claims raised by the claimants. For instance, Trafigura rejected any responsibility, stating that it did not foresee, and could not have foreseen, the illegal dumping of toxic waste in Abidjan.[313]

Fourth, the conclusion of settlements does not ensure that all victims will obtain financial compensation, especially in the context of group actions, or that the MNE is not exposed to more litigation risks. Despite Trafigura and Leigh Day reaching an out-of-court settlement for 30,000 victims, more than 100,000 Ivorian victims brought a new tort claim against Trafigura in the Netherlands in February 2015.[314] They demanded compensation for 'bodily, moral and economic injury' caused to them as well as a clean-up of the toxic waste in Ivory Coast. This highlights that settlements often neglect to remediate long-term social and environmental issues.

309 John Vidal, 'Shell Nigeria Oil Spill 60 Times Bigger Than I Claimed' *The Guardian* (London, 23 April 2012) <http://www.theguardian.com/environment/2012/apr/23/shell-nigeria-oil-spill-bigger> accessed 1 May 2021; John Vidal, 'Shell Attacked Over Four-Year Delay in Niger Delta Oil Spill Clean-Up' *The Guardian* (London, 23 September 2012) <http://www.theguardian.com/environment/2012/sep/23/shell-attacked-niger-oil-spill-clean-up-delay> accessed 1 May 2021.

310 'Shell Agrees £55m Compensation Deal for Niger Delta Community' (Leigh Day, 7 January 2015) <http://www.leighday.co.uk/News/2015/January-2015/Shell-agrees-55m-compensation-deal-for-Nigeria-Del> accessed 1 May 2021.

311 'The Toxic Truth', 162.

312 'L' Affaire du "Probo Koala" ou la Catastrophe du Déversement des Déchets Toxiques en Côte d'Ivoire' (FIDH, LIDHO and MIDH 2011) 42.

313 'Agreed Final Joint Statement' (Trafigura and Leigh Day).

314 '100,000 Victims of Ivory Coast Toxic Spill Launch Dutch Suit' *AFP* (The Hague, 20 February 2015) <http://news.yahoo.com/100-000-victims-ivory-spill-launch-164550722.html> accessed 1 May 2021.

Fifth, settlements prevent the setting of legal precedent or the adoption of legal and policy reform of corporate liability standards for MNEs. As Stephens points out, '[c]onfidential settlements and monetary payment without admission of responsibility enable the corporation and its employees, in effect, to purchase the right to commit abuses'.[315]

Out-of-court settlements between plaintiffs and corporate defendants may prove a stumbling block to the aims of the corporate accountability movement and may create potential conflicts between cause-lawyers and activists. While cause-lawyers tend to praise these agreements for allowing victims to gain effective access to remedy, corporate accountability activists have sometimes criticized them for undermining efforts to create strong corporate liability standards. For instance, Total's out-of-court agreement in France sparked tensions among the different activist groups campaigning against the MNE for its activities in Myanmar.[316] While some activists welcomed the settlement,[317] a number of observers criticized it for 'ignor[ing] responsibilities for the commission of serious violations of human rights in favour of a financial transaction allowing the Total group to clean up its act'.[318] In particular, the position of Sherpa received a lot of criticism for 'endors[ing] Total's version of its lack of responsibility for the acts alleged against the group'.[319] It should be pointed out that, in parallel, Total's lawyers also tried to reach an out-of-court settlement with another group of victims who had brought a criminal claim against the MNE in Belgium. However, the plaintiffs refused the offer on the grounds that their complaint aimed at holding Total accountable for its behaviour in Myanmar.[320] Similarly, a number of international and Ivorian CSOs insisted that the settlement between Leigh Day and Trafigura did not exonerate the MNE from its responsibility for the 'social, health, and environmental disaster' caused in Abidjan.[321] On the other hand, Leigh Day acknowledged, in

---

315 Beth Stephens, 'Making Remedies Work' in Surya Deva and David Bilchitz (eds), *Building a Treaty on Business and Human Rights: Context and Contours* (CUP 2017) 409.

316 'Info Birmanie, la Ligue des Droits de l'Homme et la FIDH Dénoncent l'Accord Intervenu entre Total et Sherpa' (Info Birmanie, LDH and FIDH 30 November 2005); Véronique Van Der Plancke and others, 'Total: Le Viol de la Démocratie en Birmanie et en Belgique' (2005)12 La Revue Nouvelle 34.

317 Ludovic François, 'Les Affrontements par l'Information entre les Entreprises et la Société Civile: L' Activisme Judiciaire en Question' (2007) 7 Market Management 65, 82.

318 'Info Birmanie, la Ligue des Droits de l'Homme et la FIDH Dénoncent l'Accord Intervenu entre Total et Sherpa' (author's translation).

319 Ibid (author's translation).

320 Frydman and Hennebel, 'Translating Unocal'.

321 'L' Accord Intervenu à Londres Entre Trafigura et Près de 31 000 Victimes Ivoiriennes ne Doit pas Occulter la Responsabilité de Trafigura!' (FIDH, 25 September 2009) <http://www.fidh.org/fr/afrique/cote-d-ivoire/Affaire-Cote-d-Ivoire-dechets/L-accord-intervenu-a-Londres-entre> accessed 1 May 2021 (author's translation).

the light of expert evidence, that 'the slops could at worst have caused a range of short-term low-level flu like symptoms and anxiety'.[322]

The conclusion of out-of-court settlements may also create tensions between plaintiffs and their local community.[323] In the *Monterrico* case, the MNE made compensation payments to 33 of the victims, without admitting liability.[324] It was reported that 'the decision by the victims to settle was seen by many as "selling out" and preventing the communities from having their day in court, although that was never the claimants' intention'.[325] Furthermore, in Peru the settlement 'resulted in a significant division among some previously tight-knit communities, resulting in a number of the victims feeling the need to move away'.[326] It also created tension among the claimants. Some victims felt pressured into settling to support the others, and others felt guilty for receiving larger sums of money. In addition, a number of victims did not receive any compensation.[327]

The tensions created by out-of-court settlements shed light on the dual nature of transnational litigation against MNEs, and the constraints imposed on cause-lawyers and corporate accountability activists by legal mobilization and the politicization of the law. Settlements may prevent the achievement of aims linked to the corporate accountability movement, such as punishing MNEs for human rights or environmental abuse, or triggering policy and legal reform. Settlements also challenge the twofold positions of cause-lawyers as private practitioners acting in their client's best interests and as activists seeking to establish a precedent that will improve the legal position of the cause.[328] Legal practice also imposes a number of financial and other constraints on lawyers. In some countries, the cost of litigation is exorbitant and lawyers, who work on the basis of market-based mechanisms, are exposed to high financial risks when they take on transnational claims against MNEs. When the legal rules governing liability and procedure limit their chances of success, cause-lawyers may be under pressure to reach a settlement with corporate defendants to avoid failure and not recovering any costs. Furthermore, lawyers must protect their clients' interests and are normally bound by their clients' decisions. As a result, they cannot prevent them from opting for a quick and easy way to obtain financial compensation.

322 'Agreed Final Joint Statement'.

323 Skinner and others, 'The Third Pillar', 93–97.

324 'Peruvian Torture Claimants Compensated by UK Mining Company'.

325 Skinner and others, 'The Third Pillar', 105.

326 Ibid.

327 Ibid, 106.

328 On partisanship and client representation, see Boon, 'Cause Lawyers and the Alternative Ethical Paradigm', 257–258.

5 Conclusions

This chapter has described the development of transnational litigation against MNEs in home countries, comparing experiences in common law and civil law jurisdictions. It also analysed the dynamics between social movements and transnational litigation against MNEs in Europe.

Transnational litigation against MNEs emerged in common law jurisdictions around two sets of cases that started in the 1990s. First of all, plaintiffs have brought civil actions based on the ATS before the US federal courts against foreign companies for their involvement in alleged violations of human rights in their foreign operations. However, recent decisions of the US Supreme Court have closed the doors of the ATS, preventing foreign companies from being held accountable for human rights violations committed abroad. Furthermore, a series of tort actions have been brought before domestic courts of various common law jurisdictions to hold MNEs accountable for wrongs committed abroad. Until recently, however, the success of this type of litigation had been limited, most notably because of jurisdictional issues and the application of the *forum non conveniens* doctrine. Nonetheless, courts are increasingly inclined to exercise jurisdiction over this type of litigation. Furthermore, by accepting in *Vedanta* and *Okpabi* that a parent company could incur a duty of care in respect of the activities of its subsidiary under certain circumstances, the UK Supreme Court opened the door to future claims for compensation against parent companies for human rights abuse and environmental pollution.

The increasing number of claims in European civil law jurisdictions may result in Europe becoming a primary venue for transnational claims against MNEs. Litigators have used diverse legal strategies to hold companies liable in the context of MNE activities. Nonetheless, while some victories have been won on procedural issues, such as court jurisdiction, a number of obstacles still exist, including access to evidence and reluctance by prosecutors and judges to hold MNEs to account. As a result, the success of transnational litigation against MNEs to hold parent companies liable in the context of their foreign activities and to secure remediation to victims remains limited in European civil law countries. However, the recent landmark ruling in *Shell* in the Netherlands, which recognized for the first time that a parent company had a duty of care to local communities affected by the activities of its foreign subsidiary, may boost transnational claims for corporate accountability.

For several decades, civil society actors concerned with business abuse have alternated between various strategies to influence corporate conduct, ranging from pressure to collaboration. However, increased corporate power and limited results of voluntary initiatives to effectively prevent business-related abuse of human rights and environmental pollution resulted in the emergence of a distinct social movement. The corporate accountability movement focuses on the role of policy-makers and courts to effectively regulate corporate conduct through binding obligations and punishment. While this movement is global, it has also developed specific characteristics in Europe as a result of the existence of regional institutional and legal frameworks. The years since 2000 have also seen the emergence of law firms and legal NGOs fully or partly dedicated to corporate accountability litigation in Europe. The interaction of these cause-lawyers with actors of the corporate accountability movement has triggered the use of legal mobilization as a strategy to hold MNEs accountable and shed light on the need for legal and policy reform. In this context, transnational litigation against MNEs is a strategic type of legal mobilization which aims to achieve remediation of corporate abuse, corporate group liability, and legal and policy reform. While victories on issues such as MNE liability or access to remedies have been rare in courts so far, litigation has produced various other legal and non-legal benefits. At the same time, the conclusion of confidential and out-of-court settlements between plaintiffs and corporate defendants has been a source of disagreement within the corporate accountability movement, revealing the constraints that legal mobilization imposes on both cause-lawyers and activists.

The next chapter provides an in-depth analysis of civil litigation against MNEs in France and the Netherlands.

Part II
Suing multinational enterprises in Europe: comparing national experiences in civil law jurisdictions

Chapter 4

Civil litigation against multinational enterprises in France and the Netherlands

1 Introduction

Transnational civil litigation against MNEs differs from traditional civil litigation. The transnational nature of civil claims against MNEs has many distinct, yet significant consequences on the procedural and substantive law that applies. In particular, these claims raise a number of legal questions regarding whether the host or the home State courts have jurisdiction to hear the case, and whether to apply the law of the host or home State. Furthermore, various procedural aspects can affect the progress and the outcome of the proceedings. For example, standing impacts the ability of victims and NGOs to participate in civil proceedings, while the availability of collective redress mechanisms can improve the opportunities for poor communities to hold MNEs liable or obtain remedy where they may not have the resources to bring individual claims. In addition, rules that restrict access to evidence held by MNEs may also complicate victims' ability to produce sufficient evidence to establish liability. Finally, litigation costs and limited availability of financial support may influence victims' decision to bring, or continue, a claim against an MNE. Ultimately, all of these procedural rules will impact the plaintiffs' ability to gain access to justice.

2 Jurisdiction of home State courts

When faced with a civil claim against an MNE for harm occurring in a host country, French and Dutch courts must assess whether they are competent to hear the claim. Rules of private international law, which govern transnational disputes that arise from the interactions between private persons, will guide judges in this exercise. In the context of this book, these rules are relevant for various reasons. First, transnational litigation against MNEs involves private parties from various countries, including host State plaintiffs and MNEs with their statutory seat, central administration, or main place of business in France or the Netherlands. Second, in some cases, the damage may have occurred in the host country while the event giving rise to the damage may have occurred in the home country. Third, litigators have brought transnational claims against

MNEs under various branches of civil law, including tort and labour law, to which private international law applies.

In the EU, a number of regulations harmonize private international rules governing jurisdiction in civil cases across Member States, including France and the Netherlands. In particular, Regulation 1215/2012 (Recast Brussels I Regulation)[1] defines the rules that domestic courts must apply when they assess whether they are competent to hear a civil or commercial claim. This instrument has a major impact on whether civil claims can be brought against MNEs in EU home countries. Under the Recast Brussels I Regulation, different rules of jurisdiction will apply to transnational claims against MNEs depending on whether the corporate defendant is domiciled in an EU Member State.

This section aims to offer an analysis of the impact of the Recast Brussels I Regulation on access to courts in France and the Netherlands in the context of transnational litigation against MNEs. Readers should nonetheless keep in mind that the Recast Brussels I Regulation repealed Regulation 44/2001 (Brussels I Regulation),[2] which, until 9 January 2015, was the instrument applicable to claims against MNEs.[3] Therefore, the following analysis may include references to the Brussels I Regulation. However, the change of Regulation has little impact on the potential determination of jurisdiction, as the rules applicable to transnational claims against MNEs are, except for the provisions on *lis pendens*, similar in both Regulations. Another aspect to keep in mind is that the Recast Brussels I Regulation applies in civil and commercial matters regardless of the court or tribunal.[4] This means that specialized civil courts, such as labour courts, must also apply the regulation.[5]

Corporate defendant domiciled in the EU

Under the Recast Brussels I Regulation, the defendant's domicile is the most relevant criteria for establishing jurisdiction, making it a general precondition for connecting a claim to an EU Member State.[6] According to Article 4(1), persons domiciled in a Member State shall, whatever their nationality, be sued

---

1   Regulation (EU) No 1215/2012 of the European Parliament and of the Council of 12 December 2012 on jurisdiction and the recognition and enforcement of judgments in civil and commercial matters [2012] OJ L351/1.

2   Council Regulation (EC) 44/2001 of 22 December 2000 on jurisdiction and the recognition and enforcement of judgments in civil and commercial matters [2000] OJ L12/1.

3   Recast Brussels I Regulation, Article 66(1).

4   Recast Brussels I Regulation, Article 1(1). Article 1(1) Brussels I Regulation had the same rule.

5   Both Regulations provide several exceptions that are not relevant in the context of this study.

6   Marta Requejo Isidro, 'Business and Human Rights Abuses: Claiming Compensation under the Brussels I Recast' (2016) 10 Hum Rts & Int'l Legal Discourse 72, 78. This was confirmed in *Owusu*.

in the courts of that Member State.[7] A company, or a legal person, is deemed to be domiciled where it has its statutory seat, central administration, or principal place of business.[8]

In France, this rule is reflected in Article 42 French Code of Civil Procedure (*Code de procédure civile*), which states that the court with territorial jurisdiction is, unless otherwise provided, that of the place where the defendant resides. If there is more than one defendant, the plaintiff can seize the court of the place where one of them resides. Furthermore, the domicile of a legal person means the place where it is established.[9] Another relevant rule is found under Article 15 French Civil Code (*Code civil*), which provides that a French person may be brought before a French court for obligations contracted by that person in a foreign country, even with a foreigner.

In the Netherlands, rules in the Dutch Code of Civil Procedure (*Wetboek van Burgerlijke Rechtsvordering*) differ depending on how civil proceedings are commenced. If the proceedings are initiated by a writ of summons, the Dutch court has jurisdiction if the defendant is domiciled or habitually resides in the Netherlands.[10] However, if they are initiated by a petition, the Dutch court has jurisdiction in three situations: where the applicant, or one of the applicants, or one of the parties is domiciled or habitually resides in the Netherlands.[11] As a result, in both types of proceedings the Dutch court has, or can have, jurisdiction if the defendant is domiciled in the Netherlands. A legal person has its domicile where it has its seat.

In the context of transnational claims against MNEs, French and Dutch courts therefore have jurisdiction to hear a civil claim against a member of an MNE which has its statutory seat in France and the Netherlands respectively. So far, this rule has not posed problems where civil claims have targeted a company domiciled in France or the Netherlands, such as the French or Dutch parent company of an MNE.[12] For instance, in *Alstom* the Nanterre Regional Court held that, pursuant to Article 42 French Code of Civil Procedure, it had jurisdiction to hear the claims against Alstom and Veolia, as both defendants had their registered offices within the jurisdiction of the court.[13] Similarly, in *Shell* both the District Court and the Court of Appeal of The Hague found that, based on the

---

7   Under the Brussels I Regulation, this rule was found under Article 2(1).

8   Recast Brussels I Regulation, Article 63(1). Under the Brussels I Regulation, this rule was found under Article 60(1).

9   French Code of Civil Procedure, Article 43.

10   Dutch Code of Civil Procedure, Article 2.

11   Ibid, Article 3(1).

12   Geert Van Calster, *European Private International Law* (2nd edn, Hart Publishing 2013) 367.

13   TGI Nanterre 15 April 2009, n° 07/2902.

then-applicable Brussels I Regulation, they had undisputed jurisdiction over RDS, the parent company, because it was headquartered in the Netherlands.[14]

Corporate defendant domiciled outside the EU

Rules on jurisdiction are different for defendants which are not domiciled in a Member State.[15] Article 6(1) Recast Brussels I Regulation provides that the law of each Member State determines the jurisdiction of its courts in such a situation (ie residual jurisdiction).[16] Therefore, France and the Netherlands will determine whether their courts can exercise jurisdiction over defendants domiciled in foreign countries, such as subsidiaries based in host States.[17] In the context of transnational claims against MNEs, there are a number of alternative grounds of jurisdiction upon which French and Dutch courts may base jurisdiction over host State subsidiaries, namely joining of co-defendants and *forum necessitatis*.

Joining of co-defendants

Both France and the Netherlands allow the joining, or joinder, of co-defendants. Under Article 42 §2 French Code of Civil Procedure, if there is more than one defendant, the plaintiff can choose to seize the court of the place where one of them is domiciled. Similarly, Article 7(1) Dutch Code of Civil Procedure provides that, if the Dutch court has jurisdiction with respect to one of the defendants, it also has jurisdiction with respect to other defendants involved in similar proceedings, provided the claims against the various defendants are connected to the extent that reasons of efficiency justify a joint hearing.

However, these claims must meet a number of criteria for French or Dutch courts to have jurisdiction in cases involving co-defendants. French courts

---

14   DC The Hague 30 December 2009, Judgement in Motion Contesting Jurisdiction, 330891/ HAZA09-579; CA The Hague 18 December 2015, C/09/337058/HAZA09-1581 + C/09/365482/ HAZA10-1665 [3.9].

15   During the review of the Brussels I Regulation, the EC suggested extending the general rules of jurisdiction to non-EU-domiciled defendants. However, this suggestion was strongly contested by corporate accountability CSOs and litigators, who claimed it would restrict the opportunities for foreign victims of business-related abuses to be heard in the courts of EU Member States. See European Commission, 'Proposal for a Regulation of the European Parliament and of the Council on Jurisdiction and the Recognition and Enforcement of Judgments in Civil and Commercial Matters' COM(2010) 748 final, 4. 'Submission on Brussels I Regulation Legislative Proposal' (Amnesty International 2011) 3.

16   Under the Brussels I Regulation, this rule was found under Article 4(1).

17   Arnaud Nuyts, 'Study on Residual Jurisdiction – Review of the Member States' Rules concerning the "Residual Jurisdiction" of their Courts in Civil and Commercial Matters Pursuant to the Brussels I and II Regulations' (Report prepared for the European Commission, 2007) 21.

require three elements to be met.[18] First, the claims against the defendants must bear 'close connected links'. Therefore, the object of the dispute has to be identical. Second, one of the defendants must be domiciled in France. As a result, French courts lack jurisdiction if the only basis for jurisdiction lies in a choice-of-court clause or if one of the defendants is a French national. Third, the defendant must be 'an actual, serious defendant in order to avoid any fraudulent choice of jurisdiction by initiating a fictitious claim against a French resident'.[19] In the Netherlands, the claims against the various defendants must be connected to the extent that reasons of efficiency justify a joinder of claims.

Both provisions reflect Article 8(1) Recast Brussels I Regulation,[20] which allows a joinder where one of the defendants is domiciled in the Member State whose courts have been seised, 'provided the claims are so closely connected that it is expedient to hear and determine them together to avoid the risk of irreconcilable judgments resulting from separate proceedings'. This alternative ground for jurisdiction aims to achieve efficiency and procedural economy to facilitate the sound administration of justice.

In the context of transnational litigation against MNEs, French and Dutch courts will therefore be competent to hear claims against various companies of an MNE, including those based in a third country, when one of these companies is domiciled in France or the Netherlands respectively, provided the above-mentioned requirements are met.

In the Netherlands, plaintiffs have strategically used the ground of jurisdiction under Article 8(1) Recast Brussels I Regulation and Article 7(1) Dutch Code of Civil Procedure to establish the Dutch court's jurisdiction over the foreign subsidiaries of Dutch companies. This approach has proved successful in both *Shell*[21] and *Kiobel*,[22] as the Dutch courts concluded they had international jurisdiction to hear the claims against the Nigerian and British subsidiaries of the Shell group.

18   Pierre Raoul-Duval and Marie Stoyanov, 'Comparative Study of "Residual Jurisdiction" in Civil and Commercial Disputes in the EU: National Report for France' (Report prepared for the European Commission, 2007) 14.

19   Ibid.

20   Under the Brussels I Regulation, this rule was found under Article 6(1).

21   In *Shell*, both the District Court and the Court of Appeal found that the Dutch court had jurisdiction to hear the claims against SPDC based on Article 7(1) and the then-Article 6(1) Brussels I Regulation. *Shell*, [2009] [3.4]–[3.7]; [2015] [3.1]–[3.8].

22   In *Kiobel*, the District Court found it had international jurisdiction to hear the claims against the British and Nigerian subsidiaries of the Shell group based on Article 8(1) Recast Brussels I Regulation and Article 7(1) Dutch Code of Criminal Procedure. DC The Hague 1 May 2019, C/09/540872/HAZA17-1048 [4.23]–[4.29].

In *Shell*, the Court of Appeal of The Hague concluded that the claims against
RDS and SPDC were connected to the extent that reasons of efficiency justified
a joint hearing based on the facts:

> (i) that between defendants, held liable as the joint and several
> parties at fault, there exists a group link, in which the acts and
> omissions of SPDC as a group company play an important role
> in the assessment of the liability/obligation, if any, of RDS as
> top holding; (ii) that the claim lodged against them is identical
> and (iii) has the same *factual* basis, in the sense that it concerns
> the same spill, while (iv) the discussion about the facts largely
> focuses on questions such as what caused the spill and whether
> enough was done to prevent it and to remedy the consequences,
> in relation to which (v) possibly further investigations are
> required, (vi) which investigation is preferably carried out by one
> single court to avoid divergent findings and assessments.[23]

Similarly, in *Kiobel*, the District Court of The Hague found that the claims against
the Dutch and foreign defendants were based on the same facts, circumstances,
and legal bases, and therefore pertained to the same situation, both factually
and at law. If these related cases were to be prosecuted separately, there was a
risk that contradictory decisions would be made.[24]

These cases show that it is in the interest of the plaintiffs to join the parent
company and its subsidiaries. Joining of co-defendants may not only 'prove
useful for establishing a shared liability, help ease the evidence issues, and
even have a bearing on the applicable law',[25] but it can also facilitate the
plaintiffs' access to home State courts when they should actually be barred
from seizing them. In the Dutch context, a significant argument for the use of
this jurisdictional ground is that the potential success of the claim against the
Dutch defendant does not determine whether the Dutch court should have
jurisdiction over the foreign defendants. In *Kiobel*, the District Court rejected
the defendants' argument that it did not have jurisdiction to hear the claims
against the British and Nigerian subsidiaries 'as the claims against "anchor"
defendant SPNV have no chance of succeeding'.[26] Furthermore, dismissal of
the liability claim against the Dutch anchor defendant at a later stage does not
preclude the Dutch courts from assessing the liability of the foreign defendants.
In *Shell*, dismissing the liability claim against RDS did not stop the District
Court from carrying on with the proceedings against SPDC and finding that

---

23   *Shell*, [2015] [3.4] (emphasis in original).

24   *Kiobel*, [4.26].

25   Requejo Isidro, 'Business and Human Rights Abuses', 81.

26   *Kiobel*, [4.23], [4.27].

the Nigeria-based subsidiary was liable for some of the oil spills. Ultimately, joinder of co-defendants is a crucial strategic tool in helping plaintiffs establish jurisdiction to seek liability of foreign companies independently of that of their parent company in European home State courts.

Forum necessitatis

Both France and the Netherlands allow their courts to assume jurisdiction in situations where it would not otherwise exist based on *forum necessitatis* or the need to guarantee access to justice.[27]

In France, the use of *forum necessitatis* is based on the prohibition of 'denial of justice' (*déni de justice*), and stems from case law.[28] French courts may exercise jurisdiction over claims for which they would normally have no jurisdiction as long as two requirements are met. First, the plaintiff must prove it is impossible for them to bring the case in a foreign court. Impossibility can be based either on factual grounds (eg the plaintiff would be seriously threatened if they returned to the foreign country) or legal grounds (eg the plaintiff can show that the foreign court has already ruled it does not have jurisdiction). If a foreign court rules that the case is inadmissible or dismisses the case on the merits, a denial of justice cannot be found, as the exercise of *forum necessitatis* would be deemed inappropriate.[29] Second, there must be some nexus with French courts.[30] This requirement is usually easily achieved, as the most stringent case law merely requires that the plaintiff has their habitual residence in France.[31]

In the Netherlands, *forum necessitatis* stems from statute. Dutch courts may exercise jurisdiction over claims that have no nexus with the Dutch legal order if legal proceedings outside the Netherlands appear to be impossible.[32] Impossibility may be based on factual or legal impossibility. Factual impossibility may include circumstances beyond the foreign country's control, such as natural disasters or war, while legal impossibility may be demonstrated by denial of access to a tribunal due to race or religion.[33] Moreover, Dutch courts may have jurisdiction if the legal proceedings have sufficient connection with the Dutch legal sphere and it would be unacceptable to demand from the

---

27   Chilenye Nwapi, 'Jurisdiction by Necessity and the Regulation of the Transnational Corporate Actor' (2014) 30 Utrecht Journal of International and European Law 24, 24.

28   Stephanie Redfield, 'Searching for Justice: The Use of Forum Necessitatis' (2014) 45 Georgetown Journal of International Law 893, 911.

29   Ibid, 912.

30   Ibid.

31   Ibid.

32   Dutch Code of Civil Procedure, Article 9(b).

33   Redfield, 'Searching for Justice', 913.

plaintiff that they submit the case to the judgment of a foreign court.[34] While Dutch courts have used *forum necessitatis* to accept jurisdiction where no sufficient connection with the Netherlands exists, they have also refused to accept jurisdiction over claims based on poverty alone or prohibitively high litigation costs in the alternative forum.[35]

The Recast Brussels I Regulation does not address the issue of *forum necessitatis*. During the review of the Brussels I Regulation, the EC proposed to incorporate a rule on *forum necessitatis* to harmonize this subsidiary jurisdiction rule among Member States. This notably aimed to guarantee access to a court as well as a level playing field for companies in the EU.[36] However, this option was excluded from the final version of the Recast Brussels I Regulation.

In transnational claims against MNEs in France, plaintiffs have asserted jurisdiction based on denial of justice. However, courts have differed in their reception to this argument. In *Alstom* in 2009, the Nanterre Regional Court held it had jurisdiction over the corporate defendants, as both companies were French and had their statutory seat in France. In addition, it took into account the risk of denial of justice. Notably, it raised the point that:

> Given the risk of a denial of justice inherent in the nature of this dispute, the French court is, *prima facie*, competent to solve the dispute in order to guarantee the free access to justice by the parties involved, in pursuance of Article 6(1) ECHR. It is well established that the risk of denial of justice is a criterion for the jurisdiction of French courts as soon as the dispute has a connection with France, which is the case in the circumstances of the present case, the defendants being French companies based in France, Alstom recognizing that its plants in La Rochelle, Ornans, Le Creusot, Villeurbanne, and Tarbes are producing 46 cars of the Jerusalem tramway.[37]

However, in *COMILOG* the plaintiffs were unsuccessful in using denial of justice as a basis for establishing jurisdiction. In this case, in 1991, COMILOG – a Gabonese mining company created in 1953 when the country was under French colonial rule – fired more than 1,000 Congolese employees without compensating them. In 1992, some of COMILOG's former employees lodged a complaint against COMILOG with the Pointe-Noire Labour Court

---

34   Dutch Code of Civil Procedure, Article 9(c).

35   Redfield, 'Searching for Justice', 914; Nwapi, 'Jurisdiction by Necessity', 37.

36   European Commission, 'Proposal for a Regulation of the European Parliament and of the Council on jurisdiction and the recognition and enforcement of judgements in civil and commercial matters' COM(2010) 748 final, Article 26.

37   TGI Nanterre 15 April 2009, n° 07/2902 (author's translation).

in the Republic of Congo in order to obtain their severance pay. In 1993, the Labour Court rejected the exception of territorial incompetence raised by COMILOG, and this judgment was confirmed by the Pointe Noire Court of Appeal in 1994. COMILOG lodged an appeal in cassation against this decision. However, at the time of writing the Congolese Court of Cassation still had not ruled on this case.[38] To date, the former employees are still waiting to obtain compensation for their dismissal.

In 2007, a group of more than 800 former employees sued COMILOG, its subsidiaries based in France, and its parent company Eramet, a French metallurgical MNE, before the Paris Labour Court, arguing that the French court had jurisdiction on various grounds.[39] First, Article 15 Civil Code, which provides that a French person may be brought before a French court for obligations contracted by that person in a foreign country, even with an alien, was applicable for the plaintiffs, since COMILOG was a French company at the time of its creation. Second, Article R 1412-1 French Labour Code (*Code du travail*) provides that an employee may bring a claim before the labour court of the place where the agreement was contracted or of the place where the employer is established. Third, the plaintiffs had been denied justice in the Republic of Congo. They alleged that, pursuant to Article 6(1) ECHR,[40] 'the right of access to a court is breached when one of the parties cannot bring a claim in front of any court. In such a situation, French courts have international jurisdiction based on the principle of denial of justice.'[41]

In 2011, the Labour Court rejected the plaintiffs' arguments and ruled it was incompetent to hear the claims against all the defendants, including COMILOG.[42] It found the case had no nexus with France, given that COMILOG was a Gabonese company and that all the plaintiffs were of Congolese nationality. Furthermore, it rejected the existence of denial of justice in the plaintiffs' country:

> The denial of justice cannot be based on the fact that French judges would have reasons to suspect foreign courts or the manner in which justice is administered in the country which normally has jurisdiction, or the fact that the outcome of the merits of the case in the way it could be obtained abroad goes against French public policy.[43]

---

38 CA Paris 28 March 2019, n° 17/21751. See also Oscar Oesterlé and Sandra Cossart, 'Pour un *forum necessitatis* concret et effectif' (2018) 1808 Semaine Sociale Lamy 5, 6.

39 Conclusions, 17 June 2010, n° 09/10495 (*Akala v COMILOG*).

40 Pursuant to its Article 6(1), in the determination of his civil rights and obligations, everyone is entitled to a fair and public hearing within a reasonable time by an independent and impartial tribunal established by law.

41 Conclusions, 17 June 2010, n° 09/10495 (*Akala v COMILOG*) 3 (author's translation).

42 Conseil des Prud'Hommes Paris 26 January 2011, n° F 08/06791.

43 Ibid (author's translation).

The Labour Court concluded that the plaintiffs had not sufficiently demonstrated that they could not materially access courts in Gabon or the Republic of Congo.

The Paris Court of Appeal overturned the Labour Court's judgment in two instances. First, it accepted that the French courts had jurisdiction over COMILOG's French subsidiaries based on Article 15 Civil Code and Article 42 §2 Code of Civil Procedure.[44] Then it accepted, on the grounds of denial of justice, that French courts had jurisdiction over COMILOG for 600 claimants who were able to prove they had brought a claim in the Republic of Congo.[45] The Court of Appeal found that the case met all the conditions required to assume jurisdiction based on denial of justice. First, the Congolese courts had still not rendered a final ruling more than 20 years after the plaintiffs had first lodged their complaint, which was contrary to the principle of achieving justice within a reasonable time. Second, the Court of Appeal found a connection with France by concluding that Eramet was COMILOG's main shareholder – it owned 63.71 per cent of its capital – at the time the complaints were brought before the French courts. The ruling of the Court of Appeal was hailed by NGOs.[46] It was significant from an access to justice perspective, as the Court of Appeal characterized denial of justice on the *objective* absence of a final ruling in the Congolese proceedings, as opposed to the *formalistic* criteria of access to a court in general.

However, in 2017 the Court of Cassation overturned this ruling.[47] It held that a foreign court was already seised of the dispute. It was therefore not impossible for the former employees to have access to a judge responsible for ruling on their claim. Furthermore, the mere acquisition by a French company of a shareholding in the capital of COMILOG was not a connecting factor by virtue of the denial of justice doctrine. In particular, 'the connection with France cannot result from simple capitalist links between several companies that are not co-employers'.[48] In 2019, the Paris Court of Appeal rejected the plaintiffs' claims, thus aligning with the Court of Cassation's position.[49]

44   CA Paris 20 June 2013, n° 08/07365. This ruling was later upheld by the Court of Cassation. See Cass soc 28 January 2015, n° 13-22.994 to 13-23.006.

45   Concepcion Alvarez, 'Devoir de vigilance: une filiale gabonaise d'Eramet condamnée par la justice française à indemniser ses ex-salaries' (*Novethic*, 14 September 2015) <http://www.novethic.fr/empreinte-sociale/sous-traitance/isr-rse/26-ans-apres-la-justice-francaise-donne-raison-aux-salaries-congolais-de-la-comilog-143600.html> accessed 1 May 2021.

46   Ibid.

47   Cass soc 14 September 2017, n° 15-26.737, 16-26.738.

48   Author's translation.

49   See CA Paris 28 March 2019, n° 17/21751. However, there are more rulings of the Paris Court of Appeal in this case, since the 868 plaintiffs had to file individual complaints as a result of the absence of collective action mechanisms in France.

The reasoning of the Court of Cassation regarding what constitutes a denial of justice is questionable from an access to justice perspective. The Court of Cassation adopted a formalistic view by focusing on the ability of the Congolese claimants to bring proceedings abroad and have access to a judge, rather than their ability to effectively obtain a ruling and therefore a remedy. This approach contradicts French statutory rules on denial of justice[50] and the right to a trial within reasonable time protected by Article 6(1) ECHR. The ECtHR recognizes that, in civil proceedings, the reasonable-time requirement usually starts from the moment the action is started before a competent court until the last decision delivered has become final and has been executed.[51] In *COMILOG*, the plaintiffs lodged a complaint in 1992. At the time of the Court of Cassation's ruling, they had been waiting for a judicial decision for 25 years. Such delay was a clear violation of the plaintiffs' right to a trial within reasonable time. Ultimately, the Court of Cassation's approach goes against the increasing recognition of the *forum necessitatis* doctrine to guarantee access to justice in a growing number of countries.[52]

Lis pendens

In a cross-border context, *lis pendens* usually applies where the same dispute has been brought before courts from two different countries which may both exercise competence. Plaintiffs may ask to apply *lis pendens* to stay proceedings in a court when another court has already been seised of the same dispute. This rule is based on the aim to reduce the possibility of concurrent proceedings and to ensure that irreconcilable judgments will not be given in different States.[53]

Provisions on *lis pendens* already existed in the Brussels I Regulation but were concerned with similar proceedings brought in the courts of different Member States. The Recast Brussels I Regulation introduced novel provisions on *lis pendens* where, in parallel to proceedings or actions before Member States' courts, similar proceedings or actions are pending before the courts of third States.[54] These provisions are directly relevant in the context of transnational litigation against MNEs.

Two situations should be distinguished. First, Article 33(1) provides for the situation when the court of a Member State is seised of an action involving

---

50   According to Oesterlé and Cossart, this vision is in opposition to that of Articles 4 French Civil Code and 434-7-1 French Criminal Code, which do characterize denial of justice as the lack of decision once the judge is seised, and not the absence of an avenue through which to obtain remediation. Osterlé and Cossart, 'Pour un *forum necessitatis* concret et effectif', 8.

51   *Poiss v Austria* (1987) 10 EHRR 231, para 50; *Bock v Germany* (1989) 12 EHRR 247, para 35.

52   Osterlé and Cossart, 'Pour un *forum necessitatis* concret et effectif', 8.

53   Recast Brussels I Regulation, Recital 21.

54   Recast Brussels I Regulation, Articles 33 and 34.

the same cause of action between the same parties as the proceedings pending before the court of a third State. In this situation, the court of the Member State *may* stay the proceedings if it is expected that the court of the third State will give a judgment capable of recognition and, where applicable, of enforcement in that Member State, and it is satisfied that a stay is necessary for the proper administration of justice. Second, Article 34(1) governs the situation where the court in a Member State is seised of an action which is *related* to an action pending in the court of a third State. Similarly, the court of the Member State *may* stay the proceedings if it is expedient to hear and determine the related actions together to avoid the risk of irreconcilable judgments resulting from separate proceedings, and if the conditions of proper administration of justice, and recognition and enforcement of judgment, are met. The court of the Member State may apply Articles 33 and 34 at the request of one of the parties or, where possible under national law, of its own motion.

Articles 33(1) and 34(1) apply only to proceedings over which the courts of Member States have jurisdiction based on specific articles of the Recast Brussels I Regulation. Some of these articles, in particular Articles 4, 7, and 8, are directly relevant in the context of transnational litigation against MNEs. The new rules on *lis pendens* could potentially interfere with the grounds of jurisdiction relied upon the most by plaintiffs to successfully establish jurisdiction in the home State. Even when it has jurisdiction to hear a claim against either an EU-domiciled parent company (based on Article 4) or an EU-domiciled parent company together with its foreign subsidiary (based on Article 8), a Member State's court can stay proceedings if similar proceedings are pending before the host State court. MNEs have already raised *lis pendens* as a tactic to avoid litigation in the home State court. For instance, in *Shell* the defendants argued that similar claims pre-existed in Nigeria.

At the same time, Articles 33 and 34 provide courts with discretion on whether to stay proceedings based on *lis pendens*. In doing so, a court must consider whether a judgment of a third State is capable of being recognized and enforced in the Member State concerned. It must also take into account the proper administration of justice and assess all the circumstances of the case before it, such as whether the third State's court can give a judgment within a reasonable time.[55] Importantly, courts of Member States may continue proceedings if the proceedings in the third State are themselves stayed, discontinued, or unlikely to be concluded within a reasonable time, if the continuation of the proceedings is required for the proper administration of justice, or when the risk of irreconcilable judgments no longer exists.[56] As such, courts may refuse

55   Recast Brussels I Regulation, Recital 24.
56   Recast Brussels I Regulation, Articles 33(2) and 34(2).

to stay proceedings when legal proceedings against MNEs are lengthy and questionable in terms of fairness and impartiality in host countries with a weak legal and judicial system.

Both France and the Netherlands recognize the application of *lis pendens* in cross-border disputes. In the *Miniera di Fragne* case, the French Court of Cassation held that *lis pendens* can be raised before the French court, by virtue of French ordinary law, where proceedings are brought before a foreign court which is also competent, but cannot be upheld where the decision to be given abroad is not likely to be recognized in France.[57] Therefore, the possible recognition in France of the foreign judgment, usually through international conventions, is an essential condition for permitting an application of *lis pendens*. In the Netherlands, pursuant to Article 12 Dutch Code of Civil Procedure, if a case has been brought before a foreign court and a judgment may be given that may be recognized and, where appropriate, enforced in the Netherlands, the Dutch court seised subsequently of a case involving the same cause of action and between the same parties may stay the proceedings until the foreign court rules on the dispute.

3 The law applicable to transnational claims against MNEs

Once French and Dutch courts have established jurisdiction, they must decide on the challenging question of whether to apply the law of the host or the home State.

At EU level, Regulation 864/2007 on the law applicable to non-contractual obligations (Rome II Regulation)[58] defines the rules domestic courts of EU Member States must apply when they assess the law applicable to non-contractual obligations in cross-border civil and commercial disputes. The Rome II Regulation generally extends the European harmonization of private international law already advanced by the Recast Brussels I Regulation.[59]

---

57 Cass civ 26 November 1974, n° 73-13.820. The Court of Cassation confirmed this position in Cass Com 19 February 2013, n° 11-28.846.

58 Regulation (EC) 864/2007 of the European Parliament and of the Council of 11 July 2007 on the law applicable to non-contractual obligations [2007] OJ L199/40.

59 European Commission, 'Proposal for a Regulation of the European Parliament and the Council on the law applicable to non-contractual obligations' COM(2003) 427 final, 4 (Proposal Rome II Regulation).

The Rome II Regulation has not yet applied to any civil claims against MNEs before French and Dutch courts due to its temporal scope. It applies to events giving rise to damage which occurs after its entry into force (11 January 2009),[60] while the majority of claims brought against MNEs have so far been concerned with events giving rise to damage that occurred before this date. Consequently, Dutch and French courts have applied previously existing domestic rules in determining the applicable law substantive to such cases.

This section provides an overview of the conflict of laws in transnational claims against MNEs before French and Dutch courts. It also describes how the Rome II Regulation will influence the choice of law in future cross-border human rights and environmental claims against MNEs.

Applicable law in transnational claims against MNEs

In the Netherlands, so far, courts have applied host State law to all transnational claims against MNEs based on Dutch domestic rules prior to the Rome II Regulation. In *Shell*, the District Court ruled that the *Wet conflictenrecht onrechtmatige daad* (WCOD),[61] which is a 2001 act governing the rules applicable in private international law matters, should determine the law applicable. One of the basic rules of the WCOD is the application of the law of the State where the act occurred in matters relating to tort, *delict*, or *quasi-delict*.[62] However, when an act has a harmful impact upon a person, property, or the natural environment outside the State where the act occurred, the law of the State where the impact occurred should apply.[63] In cases of complex *delicts* or torts with a multiple locus, such as in transnational cases against MNEs, the law of the place where the damage occurred should apply.[64] An injured party cannot choose the law of the place in which the tort occurred, even if it offers greater protection to the victim.[65]

In *Shell*, the plaintiffs argued that Dutch law should apply, whereas the defendants argued for the application of Nigerian law. The plaintiffs contended that the application of Nigerian law would be manifestly incompatible with the

---

60   Rome II Regulation, Articles 31 and 32. Furthermore, the CJEU interpreted the Rome II Regulation as applying only to events giving rise to damage occurring after 11 January 2009. See Case C-412/10 *Deo Antoine Homawoo v GMF Assurances SA* [2011] ECR I-11603.

61   On the WCOD, see Paul Vlas, 'Dutch Private International Law: The 2001 Act Regarding Conflict of Laws on Torts' (2003) 50 Netherlands International Law Review 221.

62   WCOD, Article 3(1).

63   Ibid, Article 3(2).

64   Ibid.

65   Vlas, 'Dutch Private International Law', 221.

Dutch public order. The District Court chose to apply Nigerian law in assessing the plaintiffs' claims because of their connection with Nigeria:

> In the event of a tort that has been committed by SPDC, this tort occurred on the territory of Nigeria. In the event that RDS allegedly committed tort with regard to the occurrence of these two oil spills, this tort by RDS had harmful effects in Nigeria. Therefore, the District Court is of the opinion that based on Section 3(1) and (2) of WCOD, the claims in the main action must be substantively assessed under Nigerian law, more in particular the law that applies in Akwa Ibom State, where these two oil spills occurred.[66]

In 2015, the Court of Appeal noted that the parties had finally agreed that Nigerian law would apply to all claims, even those against the parent company, since Nigerian law was 'the law of the state where (i) the spill occurred, (ii) the ensuing damage occurred and (iii) where SPDC, whose activities were allegedly monitored insufficiently, has its registered office'.[67] However, the Court of Appeal clarified that Dutch law should still apply to procedural matters as *lex fori* (law of the forum).

In *Kiobel*, the plaintiffs have acknowledged from the outset that their case is subject to Nigerian law, since the unlawful act was committed in Nigeria and the damage also occurred in Nigeria.[68]

In France, the choice of which law to apply has been slightly different, as the question was raised in claims concerning a tort that occurred in the context of valid employment contracts or resulting from the participation of companies in unlawful international contracts.

In *AREVA*, the defendants argued against the application of French law on the grounds that the employment contract between Venel, the victim, and Cominak had been executed in Niger, that it was subject to Nigerien law, and that Venel was subject to the Nigerien social security fund. However, the French courts rejected this argument based on specific French social security law and a French–Nigerien Convention.[69] French law was applicable because Venel was

---

66   DC The Hague 30 January 2013, C/09/337050/HAZA09-1580 (*Akpan*), [4.9]; C/09/330891/HAZA09-0579 (*Oguru*), [4.10]; C/09/337058/HAZA09-1581 (*Dooh*), [4.10].

67   *Shell* [2015] [1.3].

68   'Writ of Summons' (Prakken d'Oliveira 2017), para 143. In this case, the legal basis was not WCOD though, as the facts took place in 1995.

69   TASS Melun 11 May 2012, n° 10-00924/MN; CA Paris 24 October 2013, n° 12/05650, 12/05777, 12/05651.

affiliated to a compulsory social security scheme in France and had carried out his last employed activity on French territory.[70]

In *Alstom*, the court was asked to determine the lawfulness of international contracts for the construction of a tramway in Jerusalem. The plaintiffs requested that the judge find that the contracting French companies were at fault for their participation in contracts that had contributed to the violation of international law norms based on international humanitarian treaties and French law.[71] The defendants argued that the question of the lawfulness of an international contract could be examined only in the light of the law applicable to that contract, which in this case was Israeli law.[72] The District Court eventually found that French law could not be applied to a public contract concluded between the State of Israel and a company incorporated under Israeli law for a building site in the City of Jerusalem.

The Rome II Regulation

As a general rule, the Rome II Regulation provides that the applicable law should be determined on the basis of where the damage occurs. At the same time, it also provides for exceptions to the rule as well as the application of specific rules for special torts/*delicts* where the application of the general rule would be incapable of striking a reasonable balance between the interests at stake.[73] Some of these exceptions and specific rules are relevant in the context of transnational claims against MNEs.

General rule: *lex loci damni*

Lex loci damni is the cornerstone of the Rome II Regulation. Under this general rule, the law of the country in which the damage occurs must apply to a tort/*delict* claim arising out of a non-contractual obligation.[74] This rule applies irrespective of the country in which the event giving rise to the damage occurred and irrespective of the country or countries in which the indirect consequences of that event occurred. The Rome II Regulation makes it clear that, in cases of personal injury or damage to property, the country in which the damage occurs should be the country where the injury was sustained, or the property was damaged, respectively.[75] The rule of *lex loci damni* reflects

---

70   CA Paris 24 October 2013, n° 12/05650, 12/05777, 12/05651.

71   Hélène de Pooter, 'L' affaire du tramway de Jérusalem devant les tribunaux français' (2014) 60 Annuaire Français de Droit International 45, 49.

72   TGI Nanterre 30 May 2011, n° 10/02629.

73   Rome II Regulation, Recital 19.

74   Ibid, Article 4(1).

75   Ibid, Recital 17.

the pre-existing practice of some EU Member States, including France and the Netherlands.[76]

The application of the Rome II Regulation means that French and Dutch courts must apply the law of the host country in the context of transnational claims against MNEs. The host State law will apply to crucial substantive and procedural aspects of the litigation, such as corporate liability, evidence, or financial compensation.[77] This includes rules that govern not only liability standards – such as the basis and extent of liability, the grounds for exemption from liability and limitation or division of liability, and liability for the acts of another person – but also the existence, the nature, and the assessment of damage or the remedy claimed, the persons entitled to compensation for damage sustained personally, the rules of prescription and limitation,[78] and the rules raising presumptions of law or determining the burden of proof.[79] This solution is likely to be unsatisfactory for plaintiffs, as they generally pursue their case with the purpose of applying the home State law.[80] Furthermore, plaintiffs' dissatisfaction may be reinforced if such standards are less favourable to plaintiffs in comparison with those of the home country. Litigators have argued that the determination of the applicable law may constitute a legal obstacle for victims when the content of the applicable law is difficult to ascertain before a foreign court, or when it is not protective of victims.[81] The existence of exceptions to the general rule of *lex loci damni* is therefore of significant importance to plaintiffs if they allow the application of the law of an alternative forum with which the judge is more familiar, or one more protective of victims.

Residence of the parties

According to Article 4(2) Rome II Regulation, where the person claimed to be liable of causing damage and the person sustaining damage both have their habitual residence in the same country at the time the alleged damage occurs, the law of that country shall apply. This rule is unlikely to be relevant in the context of transnational litigation against MNEs, as plaintiffs often reside in

76   Ibid. The Proposal for the Rome II Regulation states that 'while the absence of codification in several Member States makes it impossible to give a clear answer for the more than fifteen systems, the connection to the law of the place where the damage was sustained has been adopted by those Member States where the rules have recently been codified'.

77   Liesbeth Enneking, *Foreign Direct Liability and Beyond: Exploring the Role of Tort Law in Promoting International Corporate Social Responsibility and Accountability* (Eleven 2012) 214.

78   Rome II Regulation, Article 15.

79   Rome II Regulation, Article 22.

80   Van Calster, *European Private International Law*, 369.

81   Sandra Cossart and Lucie Chatelain, 'Key Legal Obstacles around Jurisdiction for Victims Seeking Justice Remain in the Revised Draft Treaty' (BHRRC, 2019) <https://www.business-humanrights.org/en/key-legal-obstacles-around-jurisdiction-for-victims-seeking-justice-remain-in-the-revised-draft-treaty> accessed 1 May 2021.

the host State. If they sue the host State company, both parties reside in the host State, whose law remains applicable. If they sue the home State company, both parties reside in different countries and the exception of Article 4(2) is not applicable. Furthermore, even if the plaintiffs were to subsequently move to the home State where the parent company resides, this would not be helpful, as Article 4(2) looks at the time when the damage occurred in determining residency.[82]

Escape clause

Article 4(3) Rome II Regulation contains a general escape clause.[83] It provides that, where it is clear from all the circumstances of the case that the tort/ *delict* is manifestly more closely connected with another country, the law of that country shall apply. A manifestly closer connection with another country might be based on a pre-existing relationship between the parties, such as a contract, that is closely connected with the tort/*delict* in question. Article 4(3) can potentially open the door to the application of French and Dutch law to civil cases. However, a strong connection with the home country must be manifest, which is difficult for plaintiffs to establish when bringing a claim against MNEs in Europe. Furthermore, it is likely that the requirement of 'a manifestly closer connection' will be interpreted and applied restrictively to guarantee the Rome II Regulation's general aim of providing for legal certainty.[84]

Environmental damage

Article 7 Rome II Regulation provides for a specific rule applicable to environmental damage. Accordingly, the person seeking compensation for environmental damage can choose to base their claim on the law of the country in which the event giving rise to the damage occurred. Environmental damage should be understood as 'the adverse change in a natural resource, such as water, land or air, impairment of a function performed by that resource for the benefit of another natural resource or the public, or impairment of the variability among living organisms'.[85]

---

82   Van Calster, *European Private International Law*, 369.

83   An escape clause is 'a provision inserted in a legal instrument to supplement or cure the defect in the main rule, especially where the main rule has little or no connection with the issue to be resolved before the court'. It gives the court the discretion to locate the law of a country that is more or most closely connected with the subject matter. See Chukwuma Samuel Adesina Okoli and Gabriel Omoshemime Arishe, 'The Operation of the Escape Clauses in the Rome Convention, Rome I Regulation and Rome II Regulation' (2012) 8 Journal of Private International Law 489, 489.

84   Liesbeth Enneking, 'Judicial Remedies: The Issue of Applicable Law' in Juan José Álvarez Rubio and Katerina Yiannibas (eds), *Human Rights in Business: Removal of Barriers to Access to Justice in the European Union* (Routledge 2017) 52.

85   Rome II Regulation, Recital 24.

This exception is directly relevant in the context of transnational litigation against MNEs, as a number of past and ongoing claims have raised environmental damage (eg *Shell*; *Trafigura*). The question of when plaintiffs can choose the law of the country in which the event giving rise to the damage occurred should be determined in accordance with the law of the Member State in which the court is seised, hence French or Dutch law.[86]

However, the application of the environmental damage exception raises several issues. To choose the law of the home State, the plaintiffs must demonstrate that the event causing the damage occurred in the home State. This means convincing the court that direct instructions or negligent lack of oversight by the home State company led to the damage at issue.[87] As will be seen in Section 5, such a burden of proof is difficult to meet, since MNEs are often in possession of evidential information incriminating them, and disclosure procedures are often applied restrictively in EU Member States.

Freedom of choice

Under Article 14 Rome II Regulation, the parties are allowed to decide on the law applicable to their dispute in an agreement. However, this choice must be expressed or demonstrated with reasonable certainty by the circumstances of the case and cannot prejudice the rights of third parties. The practicality of this provision appears limited in the context of transnational litigation against MNEs. It is unlikely that victims and MNEs will agree on the rules that will govern the proceedings as they have opposing interests. MNEs are likely to be interested in applying laws that limit their liability and the potential compensation they may have to provide, whereas plaintiffs are inclined to choose laws that will give the most satisfactory level of protection and damages.

Overriding mandatory provisions

Article 16 Rome II Regulation provides that '[n]othing in the Rome II Regulation restricts the application of the provisions of the law of the forum in a situation where they are mandatory irrespective of the law otherwise applicable to the non-contractual obligation'. In exceptional circumstances, considerations of public interest justify allowing courts of Member States to apply exceptions based on overriding mandatory provisions.[88] These are provisions that are regarded as crucial by a country for safeguarding its public interests, such as its political, social, or economic organization, to such an extent that they are applicable to any situation falling within their scope, irrespective of the law

---

86   Ibid, Recital 25.
87   Van Calster, *European Private International Law*, 370.
88   Rome II Regulation, Recital 32.

otherwise applicable.[89] These provisions typically include domestic rules of a semi-public law nature that intervene in private legal relationships in order to protect the public interest, such as rules on working conditions or health and safety under labour law.[90] They can also include rules from non-domestic legal sources, such as public international law and international human rights law.[91] It is unclear how Article 16 could be relevant to transnational litigation against MNEs. As already mentioned, this article should apply in exceptional circumstances only. Furthermore, it is unlikely that a State would apply its overriding mandatory provisions outside its territory.[92]

Rules of safety and conduct

Pursuant to Article 17 Rome II Regulation, in assessing the conduct of the person claimed to be liable, account must be taken, as a matter of fact and in so far as is appropriate, of the rules of safety and conduct which were in force at the place and time of the event giving rise to the liability. The term 'rules of safety and conduct' should be interpreted as referring to all regulations having any relation to safety and conduct, including, for example, road safety rules in the case of an accident.[93] Rules on safety and hygiene in the workplace could also fall within the scope of Article 17, which would make it relevant in the context of transnational litigation against MNEs. For instance, Article 17 could potentially allow the court to take into account the home State's rules of safety and conduct, such as those related to an employer's duty of care vis-à-vis its employees, even when the law of the host State would be applicable. However, Article 17 would only impose on the court the duty *to take into account* the home State rules, not *to apply* them.[94]

Public policy of the forum

Article 26 Rome II Regulation provides that the application of the law of any country specified by the Rome II Regulation may be refused if such application is manifestly incompatible with the public policy (*ordre public*) of the forum. In exceptional circumstances, the courts of Member States may apply an exception based on public policy which is justified by considerations of public interest. This is the case, for instance, where the applicable law would result in measures which are regarded as being contrary to the public policy of the forum seised, such as the award of non-compensatory exemplary or punitive damages of an

---

89   Case C-135/15 *Republik Griechenland v Grigorios Nikiforidis* ECLI:EU:C:2016:774.

90   Enneking, 'Judicial Remedies', 55–56.

91   Ibid.

92   Ibid.

93   Rome II Regulation, Recital 34.

94   Enneking, 'Judicial Remedies', 58.

excessive nature.[95] One consequence is that the application of this provision will depend on the circumstances of the case and the legal order of the forum, which may vary from one country to another.[96] It has been suggested that, in the context of transnational litigation against MNEs, Article 26 may be a useful tool for setting aside the applicable host State law where its application would amount, for instance, to serious violations of international human rights norms.[97]

However, Article 26 may have limited practical value. First, the application of exceptions based on public policy should remain exceptional. Furthermore, courts are often reluctant to make an assessment of the well-foundedness of the law of the third country. Even if they were to make such an assessment, finding that 'the applicable rules of the host country are wrong as to their substance and conclusion, is not a sufficient reason for invoking public policy, not even if the incorrectness is manifest'.[98]

Towards a revision of the Rome II Regulation?

Litigators and NGOs have been calling for more flexibility to apply the law that best enables transnational claims against controlling companies.[99] This would suggest that a reform of the Rome II Regulation is necessary. For instance, the scope of Article 7 Rome II Regulation, on the environmental damage exception, could be extended to include human rights or health and safety damage.[100] Furthermore, the principle that the weaker party to a contract should be protected[101] could be extended to disputes involving MNEs and victims of human rights abuse in third countries. The Rome II Regulation could provide the application of conflict-of-law rules that are more favourable to the weaker party's interests than are the general rules.

Allowing the application of the home State law in specific circumstances, such as when the host State law does not sufficiently protect the rights of

95 Rome II Regulation, Recital 32. See also Angelika Fuchs, 'Article 26: Public Policy of the Forum' in Peter Huber (ed), *Rome II Regulation: Pocket Commentary* (Sellier 2011) 425.

96 Fuchs, 'Article 26', 430.

97 Enneking, 'Judicial Remedies', 60.

98 Ibid, citing Case C-38/98 *Régie Nationale des Usines Renault SA v Maxicar SpA and Orazio Formento* [2000] ECR I-02973.

99 'Creating a Paradigm Shift: Legal Solutions to Improve Access to Remedy for Corporate Human Rights Abuse' (Amnesty International and BHRRC 2017) 10.

100 Enneking, 'Judicial Remedies', 65.

101 Recital 31 of the Rome II Regulation provides the protection of the weaker party when the parties agree on the law applicable to their dispute. This idea is also found under Regulation (EC) No 593/2008 on the law applicable to contractual obligations (Rome I). Recital 23 provides that, as regards contracts concluded with parties regarded as being weaker, those parties should be protected by conflict-of-law rules that are more favourable to their interests than the general rules.

victims, seems all the more important in the current political context. As
will be seen in Chapter 7 of this book, home States are increasingly imposing
accountability standards upon business actors through, for instance, the
adoption of mandatory HRDD legislation. It is therefore crucial to ensure that
these standards are not dead letters and can effectively protect people and the
environment. In the future, the European legislator is likely to be faced with the
challenge of balancing legal certainty and the protection of parties' interests
with the need to protect victims of business-related human rights abuse.

4 The procedural framework for initiating civil proceedings

The way in which the law authorizes natural and legal persons to bring civil
claims before domestic courts has a direct effect on the ability of these persons
to gain access to remedy or to hold MNEs to account. Various types of plaintiffs
may bring a civil claim against an MNE, including individuals who suffer direct
damage from the business-related abuse, a representative of a particular group,
such as an affected village, or an organization defending a collective interest
related to the claim.[102] However, NGOs may face considerable obstacles to bring
claims.[103] Furthermore, the absence or limited access to collective redress may
be an obstacle to groups affected by business activities.

Right of action

In France, the action is the right of the plaintiff of a claim to bring an action to
be heard on the merits of their claim so that the judge may declare it founded or
unfounded.[104] The right of action is available to all those who have a legitimate
interest in the success or dismissal of a claim. However, there are situations
where the law confers the right of action solely upon persons authorized to
raise or oppose a claim, or to defend a particular interest.[105] To have a right
of action, a potential plaintiff must satisfy three criteria. First, plaintiffs must
demonstrate that they have a 'legitimate interest' to bring a civil claim (*intérêt
légitime*) against an MNE, meaning that the claim may provide an advantage

---

102 Stephen Tully, "'Never Say Never Jurisprudence'': Comparative Approaches to Corporate
Responsibility under the Law of Torts' in Stephen Tully (ed), *Research Handbook on Corporate
Legal Personality* (Edward Elgar Publishing 2005) 125.

103 Other organizations, such as trade unions, have brought claims against MNEs (eg *COMILOG*).
However, given the constraints of this book, this study focuses on NGOs.

104 French Code of Civil Procedure, Article 30.

105 French Code of Civil Procedure, Article 31.

or a benefit to the plaintiff. Such interest must already exist when the plaintiff brings the claim.[106] Importantly, French courts have progressively accepted that the interest to bring a civil claim is not subordinated to the legitimacy, or well-foundedness, of the claim.[107] Second, Article 31 implies that plaintiffs must have 'standing' to bring a civil claim (*qualité à agir*) against an MNE. However, the distinction between interest and standing to bring a claim is not always clear in French case law.[108] To have standing, plaintiffs must usually demonstrate a direct and personal interest, which may be problematic for NGOs when they seek to sue an MNE in defence of a collective or public interest (this aspect is studied in more detail below).[109] Nevertheless, the law may directly confer standing on NGOs in specific circumstances.[110] Third, 'legal capacity' is a prerequisite for the right of action.[111] However, there is no requirement as to the plaintiff's nationality and, as a result, foreign victims may be entitled to the right of action.

There are situations where a claim might be declared inadmissible for lack of a right of action (*fins de non-recevoir*), including lack of interest, lack of standing, statute of limitations, fixed time limit, or *res judicata*.[112] Furthermore, any claim raised by, or against, a person deprived of the right of action is inadmissible, and a person bringing a claim deemed abusive may be fined up to €10,000.[113] In several cases, MNEs have used this as an argument against NGOs and victims seeking civil redress for human rights or environmental abuse.

In the Netherlands, pursuant to Article 3:303 Dutch Civil Code (*Burgerlijk Wetboek*), a person has no right of action where they lack sufficient interest. However, the existence of sufficient interest is generally presumed and there is no requirement to address questions of substance before 'standing' can be granted.[114] Plaintiffs can be natural or legal persons, irrespective of whether they are Dutch nationals. However, legal personality is a prerequisite and, as a result, only companies, NGOs, and other foundations or associations that have legal personality may bring a civil claim.

---

106 Serge Guinchard, Cécile Chainais, and Frédérique Ferrand, *Procédure civile: Droit interne et droit de l'Union européenne* (32nd edn, Dalloz 2014) paras 131–136.

107 Ibid, para 137. See also Cass civ (2) 13 January 2005, n° 03-13.531.

108 Guinchard, Chainais and Ferrand, *Procédure civile*, para 122.

109 French law differentiates between individual, collective, and general interests. See ibid, para 145.

110 Ibid, paras 138–165.

111 Ibid, paras 124–124.

112 French Code of Civil Procedure, Article 122.

113 French Code of Civil Procedure, Article 32 and 32-1.

114 Cornelis Hendrik Van Rhee, 'Locus Standi in Dutch Civil Litigation in Comparative Perspective' (2014) Maastricht Faculty of Law Working Paper 2014/03, 6 <http://ssrn.com/abstract=2376162> accessed 1 May 2021.

Standing of NGOs

NGOs defending a collective or public interest often face obstacles in obtaining standing. For the purpose of this study, the words 'association' and 'NGO' are used interchangeably, as French and Dutch laws usually refer to NGOs as 'associations'.

In France, a lawfully registered association[115] can, without specific authorization, be a party to legal proceedings.[116] However, France distinguishes between two situations: whether the association is suing to protect its individual interests or collective interests.[117] For a long time, an association could only bring a claim to protect its individual interests, such as its own property. Since 1923, the Court of Cassation had rejected the idea that an association had standing to defend collective interests in the absence of direct and personal harm.[118] However, legislative and jurisprudential developments have gradually removed obstacles to the action of associations for the defence of collective interests. The French legislator has authorized some associations to act in defence of the collective interests they aim to protect in civil matters, such as consumer or environmental protection. Furthermore, the Court of Cassation has accepted that an association could act in defence of collective interests as long as they fell within the scope of its statutes[119] or its social purpose.[120]

Associations may also be a party to legal proceedings to protect the interests of their members. For a long time, the Court of Cassation has recognized that an association may bring a claim to protect the individual interests of its members.[121] This is the case for associations of local residents or of victims of a specific harmful activity.[122] However, a number of conditions are required. First, associations can only act for their members and cannot bring a claim for third parties. Second, an association's statutes must clearly provide that the association can bring a claim to protect its members' interests.[123]

---

115 Article 1 French Act of 1 July 1901 defines 'association' as the agreement between two or several persons who put together, permanently, their knowledge or their activity with a goal other than sharing profits. Loi du 1er juillet 1901 relative au contrat d'association.

116 Article 6 French Act of 1 July 1901. It is important to stress that an association which has not been lawfully registered does not have standing. Cass civ (2) 20 March 1989, n° 88-11585.

117 For a description of the concept of 'collective interest', see Jacques Héron and Thierry Le Bars, *Droit judiciaire privé* (5th edn, Domat 2012) 80.

118 Cass ch réunies 15 June 1923, DP 1924 1 153, S 1924 1 49, note Chavegrin (*Cardinal Luçon*).

119 Cass civ (3) 26 September 2007, n° 04-20636.

120 Cass civ (1) 18 Septembre 2008, n° 06-22.038.

121 Cass civ 23 July 1918, DP 1918, 1, 52; Cass civ (1) 27 May 1975, D 1976, 318, obs Viney.

122 Héron and Le Bars, *Droit judiciaire privé*, 98.

123 Ibid. See Cass civ (3) 17 July 1997, n° 95-18100.

Standing of NGOs was a major issue in *Alstom*. The corporate defendants challenged the assertion that AFPS, a French NGO that supports the rights of Palestinians, had standing in this case, arguing that AFPS had not established a personal interest or the collective interest of its members that would entitle it to bring the claim. Furthermore, AFPS had not been authorized by the legislator to bring a claim and its statutes were too vague to allow it to defend the Palestinian people. AFPS argued that, according to its statutes, it had the right to institute proceedings before national and international courts to defend the rights of the Palestinian people. The District Court ruled that AFPS was allowed to bring a claim, as its purpose was to initiate all procedures to ensure the defence of the rights of the Palestinian people.

However, the Court of Appeal reversed the District Court's ruling, rejecting the argument that AFPS could bring a civil claim.[124] It held that an association cannot act for the general interest. Without specific statutory authorization, an association can take legal action on behalf of collective interests 'insofar as its action corresponds to its social purpose'. In this instance, the Court of Appeal found that AFPS' social purpose was worded in general terms and did not allow AFPS to bring a claim to annul international contracts, to which it is a third party, on behalf of the Palestinian people.

The Court of Appeal's interpretation of NGO standing is questionable. AFPS' statutes clearly indicated that the association could sue to defend the Palestinian people, which, according to the Court of Cassation's jurisprudence, would have been enough to justify AFPS' standing. Instead, the Court of Appeal focused solely on AFPS' social purpose, which, taken together with a narrow interpretation of the purpose of the claim, led to a rejection of the possibility of an NGO challenging potential violations of international humanitarian law. This confusion is partly the result of the absence of a consistent and clear set of statutory rules on NGO standing. An intervention of the legislator therefore appears desirable to allow NGOs to play a more active role in defending societal interests and promote public interest litigation.

Alstom also demonstrates the interplay between the right of action of NGOs and the right of access to a court.[125] The Court of Appeal held that a declaration that AFPS' claim is inadmissible does not conflict with Article 6 ECHR and Article 47 EU Charter as:

> the association has been able to bring its suit, it has thus had access to a court. But this right is not unlimited. If the formal and substantive conditions for bringing a lawsuit are lacking, it

124 CA Versailles 22 March 2013, n° 11/05331.

125 Article 6 ECHR embodies the right of access to a court, which is the right to institute proceedings before civil courts. See *Golder v the UK* (1975) Series A no 18, para 36.

must be dismissed. On the facts, the AFPS fails to demonstrate that it fulfills the conditions allowing a charitable organization to bring a suit in defence of collective interests; thus, its suit must be declared inadmissible, without this prejudicing its right since it has had access to a court and a trial has taken place.[126]

This position on the right of access to a court appears inconsistent with the spirit of the ECHR. Although such a right is not absolute, limitations should not impair its very essence.[127] The Court of Appeal's view that AFPS had access to a court because it was able to bring its suit is erroneous in the light of the various interpretations given by the ECtHR of Article 6 ECHR. This approach limits the right of access to a court to the practical possibility to file a claim. However, the scope of this right is much broader, and must be practical and effective.[128] As such, the right of access to a court may be impaired by the existence of procedural rules barring certain subjects of law from bringing court proceedings[129] or by excessive formalism.[130] *Alstom* demonstrated that the complexity and formalism of rules governing NGO standing in French civil procedure affect the ability for NGOs to gain access to a court in transnational litigation against MNEs.

In the Netherlands, NGOs were traditionally barred from civil courts until the Dutch Supreme Court allowed them to bring an action to protect the public interest in a case related to environmental pollution.[131] A number of requirements must be fulfilled: (1) the NGO must be a legal person; (2) its statutes must include the protection of the public interest on which the action is based; and (3) the action must aim to protect such an interest.[132] Furthermore, since 1994, Article 3:305a Civil Code provides the possibility for an NGO to bring a representative action to protect interests similar to those that it promotes. This mechanism is addressed in the following section on collective redress.

Collective redress

In specific instances, business activities may cause damage to many victims. This can occur when, for example, a company operates a mine that pollutes

---

126 Noah Rubins and Gisèle Stephens-Chu, 'Introductory Note to AFPS and PLO v Alstom and Veolia (Versailles Ct App.)' (2013) 52 International Legal Materials 1173.

127 *Philis v Greece* (1991) Series A no 209, para 59.

128 *Bellet v France* (1995) Series A no 333-B, para 38.

129 *Philis v Greece*, para 65; *The Holy Monasteries v Greece* (1995) Series A no 301-A, para 83; *Lupsa v Romania* ECHR 2006-VII, paras 64–67.

130 *Pérez de Rada Cavanilles v Spain* (1998) 29 EHRR 109, para 49.

131 HR 17 June 1986, NJ 1987, 743.

132 Hanna Tolsma, Kars de Graaf and Jan Jans, 'The Rise and Fall of Access to Justice in the Netherlands' (2009) 21 Journal of Environmental Law 309, 311–312.

the environment, damaging local flora and fauna. The health and livelihoods of communities living nearby might be impacted, as they cannot access drinking water, farm their land, or fish for themselves or commercial purposes.

In the context of mass harm resulting from business activities, collective redress mechanisms[133] are crucial instruments in achieving justice. As the UNGPs pointed out, inadequate options for aggregating claims or enabling representative proceedings, such as class actions and other collective action procedures, constitute barriers preventing effective access to remedy for claimants.[134] In France, the absence of collective redress mechanisms has constituted a significant obstacle for plaintiffs. In *COMILOG*, victims were unable to aggregate their claims and had to file more than 800 separate applications.[135] Lodging a large number of individual claims is costly and time-consuming for victims and NGOs who, often, have limited financial resources. The absence of collective redress mechanisms can therefore prohibit the vindication of rights on a collective basis, no matter how meritorious the claims are.

In the EU, for a long time the existence of collective redress mechanisms in Member States was limited. Reluctance to allow such instruments has notably been fuelled by fears of perceived excesses in the US class action system. Nonetheless, faced with rising demands for access to justice in situations of mass harm, and as a result of EU efforts to boost the development of collective redress mechanisms, Member States are increasingly adopting such instruments. However, collective redress mechanisms vary greatly from one Member State to another. Furthermore, their effectiveness is limited and, as a result, access to justice remains unsatisfactory in the context of mass harm caused by MNEs.

EU efforts on collective redress

At EU level, collective redress is generally perceived as a potential instrument for improving access to justice. However, the lack of political consensus has

---

133 The EC defines 'collective redress' as either a legal mechanism that ensures a possibility to claim cessation of illegal behaviour collectively by two or more natural or legal persons or by an entity entitled to bring a representative action (injunctive collective redress) or a legal mechanism that ensures a possibility to claim compensation collectively by two or more natural or legal persons claiming to have been harmed in a mass harm situation or by an entity entitled to bring a representative action (compensatory collective redress). Commission Recommendation of 11 June 2013 on common principles for injunctive and compensatory collective redress mechanisms in the Member States concerning violations of rights granted under Union Law [2013] OJ L201/60, para 3(a) (Recommendation on collective redress).

134 UNHRC, 'Guiding Principles on Business and Human Rights: Implementing the United Nations "Protect, Respect and Remedy" Framework' (21 March 2011) UN Doc A/HRC/17/31 (UNGPs), Commentary to GP 26.

135 Alvarez, 'Devoir de vigilance'.

hampered the enactment of any binding instrument on collective redress.[136] Opponents to the development of EU collective redress instruments have also questioned whether the EU has competence to legislate for collective redress, as well as whether such mechanisms to ensure private enforcement are desirable. As a result, the work carried out by the EU institutions in this field has produced limited results.[137]

In 2012, the EP called for the adoption of a legally binding horizontal framework which would include a common set of principles providing uniform access to justice via collective redress within the EU.[138] Such a framework should specifically deal with consumer protection but could be extended to other sectors. However, in 2013 the EC adopted a recommendation (2013 Recommendation) containing a series of non-binding principles 'to ensure a coherent horizontal approach to collective redress in the EU without harmonising Member States' systems'.[139] Pursuant to this document, all EU Member States should have collective redress mechanisms for both injunctive and compensatory relief that respect a number of principles on, for instance, standing, admissibility, funding, or the constitution of the claimant party by 'opt-in' principle. These principles should be applied horizontally and equally in consumer protection, competition, environmental protection, protection of personal data, financial services legislation, and investor protection. As will be seen below, the 2013 Recommendation was, to a certain extent, followed in France. However, a 2018 report by the EC showed that the implementation of the 2013 Recommendation was unsatisfactory, as the availability of collective redress mechanisms was still inconsistent across the EU.[140] Furthermore, the inability of EU citizens to access collective compensatory relief in cases such as the Volkswagen Dieselgate scandal demonstrated the limits of collective redress mechanisms in the EU.[141] These developments led to the adoption of Directive 2020/1828 on representative actions for the protection of the collective interests of consumers in 2020.[142] This instrument empowers

136 Alexia Pato, *Jurisdiction and Cross-Border Collective Redress: A European Private International Law Perspective* (Hart Publishing 2019) 69.

137 Ibid, 45–46.

138 European Parliament Resolution of 2 February 2012 on 'Towards a Coherent European Approach to Collective Redress' (2011/2089(INI)).

139 Recommendation on collective redress.

140 European Commission, 'Report on the Implementation of the Commission Recommendation of 11 June 2013 on Common Principles for Injunctive and Compensatory Collective Redress Mechanisms in the Member States Concerning Violations of Rights Granted under Union Law (2013/396/EU)' COM(2018) 40 final.

141 'Volkswagen Dieselgate Four Years Down the Road' (BEUC 2019).

142 Directive (EU) 2020/1828 of the European Parliament and of the Council of 25 November 2020 on representative actions for the protection of the collective interests of consumers and repealing Directive 2009/22/EC [2020] OJ L409/1.

qualified entities (ie consumer organizations or public bodies designated by the Member States) to bring representative actions (including cross-border representative actions) on behalf of groups of consumers seeking injunctive and redress measures against traders. This directive is significant because it requires all Member States to establish a representative action mechanism to protect the collective interests of consumers. However, it does not create a general collective redress mechanism. Representative actions can only be brought against traders who violate specific EU legal instruments in areas such as financial services, travel and tourism, energy, health, telecommunications, and data protection.

The current EU collective redress framework, which focuses on consumer rights, is unhelpful in dealing with mass harm situations caused by corporations in the context of transnational litigation against MNEs. There is currently no EU legal framework requiring, or even recommending, Member States to establish a mechanism for collective redress in civil litigation. Furthermore, because of the TFEU's limitations on EU competences, existing EU initiatives have limited collective redress to specific areas of law that are not necessarily relevant for the type of damage suffered by victims of corporate mass harm. As a result, any meaningful collective redress mechanism in the context of transnational litigation against MNEs is more likely to emerge from national initiatives.

Collective redress in France

The creation of collective redress mechanisms has been much debated within political and economic circles.[143] However, France has traditionally been reluctant to allow such instruments.[144] Fears of the perceived excesses of the US class action system and a strong business lobby opposed to collective redress have been effective in delaying the adoption of mechanisms for solving mass harm.[145]

Nonetheless, France recently introduced the possibility for group action (*action de groupe*) in a limited number of sectors, in line with the 2013 Recommendation. The first step was taken in 2014 when France passed a new law that introduced a group action in the fields of consumer law and

143 Raphael Amaro and others, 'Collective Redress in the Member States of the European Union' (European Parliament 2018) 151.

144 On the subject of group action in France, see Guillaume Cerutti and Marc Guillaume, 'Rapport sur l'action de groupe' (La Documentation Française 2005); Véronique Magnier and Ralf Alleweldt, 'Evaluation of the Effectiveness and Efficiency of Collective Redress Mechanisms in the European Union: Country Report France' (Civic Consulting 2008); Angélique Legendre (ed), *L'action collective ou action de groupe: Se préparer à son introduction en droit français et en droit belge* (Larcier 2010).

145 See Thomas Clay, 'Class Actions or Not Class Actions?' [2010] Recueil Dalloz 1776. Amaro and others, *Collective Redress*, 151.

competition law.[146] France later extended the possibility for group action to other fields, namely health,[147] privacy and data protection,[148] environment,[149] and discrimination.[150] Furthermore, France adopted a set of procedural rules that apply to the above-mentioned group actions.[151] In general, a group action follows a complex two-stage procedure. First, there is the liability phase during which the court decides on the liability of the defendant based on individual model cases. At this stage, there is no group of claimants. The court then defines the group of potential claimants and the parameters that individual claimants must meet to join the group. It also specifies how the case will be publicized in the media and the deadline for plaintiffs to join the group. Second, there is the compensation phase during which claimants meeting the criteria fixed by the court can join the group via an opt-in system and receive compensation.[152]

This system has been criticized for its complexity, its hurdles to bringing claims, and its ineffectiveness in solving mass claims.[153] In particular, only accredited associations can file a group action, which means that lawyers and other public bodies cannot start group actions from their own motion. Moreover, not all associations can launch group actions, as they must meet restrictive prerequisites. Additionally, in practice only a few associations have sufficient resources to effectively initiate and handle group actions. Furthermore, the effectiveness of group actions is limited by the fact that they are usually costly, burdensome, and time-consuming. Difficulties also arise with the quantification of loss and the type of damage to be compensated (only material) for each individual within the group.[154]

In the context of transnational litigation against MNEs, the group action of some sectors, such as environment, privacy and data protection, and discrimination, could be relevant. Furthermore, some aspects of the current system offer some significant advantages. In the few group actions that have taken place so far, associations have used the media intensively to advertise proceedings. Important media coverage is likely to trigger some behavioural changes in

146 Loi n° 2014-344 du 17 mars 2014 relative à la consommation. See French Consumer Code (*Code de la consommation*), Article L623-1.

147 Loi n° 2016-41 du 26 janvier 2016 de modernisation de notre système de santé. See French Public Health Code (*Code de la santé publique*), Article L1143-1.

148 Loi n° 2016-1547 du 18 novembre 2016 de modernisation de la justice du XXIe siècle. See Loi n° 78-17 du 6 janvier 1978 relative à l'informatique, aux fichiers et aux libertés (Act 78-17), Article 37.

149 Loi n° 2016-1547.

150 Ibid.

151 French Code of Civil Procedure, Articles 848 to 849-21.

152 Amaro and others, *Collective Redress*, 154.

153 Ibid, 151–164.

154 Ibid.

businesses. Additionally, group actions have incentivized defendants and associations to settle their case, therefore providing victims with faster access to a remedy.[155] However, the current system of group action appears, at the same time, insufficient to help victims of business-related abuse gain access to justice. Not all claims against MNEs are likely to fall under the scope of the current group actions. Furthermore, the group action mechanism seems to reproduce the same flaws that have plagued transnational litigation against MNEs, such as high costs and lengthy duration. To date, claims have rarely reached stage two of the procedure. Finally, the current rules provide limited elements for the resolution of international mass claims.[156]

Collective redress in the Netherlands

Collective redress mechanisms have existed in the Netherlands since 1994. However, they are quite different from US class actions or UK group actions in order to prevent transforming the Dutch legal system into a 'perceived aggressive American litigating society'.[157] One striking aspect of the Dutch practice of collective redress is its emphasis on mediation. In the Netherlands, there are two main collective redress mechanisms: representative action and settlement.

In a representative action under Article 3:305a Civil Code, an NGO (either a foundation or an association with full legal capacity) can bring an action on behalf of a group of claimants who have suffered harm as a result of the defendant's acts. The interests of the claimants must be analogous to be suitable for protection through the representative action.[158] Furthermore, the action must aim to protect similar interests of other persons to the extent that the NGO's articles promote such interests. The representative action under Article 3:305a is frequently used for the protection of common interest issues, such as general environmental concerns. It presents a number of strengths. For instance, the NGO can be established after the dispute has arisen.[159] Moreover, Article 3:305a allows a person whose interest has been represented in the action to opt out by refusing to be bound by the ruling's effect. Furthermore, as a result of the emphasis of Dutch civil procedure on conciliation, the NGO must adequately consult with the defendant before initiating the action. This means

---

155 Ibid, 156.

156 Ibid, 159.

157 Marie-José Van Der Heijden, 'Class Actions/les actions collectives' (2010) 14.3 EJCL 3 <http://citeseerx.ist.psu.edu/viewdoc/download?doi=10.1.1.463.3430&rep=rep1&type=pdf> accessed 1 May 2021.

158 Berthy Van Den Broek and Liesbeth Enneking, 'Public Interest Litigation in the Netherlands: A Multidimensional Take on the Promotion of Environmental Interests by Private Parties through the Courts' (2014) 10 Utrecht Law Review 77, 84.

159 Marieke Van Hooijdonk and Peter Eijsvoogel, *Litigation in the Netherlands: Civil Procedure, Arbitration and Administrative Litigation* (Kluwer Law International 2013) 105.

that the NGO will have no *locus standi* if it has not made a sufficient attempt to achieve the objective of the action through consultations with the defendant.[160] Litigation should only be initiated when consultations are not possible. At the same time, some requirements under Article 3:305a limit the effectiveness of representative action. Article 3:305a is confined to injunctive relief and/or a declaratory decision. It does not allow the NGO to claim collective damages on behalf of the claimants. If the liability of the defendant is established, each claimant must bring their own claim for damages on that basis separately. This means that a successful claimant must incur extra costs and go through additional proceedings to access remedy. This aspect defeats the aim of collective redress to facilitate access to justice in the context of mass harm.

In *Shell*, Milieudefensie brought a claim on the basis of Article 3:305a. Both the District Court and the Court of Appeal of The Hague accepted the admissibility of Milieudefensie's claim. However, the corporate defendants disputed the admissibility of Milieudefensie's claim,[161] and their arguments raised important questions for collective redress in the context of cross-border private enforcement. First, Shell challenged whether Milieudefensie, a Dutch NGO, could use Article 3:305a to advocate for the protection of non-Dutch interests, namely the interests of the Nigerian victims of the oil spills, which were not linked in any way to the Dutch domestic jurisdiction.[162] Shell also argued that Milieudefensie's object clause in its articles of association was not specific enough to include the protection of the environment in Nigeria and that Milieudefensie did not perform any activities in that country. However, both the District Court and the Court of Appeal concluded that there were no valid grounds to restrict the scope of application of Article 3:305a and dismissed Shell's argument. For the courts, Milieudefensie had engaged in activities in support of the interests of the environment in Nigeria. Furthermore, the protection of the environment globally is an objective set out in Milieudefensie's charter. There was no reason to assume that this objective was not sufficiently specific, or that localized damage to the environment abroad felt outside that objective or outside the application of Article 3:305a.[163] The Court of Appeal added that 'there is a sufficient link with the Dutch domestic jurisdiction, namely to the extent that the existence and scope of the duty of care of the parent company having its headquarters in the Netherlands have been submitted for review'.[164]

---

160 Van Den Broek and Enneking, 'Public Interest Litigation in the Netherlands', 84.

161 'Motion for the Court to Decline Jurisdiction and Transfer the Case, Also Conditional Statement of Defense in the Main Action' (De Brauw Blackstone Westbroek 13 May 2009) paras 85–98.

162 Ibid, para 98.

163 DC The Hague 14 September 2011, Judgement in the Ancillary Actions Concerning the Production of Exhibits and in the Main Actions, 337050/HAZA09-1580 (*Akpan*), [4.4]; 330891/HAZA09-0579 (*Oguru*), [4.5]; 337058/HAZA09-1581 (*Dooh*), [4.5].

164 *Shell* [2015], [4.4].

Shell also challenged the representativeness of the group and the benefit of using the action under Article 3:305a in this case. For the defendants, the case at issue involved a 'purely individual representation of interests'.[165] Furthermore, the claim did not offer any advantages 'whatsoever over litigating in the name of the interested parties themselves'.[166]

However, the District Court held that the plaintiffs' claims rose above the individual interests of the parties, as the decontamination of the soil and the clean-up of the fishponds would benefit not only the plaintiffs but also the rest of the community and the environment. It also recognized that it could well be inconvenient for the interested parties to litigate as individuals, seeing as many people could now be affected. The Court of Appeal also reiterated that, for the admissibility of an action under Article 3:305a CC, it is a condition that the claim seeks to protect similar interests of other persons. This requirement is satisfied if the interests that the action seeks to protect are suitable to be joined, so that an efficient and effective safeguarding of legal rights can be promoted for the benefit of the interested parties.[167] The size of the group does not matter in this regard.

The second collective redress mechanism is a settlement-only action under the 2005 Act on collective settlements of mass claims (*Wet collectieve afhandeling massaschade* or WCAM).[168] The idea behind the WCAM is to settle cases of mass damages in a smooth manner by enabling liable and injured parties to reach a collective settlement.[169] There are two main stages. First, a foundation or an association representing victims of a mass harm reaches a collective settlement with the tortfeasor. Second, the Court of Appeal of Amsterdam approves the settlement. One advantage is that the WCAM is not restricted to a particular area of law or to certain sectors, such as competition or consumer law.[170] One disadvantage from a victim's perspective is that all injured parties, including those who have not participated in the negotiation of the settlement, are bound by the court decision approving the settlement, unless they have opted out. Although this rule aims to ensure legal certainty and prevent additional claims, it is problematic for injured parties who disapprove of the settlement or ignore the proceedings. Another disadvantage is that the WCAM does not deal with the process of reaching a settlement. It only provides that the settlement is a

165 'Motion for the Court to Decline Jurisdiction and Transfer the Case', paras 94–95.

166 Ibid, paras 96–97.

167 *Shell* [2015], [4.4].

168 Stefaan Voet, 'European Collective Redress Developments: A Status Quaestionis' (2014) 4 International Journal of Procedural Law 97, 107.

169 Marco Loos, 'Evaluation of the Effectiveness and Efficiency of Collective Redress Mechanisms in the European Union: Country Report The Netherlands' (Civil Consulting 2008) 2.

170 Van Der Heijden, 'Class Actions', 3.

prerequisite that must be reached out of court.[171] However, the requirement for a pre-trial hearing has existed since 2013. This mechanism could potentially be used by claimants seeking remediation for mass harm caused by MNEs and may provide a cheaper and faster alternative for accessing a remedy than transnational litigation against MNEs. However, only nine class settlements were successfully reached through this mechanism between 2005 and 2019, which raises questions as to the chances of success and the effectiveness of this mechanism in the context of mass harm caused by MNEs.[172]

In 2019, the Netherlands adopted new legislation called *Wet afwikkeling massaschade in collectieve actie* (WACAM),[173] which introduced changes to the mechanism under Article 3:305a. An important positive change is that the WACAM introduced the possibility to claim compensatory damages. The WACAM also established stricter standing and admissibility requirements. An NGO must now have a supervisory board, a mechanism for decision-making by the persons whose interest is represented, sufficient financial resources for the costs of the representative action, and sufficient experience and expertise to bring the action. While these new requirements aim to improve the effectiveness of the mechanism, they raise concerns that fewer NGOs will be able to bring a representative action in areas of common interest. Another potential hurdle is that new criteria are required for the representative action to be sufficiently connected to the Dutch jurisdiction: the majority of the claimants must be Dutch residents; or the events on which the action is based must have occurred in the Netherlands. The mere fact that the defendant is located in the Netherlands is now insufficient. It is unlikely that foreign victims of mass harm caused by Dutch MNEs will meet these criteria.

5 Production of evidence

Rules governing the production of evidence have a major impact on the ability of victims to gain access to justice, especially in the context of human rights abuse and environmental pollution involving MNEs. Until now, access to, and production of, evidence in transnational litigation against MNEs has been problematic for several reasons. First, collecting evidence in transnational cases is costly for plaintiffs, as evidence is usually located in both host and home countries. In cases raising complex issues, such as environmental

---

171 Loos, 'Evaluation of the Effectiveness and Efficiency of Collective Redress Mechanisms', 2.

172 Albert Knigge and Isabella Wijnberg, 'Class/Collective Action in the Netherlands: Overview' (Thomson Reuters, 1 June 2019) <https://uk.practicallaw.thomsonreuters.com/6-618-0285?transitionType=Default&contextData=(sc.Default)&firstPage=true&bhcp=1> accessed 1 May 2021.

173 This Act came into force on 1 January 2020.

pollution, the use of experts may be required, necessitating additional financial resources. Second, plaintiffs must usually prove corporate involvement in the production of the harm. Frequently, MNEs are in possession of such evidence and refuse to share compromising information with plaintiffs. Furthermore, MNEs often operate in a complex way with little transparency as to the structure, management, and operational functioning of the corporate group. Third, the rules governing the collection and admissibility of evidence may place an excessive burden on plaintiffs or fail to provide effective disclosure procedures to reduce potential inequality of arms between the parties. Ultimately, difficulties arising from the production of evidence reveal the asymmetric positions of plaintiffs and corporate defendants. These obstacles have been acknowledged in the UNGPs, which provide that unbalanced access to information and to expertise between parties in business-related human rights claims create barriers to accessing judicial remedy.[174] NGOs and scholars have also described how the lack of transparency and access to information, as well as formalistic rules on evidence, are significant obstacles for victims of corporate abuse seeking remediation.[175]

This section aims to give an overview of the rules governing burden of proof, admissibility of evidence, and disclosure and discovery procedures in France and the Netherlands, and how they impact on the ability of victims to demonstrate the merits of their liability claims against MNEs.

Burden of proof

As a result of the Rome II Regulation, French and Dutch courts are more likely to apply the host State rules governing the burden of proof. However, in a number of exceptional circumstances, they may be able to apply the law of the forum – meaning French and Dutch procedural law – to determine the burden of proof.[176] Therefore, a brief overview of French and Dutch rules is relevant here.

Both France and the Netherlands follow the principle that 'whoever asserts a fact must prove it'. In France, this principle is contained in Article 1353 French Civil Code, which provides that 'anyone claiming enforcement of an obligation must prove it'. Furthermore, each party shall bear the burden of proving the

---

174 UNGPs, Commentary to Guiding Principle 26.

175 See Gwynne Skinner and others, 'The Third Pillar: Access to Judicial Remedies for Human Rights Violations by Transnational Business' (ICAR, ECCJ & CORE 2013); Liesbeth Enneking, 'Multinationals and Transparency in Foreign Direct Liability Cases: The Prospects for Obtaining Evidence under the Dutch Civil Procedural Regime on the Production of Exhibits' (2013) 3 The Dovenschmidt Quarterly 134.

176 See Section 3 of this chapter.

facts necessary for the success of their claim.[177] However, the facts on which the resolution of the dispute depends may, at the request of the parties or *ex officio*, be the subject of any legally admissible investigative measure.[178] An investigative measure may be ordered in respect of a fact only if the party alleging it does not have sufficient evidence to prove it. However, under no circumstances may an investigative measure be ordered to make up for the party's failure to provide evidence.[179]

In the Netherlands, Article 150 Dutch Code of Civil Procedure states that the party claiming the legal consequences of facts or rights shall bear the burden of proving them. Therefore, plaintiffs initiating a civil claim against an MNE must prove the facts and circumstances to substantiate that claim. If the plaintiffs are not able to meet their evidentiary burden, it will be assumed that the facts and circumstances in question do not exist.[180] However, there are a number of exceptions to this rule, such as when the law specifically provides otherwise, or when the application of such requirement would be contrary to the principles of reasonableness and fairness.[181] Furthermore, under specific circumstances a reversal of burden of proof is possible during the proceedings or an aggravated burden of proof may be placed on the defendant to motivate their defence.[182]

As will be seen below, strict rules on the burden of proof, coupled with the absence or inadequacy of disclosure procedures and complex systems of liability within corporate groups, are challenging for plaintiffs to overcome.

Admissibility

In France, according to Article 1358 French Civil Code, proof may be provided by any means, except where the law states otherwise. However, French civil procedure is characterized by the prevalence of written evidence.[183] Parties argue their cases almost exclusively based on written evidence, and statements by parties do not count as evidence. Nonetheless, the judge may invite the parties to provide factual explanations deemed necessary for the resolution of the dispute. The judge can also appoint an independent expert to further investigate technical matters or admit evidence from third parties by affidavit or oral testimony. However, this last option is less common. In general,

---

177 French Code of Civil Procedure, Article 9.

178 French Code of Civil Procedure, Article 143.

179 French Code of Civil Procedure, Article 146.

180 Van Den Broek and Enneking, 'Public Interest Litigation in the Netherlands', 87.

181 Dutch Code of Civil Procedure, Article 150.

182 Enneking, 'Multinationals and Transparency', 138.

183 Martin Oudin, 'Evidence in Civil Law – France' (Institute for Local Self-Government and Public Procurement 2015) 15.

evidence will not be admissible if it violates the privacy of individuals or the secrecy of correspondence. Nonetheless, judges should assess whether the production of evidence is indispensable to the exercise of the right to evidence and proportionate to the conflicting interests involved before dismissing evidence.[184]

In the Netherlands, there is no restriction on the admissibility of evidence, which may be presented in any form, unless the law provides otherwise.[185] In some cases, evidence unlawfully obtained may be admissible.[186] Dutch courts usually have discretion to assess evidence.[187] The absence of restrictions on the admissibility of evidence benefits victims bringing civil claims against MNEs. The flexibility of Dutch rules allows victims to present a large range of documents to substantiate their arguments. It also reduces the inequality of arms between the parties. However, as will be seen below, the benefit of these rules appears to be limited due to inadequate disclosure procedures. Furthermore, Dutch courts sometimes reject evidence that has been lawfully obtained when, for instance, it would violate the other party's right to a private life.[188]

Disclosure

MNEs often hold information that can substantiate the plaintiff's liability arguments, such as information regarding their structure, operations, ownership, or governance. However, information is not always transparent or easily available to third parties. Therefore, disclosure is crucial in allowing plaintiffs to access necessary evidence held by MNEs.

In France, parties must respect an obligation 'to contribute to justice with a view to the manifestation of the truth'.[189] As a result, parties are required to communicate in due time and spontaneously to one another the evidence they produce or rely upon.[190] The judge may order parties to transmit evidence if communication of proof is not done spontaneously.[191]

Furthermore, French civil procedure allows parties to request the production of evidence held by the other party or third parties.[192] In this situation, the

---

184 Cass civ (1) 5 April 2012, n° 11-14.177.

185 Dutch Code of Civil Procedure, Article 152(1). See also Van Den Broek and Enneking, 'Public Interest Litigation in the Netherlands', 87.

186 Van Hooijdonk and Eijsvoogel, *Litigation in the Netherlands*, 22.

187 Dutch Code of Civil Procedure, Article 152(2).

188 Van Hooijdonk and Eijsvoogel, *Litigation in the Netherlands*, 22.

189 French Civil Code, Article 10.

190 French Code of Civil Procedure, Articles 15 and 132.

191 Ibid, Article 133.

192 Ibid, Articles 11, 142 and 138.

judge may order the issuance or production of the document or exhibit if they consider the application to be well-founded.[193] They can impose penalties on the party holding the evidence, if necessary, or may order third parties, such as other members of MNEs, to disclose documents. However, the judge has the discretion to appreciate the opportunity of such requests and controls the procedure tightly.[194] The plaintiff's request must be specific and identify existing documents that the corporate defendant possesses. Any general requests are considered inadmissible.[195]

In the context of transnational litigation against MNEs, criteria, such as the specificity of documents requested, and the discretion of French judges to consider whether a request for disclosure of evidence is well founded, have proven challenging for plaintiffs. In *COMILOG*, the plaintiffs requested the disclosure of specific documents, including corporate by-laws and minutes of meetings, in order to establish the situation of co-employment.[196] The corporate defendants challenged the request. However, the Court of Appeal ordered the companies to disclose the documents in 2013 and the Court of Cassation later upheld this decision.[197]

The plaintiffs' disclosure request has been less successful in *Bolloré* thus far. Plaintiffs have asked for the disclosure of various documents in the defendants' possession demonstrating the legal and capitalistic links between the various companies. Their disclosure request targeted specific documents (eg the concession contract between the Cambodian State and Socfin-KCD) as well as broad categories of files (eg Bolloré group's internal memos concerning the operations of Socfin and Socfin-KCD between 2008 and 2016). To support their request for disclosure, the plaintiffs alleged that Bolloré and Compagnie du Cambodge exercised, from France, operational powers in the Socfin-KCD joint venture, and that they directed and organized, on a daily basis, the activities harming them in Bu Sra, Cambodia. However, the Court found that the plaintiffs provided no evidence as to the operational power alleged or of the alleged harm, even though some information was publicly available, since the two companies are listed on the stock market. Accordingly, the Court stated that 'the request for an order of disclosure of evidence, the purpose of which should not supplement the plaintiff's failure to obtain evidence, must be rejected'.[198]

Restrictive disclosure rules under French law legitimately aim to discourage 'fishing expeditions'. At the same time, they can negatively affect equality of

193 Ibid, Article 139.

194 Cass civ (1) 6 November 2002, n° 00-15.220. See also Héron and Le Bars, *Droit judiciaire privé*, 825.

195 Héron and Le Bars, *Droit judiciaire privé*, 825.

196 Conclusions, 17 June 2010, n° 09/10495 56.

197 Cass soc 28 January 2015, n° 13-22.994 to 13-23.006.

198 TGI Nanterre (6) 10 February 2017, n° 15/10981.

arms between the parties and, ultimately, the ability of plaintiffs to have access to justice. According to lawyers and NGOs, requiring that requests for information be very specific as to the type of document or piece of evidence sought may constitute an obstacle as, in practice, this level of detail may not be fully known in advance.[199]

In the Netherlands, parties are free to submit or withhold evidence to a large extent. There is no obligation on a party to disclose documents that are damaging to its own case. Furthermore, a party has limited options to request documents from the other party, as 'fishing expeditions' are not allowed.[200] However, pursuant to Article 843a Dutch Code of Civil Procedure, anyone who has records at their disposal or in their custody must allow a person with a legitimate interest to inspect, have a copy of, or obtain an extract from those records pertaining to a legal relationship to which they or their legal predecessors are party. If necessary, the court may determine how an inspection must be conducted or how a copy or extract must be produced. However, there are several limits to the application of Article 843a. As a result, obtaining evidence from MNEs remains problematic when they are unwilling to disclose it.[201] Access to evidence using disclosure has been a major obstacle for plaintiffs in the two ongoing cases against Shell.

In *Shell*, the claimants requested disclosure, based on Article 843a, of Shell's internal documents, including management reports and internal emails. For the plaintiffs, these documents aimed to demonstrate that insufficient maintenance of the oil pipelines, and not sabotage, was the cause of the spills, and to demonstrate the control that RDS had over SPDC's environmental policy.

In 2011, the District Court rejected the plaintiffs' request. It held that Article 843a covers an exceptional obligation to produce evidence, and that 'there is no general obligation for the parties to proceedings to produce exhibits in the sense that they can be obliged as a rule to provide each other with all manner of information and documents'.[202] Therefore, and to avoid 'so-called fishing expeditions', the application of Article 843a must meet a number of conditions to be admissible:

> Firstly, the party claiming the production of an exhibit must demonstrate a genuine *legitimate interest*, which legitimate interest can be explained as *an interest in evidence*. An interest in evidence exists when an item of evidence may contribute

199 'Creating a paradigm shift', 19.

200 Van Hooijdonk and Eijsvoogel, *Litigation in the Netherlands*, 4.

201 Ibid, 30.

202 *Akpan* [2011], [4.5]; *Oguru* [2011], [4.6]; *Dooh* [2011], [4.6].

to the substantiation and/or demonstration of a concretely substantiated and disputed argument that is relevant to and possibly decisive for the claims being assessed. Secondly, the claims must concern *"certain documents"* which, thirdly, are at *the actual disposal of the respondent*, or can be put at its disposal. Fourthly, the party *claiming the production of an exhibit* must be *party to the legal relationship* covered by the claimed documents specifically. This includes legal relationship as a result of unlawful act. If all of these conditions are met, there nevertheless exists no obligation to submit if, fifthly, there are *no serious causes* or if, sixthly, it can reasonably be assumed that *due administration of justice* is also guaranteed without such provision of information.[203]

The District Court held that the demonstration of a concretely substantiated and disputed argument appears as a *sine qua non* condition to justify a legitimate interest. However, it found that the plaintiffs had insufficiently substantiated their argument and, as a result, had no legitimate interest in obtaining the items of evidence they requested.

The plaintiffs also invoked their right of disclosure on the grounds of the principle of equality of arms laid down by Article 6 ECHR. Nonetheless, the District Court rejected this argument and maintained that the conditions under Article 843a were compatible with Article 6 ECHR and the principle of equality of arms.[204]

The District Court's judgment was a major drawback for the plaintiffs, who appealed it. Furthermore, they sought a new injunction under Article 843a following the 2013 ruling of the District Court, which had found SPDC liable for some of the oil spills.[205] In 2014, new factual information became available as a result of disclosure in *Bodo*, the tort suit against SPDC in England. Documents disclosed by SPDC demonstrated that RDS and SPDC had acted negligently in preventing the oil spills that were at the heart of the Dutch court case. The plaintiffs used this new information to request access to evidence that was in the hands of RDS and SPDC.[206]

In December 2015, the Court of Appeal ordered Shell to disclose some of the documents requested by the plaintiffs. First, it found that there was insufficient cause to order Shell to produce documents to allow Milieudefensie to make

203 Ibid (original emphasis).

204 *Akpan* [2011], [4.14]; *Oguru* [2011], [4.16]; *Dooh* [2011], [4.15].

205 'Motion to Produce Documents' (Prakken d'Oliveira 10 September 2013) 200.126.843 (*Dooh*); 200.126.849 (*Milieudefensie*); 200.126.834 (*Oguru*).

206 'Statement of Appeal Regarding the Dismissal of the Motion to Produce Documents by Virtue of Section 834A DCCP (Interlocutory Judgement District Court of The Hague 14-09-2011)' (Prakken d'Oliveira 2014), para 8.

a plausible case for insufficient maintenance. Instead it suggested that an inspection might be a more appropriate way to understand the cause of the oil spills and invited the parties to agree on an expert examination. It concluded that 'there is insufficient evidence of the interest of Milieudefensie et al. in inspection of those documents', as 'it can reasonably be assumed that a proper administration of justice is safeguarded even without the submission of the information requested.'[207] Second, the Court of Appeal authorized the plaintiffs to have access to Shell's documents to understand whether RDS had failed to supervise SPDC. It held that the 'assertion by Shell that the parent company did not know about the spillage and the condition and maintenance of the pipeline locally does not seem to be an adequate defence in all cases, particularly not if sabotage ceases to be a cause of damage.'[208] Access to Shell's documents is important when

> Considering, inter alia, (i) that Shell sets itself goals and ambitions with regard to, for instance, the environment, and has defined a group policy to achieve these goals and ambitions in a coordinated and uniform way, and (ii) that RDS (like the former parent company) monitors compliance with these group standards and this group policy ... . Milieudefensie et al. have demonstrated their legitimate evidentiary interest in inspection of the documents in question, assuming for now the possibility under Nigerian law under (very) special circumstances of a parent company's liability for violation of a duty of care.[209]

Similarly, in *Kiobel* the District Court ordered the defendants to produce some internal documents while it rejected the plaintiffs' request for the release of other confidential files, including trial exhibits produced during the US proceedings in relation to the same facts (see Chapter 3). With regard to the second set of documents, it ruled that the plaintiffs had not met the requirements of 'legitimate interest' and 'specific documents' under Article 843a. The plaintiffs' request for documents was defined too broadly. Furthermore, they did not have an automatic legitimate interest to examine documents relevant to the US proceedings, even though they had brought that case, in the context of the Dutch litigation. Finally, the fact that a large number of documents in a general sense might be relevant or interesting was insufficient to meet the requirements set out in Article 843a.[210]

---

207 *Shell* [2015], [6.4].
208 Ibid.
209 Ibid [6.9], [6.10].
210 DC The Hague 1 May 2019, C/09/540872/HAZA17-1048 [4.35]–[4.36].

In the *Shell* and *Kiobel* cases, the Dutch courts adopted a restrictive interpretation of the requirements triggering disclosure. This attitude reflects the Dutch objective of balancing the legitimate interest of parties to have access to evidence to substantiate their claims with the concern to prevent so-called 'fishing expeditions' and therefore frivolous litigation. This is in stark contrast with the more liberal approach to disclosure adopted by judges in common law countries, particularly in the US and the UK.

In conclusion, from an access to justice perspective, restrictive disclosure in civil law jurisdictions is problematic in the context of transnational litigation against MNEs, as it ignores the underlying asymmetry between MNEs and victims and could potentially lead to unfair results for the weaker party. As will be seen in Chapter 6, rules applicable to corporate group liability make it difficult for victims to hold the parent company liable for the damage caused by its subsidiaries. To demonstrate the role of the parent company in the production of the damage, or the degree to which one company entity relates to another, victims need to produce evidence which is often in the MNE's possession. Therefore, flexible disclosure procedures are crucial for remedying the original asymmetry between the parties. Ultimately, disclosure and access to justice are intricately connected, as disclosure requirements can have a significant influence on the substantive outcomes of cases and, therefore, the opportunities of success for victims.

Discovery

Civil law countries traditionally show reluctance regarding the concept of discovery, which is mainly found in common law jurisdictions.[211] In the Netherlands, discovery does not exist, although it may be possible to order pre-trial hearings of parties as witnesses if a Dutch court is competent to hear the claim.[212] However, this procedure has been of little use to plaintiffs in transnational litigation against MNEs.

France allows a form of discovery with the legal regime of measures of inquiry *in futurum* provided for in Article 145 French Code of Civil Procedure.[213] Accordingly, 'if there is a legitimate reason to preserve or establish, prior to any legal proceedings, evidence of facts upon which the outcome of a dispute could depend, legally permissible measures of inquiry may be ordered at

---

211 Diana Lloyd Muse, 'Discovery in France and The Hague Convention: The Search for a French Connection' (1989) 64 New York University Law Review 1073, 1075.

212 Dutch Code of Civil Procedure, Article 186.

213 Anne-Marie Batut, 'Les mesures d'instruction "in futurum"' (Cour de Cassation 1999) <https://www.courdecassation.fr/publications_cour_26/rapport_annuel_36/rapport_1999_91/etudes_documents_93/anne_marie_5790.html> accessed 1 May 2021.

the request of any interested party, by way of application or interlocutory proceedings.' In the context of transnational litigation against MNEs,' plaintiffs can request that the judge orders measures to allow them access to items of evidence in the MNE's possession before any procedure is brought in court. However, to be admissible, such requests must be justified by the need to preserve or establish evidence for the purpose of a potential trial. The applicant must have a legitimate reason, which is assessed by judges in a discretionary manner.[214] Furthermore, the dispute must not be ongoing, which means that there must be an absence of proceedings on the merits.[215] The judge enjoys broad powers to order investigative measures. However, such measures must be legally admissible and cannot violate fundamental freedoms. For instance, an investigative measure allowing a bailiff to search the premises of a company, without having previously requested the spontaneous delivery of the documents concerned and having obtained the consent of the requested party, is not considered legally admissible.[216] Usually, French judges authorize measures under Article 145 in a restrictive manner.

To date, NGOs have struggled to make use of Article 145. In September 2020, the Paris Court of Appeal dismissed Sherpa and Friends of the Earth France's request for an investigation against the oil company Perenco SA pursuant to Article 145.[217] This request was intended to obtain evidence in order to demonstrate the involvement of the French company in environmental pollution occurring in the context of its oil activities in the DRC. Before the Court of Appeal's decision, in August 2019 the Paris Judicial Court had allowed their request and authorized them to seize, by bailiff, documents from the Paris headquarters of Perenco. However, the company's directors had opposed the execution of the court order by refusing access to the company's premises. Despite this unlawful refusal, no measures were allowed in order to force the company to comply with the order. Furthermore, the courts, including the Paris Court of Appeal, refused to proceed further when the NGOs lodged a new request in October 2019 asking the judge to impose a periodic penalty payment until the company complied with the measure.[218] This situation is in

---

214 Cass civ (2) 8 February 2006, n° 05-14.198, Bull. 2006, II, n° 44; Cass civ (2) 29 September 2011, n° 10-24.684; Cass civ (2) 12 July 2012, n° 11-18.399, Bull. 2012, II, n° 132.

215 Cass civ (2) 28 June 2006, n° 05-19.283, Bull. 2006, II, n° 173.

216 Cass civ (2) 16 May 2012, n° 11-17.229, Bull. 2012, II, n° 89.

217 CA Paris 17 September 2020, n° 19/20669. See also Sandra Cossart and Laura Bourgeois, 'L'article 145 du Code de procédure civile: un outil insuffisant pour la preuve des violations économiques de droits fondamentaux' (2020) 1923 Semaine sociale Lamy 10.

218 'La pétrolière française Perenco mise en cause pour pollution et opacité sur ses activités en RDC' (Sherpa, 18 June 2020) <https://www.asso-sherpa.org/la-petroliere-francaise-perenco-mise-en-cause-pour-pollution-et-opacite-sur-ses-activites-en-rdc> accessed 1 May 2021.

clear contrast to the discovery and/or disclosure procedure which may exist in common law countries and which allows for a genuine level playing field between the parties.

Discovery procedures in common law jurisdictions, including the US and England, have nonetheless produced information that has been useful in several cases heard against Shell in the Netherlands. In *Kiobel*, the plaintiffs submitted their complaint based on evidentiary material submitted by Shell in the context of various discovery proceedings in the US.[219] Similarly, in *Shell* plaintiffs used information disclosed by Shell in the *Bodo* tort suit against SPDC in England to request access to evidence in Shell's hands. Disclosed information demonstrated that RDS and SPDC had acted negligently in preventing the oil spills in question in the Dutch court case.

6 Remedies

The UNGPs clearly provide that States must take appropriate steps to ensure that those affected by business-related human rights abuse have access to effective remedy, notably through judicial or legislative means.[220] Remedies vary and may include apologies, restitution, rehabilitation, financial or non-financial compensation, punitive sanctions, and prevention of harm through injunctions or guarantees of non-repetition.[221]

In the context of transnational litigation against MNEs in France and the Netherlands, victims have asked for a variety of remedies, including financial compensation for personal loss or environmental damage, public apologies, condemnation as symbolic reparation (*un euro symbolique*), environmental remediation, contract annulment, publication of judgment in newspapers, or payment of salary. In *Shell*, for instance, the plaintiffs have requested that the defendants maintain their oil pipelines in good condition and implement an effective plan for avoiding and/or responding to oil leakages. However, to date, plaintiffs have rarely had access to judicial remedy. Often, courts dismiss claims before they are decided on their merits. Furthermore, courts have rarely found companies liable for human rights abuse or environmental damage in host countries.

At EU level, the Rome II Regulation applies to the determination of remedies in transnational litigation against MNEs. The general rule is that the type of remedy, including the character and amount, must be determined according

---

219 'Writ of Summons' (Prakken d'Oliveira 2017), paras 128–131.
220 UNGPs, GP 25.
221 Ibid.

to the law of the host State.[222] NGOs and scholars have criticized the effect of the Rome II Regulation on remedies available to plaintiffs.[223] They suggest that available remedies in host States might not always be appropriate to remediate corporate abuse of human rights or environmental pollution, and that the maximum amount of compensation might be too low to cover the real costs of litigation in the home country.[224]

Nonetheless, an overview of potential remedies in France and the Netherlands remains noteworthy for understanding whether effective remedies are available in practice and in law in the event of human rights abuse or environmental pollution. It is also important to consider whether remedies can realistically place victims or the environment in the same position in which they would have found themselves had the harm not occurred. Furthermore, as mentioned above, the Rome II Regulation provides for a number of situations where the home State law may apply.

Damages

Plaintiffs have asked for compensation for the personal damage they suffered in most of the claims analysed in this study. However, very few of them have been effectively compensated. In France, in *COMILOG* and *AREVA*, the plaintiffs were originally awarded damages for the loss they suffered. However, these rulings were quashed by the Court of Cassation, and the claims were eventually dismissed on jurisdictional grounds or on the merits. In the Netherlands, in *Shell*, SPDC was eventually found liable and was ordered to pay damages to some of the plaintiffs in 2021. At the time of writing, the amount of the compensation had yet to be determined in a follow-up procedure.

In French and Dutch tort law the principle behind awarding damages is generally aimed at repairing the harm suffered by the victim rather than punishing the tortfeasor.[225] In France, victims of corporate abuse can obtain damages before civil and criminal courts in order to repair and compensate them for the harm they suffered. French courts calculate damages on a case-by-case basis and there is generally no maximum limit to damages. Courts assess damages at the time of the ruling on the basis of the injury suffered by the plaintiff. French courts can order the defendant to compensate the plaintiff for the entire injury, which may comprise pecuniary loss (*dommage patrimonial*) and non-pecuniary loss (*dommage moral*), such as pain, suffering,

---

222 Skinner and others, 'The Third Pillar', 65.

223 Ibid.

224 Ibid.

225 Enneking, *Foreign Direct Liability and Beyond*, 255; Cees Van Dam, *European Tort Law* (2nd edn, OUP 2013) 352.

or loss of amenities.[226] Compensation for non-pecuniary loss may be granted for personal injury, for death or serious injuries to a loved one, or even for harm to feelings.[227] French courts tend to award generous sums to compensate non-pecuniary loss.[228] Furthermore, an extensive list of relatives are eligible to claim damages for the loss of a close relative or a loved one.[229] However, any benefits to the defendant as a result of the harm are not taken into account in the assessment of damages. In addition to reparation and compensation, French courts may award a *euro symbolique* to recognize that the victim has suffered a wrong or that their right has been infringed.[230]

In the Netherlands, compensatory damages may cover loss to property, rights, and interests, such as any loss incurred and any deprivation of profits, as well as any other damage.[231] In personal injury cases, victims may claim damages for their recovery and for other pecuniary and non-pecuniary damage, such as pain and injury.[232] As a general rule, damages shall be paid in monetary form, although Dutch courts have discretion to award them in other forms.[233] They also enjoy discretion to assess the amount of financial compensation and are not bound by rules of evidence in this regard. Nonetheless, the injured party should be placed, as far as possible, in the situation they would have been in if the event that caused the damage had never occurred.[234] Unlike France, the Netherlands allows the injured party to request that the damages be assessed according to the amount of the profit (or a part thereof) that the tortfeasor derived from committing the tort.[235] This provision could potentially be useful for plaintiffs in the context of transnational claims against MNEs. For instance, MNEs may derive a profit from the sale of goods produced by employees who did not receive the minimum wage in violation of labour law requirements.

Punitive damage awards do not exist under French and Dutch law. This limits the benefit of using litigation to deter MNEs from committing human rights or environmental abuse. In general, under French and Dutch law damages aim to repair the harm and compensate the victim rather than punish the tortfeasor. In France, courts continue to show distrust towards punitive damages, even

---

226 Van Dam, *European Tort Law*, 346, 354.

227 Ibid, 354.

228 Ibid, 352.

229 Ibid, 371.

230 Ibid, 349.

231 Dutch Civil Code, Articles 6:95 and 6:96(1).

232 Enneking, *Foreign Direct Liability and Beyond*, 255.

233 Dutch Civil Code, Article 6:103. See also Van Hooijdonk and Eijsvoogel, *Litigation in the Netherlands*, 61.

234 Van Hooijdonk and Eijsvoogel, *Litigation in the Netherlands*, 61.

235 Dutch Civil Code, Article 6:104.

though the Court of Cassation recently held that they were not contrary to public policy.[236] Nonetheless, foreign awards of punitive damage can be enforced in France when the amount awarded is not disproportionate with regard to the damage sustained.

Other remedies

France provides for various types of injunctive relief, most notably to prevent or halt ongoing infringement of the plaintiff's rights, or to order the defendant to take positive action to further limit harm that has already occurred.[237] Similarly, Dutch courts can issue injunctions that order the defendant to perform certain acts after the tort took place, or to abstain from certain acts before the tort takes place.[238] As a result, plaintiffs in transnational litigation against MNEs may ask courts to order MNEs to honour any legally enforceable obligations or to grant interim injunctions or orders.[239] However, it remains to be seen whether such remedies are applicable or effective, particularly as the harm usually takes place in host countries where there are limited means of enforcement.[240]

To date, courts have tended to focus on the award of damages to injured individuals. In *Shell*, the plaintiffs requested the Dutch courts to order the corporate defendants to clean up the oil spills in Nigeria. However, in 2013 the District Court ordered the subsidiary to compensate plaintiffs for the damage they suffered, but ignored the plaintiffs' requests to clean up the pollution. In 2021, the Court of Appeal found that SPDC was liable for damages resulting from the leakage from the pipelines, but rejected the request that it should further clean up the contaminated areas. Despite persistent pollution in the areas at stake, the Court of Appeal nonetheless held that SPDC had already remedied the areas according to the remediation standard published by the Nigerian Department of Petroleum Resources and was not required to comply with target values, meaning to return the soil to its previous state.[241] It dismissed

236 See Benjamin West Janke and François-Xavier Licari, 'Enforcing Punitive Damage Awards in France after *Fountain Pajot*' (2012) 3 American Journal of Comparative Law 775.

237 Van Dam, *European Tort Law*, 347–348.

238 Enneking, *Foreign Direct Liability and Beyond*, 255.

239 Ibid.

240 Similarly, scholars have raised potential difficulties in enforcing judgments resulting from ATS litigation overseas. See Ugo Mattei and Jeffrey Lena, 'United States Jurisdiction over Conflicts Arising outside of the US: Some Hegemonic Implications' (2001) 24 Hastings International and Comparative Law Review 381.

241 Cees Van Dam, 'Commentary: Shell Liable for Oil Spills in Niger Delta. The Hague Court of Appeal Decisions of 29 January 2021' (BHRRC, February 2021) <https://www.business-humanrights.org/de/neuste-meldungen/commentary-shell-liable-for-oil-spills-in-niger-delta/> accessed 14 July 2021.

the assertion that the residual pollution constituted an unlawful situation or a violation of the plaintiffs' right to a clean environment.[242] While the choice to apply governmental remediation standards has the merits of legal certainty, this approach is nevertheless open to criticism when such standards are so low that they fail to restore the land to the state in which it was before the pollution occurred and to address the source of the victims' deteriorating standard of living. On a positive note, one important aspect of the Court of Appeal's ruling was that it ordered both SPDC and RDS to set up a leak detection system (LDS) within one year of the ruling in order to detect future leaks more rapidly. In the event that the companies do not comply with this order, they will be obliged to pay a periodic penalty payment of €100,000 per day. This order has the benefit of preventing future oil pollution or, at the very least, reducing the damage that could result from potential oil leakage. However, the Court of Appeal could have been bolder, in particular by ordering the replacement of old and defective pipelines at the source of the pollution.

Scholars and activists have generally called for home country courts to take into account types of remedy other than financial compensation, such as injunctions or clean-up operations. They have pointed out that excessive focus on financial compensation to injured individuals does not remedy long-standing social and environmental problems.[243] Furthermore, according to the ECtHR, a remedy cannot be considered effective if, despite its theoretical existence, there is significant uncertainty as to its practical availability.[244] Therefore, plaintiffs must be able to effectively invoke other remedies.

7 The cost of civil litigation against MNEs

Transnational litigation against MNEs in France and the Netherlands is generally costly,[245] even though litigation costs in those countries are perceived

---

242 Ibid; Lucas Roorda, 'Wading through the (Polluted) Mud: The Hague Court of Appeals Rules on Shell in Nigeria' (RightsasUsual, 2 February 2021) <https://rightsasusual.com/?p=1388> accessed 1 May 2021.

243 Peter Newell, 'Access to Environmental Justice? Litigating against TNCs in the South' (2001) 32 IDS Bulletin 83, 86; Jedrzej Frynas, 'Social and Environmental Litigation against Transnational Firms in Africa' (2004) 42 Journal of Modern African Studies 363, 381.

244 *McFarlane v Ireland* App no 31333/06 (ECtHR, 10 September 2010).

245 For instance, Milieudefensie claimed it needed €180,000 per year to pursue its legal case against Shell in the Netherlands. The NGO eventually used its website to seek funding for the case through external donations, but this could only partially cover its costs. See Virginie Rouas, 'In Search of Corporate Accountability: Transnational Litigation against Multinational Enterprises in France and the Netherlands' (PhD thesis, School of Oriental and African Studies 2017) 231.

to be moderate compared to common law countries.[246] Various reasons explain such high litigation costs. First, MNEs will forcefully fight against transnational claims against them to prevent the establishment of unfavourable precedent.[247] As a result, litigation is often lengthy, lasting at least several years, with limited chances of success for plaintiffs. Second, essential evidence, including documents and witnesses, is often located in the host country and bringing it to the home country where proceedings take place increases litigation costs.[248] Third, transnational litigation against MNEs is usually complex and requires specific legal and scientific expertise, thus increasing costs.

According to the UNGPs, barriers to accessing judicial remedy arise where 'the costs of bringing claims go beyond being an appropriate deterrent to unmeritorious cases and/or cannot be reduced to reasonable levels through Government support, "market-based" mechanisms (such as litigation insurance and legal fee structures), or other means'.[249] A lack of resources may also make finding legal representation difficult for claimants.[250] In France and the Netherlands, the application of the loser pays principle, limited legal aid schemes, and absence of funding arrangement options between plaintiffs and their lawyers may prevent victims and NGOs from accessing courts.

The loser pays principle

France applies the loser pays principle, whereby the losing party bears the costs of the legal proceedings.[251] However, the judge may decide to impose the whole or part of the legal costs on the other party. Furthermore, Article 700 French Code of Civil Procedure provides that the judge can order the losing party, or the party obliged to pay the legal costs, to pay an amount determined by the judge to the other party to cover any expenses not included in the legal costs. Nonetheless, the judge must consider rules of equity and the financial condition of the party ordered to pay. On such grounds, they may free the losing party from paying other expenses in addition to the legal costs.[252] In *Alstom*,

---

246 'Collective Redress in the Netherlands' (US Chamber Institute for Legal Reform 2012) 17.

247 Enneking, *Foreign Direct Liability and Beyond*, 257.

248 Ibid.

249 UNGPs, Commentary to GP 26.

250 Ibid.

251 French Code of Civil Procedure, Article 696. Furthermore, Article 695 French Code of Civil Procedure lists the various costs.

252 French Code of Civil Procedure, Article 700.

the plaintiffs lost, and the Versailles Court of Appeal ordered them to pay the entire costs of the legal proceedings. In addition, the plaintiffs were ordered to pay €30,000 to each of the corporate defendants pursuant to Article 700. Following the ruling, AFPS stated that those sums were substantial financial penalties for an NGO.[253]

Similarly, the Netherlands applies the loser pays principle.[254] Dutch courts will also order the losing party to bear the legal costs and the costs of the prevailing party, including registry fees, compensation for witnesses and experts, and lawyer fees.[255] However, the losing party is not required to pay the full lawyer fees incurred by the prevailing party. As a rule, lawyer fees are calculated on the basis of a scale of costs set out in non-binding, but generally applied, court guidelines. In practice, this scale leads to a remuneration that does not cover the complete costs of legal representation and, as a result, the prevailing party will usually recover only a small percentage of its actual costs.[256] An important feature of Dutch civil procedure is that a claimant may request the court to order the defendant to pay the costs. The defendant can make the same request in their statement of defence.[257]

In *Shell*, the District Court ordered the plaintiffs to pay the defendants' costs concerning the production of evidence during the legal proceedings following the dismissal of the plaintiffs' request to obtain access to evidence. For two of the claims, the plaintiffs were ordered to pay jointly and severally the sum of €2,712 to the defendants within 14 days of the judgment.[258] Furthermore, in 2013 the District Court ordered Milieudefensie and the plaintiffs who had lost in the first instance to pay the defendants' costs, including their court fees and a fixed lawyer fee. However, the cost of the lawyer fees was relatively low due to the application of the above-mentioned scale. In 2021, the Court of Appeal ruled that the successful plaintiffs should be compensated for the costs of the proceedings at first instance, so that the parties bear their own costs. It also ordered SPDC to bear the costs of expertise.[259]

---

253 'Tramway Colonial: Un jugement incompréhensible de la cour d'appel' (AFPS 25 March 2013) <http://www.france-palestine.org/Tramway-colonial-un-jugement> accessed 1 May 2021.

254 Dutch Code of Civil Procedure, Article 237.

255 Van Hooijdonk and Eijsvoogel, *Litigation in the Netherlands*, 51.

256 Ibid.

257 Ibid, 52.

258 *Oguru* [2011], [6.2]; *Dooh* [2011], [6.2].

259 CA The Hague 29 January 2021, C/09/365498/HAZA10-1677 (case a) + C/09/330891/ HAZA09-0579 (case b) (*Oguru*); C/09/337058/HAZA09-1581 (case c) + C/09/365482/ HAZA10-1665 (case d) (*Dooh*).

The application of the loser pays principle is particularly problematic when one considers that victims and NGOs often have limited financial resources, if any, to pursue legal proceedings compared to the large sums spent by MNEs. Ultimately, the loser pays principle reinforces the inequality of arms between plaintiffs and MNEs. It also deters victims and NGOs from initiating legitimate legal proceedings to gain access to remedy and to hold companies to account.

Access to legal aid

In view of the high legal costs incurred by plaintiffs to bring claims against MNEs, as well as the limited financial resources of victims and NGOs, access to legal aid is therefore crucial to guarantee that plaintiffs can nonetheless use courts to seek justice. However, restrictive conditions for granting legal aid may impede effective access to justice by plaintiffs. In the EU, there is a legal framework applicable to legal aid, which is relevant to plaintiffs in transnational litigation against MNEs in France and the Netherlands.

The EU legal framework on legal aid

Access to legal aid is an important part of the right to a fair trial. Article 47(3) EU Charter, on the right to an effective remedy and to a fair trial, provides that legal aid must be made available to those who lack sufficient resources in so far as such aid is necessary to ensure effective access to justice. The CJEU has interpreted that national courts should ascertain 'whether the conditions for granting legal aid constitute a limitation of the right of access to the courts which undermines the very core of that right; whether they pursue a legitimate aim; and whether there is a reasonable relationship of proportionality between the means employed and the legitimate aim which it is sought to achieve'.[260]

The EU also enacted Council Directive 2002/8/EC (Directive on legal aid)[261] to promote access to legal aid in civil and commercial cross-border disputes for persons who lack sufficient resources, particularly where aid

---

260 Case C-279/09 *DEB Deutsche Energiehandels- und Beratungsgesellschaft mbH v Bundesrepublik Deutschland* [2010] ECR I-13849.

261 Council Directive 2002/8/EC of 27 January 2003 to improve access to justice in cross-border disputes by establishing minimum common rules relating to legal aid for such disputes [2003] OJ L26/41.

is necessary to secure effective access to justice. However, the Directive on legal aid applies only to cross-border disputes where the party applying for legal aid is domiciled or habitually resides in a Member State other than the Member State where the court is sitting or where the decision is to be enforced.[262] As a result, the Directive on legal aid does not confer rights to individuals domiciled or residing in countries outside the EU, such as victims of abuse committed by EU MNEs in host countries. This situation discriminates against foreign victims and limits their opportunities to obtain effective access to civil remedy in the EU.

National experiences

In France, legal aid (*aide juridictionnelle*) is available to natural persons who lack sufficient resources in order to secure their effective access to justice.[263] The State will cover the costs of legal assistance, including lawyer fees, and the costs of proceedings. The latter include the fees to persons mandated by the court to perform acts during the proceedings on behalf of the legal aid recipient. One advantage for plaintiffs is that legal aid can be obtained for any type of legal proceedings, including civil and criminal.

However, various restrictions apply to legal aid in France. First, the legal aid recipient may obtain either full or partial legal aid depending on their resources. Second, legal aid does not cover the costs that may be imposed if the plaintiff loses the case (eg the defendant's legal costs, damages). Third, only a natural person, who is a French national, an EU national, or a foreign national legally and habitually residing in France, may receive legal aid.[264] Moreover, legal persons are excluded from receiving legal aid. In the context of transnational litigation against MNEs, these conditions limit access to legal aid by foreign victims and NGOs. Only in exceptional cases can nationals of non-EU countries residing outside France receive legal aid, for instance where their situation appears particularly noteworthy regarding the subject matter or the costs of the proceedings.[265] In exceptional circumstances, legal aid may be available to non-profit legal persons, which have their seat in France and lack sufficient resources to bring a claim.[266]

---

262 Ibid, Article 2(1).
263 Loi n° 91-647 du 10 juillet 1991 relative à l'aide juridique (Loi sur l'aide juridique), Article 2.
264 Ibid, Articles 3(1) and 3(2).
265 Ibid, Article 3(3).
266 Ibid, Article 2(2).

The Netherlands has one of the most elaborate legal aid systems in Europe.[267] Article 18(2) Dutch Constitution provides for the granting of legal aid to persons of limited means.[268] In general, the Dutch State will cover a certain amount of the court fees and the lawyer fees paid by the legal aid recipient. Legal aid may be granted to both natural and legal persons with inadequate financial resources in relation to legal interests within the Dutch legal sphere of influence.[269] Furthermore, depending on the recipient's income, legal aid may allow for a reduction in court fees.[270] Moreover, there is no restriction of nationality or residence on obtaining legal aid, as long as legal interests within the Dutch legal sphere of influence are involved. In *Shell*, the Nigerian plaintiffs were able to receive legal aid. However, due to high litigation costs, legal aid has been insufficient to fund the whole case and other sources of funding have been necessary to initiate and continue the lawsuit.[271] Another limit of the Dutch system is that legal aid recipients must always cover part of their litigation costs according to their financial resources.[272] Moreover, legal aid will not be granted if the party's chance of winning is considered to be close to zero or if the costs incurred during the proceedings are not reasonable compared to the interest of the case.[273]

Market-based funding mechanisms

The UNGPs explicitly mention 'market-based' mechanisms, such as litigation insurance and legal fee structures, to fund legitimate cases involving business-related abuse. In contrast with common law countries, market-based mechanisms (eg contingency fees in the US or conditional fees in the UK) are less widespread in civil law countries.

---

267 Erhard Blankenburg, 'The Infrastructure for Avoiding Civil Litigation: Comparing Cultures of Legal Behavior in The Netherlands and West Germany' (1994) 28 Law & Society Review 789, 789.

268 The Constitution of the Kingdom of the Netherlands 2008 (Ministry of the Interior and Kingdom Relations 2012) <https://www.government.nl/documents/regulations/2012/10/18/the-constitution-of-the-kingdom-of-the-netherlands-2000> accessed 1 May 2021.

269 Legal Aid Act 1994, Article 12. See also 'Access to Justice: Human Rights Abuses Involving Corporations – The Netherlands' (International Commission of Jurists 2010) 33.

270 'Access to Justice', 33.

271 Rouas, *In Search of Corporate Accountability*, 238.

272 'Access to Justice', 33.

273 Legal Aid Act 1994, Article 12; 'Access to Justice', 35.

In France, the 'no win, no fee' agreement (*pacte de quota litis*) is generally considered to be 'shocking' and 'inappropriate',[274] and French law prohibits it.[275] As a result, parties, and not their lawyers, must bear the costs of legal proceedings. Nonetheless, a party and their lawyer may agree a contingency fee or a success fee in addition to the remuneration for the service.

In the Netherlands, parties and their lawyers are free to agree on how lawyers are to be paid. However, the Code of Conduct of the Dutch Bar Association imposes certain limitations.[276] As a general rule, a lawyer must take into account all the circumstances of the case when determining their fee, and they must charge a reasonable fee.[277] Furthermore, US-style contingency fees are not permitted. A lawyer should not agree to charge a proportionate part of the value of the result obtained.[278] Success fees are not allowed either. A lawyer should not agree that they will only charge for their services upon obtaining a specific result.[279] However, the Disciplinary Appeals Tribunal has accepted certain forms of success fees, such as charging fees at a higher hourly rate if the case is successful.[280] Finally, WCAM settlements can be used by plaintiffs to pay their lawyer fees, which can be substantial.[281]

8 Conclusions

This chapter has examined how French and Dutch rules of civil procedure and remedies affect the opportunities of plaintiffs to gain effective access to justice in the context of transnational litigation against MNEs. It showed that plaintiffs have faced significant procedural and practical obstacles that impede their right to a fair trial, including their right of access to a court and the respect of equality of arms, as well as their right to access an effective remedy. Some

---

274 Doris Marie Provine, 'Courts in the Political Process in France' in Herbert Jacob and others, *Courts, Law, and Politics in Comparative Perspective* (Yale University Press 1996) 237.

275 Loi n° 71-1130 du 31 décembre 1971 portant réforme de certaines professions judiciaires (Loi sur les professions judiciaires), Article 10.

276 'Collective Redress in the Netherlands', 17.

277 'English Version of the Code of Conduct of the Netherlands Bar Association: The Rules of Conduct of Advocates 1992' (CCBE 3 December 2008), Rule 25 (Clause 1) (Dutch Bar Association's Code of Conduct).

278 Dutch Bar Association's Code of Conduct, Rule 25 (Clause 3).

279 Ibid, Rule 25 (Clause 2).

280 'Collective Redress in the Netherlands', 18.

281 Ibid.

of these obstacles originate from the civil law nature of these countries (eg lack of effective collective redress mechanisms or unfit rules on production of evidence),[282] while others are the consequences of EU harmonization.

The nature of transnational civil litigation against MNEs raises a number of legal challenges with regard to the home State's competence to hear claims, and whether the law of the home or host State applies to the proceedings. Under the EU regime of private international law to which France and the Netherlands are bound, plaintiffs can successfully establish French and Dutch jurisdiction over a company domiciled in France and the Netherlands. However, the jurisdiction of French and Dutch courts to hear claims against companies domiciled outside the EU (such as host State subsidiaries) is less certain. Furthermore, the host State law will generally apply to transnational claims against MNEs in France and the Netherlands. This solution is likely to be unsatisfactory for plaintiffs, as they generally pursue their case with the purpose of applying the home State law.

France and the Netherlands have traditionally been reluctant to allow collective redress mechanisms similar to those found in common law countries. As a result, collective redress has generally not been available to plaintiffs in French and Dutch proceedings. Nonetheless, as a result of EU policy, France and the Netherlands recently reformed their legal framework on collective redress mechanisms. However, EU policy on collective redress has to date focused excessively on consumer issues and, as a result, it provides no opportunities to address mass harm situations caused by corporations in a transnational context.

Another significant procedural issue relates to the production of evidence. Plaintiffs initiating a liability claim against an MNE usually bear the burden of proof. Furthermore, although France and the Netherlands allow disclosure for the benefit of plaintiffs, their courts have been reluctant to require corporate defendants to produce evidence and have been wary of allowing 'fishing expeditions'. As a result, plaintiffs face significant obstacles to demonstrate the validity of their claims, especially since they often have limited access to crucial evidence possessed by MNEs.

Other procedural and practical issues include restrictive approaches to NGO standing in litigation, high litigation costs, and insufficient legal aid. Moreover, even though a wide range of remedies are theoretically available in France and the Netherlands, courts have tended to focus on financial compensation, neglecting other important remedies, such as environmental remediation.

---

282 For a discussion of the influence of legal culture on transnational litigation against MNEs, see Enneking, *Foreign Direct Liability and Beyond*.

As a result, it is unlikely that foreign victims of business-related abuse can hold MNEs to account and obtain remediation for the loss they have suffered. Despite the existence of these claims for more than a decade, domestic rules remain unfit to face the transnational justice challenges created by MNEs' global activities.

The next chapter provides an analysis of criminal litigation against MNEs in France and the Netherlands.

Chapter 5

Criminal litigation against multinational enterprises in France and the Netherlands

1 Introduction

Alongside transnational civil claims against MNEs, victims of business-related abuse and NGOs have sought justice by using the criminal system of home States. In France, 12 out of the 16 claims discussed in this book have been of a criminal nature. Various factors may influence the decision of victims to use national criminal proceedings instead of civil proceedings. First, from a moral viewpoint the criminal justice system may seem more suitable for holding companies accountable for their misconduct, in particular gross human rights abuses. The criminal sentencing of a company sends a stronger message of disapprobation about the corporate wrongdoing. Harm is done not only to the victim, but also to society. The symbolism that the criminal justice system conveys may be attractive to victims seeking formal punishment of corporate misbehaviour.[1] Furthermore, criminal punishment for misconduct may have a dissuasive effect on companies. This may be particularly relevant in strategic litigation where lawyers and NGOs are trying to bring about changes in the way companies behave. In this respect, criminal proceedings may be preferred in countries where the civil justice system does not impose exemplary or punitive damages, which is often the case in civil law countries. Finally, victims are more likely to use criminal proceedings to hold MNEs to account when they can play an active role in initiating criminal proceedings, for instance by triggering investigation into the alleged crimes or prosecution of the apparent perpetrator. This is the case in France where victims can request that the public prosecutor investigates the facts they bring forward or can launch a civil action before the examining magistrate in order to claim reparation for the damage suffered as a result of the criminal offence. They can also directly summon the alleged perpetrator in some instances.

However, choosing criminal law to hold MNEs accountable for their misconduct abroad is not necessarily easier for victims when compared to transnational civil claims against MNEs. Victims face similar obstacles that are likely to

---

1   Jan Wouters and Cedric Ryngaert, 'Litigation for Overseas Corporate Human Rights Abuses in the European Union: The Challenge of Jurisdiction' (2009) 40 George Washington International Law Review 939, 943.

jeopardize their quest for justice. One obstacle is whether the criminal law of the home State applies to the extraterritorial offences in question and, therefore, leads to criminal courts having jurisdiction to judge these criminal offences. Furthermore, the impossibility for prosecutors or examining magistrates to have access to evidence in the host State may lead to a dead-end for victims. Another challenge for victims is the acceptation of their role and position in the criminal proceedings. Despite the growing recognition of the rights of victims of crime at international and national levels,[2] victims still struggle to be recognized as legitimate actors of criminal proceedings. This is partly due to the dichotomous nature of criminal trials, which traditionally pit the State against the accused. Within this context, victims are seen as a third party whose interests are difficult to accommodate and who may disturb the delicate balance of power between the prosecution and the defence. The private nature of victims' interests is perceived by some to be at odds with the public character of the criminal justice system, whose main function ought to be the protection of the public interest.[3] In addition, concerns have been voiced that victims' participation in criminal proceedings threatens the guarantee of the rights of the defendant and may lead criminal judges to adopt harsher punishments.[4]

2 Prosecuting MNEs for extraterritorial crimes

In criminal law, jurisdiction concerns the reach which the State gives to its law, and addresses the question as to where and to whom that State's law is applicable.[5] Therefore, the application of criminal law and the exercise of criminal jurisdiction are intertwined. A court's exercise of jurisdiction usually follows from the application of its State's criminal law on the grounds of the 'solidarity between jurisdiction and legislative competence' principle (*principe de solidarité des compétences législative et juridictionnelle*).[6]

2   Cherif Bassiouni, 'International Recognition of Victims' Rights' (2006) 6 Human Rights Law Review 203.
3   Jonathan Doak, 'Victims' Rights in Criminal Trials: Prospects for Participation' (2005) 32 Journal of Law and Society 294, 295–300.
4   For a discussion of victims' rights in criminal proceedings, see Jonathan Doak, *Victims' Rights, Human Rights and Criminal Justice: Reconceiving the Role of Third Parties* (Bloomsbury Publishing 2008).
5   Emma van Gelder and Cedric Ryngaert, 'Dutch Report on Prosecuting Corporations for Violations of International Criminal Law' in Sabine Gless and Sylwia Broniszewska-Emdin (eds), *Prosecuting Corporations for Violations of International Criminal Law: Jurisdictional Issues* (Maklu 2017) 132.
6   Francis Desportes and Francis Le Gunehec, *Le Nouveau Droit Pénal. Tome 1: Droit Pénal Général* (Economica 1995) 298.

The territoriality principle is the cornerstone of jurisdiction in criminal law. The courts of the State on whose territory the criminal offence was committed have jurisdiction of the offence. Alternative extraterritorial jurisdictional principles also exist, such as the active and passive personality principles based on the nationality of the perpetrator or the victim, and the universal jurisdiction principle, which mainly applies to international crimes. Domestic courts tend to carefully apply some of these alternative principles in criminal matters as a result of their contentious nature and potential infringement on other States' sovereignty. However, continental European countries put far less emphasis on the territoriality principle in criminal law compared with common law countries,[7] and France and the Netherlands have, to some extent, accepted the application of alternative principles of jurisdiction.

Holding MNEs, and their parent companies in particular, accountable for crimes involving human rights violations or environmental crimes committed in the context of group activities raises complex questions from a jurisdictional perspective.[8] This is partly due to the fact that MNEs' global structure, management, and operations are intricate and lack transparency, which makes it difficult to identify the real entity that committed a criminal offence or to geographically situate the place where the crime was committed (*locus delicti*). Furthermore, attribution of jurisdiction may be problematic as a result of the criminal involvement of the MNE or the nature of the crime at stake. MNEs may be involved as direct perpetrators or accomplices of domestic crimes with an extraterritorial dimension or crimes under international law. In such a context, the jurisdictional principles mentioned above may be inadequate to grasp the reality of criminal activities within complex corporate group structures and ensure the prosecution of MNEs when they commit crimes with an extraterritorial or international dimension.

The territoriality principle

The principle of territoriality is the primary basis for the application of French and Dutch criminal law and the jurisdiction of their respective courts in criminal matters. Pursuant to Article 113-2 French Criminal Code, French criminal law applies to offences committed on the French territory, including the maritime and air spaces linked to it. Similarly, Article 2 Dutch Criminal Code (*Wetboek*

---

7   Cedric Ryngaert, *Jurisdiction in International Law* (2nd edn, OUP 2015) 101.

8   Anne Schneider, 'Corporate Criminal Liability and Conflicts of Jurisdiction' in Dominik Brodowski, Manuel Espinoza de los Monteros de la Parra, and Klaus Tiedemann (eds), *Regulating Corporate Criminal Liability* (Springer 2014); Sabine Gless and Sarah Wood, 'General Report on Prosecuting Corporations for Violations of International Criminal Law: Jurisdictional Issues' in Sabine Gless and Sylwia Broniszewska-Emdin (eds), *Prosecuting Corporations for Violations of International Criminal Law: Jurisdictional Issues* (Maklu 2017).

van Strafrecht) provides that Dutch criminal law is applicable to anyone who is guilty of any offence within the Netherlands. Furthermore, Dutch criminal law applies to anyone who is guilty of any offence outside the Netherlands on board a Dutch vessel or aircraft.

The application of the territoriality principle raises important challenges in the context of transnational litigation against MNEs. Indeed, these cases often involve criminal offences committed on the territory of a host State. A strict interpretation of the territoriality principle would therefore result in the impossibility of applying the criminal law of the home State to a criminal offence committed outside its territory. However, French and Dutch criminal law allow a flexible interpretation of the territoriality principle which may allow for the prosecution of extraterritorial crimes in France and the Netherlands.

The French Criminal Code and courts have interpreted the territoriality principle in an extensive manner. Three situations are relevant in this study: theory of ubiquity, theory of indivisibility, and complicity. First, Article 113-2 French Criminal Code provides for the application of the theory of ubiquity (*théorie de l'ubiquité*). An offence is deemed to have been committed within French territory where one of its 'constituent facts' (*faits constitutifs*) took place in France.[9] French courts have broadly interpreted the notion of constituent facts and have accepted that preparatory acts or even effects are sufficient.[10] When the perpetrator is a company, the Court of Cassation takes into account the place of the statutory seat to locate the business decisions which constitute a criminal offence.[11] As a result, French criminal law may apply when the business decisions of a company whose statutory seat is within French territory, such as the French member of an MNE, are a constituent fact of the offence. The Court of Cassation recently ruled that the French courts had jurisdiction over the offence of bribing a foreign public official committed abroad where, on the one hand, the bribery of a foreign public official was decided and organized on the national territory where the amount of the remuneration due in this respect was also paid and, on the other hand, the registered office of the company that benefited from the proceeds of the offence was located in that territory and was used to domicile the account opened abroad that was intended for the transit of the kickbacks.[12] The French Criminal Code also applies the theory of ubiquity to accomplices.

---

9   Cass crim 31 May 2016, n° 15-85920.

10   Cass crim 19 April 1983, n° 82-90.345, Bull. crim. n° 108; Cass crim 11 April 1988, n° 87-83.873, Bull.

11   Cass crim 6 February 1996, Bull crim n° 60; Cass crim 31 January 2007, Bull crim n° 28.

12   Cass crim 14 March 2018, n° 16-82117.

Second, French courts have developed the theory of indivisibility which is relevant in the context of transnational litigation against MNEs.[13] French law is applicable to a criminal offence committed abroad if this offence forms an indivisible whole with an offence committed on French territory.[14] However, the foreign acts must have a link with France or must be tried in the French courts. The Court of Cassation recently interpreted the concept of indivisibility. Accordingly, French criminal law is applicable to an offence committed abroad where there is a link of indivisibility between that offence and another offence committed on French territory, the facts being indivisible when they are linked to each other by a connection such that the existence of one would not be understood without the existence of the other. If several offences are merely connected, French courts do not have jurisdiction over offences committed abroad by a person of foreign nationality against a foreign victim.[15]

Third, under Article 113-5 French Criminal Code, French criminal law is also applicable to any person who, within the French territory, is guilty as an accomplice to a felony or misdemeanour committed abroad if: (1) it is punishable by both the French and foreign law; and (2) if it was established by a final decision of a foreign court. The application of Article 113-5 presents a number of challenges. First, it applies only to accomplices to a criminal offence committed abroad. Second, it requires 'double (or dual) criminality' (*double incrimination*), which means that the criminal offence must be punishable under the legislation of both countries. Third, a foreign court must have rendered a final judgment. In general, French courts interpret these requirements strictly, thus limiting the application of Article 113-5.[16]

Victims in *Rougier* and *DLH* relied upon Article 113-5 to justify the criminal prosecution in France of French companies for criminal offences occurring abroad. However, the *Rougier* case demonstrates that Article 113-5 provides limited opportunities as a basis to apply French criminal law to crimes involving MNEs and gain access to justice. The victims alleged that, pursuant to Article 113-5, French criminal law was applicable to the French company Rougier for complicity in the commission of various criminal offences by SFID, its Cameroonian subsidiary. However, the Paris Court of Appeal dismissed their claim on the grounds that Article 113-5 requires a final ruling from a foreign

---

13   In the past, French courts have used the theory of indivisibility to exercise territorial jurisdiction over autonomous criminal offences committed abroad that are sometimes only remotely connected with France, such as concealment abroad of goods obtained through fraud in France. See Cass crim 9 December 1933, Bull crim n° 237.

14   Cass crim 23 April 1981, n° 79-90.346.

15   Cass crim 31 May 2016, n° 15-85920.

16   Nicolas Mathey, 'La responsabilité sociale des entreprises en matière de droits de l'homme' (2010) 3 Cahiers de Droit de l'Entreprise.

court, which was missing in this instance.[17] The Court of Appeal rejected the victims' argument that they had been unable to gain access to justice in Cameroon because of corruption and lack of independence of local and judicial authorities.[18] It found that they did not demonstrate that it was impossible to obtain a final ruling in Cameroon. The legitimacy of the requirement of a final ruling from a foreign court is questionable in situations where victims are unable to obtain justice in the host country, especially in States plagued by corruption or conflict.

Article 2 Dutch Criminal Code provides that Dutch criminal law is applicable to anyone who commits any criminal offence within the Netherlands. The determining factor is *locus delicti*, meaning the place where the criminal offence was committed. Unlike the criminal codes of some other European countries, the Dutch Criminal Code does not describe the place where an offence is committed.[19] Therefore, Dutch courts have had to clarify the scope of *locus delicti* under Dutch law. On several occasions, the Supreme Court ruled that a criminal offence could be committed in more than one place.[20] Furthermore, it is not necessary that all the constituent elements of the criminal offence took place on Dutch territory to establish jurisdiction of the Dutch courts. They may exercise jurisdiction over a criminal offence when only one of its elements took place in the Netherlands.[21] Therefore, a legal person who committed a criminal offence abroad may be prosecuted in the Netherlands when one element of the criminal offence took place in the Netherlands. Moreover, the Supreme Court ruled that Dutch courts could exercise jurisdiction over accomplices acting abroad in support of crimes that took place on Dutch territory.[22] However, whether Dutch courts have jurisdiction over accomplices acting in the Netherlands for an offence committed abroad is not entirely clear.[23] Nonetheless, scholars assume that the location where the complicity

---

17   Chambre de l'Instruction, CA Paris 13 February 2004.

18   'Press Release: 7 Cameroonian Farmers Confront the French Rougier Group and its Cameroonian Affiliate SFID Before French Tribunal' (Les Amis de la Terre and Sherpa 2002).

19   Marius Teengs Gerritsen, 'Jurisdiction' in Bert Swart and André Klip (eds), *International Criminal Law in the Netherlands* (Max-Planck-Institut für Auslandisches und Internationales Strafrecht 1997) 52.

20   HR 6 April 1915, NJ 1915, 475; HR 6 April 1954, NJ 1954, 368. The 1954 decision of the Dutch Supreme Court is generally interpreted as implying that the place of the offence may also be the place where the instrument used by the perpetrator has its effect. See also 'Access to Justice: Human Rights Abuses Involving Corporations – The Netherlands' (International Commission of Jurists 2010) 19.

21   HR 14 September 1981, ECLI:NL:1981:AC3699; HR 2 February 2010, ECLI:NL:HR:2010:BK6328.

22   HR 18 February 1997, NJ 1997, 628.

23   André Klip and Harmen Van Der Wilt, 'Netherlands' Report for the International Association of Penal Law' (2004) 73 Revue Internationale de Droit Pénal 1091, 1097.

takes place can be considered the *locus delicti* for the crime of complicity.[24] As for joint wrongdoing, scholars have inferred from case law that the location where the acts of joint wrongdoing took place could be seen as the *locus delicti*.[25] In addition, Dutch courts have jurisdiction over extraterritorial acts which aggravate the territorial offence, but not over extraterritorial acts that constitute separate crimes.[26]

Alternative principles of jurisdiction

French and Dutch statutory law allows prosecution of extraterritorial crimes based on various alternative principles of jurisdiction. French and Dutch domestic courts are, however, usually reluctant to assert extraterritorial jurisdiction in criminal cases.

Under Article 689 French Code of Criminal Procedure (*Code de procédure pénale*), perpetrators of, or accomplices to, offences committed outside French territory may be prosecuted and tried by French courts in two situations: (1) when French law is applicable under Book I of the French Criminal Code or any other statute; and (2) when an international convention or an act adopted pursuant to the treaty establishing the European Community gives jurisdiction to French courts to deal with the offence. Book I of the French Criminal Code contains the principles governing the application of French criminal law to offences committed outside French territory.

Articles 3 to 8d Dutch Criminal Code govern jurisdiction and the application of Dutch criminal law over criminal offences committed abroad. These provisions apply not only to all offences under the Dutch Criminal Code, but also to those defined in other statutes, unless the statute provides otherwise.[27] In addition, the International Crimes Act (ICA),[28] which came into force in 2003, contains specific rules concerning serious violations of international humanitarian law, including the crime of genocide, crimes against humanity, war crimes, and torture.[29] The ICA replaced fragmented legislation on international crimes and incorporated crimes under the Rome Statute of the International Criminal Court (Rome Statute)[30] into Dutch law. Under the ICA, Dutch criminal law

24   Ibid.

25   HR 24 January 1995, NJ 1995, 352.

26   Ryngaert, *Jurisdiction in International Law*, 201.

27   Luc Reydams, *Universal Jurisdiction: International and Municipal Legal Perspectives* (OUP 2004) 165.

28   Wet Internationale Misdrijven 2003.

29   See Machteld Boot-Matthijssen and Richard Van Elst, 'Key Provisions of the International Crimes Act 2003' (2004) 35 Netherlands Yearbook of International Law 251.

30   Rome Statute of the International Criminal Court (adopted 17 July 1998, entered into force 1 July 2002) 2187 UNTS 3.

applies to a number of criminal offences committed outside the Netherlands in three situations: (1) if the suspect is present in the Netherlands; (2) if the crime is committed against a Dutch national; or (3) if the crime is committed by a Dutch national.[31] Criminal prosecution against a Dutch national may also take place if the suspect became a Dutch national after committing the crime.[32] Pursuant to the scope of the ICA, the crimes must have been committed after its entry into force on 1 October 2003. To date, there has been one complaint against an MNE based on the ICA. In *Riwal*, Al-Haq accused several companies of the Riwal group, and two managing directors, of contributing to war crimes and crimes against humanity in the West Bank within the meaning of ICA.[33] Following a pre-investigation, however, the public prosecutor refused to initiate criminal proceedings against the MNE and the managing directors. It should be noted that the legal framework governing extraterritorial jurisdiction in Dutch criminal law has changed considerably since 2014.[34] Therefore, the analysis below focuses on legislation existing at the time of writing.

Active personality

Under the active personality principle, a State has jurisdiction over criminal offences committed by its nationals. The active nationality principle appears to be the most justifiable basis for exercising jurisdiction to regulate MNEs' conduct abroad.[35]

Pursuant to Article 113-6 French Criminal Code, French criminal law applies to criminal offences committed by French nationals outside the French territory. However, it distinguishes between felonies and misdemeanours. French criminal law applies to any felony without any further conditions,[36] while it is applicable to any misdemeanour if the conduct is also punishable under the

---

31   ICA, Article 2(1). The ICA applies without prejudice to the Dutch Criminal Code and the Dutch Code of Military Law.

32   ICA, Article 2(3). The Dutch Criminal Code also stipulates that a person who acquires Dutch nationality after having committed a crime may be prosecuted in the Netherlands for that crime. See also HR 30 June 1950, NJ 1950, 646.

33   'Al Haq/Report of War Crimes and Crimes against Humanity by Riwal' (Complaint to National Public Prosecutor's Office) (Böhler Advocaten 15 March 2010).

34   Van Gelder and Ryngaert, 'Dutch Report on Prosecuting Corporations', 136. This change is the result of the entry into force of the Act of Amendment, Review Extraterritorial Jurisdiction (*Wijzigingswet, Herziening extraterritoriale rechtsmacht*) on 1 July 2014 and the Decision regarding International Obligations of Extraterritorial Jurisdiction.

35   Anna Triponel, 'Comparative Corporate Responsibility in the United States and France for Human Rights Violations Abroad' in Andrew Morris and Samuel Estreicher (eds), *Global Labor and Employment Law for the Practicing Lawyer* (Kluwer Law International 2010) 103; Olivier de Schutter, 'Extraterritorial Jurisdiction as a Tool for Improving the Human Rights Accountability of Transnational Corporations' (UN OHCHR Seminar, Brussels, 3–4 November 2006) 24.

36   French Criminal Code, Article 113-6(1).

legislation of the country in which it was committed.[37] Therefore, Article 113-6 requires the application of double criminality to misdemeanours committed by French nationals outside France. Another important aspect is that Article 113-6 only applies to French companies and, therefore, foreign subsidiaries are excluded. French legal experts suggest that the foreign subsidiary should be considered to be of French nationality when a number of elements, including the control that the French parent company has over the foreign subsidiary, demonstrate that, in reality, the foreign subsidiary is French.[38]

The French prosecutor has absolute discretion to decide whether to pursue prosecution of misdemeanours in the cases set out under Article 113-6. This rule, which is stated under Article 113-8 French Criminal Code, has been a major obstacle to transnational criminal litigation against MNEs, especially when the French prosecutor is reluctant to sue companies. In *Rougier*, the victims used Article 113-6 as a basis for their claim. However, the prosecutor refused to initiate criminal proceedings against the French parent company. Both the Court of Appeal and the Court of Cassation respectively dismissed the victims' appeal on the grounds that, pursuant to Article 113-8, only the prosecutor can initiate criminal proceedings based on Article 113-6.[39] Consequently, victims could not successfully use the active personality principle to establish the applicability of French law to misdemeanours committed by French companies abroad.

Moreover, the fact that the offence committed by a French national outside the French territory falls under the category of felony does not guarantee the application of Article 113-6. In *Trafigura*, victims filed a criminal complaint against two French executives of Trafigura for various criminal offences, including administration of harmful substances, manslaughter, active corruption, and violations of rules pertaining to the transboundary movements of waste. After conducting a preliminary enquiry, the prosecutor declined to investigate further. According to an NGO report, one basis for this decision was the lack of lasting attachment to the French territory of Trafigura's executives, even though both individuals were of French nationality. Furthermore, the complaint was rejected on the grounds that the companies involved were established outside the French territory and that simultaneous criminal proceedings were ongoing in Ivory Coast and the Netherlands.[40]

The rule under Article 113 8 requiring that only the prosecutor, and not a civil party, can launch prosecution is questionable in the context of transnational litigation against MNEs because it places significant power in the hands of

---

37 Ibid, Article 113-6(2).

38 Mathey, 'La responsabilité sociale des entreprises'.

39 Cass crim 12 April 2005, n° 04-82318.

40 Ibid; 'The Toxic Truth about a Company Called Trafigura, a Ship Called the Probo Koala, and the Dumping of Toxic Waste in Cote d'Ivoire' (Amnesty International & Greenpeace Netherlands 2012) 168.

one entity.[41] This discretion is even more problematic in the French context where the independence of prosecutorial authorities is debatable. In 2010, the ECtHR ruled that the French public prosecutor did not meet the guarantees of independence from the executive required by Article 5(3) ECHR because the prosecutor is under the authority of the Minister of Justice, who is a member of the government and thus part of the executive branch.[42] The Corporate Crime Principles highlight that, in some countries, prosecutors may be internally pressured into, or rewarded for, swiftly resolving corporate crimes cases.[43] In this context, one can legitimately ask whether French prosecutors should decide alone on the prosecution of cases involving French MNEs when one knows the potential political and economic pressure this type of case can produce.

Article 7 Dutch Criminal Code provides that Dutch criminal law is applicable to a Dutch national who commits an offence outside the Netherlands. However, Article 7 distinguishes between two situations. First, Article 7(1) provides that Dutch criminal law applies to Dutch nationals who are guilty of an offence committed outside the Netherlands which is considered a criminal offence under Dutch criminal law and which is punishable by the law of the country where it was committed.[44] Therefore, Article 7(1) requires the condition of double criminality. However, this condition is not interpreted strictly.[45] Double criminality is determined *in abstracto*, which means that it is sufficient that the act falls within the scope of a foreign criminal provision.[46] Second, pursuant to Article 7(2), Dutch criminal law applies to Dutch nationals who commit certain crimes outside the Netherlands. These include crimes against the security of the State or against royal dignity, human trafficking, crimes harming the International Criminal Court (ICC), sexual abuse of minors and genital mutilation, and crimes forcing someone to act under violence or the threat of violence. If the Dutch Criminal Code restricts the application of the active personality principle to crimes, specific statutes nevertheless allow for the exercise of jurisdiction over misdemeanours.[47]

The Supreme Court held that the Dutch Criminal Code applies to every Dutch legal person who commits a crime outside the Netherlands, where this act constitutes a criminal offence according to the law of the State on whose

41   Triponel, 'Comparative Corporate Responsibility', 104.

42   *Moulin v France* App no 37104/06 (ECtHR, 23 November 2010).

43   Justice Ian Binnie and others, 'The Corporate Crimes Principles: Advancing Investigations and Prosecutions in Human Rights Cases' (Amnesty International and ICAR 2016) 2.

44   See also HR 21 May 2002, NJ 2003, 316 (*Asean Explorer*).

45   Van Gelder and Ryngaert, 'Dutch Report on Prosecuting Corporations', 137.

46   An assessment of the foreign law on the issue of justifications and excuses is not necessary.

47   Van Gelder and Ryngaert, 'Dutch Report on Prosecuting Corporations', 137.

territory the crime is committed.[48] When the offender is a legal person, it is assumed that the legal person must have a link with the Netherlands, such as incorporation or registration under Dutch law.[49] The fact that a legal person is not recognized as such in the other country does not bar prosecution in the Netherlands.[50] Furthermore, it is not relevant whether the law of the State where the crime is committed recognizes the criminal liability of natural persons for crimes committed by legal persons.[51]

In the case against Trafigura in 2008, the Dutch prosecutor declined to prosecute Trafigura BV, Puma Energy International BV (Puma) (another Dutch company), and Claude Dauphin (Trafigura's chairman) for the criminal offences related to toxic waste dumping in Ivory Coast. The main reason was that it appeared impossible to conduct an investigation in Ivory Coast, most notably due to the lack of cooperation of the Ivorian authorities.[52]

In 2009, Greenpeace lodged a complaint with the Court of Appeal of The Hague against the Dutch prosecutor's decision.[53] It claimed that the Netherlands had jurisdiction to prosecute Trafigura BV and Puma under then-Article 5(1)2° (now Article 7(1)):

> The *locus delicti* of the offences is (partly) in the Netherlands, precisely because two 'suspected' legal persons have their offices in the Netherlands and the offences objected to and described in this complaint were committed entirely in the Dutch 'context' of these legal persons. The Netherlands, at any rate, has jurisdiction to try Trafigura and Puma pursuant to Article 5(1)2° of the Dutch [Criminal] Code. After all the persons who committed offences which are also punishable in Côte d'Ivoire are Dutch legal persons. In this case, the fact that Dauphin does not have Dutch nationality does not affect the jurisdiction of the Netherlands. For, if the legal person has the Dutch nationality, the executive 'in fact' can be prosecuted in the Netherlands, irrespective of his nationality.[54]

48   HR 11 December 1990, NJ 1991, 466. See also Berend Keulen and Erik Gritter, 'Corporate Criminal Liability in the Netherlands' in Mark Pieth and Radha Ivory (eds), *Corporate Criminal Liability: Emergence, Convergence, and Risk* (Springer 2011) 190.

49   Gerritsen, 'Jurisdiction', 60.

50   HR 12 February 1991, NJ 1991, 528. A Dutch person found responsible for a crime committed abroad by a foreign legal person can also be prosecuted in the Netherlands.

51   HR 18 October 1988, NJ 1989, 496. See also Keulen and Gritter, 'Corporate Criminal Liability in the Netherlands', 190.

52   'The Toxic Truth', 160.

53   'Complaint Concerning Failure to Prosecute for an Offence (Article 12 of the Dutch Code of Criminal Procedure)' (Greenpeace Nederland 16 September 2009).

54   Ibid, 19–20.

In 2011, the Court of Appeal rejected Greenpeace's complaint,[55] concluding that the Dutch courts did not have jurisdiction for several reasons. First, the facts did not take place in the Netherlands. Second, although Trafigura BV had its formal establishment in the Netherlands, the actual business of the company was carried out in the UK and Switzerland. Therefore, Trafigura BV could not be considered a Dutch legal person under Article 5 Dutch Criminal Code. Third, none of the natural persons targeted by the complaint had Dutch nationality or resided in the Netherlands. Fourth, the Court of Appeal questioned the feasibility of both an investigation and a prosecution, and raised the impossibility of conducting a proper criminal investigation in Ivory Coast. Fifth, it held that the toxic waste was dumped by Tommy Company, and not by Trafigura BV. In the court's view, Greenpeace did not demonstrate that Trafigura BV knew that Tommy Company would commit such acts.[56] Overall, there was insufficient evidence justifying an investigation into, and prosecution of, the alleged criminal offences.

Article 2(1)(c) ICA also provides that Dutch criminal law applies to Dutch nationals who commit any of the crimes defined in ICA outside the Netherlands. Therefore, Dutch courts have jurisdiction to apply Dutch criminal law to the commission of genocide, crimes against humanity, war crimes, and torture by a Dutch company in a foreign country after 2003. Importantly, it does not matter if the suspect became a Dutch national only after committing the crime.[57] In *Riwal*, Al-Haq argued that Article 2(1)(c) ICA conferred extraterritorial jurisdiction on the Dutch court, as the natural and legal persons being the subject of the report lived or resided in the Netherlands or had their principal place of business in the Netherlands. However, as mentioned above, the prosecutor refused to prosecute Riwal and the managing directors.

In the Netherlands, no Dutch company has been tried for the commission of international crimes abroad. However, two Dutch businessmen have been prosecuted for business activities directly related to international crimes.[58] In both cases, the Dutch courts held they had jurisdiction based on the active nationality principle.

In *Public Prosecutor v Van Anraat*,[59] Frans van Anraat, a Dutch businessman, was accused of complicity in genocide and war crimes before the Dutch criminal courts. From 1985 until 1988, van Anraat delivered large quantities

55   CA The Hague 12 April 2011, NJFS 2011, 137.

56   Ibid, [16].

57   ICA, Article 2(3).

58   See Wim Huisman and Elies Van Sliedregt, 'Rogue Traders: Dutch Businessmen, International Crimes and Corporate Complicity' (2010) 8 Journal of International Criminal Justice 803.

59   For a description of the case, see Harmen Van Der Wilt, 'Genocide v War Crimes in the Van Anraat Appeal' (2008) 6 Journal of International Criminal Justice 557; 'Public Prosecutor v Frans Cornelis Adrianus Van Anraat' (International Crimes Database, 2013) <http://www.internationalcrimesdatabase.org/Case/178/Van-Anraat/> accessed 1 May 2021.

of thiodiglycol, a chemical used in the production of chemical weapons, to the regime of Saddam Hussein. Later, the Iraqi regime deployed chemical weapons against Kurdish civilians in northern Iraq as part of a larger genocidal campaign to annihilate the Kurdish population.[60] In 2005, the District Court of The Hague found van Anraat guilty of complicity in war crimes, but acquitted him of complicity in genocide.[61] In 2007, the Court of Appeal of The Hague upheld the District Court's ruling, also acquitting van Anraat in respect of genocide, albeit for different reasons.[62] Ultimately, in 2009 the Supreme Court confirmed the conviction.[63]

During the trial, van Anraat challenged the jurisdiction of the Dutch criminal courts. He argued that, because of the accessory character of complicity to genocide and war crimes, the District Court was not competent as it lacked jurisdiction over the main offences. However, the District Court dismissed van Anraat's argument. First, it held that complicity in a crime, even if it concerns genocide or war crimes, is an independent indictable offence. Second, given that van Anraat was staying in the Netherlands and was a Dutch national, and that the indicted offences of complicity were considered to be criminal offences, the District Court found that van Anraat could be prosecuted in the Netherlands pursuant to Article 5 Dutch Criminal Code.

In *Public Prosecutor v Kouwenhoven*,[64] Guus Kouwenhoven, a Dutch businessman, was accused of complicity in war crimes and illegal supply of arms to Charles Taylor, the former president of Liberia, in violation of UN and Dutch embargos prohibiting arms trade with Liberia. After more than 12 years of criminal proceedings, in 2017 the Court of Appeal of 's-Hertogenbosch eventually found Kouwenhoven guilty of the above-mentioned crimes and sentenced him to 19 years' imprisonment.[65] In this instance, the Dutch courts based their extraterritorial jurisdiction on the active nationality principle. However, as will be seen later, the practical exercise of this jurisdictional basis presented difficulties regarding the collection of evidence abroad, mutual legal assistance, and the complexity for Dutch judges in forming a judgment based on the facts.[66]

---

60   Harmen Van Der Wilt, 'Corporate Criminal Responsibility for International Crimes: Exploring the Possibilities' (2013) 12 Chinese Journal of International Law 43, 61.

61   DC The Hague 23 December 2005, Case No 09/751003-04.

62   CA The Hague 9 May 2007, Case No 2200050906-2.

63   HR 30 June 2009, Case No 07/10742.

64   For a description of the case, see Larissa Van Den Herik, 'The Difficulties of Exercising Extraterritorial Criminal Jurisdiction: The Acquittal of a Dutch Businessman for Crimes Committed in Liberia' (2009) 9 International Criminal Law Review 211; 'The Public Prosecutor v Guus Kouvenhoven' (International Crimes Database, 2013) <http://www.internationalcrimesdatabase.org/Case/2238/Kouwenhoven/> accessed 1 May 2021.

65   CA 's-Hertogenbosch 21 April 2017, ECLI: NL: GHSHE: 2017: 1760. This ruling was confirmed in cassation. See HR 18 December 2018, ECLI: NL: HR: 2018: 2336.

66   See Van Den Herik, 'The Difficulties in Exercising Extraterritorial Criminal Jurisdiction'.

Passive personality

Under the passive personality principle, a State has jurisdiction over criminal offences committed by foreign nationals that affect its own citizens.

Article 113-7 French Criminal Code provides that French criminal law applies to any felony, and any misdemeanour punishable by imprisonment, which is committed by a French or a foreign national outside French territory where the victim is a French national at the time the offence took place. In transnational criminal litigation against MNEs, Article 113-7 enables French courts to exercise jurisdiction over criminal offences committed by foreign and French companies against French nationals abroad. This provision presents various advantages, as it confers automatic and exclusive jurisdiction to French criminal courts[67] and does not require double criminality. However, the above-mentioned Article 113-8 French Criminal Code also applies to Article 113-7, which means that the French prosecutor has absolute discretion to initiate criminal proceedings in cases alleging misdemeanours.

Dutch criminal law applies to anyone on foreign soil who commits certain criminal offences against a victim of Dutch nationality. The passive personality principle can apply on two main bases. First, the Dutch Criminal Code allowed, until 2014, the application of the passive personality principle to certain criminal offences, such as human trafficking and offences relating to minors, on the condition that the conduct constituted a criminal offence in the foreign state as well (double criminality). However, Article 5(1) Dutch Criminal Code now provides that Dutch criminal law applies to anyone who is guilty of a crime outside the Netherlands against a Dutch national, a Dutch civil servant, or a Dutch vehicle, vessel, or aircraft, insofar as this crime is legally punishable by at least eight years' imprisonment under Dutch law and is punishable by the law of the country where it was committed. The rationale regarding the eight year rule is that passive personality jurisdiction should only be justified for crimes of a certain gravity.[68] Second, the ICA provides that Dutch domestic law shall apply to anyone who commits the crimes it describes outside the Netherlands if the crime is committed against a Dutch national.[69] The ICA does not require double criminality.[70] In both situations, the passive personality principle extends to corporations as, under Dutch law, a 'person' is also understood as a 'legal person'.[71]

However, the usefulness of the passive nationality principle in the context of transnational criminal litigation against MNEs is limited in practice. First,

---

67   Triponel, 'Comparative Corporate Responsibility', 100.
68   Van Gelder and Ryngaert, 'Dutch Report on Prosecuting Corporations', 138.
69   ICA, Article 2(1)(b).
70   Boot-Matthijssen and Van Elst, 'Key Provisions of the International Crimes Act 2003', 280.
71   Van Gelder and Ryngaert, 'Dutch Report on Prosecuting Corporations', 139.

victims of MNE conduct in host States are often nationals of these countries. Unless the victim has dual nationality, this aspect limits the use of legislation based on the passive nationality principle to prosecute French, Dutch, and foreign companies of MNEs. Second, the passive personality principle is the most controversial of the five accepted bases of jurisdiction in international law.[72] In France, Article 113-7 has been criticized for being an incongruous basis on which to prosecute extraterritorial crimes, as it is usually seen as intruding on the sovereignty of other nations and subjecting foreign nationals to an indeterminate threat of criminal responsibility in dealings with French nationals.[73] In the Netherlands, by virtue of a long-standing tradition, domestic courts are particularly reluctant to apply jurisdiction based on the passive personality principle, thus limiting its potential benefits.[74]

Universal jurisdiction

Under the universal jurisdiction principle, a State has jurisdiction to prosecute and punish foreign nationals who commit crimes abroad against foreigners.[75] Universal jurisdiction can be regarded as the broadest ground for establishing jurisdiction.[76] In theory, it does not operate on the basis of a connecting factor linking up a situation with a State's interests.[77] Therefore, universal jurisdiction can be advantageous in establishing criminal jurisdiction in cases where the perpetrator is a foreign company with no territorial link with France and the Netherlands. However, the application of the universal jurisdiction principle is accepted only in relation to a limited number of core crimes under international law, such as war crimes, genocide, crimes against humanity, and torture. The reason for this is that jurisdiction is based solely on the egregious nature of these crimes.[78]

Both French and Dutch law provide for the application of the universal jurisdiction principle in criminal law. The French Code of Criminal Procedure provides for the exercise of universal jurisdiction through the application of a domestic enabling clause (Article 689-1) combined with international conventions enumerated in subsequent articles (Articles 689-2 to 689-14). First, Article 689-1 provides that a person guilty of committing, or attempting

---

72   Eric Cafritz and Omar Tene, 'Article 113-7 of the French Penal Code: The Passive Personality Principle' (2003) 41 Columbia Journal of Transnational Law 585, 586.

73   Ibid, 587.

74   Gerritsen, 'Jurisdiction', 58.

75   Reydams, *Universal Jurisdiction*, 1.

76   Van Gelder and Ryngaert, 'Dutch Report on Prosecuting Corporations', 140.

77   Ryngaert, *Jurisdiction in International Law*, 120.

78   Ibid; Cedric Ryngaert, 'Accountability for Corporate Human Rights Abuses: Lessons from the Possible Exercise of Dutch National Criminal Jurisdiction over Multinational Corporations' (2018) 29 Criminal Law Forum 1, 17.

to commit, any of the offences listed by the international conventions quoted in Articles 689-2 to 689-14 outside France and who happens to be in France may be prosecuted and tried by French courts. Second, Articles 689-2 to 689-14 list the criminal offences, which are attached to various international conventions, over which French courts have criminal jurisdiction under the universality principle. In the context of transnational criminal litigation against MNEs the most relevant offences and conventions are as follows:

- Torture under the Convention against Torture and other Cruel, Inhuman or Degrading Treatment or Punishment (Convention against Torture);[79]
- Acts financing terrorism under the International Convention for the Suppression of the Financing of Terrorism;[80]
- Genocide, crimes against humanity, and war crimes and misdemeanours under the Rome Statute;[81]
- Enforced disappearance under the International Convention for the Protection of All Persons from Enforced Disappearance;[82] and
- Damage to cultural property under the Convention for the Protection of Cultural Property in the Event of Armed Conflict.[83]

For all these offences, France nonetheless requires some territorial link in the form of the presence of the suspect on its territory. However, it is possible to judge the suspect *in absentia* if the proceedings were validly instituted when the accused was on national territory.[84]

The exercise of French jurisdiction over international crimes under the Rome Statute based on the universal jurisdiction principle is only possible if several conditions are met: (1) the suspect must habitually reside in France; (2) the public prosecutor has absolute discretion to prosecute; (3) no international or national court requests the surrender or extradition of the person; and (4) for crimes against humanity and war crimes and misdemeanours, the acts must be

79 Convention against Torture and other Cruel, Inhuman or Degrading Treatment or Punishment (adopted 10 December 1984, entered into force 26 June 1987) 1465 UNTS 85; French Code of Criminal Procedure, Article 689-2.

80 International Convention for the Suppression of the Financing of Terrorism (adopted 9 December 1999, entered into force 10 April 2002) 2178 UNTS 197; French Code of Criminal Procedure, Article 689-10.

81 French Code of Criminal Procedure, Article 689-11.

82 International Convention for the Protection of All Persons from Enforced Disappearance (adopted 20 December 2006, entered into force 23 December 2010) 2716 UNTS 3; French Code of Criminal Procedure, Article 689-13.

83 Hague Convention for the Protection of Cultural Property in the Event of Armed Conflict (adopted 14 May 1954).

84 Blanco Cordero Isidoro, 'Compétence universelle. Rapport général' (2008) 79 Revue internationale de droit pénal 13, 28.

punishable under the law of the State where they were committed, or that State or the State of which the suspected person is a national is a party to the Rome Statute. NGOs have criticized the way France applies the universal jurisdiction principle to international crimes under the Rome Statute. They argue that the four conditions attached to the application of universal jurisdiction are so restrictive that it is almost impossible to use this jurisdictional ground.[85]

French courts have agreed to exercise universal jurisdiction over the commission of criminal offences by foreigners abroad in a few cases only. For instance, in July 2005 a Mauritanian army officer was sentenced to imprisonment for committing acts of torture and barbarity in Mauritania in the 1990s.[86] Pursuant to Articles 689, 689-1, and 689-2, and Article 7(2) Convention against Torture, French courts held that they had jurisdiction to try the case and apply French law. They also overrode a Mauritanian amnesty law, as application of that law would have resulted in a breach of France's international obligations and rendered the principle of universal jurisdiction totally ineffective.[87]

To date, France has not used the universal jurisdiction principle to assert jurisdiction over international crimes committed by companies. However, the requirement of presence on French territory is likely to create problems when prosecuting companies based on the universal jurisdiction principle. The law provides no guidance on how to characterize the presence of a foreign legal person on French territory. A solution may be to require that the company possesses property or has an economic activity in France. To date, there has been no illustration of a corporation's prosecution under the universal jurisdiction principle.[88] Whether such a rule may apply to legal persons, and under which conditions, needs to be clarified.

In the Netherlands, the legal rationale underlying the principle of universal jurisdiction is the fulfilment of the State's international obligations, combined with the nature of the crime directed against the interests of the international community as a whole. As a result, the international community has an interest in repressing the crime.[89] Both the Criminal Code and the ICA provide for the exercise of universal jurisdiction. First, Article 4 Criminal Code provides for the exercise of universal jurisdiction for a limited number of criminal offences,

85 'Qu'est-ce que la compétence universelle?' (Amnesty International) <https://www.amnesty.fr/focus/competence-universelle> accessed 1 May 2021.

86 Cour d'assises Nîmes 1 July 2005 (*Ould Dah*).

87 CA Nîmes 8 July 2002; Cass crim 23 October 2002 (*Ould Dah*). For a description of the French proceedings, see *Ould Dah v France* App no 13113/03 (ECtHR, 17 March 2009).

88 Juliette Lelieur, 'French Report on Prosecuting Corporations for Violations of International Criminal Law' in Sabine Gless and Sylwia Broniszewska-Emdin (eds), *Prosecuting Corporations for Violations of International Criminal Law: Jurisdictional Issues* (Maklu 2017) 204.

89 Cordero Isidoro, 'Compétence universelle', 16.

such as piracy, terrorism, or counterfeiting currency. Most of these crimes are, however, irrelevant in the context of this study. Second, under Article 2(1)(a) ICA, Dutch domestic law applies to anyone who commits the crimes it describes outside the Netherlands if the suspect is present in the Netherlands. In the same way as in France, the ICA requires that the alleged offender be present in the Netherlands. Furthermore, Dutch courts will only exercise universal jurisdiction if neither the territorial courts nor the ICC is exercising jurisdiction. Dutch courts have, on several occasions, been confronted with the application of universal jurisdiction. In the notorious *Bouterse* case, the Dutch Supreme Court rejected the application of universal jurisdiction based on the Convention against Torture. It opined that prosecution and punishment in the Netherlands of a person suspected of an offence under the Dutch Act Implementing the Torture Convention was only possible if one of the links mentioned in the Convention existed, for example when the offender or victim is a Dutch citizen, or when the suspect is present in the Netherlands at the time of their arrest.[90] Since *Bouterse*, a number of cases have nonetheless been successfully prosecuted in the Netherlands based on universal jurisdiction.[91]

To date, there has been no prosecution of a company using universal jurisdiction. In *Riwal*, Al-Haq argued that Article 2(1)(a) ICA conferred extraterritorial jurisdiction on Dutch courts. However, the prosecutor did not address this point, as he refused to prosecute the companies and managing directors for expediency reasons. Just as in France, the application of the transitory presence requirement to companies is nonetheless likely to create problems. Notably, scholars have argued that companies are more likely to be prosecuted under the territoriality or personality principle.[92]

3 The participation of victims and NGOs in criminal proceedings

More recently, it has become increasingly accepted that justice cannot be administered effectively without due recognition of the rights and interests of victims during criminal proceedings.[93] The ability of victims and NGOs to participate in the proceedings is now crucial to guarantee their rights and interests in the context of transnational criminal litigation against MNEs.

In France, victims have traditionally been able to play a significant role in the initial phases of criminal proceedings. However, this participation has

---

90   HR 23 October 2001, NJ 2002, 77.

91   Elies van Sliedregt, 'International Crimes before Dutch Courts: Recent Developments' (2007) 20 Leiden Journal of International Law 895.

92   Van Gelder and Ryngaert, 'Dutch Report on Prosecuting Corporations', 140.

93   Doak, *Victims' Rights, Human Rights and Criminal Justice*, 1.

produced limited outcomes in the context of transnational criminal claims against MNEs. In the EU, the acknowledgement of victims' rights through the adoption of various directives has led to changes in French and Dutch legal frameworks governing the participation of victims in criminal proceedings. In theory, such changes should help victims in the context of criminal proceedings against corporations.

Initiating criminal proceedings

The French and Dutch criminal systems recognize the principle of opportunity, under which the public prosecutor has discretion whether to initiate criminal proceedings. This principle applies to all criminal offences.

In France, the Code of Criminal Procedure distinguishes between public action (*l'action publique*), which is the legal action brought before a criminal court for the application of criminal law to offenders, and civil action (*l'action civile*), which is a legal action brought before a criminal court for compensation of the damage resulting from the commission of a criminal offence. Under Article 1 Code of Criminal Procedure, judges and prosecutors have the power to initiate and exercise public action for the imposition of penalties. However, this power is not exclusive, as the injured party may also initiate public action under the conditions determined by the Code of Criminal Procedure. This form of action is an important way of getting around unwilling prosecutors and its use has increased in France in recent years.[94] As a result, victims of corporate abuse have been able to directly initiate criminal proceedings against MNEs.

Generally, victims have three options to initiate criminal proceedings. First, they can file a criminal complaint with, or denunciate alleged crimes to, law enforcement authorities or the public prosecutor.[95] In general, the prosecutor decides whether it is appropriate to prosecute, to implement an alternative procedure to prosecution, or to discontinue the proceedings if the particular circumstances relating to the commission of the facts justify it.[96] The prosecutor enjoys a significant discretion in that decision. However, when the prosecutor decides to discontinue the proceedings, they must notify the victims of the decision and indicate the legal or expediency reasons for doing so.[97] When the criminal complaint is dismissed or no action is taken by the prosecutor, victims can file a criminal complaint and bring a civil action at the same time (*dépôt de plainte avec constitution de partie civile*). In this situation,

94   Jacqueline Hodgson, *French Criminal Justice: A Comparative Account of the Investigation and Prosecution of Crime in France* (Hart Publishing 2005) 31.

95   French Code of Criminal Procedure, Article 40.

96   Ibid, Article 40-1.

97   Ibid, Article 40-2.

an examining magistrate will take over the case and open an investigation to decide whether prosecution is possible, which may result in a judicial enquiry (*information judiciaire*). This procedure prevents the case from being closed without immediate follow-up.

Until now, in most cases filing a complaint with the public prosecutor has been an unsuccessful strategy in bringing transnational litigation against MNEs. The majority of the complaints submitted to public prosecutors have eventually been dismissed. In some cases, however, examining magistrates have continued criminal proceedings in spite of the prosecutor's refusal to prosecute MNEs. In *Amesys*, the prosecutor dismissed the complaint on the grounds that the alleged acts did not qualify as crimes. However, an examining magistrate of the Crimes against Humanity Unit subsequently ordered a criminal investigation. The prosecutor appealed this decision, but the Paris Court of Appeal rejected this appeal.[98] The prosecutor's reluctance to investigate an MNE was also visible in *Total* where the prosecutor sought the dismissal of the complaints even though victims had brought these complaints directly before an examining magistrate. After an examining magistrate rejected the initial request of the prosecutor to dismiss the civil action, the prosecutor appealed the decision before the Versailles Court of Appeal. The Court eventually rejected the prosecutor's appeal on the grounds that the prosecutor did not have jurisdiction to request the dismissal of the case at the judicial enquiry stage.

As a second option, victims may initiate criminal proceedings by bringing a civil action directly before the examining magistrate. One advantage of this procedure is that victims can trigger formal criminal investigation by a judge while simultaneously claiming financial compensation. In several cases, victims have used this procedure after a prosecutor had dismissed their complaint. In such a situation, bringing a civil action directly before the examining magistrate offers a second chance to trigger the public action as well as an opportunity to get around prosecutors' reluctance to try MNEs. In *DLH*, the plaintiffs initiated new criminal proceedings before the examining magistrate for Montpellier after the first complaint with the prosecutors for Nantes and Montpellier was unsuccessful.[99] Plaintiffs in the cases against Auchan and Vinci adopted the same strategy. To date, victims' claims have been more successful with examining magistrates than with prosecutors.

Third, victims can directly summon the alleged perpetrator to court for misdemeanours or crimes where there is sufficient evidence and where the court can try the case without prior investigation (*citation directe*).[100] In that

98 'The Amesys Case' (FIDH 2015).

99 In the *DLH* case, Sherpa and the other plaintiffs considered the second option after the first option was unsuccessful. In the *Auchan* case, Sherpa and the other plaintiffs adopted this strategy. See 'Sherpa: Rapport d'Activités 2013' (Sherpa 2014) 7.

100 French Criminal Code of Procedure, Articles 389 to 392-1 and 550 to 566.

situation, the victim must provide the evidence necessary to establish the alleged perpetrator's guilt and to demonstrate the extent of the harm suffered. Furthermore, the victim must bear the costs of the deposit, in order to guarantee the possible payment of a civil fine in the event of abuse proceedings, and the bailiff's fee, which will be reimbursed by the perpetrator if they are found guilty. To date, this situation has not occurred in the context of transnational claims against MNEs.

In the Netherlands, victims cannot initiate criminal proceedings. Contrary to the French system, the Dutch public prosecutor holds a monopoly on prosecution and is not obliged to prosecute. The prosecutor may decide not to prosecute under the expediency principle, as laid down in Article 167 Code of Criminal Procedure (*Wetboek van Strafvordering*). Accordingly, they may waive prosecution for reasons of public interest.[101] The Dutch prosecutor tends to deal with some criminal offences – such as environmental offences – through transaction, settlement, or dismissal.[102] Furthermore, the Code of Criminal Procedure does not provide the criteria for the exercise of this power, and no other authority will check whether discretion by the prosecutor was properly used. Nonetheless, the prosecution service is still bound by its own policies.[103]

However, Article 12 Code of Criminal Procedure gives victims and NGOs a right to appeal the prosecutor's decision not to initiate criminal proceedings. Accordingly, parties with a direct interest in the prosecution of criminal offences can apply to the Court of Appeal against the prosecutor's decision. Article 12 is 'the only way in which a private person (natural or otherwise) can formally influence the decision on prosecution'.[104] The Court of Appeal's decision is final. If it considers the complaint to be reasonable, it will order the prosecutor to launch the prosecution, but this is done only in exceptional cases.[105]

NGOs used this approach in the Dutch proceedings against Trafigura, but it produced unsuccessful results. In 2009, Greenpeace appealed the prosecutor's decision not to prosecute Trafigura BV, as well as the chairman and various employees of the Trafigura group. In 2011, the Court of Appeal of The Hague rejected Greenpeace's complaint on the grounds that the NGO lacked standing. Greenpeace had an insufficient direct interest to request prosecution of

101 Sanne Taekema (ed), *Understanding Dutch Law* (Boom Juridische Uitgevers 2004) 152.

102 Jonathan Verschuuren, 'The Netherlands' in Louis Kotzé and Alexander Paterson (eds), *The Role of the Judiciary in Environmental Governance: Comparative Perspectives* (Wolters Kluwer 2009) 67.

103 Keulen and Gritter, 'Corporate Criminal Liability in the Netherlands'.

104 Chrisje Brants-Langeraar, 'Consensual Criminal Procedures: Plea and Confession Bargaining and Abbreviated Procedures to Simplify Criminal Procedure' (2007) 11.1 EJCL 10.

105 J.F. Nijboer, 'The Criminal Justice System' in Jeroen Chorus, Piet-Hein Gerver, and Ewoud Hondius, *Introduction to Dutch Law* (4th edn, Kluwer Law International 2006) 411.

Trafigura BV, and the criminal acts in question were beyond the scope of Greenpeace's purpose as an organization. In addition, the Court of Appeal held that the prosecutor had a margin of discretion in deciding which offences are in the public interest to investigate and prosecute, and that they had sole authority to decide which cases to pursue.[106]

The rights of victims of crimes under EU law

The EU recently adopted a number of instruments that aim to support and protect victims of crime.[107] The most significant one is Directive 2012/29/EU (Victims' Rights Directive), which aims 'to ensure that victims of crime receive appropriate information, support and protection and are able to participate in criminal proceedings'.[108] The Victims' Rights Directive acknowledges that '[c]rime is a wrong against society as well as a violation of the individual rights of victims'.[109] Therefore, Member States must ensure that during criminal proceedings, victims are recognized and treated in a respectful, sensitive, tailored, professional, and non-discriminatory manner in all contacts with victim support, or restorative justice services, or a competent authority.

The Victims' Rights Directive is directly relevant in the context of transnational criminal litigation against MNEs for several reasons. First, the rights it sets out apply to victims in a non-discriminatory manner, regardless of their residence status.[110] The Victims' Rights Directive does not require victims of crime to reside in, or to be a national of, EU Member States. Therefore, Member States should ensure that the rights set out in the directive are not made conditional on the victim's residence status, citizenship, or nationality.[111] Second, the Victims' Rights Directive applies to criminal offences committed in the EU and to criminal proceedings taking place in the EU. It confers rights on victims of extraterritorial offences in relation to criminal proceedings that take place in the EU.[112] As a result, the Victims' Rights Directive is directly applicable to transnational criminal litigation against MNEs. Finally, the Victims' Rights Directive deals with various aspects of criminal proceedings which have posed

---

106 'The Toxic Truth', 160–161.

107 Theo Gavrielides, 'The Victims' Directive and What Victims Want from Restorative Justice' (2017) 12 Victims & Offenders 21.

108 Directive 2012/29/EU of the European Parliament and of the Council of 25 October 2012 establishing minimum standards on the rights, support and protection of victims of crime, and replacing Council Framework Decision 2001/220/JHA [2012] OJ L315/57, Article 1(1).

109 Victims' Rights Directive, Recital 9.

110 Ibid, Article 1(1).

111 Ibid, Recital 10.

112 Ibid, Recital 13.

significant obstacles to victims in past and ongoing claims against MNEs. Importantly, it recognizes and strengthens the rights of victims in order to guarantee their effective participation in criminal proceedings against MNEs.

The Victims' Rights Directive lists several rights that Member States must guarantee to victims of crime in relation to provision of information and support, participation in criminal proceedings, and protection of victims and recognition of victims with specific protection needs. The implementation of a large number of these rights is significant in the context of transnational litigation against MNEs, including the right to interpretation and translation, the right to be heard, or the right to protection. However, the analysis below pays particular attention to the rights to receive information about the case; the rights in the event of a decision not to prosecute; the rights to legal aid and to reimbursement of expenses; and the right to decision on compensation from the offender during criminal proceedings. It should be mentioned that 'victims' within the scope of the Victims' Rights Directive means natural persons who have suffered harm and family members of a person whose death was caused by a criminal offence and who have suffered harm resulting from that person's death.[113] As a result, NGOs are excluded from the scope of the Victims' Rights Directive. This means that, despite the preponderant role NGOs have so far played in criminal proceedings against MNEs, they cannot enjoy the guarantees provided by this directive.

Victims' right to receive information about their case

In the context of transnational litigation against MNEs, access to information about the progress of criminal proceedings is often strewn with obstacles. In *DHL*, it was difficult for complainants to obtain information on the status of their case from prosecutorial authorities. The complainants were given little information about the reasons for the prosecutor's decision to dismiss the complaint. As a result, Sherpa repeatedly requested the case documents to understand the prosecutor's decision. However, it was refused access to such documents without explanation.[114]

The Victims' Rights Directive acknowledges that providing information to victims means that:

> sufficient detail should be given to ensure that victims are treated
> in a respectful manner and to enable them to make informed
> decisions about their participation in the proceedings. In this

---

113 Ibid, Article 2(1)(a).

114 'DLH – Liberia: A Dismissal without Further Action or Explanation' (Sherpa, 6 April 2014) <https://www.asso-sherpa.org/dlh-liberia-dismissal-without-further-action-or-explanation> accessed 1 May 2021.

respect, information allowing the victim to know about the current status of any proceedings is particularly important. This is equally relevant for information to enable a victim to decide whether to request a review of a decision not to prosecute.[115]

Article 6 provides various rights of victims to receive information about their case. One of the most relevant rights in the context of this study is that of victims to receive, upon request, information on any decision not to proceed with or to end an investigation, or not to prosecute the offender.[116] In this situation, information must include the reasons or a brief summary of reasons for the decision concerned.[117] However, the benefits conferred upon victims by this rule are limited by the fact that victims must request this information. There is no obligation on Member States to automatically provide this information. Furthermore, where the reasons are confidential, Member States are not obliged to provide them as a matter of national law. Another important right is that victims should receive, upon request, information enabling regarding the stage that the criminal proceedings have reached.[118] Similarly, the added-value of this provision is restricted by the fact that victims must expressly request such information. Moreover, they will not be able to receive this information where the proper handling of the case may be adversely affected by such notification. This provision also depends on the role of victims in the criminal justice system of the State. Where victims are not provided a legal status as a party to criminal proceedings or a legal entitlement to participate in the proceedings, it should be inferred that this provision does not apply.

In France, the prosecutor had the obligation to notify victims of the decision to discontinue proceedings and to provide the legal or expediency justifications for this decision prior to the adoption of the Victims' Rights Directive. Furthermore, since around 2010 France has opened victim support offices (*bureau d'aide aux victimes*, or BAV) in each regional court (*Tribunal de Grande Instance*). Among their missions, BAVs are charged with providing information about the status of criminal proceedings to victims. Despite the existence of this framework, victims still experience difficulties in accessing information about their case.

In the Netherlands, Article 51ac(2) Code of Criminal Procedure provides that victims are automatically notified when a case starts, and then of its progress when they request this information. Furthermore, they should be contacted if criminal investigations are discontinued or stopped and the alleged offence is not prosecuted.

---

115 Victims' Rights Directive, Recital 26.

116 Ibid, Article 6(1)(a).

117 Ibid, Article 6(3).

118 Ibid, Article 6(2)(b).

Victims' rights in the event of a decision not to prosecute

Pursuant to the Victims' Rights Directive, Member States must ensure that victims, in accordance with their role in the relevant criminal justice system, have the right to a review of a decision not to prosecute.[119] Where the role of the victim in the relevant criminal justice system is established only after a decision to prosecute the offender has been taken, the Member States must guarantee that the victims of serious crimes have the right to a review of a decision not to prosecute.[120] In this event, EU criminal legislation and international criminal justice standards may be taken into account to interpret the term 'serious crimes'.[121] Generally, Member States should develop a clear, transparent, and simple procedure that ensures victims are able to ask for a review.[122]

In France, persons who have denunciated facts to the prosecutor may lodge an appeal with the General Prosecutor against the decision of dismissal taken as a result of this denunciation. The General Prosecutor may enjoin the prosecutor to institute proceedings or reject the appeal if they consider the appeal unfounded, in which case they must inform the person concerned.[123] Similarly, a civil party may file an appeal against the investigative judge's orders of non-investigation, dismissal, and orders adversely affecting its civil interests.[124] A special judicial body called the Investigating Chamber will then review the appeal.

In the Netherlands, as already mentioned, Article 12 Code of Criminal Procedure gives victims and NGOs a right to appeal the prosecutor's decision not to initiate criminal proceedings.

Victims' rights to legal aid and reimbursement of expenses

There are no judicial costs for criminal proceedings in France and the Netherlands. Unlike civil proceedings, victims do not have to pay for court fees when they bring a civil action (France)[125] or join criminal proceedings (Netherlands) against an MNE. However, France allows that a civil party may be ordered to pay some legal costs (such as experts' costs) where the

---

119 Ibid, Article 11(1).

120 Ibid, Article 11(2).

121 European Commission, 'DG Justice guidance document related to the transposition and implementation of Directive 2012/29/EU of the European Parliament and of the Council of 25 October 2012 establishing minimum standards on the rights, support and protection of victims of crime, and replacing Council Framework Decision 2001/220/JHA' (2013), 30 (DG Justice Guidance).

122 Ibid, 30–31.

123 French Code of Criminal Procedure, Article 40-3.

124 Ibid, Article 186.

125 Ibid, Article 800-1.

constitution as civil party has been judged to be abusive or dilatory.[126] This rule does not apply where criminal proceedings are concerned with crimes or misdemeanours against persons, or where the civil party has obtained legal aid.

Victims still have to pay for their lawyer's fees when they join criminal proceedings. Access to financial assistance is therefore crucial for victims who are unable to afford legal representation and access to the criminal justice system. The Victims' Rights Directive recognizes a right to legal aid. Member States have the obligation to ensure that victims have access to legal aid where they have the status of parties to criminal proceedings.[127] Legal aid should cover at least legal advice and legal representation should be free of charge.[128] As a result, foreign victims should have access to legal aid in transnational criminal litigation against MNEs. However, the provision of legal aid remains subject to national conditions or procedural rules.[129]

In France, rules on legal aid do not distinguish between civil or criminal matters, or the nature of the dispute. Furthermore, the status of the party to the proceedings (eg victim or accused) is not taken into account when deciding whether or not to grant legal aid.[130] As a general rule, legal aid is available to natural persons whose resources are insufficient to enforce their rights in court. Such aid may be total or partial.[131] French nationals, nationals of other Member States, and persons of foreign nationality habitually and regularly residing in France are eligible for legal aid. However, legal aid must be granted without considering the residence status of foreigners when they are civil parties to criminal proceedings.[132] Therefore, foreign victims can obtain legal aid when they take part as civil parties in criminal proceedings against MNEs. Furthermore, legal aid may be exceptionally granted to non-profit legal persons, such as NGOs, that are registered in France and lack sufficient resources. Another important aspect is that victims and their dependants are exempt from having to prove their resources when they bring a civil action in support of the public prosecution or for damages arising out of a number of serious crimes, namely intentional attacks against life or personal integrity.[133] Furthermore, in exceptional circumstances, the means condition may be waived where the circumstances of the legal aid applicant are of particular interest having regard to the object of the litigation or the foreseeable costs of the proceedings.

126 Ibid, Article 800-1.
127 Victims' Rights Directive, Article 13.
128 DG Justice Guidance, 34.
129 Victims' Rights Directive, Article 13.
130 Loi n° 91-647 du 10 juillet 1991 relative à l'aide juridique, Article 10.
131 Ibid, Article 2.
132 Ibid, Article 3.
133 Ibid, Article 9-2.

In the Netherlands, victims of crime are not automatically entitled to legal aid. They can use the assistance of a lawyer during the criminal trial,[134] and part of their lawyer's fees may be reimbursed by the State depending on the victim's income. Victims of a violent crime or a sexual crime and their surviving relatives may, under certain circumstances, qualify for free legal assistance from a lawyer regardless of their income. In such cases, a prosecution must have been instituted and the victim or surviving relative needs to qualify for benefits in accordance with Article 3 Violent Crime Compensation Fund Act (*Wet schadefonds geweldsmisdrijven*).

The Victims' Rights Directive also provides that Member States must afford victims the possibility of reimbursement of expenses incurred as a result of their active participation in criminal proceedings.[135] This rule aims to guarantee that victims are not prevented from actively participating in criminal proceedings due to their own financial limitations. Reimbursement will nonetheless depend on their role in the proceedings, whether as parties, witnesses, or in another role, as well as national conditions or procedural rules. In practice, reimbursement should at least cover travel expenses and loss of earnings.[136] Both France and the Netherlands provide that the State will reimburse victims' expenses.[137] In France, judges can also sentence the offender to pay costs incurred by the civil party and not covered by the State. In this case, judges will take into account the equity or economic situation of the convicted party.[138]

Victims' right to decision on compensation from the offender in the course of criminal proceedings

Pursuant to the Victims' Rights Directive, Member States must ensure that, in the course of criminal proceedings, victims are entitled to obtain a decision on compensation by the offender, within a reasonable time, except where national law provides for such a decision to be made in other legal proceedings. They must also promote measures to encourage offenders to provide adequate compensation to victims.[139]

In France, victims are entitled to bring a civil action (*constitution de partie civile*) at various stages of the criminal proceedings. A civil action aims at the reparation of the damage suffered because of a criminal offence. It is open to all those who have personally and directly suffered damage resulting from a

---

134 Dutch Code of Criminal Procedure, Article 51c.

135 Ibid, Article 14.

136 DG Justice Guidance, 35.

137 French Code of Criminal Procedure, Article R92(4); Dutch Code of Criminal Procedure, Article 592.

138 French Code of Criminal Procedure, Articles 375 and 475-1.

139 Victims' Rights Directive, Article 16.

criminal offence.[140] The civil action may be brought at the same time as the public action and before the same court.[141]

Under certain circumstances, French law allows NGOs to bring a civil action on behalf of victims of specific criminal offences. Articles 2-1 to 2-23 Code of Criminal Procedure list the types of associations that can exercise the rights granted to a civil party. In the context of this study, the most relevant associations focus on the following topics:

- Racism or discrimination (Article 2-1);
- Sexual violence and harassment, and spousal abuse (Article 2-2);
- Violence committed against children (Article 2-3);
- War crimes and crimes against humanity (Article 2-4);
- Sexual discrimination (Article 2-6);
- Discrimination of persons with disabilities (Article 2-8);
- Support to victims of criminal offences (Article 2-9);
- Social exclusion and poverty (Article 2-10);
- Protection of the individual and collective rights and liberties (Article 2-17);
- Occupational disease (Article 2-18);
- Human trafficking and slavery (Article 2-22); and
- Corruption and money laundering (Article 2-23).

Associations must have been lawfully registered for at least five years at the time of the criminal offence in order to bring a civil action in criminal proceedings. Similarly, Article L142-2 French Environmental Code provides that lawfully registered environmental NGOs can exercise the rights granted to a civil party in respect of facts creating direct or indirect damage to the collective interests they defend and constituting a criminal offence according to environmental legislation. However, environmental NGOs are not subject to the five-year registration condition.

French NGOs have played a crucial role in the emergence and development of transnational litigation against MNEs. For instance, Sherpa has been involved as adviser or litigator in most claims brought against MNEs. In parallel to its work on corporate accountability, Sherpa has also been involved in strategic litigation related to corruption, probity, and public embezzlement. However, Sherpa has recently faced a number of obstacles in bringing civil actions against MNEs in criminal cases. In 2019, Sherpa reported that French authorities had implicitly refused to renew its licence (*agrément*) to bring civil actions alleging

140 French Code of Criminal Procedure, Article 2.
141 Ibid, Article 3.

crimes of corruption. For the NGO, this refusal was an important obstacle to its ability to participate in criminal proceedings. Ultimately, Sherpa was granted its licence following a public campaign on the topic.

Moreover, in the case against Lafarge, the Investigating Chamber of the Paris Court of Appeal rejected Sherpa and the ECCHR's civil action on the ground that they did not have the necessary licence to participate in the criminal proceedings as civil parties.[142] As a result, the Investigating Chamber also rejected the admissibility of all the legal briefs submitted by the NGOs.[143] Ultimately, in September 2021, the Court of Cassation ruled that only the ECCHR could bring a civil action, and only in relation to the offence of complicity in crimes against humanity for which Lafarge was charged.[144] The ECCHR promotes international humanitarian law, allowing it to act against both war crimes and crimes against humanity. As a result, the ECCHR can be a civil party in cases of complicity in crimes against humanity. Sherpa's statutes, on the other hand, indicate that the NGO fights against economic crimes, implying that its action does not include crimes against humanity. Therefore, Sherpa cannot be a civil party in a case of complicity in crimes against humanity. The Court of Cassation's decision serves as a reminder of the restrictive conditions under which NGOs can participate in criminal proceedings. The law does not recognize a general right of action for NGOs in criminal court. However, in derogation to the principle that only persons who have suffered direct and personal loss as a result of a criminal offence can bring a civil action before the criminal court, the law allows NGOs that defend certain collective interests mentioned in their statutes to bring a civil action for specific categories of offences related to these interests, and under strict conditions. This means that, in the context of transnational litigation against MNEs, only NGOs that explicitly defend the collective interests harmed by the corporate criminal offence can bring a civil action. Given that an NGO's statutes can only cover a limited field of action, French law on NGOs in criminal proceedings limits the ability of corporate accountability NGOs, such as Sherpa, to effectively participate in criminal proceedings against corporations.

In the Netherlands, persons who have suffered direct damage as a result of a criminal offence are nonetheless authorized to join criminal proceedings to bring a claim for damages.[145] If the public prosecutor initiates or continues a

---

142 'French Court Rejects ECCHR and SHERPA's Admissibility in the Lafarge/Syria Case: Organizations to Appeal Decision at French Supreme Court' (Sherpa, 24 October 2019) <https://www.asso-sherpa.org/10533-2> accessed 1 May 2021.

143 'French Court Narrows Charges against Lafarge' (Sherpa, 7 November 2019) <https://www.asso-sherpa.org/french-court-narrows-charges-against-lafarge> accessed 1 May 2021.

144 Cass crim 7 September 2021, n° 19-87.031, 19-87.036, 19-87.040, 19-87.367, 19-87.376 and 19-87.662.

145 Dutch Code of Criminal Procedure, Article 51f, 1A.

prosecution, they must inform the injured party in writing as soon as possible. They must also inform the injured party of the time of the hearing in good time.[146] However, the victim's claim for damages is ancillary to the assessment of the crime, and the court will assess whether the victim should institute civil proceedings instead. The admissibility of the victim's claim depends on an evaluation as to whether or not the ruling represents an undue burden for the criminal proceedings.[147] However, this criterion, which was introduced in 2011, is rather vague.[148] If a court determines that the claim is inadmissible, the victim must submit the claim for damages before a civil court.

In *Public Prosecutor v Van Anraat*, a group of victims joined the proceedings to claim damages. However, the Court of Appeal of The Hague declared these claims inadmissible on the grounds that they were not 'easy in nature.' This was the admissibility criterion for joining a procedure to claim damages until the end of 2010. For the Court of Appeal, a criminal trial should not be burdened with complex civil cases, and the Supreme Court upheld this ruling in cassation.[149]

4 Production of evidence

In criminal proceedings, the burden of proof for establishing the guilt of suspects is on the prosecution. Therefore, prosecutorial authorities are generally in charge of seeking both inculpatory and exculpatory evidence, often with the help of the police. In some States, such as France, investigating magistrates are also in charge of gathering evidence related to some criminal offences.

As a consequence of this burden of proof, prosecutorial authorities often conduct a preliminary investigation to determine whether to prosecute or not. In the Netherlands, public prosecutors take several factors into account, including 'the feasibility of a case, the possibilities to conduct an investigation, the availability of, and access to, evidence in foreign countries, the safety of witnesses, and the possibility of doing independent research in foreign countries'.[150] For international crimes, public prosecutors must inquire whether there is sufficient information to treat the case as a reasonable prima facie case and whether there is a reasonable prospect of successful prosecution.[151]

---

146 Ibid, Article 51f, 5.

147 Ibid, Article 361, §3.

148 Renée S.B. Kool, Jessy M. Emaus, and Daan P. van Uhm, 'The Victim's Right to Intervene as an Injured Party in Criminal Proceedings: A Multidimensional and Interdisciplinary Assessment of Current Dutch Legal Practice' (2017) 13 Utrecht Law Review 77, 82.

149 Van Gelder and Ryngaert, 'Dutch Report on Prosecuting Corporations', 127.

150 Ibid, 123.

151 Ibid.

The primary responsibility of prosecutorial and judicial authorities in finding evidence, and the powers they can use for fact-finding, could, in theory, encourage victims to use the criminal justice system to hold MNEs accountable, especially when they cannot access evidence in the MNE's possession or have limited financial resources to conduct an extensive investigation. In practice however, prosecutorial and judicial authorities often struggle to find a sufficient amount of evidence in transnational cases against MNEs. Various reasons explain this situation. Evidence in third countries may be difficult to access as a result of the foreign authorities' refusal to cooperate with the home State's authorities. Prosecutorial and judicial authorities may also lack the financial resources or the technical expertise to gather evidence abroad.

Until now, most prosecutors have declined to prosecute MNEs on the grounds that access to evidence was, or was likely to be, unfeasible. In France, prosecutors have dismissed complaints for lack of evidence in several criminal claims against companies or executives of MNEs, including *DLH*. In the Netherlands, in *Riwal*, the Dutch prosecutor decided not to prosecute the companies and individuals targeted by the report for various reasons, including the difficulty of accessing evidence in Israel. In this respect, the prosecutor stated that:

> Necessary follow-up investigations would – also given the complexity of the case – consume a significant amount of resources of the police and/or the judiciary. It has been considered that further investigations in Israel would most probably not be possible due to lack of cooperation from the Israeli authorities. Given the above, the Public Prosecution Service will not conduct further investigations or prosecution of Lima Holding B.V. and its two managing directors for reasons of expediency. Their cases will be dismissed.[152]

In this case, the relevant information was held by a subsidiary of the corporation in Israel, and the Israeli authorities had refused to act on requests for legal assistance sent by the Dutch Public Prosecutor.[153]

In this context, the onus remains on victims to gather the evidence necessary for criminal litigation to take place. The role of victims in finding evidence is reinforced by the fact that they usually initiate criminal proceedings in transnational criminal claims against MNEs. Therefore, they must ensure that they have sufficient inculpatory evidence from the moment they report allegations of crimes to prosecutorial authorities or bring a civil action to join criminal proceedings. Often, victims have limited financial resources to

152 Letter of Dismissal from National Public Prosecutor's Office to Mr Van Eijck (14 May 2013).
153 Van Gelder and Ryngaert, 'Dutch Report on Prosecuting Corporations', 129.

gather evidence. As such, the intervention of NGOs in finding incriminatory information is crucial for ensuring that criminal proceedings can go ahead. However, it can create problems from an admissibility perspective.

NGOs have played an important role in gathering evidence that will be used in the context of criminal proceedings. However, scholars have suggested that prosecutorial authorities' reliance on information provided by NGOs is not without risk, especially for the admissibility of evidence.[154] This reflection resulted from the handling of evidence in *Kouwenhoven*. In this case, the National Police Agency, which conducted the criminal investigation, and the public prosecutor relied on information supplied by the NGO Global Witness. The Court of Appeal rebuked the prosecution for failing to test the dependability and accuracy of the witness statements and for having uncritically adopted the information provided by Global Witness. Because of the lack of transparency with regard to witness selection, there was a risk of manipulation of the investigation. Kouwenhoven's lawyer criticized the prosecutor for exclusively relying on witnesses provided by the same anonymous confidants used for the Global Witness Report.[155] As a result, the Court of Appeal acquitted Kouwenhoven. Huisman and van Sliedregt point out that

> the acquittal of Kouwenhoven by the Court of Appeal can be interpreted as a serious message to NGOs to be cautious when pointing the accusatory finger to individuals in public reports. This message should be taken to heart by national and international prosecutors and adjudicators as well, in particular the ICC where NGOs have been given an important role through the trigger mechanism and victim's participation. NGO reports provide a useful source of information, yet the risk of manipulation is very real.[156]

5 Punishment for corporate crime and remedies for victims

Until recently, criminal trials involving MNEs had never reached the trial phase. Therefore, no French or Dutch courts have ruled on the imposition of criminal punishments on companies or compensation for victims. However, an overview of potential criminal punishments imposed on companies and remedies for victims remains relevant for identifying the potential dissuasive

154 Huisman and van Sliedregt, 'Rogue Traders', 813.

155 Ibid.

156 Ibid.

effect of criminal sanctions incurred by companies and the remedies to which victims might be entitled. Other mechanisms, such as restorative justice, plea bargaining, and settlements, may constitute valuable alternatives to obtain remediation. They may however raise questions whether they interfere with the victims' quest for accountability and justice.

Criminal punishment for companies

Both France and the Netherlands recognize the criminal liability of legal persons, which include companies, and provide sanctions specifically applicable to them.

In France, when a company is found guilty of a crime or misdemeanour, it will generally incur a fine.[157] The maximum rate applicable to companies is five times that provided for natural persons by the law punishing the offence. In the case of a crime for which no fine is provided for natural persons, the fine incurred by legal persons must be €1 million. In some situations, companies can also incur other penalties, including dissolution where the legal person has been established or diverted from its purpose to commit the offence; prohibition from directly or indirectly exercising one or more professional or social activities; placement under judicial supervision; closure of one or more of the establishments of the company that were used to commit the incriminated acts; exclusion from public contracts; prohibition to make a public offer of financial securities or to have financial securities admitted to trading on a regulated market; prohibition on issuing cheques; confiscation; posting of the decision pronounced or its dissemination either by the written press or by any means of communication to the public by electronic means; or prohibition on receiving any public aid.[158] Most of these sanctions will apply either temporarily or permanently.

When the company commits corruption-related offences, it can be sentenced to submit to a compliance programme, under the supervision of the French Anti-Corruption Agency, for a maximum period of five years.[159] Furthermore, when a company commits a misdemeanour, the penalty of sanction-reparation may be imposed instead of, or at the same time as, the fine normally incurred.[160] This punishment is relevant in the context of transnational litigation against MNEs. Where it is imposed, the company will directly compensate the victim's loss. The victim and the company can agree that the reparation may be made in kind,

---

157 French Criminal Code, Article 131-37(1).
158 Ibid, Articles 131-37(2) and 131-39.
159 Ibid, Articles 131-37(2) and 131-39-2.
160 Ibid, Articles 131-37 and 137-39-1.

which may then consist of restoring property damaged during the commission of the offence.[161] However, the penalty of sanction-reparation cannot exceed €75,000 or the fine incurred by the legal person for the offence in question.

In the Netherlands, companies will often incur a fine when they are convicted of a criminal offence. Article 23 Criminal Code generally provides for six categories of fines ranging from €435 to €870,000. However, when legal persons, including companies, are convicted, the judge can impose a fine up to the amount of the next higher category if the category of fines determined for the offence does not allow suitable punishment. When the sixth category of fines is applicable and that category does not allow appropriate punishment, a fine may be imposed up to a maximum of 10 per cent of the company's annual turnover in the financial year prior to the judgment or penalty decision.[162] Other sanctions may be imposed on companies, such as withdrawal of certain rights, confiscation, and disclosure of the court judgment.[163] The Economic Offences Act (EOA) imposes a similar range of criminal sanctions for economic crimes.[164] It also provides additional penalties, such as the total or partial cessation of the business, forfeiture of objects, or confiscation of property belonging to the company.[165] Dutch courts can also impose interim measures, such as seizure of goods to safeguard the enforcement of payment of a fine or the confiscation of goods following a conviction by the court. Importantly, when a legal person commits a criminal offence, criminal punishments may be pronounced against not only the legal person but also the person(s) who ordered the offence, as well as those who gave actual direction for the prohibited conduct.[166]

France and the Netherlands offer a broad range of criminal sanctions against companies. Of interest here is the possibility to impose a fine up to a maximum of 10 per cent of the company's annual turnover in the financial year in the Netherlands. Furthermore, both countries allow for the punishment of the companies as well as the person(s) who ordered the offence. At the same time, the dissuasive effect of these sanctions is likely to be limited in the context of transnational litigation against MNEs. For instance, the highest level of fines remains low when compared with the benefits MNEs gain from committing crimes. Moreover, judges will not necessarily impose the highest penalty on the corporate perpetrator. These aspects raise the question whether existing punishments against companies are proportionate, and therefore appropriate, to dissuade MNEs from engaging in economically attractive criminal activities in the context of their group activities.

161 Ibid, Article 131-8-1.
162 Dutch Criminal Code, Article 23(7).
163 Ibid, Article 9(1)(b).
164 *Wet op de economische delicten*, Articles 5–16.
165 Ibid, Article 7.
166 Dutch Criminal Code, Article 51(2).

Remedies for victims

Criminal judges will generally focus on the remediation of the harm suffered by victims through awarding financial compensation.

In France, as previously mentioned, victims can bring a civil action to obtain reparation for damage suffered as a result of a criminal offence. This action is open to all those who have personally and directly suffered loss resulting from a criminal offence. A civil action is admissible on all counts of loss whether material, bodily, or moral, resulting from the facts which are the subject of the proceedings.[167] If the convicted offender does not voluntarily compensate the victim, the victim can seize the Victims of Crime Recovery Assistance Service (*Service d'Aide au Recouvrement des Victimes d'Infractions*, or SARVI). SARVI will pay the victim damages up to €1,000. Above that amount, it will pay an advance of 30 per cent, up to a ceiling of €3,000. SARVI then recovers the damages from the convicted person. The French State has also established a compensation fund for victims of crimes. The Compensation Fund for Victims of Acts of Terrorism and Other Offenses (*Fonds de Garantie des Victimes des Actes de Terrorisme et d'Autres Infractions*, or FGTI) originally compensated victims of terrorist acts. However, since 1990 it has also compensated victims of ordinary criminal offences, such as murder, rape and sexual assault, or offences resulting in permanent disability. To receive compensation from FGTI, a victim must meet specific conditions. If the offence was committed in France, compensation can be awarded to persons of French nationality, nationals of another EU Member State, or foreigners legally residing in France on the day of the events or of the application submitted to the FGTI. If the offence took place abroad, only French nationals can be compensated. This condition therefore limits the use of the FGTI in the context of transnational claims against MNEs.

Victim compensation in the context of criminal proceedings has been a focal point in Dutch criminal justice policy since 2000.[168] In principle, victims can only claim monetary compensation.[169] When the criminal court finds an offender guilty, it orders the convicted offender to pay the victim compensation. This compensation is usually financial, and the court specifies the exact amount victims must receive. Compensation should cover all property damage and any psychological damage that the court considers to be fair. Since 2011, the Dutch State has guaranteed full compensation to victims of a violent or sexual crime, and if the convicted offender has not compensated the victims within eight months, the State will then recover the amount from the convicted offender. Victims of violent crime can also apply for financial compensation from the State through the Compensation Fund for Violent Crime (*Schadefonds Geweldsmisdrijven*) within three years of the crime. There is no restriction

---

167 French Code of Criminal Procedure, Article 3.

168 Kool, Emaus, and van Uhm, 'The Victim's Right to Intervene', 82.

169 Dutch Criminal Code, Article 36f.

on third country nationals applying for compensation through the Fund. An interesting feature of compensation under the Dutch criminal system is that, since 2014, the State can seize assets, such as money and goods, from those suspected of a serious crime at an early stage of an investigation. These assets can subsequently be used to compensate the victims for damage suffered once the offender has been convicted (by a final conviction).

Alternative mechanisms

Restorative justice

Restorative justice has emerged as an alternative to the classical retributive model of court-based criminal justice.[170] A restorative justice process is any process in which the victim, the offender, and, where appropriate, any other individuals or community members affected by a crime participate together actively in the resolution of matters arising from the crime, generally with the help of a facilitator.[171] Restorative justice offers a number of benefits for the victim and the offender, as well as the State. It is likely to lead to lower rates of subsequent offending, and to be cost-effective in comparison to incarceration.[172] Restorative justice is well known in Canada and the US, where it has been in use for several decades.[173] Furthermore, restorative justice has shown to be relevant in post-conflict countries or countries which have experienced the commission of gross human rights violations on a large scale. In such countries, authorities may be faced with the difficult mission of achieving national reconciliation while answering legitimate demands for justice and reparation. Restorative justice may provide an adequate framework for restoring a balance between these competing demands.[174] Similarly, it has been argued that restorative justice is well positioned to address environmental crime.[175] Within the BHR field, there is emerging scholarship also arguing that restorative justice could be a suitable framework for providing effective remedies in the context of

170 On restorative justice, see Gerry Johnstone and Daniel Van Ness (eds), *Handbook of Restorative Justice* (Routledge 2013).

171 Yvon Dandurand and others, *Handbook on Restorative Justice Programmes* (UN 2006) 6.

172 'Restorative Justice: Investment Brief' (NZ, 2016).

173 Joanne Katz and Gene Bonham Jr, 'Restorative Justice in Canada and the United States: A Comparative Analysis' (2006) 6 Journal of the Institute of Justice and International Studies 187.

174 For a critical perspective on restorative justice in post-conflict countries or countries which have experienced gross human rights violations, see Lars Waldorf, 'Rwanda's Failing Experiment in Restorative Justice' in Dennis Sullivan and Larry Tifft (eds), *The Handbook of Restorative Justice: A Global Perspective* (Routledge 2006); Chris Cunneen, 'Exploring the Relationship between Reparations, the Gross Violation of Human Rights, and Restorative Justice' in Dennis Sullivan and Larry Tifft (eds), *The Handbook of Restorative Justice: A Global Perspective* (Routledge 2006).

175 Femke Wijdekop, 'Restorative Justice Responses to Environmental Harm' (IUCN, 2019).

corporate-related human rights abuses.[176] In Europe, the picture of restorative justice mechanisms varies among States.[177] While some countries have had restorative justice processes in place for some years (eg Belgium),[178] others have only recently started to experiment with restorative justice, such as France.

At the EU level, the Victims' Directive has been a game changer, as it requires all Member States to introduce restorative justice into their criminal justice system.[179] As a result, France amended its Code of Criminal Procedure in 2014 to include a provision on restorative justice. Article 10-1 now provides that, in the course of any criminal proceedings and at all stages of those proceedings, including the execution of the sentence, the victim and the perpetrator of an offence may be offered restorative justice measures provided that the facts have been established. A restorative justice measure is defined as 'any measure enabling a victim as well as the perpetrator of an offence to participate actively in the resolution of difficulties arising from the offence, including compensation for damage of any kind resulting from its commission'. Such a measure may only be taken after the victim and the perpetrator of the offence have received full information about it and have expressly consented to participate in it. It must be implemented by an independent and trained third party, under the supervision of the judicial authority or, at the request of the latter, the prison administration. It is confidential, unless otherwise agreed by the parties and except in cases where an overriding interest linked to the need to prevent or punish offences justifies that information relating to the progress of the measure be brought to the attention of the public prosecutor. Similarly, the Netherlands now provides the possibility of restorative justice.[180] Pursuant to Article 51a(1)(d) Dutch Code of Criminal Procedure, restorative justice enables the victim and the suspect or the convicted person, if they voluntarily agree, to actively participate in a process aimed at solving the consequences of the offence, with the help of an impartial third party.

---

176 Maximilian Schormair and Lara Gerlach, 'Corporate Remediation of Human Rights Violations: A Restorative Justice Framework' (2019) Journal of Business Ethics <https://doi.org/10.1007/s10551-019-04147-2> accessed 14 July 2021.

177 On restorative justice in Europe, see Christa Pelikan and Thomas Trenczek, 'Victim Offender Mediation and Restorative Justice: The European Landscape' in Dennis Sullivan and Larry Tifft (eds), *The Handbook of Restorative Justice: A Global Perspective* (Routledge 2006).

178 Ivo Aertson and Tony Peters, 'Mediation and Restorative Justice in Belgium' (1998) 6 European Journal on Criminal Policy and Research 507.

179 Victims' Directive, Article 12. For a critical perspective on restorative justice in the Victims' Directive, see Katrien Lauwaert, 'Restorative Justice in the 2012 EU Victims Directive: A Right to Quality Service, but No Right to Equal Access for Victims of Crime' (2013) https://doi.org/10.5235/20504721.1.3.414.

180 Antony Pemberton, 'Changing Frames? Restorative Justice in the Netherlands' in Inge Vanfraechem, Daniela Bolívar Fernández, and Ivo Aertsen, *Victims and Restorative Justice* (Routledge 2015).

Plea bargaining

A plea bargain, also called a guilty plea, is an arrangement between a prosecutor and a suspect and/or defendant in which the offender pleads guilty in exchange for an agreement by the prosecutor to recommend a more lenient sentence, to drop one or more charges, or to reduce the charge to a less serious offence. This agreement may allow both the prosecutor and the offender to avoid a trial. While plea bargaining has been praised for reducing enforcement costs and caseloads of courts, it has also been criticized for impairing the presumption of innocence and the rights of the defence.[181] Originally an American procedure, plea bargaining has become an important feature of some common law countries (UK) and has been transplanted in several civil law countries, such as France. Informal versions based on non-trial settlement also exist in various countries, including the Netherlands.[182]

In France, two types of plea bargains exist that may be relevant for transnational litigation against MNEs. First, the procedure of 'appearance on prior admission of guilt' (*comparution sur reconnaissance préalable de culpabilité*, or CRPC) was introduced in 2004.[183] The prosecutor may, of their own motion or at the request of the suspect, offer a CRPC where the suspect acknowledges the acts of which they are accused. This means the prosecutor will suggest that the suspect be subject to the standard criminal sanctions. If the suspect accepts the offer, a hearing takes place before a judge who will then decide to validate, refuse, or modify the sanctions. Victims must be informed of the CRPC, and they are invited to attend the hearing. They can join the proceedings as a civil party and ask for compensation for the loss they have suffered. The scope of CRPC is limited to specific misdemeanours; crimes are therefore excluded. Furthermore, offences pertaining to intentional and unintentional attacks on personal integrity and sexual assaults are also excluded. Importantly, the CRPC can apply to a legal person, which then has to be represented by a natural person in accordance with Article 7064-3 Code of Criminal Procedure.

The second type of plea bargain is called 'judicial agreement in the public interest' (*convention judiciaire d'intérêt public*, or CJIP).[184] It was introduced in 2016 to allow prosecutors to conclude an agreement with legal persons accused of offences against probity. A CJIP may impose one or more obligations upon the legal person. First, the legal person may be obliged to pay a fine set in proportion to the benefits derived from the criminal offences. This fine should

---

181 Nuno Garoupa and Stephen Frank, 'Why Plea-Bargaining Fails to Achieve Results in So Many Criminal Justice Systems: A New Framework for Assessment' (2008) 15 Maastricht Journal of European and Comparative Law 323.

182 Ibid.

183 French Code of Criminal Procedure, Articles 495-7 to 495-16.

184 Loi n° 2016-1691 du 9 décembre 2016 relative à la transparence, à la lutte contre la corruption et à la modernisation de la vie économique, Article 22; Article 41-1-2 French Code of Criminal Procedure governs CJIPs.

be up to a limit of 30 per cent of the average annual turnover calculated on the last three annual turnover figures known on the date of the observation of such breaches. Second, the legal person must submit, for a maximum period of three years and under the supervision of the French Anti-Corruption Agency, to a compliance programme designed to ensure the existence and implementation of various measures to prevent criminal activities by the legal person.[185] Importantly, the procedure leading to a CJIP allows for victim participation. Where the victim is identified, and unless the legal person can prove that it has already remedied the damage, the CJIP must provide compensation for the damage caused by the offence within one year. The victim is informed of the public prosecutor's decision to propose the conclusion of a CJIP to the legal person in question, and must transmit to the public prosecutor any information to establish the reality and extent of the loss. Following the hearing of both the legal person and the victim, a judge then decides whether to validate or reject the CJIP. The public prosecutor must launch criminal proceedings in a situation where the judge rejects the CJIP.

Both CRPC and CJIP allow victims to claim compensation for the loss they suffered as a result of the criminal offence. They can provide victims with a fast-track route for obtaining remediation in comparison with traditional criminal proceedings, which can last for years. While the limited scope of the CRPC to certain misdemeanours is likely to limit its pertinence to transnational litigation against MNEs, CJIPs apply to a number of white-collar crimes – mainly bribery and influence-peddling, obstruction of justice, tax fraud, laundering of tax money, or falsifying business records – which are relevant for crimes committed by MNEs. In past criminal claims, victims have accused companies of committing some of these white-collar crimes (eg *Rougier*). In addition, one interesting feature of CJIPs is that they must be made public on the website of the French Anti-Corruption Agency. This provision guarantees that corporate wrongdoing does not go unnoticed. However, the very nature of CRPC and CJIP may limit their added-value for victims mainly interested in holding MNEs liable for their wrongdoing. A validation of a CRPC or a CJIP does not result in a conviction and does not have the nature or the effects of a conviction judgment. Furthermore, they carry more lenient sentences for legal persons, which limits the deterrent effect of criminal enforcement. More generally, plea bargaining may impair the public interest in effective punishment of crime.[186]

In the Netherlands, there is no plea bargaining as such. However, criminal cases may be settled out of court through a so-called 'transaction' (*transactie*). The prosecutor will negotiate an out-of-court settlement with a suspect in which the suspect agrees to meet certain conditions, such as to pay a fine and/ or to compensate the victim, in order to avoid being prosecuted and tried

---

185 French Code of Criminal Procedure, Article 131-39-2.

186 Stephen J. Schulhofer, 'Plea Bargaining as Disaster' (1992) 101 The Yale Law Journal 1979.

by a court. A transaction is a consensual agreement between two parties to avoid prosecution; it does not involve an admission of guilt or the approval of a court. If the offer of an out-of-court settlement by means of a transaction is rejected or ignored by the suspect, the prosecutor must charge the defendant and bring them to trial.[187]

Out-of-court settlements

To date, plaintiffs and MNEs have rarely concluded out-of-court settlements in France or the Netherlands, unlike parties in various transnational claims against MNEs in common law countries. The only existing instance of out-of-court settlement took place in the context of the French criminal litigation brought against Total for gross human rights abuse in Myanmar.[188] Total agreed to pay €10,000 to each plaintiff in exchange for the withdrawal of the complaint. In addition, the company pledged to create a fund of €5.2 million to implement humanitarian and development projects.[189] Although out-of-court settlements allow for rapid remediation for victims, they are nevertheless problematic from the point of view of access to justice. This aspect is explored in Chapter 3 of this book.

6 Conclusions

This chapter has explored how French and Dutch criminal law and procedure affect opportunities for victims of extraterritorial crimes involving businesses to seek justice in France and the Netherlands. It showed that victims of extraterritorial or international crimes committed by MNEs face important procedural obstacles when seeking justice through criminal courts.

In general, the traditional jurisdictional principles under criminal law appear to be inadequate to ensure the prosecution of MNEs when they commit crimes in an extraterritorial or transnational context. In France and the Netherlands, the territoriality principle remains relevant when one of the constituent elements of the crime was committed on their territory or when a domestic company was complicit in a crime committed in a host country. However, a number of requirements must be met, including double criminality and a foreign court's final judgment, which have made the prosecution of companies difficult so far. French and Dutch laws also recognize the existence of alternative principles of jurisdiction based on the nationality of the perpetrator or of the victim, or the

---

187 Pauline Jacobs and Petra van Kampen, 'Dutch "ZSM Settlements" in the Face of Procedural Justice: The Sooner the Better?' (2014) 10 Utrecht Law Review 73, 73.

188 Olivier de Schutter, 'Les affaires Total et Unocal: complicité et extraterritorialité dans l'imposition aux entreprises d'obligations en matière de droits de l'homme' (2006) 52 Annuaire français de droit international, 70.

189 'Annual Report 2006' (Sherpa 2 May 2007) 2.

necessity to prosecute perpetrators of gross human rights abuses. Among them, the active nationality principle appears to be the most justifiable jurisdictional ground for regulating the conduct of French and Dutch companies in host countries. Nonetheless, procedural requirements and institutional obstacles limit the opportunities offered by the French and Dutch criminal systems to hold members of MNEs accountable for crimes in host States.

As a result of the application of the principle of opportunity, the public prosecutor enjoys broad discretion to initiate prosecution in France and the Netherlands. This may be problematic, as prosecutors are generally reluctant to sue MNEs for human rights abuse or environmental pollution taking place in host countries. However, French law allows victims and NGOs to play a predominant role in criminal proceedings. At EU level, the Victims' Rights Directive has reinforced the role and ability of victims to participate in criminal proceedings.

As in civil cases, access to evidence remains a thorny problem in the context of transnational criminal litigation against MNEs. As a result of the burden of proof on prosecutorial authorities, the prosecutor usually has the main role in gathering and requesting evidence. However, in practice this does not relieve victims of the burden of gathering the evidence necessary to demonstrate a company's involvement in a crime. The difficulty in accessing relevant incriminatory evidence will often result in the prosecutor deciding not to investigate further or to prosecute alleged crimes committed by MNEs abroad. Victims and NGOs must therefore play an important role in gathering evidence before and during criminal proceedings in order to ensure the prosecution of MNEs. However, evidence gathered by victims and NGOs may not meet admissibility standards required under criminal procedure.

France and the Netherlands offer a broad range of criminal sanctions against companies. However, the dissuasive effect of these sanctions is likely to be limited in the context of transnational litigation against MNEs, as the highest level of fines remains low when compared with the benefits that some crimes committed by MNEs can generate. Furthermore, remedies for victims tend to focus on the award of financial compensation to the detriment of other relevant remedies, such as environmental remediation. These two aspects show that a reflection of appropriate sanctions and remedies under criminal law might be needed in France and the Netherlands. Finally, other mechanisms, such as restorative justice, plea bargaining, and settlements, may constitute valuable alternatives for obtaining remediation. They may, however, raise questions regarding their interference with the victims' quest for accountability and justice.

In conclusion, French and Dutch criminal law and procedure are currently insufficient to address the challenges posed by economic actors committing crimes in a transnational context.

The next chapter analyses the rules governing the liability of corporate groups in areas directly relevant to human rights and environmental protection.

Chapter 6
Holding multinational enterprises liable in France and the Netherlands

1 Introduction

Corporate liability standards for punishing human rights abuse and environmental damage occurring in the context of corporate group activities are crucial to the success of transnational claims against MNEs. However, legal barriers can arise where the way in which liability is attributed among members of a corporate group under domestic laws facilitates the avoidance of appropriate accountability.[1] As a result, such barriers may prevent legitimate cases from being addressed, thus leading to corporate impunity. In France and the Netherlands, a number of plaintiffs have sought to hold parent companies liable for their direct or indirect involvement in activities harmful to humans and the environment in host countries. In most instances, cause-lawyers and CSOs litigating these cases have attempted to demonstrate the absence of an effective regime of liability applying to MNEs. They have also demonstrated the inequality arising from the benefits relating to the corporate form, such as 'the limited liability for its members and a legal personality separate from that of its members',[2] when business-related abuse occurs in the context of corporate groups.

It is important to make a few clarifications before starting the analysis. First, this chapter mainly explores how liability can be attributed to the parent company for harm resulting from its subsidiaries' activities. It does not specifically investigate the liability of a company which may arise as a result of damage occurring in the context of its subcontractor's activities or in joint ventures. Second, in the context of transnational civil litigation against MNEs, the law of the host State generally applies to the facts of the claim as a result of the Rome II Regulation. Consequently, it is less likely that French or Dutch corporate liability standards will apply to these claims. Nonetheless, the

---

1   UNHRC, 'Guiding Principles on Business and Human Rights: Implementing the United Nations "Protect, Respect and Remedy" Framework' (21 March 2011) UN Doc A/HRC/17/31, GP 26, Commentary.

2   UNHRC, 'Human Rights and Corporate Law: Trends and Observations from a Cross-National Study Conducted by the Special-Representative' (2 May 2011) UN Doc A/HRC/17/31/Add.2, para 29.

Rome II Regulation creates a number of exceptions which allow plaintiffs to choose the law of the home State (ie French or Dutch law) as the applicable law. As a result, the study of corporate liability standards in France and the Netherlands remains relevant. Third, France and the Netherlands have recently enacted legislation imposing mandatory HRDD obligations on companies that may be directly relevant to corporate liability standards. A detailed analysis of these new legal regimes is provided in Chapter 7 of this book.

2 Challenges to establishing the liability of MNEs

In order to understand the issues surrounding MNE's liability for human rights violations and environmental pollution, one must understand the legal complexity of corporate groups under French and Dutch company law. The absence of a legal definition of the 'corporate group' as well as the existence of the separate legal personality of a company and the nature of limited liability companies pose problems in holding MNEs liable.

MNEs as corporate groups

Before delving into the subject of corporate group liability, it is important to first define what the corporate group is. Vandekerckhove broadly defines the corporate group as 'an aggregate of legally independent corporations that are related to each other through patrimonial, contractual or personal links and that come under a common centre of control'.[3] She explains that:

> the corporate group is one of the forms of concentration of companies. Such a concentration may be the result of very different evolutions. The group may have grown through new incorporations or other forms of establishment abroad. It may also have grown by way of international mergers and acquisitions or through joint ventures. Groups are further characterised by their organisational structure, the territorial distances between group members, ownership pattern, intensity of intra-group transactions, profitability, and technical circumstances. This results in the existence of very different types of groups, from highly centralised to decentralised, from very specialised to largely diversified.[4]

---

3   Karen Vandekerckhove, *Piercing the Corporate Veil* (Kluwer Law International 2007) 17.
4   Ibid.

There is no statutory definition of the 'corporate group' in France,[5] and the responsibility to define or deal with the corporate group has been left to the French courts. In general, French courts recognize the 'interest of the group.' However, different definitions have been adopted by the courts in different areas of law. For example, the Commercial Chamber of the Court of Cassation has held that a corporate group is characterized by economic unity and a community of indivisible interests led by one person.[6] On the other hand, for the Criminal Chamber of the Court of Cassation, a corporate group exists when its companies share a common economic, social, or financial interest (*intérêt économique, social, ou financier commun*), which must be appreciated with regard to the policies developed for the whole group.[7] While these definitions reflect the priorities of the various legal branches, they show a lack of consistency.

Although there is no statutory definition of the corporate group, the French Commercial Code describes how companies may be linked to each other through financial ownership or control.[8] Generally, where a company owns more than 50 per cent of the capital of another company, the second company is to be regarded as a subsidiary (*filiale*) of the first company (Article L233-1). Furthermore, where a company owns between 10 and 50 per cent of the capital of another company, the first company shall be regarded as having a participation (*ayant une participation*) in the second company (Article L233-2).

In the context of listed companies and for specific purposes,[9] any person, whether natural or legal (such as a company), is deemed to control another one in various situations, namely where: (1) it directly or indirectly holds a fraction of the capital that gives it a majority of the voting rights at that company's general meetings; (2) it holds a majority of the voting rights in that company by virtue of an agreement; (3) it effectively determines the decisions taken at that company's general meetings through its voting rights; or (4) it is a partner in or shareholder of that company and has the power to appoint or dismiss the majority of the members of that company's administrative, management, or supervisory structures (Article L233-3(I)). Furthermore, a person is presumed

---

5   Pierre-Henri Conac, 'National Report on France' in Rafael Mariano Manóvil (ed), *Groups of Companies: A Comparative Law Overview* (Springer 2020) 87–88.

6   Cass com 5 February 1985, n° 82-15.119.

7   Cass crim 4 February 1985, n° 84-91581 (*Rozenblum*). See also Clarisse Le Gunehec, 'Le fait justificatif tiré de la notion de groupe de sociétés dans le droit pénal français de l'abus de biens sociaux' (1987) 58 Revue internationale de droit pénal 117.

8   See Chapter III of Title III of Book II of the Legislative Part of the French Commercial Code, which governs subsidiaries, participations, and controlled companies.

9   Article L233-3 applies for the purposes of Section 2 on notifications and information and Section 4 on cross-shareholding of Chapter III of Title III of Book II of the Legislative Part of the French Commercial Code.

to exert control when it directly or indirectly holds a fraction of the voting rights above 40 per cent and no other partner, member, or shareholder directly or indirectly holds a fraction larger than its own (Article L233-3(II)). Finally, two or more persons acting in concert shall be regarded as jointly controlling another when, in fact, they determine the decisions taken at the general assembly (Article L233-3(III)). Ultimately, Article L233-3 deals with different types of control: *de jure* or de facto control, exclusive or with other partners.[10]

There is also a definition of control applicable to accounting matters. Article L233-16(I) French Commercial Code provides that companies must, on an annual basis, draw up and publish consolidated accounts and a group management report for any company which they control, either solely or jointly. Article L233-16(II) provides that sole control of a company exists where: (1) a majority of its voting rights are held by another company; (2) a majority of the members of its board of directors, management board, or supervisory board are appointed by another company for two consecutive financial years;[11] and (3) a dominant interest is exerted over the company by virtue of a contract or the terms and conditions of its memorandum and articles of association, when the applicable law allows this. Furthermore, according to Article L233-16(III), joint control exists where the control of a company operated jointly by a limited number of partners or shareholders is shared and decisions are made on the basis of an agreement between them.

In contrast to French law, Dutch company law provides a general definition of the 'group' in Article 2:24b Dutch Civil Code. According to this provision, a 'group is an economic unit in which legal persons and commercial partnerships are organizationally interconnected. Group companies are legal persons and commercial partnerships interconnected in one group.'[12] This definition applies to all types of legal persons, and foreign company types may also form part of a group.[13] According to Dutch scholars, an important feature of a group, which is not included in this definition, is central management.[14] This concept is difficult to define, as it depends on factual circumstances. However, central management will generally be present 'when there is a joint strategy that forms the basis for the dissemination of plans and coordination of a strategy at lower levels within the group'.[15] The definition found under Article 2:24b is referred

10   Conac, 'National Report on France', 90.

11   In this situation, the consolidating company is deemed to have made this designation when, during that period, it held more than 40 per cent of the voting rights and no other partner or shareholder held, directly or indirectly, a fraction greater than its own.

12   Author's translation.

13   Mieke Olaerts, 'National Report on the Netherlands' in Rafael Mariano Manóvil (ed), *Groups of Companies: A Comparative Law Overview* (Springer 2020) 426.

14   Ibid.

15   Ibid, 426–427.

to as the economic definition of the group concept in Dutch law, as it refers to actual control being exercised and economic unity within the group, rather than the power to control merely being available.

In contrast, the definition of 'subsidiary' refers to the power to control and therefore provides a more legal definition.[16] Article 2:24a(1) Dutch Civil Code defines a subsidiary (*dochtermaatschappij*) as a legal person:

(1)   in which another legal person, either directly or through one or more subsidiaries, whether or not on the basis of a contract with others entitled to vote, may exercise, solely or jointly, more than half of the voting rights at the general meeting; or

(2)   of which another legal person, either directly or through one or more subsidiaries, whether or not on the basis of a contract with others entitled to vote, is a member or shareholder that may appoint or dismiss, solely or jointly, more than half of the managing directors or supervisory board (assuming all votes are cast).

Based on this definition, most legal persons can qualify as a subsidiary, and foreign companies can also qualify as subsidiaries.[17] It is generally accepted that, in most cases, there will be a group relationship where there is a subsidiary.[18] Importantly, a group relationship does not require a capital investment. It may be established by means of a contractual relationship (eg on the basis of a contract establishing personal unions between two legal persons).[19]

In addition, Dutch company law provides a definition of 'participation' (or participating interest). Pursuant to Article 2:24c(1) Dutch Civil Code, a legal person has a participation in another legal person where it, either directly or through one or more subsidiaries for its own account, solely or jointly, has provided or has caused the provision of the capital of the second legal person with the aim of having a long-term association with the second company for the benefit of its own activities. Participation is presumed where the legal person holds one-fifth or more of the issued capital.

Finally, Dutch company law provides the existence of dependent companies, which are legal persons to which a public or private limited liability company or one of its dependent companies has provided, for its own account, either solely or jointly, at least one-half of the issued share capital.[20] Here, participation

---

16   Ibid, 427.
17   Ibid, 428.
18   Ibid.
19   Ibid.
20   Dutch Civil Code, Articles 2:152 and 2:262.

through share capital is required, and providing half of the issued capital is sufficient.[21]

This overview of the definition(s) of the 'group' in France and the Netherlands shows that French and Dutch company legislation generally lacks a definition of the group that takes into account its legal reality. That being said, French and Dutch law addresses the group through various capital or control relationships that may develop between companies. For example, they recognize the existence of subsidiaries or controlled or dependent companies. They do not, however, define the parent company. More importantly, the group is not recognized as a separate legal entity in both countries. In France, the Court of Cassation recognized that the group has no legal personality,[22] which means that the group is not recognized as a unified business legal entity.[23] In the Netherlands, the single entity is the starting point of Dutch company law, and the group is not recognized as a separate legal entity.[24] One consequence of this lack of legal personality is that groups cannot have rights and obligations or be bound to pay damages. Therefore, the liability resulting from any obligations belonging to entities of the group shall be borne by those entities.

Separate legal personality and limited liability within MNEs

The principles of separate legal personality of the company and limited liability of shareholders are two important aspects of modern company law.[25] They are applied at national level by a large number of jurisdictions through either domestic legislation and/or case law.[26] In the context of this book, 'separate legal personality' means that some types of companies become autonomous legal entities once they are incorporated. As such, they exercise rights and assume certain obligations. The law ignores the artificial nature of these companies by giving them a legal personality which is separate from that of the persons who manage it (directors) or own it (shareholders when the company is limited by shares).[27] Furthermore, there is 'limited liability' when, for certain types of companies, the liability of investors, owners, or shareholders

21   Olaerts, 'National Report on the Netherlands', 430.

22   Cass com 2 April 1996, n° 94-16.380; Cass com 15 November 2011, n° 10-21.701 (*Sté JCB Service (FD)*).

23   Conac, 'National Report on France', 91.

24   Olaerts, 'National Report on the Netherlands', 423, 426.

25   Alan Dignam and John Lowry, *Company Law* (5th edn, OUP 2009) 14. See also John Birds and others, *Boyle & Birds' Company Law* (8th edn, Jordans 2011); Brenda Hannigan, *Company Law* (3rd edn, OUP 2012).

26   UNHRC, 'Human Rights and Corporate Law', para 32.

27   On the separate legal personality of the company, see Paddy Ireland, 'Capitalism without the Capitalist: The Joint Stock Company Share and the Emergence of the Modern Doctrine of Separate Corporate Personality' (1996) 17 Legal History 40.

is limited to the amount of their investment, contribution, or shares in the company.[28] Both principles are of crucial importance for companies, especially MNEs. The principle of separate legal personality allows the company to act on its own while insulating the persons participating in the business (whether natural or legal persons) from personal liability. Furthermore, the principle of limited liability is essential to the proper operation of corporations in the market. Muchlinski states:

> Given its capacity to reduce investment risk through the separation of corporate assets and those of its owners and promoters, limited liability is said to encourage entrepreneurship, to reduce monitoring costs for investors and creditors and to ensure the promotion of the market for corporate control by reducing the cost of shares.[29]

However, both separate legal personality and limited liability may pose problems in the context of corporate groups – including MNEs – especially where one company owns and controls another.[30] They generally prevent one MNE member from being held liable for the activity of another member of the same MNE, even when the former member owns and controls the latter one. For instance, the parent company may be the shareholder, or one of the shareholders, of a subsidiary and, at the same time, control or be engaged in the business activities of that subsidiary. In such a situation, the application of separate legal personality and limited liability often shield the parent company from liability for human rights abuse and environmental damage committed through its subsidiary.[31] A parent company will not be liable for the harm caused by its subsidiary, even when the parent company owns and controls the subsidiary.[32] MNEs may use complex and confusing corporate structures to distance and separate the parent company from the local operating subsidiaries, thereby protecting the MNE from legal liability.[33]

28   There is no general definition of limited liability and the application of this principle varies across jurisdictions. Furthermore, limited liability is not unique to corporations. On the subject, see Phillip Blumberg, 'Limited Liability and Corporate Groups' (1986) 11 Journal of Corporate Law 573; Frank Easterbrook and Daniel Fischel, 'Limited Liability and the Corporation' (1985) 52 The University of Chicago Law Review 89.

29   Peter Muchlinski, 'Limited Liability and Multinational Enterprises: A Case for Reform?' (2010) 34 Cambridge Journal of Economics 915, 915.

30   On the interplay between corporate groups, separate legal personality, and limited liability, see Phillip Blumberg, *The Multinational Challenge to Corporation Law: The Search for a New Corporate Personality* (OUP 1993); Janet Dine, *The Governance of Corporate Groups* (CUP 2005).

31   Muchlinski, 'Limited Liability and Multinational Enterprises', 917.

32   Ibid.

33   Richard Meeran, 'The Unveiling of Transnational Corporations: A Direct Approach' in Michael Addo (ed), *Human Rights Standards and the Responsibility of Transnational Corporations* (Kluwer Law International 1999) 162; Charley Hannoun, 'La responsabilité environnementale des sociétés-mères' (2009) 6 Environnement 33.

Scholars have criticized the strict application of separate legal personality and limited liability where human rights abuse or environmental damage are involved.[34] They have also suggested that the traditional image of the company as 'an isolated and free-standing commercial entity with a sole aim of making profit, often at any cost' should be revised. Policy-makers should recognize that companies are integrated parts of society and that their economic persona should not be separated from their social and political persona.[35] Problems with the application of separate legal personality and limited liability have been particularly visible in the context of transnational claims against MNEs, where plaintiffs have repeatedly challenged the relationship between the parent company based in a home country and foreign subsidiaries under its control or ownership operating in host countries.[36]

The technique of piercing the corporate veil may provide a solution for limiting unfair consequences for victims of MNE abuse. The expression 'piercing the corporate veil', or corporate veil piercing, emerged from the lexicon of company law. It refers to the situation where a corporate shareholder is held liable for the debts of the company of which it is a shareholder notwithstanding separate legal personality and limited liability.[37] Some commentators have argued that corporate veil piercing should be extended to cases raising human rights abuse or environmental damage by MNEs through amendments to national company laws.[38] However, piercing the corporate veil is a problematic solution for a number of reasons. First, it involves judicial discretion,[39] and scholars have argued that criteria for corporate veil piercing are not very clear-cut. It may also be very difficult to establish the factual relation required to pierce the corporate veil.[40] Furthermore, complex corporate structures, coupled with the use of separate legal personality and limited liability, have

34   See Paddy Ireland, 'Limited Liability, Shareholder Rights and the Problem of Corporate Irresponsibility Limited Liability' (2010) 34 Cambridge Journal of Economics 837; Ian Lee, 'Corporate Criminal Responsibility as Team Member Responsibility' (2011) 31 Oxford Journal of Legal Studies 755. For a study of transnational asbestos companies' use of corporate law to escape liability, see also Andrea Boggio, 'Linking Corporate Power to Corporate Structures: An Empirical Analysis' (2012) 22 Social and Legal Studies 107.

35   Michael Addo, 'Human Rights and Transnational Corporations: An Introduction' in Michael Addo (ed), *Human Rights Standards and the Responsibility of Transnational Corporations* (Kluwer Law International 1999) 8.

36   In some claims, plaintiffs have challenged the liability of a company in the context of business relationships different from that existing between a parent company and its subsidiary.

37   Vandekerckhove, *Piercing the Corporate Veil*, 11.

38   Peter Muchlinski, 'Implementing the New UN Corporate Human Rights Framework: Implications for Corporate Law, Governance, and Regulation' (2011) 22 Business Ethics Quarterly 145, 152.

39   Ibid.

40   Nicola Jägers and Marie-José Van Der Heijden, 'Corporate Human Rights Violations: The Feasibility of Civil Recourse in the Netherlands' (2008) 33 Brooklyn Journal of International Law 833, 842.

an influence on the legal strategies used by plaintiffs to hold MNEs to account. For instance, limited liability forces plaintiffs to focus on acts or omissions of parent companies rather than seeking to pierce the corporate veil. However, an emphasis on parent companies limits the potential for holding accountable corporate groups that operate under a vertically hierarchical management structure. In more complex management structures, it is even harder to match existing legal principles of negligence to the reality of control.[41] In addition, there is a lot of confusion as to the exact meaning of corporate veil piercing. For instance, courts often do not distinguish between statutory rules and corporate veil piercing theories when they hold parent companies liable. As a result, parent companies are sometimes held liable based on corporate veil piercing theories where the case could have been solved by reference to existing rules of company or civil law.[42] Finally, corporate veil piercing theories are less developed outside common law countries.

Separate legal personality and limited liability in France and the Netherlands

Both France and the Netherlands apply these principles through statutory law. First of all, pursuant to French and Dutch law, a number of business forms, including corporate entities, have their own legal personality. In France, Article 1842 French Civil Code states that partnerships (*sociétés*)[43] enjoy legal personality from the time of their registration.[44] Furthermore, Article L210-6 French Commercial Code (*Code de commerce*) provides that trading companies (*sociétés commerciales*), which include limited liability companies (*sociétés à responsabilité limitée*) and joint-stock companies (*sociétés anonymes*),[45] shall have legal personality with effect from their registration in the commercial and companies register. Therefore, once a trading company is registered, it has a legal personality separate from that of its shareholders, directors, or officers. In the Netherlands, Article 2:3 Dutch Civil Code provides that a number of companies possess legal personality, including public limited companies

---

41   Halina Ward, 'Securing Transnational Corporate Accountability through National Courts: Implications and Policy Options' (2001) 24 Hastings International and Comparative Law Review 451, 470.

42   Vandekerckhove, *Piercing the Corporate Veil*, 11.

43   Pursuant to Article 1832 French Civil Code, a 'partnership is created by two or several persons who agree by a contract to appropriate property or their industry for a common venture with a view to sharing the benefit or profiting from the saving which may result therefrom' (author's translation). The partners bind themselves to contribute to the losses.

44   However, partnerships that are not registered do not enjoy legal personality. See French Civil Code, Article 1871.

45   French Commercial Code, Article L210-1.

(*naamloze vennootschappen* or NV) and private limited companies (*besloten vennootschappen* or BV). Both types of companies are legal persons with an authorized capital divided into transferable shares.[46]

The application of separate legal personality to MNEs means that a (parent) company that owns or controls another company belonging to the same group, whether a subsidiary or a controlled or dependent company, or through a participation in that company, cannot be held liable for the obligations of that company. According to French case law, companies operating as part of a corporate group remain separate legal persons.[47] Courts have held that a subsidiary must be regarded as an autonomous company, solely responsible for the consequences of its activities. Despite the close links that may exist between a parent company and its subsidiary, the latter is legally distinct from the natural and legal persons of which it is composed, irrespective of the size of the participation of the parent company in the capital of its subsidiary or the existence of common directors.[48] Similarly, under Dutch law, each company within the group has separate legal personality and is therefore responsible for its own obligations.[49]

Moreover, in France and the Netherlands, for certain types of companies, the liability of investors, owners, or shareholders is limited to the amount of their investment, contribution, or shares in the company. In France, Article L223-1 French Commercial Code states that a limited liability company may be established by one or more persons who shall bear their losses only up to their contributions. Furthermore, Article L225-1 French Commercial Code provides that a joint-stock company is a company whose capital is divided into shares and which is formed among members who shall bear any losses only up to their contributions. In the Netherlands, in both public and private limited companies, shareholders shall not be personally liable for acts performed on behalf of the company and shall not be liable to contribute to company losses exceeding the amount to be paid on their shares.[50]

One potential issue with limited liability entities is that they may be used to avoid liabilities. For example, an operator of a hazardous activity may carry out its activity through a limited liability entity in order to avoid having to bear the full cost of environmental damage. This problem may be exacerbated in the context of corporate groups. The use of limited liability entities in corporate group structures, where a (parent) company may be a shareholder

---

46   Dutch Civil Code, Articles 2:64(1) and 2:175(1).
47   Cass com 18 October 1994, n° 92-21.199.
48   CA Paris, 31 May 1989 D 1989 IR 227.
49   Olaerts, 'National Report on the Netherlands', 442.
50   Dutch Civil Code, Articles 2:64(1) and 2:175(1).

of another company of the group, may create difficulties for voluntary or involuntary creditors seeking to recover losses or obtain compensation.[51] If the company does not have sufficient assets to cover its liability, the assets of its shareholders, whether natural or legal persons, may be affected only to the extent of the value of their shares in the company.[52] This situation may create an incentive for corporate groups to externalize risks and, therefore, avoid liability by organizing themselves in such a way that the burden of hazardous or unsafe activities is borne by companies that might turn out to be insolvent.

Nonetheless, there may be specific circumstances where courts may disregard separate legal personality and limited liability in order to hold the parent company liable for the obligations of the companies it owns or controls.

3 Bases for liability of the parent company

There are several situations in which a parent company may be held liable for the obligations of its subsidiary in the context of MNEs' activities. This section explores the legal grounds for holding parent companies liable in different areas of law and, where relevant, describes how these grounds have applied in transnational cases against MNEs for human rights violations and environmental pollution.

Corporate veil piercing

In certain situations, courts may set aside separate legal personality and limited liability to hold the shareholder, which may be the parent company, liable for the actions or debts of the company of which it is a shareholder. This situation is called 'corporate veil piercing.'[53] While corporate veil piercing may be accepted in exceptional cases under company law, it is generally applied where a subsidiary is wholly-owned by its parent company under competition law.

Company law

In French and Dutch company law, courts may exceptionally pierce the corporate veil to hold the parent company liable for the obligations of its subsidiary, most notably to protect the creditors of the subsidiary in the

51   Muchlinski distinguishes between *voluntary* creditors, who entered into a contract with the company, and *involuntary* creditors, who suffered injury caused by the actions of the company. See Muchlinski, 'Limited Liability and Multinational Enterprises', 918.

52   Ibid.

53   Vandekerckhove, *Piercing the Corporate Veil*, 11; Lucas Bergkamp and Wan-Q Pak, 'Piercing the Corporate Veil: Shareholder Liability for Corporate Torts' (2001) 8 Maastricht Journal of European and Comparative Law 167, 168.

context of insolvency or bankruptcy proceedings. However, courts are usually reluctant to do so.

France

In France, corporate veil piercing may, in certain circumstances, be possible on the basis of statutory law and theories developed by the courts.

One statutory provision for piercing the corporate veil is Article L621-2 French Commercial Code on safeguarding proceedings (*procédures de sauvegarde*) under insolvency law.[54] These proceedings may be extended to one or more other persons where their assets are intermingled with those of the debtor, or where the legal entity is a sham. Article L621-2 provides for the application of two types of corporate veil piercing theories. The first one is the theory of 'commingling of assets' (*confusion de patrimoine*), which applies when it is no longer possible to distinguish between the assets of the parent company and those of its subsidiary.[55] The second one is the theory of the 'fictitious legal person' (*fictivité de la personne morale*), which provides that a legal person is deemed to be fictitious where its sole purpose is to serve the interests of the natural or legal person behind it, and that person is engaging in high-risk activities under the cover of separate legal personality and limited liability.[56] Both theories involve the notion of fraud.[57]

French courts have shown a strong reluctance to pierce the corporate veil on the basis of commingling of assets in cases of relationships within a group. The Court of Cassation usually requires the existence of 'abnormal financial relationships'.[58] For example, it refused to pierce the corporate veil in *Theetten v SA Metaleurop* on the grounds that cash-pooling, staff exchanges, and fund advances by the parent company did not automatically reveal abnormal financial relationships that constituted a commingling between the assets and liabilities of the parent company and those of its subsidiary.[59] In a corporate group, these acts may be justified. This case law is likely to make it even more difficult to prove a commingling of assets in a transnational case.[60]

---

54 'Safeguarding proceedings' are insolvency proceedings that protect companies with debt problems by suspending the payment of debts and facilitating the reorganization of the business.

55 Cass com 13 February 2001, n° 98-15190.

56 Vandekerckhove, *Piercing the Corporate Veil*, 42. See Cass com 2 December 1997, n° 95-17.624; Cass com 5 April 1994, n° 93-15.956.

57 Juan Dobson, 'Lifting the Veil in Four Countries: The Law of Argentina, England, France and the United States' (1986) 35 International and Comparative Law Quarterly 839, 841.

58 Conac, 'National Report on France', 101–102.

59 Cass com 19 April 2005, n°05-10.094.

60 Vandekerckhove, *Piercing the Corporate Veil*, 439.

French courts may also ignore the application of separate legal personality and limited liability in the context of a corporate group on the basis of the theory of 'interference' (*immixtion*). A parent company can be held liable in respect of its subsidiary's creditors when it has interfered in the activities and the management of its subsidiary.[61] If a parent company makes decisions for its subsidiary, the latter cannot be considered an autonomous legal entity. Generally, French courts use 'indicators' (*faisceau d'indices*) to determine, on a case-by-case basis, whether there is interference. In one case, the Court of Cassation found that similarities between two companies (such as telephone numbers, email addresses, head offices, or managers), important cash flows between them, and the intervention of the parent company's technicians in the context of a contract between the subsidiary and a third party pointed to interference.[62] However, French courts are reluctant to recognize such interference.[63] Corporate groups often share a common strategy, which makes it difficult to assess the degree of the parent company's interference in the management of its subsidiary.[64]

In addition, French courts may use the theory of 'appearance' (*apparence*) to hold the parent company liable for its subsidiary's acts. This theory enables the contractual commitment made by one group company to be binding on another in order to protect the co-contracting third party who acted in good faith. In the event of insolvency, a parent company may be liable to the creditors of its subsidiary if the creditor has a good faith reason to believe that the two companies are the same entity. Two conditions must be met to apply the theory of appearance: a sufficiently strong deceptive appearance and the good faith of the contracting third party. French courts also use indicators to determine, on a case-by-case basis, whether a parent company may have led a third party to believe that it formed a single entity with a subsidiary or that it wanted to enter into a commitment alongside a subsidiary (eg similar head offices or managers).[65]

Practice shows that French courts are often inconsistent in applying these theories or mix them.[66] For example, the Court of Cassation seems to require the criteria used for interference to pierce the corporate veil on the basis of

61   Cass com 4 March 1997, n° 95-10756; Cass com 26 February 2008, n° 06-20.310.

62   Cass com 26 February 2008, n° 06-20.310.

63   Cass civ (3) 25 February 2004, n° 01-11764.

64   Sandrine Clavel, 'Conflits de lois: loi applicable aux obligations non contractuelles' (2012) 2 Journal du droit international Clunet 684.

65   Jasmin Schmeidler, 'La responsabilité de la société mère pour les actes de sa filiale' (2013) Recueil Dalloz 584.

66   Ibid; Thibaud d'Alès and Laura Terdjman, 'L'écran sociétaire, rempart face à la mise en cause d'une société mère du fait de sa filiale' (2014) 47 La Semaine juridique – Entreprise et affaires 1584.

appearance.[67] This approach is, however, more demanding in terms of proof, while being less protective of third parties.[68] Furthermore, similar facts in separate cases may sometimes lead to different outcomes, as a result of the arbitrary application of these theories.[69] Scholars have criticized the French courts for being more concerned with the result of corporate veil piercing than with its legal underpinning. However, French courts are generally reluctant to hold parent companies liable for the activities of their subsidiaries, and these theories continue to be used only in exceptional circumstances.[70]

The Netherlands

In the Netherlands, corporate veil piercing takes place through the application of the identification theory developed by Dutch courts. According to Vandekerckhove, identification applies mostly in cases of statutory and contract interpretation. In these cases, courts may decide to set aside the separate legal personality of the different actors involved when the application of a legal or contractual rule that does not explicitly deal with legal persons requires that abstraction be made of the separate identity of the persons concerned. Identification occurs in cases where two persons have acted where only one should have acted. As a result of identification, affiliated corporations are considered to be one legal person, and the acts and liabilities of one corporation may be attributed to another corporation. Identification depends on the factual circumstances of the case. Dutch courts have identified various circumstances or factors that may give rise to identification, such as dominance of one company over another, intensive involvement in the management of a company, creation of expectations vis-à-vis third parties, commingling of assets, or close intermingling. In general, courts will identify affiliated corporations when respecting the formal, separate existence of both would lead to consequences that would be contrary to good faith. Courts should strike a balance between the purpose and the content of the contractual or legal norm and the rule that each affiliated corporation has its own dependent legal personality. However, the Dutch Supreme Court is reluctant to apply the identification theory and requires sufficient reasons to conclude the existence of identification (eg a close commingling of assets is not enough). In the opinion of the Supreme Court, the fact that affiliated corporations are closely related legally and economically and commingle their affairs does not provide a sufficient reason to conclude the existence of identification. In most cases, identification concerns parent and subsidiary corporations.[71]

---

67 Cass com 12 June 2012, n° 11-16-109. See Schmeidler, 'La responsabilité de la société mère'.
68 Schmeidler, 'La responsabilité de la société mère'.
69 Vandekerckhove, *Piercing the Corporate Veil*, 457.
70 D'Alès and Terdjman, 'L'écran sociétaire', 1584.
71 Vandekerckhove, *Piercing the Corporate Veil*, 36–38, 410–411.

The single economic entity in competition law

Over the years, EU competition law, which largely influences French and Dutch competition rules, has gradually accepted the recognition of parent companies' liability for their subsidiaries' acts in specific circumstances.[72] In the landmark *Akzo Nobel NV* case,[73] the CJEU held that where a parent company had a 100 per cent shareholding in a subsidiary, the parent company could be held jointly and severally liable for the payment of the fine imposed on its subsidiary.[74] The fact that the subsidiary is wholly-owned by the parent company is sufficient to presume that the parent exercises a decisive influence over the commercial policy of the subsidiary.[75] The parent company has the burden of rebutting that presumption by adducing sufficient evidence to show that its subsidiary acts independently on the market.[76] This solution is seen as an application of the 'single economic entity' doctrine, which sees the parent company and its subsidiary form a single economic unit and therefore form a single undertaking.[77] When the parent company does not wholly own the subsidiary, the CJEU must seek additional evidence of the absence of the subsidiary's autonomy and of the determining influence of the parent company on its subsidiary's behaviour on the market. Such evidence can be demonstrated by showing the parent company's influence on fixing prices or on the subsidiary's management and commercial strategy.[78]

The reception of EU case law by domestic courts is relevant here. In France, courts have adopted an interpretation that slightly departs from the *Akzo Nobel NV* judgment,[79] seeking additional proof of the lack of autonomy of the wholly-owned subsidiary.[80] For example, French courts will take into account

---

72   Clarisse Le Corre and Emmanuel Daoud, 'La présomption d'influence déterminante: l'imputabilité à la société mère des pratiques anticoncurrentielles de sa filiale' (2012) 4334 Revue Lamy de droit des affaires 83.

73   Case C-97/08 *Akzo Nobel NV v Commission* [2009] ECR I-8237.

74   Ibid, paras 60–61.

75   For a later confirmation, see Case C-508/11 *ENI SpA v Commission* [2013] OJ 225/11. See also D'Alès and Terdjman, 'L'écran sociétaire'.

76   Case C-90/09 P *General Química e.a. v Commission* [2011] ECR I-00001; Joined Cases C-201/09 P and C-216/09 P *ArcelorMittal Luxembourg SA v Commission* [2011] ECR I-2239. For a discussion of these cases, see Antoine Winckler, 'Parent's Liability: New Case Extending the Presumption of Liability of a Parent Company for the Conduct of Its Wholly Owned Subsidiary' (2011) 2 Journal of European Competition Law & Practice 231; Georges Decocq, 'Présomption de responsabilité de la société mère des infractions commises par ses filiales détenues à 100%' (2011) 3 Revue contrats concurrence consommation 31.

77   *Akzo*, para 59.

78   Case C-48/69 *Imperial Chemical Industries Ltd v Commission* [1972] ECR 619; Case C-73/95 P *Viho European BV v Commission* [1996] ECR I-5457.

79   Frédérique Chaput, 'L'autonomie de la filiale en droit des pratiques anticoncurrentielles' [2010] Contrats Concurrence Consommation 11, 12; Le Corre and Daoud, 'La présomption d'influence déterminante', 84.

80   Cons Conc, Décision n° 05-D-49 du 28 juillet 2005 relative à des pratiques mises en œuvre dans le secteur de la location entretien des machines d'affranchissement postal; Cons Conc, Décision n° 07-D-12 du 28 mars 2007 relative à des pratiques mises en œuvre dans le secteur du chèque-cinéma.

the parent company's financial participation in the capital of the subsidiary, the nomination of the managing body, or the possibility for the subsidiary's managing body to freely determine an autonomous industrial, financial, and commercial strategy.[81] In the Netherlands, Dutch courts have established that, if a parent company exercises 'decisive influence' over its subsidiary's commercial behaviour, then both form part of the same economic undertaking. As a result, the parent company and the subsidiary can be fined for infringement of competition law.[82]

Voluntary liability

Both France and the Netherlands accept 'voluntary piercing', which occurs when the parent company, as the shareholder of its subsidiary, voluntarily abandons its right to limited liability and agrees to be held jointly liable for its subsidiary's acts.[83] In that event, the parent itself lifts the corporate veil, mostly vis-à-vis one particular creditor or group of creditors.[84]

In company law, voluntary piercing in France may result from a guarantee by the parent company for liabilities of its subsidiaries to the benefit of third parties.[85] One example of voluntary piercing allows a parent, holding, or controlling company to assume liability for the environmental obligations of its subsidiary or controlled company where the latter has defaulted. More specifically, Article L233-5-1 French Commercial Code provides that a company which holds more than 50 per cent of the capital of another company,[86] or has a participation in[87] or controls another company,[88] may choose, in the event of the failure of the subsidiary or controlled company, to bear liability for all or part of the obligations to prevent and restore environmental damage caused by the subsidiary or controlled company.[89] Article L233-5-1 does not call the principles of separate legal personality and limited liability into question. It only makes it possible for a parent company to adopt 'virtuous behaviour' for reasons that are consistent with the protection of its image or with ethical rules or social commitments without creating a risk for the parent company

---

81   Le Corre and Daoud, 'La présomption d'influence déterminante', 85.

82   See Pieter Van Osch, 'Private Equity Companies and Parental Liability – Appeal Court Hands Down Judgement in the Dutch Flour Cartel' (2018) 9 Journal of European Competition Law & Practice 37.

83   Vandekerckhove, *Piercing the Corporate Veil*, 16.

84   Ibid, 16.

85   Ibid, 45.

86   French Commercial Code, Article L233-1.

87   Ibid, Article L233-2.

88   Ibid, Article L233-3.

89   The French Court of Cassation had previously accepted that a parent company could voluntarily bear responsibility for its subsidiary's environmental obligations. See Cass com 26 March 2008, n° 07-11.619.

of being accused of misuse of corporate assets.[90] Its added-value is therefore limited as it does not create an *obligation* on the parent company. Moreover, it targets only a limited number of environmental damages.[91]

In the Netherlands, the parent company can declare that it assumes joint and several liability for any obligations arising from the legal acts of its subsidiary in order to allow the latter to obtain an exemption from the duty to publish its annual accounts (Article 2:403(f) Dutch Civil Code).

Fault-based liability

A parent company may be held liable for the obligations of its subsidiary on the basis of a 'fault' or wrongful act. This fault-based liability is based on the traditional principles of tort law and applies in different areas of law, from company law to environmental law.

Tort law

Under general tort law, persons may be liable for harm caused by their own act (ie personal or direct liability). In certain circumstances, persons may also be liable for harm caused by the act of others (ie vicarious liability). In the context of corporate groups, while a parent company could potentially be held directly liable for harm caused by its subsidiary's activities on the basis of its own misconduct, its liability for harm caused solely by the misconduct of its subsidiary is generally excluded.

Direct liability

In France, Articles 1240 and 1241 French Civil Code govern liability for one's own act (*responsabilité du fait personnel*).[92] First of all, Article 1240 lays down the basic principle of civil liability for misconduct. It states that 'Any act whatever of man, which causes damage to another, obliges the one by whose fault it occurred to provide compensation for it'. Moreover, Article 1241 provides for civil liability where the damage is caused by negligence. It reads as follows: 'Everyone is liable for the damage they cause not only by their act, but also by their negligence or imprudence.' Both articles establish a fault-based liability regime (ie resulting from unlawful conduct). Initially, Article 1240 dealt with intentional faults (*delicts*), while Article 1241 governed imprudent or negligent faults (*quasi-delicts*), but this distinction has lost its meaning in practice.[93]

---

90   Gilles Martin, 'Commentaire des articles 225, 226 et 227 de la loi n° 2010-788 du 12 juillet 2010 portant engagement national pour l'environnement (dite « Grenelle II »)' [2011] Revue des sociétés 75, paras 49–50.

91   Sabrina Dupouy, 'La responsabilisation environnementale des groupes de sociétés par le grenelle: enjeux et perspectives' (2012) 11 Droit des sociétés étude 16.

92   Until 2016, this liability was found in Articles 1382 and 1383 Civil Code.

93   Philippe le Tourneau, 'Responsabilité: généralités', Répertoire civil Dalloz (2nd edn, 2009), para 63.

Articles 1240 and 1241 lay down common rules that apply to all areas of liability for one's own act. Furthermore, they apply to natural and legal persons (including companies), and to all protected rights and interests. Therefore, Articles 1240 and 1241 may be invoked as a legal basis in civil actions for the damage resulting from human rights violations and environmental pollution, such as in transnational litigation against MNEs. They require the satisfaction of three elements to give rise to liability: damage, fault (*faute*), and causation. In order to establish a fault, the judge will assess the unlawfulness (*illicéité*) of the tortfeasor's conduct. A fault may result from the infringement of a number of pre-existing obligations, most likely a written rule contained in a statute or regulation (*obligation légale ou réglementaire*). However, in some cases, it can result from the infringement of an unwritten duty derived from custom practised in a particular region, sector, or profession, or private norms (eg codes of conduct or guidelines). The commission of a criminal offence causing harm to another person is also considered to be a fault in the sense of Article 1240.[94] Finally, a person commits a fault if they abuse a right (*abus de droit*), meaning they used a right to which they are entitled with the intent to cause harm. In general, judges have a broad power of appreciation for the standard of conduct. In most situations, courts will use a standard of reference (eg *bonus pater familias*). The Court of Cassation has recognized that a civil fault may result from the positive act or the mere omission of the tortfeasor.[95]

In theory, Articles 1240 and 1241 provide a basis for holding a parent company liable in the context of corporate group activities. However, victims must show that the parent company has committed a fault, either intentionally or negligently, that has caused the damage.[96] They must also prove causation between the parent company's fault and the damage, which is challenging when the damage occurs as a result of corporate group activities. While judges may accept the parent company's fault in cases involving abuse of legal personality or mismanagement of the controlled company,[97] it is unclear whether they will accept the parent company's fault in other cases.

In the Netherlands, Article 6:162 Dutch Civil Code lays down a general rule on fault-based liability under which both natural and legal persons can be held liable for their own intentional or negligent conduct. This provision requires

---

94   At the same time, the absence of a criminal fault does not preclude the characterization of a civil fault. Civ (2) 15 November 2001, n° 99-21.636.

95   Civ 27 February 1951 (*Branly*).

96   T com Orléans 1 June 2012, n° 2010-11170. See also Alain Couret and Bruno Dondero, 'Condamnation d'un fonds d'investissement étranger à réparer le préjudice causé par une opération de restructuration' (2012) 35 La semaine juridique entreprise et affaires 1494, 85.

97   Schmeidler, 'La responsabilité de la société mère'.

a wrongful act or omission, imputability, causation, and damage.[98] Under
Article 6:162(1), a person who commits a tort against another that is attributable
to him must repair the damage suffered by the other in consequence thereof.
Furthermore, Article 6:162(3) provides that a tortfeasor is responsible for the
commission of a tort if it is their fault or results from a cause for which they
are accountable by law or pursuant to generally accepted principles. As a result,
tortious liability is incurred not only through subjective fault, but also through
objective 'answerability'. Article 6:162(2) Dutch Civil Code specifies the types of
acts which are deemed tortious. There are three main categories: (1) the violation
of a right; (2) an act or omission breaching a duty imposed by law; and (3) an
act or omission breaching a rule of unwritten law pertaining to proper social
conduct. Some of these acts may be more relevant than others in the context
of transnational litigation against MNEs. First, there is a tort where the right of
a person is infringed, such as the right to life, the right to physical integrity, or
the right to freedom.[99] This category is directly relevant to transnational tort
claims against MNEs in which plaintiffs raise human rights abuse claims. Second,
liability arises where a wrongful act or omission violates a clear legal norm, such
as Dutch laws and regulations or directly applicable norms of public international
law.[100] However, few Dutch statutory norms apply in the context of transnational
tort claims against MNEs.[101] Third, transnational claims raising the liability of a
parent company for its subsidiary's activities abroad might also be built on the
breach of unwritten norms pertaining to acceptable social behaviour.[102]

In the context of transnational claims against MNEs, tort may be a valid way
to hold parent companies liable when human rights violations occur in the
context of their subsidiaries' activities. Scholars have notably suggested that a
parent company may have a general duty of care to prevent foreseeable harm to
stakeholders caused by the actions of its subsidiaries.[103] However, courts have
not yet relied on Dutch law to establish the liability of a parent company in the
context of transnational claims against MNEs. Having said that, in *Milieudefensie
v RDS*,[104] the high-profile climate change litigation case against Shell, the District
Court of the Hague ruled that RDS, Shell's parent company, owes an obligation,
under the unwritten standard of care enshrined in Article 6:162 Dutch Civil

---

98   Berthy Van Den Broek and Liesbeth Enneking, 'Public Interest Litigation in the Netherlands: A
Multidimensional Take on the Promotion of Environmental Interests by Private Parties through
the Courts' (2014) 10 Utrecht Law Review 77, 85.

99   International Commission of Jurists, '*Access to Justice: Human Rights Abuses Involving
Corporations – The Netherlands*' (BHRRC 2010) 10, <https://www.icj.org/access-to-justice-
human-rights-abuses-involving-corporations-2/> accessed 15 July 2021.

100 Liesbeth Enneking, *Foreign Direct Liability and Beyond: Exploring the Role of Tort Law in
Promoting International Corporate Social Responsibility and Accountability* (Eleven 2012) 230.

101 Ibid.

102 Dutch Civil Code, Articles 6:162 and 6:163.

103 Jägers and Van Der Heijden, 'Corporate Human Rights Violations', 859.

104 DC The Hague 26 May 2021, C/09/571932/HAZA19-379.

Code, to reduce the Shell group's CO_2 emissions by net 45 per cent in 2030, compared to 2019 levels, through the Shell's group corporate policy. This decision demonstrates that Dutch tort law can be a legitimate and effective tool for holding parent companies accountable for human rights and environmental violations that occur in the context of corporate groups activities.

Exclusion of vicarious liability

Both France and the Netherlands recognize vicarious liability under tort law. This means that a person may be held liable to repair the damage caused by a third party, not because of their own wrongdoing, but because of their relationship with the tortfeasor. However, the French and Dutch vicarious liability regimes do not recognize that a parent company may be liable for the torts of its subsidiary or, more broadly, any entity under its control or business partners of its supply chain.

In France, Article 1242 French Civil Code provides that a person is liable not only for the damage they cause by their own act, but also for the damage caused by the acts of persons for whom they are responsible (*responsabilité du fait d'autrui*).[105] However, Article 1242 does not establish a general vicarious liability regime and applies only to a limited number of relationships (ie liability of parents for damage caused by their children; liability of teachers and craftsmen for damage caused by their students and apprentices; liability of masters for damage caused by their servants;[106] and liability of principals (or employers) for damage caused by their agents (or employees)).[107] The relationship between a parent company and its subsidiary is not defined as one that could give rise to vicarious liability. Consequently, this absence prevents parent companies from being held liable for the acts of their subsidiaries pursuant to Article 1242.

Nonetheless, it has been suggested that vicarious liability could be imposed on the parent company for the wrongdoing of its subsidiary. There are two main reasons. First, the Court of Cassation has accepted that more relationships could give rise to vicarious liability under Article 1242.[108] For example, institutions dealing with minors and sport associations have been held strictly liable for the torts of persons under their control or whose activities they control.[109] However, the existence of a general vicarious liability regime has not yet been recognized by the Court of Cassation. Second, it has been argued that the principles of

105 Until 2016, this rule was found under Article 1384 Civil Code. Article 1242 also governs liability arising from damage caused by objects.

106 In French, '*responsabilité des maîtres du fait de leurs domestiques*'.

107 In French, '*responsabilité des commettants du fait de leurs préposés*'.

108 Ass plén 29 March 1991, n° 89-15.231 (*Blieck*).

109 Cass civ (2) 22 May 1995, n° 92-21871; Cass civ (2) 20 November 2003, n° 02-13.653; Cass civ (2) 22 September 2005, n° 04-14.092.

vicarious liability applying to the principals/agents relationship could be extended to 'any relationships capable of meeting the tests of subordination or the right to give instructions'.[110] To date, however, French courts have been reluctant to extend vicarious liability to the relationship between a parent company and its subsidiary.

Since the beginning of the 21st century, a number of official studies, which aimed to inform the reform of French tort law, have made various proposals regarding parent company liability for its subsidiaries. For instance, in 2005 the Catala report[111] suggested that the category of persons under now Article 1242 should be extended to natural or legal persons who organize and have an interest in the activity of professionals or businesses (not being their employees). Furthermore, it suggested that a new Article 1360 extend such liability to the relationship between parent companies and subsidiaries. Interestingly, the Catala report promoted the creation of a strict liability regime. Similarly, in 2012 the working group led by Professor Terré suggested the creation of a fault-based liability regime for corporate groups (ie Article 7).[112] However, to date, the French Government has not followed up on these suggestions.

The Dutch Civil Code provides vicarious liability for damage caused by the acts of a number of other persons (ie children, subordinates, non-subordinates, and representatives).[113] However, similar to the French Civil Code, there is no specific mention of the relationship between a parent company and its subsidiary.

The Shell case in the Netherlands

In *Shell*, the Dutch courts applied Nigerian law and English tort law, and not Dutch tort law, to the facts. Nonetheless, an analysis of this case remains relevant as *Shell* highlights the substantive legal challenges plaintiffs face when seeking to establish the liability of the parent company in the context of corporate group activities.

In *Shell*, the plaintiffs sued the parent company, RDS, and its Nigerian subsidiary, SPDC, for damage resulting from oil spills from pipelines and a wellhead at various locations in the Niger Delta (Oruma, Goi, and Ikot Ada Udo) between 2004 and 2007. They alleged that RDS violated its duty of care by failing to properly oversee its Nigerian subsidiary SPDC.[114] RDS had an obligation to act

---

110 Paula Giliker, *Vicarious Liability in Tort: A Comparative Perspective* (CUP 2010) 101.

111 Pierre Catala, *Avant-projet de réforme du droit des obligations et de la prescription* (La documentation française 2006).

112 François Terré, 'Groupe de travail sur le projet intitulé "pour une réforme du droit de la responsabilité civile"' (Cour de cassation 2012).

113 Dutch Civil Code, Articles 6:169 to 6:172.

114 'Writ of Summons: Oguru, Efanga & Milieudefensie vs Shell plc and Shell Nigeria' (Böhler Advocaten 7 November 2008) 23, 47.

in a socially responsible manner and 'should exert its influence and control over its subsidiary [SPDC] in such a way that it is prevented as much as possible that its subsidiary [SPDC] causes damages to human beings and the environment during the oil extraction'.[115] RDS and SPDC claimed that the oil spills were the result of sabotage.

In 2013, in one of the claims the District Court found that SPDC was liable for damage resulting from the oil spills because it failed to take appropriate preventative and remedial action against the spills.[116] However, it dismissed all the claims against RDS.[117] It ruled that, pursuant to Nigerian law, 'there is no general duty of care to prevent third parties from inflicting damage on others'. This implies that parent companies like RDS have no general obligation to prevent their (sub-) subsidiaries, such as SPDC, from inflicting damage on others through their business operations.[118] The District Court also ruled that RDS did not have a duty of care to prevent oil spills occurring in the context of SPDC's activities based on the English *Chandler* precedent (see Chapter 3 of this book).[119] It found that the proximity between a parent company and its subsidiary's employees when both companies operate in the same country, which was the situation in *Chandler*, 'cannot be unreservedly equated with the proximity between the parent company of an international group of oil companies and the people living in the vicinity of oil pipeline and oil facilities of its (sub-) subsidiaries in other countries'. In the latter situation, 'the requirement of proximity will be fulfilled less readily'. As a result, the District Court held that:

> The duty of care of a parent company in respect of the employees of a subsidiary that operates in the same country further only comprises a relatively limited group of people, whereas a possible duty of care of a parent company of an international group of oil companies in respect of the people living in the vicinity of oil pipelines and oil facilities of (sub-) subsidiaries would create a duty of care in respect of a virtually unlimited group of people in many countries. The District Court believes that in the case at issue, it is far less quickly fair, just and reasonable than it was in *Chandler v Cape* to assume that such a duty of care on the part of RDS exists.[120]

115 Ibid, 47.
116 DC The Hague 30 January 2013, C/09/337050/HAZA09-1580 (*Akpan*).
117 Ibid; DC The Hague 30 January 2013, C/09/330891/HAZA09-0579 (*Oguru*); C/09/337058/HAZA09-1581 (*Dooh*).
118 *Akpan* [2013], [4.26].
119 *Chandler v Cape* [2012] EWCA Civ 525.
120 *Akpan* [2013], [4.29]; *Dooh* [2013], [4.33]; *Oguru* [2013], [4.36].

The District Court concluded that the special circumstances that can create a duty of care on the part of the parent company according to *Chandler* did not occur in this case.

The District Court adopted a narrow view of the duty of care of parent companies towards third parties in the context of MNE activities. Enneking questioned whether this narrow focus on the facts of the *Chandler* case and the criteria set out in that case was justified. In particular, she argued that it may be possible that under different circumstances, parent companies of MNEs may owe a duty of care to third parties in host countries who are adversely affected by the activities of groups there.[121]

Having said that, the District Court, and later the Court of Appeal of The Hague, also signalled that they would not exclude potential parent company liability in the context of corporate groups in this type of litigation, and in *Shell* in particular.[122] In an interlocutory judgment, the Court of Appeal stated:

> Considering the foreseeable serious consequences of oil spills to the local environment from a potential spill source, it cannot be ruled out from the outset that the parent company may be expected in such a case to take an interest in preventing spills (or in other words, that there is a *duty of care* in accordance with the criteria set out in *Caparo v Dickman* [1990] UKHL 2, [1990] 1 All ER 56), the more so if it has made the prevention of environmental damage by the activities of group companies a spearhead and is, to a certain degree, actively involved in and managing the business operations of such companies, which is not to say that without this attention and involvement a violation of the duty of care is unthinkable and that culpable negligence with regard to the said interests can never result in liability. This is not altered by the fact that, as [RDS] argues, there are no decisions by Nigerian courts in which group liability is accepted on these grounds, for this does not mean that Nigerian law by definition provides no basis for assuming (a violation of) a duty of care to the parent company under those circumstances, for instance in the context of cleaning up pollution and preventing repeated spills.[123]

This approach turned out to be true. In January 2021, the Court of Appeal of The Hague overturned the 2013 decisions of the District Court. It delivered

121 Liesbeth Enneking, 'Paying the Price for Socially Irresponsible Business Practices?' (2017) 8 AJP/PJA 988, 992.

122 Ibid.

123 CA The Hague 18 December 2015, C/09/337058/HAZA09-1581 + C/09/365482/HAZA10-1665 [3.2] (emphasis in original).

three judgments in the case against RDS and SPDC.[124] In two of them, it found that SPDC was strictly liable for the damage resulting from the leakages from the pipelines on the basis of Article 11(5)(c) of the Nigerian Oil Pipeline Act (OPA). Although SPDC had argued that the leakages were the result of sabotage, it did not meet the high evidence threshold that exists under the OPA (ie sabotage must be proved beyond any reasonable doubt). However, the Court of Appeal rejected that RDS could be held liable for the damage resulting from the leakages, since the strict liability regime under the OPA only applies to the holder of the oil pipeline licence (ie SPDC) and it could not be established that SPDC had acted negligently or unreasonably.

Furthermore, in two of the judgments, the Court of Appeal found SPDC liable for its failure to provide a timely and adequate response to the leakages on the basis of the tort of negligence. In one judgment, SPDC was found liable for neglecting to install a leak detection system (LDS) on the pipeline in Oruma. Importantly, the Court of Appeal found that RDS owed a common law duty of care to the people living in the vicinity of the Oruma pipeline. Influenced by the 2019 UK Supreme Court's ruling in *Vedanta*[125] (see Chapter 3 of this book), the Court of Appeal held that 'if the parent company knows or should know that its subsidiary is unlawfully causing damage to third parties in an area in which the parent company is interfering with the subsidiary, then, as a starting point, the parent company has a duty of care towards those third parties to intervene'.[126] Furthermore, whether RDS, as the parent company, owed a duty of care depended on 'the extent to which, and the way in which, the parent availed itself of the opportunity to take over, intervene in, control, supervise or advise the management of the relevant operations ... of the subsidiary'.[127] The Court of Appeal took the view that, at least from 2010, RDS had quite intensively interfered with the decision to equip the Oruma pipeline with an LDS. It considered several aspects, such as RDS' substantial financial interest in Nigeria, its awareness of previous oil spills in the area, the bonus of members of RDS' executive committee being partly dependent on the number of oil spills, specific documents and witness testimonies discussing the possibility of installing an LDS, and the structure/governance of the Shell MNE.[128] In addition, RDS was aware that SPDC was not able to respond adequately to leaks resulting

---

124 CA The Hague 29 January 2021, C/09/365498/HAZA10-1677 (case a) + C/09/330891/HAZA09-0579 (case b) (*Oguru*); C/09/337058/HAZA09-1581 (case c) + C/09/365482/HAZA10-1665 (case d) (*Dooh*); C/09/337050/HAZA09-1580 (cases e + f) (*Akpan*). At the time of writing, the *Akpan* case was still pending.

125 [2019] UKSC 20.

126 *Oguru* [2021] [3.31]; *Dooh* [2021] [3.29].

127 *Oguru* [2021] [3.29].

128 Ulrike Verboom and Eleonora Di Pangrazio, 'Dutch Court Rules on Parent Companies' Responsibility for Overseas Subsidiaries' (Lexology, 22 February 2021) <https://www.lexology.com/library/detail.aspx?g=02939345-2e64-4b21-8d70-a0dd054ac720> accessed 1 May 2021.

from the Oruma pipeline due to the lack of an LDS. Therefore, RDS had a duty of care. By ignoring this duty and not compelling SPDC to install an LDS, RDS acted in tort. In the second judgment, the Court of Appeal dismissed the claim against RDS on the ground that it had not been made aware of the oil spill.

The judgments of the Court of Appeal mark a turning point in the search for the liability of the parent company in the context of its group activities in Europe. While in the past, courts in other countries have agreed to hold parent companies liable for damage resulting from the activities of their foreign subsidiary in a limited number of cases (eg COMILOG, AREVA), all of these decisions have ended up being reversed upon appeal. In *Shell*, the judgments of the Court of Appeal are likely to be final,[129] which means that they are the first judicial decisions in Europe to hold a parent company accountable for harm caused by its subsidiary. More importantly, it is the first time that a parent company has been found to owe a common law duty of care to the local communities affected by the operations of its subsidiary. According to Roorda:

> Until this case, however, no court had concluded on the merits that a parent company was in sufficient proximity to its employees or local communities to incur such a duty. This holding thus staves off the fears that transnational corporate duties of care are a mere hypothetical, theoretically possible but never actually occurring in the real world.[130]

However, the possible impacts of the Court of Appeal's judgments on future litigation against parent companies should be taken with a grain of salt. The Court of Appeal interpreted that the parent company's duty of care is based on two main elements: interference and knowledge. RDS was found to have a duty of care because it had sufficiently interfered with the decision to equip the Oruma pipeline with an LDS. However, as Roorda argues, this duty of care stems from RDS' actual intervention in SPDC's operations 'rather than from its central position of authority in the corporate group' or 'its capacity to intervene'.[131] This could create an incentive for parent companies not to interfere, or to limit signs of interference, in the activities of their foreign subsidiaries in order to avoid liability claims.[132] In that event, victims may find themselves without the possibility of seeking redress against the parent company.

129 According to Cees van Dam, appeal to the Dutch Supreme Court is possible only on points of law. However, the application of foreign law is considered to be a matter of fact in Dutch law. It is therefore unlikely that the defendants could be given permission to appeal to the Supreme Court. See Cees Van Dam, 'Shell Liable for Oil Spills in Niger Delta. The Hague Court of Appeal Decisions of 29 January 2021' (February 2021).

130 Lucas Roorda, 'Wading through the (Polluted) Mud: The Hague Court of Appeals Rules on Shell in Nigeria' (RightsasUsual, 2 February 2021) <https://rightsasusual.com/?p=1388> accessed 1 May 2021.

131 Ibid.

132 Ibid.

Company law

In disputes relating to company law, French and Dutch courts may hold the parent company liable for the damage caused by its subsidiary on the basis of the parent company's fault or misconduct. They may do so on the basis of general tort liability or specific statutory schemes, such as directors' liability in bankruptcy.

In France, the courts may accept the liability of the parent company for its subsidiary's acts on the basis of Article 1240 French Civil Code. For example, in insolvency law, courts have found that a parent company had committed a fault where it maintained its subsidiary's operations even though insolvency was clearly inevitable or where it gave harmful instructions to its subsidiary.[133] It is worth mentioning that the recently adopted Act on the Duty of Vigilance creates a fault-based liability regime for the parent company where its failure to comply with its mandatory HRDD obligations results in human rights or environmental damage in the context of its activities, as well as those of its subsidiaries and subcontractors (see Chapter 7 of this book for a detailed analysis).

In the Netherlands, tort is usually the principal basis for establishing the liability of parent companies for their subsidiaries' debts under company law.[134] In the landmark *Osby* case of 1981,[135] the Dutch Supreme Court found that a parent company may commit a tort vis-à-vis its subsidiary's creditors when it has such an influence over the management of the subsidiary that, at the time of the creation of the security, the parent company knew, or should have foreseen, that new creditors would be harmed by the lack of the subsidiary's assets but nevertheless failed to satisfy the debts of those creditors.[136] Since this case, Dutch courts have refined the idea that a parent company may have a legal duty of care towards its subsidiary's creditors. As such, it must prevent a subsidiary from taking on a new debt if it is clear that this debt will not be satisfied.[137] Dutch courts usually ask two questions. First, did the parent company know, or should it have known, that its act or omission would harm the creditors of the subsidiary (duty of care)? Second, what was the degree of involvement of the parent company in the management of its subsidiary (control)? When the parent company intensively influences the subsidiary's daily management, it

---

133 Vandekerckhove, *Piercing the Corporate Veil*, 44.

134 Ibid 34; Olaerts, 'National Report on the Netherlands', 443.

135 HR 25 September 1981, NJ 1982, 443 (*Osby-Pannan A/B v Las Verkoopmaatschappij BV*).

136 In this instance, the parent company had provided credit to the subsidiary and had received all the assets of the latter, actual and future, as collateral. As a result, the subsidiary appeared to be a financially sound corporation whereas, in reality, it had no assets for the satisfaction of its debts. See Vandekerckhove, *Piercing the Corporate Veil*, 34.

137 HR 19 February 1988, NJ 1988, 487; HR 21 December 2001, NJ 2005, 96. See also Jägers and Van Der Heijden, 'Corporate Human Rights Violations', 858.

may be considered as a quasi-director and it may incur the same liabilities in the event of a breach of duty of care.[138]

Both France and the Netherlands allow their courts to hold a company, acting as a *de jure* or de facto director of its subsidiary, liable for the debts of the subsidiary where the company has committed a fault. Article L651-2(1) French Commercial Code provides that, in the context of proceedings for insufficient assets (*responsabilité pour insuffisance d'actif*), the court may, in the event of a fault in management (*faute de gestion*) that has contributed to insufficiency of assets, decide that the debts of the legal entity will be borne, in whole or in part, by all or some of the *de jure* or de facto directors who have contributed to the fault. This type of liability is interesting in the context of groups, as legal persons can be considered directors. As a result, a parent company acting as the *de jure* or de facto manager of its subsidiary may be required to pay the debts of its subsidiary.[139] French courts appear to have considerable flexibility in finding parent companies liable in such cases.[140] A controlling shareholder and/or a parent company can be held to be a de facto director if they directly manage or take part in the management of the company.[141] However, simple negligence on the part of the directors in the management of the company is not sufficient for them to be liable.

Similarly, the Dutch Civil Code provides that, when public and private limited companies become bankrupt, their director(s) shall be held liable for the amount of liabilities that cannot be satisfied out of the liquidation of the other assets if the director(s) have manifestly performed their duties improperly and it is plausible that the improper management was an important cause of the bankruptcy.[142] This rule applies to a parent company acting as a *de jure* or a de facto director of its subsidiary. A parent company may be considered as a de facto manager when it has had a direct influence over the subsidiary's management and when, in reality, the subsidiary's formal management has been set aside.[143] This rule also applies to a foreign company acting as director of a Dutch company.[144]

138 Vandekerckhove, *Piercing the Corporate Veil*, 35.

139 CA Paris 15 January 1999, n° 1998/04408.

140 Michael Bode, *Le groupe international de sociétés: le système de conflit de lois en droit comparé français et allemand* (Peter Lang 2010) 157.

141 Conac, 'National Report on France', 101.

142 Dutch Civil Code, Articles 2:138(1) and 2:248.

143 Vandekerckhove, *Piercing the Corporate Veil*, 35.

144 HR 18 March 2011, RvdW 2011, 392.

Environmental law

Similarly, the French and Dutch courts may hold a parent company liable for the environmental damage caused by its subsidiary on the basis of the parent company's own fault or misconduct. They may do so on the basis of general tort liability rules or specific statutory schemes.

France

Legal framework

Under Articles 1240 and 1241, French courts may hold a parent company liable for the environmental damage caused by its subsidiary if the parent company has committed a fault that has caused the damage. However, courts are strict about the existence of the parent company's fault. In the *Ademe v Elf Aquitaine* case,[145] the Court of Cassation rejected a claim to extend the liability of a subsidiary to its parent company for the clean-up of a landfill site. In the court's view, there was no evidence that the parent company had committed a fault that would have justified making it liable pursuant to Article 1240. The simple fact of controlling or having a participation in another company is not sufficient to demonstrate the parent company's fault. This rule applies even if the subsidiary is responsible for a public service that could pose a risk to the public interest.

Article L512-17 French Environmental Code is a specific statutory scheme creating a fault-based liability regime for the parent company. Where a subsidiary[146] enters liquidation proceedings, a court may hold its parent company liable for the cleaning up of the subsidiary's operation site if the parent company has committed a 'characterized fault' (*faute caractérisée*) which has contributed to the lack of assets of the subsidiary. When the parent company is itself insolvent, the tribunal can hold the 'grand-parent' or the 'great-grand-parent' company liable, provided that it has committed a characterized fault. This provision prevents parent companies from using shell companies or insolvent subsidiaries as a means of avoiding liability. However, scholars have criticized the requirement of characterized fault, arguing that it does not exist in bankruptcy proceedings.[147] As a result, the necessary criteria for proving that the parent company committed a characterized fault, which contributed to the subsidiary's insufficient assets, are uncertain.[148] Furthermore, only a limited

---

145 Cass com 26 March 2008, n° 07-11619.

146 The company must be a subsidiary according to Article L233-1 French Commercial Code.

147 François-Guy Trébulle, 'Entreprise et développement durable (1ère partie) Juin 2009/Juillet 2010' (2010) 12 Environnement, para 25.

148 Dupouy, 'La responsabilisation environnementale'.

number of individuals, such as the liquidator or the State, can apply for such a procedure, thus limiting opportunities for other actors, such as environmental NGOs, to bring a claim before a tribunal.

France recently created a civil regime aimed specifically at repairing 'pure environmental damage'.[149] Under the new Article 1246 French Civil Code, 'Any person responsible for ecological loss is obliged to repair it'. Ecological loss is defined as the 'non-negligible harm to the elements or functions of ecosystems or to the collective benefits derived by man from the environment'.[150] Therefore Article 1246 aims to repair damage to the environment itself, not to humans or their property. Importantly, Article 1246 is applicable to both natural and legal persons responsible for ecological loss. In theory, it may be possible for a parent company to be held liable for the ecological loss arising in the context of its subsidiary's activities. However, the parent company must have committed a fault leading to such damage. Another obstacle is that only a limited number of public authorities and environmental NGOs have standing to bring a claim under Article 1246.[151] In practice, this means that affected local communities cannot invoke Article 1246 on their own. The concept of ecological loss was first introduced in the landmark *Erika* case, which deserves attention for its contribution to the liability of the parent company in the context of corporate group activities.

The *Erika* case

The *Erika* case was a landmark case for a number of reasons. Not only did the courts recognize the concept of ecological loss for the first time, they also held the parent company of Total, an oil MNE, liable for environmental pollution caused by its subsidiary on breaking grounds.[152] *Erika* was concerned with oil pollution on the high seas, which is an area governed by specific rules of international law. The International Convention on Civil Liability for Oil Pollution Damage (CLC)[153] establishes a specific system of civil liability that deals with damage resulting from maritime casualties involving oil-carrying ships. *Erika* was a complex case raising various legal and procedural issues. However, the following summary focuses mainly on the search for criminal and civil liability of Total SA, the French parent company.

---

149 Loi n° 2016-1087 du 8 août 2016 pour la reconquête de la biodiversité, de la nature et des paysages.

150 French Civil Code, Article 1247.

151 Article 1248 Civil Code lists the persons who have standing: the State, the French Biodiversity Office, local authorities, public establishments, and environmental NGOs approved or established for at least five years.

152 See Corinne Lepage, 'Erika: "une avancée tout à fait considérable du droit de l'environnement"' (2012) 11 Environnement.

153 International Convention on Civil Liability for Oil Pollution Damage (adopted 29 November 1969, entered into force 19 June 1975) 973 UNTS 3.

In 1999, the 25-year-old Maltese-flagged tanker *Erika* sank off the coast of Brittany and spilled 31,000 tons of heavy fuel oil belonging to the Panama subsidiary of Total SA along 400 kilometres of French coastline.[154] Following the oil spill, several natural and legal persons, including the parent company, Total SA, were prosecuted on various grounds. Victims, including local communities, fishermen, and NGOs, also introduced ancillary civil actions in order to obtain compensation for the damage caused by oil pollution. In this case, the Paris Regional Court and Court of Appeal, and the Court of Cassation successively ruled on criminal and civil proceedings.[155]

The French courts found Total SA guilty of the criminal offence of involuntary ship pollution for having exercised de facto control and direction in the management or operation of the ship. This offence normally applies to the person responsible for the operation of the ship, which in this instance was Total SA's subsidiary. Nonetheless, the courts concluded that Total SA had control over the management of the tanker. First, although it was not a contracting party to the charter party,[156] Total SA had to enforce a number of the obligations in the contract. For example, in the event of an accident the captain of the ship had to inform Total SA immediately. Second, Total SA had retained a right to check vessel compliance under its vetting procedure. The charter party allowed Total SA to verify the care and the diligence with which the shipment was transported, as well as the ways in which the ship and the crew were managed. The courts concluded that Total SA was the real decision-maker and that the Panama subsidiary was 'an empty shell', as it did not have any team or building in Panama where it was registered and lacked legal and financial autonomy. Furthermore, the courts found that Total SA had made an abusive use of the charter party to separate the legal and financial risks of the tanker management and, therefore, avoid liability. An important aspect of *Erika* is that the courts assessed Total SA's behaviour on the basis of its own internal rules of control. Total SA had voluntarily set up a number of procedures for its own activities, including a specific vetting procedure to control the quality of tankers. The courts concluded that, by ignoring this procedure and not vetting the *Erika*, Total SA had neglected its duty of care. Total SA's voluntary

---

154 On the *Erika* litigation, see Vincent Foley and Christopher Nolan, 'The Erika Judgment – Environmental Liability and Places of Refuge. A Sea Change in Civil and Criminal Responsibility that the Maritime Community Must Heed' (2009) 33 Tulane Maritime Law Journal 41; Laurent Neyret, 'L' affaire Erika: Moteur d'évolution des responsabilités civile et pénale' [2010] Recueil Dalloz 2238; Sophia Kopela, 'Civil and Criminal Liability as Mechanisms for the Prevention of Oil Marine Pollution: The *Erika* Case' (2011) 20 RECIEL 313; Emmanuel Daoud and Clarisse Le Corre, 'Arrêt Erika: marée verte sur le droit de la responsabilité civile et pénale des compagnies pétrolières' (2012) 122 Bulletin Lamy droit pénal des affaires.

155 TGI Paris (11) 16 January 2008, n° 9934895010; CA Paris 30 March 2010, n° 08/02278; Cass crim 25 September 2012, n° 10-82938.

156 A charter party is the hire or lease contract between the owner of a vessel and the hirer or lessee (charterer) for the use of the vessel.

commitment to control the quality of tankers became a norm upon which the company's misconduct was assessed.

However, the Court of Appeal rejected the claim that Total SA could be held liable in tort for the damage caused by the pollution.[157] It held that the CLC places the liability for damage resulting from maritime casualties involving oil-carrying ships on the owner of the ship from which the polluting oil escaped or was discharged. This liability is strict and exonerates other potential parties from being held civilly liable unless these parties committed gross negligence. The Court of Appeal did not find that Total SA had committed any gross negligence, as it had not expected that pollution would occur, even though it did not respect its own vetting rules. However, the Court of Cassation overturned this point of the ruling, holding that Total SA had acted recklessly (*faute de témérité*) within the meaning of the CLC and that it was necessarily aware that damage would probably result from such behaviour. Ultimately, Total SA was held criminally and civilly liable for the oil pollution caused by the activities of its subsidiary on the basis of its own fault.

The Netherlands

In the Netherlands, the courts have held parent companies liable for environmental pollution caused by the activities of their subsidiaries on the basis of their own fault. It is worth mentioning two important environmental cases where general tort law was applied. First, in the *Roco BV v De Staat der Nederlanden* case, Rouwenhorst was the owner of premises that were heavily polluted. In order to escape liability, he transferred the business to a newly incorporated limited liability company, Roco BV (Roco), which continued to operate at another location. Rouwenhorst's spouse and Hoekstra BV (a holding controlled by Rouwenhorst and his spouse and of which Rouwenhorst was the sole director) held the shares of Roco. The Dutch State claimed reimbursement for costs related to the environmental clean-up. At first instance, the District Court dismissed the State's claim because Roco had been incorporated after the pollution had been caused and it had not accepted liability for the pollution upon the business transfer.[158] However, the Court of Appeal held Roco liable since the sole purpose of the transfer was to evade potential claims by the State, as Roco continued the business of its predecessor.[159] Eventually, the Supreme Court upheld that Roco was liable for the environmental clean-up.[160] However,

---

157 The French doctrine has used the expression 'guilty but not liable' to highlight the lack of consistency between civil and criminal liability. See Neyret, 'L' affaire Erika', 2239; Christine Carpentier, 'Société mère et droit de l'environnement' (2012) 4333 Revue Lamy droit des affaires 79.

158 DC Zutphen 1 August 1991, Vermande D-8-85.

159 CA Arnhem 10 May 1994, TMA 94-6, 155 et seq.

160 HR 3 November 1995, NJ 1996, 215.

it rejected the use of the theory of identification as a basis for liability since 'the case did not concern an identification of two legal or natural persons but rather an identification of an "enterprise" with the company'.[161] Furthermore, Roco could not be held liable on the basis of a successor liability theory, as this did not exist under Dutch law. Ultimately, the Supreme Court held Roco liable in tort for having continued the business with the clear intent of frustrating the State's claim for damages.[162]

Second, in the *Bato's Erf BV v De Staat der Nerderlanden* case,[163] which concerned soil and groundwater pollution, the parent company had modified its charter and name, and had transferred its operations to a newly incorporated wholly-owned subsidiary in order to avoid liability. The Court of Appeal held that the parent company and the subsidiary had to be identified because the two companies were closely intermingled. In doing so, it took into account the following factors: the parent company had incorporated the subsidiary; it had transferred most of the assets and liabilities; the subsidiary was the true operator conducting the business of the parent company, which controlled the activities of the subsidiary; both companies had the same directors; the subsidiary was wholly-owned; and the financial statements of both companies were consolidated.[164] However, the Dutch Supreme Court overturned this decision, holding that the mere fact that a parent company determines the business policy of the subsidiary and directs or influences its implementation, either by having its managing directors also act as managing directors of the subsidiary, or in its capacity as managing director and/or sole shareholder, does not mean that these activities become the activities of the parent company, as a result of which the parent company would automatically be held liable for the tortious activities of the subsidiary.[165] This case showed that mere directorship is insufficient for liability, and that negligence or gross negligence must be established.[166]

Labour law

In many countries, labour law plays an important role in protecting workers from harmful or unfair working conditions and ensuring that workers can exercise their labour rights. It often lays down the rules on liability to ensure that employers comply with labour law standards designed to protect workers. In France, the theory of 'co-employment' (or 'co employers') is a relevant basis for finding parent companies liable to employees of their subsidiaries in the context of MNEs.

161 Ibid.
162 Ibid.
163 HR 16 June 1995, NJ 1996, 214.
164 Vandekerckhove, *Piercing the Corporate Veil*, 424.
165 Bergkamp and Pak, 'Piercing the Corporate Veil', 169.
166 Ibid.

Co-employment

The theory of co-employment is a judicial creation that has prompted renewed interest in France over the last few years.[167] It challenges not only the legal principles of separate legal personality and limited liability in corporate groups, but also the contractual foundation of employment relationships.[168] Co-employment generally enables employees of a loss-making company to hold their employer and its parent company jointly and severally liable for financial compensation for the loss of their jobs. French courts have applied the co-employment theory to protect employees and to punish abnormal practices within corporate groups, especially when parent companies are also holding companies that benefit from an advantageous tax regime.[169] In general, the co-employment theory applies to situations in which a (parent) company owns some of the capital of another company.[170] Furthermore, the Court of Cassation has accepted that it could apply to MNEs.[171]

In general, the fact that two companies belong to the same group is not enough to justify co-employment.[172] French courts accept that there is co-employment in two situations. First, there is co-employment where there is a relationship of subordination between the parent company and the subsidiary's employee. This relationship of subordination may be demonstrated by the parent company's interference in the management of the subsidiary's employees.[173] Second, there is co-employment where there is a 'commingling of interests, activities, and management' (*confusion d'intérêts, d'activités, et de direction*) between the two companies.[174] In this second situation, French courts consider various indicators, such as the economic control of the subsidiary by the parent company or the lack

---

167 See Laure Calice and Marie-Charlotte Diriart, 'Les nouveaux fronts contentieux du licenciement économique: l'impossible équation entre l'existence du groupe et l'autonomie juridique de la société' (2012) 5 Cahiers de droit de l'entreprise; Patrick Morvan, 'L'identification du co-employeur' (2013) 46 La semaine juridique social 1438.

168 Jacques Perotto and Nicolas Mathey, 'La mise en jeu de la responsabilité de la société mère est-elle une fatalité? Regards croisés sur les groupes de sociétés et le risque de coemploi' (2014) 25 La semaine juridique social 1262, 1262.

169 Ibid.

170 However, a recent decision of the Grenoble Court of Appeal recognized co-employment in the context of the relationship between a franchisor and its franchisee. CA Grenoble 24 September 2019, n° 17/03329.

171 Cass soc 30 November 2011, n° 10-22.964. In this case, a German parent company was recognized as the co-employer of its French subsidiary's employees.

172 Cass soc 25 September 2013, n° 11-25.733.

173 Cass soc 19 June 2007, n° 05-42.570.

174 Cass soc 30 November 2011, n° 10-22.964; Cass soc 28 September 2011, n° 10-12.278; Cass soc 18 January 2011, n° 09-69.199.

of the subsidiary's independence to define its own strategy.[175] In recent years, however, the Court of Cassation has adopted a strict approach to co-employment where there is a commingling of interests, activities, and management. It held that 'a company belonging to a corporate group cannot be considered the co-employer of the employees of another company, outside the existence of a relationship of subordination, unless there is between them, beyond the necessary coordination of economic actions between companies belonging to a same group and the state of economic domination that belonging to the same group may produce, a commingling of interests, activities, and control demonstrated by the interference in the economic and social management of the latter'.[176] French courts seem to require strict criteria to prove such interference.[177] It should also be noted that the Court of Cassation has rejected the possibility that co-employment might be deduced from the sole ownership of a wholly-owned subsidiary. In a situation of co-employment, the subsidiary must not have autonomy in the management of its human resources.[178]

The AREVA case

The *AREVA* case showed the limits of the co-employment theory as a basis for parent company liability. Pursuant to Article L4541 French Code of Social Security (*Code de la sécurité sociale*), the plaintiffs brought a compensation claim for occupational disease against AREVA for gross negligence (*faute inexcusable*)[179] in respect of Venel, an employee of its Nigerien subsidiary AREVA NC.

In 2012, the Melun Social Security Tribunal (TASS) held that AREVA, as the co-employer of Venel, was liable for gross negligence. The TASS proceeded to apply a two-stage analysis. First, it found that AREVA and AREVA NC were co-employers since they 'pursued, in collaboration, simultaneously, indivisibly, and permanently, a common activity in a common interest, under a single authority'.[180] Indicators included AREVA NC's charter, the identity of its main

---

175 Cass soc 18 January 2011, n° 09-69.199. See Marie Hautefort, 'Co-employeur: le véritable employeur est celui qui détient les pouvoirs' (2012) 314 Jurisprudence sociale Lamy.

176 Cass com 2 July 2014, n° 13-15.208 (*Molex*) (author's translation).

177 Ibid; Cass soc 24 May 2018, n° 17-15.630, n° 16-18.621. See also D'Alès and Terdjman, 'L'écran sociétaire', 1584.

178 Cass soc 25 September 2013, n° 11-25.733.

179 The TASS described the gross negligence of the employer as follows: '[P]ursuant to the employment contract with its employee, the employer has towards [the employee] an obligation of result to ensure their safety, most notably for the occupational disease developed by this employee as a result of the products manufactured or used by the company, and the breach of that obligation constitutes gross negligence within the meaning of Article L452-1 Code of Social Security where the employer knew or ought to have known the danger to which the employee was exposed and did not take the necessary measures to protect the employee.' TASS Melun 11 May 2012, n° 10-00924/MN (author's translation).

180 Ibid (author's translation).

shareholder, and interconnections between AREVA and its subsidiary (same address, same activities, same involvement in the exploitation of the same mining site). Moreover, AREVA appeared to assume technical, economic, social, and financial liability for the potential impact on the health and safety of individuals working in its uranium mines by setting up 'health observatories' and signing a memorandum of understanding on occupational disease caused by ionizing radiation with Sherpa in 2009.[181] AREVA's voluntary commitment demonstrated that, while its subsidiary acted as the contractual employer of Venel, AREVA acted as the employer with the authority and power to control and organize working conditions, especially with regard to occupational risk management. Therefore, a subordinate relationship existed between AREVA and the employee. Second, the TASS found that AREVA had committed gross negligence by not setting up safety measures to protect workers in its mines, which caused the development of the disease.

However, in 2013, the Paris Court of Appeal overturned the TASS' judgment, rejecting the claim that AREVA was the co-employer of Venel.[182] It found that there was no subordinate relationship between AREVA and Venel, as there was no evidence that AREVA had exerted any power of direction, control, or discipline over Venel. Furthermore, it held that there was no commingling of activities, interests, and control between AREVA and its subsidiary. First, AREVA NC could not be considered AREVA's subsidiary pursuant to Article L233-1 French Commercial Code, which requires that a company owns more than 50 per cent of the capital of another company in order for the second company to be regarded as a subsidiary; AREVA owned only 34 per cent of AREVA NC's shares while the Nigerien State and other foreign companies owned the rest. Second, there was no evidence demonstrating that AREVA NC had lost the autonomy to manage its own activities. The fact that both companies shared a common interest, as a result of AREVA being AREVA NC's shareholder, did not constitute a commingling of management or activities. Third, even though AREVA owned AREVA NC's mining concession, the Court of Appeal rejected the claim that there were interconnections between both companies demonstrating dependence. Fourth, the Court of Appeal rejected the claim that AREVA's voluntary commitment made it the co-employer of Venel. The Court of Cassation upheld this ruling in 2015.[183]

The position of the French courts in *AREVA* is in line with the approach adopted by the Court of Cassation, which requires the demonstration of strict criteria showing the existence of co-employment. However, a lack of consistency, clarity, and certainty remains as to the exact criteria required. Furthermore, this approach restricts the situations that may qualify as co-employment.

181 AREVA NC agreed to monitor the impacts of its activities on its employees and to compensate them for any cases of occupational disease.
182 CA Paris 20 June 2013, n° 08/07365.
183 Cass civ 22 January 2015, n° 13-28.414.

For instance, it appears that a parent company must own 50 per cent of its subsidiary's capital within the meaning of the French Commercial Code in order for the relationship between the parent company and the subsidiary to qualify for co-employment. This criterion does not allow a parent company to be held liable in the context of a joint venture, such as in *AREVA*. Ultimately, such a position reduces the possibilities the co-employment theory could potentially provide to victims of labour rights abuse by MNEs in host countries.

Criminal liability

Under French and Dutch criminal law, the parent company may, in theory, be liable for a crime committed by its subsidiary if it is itself a primary or, in some situations, a secondary perpetrator of the crime or an accomplice to it. It should be noted that, to date, no transnational case has yet reached the merits stage.

Corporate criminal liability

The concept of the criminal liability of legal persons is relatively new in France and the Netherlands. Both countries were among the first European countries with a civil law tradition to adopt a comprehensive regime of corporate criminal liability.[184]

In France, discussions over the use of criminal sanctions to regulate corporate misconduct emerged in the 1980s after the country was confronted with the increase in MNEs' power and their ability to evade local regulatory requirements.[185] The new Criminal Code introduced corporate criminal liability in 1994. At that time, companies could be held criminally liable only if such liability existed under statutory law. This legal restriction had a direct impact on transnational claims against MNEs. In *Total*, the plaintiffs targeted Total's executives, and not the company, as the Criminal Code did not provide for corporate criminal liability for the alleged offences.[186] It was not until 2004 that the criminal liability of legal persons was extended to all criminal offences.[187] Article 121-1 French Criminal Code now provides that legal persons are criminally liable for offences committed on their behalf by their organs or representatives. Furthermore, the criminal liability of legal persons does not exclude that of natural persons who are perpetrators or accomplices of the same acts.

In the Netherlands, in 1951 the Economic Offences Act (*Wet economische delicten*) recognized that legal persons, including companies, could be

184 Sara Sun Beale and Adam Safwat, 'What Developments in Western Europe Tell Us about American Critiques of Corporate Criminal Liability' (2004) 8 Buffalo Criminal Law Review 89, 109.

185 Ibid.

186 Benoît Frydman and Ludovic Hennebel, 'Translating Unocal: The Liability of Transnational Corporations for Human Rights Violations' in Manoj Kumar Sinha (ed), *Business and Human Rights* (SAGE 2013).

187 Loi n° 2004-204 du 9 mars 2004 portant adaptation de la justice aux évolutions de la criminalité.

criminally liable for a number of economic crimes. However, in 1976 a major criminal reform introduced general corporate criminal liability. Since then, Article 51(1) Dutch Criminal Code provides, in broad terms, that criminal offences may be committed by natural and legal persons. Furthermore, Article 51(2) Dutch Criminal Code states that when a legal person commits a criminal offence, criminal proceedings may be instituted and punishments may be imposed not only on the legal person but also on persons who ordered the commission of the criminal offence or directed the unlawful acts.

Criminal liability in corporate groups

Corporate groups cannot be held criminally liable in France and the Netherlands. Pursuant to Article 121-2 French Criminal Code, only business entities that have legal personality can be held criminally liable. Since corporate groups do not enjoy legal personality, they cannot be criminally liable.[188] Similarly, in the Netherlands, only business entities with legal personality can be criminally liable. Nonetheless, Article 51(3) Dutch Criminal Code states that criminal offences may also be committed by certain entities without legal personality, such as unincorporated companies or partnerships. However, the corporate group is excluded from this provision. Ultimately, only group entities may be liable for criminal activities, such as those related to human rights violations and pollution, in France and the Netherlands.

In general, under French and Dutch criminal law, the parent company will be held liable for the offences it perpetrated. In France, Article 121-1 French Criminal Code states that no one is criminally liable except for their own conduct. Therefore, this principle of personal liability prevents the emergence of criminal vicarious liability in the context of corporate group activities.[189] This is reinforced by the fact that it may be difficult to determine which company of the group committed the offence.[190] At times, French courts may take into account the economic reality of the corporate group to hold the parent company criminally liable for criminal offences involving its subsidiary. However, even where this is the case, the liability of the parent company is always based on its own misconduct. For example, in *Erika*, the parent company was held criminally liable for involuntary pollution caused by the oil tanker chartered by its subsidiary, because while the parent company had an effective power of control over the tanker, it did not carry out

---

188 See Frédéric Desportes, 'La responsabilité pénale des personnes morales' [2002] JurisClasseur sociétés traité, fasc. 28–70; Katrin Deckert, 'Corporate Criminal Liability in France' in Mark Pieth and Radha Ivory (eds), *Corporate Criminal Liability: Emergence, Convergence, and Risk* (Springer 2011) 156.

189 Emmanuel Daoud and Clarisse Le Corre, 'À la recherche d'une présomption de responsabilité des sociétés mères en droit français' (2012) 4330 Revue Lamy droit des affaires 63, 63.

190 Maggy Pariente, 'Les groupes de sociétés et la responsabilité pénale des personnes morales' (1993) 2 Revue des sociétés 247; Marc Segonds, 'Frauder l'article 121-2 du code pénal' (2009) 9 Droit pénal 19, 19.

controls that would have prevented an unseaworthy tanker that subsequently sank being used for the shipment.[191]

The *Lafarge* case is relevant here because the Court of Cassation addressed the parent company's potential criminal liability for interfering with the management of its foreign subsidiary. In 2019, the Investigating Chamber upheld Lafarge's indictment for endangering others through a manifestly deliberate breach of the employer's safety obligation under the French Labour Code on the grounds that the Syrian employees who ensured the continuity of the plant's operations had been exposed to a risk of death or injury even though they had not received adequate training in the event of an attack. Lafarge challenged this decision, in particular the fact that the employees of the foreign subsidiary could be considered as employees of the French parent company, as well as the application to this specific case of the employer's safety obligation imposed by French law. In 2021,[192] the Court of Cassation ruled that the Investigating Chamber was correct in finding evidence of a subordinate relationship between the Syrian employees and Lafarge, or of permanent interference by Lafarge in the management of the employing company, resulting in the latter's total loss of action autonomy. On the other hand, it considered that the Investigating Chamber could not deduce the applicability of the French Labour Code and should have examined, in the light of international law, the provisions applicable to the employment relationship between the French company and the Syrian employees, and then determined whether these provisions provided for a specific safety obligation that had been breached. As a result, the Court of Cassation overturned the Investigating Chamber's decision to uphold Lafarge's indictment for endangering the lives of Syrian employees.

In the context of mergers and acquisitions, the Court of Cassation has consistently rejected the possibility that the acquiring company could be held liable for the criminal offences committed by the acquired company prior to acquisition based on the principle of personal liability found under Article 121-1.[193] However, in a recent landmark ruling, the Court of Cassation reversed its position on the transfer of criminal liability of a legal person in the event of a merger of one company into another.[194] It ruled that, under certain conditions, the acquiring company may be subject to a fine or confiscation for acts constituting an offence committed by the acquired company prior to acquisition. The Court of Cassation's new interpretation may prevent future mergers from impeding corporate criminal liability.

---

191 Emmanuel Daoud and Annaëlle André, 'La responsabilité pénale des entreprises transnationales françaises: fiction ou réalité juridique?' [2012] AJ pénal 15, 19.

192 Cass crim 7 September 2021, n° 19-87.031, 19-87.036, 19-87.040, 19-87.367, 19-87.376 and 19-87.662.

193 Cass crim 20 June 2000, n° 99-86-742.

194 Cass crim 25 November 2021, n° 18-86.955.

The Dutch Criminal Code provides possible grounds for the criminal liability of the parent company in the context of corporate group activities. Pursuant to Article 51(2), a parent company may be liable if it has committed the criminal offence (primary liability). Importantly, Article 51(2) provides for secondary liability where an offence is committed by a legal person. It applies to persons who have ordered the commission of the offence and to persons who have actually directed the commission of the offence.[195] This provision does not distinguish between natural and legal persons, which means that, theoretically, a parent company may be liable if it has ordered or actually directed the commission of an offence by its subsidiary. In addition, this secondary liability makes it possible to punish a merely passive involvement in an offence committed by a legal person. The Dutch Supreme Court has ruled that 'conditional intent' (*dolus eventualis*) is sufficient for this form of secondary liability.[196]

Importantly, a parent company may, in theory, be held liable as an accomplice to a crime in both France and the Netherlands. Article 121-7(1) French Criminal Code provides that an accomplice to a crime or misdemeanour is a person who knowingly, by aid or assistance, has facilitated the preparation or commission of a crime or misdemeanour. Furthermore, Article 121-7(2) French Criminal Code states that an accomplice is also the person who by gift, promise, threat, order, abuse of authority or power, has provoked an offence or given instructions to commit an offence. Therefore, a parent company must have committed these acts in order to be held liable as an accomplice to a crime committed by its subsidiary. Where crimes are committed by its foreign subsidiary abroad, the parent company may be held criminally liable as an accomplice under the conditions laid down in Article 113-5 French Criminal Code. However, Chapter 5 of this book has shown that these conditions are generally restrictive. A number of transnational cases against MNEs have raised the criminal liability of the parent company as an accomplice in crimes committed abroad, including crimes under international law (ie *Rougier, Amesys, Qosmos, Lafarge, BNP Paribas*). It should be noted, however, that the parent company has been accused of complicity in crimes committed not only by its subsidiary but also by foreign governments.

In the *Lafarge* case, the Court of Cassation issued a landmark decision on the definition of complicity in crimes against humanity.[197] In this case, the Investigating Chamber determined in 2019 that there was sufficient evidence to conclude that the armed groups committed crimes against humanity (concerted plan of abuses, widespread and systematic attack on the civilian population) and that Lafarge paid them funds despite being aware of the nature

195 Berend Keulen and Erik Gritter, 'Corporate Criminality in the Netherlands' in Mark Pieth and Radha Ivory (eds), *Corporate Criminal Liability: Emergence, Convergence, and Risk* (Springer 2011) 181.

196 Ibid.

197 Cass crim 7 September 2021, n° 19-87.031, 19-87.036, 19-87.040, 19-87.367, 19-87.376 and 19-87.662.

of the abuses. The Investigating Chamber concluded, however, that there was no serious or corroborating evidence of Lafarge's complicity because the financing of the armed groups was intended to allow it to continue its activity in the middle of a war zone, rather than to be associated with the crimes committed. In September 2021, the Court of Cassation overturned the Investigating Chamber's decision to annul Lafarge's indictment for complicity in crimes against humanity. It considered that one can be an accomplice to crimes against humanity, even if they do not intend to be associated with the commission of these crimes. It is necessary and sufficient to have knowledge of the preparation or commission of these acts, as well as that aid or assistance facilitated them. It is therefore not necessary to belong to the criminal organization or to participate in the conception or execution of the criminal plan. In this case, the knowing payment of several million dollars to an organization with an exclusively criminal purpose qualifies as complicity, regardless of whether the person is acting in furtherance of a commercial activity.

In the Netherlands, on the basis of Article 48 Dutch Criminal Code a parent company may be held criminally liable as an accomplice to a criminal offence committed by its subsidiary if it either intentionally aides and abets in committing a crime or provides opportunity, means, or information to commit a crime. Article 48 applies to the most serious criminal offences. Article 52 Dutch Criminal Code provides that complicity is not punishable for minor offences.

Elements of corporate criminal liability

In general, corporate criminal liability will be established when the objective element (*actus reus*) and, in some circumstances, the subjective element (*mens rea*) of the criminal offence are gathered.

Actus reus

In France, Article 121-2 French Criminal Code provides that legal persons are criminally liable for the offences committed on their account by their organs or representatives. Two conditions are therefore required. First, the criminal offence must have been committed on behalf of the company.[198] This means that the criminal offence must have been committed for the benefit of the company and not just for the individual benefit of the organ or the representative. Importantly, it is not required that the company gained a financial benefit from the criminal offence.[199] Second, an organ or a representative of the company must have committed the criminal offence. An organ may be defined as the person, either an individual or a group, who has the power of direction or

---

198 See also Cass crim 1 April 2008, n° 07-84839; Cass crim 22 January 2013, n° 12-80022.

199 Emmanuel Mercinier, 'La dégénérescence de l'article 121-2 du code pénal' (2011) 3681 Revue Lamy droit des affaires 91, 91.

organization within the company, such as a director, a board of directors, or a general assembly.[200] A company can also be liable when the criminal offence was committed by a de facto director.[201]

The situation is more complex when a representative commits the criminal offence. Previously, French courts held that a representative was an individual possessing the power, either general or special, to represent the company. Nonetheless, French courts recently extended the concept of representative to individuals, whether employees or not, who intervene on behalf of the company.[202] They also accept that a company may be liable, even though it is not possible to identify the perpetrator[203] or the company's representatives did not commit a fault.[204] Furthermore, French courts accept that the person who holds a delegation of authority is a representative of the legal person. As a result, a legal person can be held criminally liable for any offences a delegatee commits on its behalf. It is worth mentioning the situation where several companies appoint a joint delegatee in the context of a common project. In the event of a violation of health and safety standards committed by the joint delegatee, the Court of Cassation has consistently held that the violation only engages the criminal liability of the company which is the employer of the victim. In the context of transnational litigation against MNEs, this means that only the company that has hired the victim can be held liable. Even if another company has benefited from the delegation, such as the parent company, it cannot be held liable.

In the Netherlands, a legal person will be liable for criminal offences if the relevant behaviour can be reasonably attributed to that legal person. In *Drijfmest*, the Dutch Supreme Court ruled that a corporation could be held criminally liable only if there was an illegal act or omission that could be reasonably imputed to that corporation.[205] The Supreme Court provided a guiding principle to assess this 'reasonable attribution': 'the attribution of certain (illegal) conduct to the corporation may under certain circumstances be reasonable if the (illegal) conduct took place within the "scope" of the corporation.'[206] There are four situations in which conduct will, in principle, be carried out 'within the scope of a corporation'. First, the act or omission

---

200 Ibid, 91.

201 Cass crim 13 April 2010, n° 09-86429.

202 Deckert, 'Corporate Criminal Liability in France', 161; Mercinier, 'La dégénérescence de l'article 121-2 du code pénal', 93.

203 Cass crim 20 June 2006, n° 05-85255; Cass crim 25 June 2008, n° 07-80261. For a critique of this case law, see Alexandre Gallois, 'La responsabilité pénale des personnes morales: une responsabilité à repenser' [2011] Bulletin Lamy droit pénal des affaires 1.

204 Cass crim 27 October 2009, n° 09-80490. See also Mercinier, 'La dégénérescence de l'article 121-2 du code pénal', 94.

205 HR 21 October 2003, NJ 2006, 328. See also Keulen and Gritter, 'Corporate Criminality in the Netherlands', 183.

206 Ibid.

was allegedly committed by someone who works for the corporation, whether or not under a formal contract of employment. Second, the conduct was part of the everyday 'normal business' of the corporation. Third, the corporation profited from the relevant conduct. Fourth, the alleged course of conduct was at the 'disposal' of the corporation that 'accepted' the conduct. In the latter situation, the failure to take reasonable care to prevent the conduct from being carried out may establish acceptance.[207] Furthermore, any employee can cause its employer to commit an offence as long as the facts can be construed to show that the corporation ultimately 'committed' the offence.

Dutch scholars suggest that the Supreme Court's approach towards corporate criminal liability can be characterized as flexible and 'open', as there is no rigorous theory to turn to for guidance.[208] This approach has several advantages, as it 'leaves room for "tailor-made" jurisprudence, in which the courts are free to weigh relevant circumstances and factors. It acknowledges that the possible variation in cases is, in fact, endless'.[209] As a result, the Dutch approach may leave room for relevant jurisprudential developments in the context of transnational litigation against MNEs.

Mens rea

Specific categories of criminal offences require proof of a subjective element (intent). While French criminal law requires proof of the subjective element for both crimes and misdemeanours, Dutch criminal law requires this proof only for crimes (*misdrijven*) and excludes it for misdemeanours and contraventions (*overtredingen*).[210] As a result, where intent is required, there can be no liability without the intent of committing a crime. This rule creates difficulties in the context of corporate criminal liability, as legal persons are incapable of possessing intent to commit a crime. Therefore, courts have adopted creative approaches to adapting *mens rea* in a company context.

Under French law, corporate criminal liability does not depend on the commission of a fault by the legal person. The Court of Cassation has clearly stated that the criminal misconduct of the organ or representative of the legal person is sufficient to engage the criminal liability of the legal person, when

---

207 Ibid.

208 Emma van Gelder and Cedric Ryngaert, 'Dutch Report on Prosecuting Corporations for Violations of International Criminal Law' in Sabine Gless and Sylwia Broniszewska-Emdin (eds), *Prosecuting Corporations for Violations of International Criminal Law: Jurisdictional Issues* (Maklu 2017) 114.

209 Ibid.

210 Ibid, 114–116. In the context of misdemeanours and minor offences, it is generally sufficient for the public prosecutor to prove only the existence of *actus reus* in order to establish corporate criminal liability. The absence of intent is significant in the context of criminal claims brought against MNEs, as plaintiffs have raised commission of misdemeanours in past claims.

it is committed on behalf of the legal person, without the need to establish a separate fault on the part of the legal person.[211]

In the Netherlands, in order to establish corporate criminal liability, it is necessary to prove that the corporation has acted intentionally, recklessly, or with gross negligence. Dutch case law demonstrates two main approaches for proving corporate intent and negligence in the Netherlands.[212] First, the *mens rea* of a natural person is attributed to the company (*indirect* approach).[213] Such imputation is dependent on the internal organization of the corporation, and the position and responsibilities of the natural person within the corporation. It is also possible to combine the intent of multiple natural persons and impute such 'united intent' to the corporation.[214] Second, the *mens rea* of the corporation is established by the existence of intent or negligence of the corporation itself (*direct* approach). Corporate *mens rea* can be derived from circumstances closely related to the company itself, such as its policies and decisions. A company may confess by means of its agents,[215] for example stating in court that management did not act to prevent fraudulent acts that it knew were taking place within the company.[216] The latter approach is particularly suited to cases of gross negligence, which can be derived 'objectively' from the failure of a person to act in accordance with standards of conduct. According to this approach, corporate criminal liability is established based on deficiencies within the structures, policies, and culture of the corporation itself.[217]

4 Corporate social responsibility: an increasing source of liability?

The proliferation of soft law instruments and the trend towards corporate self-regulation may inadvertently contribute to the development of liability regimes.[218] Some NGOs and scholars argue that CSR instruments, whether soft law instruments or voluntary commitments of companies, are capable of creating obligations for MNEs, the breach of which may trigger corporate

---

211 Cass crim 26 June 2001, Bull Crim (2001) 161 (*Sté Carrefour*). See also Deckert, 'Corporate Criminal Liability in France', 164.

212 Keulen and Gritter, 'Corporate Criminality in the Netherlands', 183.

213 HR 15 October 1996, NJ 1997, 109.

214 Van Gelder and Ryngaert, 'Dutch Report on Prosecuting Corporations', 115.

215 HR 14 March 1950, NJ 1952, 656.

216 Keulen and Gritter, 'Corporate Criminality in the Netherlands', 184.

217 Van Gelder and Ryngaert, 'Dutch Report on Prosecuting Corporations', 115.

218 Emmanuel Daoud and Clarisse Le Corre, 'La responsabilité pénale des personnes morales en droit de l'environnement' (2013) 44 Bulletin du droit de l'environnement industriel 53, 55.

liability.[219] In practice, CSR instruments may be useful to courts in assessing misconduct of companies. Plaintiffs in transnational litigation against MNEs have used the CSR commitments of MNEs to support liability claims for human rights abuse and environmental damage. However, their arguments have been met with a mixed reception from the courts.

In France, labour courts have sometimes used ethical codes to demonstrate the employer's management power or to assess the gravity of the employee's failure to comply with a professional duty.[220] In some transnational cases against MNEs, judges have creatively used CSR instruments to assess MNEs' breach of their duty of care. In *AREVA*, the TASS held that by setting up health observatories and signing a memorandum of understanding on occupational diseases caused by ionizing radiation with Sherpa, the parent company AREVA appeared to assume liability for the potential impact on the health and safety of individuals working in its uranium mines. The TASS used AREVA's voluntary CSR commitments to find that AREVA had acted as the employer of Venel with the authority and the power to control and organize his working conditions. In addition, in *Erika*, the parent company Total SA had voluntarily set up a specific vetting procedure to control the quality of its tankers. The French courts found that by ignoring this procedure, Total SA had neglected its duty of care. Total SA's voluntary commitment to control the quality of tankers became a norm for assessing the faulty conduct of the company.[221]

However, courts do not automatically accept that a company's voluntary commitments create enforceable obligations or that a breach of a company's voluntary CSR commitments may give rise to liability. In the same *AREVA* case, the Court of Appeal ultimately rejected that AREVA's voluntary commitments led, either directly or through its subsidiaries, to a situation where AREVA automatically became the employer, or co-employer, of Venel. The argument that soft law instruments may lead to enforceable obligations, or that the breach of voluntary commitments may give rise to liability, has also revealed its limits in *Alstom*. In this case, the plaintiffs argued that the defendant companies had failed to fulfil their commitments to comply with the relevant rules of public international law enshrined in their code of ethics and the UN Global Compact that they had signed.[222] In particular, they insisted upon the

---

219 For a discussion of the legal effects of company voluntary commitments, see Stéphane Béal and others, 'Les risques juridiques liés à la mise en place d'une démarche éthique dans l'entreprise' (2012) 4 Cahiers de droit de l'entreprise; Laurence Pinte, 'La responsabilité sociale des entreprises: un nouvel enjeu fiscal' (2012) 9 Revue de droit fiscal; Julie Ferrari, 'La société mère peut-elle voir sa responsabilité engagée dans le cadre de la RSE?' (2012) 4332 Revue Lamy droit des affaires 72.

220 Béal and others, 'Les risques juridiques'.

221 Neyret, 'L' affaire Erika', 2239; Daoud and Le Corre, 'Arrêt Erika', 5.

222 The UN Global Compact is a voluntary initiative by which businesses commit to implement a principle-based framework in areas such as human rights, labour rights, the environment, or corruption. See 'UN Global Compact' (UN) <https://www.unglobalcompact.org/about> accessed 1 May 2021.

binding nature of the norms contained in the CSR instruments the companies had committed to respect. In 2013, however, the Versailles Court of Appeal rejected their argument on the basis of the non-voluntary nature of the soft law instruments relied on. First, it held that the UN Global Compact's application is 'based solely on the goodwill of the corporations. It has no binding effect ... The Global Compact being no more than a point of reference, non-compliance with its principles cannot be invoked to justify a claim for violation of international rights.'[223] Second, the Court of Appeal found that the companies' codes of ethics stated that they are of a 'strictly voluntary' and non-binding character. As these codes stemmed from a personal initiative and provided no sanction, they could not be considered binding, nor could they be relied upon by third parties. Ultimately, the Court of Appeal concluded:

> The Global Compact, as well as the codes of ethics, express values that the corporations wish their staff to apply in the exercise of their activities for the company. They are 'framework' documents which contain only recommendations and rules of conduct, without creating obligations or commitments for the benefit of third parties who may seek compliance [with such documents]. Thus, the appellant cannot rely on a breach of the Global Compact or of the standards of conduct provided for in the codes of ethics to claim that Alstom, Alstom Transport and Veolia Transport have committed a breach of international law.[224]

In the Netherlands, the question whether soft law instruments could create enforceable obligations was raised in the *BATCO* case.[225] The Amsterdam Court of Appeal annulled an English parent company's decision to close down its Dutch subsidiary in order to concentrate production at a Belgian subsidiary. It held that the lack of appropriate consultation with the trade unions and the work council by the Dutch subsidiary amounted to mismanagement in breach of the OECD Guidelines, to which the English parent was committed. For some authors, *BATCO* has shown that Dutch courts may consider the OECD Guidelines when determining the duty of care of companies under Dutch tort law.[226]

In *Shell*, the plaintiffs have argued that the parent company, RDS, had a duty of care to influence and control its subsidiary, SPDC, to prevent damage to humans and the environment in Nigeria.[227] It is worth noting that they have argued that this obligation is reinforced by the fact that the MNE committed to implement

---

223 See Noah Rubins and Gisèle Stephens-Chu, 'Introductory Note to AFPS and PLO v Alstom and Veolia (Versailles Ct App.)' (2013) 52 International Legal Materials 1157, 1181.

224 Ibid, 1182.

225 CA Amsterdam 21 June 1979, NJ 1980, 217.

226 Jägers and Van Der Heijden, 'Corporate Human Rights Violations', 857–858.

227 'Writ of Summons: Oguru, Efanga & Milieudefensie vs Shell plc and Shell Nigeria' [195].

various CSR instruments, such as the OECD Guidelines, the UN Global Compact, and the Global Reporting Initiative, which prescribe an active duty of care for parent companies.[228] For instance, pursuant to the OECD Guidelines, RDS should have set up and maintained a suitable environmental management system, including the development of emergency plans, and best practices procedures and technologies to be available in the event of oil spills.[229] Furthermore, the plaintiffs alleged that RDS failed to respect precautionary measures set in the UN Global Compact[230] and to report the oil spills in accordance with the Global Reporting Initiative.[231] However, in its 2021 decision, the Court of Appeal did not address these arguments.

5 Conclusions

This chapter has discussed the challenges to and opportunities for holding MNEs liable for damage arising in the context of group activities under French and Dutch law.

The first difficulty arises from the fact that the corporate group is not recognized as a legal entity in France and the Netherlands. As a result, groups cannot have rights and obligations or be liable to pay damages. Consequently, the liability arising from any obligations of the entities of the group shall be borne by those entities. Another difficulty arises from the fact that French and Dutch law recognizes the separate legal personality of the company and provides for limited liability of shareholders for certain companies. In the context of MNE activities, separate legal personality and limited liability generally prevent the parent company from being held liable for a subsidiary, even where the parent company owns or controls that subsidiary.

However, French and Dutch law lay down a number of bases on which to hold the parent company to account for its subsidiary's obligations. First, courts may, in some circumstances, disregard the application of separate legal personality and limited liability by piercing the corporate veil. In company law, this practice is accepted in exceptional cases. French and Dutch courts are generally reluctant to pierce the corporate veil and require strict conditions to do so. At the same time, corporate veil piercing is generally accepted in competition law where a parent company with a 100 per cent shareholding in a subsidiary can be held jointly and severally liable for the payment of the fine imposed on its subsidiary.

228 Ibid, [199]–[211].
229 Ibid, [216].
230 Ibid, [220].
231 Ibid, [221]–[223].

Furthermore, voluntary corporate veil piercing may take place where a parent company accepts liability for the obligations entered into by its subsidiary.

In addition, courts may hold a parent company liable for damage resulting from its subsidiary's activities where the parent company has committed a fault that has caused or contributed to the damage. This fault-based liability can be found in various situations across legal fields, including tort law, environmental law, and labour law. In the context of transnational litigation against MNEs, this means that a parent company could potentially be held liable for human rights violations or environmental pollution occurring as a result of its subsidiary's activities where its misconduct has contributed to the damage. To date, however, few cases have been brought or heard on the basis of the fault of the parent company under French or Dutch law. Moreover, courts tend to require gross negligence on the part of the parent company to find it liable for damage arising from its subsidiary's activities. This requirement, coupled with the lack of access to relevant evidence to demonstrate the involvement of the parent company in the damage, makes it difficult for plaintiffs to hold the parent company liable on that basis.

Finally, a parent company may, in theory, be held liable for a criminal offence committed in the context of group activities if it has committed a criminal offence either as a primary or secondary perpetrator. It may also be possible to engage the criminal liability of the parent company where it has acted as an accomplice. However, the procedural and substantive conditions to engage criminal liability limit the potential opportunities provided by criminal law.

In a limited number of cases, French and Dutch courts have taken into account the voluntary CSR commitments of the parent company to assess its misconduct in liability claims. Given the current predominance of soft norms and CSR policies to regulate business activities, this approach could be an important step in ensuring corporate accountability. However, this practice remains too rare to conclude that voluntary commitments can have legally enforceable consequences.

Ultimately, the current French and Dutch legal framework on the liability of the parent company for its subsidiary's obligations is fragmented, and it remains uncertain as to whether victims can hold the parent company accountable. A legislative intervention is necessary to establish a specific regime governing the liability of parent companies for human rights abuses and environmental pollution in the context of group activities.

The next chapter discusses the possibility of holding MNEs liable for human rights abuse and environmental pollution through the emergence of mandatory HRDD legislation across Europe.

Part III
Future pathways for access to justice
in business and human rights

Chapter 7

Achieving access to justice in Europe through mandatory due diligence legislation

1 Introduction

In 2011, the UNHRC endorsed the UNGPs, which recognize that: (1) States have a duty to respect, protect, and fulfil human rights; (2) business enterprises have an independent responsibility to respect human rights; and (3) appropriate and effective remedies must be available when rights and obligations are breached. As part of their responsibility to respect human rights, business enterprises should exercise HRDD, meaning they should undertake processes to identify, prevent, mitigate, and account for how they address potential and actual impacts on human rights caused or contributed to by their own activities, or which are directly linked to their operations, products or services resulting from their business relationships.[1]

Following the endorsement of the UNGPs, corporate HRDD has become a norm of expected conduct.[2] It has been integrated into relevant international instruments, such as the OECD Guidelines for Multinational Enterprises and the revised Tripartite Declaration of Principles concerning Multinational Enterprises and Social Policy of the International Labour Organization (ILO). A growing number of countries, especially in Europe, have also adopted or taken steps to adopt legislation imposing human rights and environmental due diligence on corporate groups. Besides these legal developments, a growing number of investors now ask companies to disclose how they handle their human rights risks.[3] A small but increasing number of large corporations in different sectors have also expressed their commitment to respect human rights and, in some cases, have called for the adoption of mandatory HRDD standards.[4] Some actors, including the UNWG, have called these developments 'the beginning of a paradigm shift'.[5] Nonetheless, the UNWG recently stated that

---

1   UNWG, 'Corporate Human Rights Due Diligence – Emerging Practices, Challenges and Ways Forward' (16 July 2018) UN Doc A/73/163, para 2.

2   Ibid, para 20.

3   Ibid, para 22.

4   'Companies & Investors in Support of mHRDD' (BHRRC) <https://www.business-humanrights.org/en/big-issues/mandatory-due-diligence/companies-investors-in-support-of-mhrdd/> accessed 1 May 2021.

5   UNWG, 'Corporate Human Rights Due Diligence', para 20.

while the global diffusion of HRDD as a norm of conduct in various frameworks is noteworthy, more remains to be done to translate the norm into actual practice.[6]

In the UNGPs, HRDD is undertaken first and foremost to prevent adverse human rights impacts.[7] However, in practice it can have a significant impact on access to justice,[8] especially when States design HRDD as a legal standard of conduct. Where this is the case, the way in which HRDD is designed and implemented can make it easier or more difficult for victims of business-related human rights abuses to seek liability or obtain redress from corporations.[9] For example, failure to comply with HRDD raises the prospect of legal liability. Furthermore, a legal HRDD regime may require businesses to provide redress where damage results from the failure to conduct reasonable HRDD. At the same time, companies may rely on HRDD as a defence to show that they have done everything they could to prevent the harm. If such a defence is acceptable, there may be a greater burden on victims to demonstrate that the company should still be held liable.

2 Unpacking human rights due diligence

Due diligence existed in national and international law long before the UNGPs introduced the concept of HRDD. Due diligence has different meanings, ranging from a standard of conduct for assessing liability to a process for identifying and managing risks in commercial transactions, including legal liability risks. In the UNGPs, HRDD borrows characteristics from these distinct understandings of due diligence. It is seen first and foremost as a process undertaken by businesses to prevent the occurrence of human rights abuses. However, HRDD may have a significant impact on what happens once human rights abuses have taken place, especially when victims of such abuse are seeking to gain access to justice. This section explores the relationship between HRDD and access to justice, particularly in the context of the UNGPs.

---

6   Ibid, para 24.

7   Ibid, para 13.

8   UN High Commissioner for Human Rights (UNHCHR), 'Improving Accountability and Access to Remedy for Victims of Business-Related Human Rights Abuse: The Relevance of human rights Due Diligence to Determinations of Corporate Liability' (1 June 2018) UN Doc A/HRC/38/20/Add.2.

9   The OHCHR's Accountability and Remedy Project has already identified the need for greater clarity on the different ways in which HRDD and corporate liability can be interlinked. See UNHCHR, 'Improving Accountability and Access to Remedy for Victims of Business-Related Human Rights Abuse: Explanatory Notes for Guidance' (12 May 2016) UN Doc A/HRC/32/19/Add.1, paras 21–23, 55–56.

The concept of due diligence

The concept of due diligence is not new and has various legal meanings at both national and international level.

Many domestic legal systems have standards that require private actors to conduct due diligence in various settings. In tort law, due diligence is usually understood as a standard of conduct required to discharge an obligation.[10] This concept can be traced to Roman law under which 'a person was liable for accidental harm caused to others if the harm resulted from the person's failure to meet the standard of conduct expected of a *diligens* (or *bonus*) *paterfamilias* – a phrase that translates roughly as a prudent head of a household'.[11] The *diligens paterfamilias* standard influenced the development of the tort of negligence in many legal systems. It was directly incorporated into Roman–Dutch tort law as the relevant standard of conduct. It also became the basis for the development of the 'reasonable man' test under the English common law concept of negligence and for similar standards in civil law legal systems.[12] Due diligence also has specific meanings in the context of business activities. In corporate law, due diligence generally refers to the process of detailed investigation carried out by a business before becoming involved in a business transaction to identify and manage commercial risks. For instance, in the area of mergers and acquisitions, a company will undertake a detailed examination of another company, including its assets, contracts, customers, markets, or financial records, as one of the first steps in a pending merger or acquisition.[13] In this context, the risk of legal liability is another commercial consideration to be identified and managed through due diligence in the context of a particular transaction.[14]

Due diligence takes on a different meaning in international law[15] where it functions primarily as a norm of conduct that defines and circumscribes the responsibility of a State for the conduct of third parties.[16] Under international law, States are normally responsible for the acts or omissions of persons exercising the authority of the State, since these actions are attributed to the

---

10   Jonathan Bonnitcha and Robert McCorquodale, 'The Concept of "Due Diligence" in the UN Guiding Principles on Business and Human Rights' (2017) 20 EJIL 899, 902.

11   Ibid.

12   Ibid, 903.

13   Ibid, 901. See also Olga Martin-Ortega, 'Human Rights Due Diligence for Corporations: From Voluntary Standards to Hard Law at Last?' (2014) 32 Netherlands Quarterly of Human Rights 44, 51.

14   Bonnitcha and McCorquodale, 'The Concept of "Due Diligence"', 901.

15   For a comprehensive analysis of due diligence in international law, see Joanna Kulesza, *Due Diligence in International Law* (Brill 2016).

16   Bonnitcha and McCorquodale, 'The Concept of "Due Diligence"', 903.

State, even if the acts exceeded the authority given by the State. As a result, acts or omissions of non-State actors are themselves generally not attributable to the State. However, the State may incur responsibility for the conduct of third parties if it fails to exercise due diligence in preventing or reacting to such acts or omissions.[17] This broad principle applies to various areas of international law, including in the fields of investment and environmental protection.[18] Due diligence also plays a significant role in international human rights law in defining the extent of a State's obligations to prevent and respond to human rights infringements by private actors within its territory or jurisdiction.[19] Bonnitcha and McCorquodale summarise due diligence in international law as follows:

> In summary, in international law, 'due diligence is concerned with supplying a standard of care against which fault can be assessed' that is relevant in some circumstances but not in others. As a standard of conduct, it defines the extent of states' responsibility, for example, for infringements of human rights, damage to foreign property and transboundary pollution. It imposes an external, 'objective' standard of conduct to take reasonable precaution to prevent, or to respond to, certain types of harm specified by the rule in question.[20]

It is worth noting that States have imposed due diligence obligations upon businesses in various legal fields, including labour law, consumer law, and environmental law. However, States have neglected to adopt similar obligations in order to ensure that businesses respect human rights. There is little explicit reference to human rights in the variety of due diligence regimes that exist in the legal systems of most States.[21] That said, the inclusion of HRDD within the UNGPs has led to a change in the way States treat corporate HRDD.

Human rights due diligence in the UNGPs

The UNGPs clearly provide that in order for business enterprises to meet their responsibility to respect human rights, they should have an HRDD process in place 'to identify, prevent, mitigate, and account for how they address their

---

17   Jan Arno Hessbruegge, 'The Historical Development of the Doctrines of Attribution and Due Diligence in International Law' (2003) 36 NYU Journal of International Law and Policy 265, 268.

18   Bonnitcha and McCorquodale, 'The Concept of "Due Diligence"', 904.

19   Ibid.

20   Ibid, 905.

21   Olivier de Schutter and others, 'Human Rights Due Diligence: The Role of States' (ICAR, ECCJ and CNCA 2012).

impacts on human rights'.[22] According to the UNWG, HRDD 'provides the backbone of the day-to-day activities of a business enterprise in translating into practice its responsibility to respect human rights'.[23] In its Interpretive Guide of the corporate responsibility to respect human rights,[24] the Office of the United Nations High Commissioner for Human Rights (OHCHR) provides that:

> It is through human rights due diligence that an enterprise identifies the information it needs in order to understand its specific human rights risks at any specific point in time and in any specific operating context, as well as the actions it needs to take to prevent and mitigate them.[25]

GP 17 defines the parameters of what the HRDD process should include. In particular, it should include assessing actual and potential human rights impacts, integrating and acting upon the findings, tracking responses, and communicating how impacts are addressed. Furthermore, GP 17 clarifies that HRDD:

> (a) Should cover adverse human rights impacts that the business enterprise may cause or contribute to through its own activities, or which may be directly linked to its operations, products or services by its business relationships;
>
> (b) Will vary in complexity with the size of the business enterprise, the risk of severe human rights impacts, and the nature and context of its operations;
>
> (c) Should also be ongoing, recognizing that the human rights risks may change over time as the business enterprise's operations and operating context evolve.

The HRDD process includes a number of interrelated processes, which should include four essential components.[26] In a nutshell, business enterprises should:

- identify and assess any actual or potential adverse human rights impacts with which they may be involved to gauge human rights risks (GP 18);
- integrate the findings from their impact assessments and take appropriate action to prevent and mitigate adverse human rights impacts (GP 19);

---

22   UNHRC, 'Guiding Principles on Business and Human Rights: Implementing the United Nations "Protect, Respect and Remedy" Framework' (21 March 2011) UN Doc A/HRC/17/31 (UNGPs), GP 15(b).

23   UNWG, 'Corporate Human Rights Due Diligence', para 10.

24   OHCHR, 'The Corporate Responsibility to Respect Human Rights: An Interpretive Guide' (UN 2012).

25   Ibid, Q26.

26   UNWG, 'Corporate Human Rights Due Diligence', para 10.

- track the effectiveness of their response to verify whether adverse human rights impacts are being addressed (GP 20); and
- be prepared to communicate externally to account for how they address their human rights impacts (GP 21).

The HRDD process also needs to be complemented by appropriate policies that elaborate the business enterprise's commitment to respect human rights and incorporate HRDD at all levels and functions, together with its active involvement in remedying adverse human rights impacts caused or contributed to by its activities.[27]

In the UNGPs, HRDD refers interchangeably to a process and a standard of care expected of companies to meet their responsibility to respect human rights.[28] However, the way in which HRDD was formulated led some authors to suggest that the UNGPs failed to explain what due diligence means in practice. According to Bonnitcha and McCorquodale, the use of the term 'due diligence' appears to be 'a clever and deliberate tactic' to build consensus among businesspeople, human rights lawyers, and States.[29] Yet 'due diligence' has a different meaning for these actors. Human rights lawyers usually understand 'due diligence' as 'a standard of conduct required to discharge an obligation', while businesspeople generally see it as 'a process to manage business risks'.[30] Bonnitcha and McCorquodale contend that the UNGPs invoke both understandings of due diligence without clarifying how they relate to each other. The confusion arising from this situation is problematic in practice because it creates uncertainty about the extent of businesses' responsibility to respect human rights and how that responsibility relates to businesses' correlative responsibility to provide a remedy where they have infringed human rights.[31] This confusion raises questions about the possible effects that HRDD may have on access to justice.

Human rights due diligence and access to justice

HRDD may have a significant impact on access to justice, particularly when States design legal HRDD regimes. The way in which HRDD is designed and implemented can make it easier or harder to establish corporate liability or obtain redress for victims of business-related human rights abuses. For instance, HRDD may be defined as an expected commitment of businesses

---

27   Ibid, para 11.

28   Lise Smit and others, 'Study on Due Diligence Requirements through the Supply Chain – Final Report' (European Commission 2020) 157, citing Bonnitcha and McCorquodale, 'The Concept of "Due Diligence"'.

29   Bonnitcha and McCorquodale, 'The Concept of "Due Diligence"', 900.

30   Ibid.

31   Ibid, 901.

or as a mandatory obligation. While the infringement of the former does not have enforceable legal consequences, the violation of the latter may lead to corporate liability and provide a cause of action for victims of human rights abuses resulting from the failure to comply with due diligence. Furthermore, HRDD may create an obligation of *conduct* (ie the duty-bearer must behave in a certain manner) or of *result* (ie the outcome of that behaviour) for companies. In the context of legal proceedings, the nature and extent of the evidence required to trigger corporate liability will vary depending on the nature of the HRDD obligation. An obligation of *conduct* will either require victims to prove that the business has failed to exercise reasonable due diligence or require the business to prove that it has carried out reasonable due diligence. In the context of an obligation of *result*, proof of the damage is likely to be sufficient. In addition, under certain circumstances, HRDD may require businesses to provide remedies when human rights abuses occur. HRDD may also be relevant for determining the type and severity of sanctions and remedies once liability is established. Judges often have a significant amount of discretion and can increase or reduce sanctions and remedies depending on the level of the company's culpability.[32] In some situations, such as in criminal proceedings or civil cases where punitive damages may apply, the fact that a company has conducted serious and thorough HRDD may be seen as a mitigating factor. As such, a judge may decide to impose less severe penalties if the business has engaged in HRDD activities.[33] If a company fails to exercise HRDD, a court could also mandate such activities as part of a sanction or remedy, or as part of a plea agreement.[34]

In the UNGPs, HRDD interacts with access to justice in a number of ways. First, the UNGPs do not address corporate liability in the context of HRDD. This is not surprising since the UNGPs distinguish between the corporate responsibility to respect human rights and corporate liability. The Commentary to GP 13 states that '[t]he responsibility of business enterprises to respect human rights is distinct from issues of legal liability and enforcement, which remain defined largely by national law provisions in relevant jurisdictions'. The corporate responsibility to respect is 'a global standard of expected conduct for all business enterprises wherever they operate', which 'exists over and above compliance with national laws and regulations protecting human rights',[35] while corporate liability is a national standard defined and applicable in a specific domestic context. According to the OHCHR, the corporate responsibility to respect means that '[b]usiness enterprises should therefore not wait for legal regimes on human rights due diligence to emerge before establishing and developing

---

32 UNHCHR, 'Improving Accountability' (June 2018), para 32.
33 Ibid, para 33.
34 Ibid, para 34.
35 UNGPs, Commentary to GP 11.

their own human rights due diligence processes, nor should they consider that mere compliance with legal requirements on human rights due diligence will necessarily be consistent with their responsibility to respect human rights'.[36]

Nonetheless, the UNGPs consider whether HRDD can provide businesses with a defence against liability claims. The Commentary to GP 17 states that:

> Conducting appropriate human rights due diligence should help business enterprises address the risk of legal claims against them by showing that they took every reasonable step to avoid involvement with an alleged human rights abuse. However, business enterprises conducting such due diligence should not assume that, by itself, this will automatically and fully absolve them from liability for causing or contributing to human rights abuses.

Accordingly, a business that demonstrates that it has conducted appropriate HRDD should be more likely to 'address the risk of legal claims' against it. This suggests that a business that conducts appropriate HRDD is less likely to be subjected to lawsuits or be held liable where a lawsuit is brought. At the same time, a business enterprise that conducts appropriate due diligence can still be held liable for causing or contributing to human rights abuses.

Stakeholders have suggested that allowing an HRDD defence to liability could incentivize companies to meaningfully engage in HRDD activities and have important preventative effects.[37] At the same time, there are serious concerns with the appropriateness of an HRDD defence and whether such a defence is fair to victims.[38] An HRDD defence might be particularly inappropriate and unfair 'in cases where superficial "check box" approaches to human rights due diligence might be used as a reference point instead of genuine attempts to identify, mitigate, and address human rights risks as contemplated in the UNGPs'.[39] If the courts are to accept an HRDD defence, it is therefore crucial to ensure that companies are obliged to set up and implement effective and robust HRDD measures. Otherwise, there is a twofold risk that companies will be, or will remain, involved in human rights abuses, while victims will struggle even more to prove corporate liability for the harm they have suffered and obtain access to remedies.

Although the UNGPs do not address corporate liability, they recognize accountability as one of the objectives of HRDD. In the context of their responsibility to respect human rights, business enterprises should carry out

36   UNHCHR, 'Improving Accountability' (June 2018), para 9.
37   Ibid, para 29.
38   Ibid.
39   Ibid.

HRDD in order to identify, prevent, mitigate, and *account* for how they address their adverse human rights impacts.[40] In particular, GP 21 states:

> In order to account for how they address their human rights impacts, business enterprises should be prepared to communicate this externally, particularly when concerns are raised by or on behalf of affected stakeholders. Business enterprises whose operations or operating contexts pose risks of severe human rights impacts should report formally on how they address them.

Businesses should have policies and processes in place through which they 'know and show that they respect human rights in practice'. 'Showing involves communication, providing a measure of transparency and accountability to individuals or groups who may be impacted and to other relevant stakeholders, including investors.'[41] Accountability in the context of HRDD is close to accounting or disclosure obligations of companies, where companies must report on their financial and non-financial performance and the risks associated with their activities. However, GP 21 seems to restrict accountability to 'communicating how impacts are addressed'. It does not indicate whether, as part of its accountability, a company should be answerable for the consequences of its actions and face potential legal and non-legal sanctions and the provision of remedies. Nevertheless, business accountability for such consequences can be derived from GP 22 on remediation.

The UNGPs do not address the question of remediation in the context of HRDD. The reason is that HRDD and remediation are seen as separate processes that business enterprises must have in place in order to meet their responsibility to respect human rights. On the one hand, businesses should set up an HRDD process to identify, prevent, mitigate, and account for how they address their impacts on human rights. On the other hand, processes should also be established to allow for the remediation of any adverse human rights impacts businesses cause or contribute to.[42] HRDD and remediation are independent processes because they address different stages of human rights abuse. The UNGPs differentiates between *potential* adverse human rights impacts (ie abuse that could occur in the future) and *actual* adverse human rights impacts (ie abuse that has already occurred). HRDD must be undertaken first and foremost to prevent *potential* impacts,[43] while remediation processes should seek to redress *actual* impacts. Nonetheless, the OHCHR points out that

---

40   UNGPs, GPs 15 and 17.
41   Ibid, Commentary to GP 21.
42   Ibid, GP 15.
43   UNWG, 'Corporate Human Rights Due Diligence', para 13.

although HRDD and remediation are two separate processes, they remain 'interrelated'.[44]

Under Pillar II, on the corporate responsibility to respect, and subsequent to describing HRDD in the UNGPs, GP 22 deals with remediation processes. Accordingly:

> Where business enterprises identify that they have caused or contributed to adverse impacts, they should provide for or cooperate in their remediation through legitimate processes.

The Commentary to GP 22 specifies that:

> Even with the best policies and practices, a business enterprise may cause or contribute to an adverse human rights impact that it has not foreseen or been able to prevent. Where a business enterprise identifies such a situation, whether through its human rights due diligence process or other means, its responsibility to respect human rights requires active engagement in remediation, by itself or in cooperation with other actors.

The performance of HRDD may not always prevent the occurrence of business-related human rights abuse. In that event, remediation should then take place. When a business identifies, through its HRDD process, that it has caused or contributed to such abuse, it should be actively involved in its remediation through legitimate processes.[45] Therefore, the business enterprise should play a direct role in providing timely and effective remedy.[46] Companies may provide remediation through operational-level grievance mechanisms, meaning procedures typically administered by enterprises and accessible directly to individuals and communities. However, these mechanisms must meet certain core criteria.[47] In particular, they should be legitimate, accessible, predictable, equitable, transparent, rights-compatible, a source of continuous learning, and based on engagement and dialogue.[48] In some circumstances, it may be most appropriate for remediation to be provided by an entity other than the enterprise, such as a court or another State-based proceeding.[49] In

---

44   OHCHR, 'The Corporate Responsibility to Respect Human Rights', Q32.

45   The UNWG has clarified that 'legitimate processes' may involve State-based judicial and non-judicial mechanisms, as well as non-State-based grievance mechanisms. UNWG, 'Corporate Human Rights Due Diligence', para 12.

46   OHCHR, 'The Corporate Responsibility to Respect Human Rights', Q64.

47   UNGPs, Commentary to GP 22.

48   Ibid, GP 31.

49   OHCHR, 'The Corporate Responsibility to Respect Human Rights', Q64.

some situations, cooperation with judicial mechanisms may be required, in particular where crimes are alleged.[50]

GP 22 is limited to situations where the business enterprise *itself* recognizes that it has caused or contributed to an adverse human rights impact.[51] If an enterprise contests an allegation that it has caused or contributed to an adverse impact, it cannot be expected to provide for remediation itself unless and until it is obliged to do so (for instance, by a court).[52] In that event, the UNGPs lack guidance on how HRDD, as a standard of conduct, can be interpreted in order to establish corporate liability. Another limitation of GP 22 is that where adverse impacts have occurred that the business enterprise has not caused or contributed to, but which are directly linked to its operations, products, or services by a business relationship, the responsibility to respect human rights does not require that the enterprise itself provide for remediation, though it may take a role in doing so.[53]

Ultimately, '[HRDD] is fundamentally a concept that encapsulates a series of good practices without necessary or clear legal implications.'[54] A company's failure to carry out HRDD does not entail any legal responsibility. HRDD also plays a limited role in ensuring that businesses provide for the remediation of adverse human rights impacts. These characteristics of HRDD stem from the fact that the corporate responsibility to respect is formulated in a manner that produces barely enforceable legal consequences[55] and gives companies a wide margin of manoeuvre to decide whether to remedy adverse human rights impacts.

3 Mandatory human rights due diligence in national legislation

In the UNGPs, HRDD is seen first and foremost as a standard and/or process aimed at companies. The UNGPs define HRDD as part of the corporate responsibility to respect, which is a standard of expected business conduct. Furthermore, they do not explicitly require States to impose a general HRDD

---

50   UNGPs, Commentary to GP 22.

51   OHCHR, 'The Corporate Responsibility to Respect Human Rights', Q63.

52   Ibid, Q68.

53   UNGPs, Commentary to GP 22.

54   Carlos López, 'The "Ruggie Process": From Legal Obligations to Corporate Social Responsibility?' in Surya Deva and David Bilchitz (eds), *Human Rights Obligations of Business: Beyond the Corporate Responsibility to Respect?* (CUP 2013) 61.

55   The corporate responsibility to respect is not in itself a legal standard. See UNHCHR, 'Improving Accountability' (June 2018), para 11.

obligation on companies. In the context of the State duty to protect human rights, the UNGPs only recommend that States should adopt HRDD standards in certain situations: when providing effective guidance to business enterprises on how to respect human rights throughout their operations;[56] in the context of activities conducted by business enterprises owned or controlled by the State or that receive substantial support and services from State agencies;[57] and in the context of business enterprises operating in conflict-affected areas.[58] At the same time, the UNGPs suggest that in order to meet their duty to protect, States should enforce laws that are aimed at, or have the effect of, requiring business enterprises to respect human rights. Such legislation could impose HRDD obligations on companies. More recently, the UNWG acknowledged that although a number of business enterprises have taken steps to implement HRDD, considerable efforts by various actors, including States, are still required to make HRDD part of standard business practice.[59]

Following the adoption of the UNGPs, a number of countries have taken significant steps to impose mandatory HRDD on companies in recent years. In Europe, the French Act on the Duty of Vigilance and the Dutch Child Labour Due Diligence Act are currently the most notable instruments on HRDD. In July 2021, Germany enacted its own human rights due diligence law, which should enter into force in 2023.[60] These instruments effectively require companies to identify human rights risks and prevent them from occurring in the context of their activities. Other EU and non-EU States, including Norway,[61] Finland,[62] and the UK,[63] are currently considering, or are in the process of adopting, mandatory HRDD measures.[64] While these initiatives vary in scope and

56   UNGPs, GP 3.

57   Ibid, GP 4.

58   Ibid, GP 7.

59   UNWG, 'Corporate Human Rights Due Diligence', para 3.

60   Gesetz über die unternehmerischen Sorgfaltspflichten zur Vermeidung von Menschenrechtsverletzungen in Lieferketten vom 16. Juli 2021.

61   'Norway: Govt.-Appointed Committee Proposes Human Rights Transparency and Due Diligence Regulation' (BHRRC, 3 December 2019) <https://www.business-humanrights.org/en/latest-news/norway-govt-appointed-committee-proposes-human-rights-transparency-and-due-diligence-regulation/> accessed 1 May 2021.

62   'Finnish Government Commits to HRDD Legislation' (BHRRC, 3 June 2019) <https://www.business-humanrights.org/en/latest-news/finnish-government-commits-to-hrdd-legislation/> accessed 1 May 2021.

63   The UK is planning to adopt a narrow type of due diligence legislation to curb illegal deforestation. PA Media, 'UK Sets Out Law to Curb Illegal Deforestation and Protect Rainforests' *The Guardian* (London, 25 August 2020) <https://www.theguardian.com/environment/2020/aug/25/uk-sets-out-law-to-curb-illegal-deforestation-and-protect-rainforests> accessed 1 May 2021.

64   'Mapping mHRDD Legislative Progress in Europe: Map and Comparative Analysis of mHRDD Laws and Legislative Proposals' (ECCJ, 28 May 2020) <https://corporatejustice.org/eccj-publications/16807-mapping-mhrdd-progress-in-europe-map-and-comparative-analysis-of-mhrdd-laws-and-legislative-proposals> accessed 1 July 2021.

content, they share the same goal of creating legally enforceable obligations for companies to identify risks to human rights and prevent such risks from materializing within their activities. However, such legislative processes are complex, can provoke controversy, and do not guarantee the successful adoption of HRDD norms. For example, in 2020, after years of debate on the adoption of a groundbreaking legislative proposal on HRDD,[65] Switzerland ultimately opted for a less ambitious counter-proposal requiring sustainability reporting with limited due diligence.[66]

The adoption of national mandatory HRDD standards may potentially lead to corporate accountability and achieve, to some extent, access to justice. This section sets out the main features of the French Act on the Duty of Vigilance and the Dutch Child Labour Due Diligence Act and assesses their added-value from an access to justice perspective. However, before describing the French and Dutch HRDD legislation, it is important to consider what mandatory HRDD standards mean in the context of this book.

Mandatory human rights due diligence standards

Mandatory HRDD standards require companies to conduct and/or exercise due diligence to prevent and/or mitigate human rights abuses in their operations. The scope and obligations of HRDD standards may be articulated in a variety of ways. In terms of scope, HRDD norms may create obligations for all companies or specific groups of companies, or differentiated obligations that take into account the size and structure of companies. They may also require that companies conduct due diligence in the context of a variety of activities, such as their direct activities, the activities of companies they own and/or control, or the activities of companies with which they have a business relationship (eg suppliers, subcontractors). In addition, a legal HRDD regime may require businesses to exercise due diligence in order to respect human rights in general or to address specific human rights challenges, such as child labour or slavery. With respect to obligations, HRDD standards can impose different duties on companies. Typically, they should require that businesses identify potential risks of human rights abuses that may occur in the context of their activities, and take specific

---

65 'Initiative populaire fédérale "Entreprises responsables – pour protéger l'être humain et l'environnement"' (Chancellerie Fédérale Suisse) <https://www.bk.admin.ch/ch/f/pore/vi/vis462t.html> accessed 1 May 2021. For a discussion on the Swiss Responsible Business Initiative, see Nicolas Bueno, 'Diligence en matière de droits de l'homme et responsabilité de l'entreprise: le point en droit suisse' (2019) 29 Swiss Review of International and European Law 345.

66 Christelle Coslin and Margaux Renard, 'Switzerland: Responsible Business Initiative Narrowly Rejected Despite Gaining 50.7% of Popular Vote' (Lexology, 7 December 2020) <https://www.lexology.com/library/detail.aspx?g=0cc7c0cb-8f17-4c48-93be-f549a2321e4c> accessed 1 May 2021.

actions to prevent such abuse. In some cases, HRDD standards may force businesses to communicate how they address human rights risks in their activities. Finally, a legal HRDD regime may impose sanctions on companies that do not comply with their HRDD obligations. It may also force companies to provide remedies when human rights abuses occur in the context of their activities, depending on whether the companies have failed to exercise due diligence or have carried out insufficient or inadequate due diligence. In some cases, companies may be required to provide remedies even if they have conducted sufficient and adequate HRDD. Notwithstanding the various ways in which HRDD can be implemented, HRDD standards are ultimately aimed at avoiding the occurrence of human rights abuses by requiring companies to actively prevent them.

On the basis of this interpretation, HRDD norms should be distinguished from transparency standards that require companies to disclose how they identify and address human rights risks in their activities. Disclosure obligations are usually intended to ensure that a specific type of information is made public in order to enable stakeholders, such as investors, consumers, or NGOs, to evaluate and/ or monitor the social and environmental performance of companies and make informed decisions. While disclosure obligations may encourage companies to respect human rights, they do not ultimately require companies to prevent human rights abuses in their activities. On the other hand, prevention of human rights abuses by companies is the main objective of HRDD.

However, businesses may be required to communicate how they address their human rights impacts as part of their HRDD.[67] In the UK, the Modern Slavery Act 2015 (MSA) falls under the category of legislation imposing disclosure obligations upon companies.[68] Under Section 54 MSA, large companies that carry out business in the UK must prepare a slavery and human trafficking statement each financial year, which should be published on their website or made available to anyone requesting it. This statement may take two forms. It may either describe the steps that the company has taken to ensure that slavery and human trafficking is not taking place in any of its supply chains and in any part of its own business, or it may simply declare that the company has taken no such steps. Therefore, the MSA only requires companies to disclose whether and, if applicable, how they address the risks of slavery and human trafficking. It does not oblige companies to actively address such risks. This can be inferred from the fact that a company does not risk legal sanctions if it declares that it has not taken any measures to prevent slavery or trafficking in human beings.[69]

---

67   UNGPs, GP 21.

68   Anne Triponel, 'Business and Human Rights Legislation: An Overview' (Triponel Consulting, 14 October 2019) <https://triponelconsulting.com/business-and-human-rights-legislation/> accessed 1 May 2021.

69   For a critical assessment of the MSA, see Virginia Mantouvalou, 'The UK Modern Slavery Act 2015 Three Years On' (2018) 81 Modern Law Review 1017.

The French Act on the Duty of Vigilance

In France, several national deputies introduced a bill in 2013 to create a 'duty of vigilance' (*devoir de vigilance*) of parent and controlling companies towards their subsidiaries, subcontractors, and suppliers.[70] This bill sought to hold MNEs accountable 'to prevent the occurrence of tragedies in France and abroad and to obtain reparations for victims of damage detrimental to human rights and the environment'.[71] However, it stirred up a lot of opposition, most notably from businesses, and the French government was anxious about the initiative. After years of contentious debate, in 2017 France adopted the Act on the Duty of Vigilance,[72] which creates new due diligence obligations in the context of MNE activities. This landmark instrument is the first statute to establish a general obligation for parent or controlling companies to implement HRDD. It also imposes a duty of due diligence in other areas, such as environmental protection and human health and safety. That said, its content was trimmed of controversial points, such as the existence of a duty of care per se, the possibility of holding parent companies liable under criminal law, and the reversal of the burden of proof on parent companies, which would have made the Act on the Duty of Vigilance a more robust instrument for corporate accountability.[73]

The Act on the Duty of Vigilance inserted two new articles into the Commercial Code: Article L225-102-4, which describes the HRDD obligations of companies, and Article L225-102-5, which provides for tort liability where companies fail to comply with those obligations.

The HRDD obligations of companies

Article L225-102-4(I) provides that parent and controlling companies of corporate groups (including MNEs) that are headquartered or registered in France and are above a certain size must draft and effectively implement a 'vigilance plan' (*plan de vigilance*).[74] This plan must contain due diligence

---

70 Proposition de loi n° 1524 & Proposition de loi n° 1519 du 6 novembre 2013 relatives au devoir de vigilance des sociétés mères et des entreprises donneuses d'ordre.

71 Ibid (author's translation).

72 Loi n° 2017-399 relative au devoir de vigilance des sociétés mères et entreprises donneuses d'ordre.

73 Sandra Cossart, Jérôme Chaplier, and Tiphaine Beau de Loménie, 'The French Law on Duty of Care: A Historic Step Towards Making Globalization Work for All' (2017) 2 Business and Human Rights Journal 317, 317.

74 Two types of companies are subject to the obligation to establish and effectively implement a vigilance plan:

   (1) Any company which employs, at the end of two consecutive financial years, at least five thousand employees within the company and in its direct or indirect subsidiaries whose registered office is in French territory; or

   (2) Any company which employs, at the end of two consecutive financial years, at least ten thousand employees within the company and in its direct or indirect subsidiaries whose registered office is in French territory or abroad.

measures to identify risks and prevent serious violations of human rights and fundamental freedoms, human health and safety, and the environment in their business activities. A significant feature of this vigilance plan is that it must cover risks and violations arising not only from the activities of the company, but also from those of the companies it directly or indirectly controls and of subcontractors or suppliers with which it has an established business relationship, where these activities are related to this relationship. As a result, the mapping of risks must cover a broad range of business relationships and corporate structures, including parent companies and their subsidiaries, as well as supply chains involving subcontractors or suppliers.[75]

Article L225-102-4(I) also lists the measures that must be included in the vigilance plan. They consist of:

(1)   A mapping of risks for their identification, analysis and prioritisation;

(2)   Procedures for the regular assessment of the situation of subsidiaries, subcontractors, or suppliers with whom an established commercial relationship is maintained, with regard to the risk mapping referred to above;

(3)   Appropriate actions to mitigate risks or prevent serious violations;

(4)   A mechanism for alerting and collecting reports relating to the existence or occurrence of risks, established in consultation with representative trade union organizations in the company; and

(5)   A system for monitoring the measures implemented and evaluating their effectiveness.

The Act provides that a decree may complement the vigilance measures already provided for and may specify procedures for drawing up and implementing a vigilance plan. To date, however, no such decree has been adopted by the government. As a result, there are some uncertainties as to the content of the vigilance plan.[76]

Another important aspect is that the company must make the vigilance plan and the report on its effective implementation public and include them

---

75   In the context of former Article L442-6(I)(5) Commercial Code, the Court of Cassation has defined 'established business relationship' as a 'regular, stable and meaningful' relationship (Cass com 6 September 2011, n° 10-30679). In the context of the Act on the Duty of Vigilance, the link with the subcontractor or supplier must be sufficiently significant. Occasional contractors seem to be excluded from its scope. See Gérard Jazottes, 'La sous-traitance saisie par la RSE' in Sandrine Tisseyre (ed), *Sécuriser la sous-traitance: quels nouveaux outils?* (Presses de l'Université Toulouse 1 Capitole 2019).

76   Academics and lawyers have raised concerns about the uncertainties regarding the entities included within the ambit of the vigilance plan and the content of the plan. See Stéphane Brabant, Charlotte Michon, and Elsa Savourey, 'The Vigilance Plan: Cornerstone of the Law on the Corporate Duty of Vigilance' (2017) 93 Revue internationale de la compliance et de l'éthique des affaires 1.

in its management report. Furthermore, the vigilance plan is intended to be developed in association with the company's stakeholders and, where appropriate, within the framework of multi-stakeholder initiatives within sectors or at the territorial level. Although the Act on the Duty of Vigilance neither defines the concept of 'stakeholders' nor makes their participation imperative, the involvement of stakeholders seems to be a prerequisite for the proper execution of the duty of vigilance. This results from the fact that, in line with the UNGPs, the Act 'uniquely combines mechanisms stemming from soft and hard law and aims to strengthen the accountability of parent companies in allowing them to self-regulate, under the control of both the judge and stakeholders'.[77]

The legislator provided several enforcement mechanisms to ensure that companies comply with their HRDD obligations. A company may be issued with a formal three month notice by a relevant stakeholder to comply with its obligations. Under Article L225-102-4(II), if the company does not comply, at the request of any person proving an interest, a court may issue an injunction ordering compliance subject to periodic penalty payments (*astreintes*).[78] A court may also be seised to rule in summary proceedings for the same purpose.

To date, NGOs have played an important role in sending formal notices to companies in order to force them to comply with their HRDD obligations.[79] They have also brought several complaints to the courts to enjoin companies

---

77 Tiphaine Beau de Loménie and Sandra Cossart, 'Stakeholders and the Duty of Vigilance' (2017) 94 Revue internationale de la compliance et de l'éthique des affaires 1.

78 Periodic penalty payments are injunctive fines payable on a daily or per-event basis until the defendant satisfies a given obligation. See Ibid, 5.

79 At the time of writing, at least five formal notices had been sent by NGOs to four companies: Total (for two different cases), Teleperformance, EDF, and Casino. See Concepcion Alvarez, 'Total mis en demeure de s'aligner avec l'Accord de Paris, avant une attaque en justice' (Novethic, 24 June 2019) <https://www.novethic.fr/actualite/environnement/climat/isr-rse/total-mise-en-demeure-de-s-aligner-avec-l-accord-de-paris-avant-une-attaque-en-justice-147392.html> accessed 1 May 2021; 'UNI Global Union and Sherpa Send Formal Notice to Teleperformance—Calling on the World Leader in Call Centres to Strengthen Workers' Rights' (UNI Global Union, 18 July 2019) <https://www.uniglobalunion.org/news/uni-global-union-and-sherpa-send-formal-notice-teleperformance-calling-world-leader-call> accessed 1 May 2021; Concepcion Alvarez, 'Devoir de vigilance: EDF mis en demeure pour violation des droits humains' (Novethic, 3 October 2019) <https://www.novethic.fr/actualite/gouvernance-dentreprise/entreprises-controversees/isr-rse/devoir-de-vigilance-edf-mis-en-demeure-pour-violation-des-droits-humains-147763.html> accessed 1 May 2021; 'Indigenous Organisations and NGO Coalition Warn Top French Supermarket Casino: Do Not Sell Beef from Deforestation in Brazil and Colombia – or Face French Law' (Sherpa, 21 September 2020) <https://www.asso-sherpa.org/indigenous-organisations-and-ngo-coalition-warn-top-french-supermarket-casino-do-not-sell-beef-from-deforestation-in-brazil-and-colombia-or-face-french-law-stop-gambling-with-our-forests> accessed 1 May 2021.

to respect their obligations.[80] For example, in one case several NGOs contended that the French oil company Total had not sufficiently developed and implemented its vigilance plan for its oil operations in one of Uganda's natural parks, which, they argued, had major environmental and social impacts. They sent a formal notice to Total requesting that it review its vigilance plan.[81] When the company refused to do so,[82] the NGOs subsequently brought summary proceedings asking the civil court to order Total to fulfil its obligations under Article L225-102-4, and for injunctive relief.[83]

Until now, the HRDD mechanism set up under the Act on the Duty of Vigilance has proved difficult to enforce. It is currently challenging to establish the exact number of companies subject to the Act on the Duty of Vigilance. Over the last few years, the French government has persistently refused to establish a formal list of all companies that are subject to HRDD obligations, preferring to leave the role of law enforcement to civil society.[84] NGOs took the bull by the horns and created a public website listing companies that are, in theory, subject to the Act on the basis of publicly available data.[85] In June 2020, they identified 265 companies subject to the duty of vigilance. However, 72 of them (27 per cent) had not published a vigilance plan since the act came into

---

80   At the time of writing, there were at least four ongoing legal proceedings against three companies (Total, EDF, and Casino) under the Act on the Duty of Vigilance. See 'Premier contentieux climatique contre une multinationale du pétrole en France: 14 collectivités et 5 associations assignent Total en justice pour manquement à son devoir de vigilance' (Sherpa, 28 January 2020) <https://www.asso-sherpa.org/premier-contentieux-climatique-contre-total> accessed 1 May 2021; 'Loi devoir de vigilance: première saisine d'un tribunal français pour le cas de Total en Ouganda' (Les Amis de la Terre, 23 October 2019) <https://www.amisdelaterre.org/communique-presse/loi-devoir-de-vigilance-premiere-saisine-dun-tribunal-francais-pour-le-cas-de-total-en-ouganda/> accessed 1 May 2021; 'EDF assigné en justice pour ses activités au Mexique' (Sherpa, 13 October 2020) <https://www.asso-sherpa.org/edf-assigne-en-justice-pour-ses-activites-au-mexique#pll_switcher> accessed 1 May 2021; 'Déforestation et atteintes aux droits humains en Amazonie: des représentants des peuples autochtones et associations assignent Casino en justice' (Sherpa, 3 March 2021) <https://www.asso-sherpa.org/deforestation-et-atteintes-aux-droits-humains-en-amazonie-des-representants-des-peuples-autochtones-et-associations-assignent-casino-en-justice> accessed 1 May 2021.
81   Amis de la Terre France et Survie, 'Devoir de vigilance: total mise en demeure pour ses activités en Ouganda' (25 June 2019).
82   'Total Responds to Questions from NGOs about its Projects in Uganda' (Total, 9 September 2019) <https://www.total.com/info/statement-09302019> accessed 1 May 2021.
83   'Oil Company Total Faces Historic Legal Action in France for Human Rights and Environmental Violations in Uganda' (Friends of the Earth International, 23 October 2019) <https://www.foei.org/news/total-legal-action-france-human-rights-environment-uganda> accessed 1 May 2021.
84   CCFD-Terre Solidaire and Sherpa, 'Le radar du devoir de vigilance: Identifier les entreprises soumises à la loi' (2020) 5 <https://ccfd-terresolidaire.org/actualites/radar-du-devoir-de-7047> accessed 16 July 2021.
85   Sherpa, CCFD-Terre Solidaire and BHRRC, 'Le projet' (Le radar du devoir de vigilance) <https://plan-vigilance.org/> accessed 1 May 2021.

force.[86] The absence of a list of companies concerned enables them to escape the application of the Act. This factual impunity is reinforced by the fact that the French government has not taken any action to ensure the effective enforcement of the Act on the Duty of Vigilance. Furthermore, in the absence of an official enforcement mechanism, NGOs are obliged to take the lead in challenging companies to fulfil their obligations. However, NGOs do not have the financial and human resources to play such a role. A recent report commissioned by the government called for the creation of a governmental unit that would have an enforcement role.[87]

At the time of writing, one issue arises as to whether civil or commercial courts are the competent courts to require companies to comply effectively with their due diligence obligations. NGOs have raised concerns about the suitability of commercial courts, whose judges are company directors and elected by traders, to rule on cases involving human rights and environmental violations.[88] Recent rulings have created uncertainty regarding which court is competent. In the case against Total for its activities in Uganda, the Nanterre Civil Court declined jurisdiction in January 2020 and referred the case to the commercial court.[89] This decision was upheld on appeal in December 2020.[90] The Versailles Court of Appeal considered that there was a direct link between the vigilance plan, its establishment and implementation, and the management of the company's operations. This link was necessary and sufficient to retain the jurisdiction of the commercial court. However, in another case against Total for the inadequacy of its measures to combat climate change, in February 2021 a pre-trial judge of the Nanterre Civil Court (ie the same court as the one in the case against

---

86   Sherpa, CCFD-Terre Solidaire and BHRRC, 'Édition 2020 du radar du devoir de vigilance: Yves Rocher, Castorama, Picard, McDonald's, France Télévisions, Bigard … 27% des entreprises hors la loi?' (Le radar du devoir de vigilance) <https://plan-vigilance.org/edition-2020-du-radar-du-devoir-de-vigilance-yves-rocher-castorama-picard-mcdonalds-france-televisions-bigard-27-des-entreprises-hors-la-loi/> accessed 1 May 2021.

87   Anne Duthilleul and Matthias de Jouvenel, 'Evaluation de la mise en œuvre de la loi n° 2017-399 du 27 mars 2017 relative au devoir de vigilance des sociétés mères et des entreprises donneuses d'ordre' (Conseil général de l'économie 2020).

88   'Total Abuses in Uganda: French High Court of Justice Declares Itself Incompetent in Favour of the Commercial Court' (Friends of the Earth International, 30 January 2020) <https://www.foei.org/no-category/total-abuses-uganda-french-high court of justice declares-itself-incompetent-duty-vigilance-law> accessed 1 May 2021; Almut Schilling-Vacaflor, 'Putting the French Duty of Vigilance Law in Context: Towards Corporate Accountability for Human Rights Violations in the Global South?' [2020] Human Rights Review <https://link.springer.com/article/10.1007%2Fs12142-020-00607-9> accessed 1 May 2021.

89   TJ Nanterre (ord réf) 30 January 2020, n° 19/02833. See also 'Méga-projet pétrolier de Total en Ouganda: une décision de justice décevante' (Amis de la Terre France, 3 February 2020) <https://www.amisdelaterre.org/mega-projet-petrolier-total-decision-de-justice-decevante/> accessed 1 May 2021.

90   CA Versailles 10 December 2020, n° 20/01692 & 20/01693.

Total for its activities in Uganda) reached a different conclusion.[91] He ruled that the plaintiffs benefited from a right of option, which they could exercise at their convenience, between the judicial court which they had validly seised and the commercial court. To reach that conclusion, the judge relied on the lack of provision in the Act on the Duty of Vigilance for the exclusive jurisdiction of the commercial court and the non-trader status of the plaintiffs. Importantly, he held that while the vigilance plan undoubtedly affects the operation of Total, its purpose and the risks it seeks to prevent are far greater than the strict framework of the management of the company. Therefore, the exclusive jurisdiction of the commercial court is not justified. The case was pending at the time of writing. However, it is expected that the case will be heard on appeal before the Versailles Court of Appeal, which has, in the past, ruled on the exclusive jurisdiction of the commercial court in this type of litigation.[92] However, the uncertainty should soon be lifted by the Parliament. In the context of the adoption of an act on confidence in the judiciary, French deputies and senators are expected to decide whether the judicial courts have jurisdiction to hear duty of vigilance actions based on Articles L225-102-4 and L225-102-5. While the competence of the judicial courts appears to be preferred, some senators have expressed a preference for the jurisdiction of the commercial court. This question should be resolved by 2021–2022.[93]

Liability regime

The Act on the Duty of Vigilance also contains a liability regime for where companies breach their due diligence obligations. Article L225-102-5 Commercial Code states that:

> Under the conditions provided for in Articles 1240 and 1241 of the Civil Code, failure to comply with the obligations laid down in Article L225-102-4 of this Code shall engage the liability of its author and oblige them to compensate for the loss that the performance of those obligations would have made it possible to avoid.[94]

---

91   TJ Nanterre (ord réf) 11 February 2021, n° 20/00915.

92   Philippe Métais and Elodie Valette, 'Devoir de vigilance: vers une option de compétence?' (Dalloz Actualités, 17 February 2021) <https://www.dalloz-actualite.fr/flash/devoir-de-vigilance-vers-une-option-de-competence#.YDkRzGj0mUk> accessed 1 May 2021.

93   Miren Lartigue, 'Contentieux relatif au devoir de vigilance : vers la désignation de tribunaux judiciaires dédiés' (Dalloz Actualités, 4 May 2021) <https://www.dalloz-actualite.fr/flash/contentieux-relatif-au-devoir-de-vigilance-vers-designation-de-tribunaux-judiciaires-dedies#.YXf3AJ7P2Uk> accessed 26 October 2021; 'Action en justice contre Total : le Sénat met en danger la loi pionnière sur le devoir de vigilance' (Notre Affaire à Tous, 6 October 2021) <https://notreaffaireatous.org/action-en-justice-contre-total-le-senat-met-en-danger-la-loi-pionniere-sur-le-devoir-de-vigilance/?utm_source=sendinblue&utm_campaign=Les_actualits_doctobre__Affaire_du_Sicle_mise_en_danger_du_devoir_de_vigilance_bote__outils_pdagogique&utm_medium=email> accessed 26 October 2021.

94   Author's translation.

Article L225-102-5 enables courts to hold parent companies of MNEs liable in tort law for any damage to humans or the environment arising from their failure to draft and/or implement a vigilance plan. It establishes a regime of direct liability of the parent or controlling company (as opposed to a regime of vicarious liability).[95] It also creates a cause of action for individuals and organizations that have suffered loss resulting from the parent company's failure to perform its due diligence obligations. This provides an opportunity for any person proving an interest, including victims of business abuse and potentially NGOs and communities, to bring a tort claim and seek redress. In this way, the Act on the Duty of Vigilance establishes a clear link between due diligence, liability, and remediation. Furthermore, the Act on the Duty of Vigilance has a distinct extraterritorial scope by creating the liability of the parent company in the context of its activities, the activities of companies it owns or controls, and of its subcontractors and suppliers.

To date, French judges have not yet ruled on the application of the new liability regime established pursuant to Article L225-102-5. However, potential plaintiffs are likely to face some barriers in establishing liability and obtaining compensation. As a result of the reference to Articles 1240 and 1241 Civil Code, the cause of action under Article L225-102-5 implicitly requires the existence of fault, loss, and a direct causal link between the two.[96] Demonstrating the existence of fault on the part of the company and the direct causal link between that fault and the loss suffered is likely to raise some challenges for the plaintiffs.

The Act of the Duty of Vigilance creates a fault-based liability regime. Pursuant to Article L225-102-5, the company's failure to comply with the obligations laid down in Article L225-102-4 triggers liability. This means that liability will be incurred where the company has failed to draw up and/or effectively implement a vigilance plan. To date, what characterizes the company's failure to draw up and/or effectively carry out a vigilance plan remains unclear. Apart from the obvious situation where a company does not draft a plan, which would assume an infringement of the company's obligations, which other acts and/or omissions could lead to liability? One question is whether the fault of the company can be demonstrated by a vigilance plan that has been insufficiently elaborated and/or implemented. The Act on the Duty of Vigilance sets out a number of measures that must be included in the plan and mentions the obligation to 'effectively implement' it, but provides little indication of what these measures actually consist of and what effective implementation means. These questions are important, as compliance with HRDD obligations is likely to act as a virtual defence to liability claims.

---

95 Cons const 23 March 2017, Décision n° 2017-750, para 27.

96 Ibid, para 21.

Furthermore, a company will be held liable for 'the loss that the performance of those obligations would have made it possible to avoid'. According to Article L225-102-4(I), vigilance measures are intended to prevent serious infringements of human rights and fundamental freedoms, human health and safety, and the environment resulting from the activities of the company and the companies it controls, and from the activities of subcontractors or suppliers in specific circumstances. Companies should therefore be liable if their failure to draft and/or effectively implement their vigilance plan has led to serious violations of human rights and human health and safety, and environmental pollution. This point raises several issues. First, it is unclear which infringements will be serious enough to justify the liability of the company. Furthermore, there must be a causal link between the company's failure to prepare and/or effectively implement a vigilance plan and the loss suffered as a result of the serious violations of human rights and fundamental freedoms, human health and safety, and the environment. Courts are left to decide how to establish such a causal link. The criteria that will be required to establish causality are currently unknown. However, the Constitutional Court has clearly stated that the liability of the company will be incurred where there is a direct causal link between the infringement and the losses.[97]

As mentioned earlier, the original Bill foresaw a reversal of the burden of proof from victims to companies. In the end, however, this reversal was rejected. As a result, plaintiffs will have the burden of establishing a direct causal link between the failure of the company to draft and/or implement its vigilance plan and the loss they have suffered. As this book has shown, in past cases brought against MNEs to hold them liable for human rights abuses occurring in the context of their global activities, victims have struggled to have access to evidence to demonstrate the liability of parent companies and, more generally, to information relevant for their case. In light of this experience, it is likely that claimants will struggle to establish a direct causal link between the loss they have suffered and the failure of the parent company to comply with its 'vigilance' obligations. In order to ensure that the Act on the Duty of Vigilance does not become a dead letter, some authors have argued for a relaxation of the causal link, or even a presumption of causality.[98]

Finally, no further indication is given as to the nature of the damage required to trigger liability. This lack of detail can be interpreted as leaving the door open to compensation for various types of loss (including bodily, material, or non-material loss). Some authors have also suggested that the failure of a company

---

97   Cons const, Décision n° 2017-750.

98   Anne Danis-Fatôme and Geneviève Viney, 'La responsabilité civile dans la loi relative au devoir de vigilance des sociétés mères et des entreprises donneuses d'ordre' [2017] Recueil Dalloz 1610.

to comply with the obligation *to identify risks* referred to in Article L225-102-4 may be regarded as a failure to comply with a safety standard. This infringement could make it possible for the company to be held liable without resulting material or bodily damage.[99]

In conclusion, the Act on the Duty of Vigilance marks an important political step to ensure 'a fair correlation between the economic power of multinationals and their legal responsibility'.[100] In particular, it does so by facilitating the conditions for civil action against MNEs. However, the contribution of the Act on the Duty of Vigilance to improving access to justice remains limited for several reasons.

First, it applies to a limited number of companies (ie the largest MNEs) whose number is currently uncertain. As a result, victims cannot hold smaller corporate groups and other types of companies liable under the Act. Furthermore, it is difficult for NGOs to identify which companies fall within the Act's scope.

Second, the Act on the Duty of Vigilance creates a specific cause of action in the context of the implementation of HRDD obligations. This means that, in other circumstances, victims of business-related human rights abuses or environmental pollution must rely on the current framework for liability, which, as noted in Chapter 6 of this book, is currently fragmented and insufficient. Therefore, legal reform remains necessary to improve access to justice in situations which do not fall within the scope of the Act.

Third, it will be difficult for victims to meet the Act's requirements for triggering liability. These requirements do not address the substantive and procedural issues that victims have faced in the context of transnational litigation against MNEs. One example of this potential difficulty is the refusal to reverse the burden of proof for the benefit of victims. Finally, the Act on the Duty of Vigilance does not address the issue of remedies in the context of human rights abuses or environmental pollution. It only provides that the court may order the publication, dissemination, or posting of its decision, and the execution of its decision by means of a periodic penalty payment. The Bill originally provided that the company could be condemned to a fine of up to €10 million, which could be increased up to three times that amount depending on the seriousness and circumstances of the breach and the damage caused. However, this provision was quashed by the Constitutional Court.

---

99 Ibid.

100 Dominique Potier, 'Rapport n° 2628 sur la proposition de loi (n° 2578) relative au devoir de vigilance des sociétés mères et des entreprises donneuses d'ordre' (Assemblée Nationale, 11 March 2015) <http://www.assemblee-nationale.fr/14/rapports/r2628.asp#P252_90424> accessed 1 May 2021.

The Dutch Child Labour Due Diligence Act

In October 2019, the Netherlands passed the Child Labour Due Diligence Act, which imposes a duty of care on companies to prevent the supply of goods and services produced using child labour on the Dutch market.[101] Specifically, companies falling within the scope of the Child Labour Due Diligence Act are required to exercise due diligence in their supply chains by investigating whether there is a reasonable suspicion that the goods or services they provide were produced through child labour. This investigation should focus on sources that are reasonably identifiable and available to the company. If there is a reasonable suspicion, the company must adopt and implement an action plan. The Act suggests the observance of the ILO–International Organisation of Employers (IOE) Child Labour Guidance Tool for Business during the investigation, as well as the adoption and implementation of the action plan. In addition, companies must issue a declaration that they have conducted due diligence to prevent the use of child labour in the production of goods and services to Dutch consumers. However, the Act does not specify the form or the content of the declaration that companies must submit. This gap creates the risk that companies will submit declarations with insufficient information on how due diligence has been carried out. However, further rules may be laid down by regulatory acts in this regard.[102] A supervisor is in charge of monitoring compliance with the Act by companies.

In terms of scope, the Child Labour Due Diligence Act applies to both Dutch and foreign companies providing goods and/or services to Dutch end-users (ie the natural or legal person who uses or purchases the good or service). However, it excludes Dutch companies operating abroad that do not provide goods and/or services on the Dutch market. Although the Act targets the last tier of the supply chain, companies under the obligation to investigate must consider the risk of child labour in the entire supply chain involved in the production of the goods or services.[103] Moreover, the Child Labour Due Diligence Act applies only to child labour and is therefore not a general piece of HRDD legislation. The Child Labour Due Diligence Act is due to enter into force in mid-2022.[104]

---

101 Wet van 24 oktober 2019 houdende de invoering van een zorgplicht ter voorkoming van de levering van goederen en diensten die met behulp van kinderarbeid tot stand zijn gekomen (Wet zorgplicht kinderarbeid).

102 Ibid, Article 4(3).

103 Liesbeth Enneking, 'The Netherlands Country Report' in Lise Smit and others, *Study on Due Diligence Requirements through the Supply Chain. Part III: Country Reports* (European Commission 2020) 170, 175.

104 Suzanne Spears, Olga Owczarek, and Rose Fernando, 'Mandatory Human Rights Due Diligence Laws: The Netherlands Led the Way in Addressing Child Labour and Contemplates Broader Action' (Allen & Overy, 2 September 2020) <https://www.allenovery.com/en-gb/global/news-and-insights/publications/mandatory-human-rights-due-diligence-laws-the-netherlands-led-the-way-in-addressing-child-labour-and-contemplates-broader-action> accessed 1 May 2021.

The Child Labour Due Diligence Act provides for the imposition of administrative and/or criminal sanctions on companies for non-compliance with their investigation, action plan, and declaration obligations. However, it does not contain provisions allowing access to remedies for actual victims of child labour. One reason is that 'the stated aim of the Act is the protection of Dutch consumers, rather than the protection of the actual victims of child labour'.[105] As a result of the relativity requirement in Dutch tort law,[106] when victims of child labour bring a tort claim based on Dutch law, they will not be able to base their claim directly on the violation of the Child Labour Due Diligence Act. Therefore, victims will have to rely on existing general civil law and, where possible, criminal law to seek redress. In some circumstances, they may nonetheless be able to rely on the Act indirectly. This should be the case where violation of the Act can be constructed as an indication that an unwritten norm pertaining to proper societal conduct has been violated by the company.[107]

Nonetheless, the Act provides that any person, whether natural or legal, whose interests have been affected by a company's action or failure to comply with the Child Labour Due Diligence Act may file a complaint with the Supervisor. However, this opportunity is limited by the fact that only a concrete indication of non-compliance by an identifiable party provides grounds for submitting a complaint. However, it is likely that it will be difficult to prove that a person has been affected by non-compliance with the Child Labour Due Diligence Act. Non-compliance should cover situations where a company has not issued a declaration and where it has adopted inadequate measures. Given that the act does not define the criteria setting out what is expected of the quality of risk assessment or of a company's action plan to prevent and mitigate child labour in its supply chains, it is likely that complaints will focus on failure to provide a declaration.[108] In addition, a complaint may only be dealt with by the Supervisor either after it has been dealt with by the company or six months after the complaint has been lodged with the company without it having been addressed.

The Child Labour Due Diligence Act is likely to be complemented by more comprehensive HRDD legislation in the coming years. In March 2021, several political parties submitted a Bill on Responsible and Sustainable International Business Conduct to the Dutch Parliament. This bill aims to impose a due

---

105 Enneking, 'The Netherlands Country Report', 177.

106 Relativity requires that the norm breached served to protect against damage such as that suffered by the person sustaining the loss.

107 Enneking, 'The Netherlands Country Report', 178.

108 Anya Marcelis, 'Dutch Take the Lead on Child Labour with New Due Diligence Law' (Ergon, 17 May 2019) <https://ergonassociates.net/dutch-take-the-lead-on-child-labour-with-new-due-diligence-law/> accessed 1 May 2021.

diligence obligation on companies with more than 250 employees to address human rights violations and environmental damage in their value chains.[109] The legislative process was ongoing at the time of writing.

4 Towards mandatory human rights due diligence in the EU

States are not the only actors that have adopted mandatory HRDD standards. The EU has also introduced a number of instruments that require companies to exercise due diligence towards humans and the environment in specific contexts. More recently, a number of studies on due diligence commissioned by the EU institutions have shown an increasing interest in the adoption of a mandatory EU HRDD instrument.[110] In April 2020, the EC announced its intention to propose a legal instrument that would impose mandatory HRDD in the EU (EU Initiative). This section discusses current EU due diligence standards and how a potential EU instrument on mandatory HRDD could further improve access to justice.

Existing EU due diligence standards

The EU has adopted a number of instruments that impose 'certain due diligence-related obligations for human rights and environmental impacts'.[111]

In 2010, the EU adopted Regulation 995/2010 laying down the obligations of operators who place timber and timber products on the market (EU Timber Regulation).[112] This instrument aims to combat illegal logging by preventing the import and placing of illegally harvested timber on the EU market. In

---

109 'Dutch Bill on Responsible and Sustainable International Business Conduct a Major Step towards Protecting Human Rights and the Environment Worldwide' (MVO Platform, 11 March 2021) <https://www.mvoplatform.nl/en/dutch-bill-on-responsible-and-sustainable-international-business-conduct-a-major-step-towards-protecting-human-rights-and-the-environment-worldwide/> accessed 1 May 2021.

110 Smit and others, 'Study on Due Diligence Requirements – Final Report'; Markus Krajewski and Beata Faracik, 'Briefing 1 – Substantive Elements of Potential Legislation on Human Rights Due Diligence' (European Parliament 2020); Claire Methven O'Brien and Olga Martin-Ortega, 'Briefing 2 – EU Human Rights Due Diligence Legislation: Monitoring, Enforcement and Access to Justice for Victims' (European Parliament 2020).

111 Lise Smit and others, 'Study on Due Diligence Requirements through the Supply Chain. Part I: Synthesis Report' (European Commission 2020) 26.

112 Regulation (EU) No 995/2010 of the European Parliament and of the Council of 20 October 2010 laying down the obligations of operators who place timber and timber products on the market [2010] OJ L295/23 (EU Timber Regulation).

particular, the EU Timber Regulation imposes due diligence obligations on specific players in the timber industry. On the basis of a systemic approach, operators should take appropriate steps to ensure that illegally harvested timber and timber products derived from such timber are not placed on the internal market. To that end, operators should exercise due diligence through a system of measures and procedures to minimize the risk of illegally harvested timber and timber products derived from such timber being place on the internal market.[113] Due diligence is seen as a risk management exercise in the context of the EU Timber Regulation. The due diligence system includes three elements inherent to risk management: access to information, risk assessment, and risk mitigation. The due diligence system should provide access to information about the sources and suppliers of the timber and timber products being placed on the internal market, including relevant information such as compliance with applicable legislation, country of harvesting, species, quantity, and, where applicable, sub-national regions and concessions for harvesting. Operators should carry out a risk assessment on the basis of this information. Where a risk is identified, operators should mitigate that risk in a manner that is proportionate to the identified risk in order to prevent illegally harvested timber and timber products derived from such timber from being placed on the internal market.[114]

An important aspect of the EU Timber Regulation is that Member States must punish operators, traders, and monitoring organizations for any infringements of the Regulation. Penalties may include fines proportionate to the damage to the environment, the value of the timber or timber products concerned, and any tax losses and economic detriment resulting from the infringement. These fines should be calculated 'in such way as to make sure that they effectively deprive those responsible of the economic benefits derived from their serious infringements'.[115] However, the EU Timber Regulation does not refer to the possibility for third parties, whether consumers in the EU or local communities where the timber was illegally harvested, to seek redress for damage they may have suffered, either as a result of the placing of illegal timber on the internal market (for EU consumers) or as a result of environmental degradation and/or related human rights abuses (for local communities).

More recently, the EU decided to impose due diligence obligations on EU-based importers of certain minerals and metals through Regulation 2017/821 (EU Conflict Minerals Regulation).[116] This instrument 'establishes a Union

113 Ibid, Recital 16.

114 Ibid, Recital 17.

115 Ibid, Article 19.

116 Regulation (EU) 2017/821 of the European Parliament and of the Council of 17 May 2017 laying down supply chain due diligence obligations for Union importers of tin, tantalum and tungsten, their ores, and gold originating from conflict-affected and high-risk areas [2017] OJ L130/1 (EU Conflict Minerals Regulation).

system for supply chain due diligence ... in order to curtail opportunities for armed groups and security forces to trade in tin, tantalum and tungsten, their ores, and gold. [It] is designed to provide transparency and certainty as regards the supply practices of Union importers, and of smelters and refiners sourcing from conflict-affected and high-risk areas.'[117] More specifically, EU importers of specific minerals and metals must comply with 'supply chain due diligence obligations',[118] which involve 'their management systems, risk management, independent third-party audits and disclosure of information with a view to identifying and addressing actual and potential risks linked to conflict-affected and high-risk areas to prevent or mitigate adverse impacts associated with their sourcing activities'.[119]

In contrast to the EU Timber Regulation, the EU Conflict Minerals Regulation does not require Member States to punish EU importers for non-compliance. This lack of sanctions creates a risk of failure to comply, with the result that the EU Conflict Minerals Regulation is a toothless instrument. While Member States are not prevented from punishing infringements of the Regulation, they may be reluctant to punish infringements if other States do not provide for similar sanctions. Furthermore, the EU Conflict Minerals Regulation does not provide for the possibility for third parties to seek redress where the failure of importers to comply with their due diligence obligations results in damage.

In addition to these instruments, the EU has sought to increase transparency by imposing a corporate obligation to disclose information on human rights and environmental risks. As discussed above, disclosure obligations are not due diligence obligations. However, companies may have to assess and communicate their human rights impacts as part of their due diligence obligations. Directive 2014/95/EU (NFRD) lays down rules on disclosure of non-financial and diversity information by large companies.[120] It amends Directive 2013/34/EU (EU Accounting Directive),[121] which harmonizes the reporting standards of companies' financial statements. The NFRD requires large public interest companies – primarily listed companies, banks, insurance companies, and designated public interest entities – to include a non-financial

---

117 Ibid, Article 1(1).

118 Ibid, Article 3.

119 Ibid, Article 2(d).

120 Directive 2014/95/EU of the European Parliament and of the Council of 22 October 2014 amending Directive 2013/34/EU as regards disclosure of non-financial and diversity information by certain large undertakings and groups [2014] OJ L330/1 (NFRD).

121 Directive 2013/34/EU of the European Parliament and of the Council of 26 June 2013 on the annual financial statements, consolidated financial statements and related reports of certain types of undertakings, amending Directive 2006/43/EC of the European Parliament and of the Council and repealing Council Directives 78/660/EEC and 83/349/EEC [2013] OJ L 182/19 (EU Accounting Directive).

statement in their management report. This statement must contain 'information to the extent necessary for an understanding of the undertaking's development, performance, position and impact of its activity, relating to, as a minimum, environmental, social and employee matters, respect for human rights, anti-corruption and bribery matters'.[122] Ultimately, the NFRD aims to increase the consistency and comparability of non-financial information disclosed by certain large undertakings and groups across the EU in order to provide a more complete picture of their development and performance, as well as the impact of their activities on humans and the environment.

The implementation of the NFRD has so far failed to achieve this objective. In 2020, the Alliance for Corporate Transparency, a group of NGOs and experts, published a study analysing the sustainability reports of 1,000 companies under the NFRD.[123] It found out that:

> while there is a minority of companies providing comprehensive and reliable sustainability-related information, at large quality and comparability of companies' sustainability reporting is not sufficient to understand their impacts, risks, or even their plans.[124]

The lack of comparability found by the study appears, to some extent, to result from the considerable flexibility given to Member States and companies by the NFRD.

Another important flaw in the NFRD is that it excludes the review of the information contained in the non-financial statement. According to the EU Accounting Directive, the annual financial statements of large and medium-sized companies and public interest entities should be audited by statutory auditors to ensure that they provide 'a true and fair view' of assets, liabilities, financial position, and profit or loss of the company.[125] However, an equivalent requirement for annual non-financial statements is missing from the NFRD, which merely requires that statutory auditors and audit firms should check whether a non-financial statement or a separate report has been provided. Furthermore, Member States have the option, not the obligation, of requiring that the information included in a non-financial statement or a separate report be verified by an independent assurance services provider.[126] This means that,

---

122 NFRD, Article 1.

123 Alliance for Corporate Transparency, '2019 Research Report: An analysis of the sustainability reports of 1,000 companies pursuant to the EU Non-Financial Reporting Directive' (2020).

124 Ibid, 10.

125 EU Accounting Directive, Article 4(3).

126 Ibid, Article 19a(6).

in practice, companies may include irrelevant or inaccurate information in their non-financial statements without being punished for it.

In April 2021, the EC adopted a proposal for a Corporate Sustainability Reporting Directive (CSRD), which would amend the NFRD's existing reporting requirements.[127] The proposed CSRD addresses some of the above-mentioned loopholes. It broadens the scope of the reporting requirements to include all large companies and listed companies. It also mandates the auditing of sustainability information, and introduces more detailed reporting requirements and the obligation to report in accordance with mandatory EU sustainability reporting standards. Another novel feature is that it requires all information to be published as part of companies' management reports and disclosed in a digital, machine-readable format. However, NGOs have claimed that the proposed CSRD falls short on several key points. For example, a number of companies are still excluded from the scope of the proposed CSRD (eg all companies from high-risk sectors). The exemption for large companies that are members of corporate groups is also problematic.[128] At the time of writing, the legislative process for adopting the proposed CSRD was still in progress.

Ultimately, the shortcomings of the current EU Framework on corporate conduct vis-à-vis human rights and the environment have resulted in calls by a number of CSOs for the adoption of more robust standards on corporate accountability.[129]

Options for an EU instrument on mandatory human rights due diligence

In April 2020, Didier Reynders, the European Commissioner for Justice, announced that the EC would introduce legislation to impose mandatory HRDD on companies in 2021.[130] Reynders said the proposed instrument would contain, in particular, provisions to ensure corporate liability and access to remedies for victims of abuses. This announcement sparked a great deal of

127 European Commission, 'Proposal for a Directive of the European Parliament and of the Council Amending Directive 2013/34/EU, Directive 2004/109/EC, Directive 2006/43/EC and Regulation (EU) No 537/2014, as regards corporate sustainability reporting' COM(2021) 189 final.

128 'On the Corporate Sustainability Reporting Directive (NFRD reform) Proposal: Most Promising Changes and Caveats' (Alliance for Corporate Transparency, 21 April 2021) <https://www.allianceforcorporatetransparency.org/news/on-the-draft-sustainability-reporting-directive-nfrd-reform-proposal-most-promising-changes-and-caveats.html> accessed 1 May 2021.

129 'Key Features of Mandatory Human Rights Due Diligence Legislation' (ECCJ, June 2018) <https://corporatejustice.org/publications/key-features-of-mandatory-human-rights-due-diligence-legislation/> accessed 16 July 2021.

130 'European Commission Promises Mandatory Due Diligence Legislation in 2021' (RBC, 30 April 2020) <https://responsiblebusinessconduct.eu/wp/2020/04/30/european-commission-promises-mandatory-due-diligence-legislation-in-2021/> accessed 1 May 2021.

interest and commentary from various actors in the BHR sector, including CSOs, companies, governments, and academics.[131] Furthermore, in March 2021 the EP adopted a resolution in which it requested the EC to submit without undue delay a legislative proposal on mandatory supply chain due diligence.[132] This resolution also includes non-binding recommendations for the future instrument (EP Proposal).

If successful, the adoption of an EU instrument on mandatory HRDD (EU Instrument) would be a significant normative development for corporate accountability. First of all, such an instrument would be the first regional legislation to translate the HRDD concept into hard law. Given the EU's economic and political leverage, this instrument could have a significant impact on respect of human rights by companies around the world. It could encourage, if not compel, companies in third countries to establish and implement HRDD in their operations, as well as prompt non-EU countries to follow the EU's lead and enact similar legislation. A legally binding EU instrument on HRDD would also mark a fundamental shift in the EU's approach to corporate responsibility for human rights. To date, the EU has primarily encouraged businesses to respect human rights through voluntary, or CSR, initiatives rather than legally binding rules (eg 2011 CSR Strategy).[133] However, in the Inception Impact Assessment of the future instrument,[134] the EC acknowledged that the current legal framework, in particular corporate legislation, fails to foster accountability towards stakeholders and 'lags behind the development of global value chains and corporate structures when it comes to the responsibility of a limited liability company for identifying and preventing harm in its group-wide operations and production channels'.[135] Ultimately, regulatory failure has been a driving force behind corporate short-termism and a lack of consideration for environmental, social, and human rights interests.

---

131 'Commissioner Reynders Announces EU Corporate Due Diligence Legislation' (ECCJ, 30 April 2020) <https://corporatejustice.org/news/16806-commissioner-reynders-announces-eu-corporate-due-diligence-legislation> accessed 1 May 2021; Adidas and others, 'Support for EU Framework on Mandatory Human Rights and Environmental Due Diligence' (BHRRC, 2 September 2020) <https://www.business-humanrights.org/en/latest-news/support-for-eu-framework-on-mandatory-human-rights-and-environmental-due-diligence/> accessed 1 May 2021; 'Towards EU Mandatory Due Diligence Legislation: Perspectives from Business, Public Sector, Academic and Civil Society' (BHRRC, 11 November 2020) <https://www.business-humanrights.org/en/from-us/briefings/towards-eu-mandatory-due-diligence-legislation/> accessed 1 May 2021.

132 European Parliament resolution of 10 March 2021 with recommendations to the Commission on corporate due diligence and corporate accountability (2020/2129(INL)).

133 European Commission, 'A Renewed EU Strategy 2011–2014 for Corporate Social Responsibility' (Communication) COM/2011/0681 final.

134 European Commission, 'Sustainable Corporate Governance' (Inception Impact Assessment) Ref. Ares(2020)4034032.

135 Ibid.

There would be several benefits in the adoption of an EU Instrument on mandatory HRDD. First, it would ensure that HRDD standards are implemented throughout the EU internal market. As previously stated, some Member States have already passed HRDD legislation, while others are considering doing so. However, the majority of Member States still lack HRDD requirements. As a result, the adoption of an EU legal instrument would ensure that HRDD is in effect in all Member States. Second, as more EU Member States enact HRDD legislation, the risk of fragmentation increases, leading to legal uncertainty and the need for EU-wide harmonization.[136] The adoption of an EU Instrument would ensure that common HRDD requirements are applied across Member States, creating a level playing field in which businesses in all Member States would be required to follow the same rules. Third, enacting mandatory HRDD standards at EU level would reduce regulatory and compliance burdens for businesses operating across Member States, while ensuring greater legal certainty for companies. Finally, effective due diligence standards could address some of the barriers that prevent victims from seeking justice (eg attribution of liability to parent companies in corporate groups)[137] and improve access to remedy.[138]

The remaining sections of this chapter discuss how the future EU Instrument on mandatory HRDD should be designed to achieve meaningful corporate accountability and access to justice. This discussion focuses on four key elements: scope, HRDD obligations, enforcement, and access to justice. It also points out how these issues were addressed in relevant EU preparatory documents,[139] such as the Inception Impact Assessment and the EP Proposal.[140] In order to ensure coherence with the current international BHR framework, the future EU Instrument should align with the UNGPs. However, where regulatory gaps exist, the EU should take the opportunity to go beyond the UNGPs in order to address those gaps.

Scope

The scope of the future EU instrument on mandatory HRDD raises several crucial questions. First, as part of their due diligence obligations, which human

---

136 Axel Marx and others, 'Access to Legal Remedies for Victims of Corporate Human Rights Abuses in Third Countries' (European Parliament 2019).

137 Ibid, 107–110.

138 EU FRA, 'Improving Access to Remedy in the Area of Business and Human Rights at the EU Level' FRA Opinion – 1/2017 [B&HR], Opinion 21.

139 It should be noted that these texts are intended to assist in the preparation of the future instrument and are not, in themselves, binding.

140 The EC's proposal was due to be published by the end of 2021, after the completion of this book, and thus could not be considered in the analysis.

rights should companies be required to respect? Businesses can have an impact on the full range of human rights. As a result, an EU Instrument should theoretically apply to all human rights.[141] Nonetheless, there are significant practical difficulties with this approach. First, requiring businesses to exercise due diligence on all human rights would entail significant financial and technical resources, which not all companies may have. Moreover, there is a broad list of existing human rights, and one right can be expressed in a variety of ways in human rights instruments. MNEs, which operate in more than one country, and sometimes in different regions, are likely to be confronted with differing human rights standards. They may find it difficult to consider their impacts on all human rights enshrined in international, regional, and national instruments if the EU Instrument's human rights scope is not delineated. This approach can also be counterproductive, since businesses can overlook human rights impacts that are most likely to occur in their activities. On the other hand, limiting the scope of the EU Instrument to an insufficient number of human rights may lead to businesses being unaware of less evident, but equally important, human rights violations. As a result, it is critical that the EU Instrument applies to a broad but realistic set of human rights. Businesses should be required by the EU Instrument to consider the human rights that are likely to be impacted by their operations. In order to determine the most relevant human rights, businesses should identify potential and actual human rights impacts. In accordance with the UNGPs, this exercise should be 'ongoing' as 'human rights risks may change over time'.[142]

The EU Instrument should include a list of the human rights instruments that businesses must respect. To ensure consistency with international standards and practices, the EU Instrument should, at a minimum, reflect the internationally recognized human rights reflected in the UNGPs. GP 12 refers to the International Bill of Human Rights and the principles concerning fundamental rights set out in the International Labour Organization's Declaration on Fundamental Principles and Rights at Work. However, the EU Instrument should go further and require companies to also respect rights enshrined in European instruments, such as the EU Charter and the ECHR. When HRDD applies to activities taking place in foreign countries, the EU Instrument may oblige businesses to comply with applicable national and regional human rights instruments. In these circumstances, companies should exercise HRDD suited to the local context. The EU Instrument should also demand that businesses pay attention to the human rights of vulnerable groups like children, indigenous peoples, women, migrant workers, or people with disabilities.

---

141 Krajewski and Faracik, 'Briefing 1', 5.
142 UNGPs, GP 17(c).

Article 1 of the EP Proposal vaguely refers to 'human rights, the environment and good governance' without delimiting their scope. However, the Recital in the EP Proposal states that the EC should include an annex[143] setting out 'a list of types of business-related adverse impacts on human rights' expressed in various human rights instruments, including 'the international human rights conventions that are binding upon the Union or the Member States', the International Bill of Human Rights, international humanitarian law, UN instruments on the rights of vulnerable persons or groups, and the ILO Declaration on Fundamental Principles and Rights at Work and various ILO conventions.[144] The Recital also suggests including regional human rights instruments and national human rights instruments. The EP Proposal attempts to strike a balance between the need to protect human rights and the conduct of appropriate HRDD by stating that 'the Commission should ensure that those types of impacts listed are reasonable and achievable'.[145]

The second issue with the scope of the future EU Instrument concerns the types of businesses, or 'undertakings', that should carry out HRDD. Should the EU Instrument apply to all companies, regardless of size (whether small and medium-sized enterprises (SMEs) or large corporate groups)? In general, the UNGPs apply to 'all business enterprises, both transnational and others, regardless of their size, sector, location, ownership and structure'.[146] More specifically, the responsibility of business enterprises to respect human rights applies 'fully and equally' to all enterprises 'regardless of their size, sector, operational context, ownership and structure'.[147] However, the UNGPs stress that 'the scale and complexity of the means through which enterprises meet [their] responsibility may vary according to these factors and with the severity of the enterprise's adverse human rights impacts'.[148] On this basis, all business enterprises should establish an HRDD process that is proportional to their size, unless they have severe human rights impacts, in which case corresponding measures to the impacts must be adopted. To date, only large companies have been subject to the few domestic statutes requiring mandatory HRDD (eg France). Legislators are cautious of imposing due diligence requirements that would be too onerous for small businesses.[149] However, while SMEs cannot carry the same HRDD obligations as large companies, such as MNEs, the fact

---

143 The EP Proposal also refers to additional similar annexes listing the types of business-related adverse impacts on the environment and good governance that fall within its scope. Ibid, Recitals 22 and 25.

144 EP Proposal, Recital 21.

145 Ibid.

146 UNGPs.

147 Ibid, GP 14.

148 Ibid.

149 Krajewski and Faracik, 'Briefing 1', 8.

that SMEs can be involved in human rights abuses should not be ignored.[150] Furthermore, SMEs constitute an overwhelming majority of enterprises in the EU.[151] Therefore, the future EU instrument should require all companies operating in the EU to carry out HRDD that is proportionate to their size and/or leverage in the supply chain, and commensurate with the nature of the adverse human rights impact. In particular, the instrument should address the specific challenges faced by SMEs when carrying out HRDD.[152]

In the Inception Impact Assessment, only limited liability companies appeared to be the target of the EU Initiative. This option risks leaving a large number of companies outside the scope of future HRDD obligations. The EP Proposal suggests a wider scope. It would apply to large undertakings governed by the law of the Member States or established in the EU,[153] publicly listed SMEs, and SMEs operating in high-risk sectors presumably established in the EU[154] or, in some circumstances, established outside the EU 'when they operate in the internal market selling goods or providing services'.[155] However, the EP Proposal excludes a significant number of SMEs from the scope of HRDD obligations. On the other hand, the EP Proposal would require undertakings to 'carry out value chain due diligence which is proportionate and commensurate to the likelihood and severity of their potential or actual adverse impacts and their specific circumstances, particularly their sector of activity, the size and length of their value chain, the size of the undertaking, its capacity, resources and leverage'.[156] Technical assistance would also be provided to the obliged undertakings. The EC would be required to publish non-binding guidelines for undertakings on 'how best to fulfil the due diligence obligations', which would provide 'practical guidance on how proportionality and prioritization' may be applied to HRDD obligations 'depending on the size and sector of the undertaking'.[157] Furthermore, the EP Proposal would include support for SMEs, such as financial assistance.[158]

In addition, there is a question whether the EU Initiative should apply to all sectors or to limited sectors. Businesses are already subject to various due

---

150 To date, the role of SMEs as perpetrators of human rights abuses has been largely neglected in the BHR debate. See Ceyda Ilgen, 'The Implementation of the UNGPs on Business and Human Rights for SMEs: Challenges and Opportunities' (LLM Dissertation, University of Essex 2019).

151 Krajewski and Faracik, 'Briefing 1', 9.

152 Ibid, 9.

153 EP Proposal, Article 2(1).

154 Ibid, Article 2(2).

155 Ibid, Article 2(3).

156 Ibid, Article 4(7).

157 Ibid, Article 14.

158 Ibid, Article 15.

diligence requirements. However, these expectations are 'often fragmented according to certain issues, sectors, or commodities, which can create legal uncertainty for businesses having to comply with different standards'.[159] The EU institutions should take into account this aspect when drafting HRDD obligations for businesses and consider whether the adoption of a general obligation is better suited to prevent business abuse and ensure accountability. One of the advantages of a general approach is that it would minimize the risk of conflict between different due diligence standards, while, at the same time, facilitating the efforts of companies to fulfil their obligations and ensuring a comprehensive and consistent approach to due diligence. The EP Proposal takes a general approach and would apply to undertakings from all economic sectors, including the financial sector.

Another question with regard to the scope of the future EU Instrument is whether companies should conduct HRDD only for their own activities or also for the activities of their subsidiaries, contractors and subcontractors, and suppliers.[160] This question is particularly relevant in the context of MNEs' activities and raises the possibility of HRDD obligations having extraterritorial reach. GP 13 provides that the responsibility to respect human rights requires that business enterprises avoid causing or contributing to adverse human rights impacts *through their own activities* and seek to prevent or mitigate adverse human rights impacts that are *directly linked to their operations, products or services by their business relationships*, even if they have not contributed to those impacts. The Commentary to GP 13 clarifies that 'a business enterprise's "activities" are understood to include both actions and omissions; and its "business relationships" are understood to include relationships with business partners, entities in its value chain, and any other non-State or State entity directly linked to its business operations, products or services'. The UNWG has clarified that the HRDD of a business enterprise 'extends not only to its relationships with first-tier suppliers, but to business relationships along the whole of its value chain, including business connections in the extended supply chain, business relations using products and services, joint venture partners, corporate lenders, project financers, investors, and governments'.[161] HRDD should not be limited to an enterprise's own activities and first-tier suppliers.[162] Similarly, CSOs have suggested that businesses should conduct

---

159 Lise Smit and others, 'Business Views on Mandatory Human Rights Due Diligence Regulation: A Comparative Analysis of Two Recent Studies' [2020] Business and Human Rights Journal 1, 4.

160 Krajewski and Faracik, 'Briefing 1', 10.

161 Letter from the UNWG to European Commissioner for Justice Didier Reynders, Ref SPB/SHD//NF/GF/ff (22 October 2020).

162 Ibid.

HRDD in their own operations, in their global value chains, and within their business relationships.[163]

The EP Proposal adopts a broad approach. Pursuant to Article 1(1) of the EP Proposal, obliged undertakings would 'fulfil their duty to respect human rights, the environment and good governance' and 'not cause or contribute to potential or actual adverse impacts on human rights, the environment and good governance through their own activities or those directly linked to their operations, products or services by a business relationship or in their value chains, and that they prevent and mitigate those adverse impacts'. Therefore, undertakings would exercise HRDD for their own activities as well as for activities directly related to their operations, products, or services through a business relationship or through their value chains. In practice, this means that undertakings should respect, avoid causing or contributing to, prevent, and mitigate human rights abuses in a large number of situations (ie direct activities and activities of a business relationship or in its value chains directly linked to its operations, products, or services).

HRDD obligations

As far as the obligations of companies are concerned, an EU mandatory HRDD instrument should not be limited to reporting requirements, as these already exist under the NFRD. The UNWG has also clarified that a 'comply or explain' approach is not a sufficient mandatory HRDD regime under the UNGPs.[164] The EU should adopt a substantive due diligence model, which, at the very least, requires businesses to carry out a risk assessment to identify the potential risks of human rights abuses that may arise in the context of their activities and those of companies with which they have a business relationship, and to take specific actions to prevent such abuses. Furthermore, when human rights abuse occurs, companies should be required to mitigate and remedy the resulting adverse impacts.

In general, the EP Proposal adopts a substantive due diligence model. It provides that the exercise of due diligence would require undertakings 'to identify, assess, prevent, cease, mitigate, monitor, communicate, account for, address and remediate the potential and/or actual adverse impacts on human rights, the environment and good governance that their own activities and those of their value chains and business relationships may pose'.[165] More specifically, undertakings would have to conduct a 'risk based

---

163 'Joint Open Letter: An EU Mandatory Due Diligence Legislation to Promote Businesses' Respect for Human Rights and the Environment' (ActionAid and others 1 September 2020).

164 Letter from the UNWG to European Commissioner for Justice Didier Reynders.

165 EP Proposal, Article 1(2).

monitoring methodology' to identify and assess potential or actual impacts on human rights, the environment, and good governance.[166] They would also be obliged to establish and implement 'a due diligence strategy' effectively. This document would specify potential actual adverse impacts, map the value chain of the undertaking, adopt and indicate 'all proportionate and commensurate policies and measures with a view to ceasing, preventing or mitigating potential or actual adverse impacts'. In their due diligence strategy, undertakings would also be required to set up 'a prioritisation strategy' where they are unable to deal with all the potential or actual adverse impacts at the same time.[167] Importantly, undertakings would be required to engage with relevant stakeholders when establishing and implementing their due diligence strategy[168] and to publish and communicate that strategy.[169] The EP Proposal would also require undertakings to provide a grievance mechanism 'both as an early-warning mechanism for risk-awareness and as a mediation system'.[170] Where an adverse impact occurs, the undertaking would be required to provide for or cooperate with the remediation process depending on whether it has caused or contributed to the adverse impact or whether it is directly linked to the adverse impact.[171]

Enforcement

The French experience with the implementation of the Act on the Duty of Vigilance has shown the importance of having in place monitoring and enforcement mechanisms.[172] The future EU mandatory HRDD instrument should include monitoring mechanisms to ensure that all obliged undertakings have an HRDD process in place and that they effectively comply with its requirements. In this respect, injunctive procedures could be useful, especially to prevent harm. Monitoring will only be effective if it is accompanied by each Member State's publication of a list of obliged undertakings that fall under the scope of the EU Instrument. Businesses that do not comply with their HRDD obligations should also be subject to sanctions. The EU Instrument should suggest a list of adapted penalties.

The EP Proposal provides for both monitoring and sanctions. According to Article 13, competent authorities in Member States would have 'the power to

---

166 Ibid, Article 4(2).

167 Ibid, Article 4(4).

168 Ibid, Article 5.

169 Ibid, Article 6.

170 Ibid, Article 9.

171 Ibid, Article 10(1).

172 See Elsa Savourey and Stéphane Brabant, 'The French Law on the Duty of Vigilance: Theoretical and Practical Challenges Since Its Adoption' (2021) 6 Business and Human Rights Journal 141.

carry out investigations' in order to ensure that undertakings comply with their due diligence obligations. In particular, they should be authorized to carry out checks on undertakings, such as an examination of their due diligence strategy and of the functioning of the grievance mechanism, on-the-spot checks, and interviews with affected stakeholders.[173] Moreover, Member States would be required to provide for effective, proportionate, and dissuasive sanctions, which take into account 'the severity of the infringements committed and whether or not the infringement has taken place repeatedly'.[174] They would also be allowed to 'impose proportionate fines calculated on the basis of an undertaking's turnover, temporarily or indefinitely exclude undertakings from public procurement, from state aid, from public support schemes including schemes relying on Export Credit Agencies and loans, resort to the seizure of commodities and other appropriate administrative sanctions'.[175]

Access to justice

The EU mandatory HRDD instrument represents a timely opportunity to enhance the ability of victims of business-related abuse to seek redress. In order to ensure access to justice, the future instrument should address the main substantive and procedural barriers that victims, in particular foreign ones, face when bringing complaints against MNEs in EU Member States.[176] On the basis of the obstacles described in Part II of this book, and taking into account the original purpose of due diligence norms, it is suggested that an EU mandatory HRDD instrument should: (1) create corporate liability where damage results from a company's failure to comply with its HRDD obligations; (2) address obstacles hindering access to justice in the context of transnational business-related abuses, most notably by addressing relevant private international law issues; (3) place the burden of proof on companies; and (4) ensure the availability of appropriate remedies for victims.

The EU mandatory HRDD instrument should impose liability on companies that fail to comply with their due diligence obligations. There are several options possible. Liability could arise where: (1) the company does not conduct due diligence; (2) the company does not conduct due diligence in a sufficient or adequate (or reasonable) manner; (3) damage arises as a result of lack of due diligence and/or the conduct of insufficient or inadequate due diligence; and (4) damage arises in spite of sufficient and adequate due diligence. Since due

173 EP Proposal, Article 13(1).

174 Ibid, Article 18(1).

175 Ibid, Article 18(2).

176 This approach has been suggested by NGOs and academics active in the BHR field. See, for instance, Robert McCorquodale and Martijn Scheltema, 'Core Elements of an EU Regulation on Mandatory Human Rights and Environmental Due Diligence' (August 2020); Methven O'Brien and Martin-Ortega, 'Briefing 2'.

diligence standards often create an obligation of *conduct* (as opposed to an obligation of *result*) for the duty-holder, option 4, which would create a type of strict liability regime that does not involve a fault element, is likely to be controversial and unfeasible in the context of an EU mandatory HRDD instrument.

The French approach to liability under the Act on the Duty of Vigilance could serve as an inspiration. Accordingly, the future EU Instrument should require that companies be held liable for damage resulting from their activities that could have been avoided if sufficient and appropriate due diligence had been conducted by the company. It is essential, from the point of view of victims, for the instrument to provide a legal basis upon which they can base their legal claims for redress. However, in doing so, the EU mandatory HRDD instrument should provide guidance on how liability should be triggered, such as the type of misconduct that would constitute failure to comply with HRDD obligations. Furthermore, it should take into account aspects that may hinder the ability of victims, in particular foreign ones, to hold companies liable, such as conflict of laws or access to evidence.

It has been suggested that the conduct of sufficient and appropriate due diligence could serve as a defence against liability.[177] This argument is consistent with the idea that due diligence essentially imposes an obligation of conduct. Furthermore, the use of due diligence as a defence would provide an incentive to comply with the EU legislation. However, as discussed earlier, it could create a major obstacle for victims, particularly if it is unclear what companies need to do in order to conduct sufficient and appropriate due diligence. This uncertainty could create a loophole that allows companies to overcome any liability claims against them. If the EU intends for due diligence to act as a defence against liability, in particular to encourage compliance and to guarantee legal security to companies that comply with their obligations, it should, at the same time, ensure that the burden of proof is on companies. This means that, in the context of a civil claim for damages, companies should prove that they have carried out sufficient and appropriate due diligence to ensure that no human rights violations occur in their value chain instead of victims having to demonstrate lack of due diligence on the part of the company. However, it is likely that, as in the French context, the inclusion of a provision for reversing the burden of proof will be met with resistance. Furthermore, litigators have suggested that such a defence should not be available 'in case of control over the entity that caused the harm because victims should not bear the consequences of internal corporate structure decisions'.[178]

---

177 McCorquodale and Scheltema, 'Core Elements of an EU Regulation on Mandatory Human Rights'.

178 Lucie Chatelain, 'Corporate Due Diligence and Civil Liability: Comment from Multi-Stakeholders' (NOVA BHRE, 3 March 2021) <https://novabhre.novalaw.unl.pt/corporate-due-diligence-civil-liability-comment-from-multi-stakeholders/> accessed 1 May 2021.

The availability of appropriate remedies is another crucial issue. Victims should have access to a wide range of remedies. While the award of damages, or financial compensation, should always be guaranteed, other remedies, such as injunctive relief, rehabilitation or account of profits, should also be available options. An EU mandatory HRDD instrument should also contain provisions that require Member States to guarantee adequate remedy mechanisms,[179] whether these mechanisms are of a judicial or non-judicial nature. Member States could be given the opportunity to choose whether civil, criminal, or administrative mechanisms are the most appropriate for the domestic context. In any case, such mechanisms should be low-cost (or made affordable through the provision of legal aid), expeditious, and effective for victims.[180] Furthermore, some authors have suggested that an EU mandatory HRDD instrument should require companies to engage actively in remedying any adverse impacts on human rights resulting from their activities or connected to them in their business relations.[181] They could do so by setting up corporate grievance mechanisms as part of their HRDD procedures.[182] This is one of the approaches adopted by the EP, where emphasis is put on corporate grievance mechanisms. Another solution would be to promote access to remedies through the use of alternative dispute resolution (ADR) mechanisms outside the corporate sphere, such as mediation, conciliation, or arbitration. However, the existence of non-judicial mechanisms, such as corporate grievance and ADR mechanisms, should not preclude the possibility for victims to bring their claims before the courts.

It is likely that provisions on civil liability will be included in the future instrument. Commissioner Reynders has stated on several occasions that there is a need to provide for civil liability in the context of the EU HRDD instrument. In particular, he has referred to EU rules on collective redress.[183] The EP Proposal also suggests including provisions on civil liability. Article 19(2) would require Member States to 'ensure that they have a liability regime in place under which undertakings can ... be held liable and provide remediation for any harm arising out of potential or actual adverse impacts on

179 Krajewski and Faracik, 'Briefing 1', 15.
180 Ibid.
181 Ibid, 14–15.
182 Methven O'Brien and Martin-Ortega, 'Briefing 2'.
183 'Commissioner Reynders Announces EU Corporate Due Diligence Legislation'; Mirjam Erb and Julia Grothaus, 'EU Commissioner for Justice Reveals Details of Forthcoming EU Legislative Proposal on Human Rights Supply Chain Due Diligence' (Lexology, 3 March 2021) <https://www.lexology.com/library/detail.aspx?g=76345b5f-b3a7-4035-b5dd-8f0c0d89f56e> accessed 1 May 2021.

human rights, the environment or good governance that they, or undertakings under their control, have caused or contributed to by acts or omissions'. The inclusion of civil liability in the future instrument would make a significant contribution to access to justice. It would recognize the link between HRDD and access to justice, provide an incentive for companies to exercise due diligence, and ensure that victims have access to judicial redress. However, the future instrument must also contain the necessary safeguards to ensure that potential victims can effectively hold an undertaking which has failed to comply with its due diligence obligations to account. At the time of writing, it was unclear how the suggestions made so far by Commissioner Reynders and the EP contain the necessary safeguards to ensure access to justice.

First of all, while it is important that collective redress mechanisms are taken into account, the future instrument should not rely solely on them to provide redress, particularly as current EU rules on collective redress are currently inadequate.[184] Another aspect to consider is how HRDD should provide undertakings with a defence against liability claims. On this point, the EP Proposal is ambiguous. On the one hand, it provides that an undertaking which respects its due diligence obligations shall not be absolved of any liability which it may incur pursuant to national law.[185] On the other hand, Member States would have an obligation to ensure that their liability regime is such that 'undertakings that prove that they took all due care in line with this Directive to avoid the harm in question, or that the harm would have occurred even if all due care had been taken, are not held liable for that harm'.[186] Here the relationship between the exercise of due diligence and liability would require clarification. In particular, it would be important to clarify the situations in which an undertaking is considered to have failed to comply with its obligations under the future instrument and how such situations may lead to its liability. In addition, where damage is caused by the direct activities of the undertaking, it is questionable whether an HRDD-based defence could interfere with the application of existing liability regimes which provide for strict liability rules.

On a positive note, the EP Proposal addresses several important issues which may limit the application of the civil liability regime. The first is the contentious issue of the burden of proof. In certain circumstances, the EP Proposal provides for a reversal of the burden of proof to the undertaking. For instance, the burden of proof 'would be shifted from a victim to an undertaking to prove that an undertaking did not have control over a business entity involved in the human rights abuse'.[187] However, victims would still have to demonstrate

---

184 See Chapter 4 of this book for a discussion on collective redress mechanisms in the EU.

185 EP Proposal, Article 19(1).

186 Ibid, Article 19(3).

187 Ibid, Recital 53.

causation between the acts or omissions of the undertaking, or those under its control, and the harm arising out of potential or actual adverse impacts. Furthermore, the limitation period for bringing civil liability claims concerning harm arising out of adverse impacts on human rights and the environment should be reasonable.[188] In particular:

> [l]imitation periods should be deemed reasonable and appropriate if they do not restrict the right of victims to access justice, with due consideration for the practical challenges faced by potential claimants. Sufficient time should be given for victims of human rights, environmental and governance adverse impacts to bring judicial claims, taking into account their geographical location, their means and the overall difficulty to raise admissible claims before Union courts.[189]

Furthermore, the EP Proposal's provisions would be regarded as overriding mandatory provisions in line with Article 16 Rome II Regulation.[190] This would ensure that the law of the Member State implementing the EU Instrument, rather than the law of a third country, applies to transnational claims. Finally, the EP Proposal provides for various types of remedies, including 'financial or non-financial compensation, reinstatement, public apologies, restitution, rehabilitation or a contribution to an investigation'.[191] However, this reference to remedies is made in the context of extrajudicial remedies and it is unclear whether such remedies could be applied in the context of judicial proceedings.

5 Conclusions

This chapter has discussed whether the adoption of mandatory HRDD legislation offers some opportunities to address some of the barriers identified in this book and improve access to justice for victims of business-related human rights abuses in Europe.

Due diligence has gained momentum following the adoption of the UNGPs. As part of their responsibility to respect human rights, companies should undertake processes to identify, prevent, mitigate, and account for how they address potential and actual impacts on human rights caused by or contributed to through their own activities, or those that are directly linked to their operations, products, or services by their business relationships. Under

188 Ibid, Article 19(4).
189 Ibid, Recital 54.
190 Ibid, Article 20.
191 Ibid, Article 10(3).

the UNGPs, HRDD borrows characteristics from a different understanding of due diligence under national and international law, and refers interchangeably to the process and standard of care expected of companies to fulfil their responsibility to respect human rights. However, the way in which HRDD is formulated in the UNGPs does not explain what due diligence means in legal terms. This confusion is problematic in practice because it creates uncertainty regarding the extent of responsibility of businesses to respect human rights and how that responsibility relates to correlative responsibility to provide a remedy in situations where they have infringed human rights.

HRDD is seen first and foremost as a process undertaken by businesses to prevent human rights abuses from occurring. At the same time, HRDD may have a significant impact on what happens once human rights abuses have taken place, especially when victims of such abuses seek access to justice. However, the fact that the UNGPs do not clearly address the legal dimension of HRDD creates legal uncertainty and puts victims in a precarious situation. For example, while it is unclear how HRDD can be interpreted as a standard of conduct to establish corporate liability, in some circumstances it may provide businesses with a defence against liability claims.

Following the adoption of the UNGPs, a number of countries have taken important steps to impose mandatory HRDD on companies. In Europe, the French Act on the Duty of Vigilance and the Dutch Child Labour Due Diligence Act are currently the most significant instruments on HRDD. However, they differ greatly on liability and remedy. In France, courts may hold parent companies of MNEs liable in tort law for any damage to humans or the environment arising from their failure to draw up and/or implement a vigilance plan. However, potential plaintiffs are likely to face some barriers in establishing liability and obtaining compensation. Demonstrating the existence of a fault and a causal connection may, in particular, give rise to certain challenges. The Dutch Child Labour Due Diligence Act provides for the imposition of administrative and/or criminal sanctions on companies for non-compliance with their investigation, action plan, and declaration obligations. However, it does not contain provisions allowing access to remedies for actual victims of child labour. In both acts, the interests of victims in the context of mandatory HRDD obligations remain insufficiently protected.

The EU has adopted a number of instruments that impose certain due diligence-related obligations for human rights and environmental impacts. However, these instruments may not provide the possibility for third parties to seek redress for damage they have suffered as a result of a business' failure to conduct due diligence. The EU has also adopted an important instrument imposing non-financial disclosure obligations on companies, which has proved to be ineffective in improving corporate reporting of sustainability-related information. The shortcomings of the current EU framework have led to calls for the adoption of standards which effectively require companies to respect human rights. The EC is expected to introduce legislation to impose mandatory HRDD on companies in 2021. The scope and obligations of this future EU instrument could be articulated in a variety of ways. However, this chapter has suggested that, in order to improve victims' ability to seek redress for business-related abuses, an EU mandatory HRDD instrument should at least create liability for businesses that failed to comply with their due diligence obligations, place the burden of proof on companies, and ensure that appropriate remedies are available to victims. Nonetheless, the inclusion of such provisions is likely to be met with opposition from the business community.

The next chapter attempts to answer the question whether an international instrument on BHR could similarly contribute to improving access to justice.

Chapter 8

Achieving access to justice through an international treaty on business and human rights

1 Introduction

In June 2014, the UNHRC adopted Resolution 26/9, in which it decided 'to establish an open-ended intergovernmental working group on transnational corporations and other business enterprises with respect to human rights' (OEIGWG).[1] This working group has a mandate 'to elaborate an international legally-binding instrument to regulate, in international human rights law, the activities of transnational corporations and other business enterprises' (BHR Treaty). The first two sessions of the OEIGWG were dedicated to 'conducting constructive deliberations on the content, scope, nature, and form of the future international instrument'.[2] Since 2018, the OEIGWG has annually released a draft version of a potential BHR Treaty: the Zero Draft,[3] along with a Draft Optional Protocol to the legally binding instrument;[4] the Revised Draft (2019 Draft);[5] and the Second Revised Draft (2020 Draft).[6]

---

1   UNHRC Res 26/9 (2014) UN Doc A/HRC/RES/26/9.

2   OEIGWG, 'Report of the First Session of the Open-ended Governmental Working Group on Transnational Corporations and Other Business Enterprises with Respect to Human Rights. with the Mandate of Elaborating an International Legally Binding Instrument' (5 February 2016) UN Doc A/HRC/31/50; OEIGWG, 'Report of the Second Session of the Open-ended Governmental Working Group on Transnational Corporations and Other Business Enterprises with Respect to Human Rights. with the Mandate of Elaborating an International Legally Binding Instrument' (4 January 2017) UN Doc A/HRC/34/47; OEIGWG, 'Elements for the Draft Legally Binding Instrument on Transnational Corporations and Other Business Enterprises with Respect to Human Rights' (29 September 2017).

3   OEIGWG, 'Legally Binding Instrument to Regulate, in International Human Rights Law, the Activities of Transnational Corporations and Other Business Enterprises – Zero Draft' (16 July 2018).

4   OEIGWG, 'Draft Optional Protocol to the Legally Binding Instrument to Regulate, in International Human Rights Law, the Activities of Transnational Corporations and Other Business Enterprises' (2018).

5   OEIGWG, 'Legally Binding Instrument to Regulate, in International Human Rights Law, the Activities of Transnational Corporations and Other Business Enterprises – Revised Draft' (16 July 2019).

6   OEIGWG, 'Legally Binding Instrument to Regulate, in International Human Rights Law, the Activities of Transnational Corporations and Other Business Enterprises – Second Revised Draft' (6 August 2020).

As Bilchitz argues, the proposed BHR Treaty will be unique among human rights treaties.[7] In general, human rights treaties outline rights that all individuals or particular vulnerable groups, such as women or children, are entitled to, and impose obligations on States to respect, protect, or realize these rights. In contrast, the BHR Treaty is likely to focus on the regulation of a specific class of non-State actors, meaning businesses, to ensure that they do not harm human rights and that they potentially play their part in contributing to the realization of human rights.[8] Furthermore, the adoption of the BHR Treaty would offer a significant opportunity not only to extend the scope of international human rights law to business actors, but also to 'envision a system that could actually offer effective remedies for corporate human rights violations'.[9] In particular, it could address procedural, substantive, and practical barriers that victims of business-related human rights abuse face when seeking redress, especially against MNEs. However, due to long-standing State and business opposition towards binding international human rights standards for corporate actors and the complexity of the topic, negotiating, adopting, and implementing a BHR Treaty will be challenging.

2 The contentious road to an international treaty on BHR

This section examines the reasons that led to the BHR Treaty initiative, especially the UNGPs' inability to effectively achieve corporate accountability and access to remedy. It also describes the position of key players on the BHR Treaty initiative and the existing arguments in support of or against the adoption of a BHR Treaty.

The UNGPs' failure to achieve access to justice

Since their adoption in 2011, the UNGPs have often been described as having achieved a long-awaited consensus on BHR issues among a majority of

---

7   David Bilchitz, 'Corporate Obligations and a Treaty on Business and Human Rights' in Surya Deva and David Bilchitz (eds), *Building a Treaty on Business and Human Rights: Context and Contours* (CUP 2017) 185.

8   Ibid.

9   Beth Stephens, 'Making Remedies Work' in Surya Deva and David Bilchitz (eds), *Building a Treaty on Business and Human Rights: Context and Contours* (CUP 2017) 409.

stakeholders.[10] However, a significant number of stakeholders, most notably CSOs and academics, have been critical of the UNGPs or have opposed their adoption.[11] Similarly, some States from the Global South have expressed misgivings either publicly or privately.[12]

In general, actors have been dissatisfied with the development, content, and implementation of the UNGPs.[13] First, the development of the UNGPs has been criticized for excluding the voices of those most likely to be impacted by business human rights abuse.[14] Deva explains how the SRSG made the conscious decision not to engage directly with victims of business human rights abuse while at the same time holding face-to-face consultations with businesses.[15] Furthermore, the SRSG did not adequately articulate the dissenting voices from NGOs and scholars in his consultation papers and reports.[16] For Deva, 'the SRSG bypassed controversial issues and ignored dissenting voices in an attempt to sustain a façade of consensus'.[17]

Second, there is discontent with the content and normative value of the UNGPs. For Penelope Simons, the UNGPs failed to adequately address some of the most controversial BHR issues, such as whether companies should have obligations under international human rights law. They also misrepresented international human rights law, especially with regard to the State extraterritorial obligation to protect from business human rights abuse.[18] Moreover, as noted earlier in this book, a significant number of CSOs and scholars have regularly expressed

10   For a critical discussion of the consensus-building approach of the SRSG, see Surya Deva, 'Treating Human Rights Lightly: A Critique of the Consensus Rhetoric and the Language Employed by the Guiding Principles' in Surya Deva and David Bilchitz (eds), *Human Rights Obligations of Business: Beyond the Corporate Responsibility to Respect?* (CUP 2013).

11   Douglass Cassel and Anita Ramasastry, 'White Paper: Options for a Treaty on Business and Human Rights' (2016) 6 Notre Dame Journal of International Comparative Law 1, 9. For instance, see Misereor, Global Policy Forum, Brot für die Welt, 'Working Paper: Corporate Influence on the Business and Human Rights Agenda of the United Nations' (June 2014); Carlos López, '"The 'Ruggie Process": From Legal Obligations to Corporate Social Responsibility?' in Surya Deva and David Bilchitz (eds), *Human Rights Obligations of Business: Beyond the Corporate Responsibility to Respect?* (CUP 2013).

12   López, 'The "Ruggie Process"', 58–59.

13   David Bilchitz, 'The Necessity for a Business and Human Rights Treaty' (2016) 1 Business and Human Rights Journal 203.

14   López, 'The "Ruggie Process"', 69–70.

15   Deva, 'Treating Human Rights Lightly', 83–86.

16   López, 'The "Ruggie Process"', 69–70.

17   Deva, 'Treating Human Rights Lightly', 86.

18   Penelope Simons, 'The Value-Added of a Treaty to Regulate Transnational Corporations and Other Business Enterprises' in Surya Deva and David Bilchitz (eds), *Building a Treaty on Business and Human Rights: Context and Contours* (CUP 2017) 58–63. See also Olivier de Schutter, 'Towards a New Treaty on Business and Human Rights' (2015) 1 Business and Human Rights Journal 41, 45–47; López, 'The "Ruggie Process"', 60.

their dissatisfaction with the formulation of Pillar III on access to remedy in the UNGPs. For Deva, the UNGPs do not adequately reflect the rich international human rights jurisprudence concerning the right to remedy because the UNGPs recognize Pillar III as flowing from the State duty to protect human rights rather than imposing a self-standing obligation.[19] In addition, Principle 26 on State-based judicial mechanisms only recommends that States 'should' take appropriate steps to ensure the effectiveness of domestic judicial mechanisms when addressing business-related human rights abuses, therefore departing from the obligatory 'must' language.[20]

Third, the implementation of the UNGPs is deemed insufficient by some CSOs and scholars. For instance, Simons criticizes State uptake of the UNGPs, describing it as 'far from spectacular'.[21] To date, the development and implementation of NAPs by States have been disappointing.[22] Furthermore, according to Deva, even if the UNGPs have achieved 'alignment of standards and actions in line with a commonly accepted framework' and have 'facilitated the socialisation of human rights norms among businesses', at the same time 'not much has yet changed for the rightsholders on the ground'.[23] Regarding access to remedy, various CSOs and scholars contend that Pillar III has not made meaningful progress. Legal and practical hurdles continue to thwart access to justice for victims of business abuse of human rights, especially in the transnational context.[24] Furthermore, victims and their litigators have suffered significant setbacks in lawsuits against MNEs in some jurisdictions, such as the US, since the adoption of the UNGPs.[25] At the same time, recent cases, such as *Vedanta* and *Okpabi* in England, *Shell* in the Netherlands, or *Nevsun* in Canada, raise a number of interesting prospects for potential future success.

Dissatisfaction with the UNGPs, and the recurring preference for soft law or CSR initiatives more generally, ultimately led some States, especially from the Global South, and CSOs to advocate for the adoption of binding international standards on BHR.

19   Deva, 'Treating Human Rights Lightly', 102.

20   Ibid.

21   Simons, 'The Value-Added of a Treaty', 61.

22   In the closing plenary of the 2017 UN Forum on Business and Human Rights, the Chairperson of the UN Working Group stated: 'The quality of existing National Action Plans, especially when it comes to Pillar III, is a matter of concern for the Working Group. The word "action" in National Action Plans should be taken more seriously. We strongly encourage all states to develop forward-looking National Action Plans and implement these in a robust manner.'

23   Surya Deva, 'From "Business or Human Rights" to "Business and Human Rights": What Next?' in Surya Deva and David Birchall (eds), *Research Handbook on Human Rights and Business* (Edward Elgar 2020) 4.

24   Cassel and Ramasastry, 'White Paper', 9.

25   Ibid, 10. See Chapter 2 of this book for a description of cases in the US.

The positions of the main stakeholders on a BHR Treaty

The decision to establish the OEIGWG and the negotiations of the BHR Treaty have been highly contentious.

While the decision to negotiate the BHR Treaty has generally received support from States from the Global South and a large number of CSOs, it has received a cold reception from MNEs and their home countries, including the US, the UK, France, and Germany.[26] The vote on Resolution 26/9 was representative of this divide. The resolution was adopted by a recorded vote of 20 to 14, with 13 abstentions. While most of the 20 countries in favour came from the Global South,[27] the 14 countries opposed to Resolution 26/9 came mainly from the EU,[28] along with Japan, Montenegro, South Korea, what is now the Republic of North Macedonia, and the US.

To date, the negotiations have been crippled by a lack of participation by key stakeholders, such as the US and the EU. The US has repeatedly expressed its opposition to the BHR Treaty initiative and decided not to take part in the sessions of the OEIGWG in Geneva.[29] Many observers have raised concerns that the US opposition to the negotiations could have a negative impact subsequent to the adoption and during the implementation of the BHR Treaty.[30]

The EU originally opposed the establishment of the OEIGWG. During the UNHRC session in which Resolution 26/9 was adopted, the EU and its Member States questioned whether the OEIGWG would be the most effective response for tackling BHR challenges. Furthermore, all the EU Member States in the UNHRC voted against Resolution 26/9. Since 2014, the EU has regularly criticized the treaty negotiations.[31] During the first session of the OEIGWG,

26   Simons, 'The Value-Added of a Treaty', 48.

27   Algeria, Benin, Burkina Faso, China, Congo, Côte d'Ivoire, Cuba, Ethiopia, India, Indonesia, Kazakhstan, Kenya, Morocco, Namibia, Pakistan, Philippines, Russia, South Africa, Venezuela, and Vietnam.

28   Austria, the Czech Republic, Estonia, France, Germany, Ireland, Italy, Romania, and the UK.

29   US Mission to International Organizations in Geneva, 'The United States' Opposition to the Business and Human Rights Treaty Process' (15 October 2018) <https://geneva.usmission.gov/2018/10/15/the-united-states-opposition-to-the-business-and-human-rights-treaty-process/> accessed 1 May 2021; US Mission to International Organizations in Geneva, 'The U.S. Government's Opposition to the Business and Human Rights Treaty Process' (26 October 2020) <https://geneva.usmission.gov/2020/10/26/the-u-s-governments-opposition-to-the-business-and-human-rights-treaty-process/> accessed 1 May 2021.

30   For example, see John Ruggie, 'Get Real or We'll Get Nothing: Reflections on the First Session of the Intergovernmental Working Group on a Business and Human Rights Treaty' (BHRRC, 22 July 2015) <https://www.business-humanrights.org/en/blog/get-real-or-well-get-nothing-reflections-on-the-first-session-of-the-intergovernmental-working-group-on-a-business-and-human-rights-treaty/> accessed 1 May 2021.

31   EU, 'Inter-Governmental Working Group (IGWG) on the elaboration of an international legally-binding instrument on transnational corporations and other business enterprises with respect to human rights – Submission of the European Union' (2015).

the EU participated in the first meetings, but left the negotiations during the second day after it had failed to alter the programme of work.[32] This departure was strongly criticized by NGOs.[33] Moreover, only eight out of the then-28 EU Member States attended the first session.[34] Nonetheless, since then the EU and a growing number of EU Member States have attended the OEIGWG's sessions, although the EU has not actively participated in the sessions on the ground that it does not have a formal negotiation mandate under EU law.[35] In addition, for some time, it refused to participate actively in the negotiations as long as the scope of the BHR Treaty did not include domestic companies. However, the EU remained reserved even after the OEIGWG extended the scope of the BHR Treaty to all business activities. While some NGOs have accused the EU of obstructing the BHR Treaty negotiations,[36] other stakeholders have called for the EU to effectively engage in the negotiations.[37]

At the same time, some EU institutions have endorsed the BHR Treaty negotiations. Among them, the EP has repeatedly expressed its support for

32   Carlos López and Ben Shea, 'Negotiating a Treaty on Business and Human Rights: A Review of the First Intergovernmental Session' (2016) 1 Business and Human Rights Journal 111, 112.

33   Amis de la Terre France and others, 'The EU and the Corporate Impunity Nexus: Building the UN Binding Treaty on Transnational Corporations and Human Rights' (October 2018) <https://www.tni.org/en/publication/the-eu-and-the-corporate-impunity-nexus>.

34   López and Shea described how many States were absent during the first session and others (including some European States) were represented only by low-ranking officials or summer interns. López and Shea, 'Negotiating a Treaty on Business and Human Rights', 112–113.

35   European External Access Service (EEAS), 'HRC – Open-ended Intergovernmental Working Group on Transnational Corporations and Other Business Enterprises with Respect to Human Rights: Opening Remarks' (14 October 2019) <https://eeas.europa.eu/delegations/fiji/12928/hrc-open-ended-intergovernmental-working-group-transnational-corporations-and-other-business_en> accessed 1 May 2021.

36   Friends of the Earth Europe, 'The EU's Double Agenda on Globalisation: Corporate Rights vs People's Rights' (2018) <https://friendsoftheearth.eu/publication/the-eus-double-agenda-on-globalisation-corporate-rights-vs-peoples-rights/> accessed 17 July 2021.

37   CNCD-11.11.11 (Belgium) and others, 'Time for Constructive Engagement from the EU and Member States on the Content of the Revised Draft of the UN Binding Treaty' (BHRRC, 14 October 2019) <https://www.business-humanrights.org/en/latest-news/time-for-constructive-engagement-from-the-eu-and-member-states-on-the-content-of-the-revised draft of the un binding treaty/> accessed 17 July 2021; 'Are the EU Going to Miss the Boat on the UN Binding Treaty?' (CISDE, 18 October 2019) <https://www.cidse.org/are-the-eu-going-to-miss-the-boat-on-the-un-binding-treaty/> accessed 1 May 2021; Letter from Manon Aubry and Marie Arena to Ursula von der Leyen and others, 'The EU Must Adopt a Negotiation Mandate to Participate in the UN Negotiations for a Binding Treaty on Business and Human Rights' (16 July 2020); Markus Krajewski, 'Aligning Internal and External Policies on Business and Human Rights – Why the EU Should Engage Seriously with the Development of the Legally Binding Instrument' (OpinioJuris, 11 September 2020) <http://opiniojuris.org/?s=Aligning+Internal+and+External+Policies+on+Business+and+Human+Rights+%E2%80%93+Why+the+EU+Should+Engage+Seriously+with+the+Development+of+the+Legally+Binding+Instrument%E2%80%99+> accessed 17 July 2021.

the negotiations of a binding BHR Treaty.[38] In 2018, it adopted a resolution specifically on the EU's input on the BHR Treaty in which it highlighted 'the paramount importance of the EU constructively contributing to the achievement of a Binding Treaty'.[39] In general, the EP has lamented 'that a global approach is still lacking to the way in which transnational corporations (TNCs) abide by human rights law and ensure other remedy mechanisms, which may contribute to TNCs' impunity for cases of human rights abuses and thus be detrimental to people's rights and dignity'.[40] It has also regretted 'any obstructive behaviour in relation to this process' and has called on the EU and Member States 'to constructively engage in the negotiations'.[41] Similarly, the European Economic and Social Committee (EESC) explicitly endorsed an international treaty on BHR,[42] and called for the EU's full commitment to the development of such an instrument.[43]

Among non-State actors, a significant number of human rights and environmental NGOs, trade organizations, and scholars have signalled their support for the BHR Treaty project.[44] In fact, the creation of the Treaty Alliance, an NGO coalition on the BHR Treaty, proved crucial for the establishment of the OEIGWG.[45] A group of parliamentarians and local authorities from

38   See, for instance, European Parliament resolution of 12 March 2015 on the EU's priorities for the UN Human Rights Council in 2015 (2015/2572(RSP)); European Parliament resolution of 17 December 2015 on the Annual Report on Human Rights and Democracy in the World 2014 and the European Union's policy on the matter (2015/2229(INI)); European Parliament resolution of 21 January 2016 on the EU's priorities for the UNHRC sessions in 2016 (2015/3035(RSP)); European Parliament resolution of 25 October 2016 on corporate liability for serious human rights abuses in third countries (2015/2315(INI)); European Parliament resolution of 14 December 2016 on the Annual Report on human rights and democracy in the world and the European Union's policy on the matter 2015 (2016/2219(INI)).

39   European Parliament resolution of 4 October 2018 on the EU's input to a UN Binding Instrument on transnational corporations and other business enterprises with transnational characteristics with respect to human rights (2018/2763(RSP)), para 19.

40   Ibid, para 8.

41   European Parliament resolution of 25 October 2016, para 12.

42   EESC, 'Binding UN Treaty on Business and Human Rights (Own-Initiative Opinion)' (REX/518-EESC-2019).

43   Ibid, para 1.13.

44   See the written contributions for the first session of the OEIGWG. 'First Session of the Open-Ended Intergovernmental Working Group on Transnational Corporations and Other Business Enterprises with Respect to Human Rights' (OHCHR, 2015) <https://www.ohchr.org/EN/HRBodies/HRC/WGTransCorp/Session1/Pages/Session1.aspx> accessed 1 May 2021.

45   Nadia Bernaz and Irene Pietropaoli, 'The Role of Non-Governmental Organizations in the Business and Human Rights Treaty Negotiations' (2017) 9 Journal of Human Rights Practice 287, 288.

around the world has also expressed its support for Resolution 26/9.[46] On the other hand, the business community has generally rejected the idea of a BHR Treaty that imposes binding obligations on businesses, and has criticized the negotiations and the various drafts produced so far.[47]

Pros and cons of a BHR Treaty

The idea of a BHR Treaty has attracted a great deal of attention and comment from CSOs, academics, States, and businesses over the last few years. Questions on the BHR Treaty project, such as whether there is a need for an international legally binding instrument to regulate corporate conduct, and what content such an instrument should contain, have been vigorously debated and have not yet been settled. This section provides an overview of the main arguments put forward in support of, and against, a BHR Treaty.

Arguments in support of a BHR Treaty

The most prominent argument in favour of a BHR Treaty is the necessity to adopt legally binding standards governing corporate conduct towards human rights.[48] Bilchitz contends that there is a need to expressly recognize and clarify that businesses have legal obligations flowing from international human rights law. In his opinion, only an international treaty has the authoritative nature to do so.[49] A BHR Treaty would 'provide a clear recognition and articulation of the important normative position that fundamental rights under international law impose legally-binding obligations upon businesses'. He adds that the 'increased capacity of businesses in recent years to impact upon fundamental rights provides added impetus for this development'.[50]

As mentioned earlier in this book, an international instrument seems to be an appropriate instrument for addressing the transnational nature of human rights abuse involving MNEs. Deva argues that, in order to add value to the

---

46   'Representatives Worldwide Supporting the UN Binding Treaty on Transnational Corporations with Respect to Human Rights' (BindingTreaty.org) <https://bindingtreaty.org> accessed 1 May 2021.

47   See IOE and others, 'Business Response to the Zero Draft Legally Binding Instrument to Regulate, in International Human Rights Law, the Activities of Transnational Corporations and Other Business Enterprises ("Zero Draft Treaty") and the Draft Optional Protocol to the Legally Binding Instrument ("Draft Optional Protocol") Annex' (October 2018); ICC, 'ICC Briefing: The United Nations Treaty Process on Business and Human Rights' (14 October 2019).

48   See Bilchitz, 'The Necessity for a Business and Human Rights Treaty'; ICJ, 'Needs and Options for a New International Instrument in the Field of Business and Human Rights' (June 2014).

49   Bilchitz, 'The Necessity for a Business and Human Rights Treaty', 205–210.

50   Ibid, 206.

existing regulatory landscape, the future BHR Treaty should accomplish key normative objectives, such as addressing the asymmetry between transnational operations of companies and the predominantly territorial nature of human rights law.[51]

In line with this view, a more recent argument links the need for a BHR Treaty with the growing adoption of mandatory HRDD standards at national and regional level. As discussed earlier, an increasing number of countries and the EU are imposing or considering imposing mandatory HRDD requirements on companies. This situation may place an unfair burden on domestic companies which are subject to mandatory HRDD requirements vis-à-vis their foreign competitors who are not subject to such requirements. Krajewski argues that the adoption of an international treaty mandating HRDD legislation could contribute to a level playing field among the States Parties to such a treaty.[52] It would certainly encourage more States to adopt mandatory HRDD standards.

Deva also claims that a BHR Treaty is needed 'to fill certain governance gaps left by existing regulatory initiatives, including the [UNGPs]'.[53] It has been argued that soft law or CSR instruments have proved ineffective in stopping businesses from committing or being involved in human rights abuse.[54] Moreover, they have been of little help to victims seeking redress because they do not create legally enforceable obligations whose infringement could lead to liability. For instance, Stephens argues that the State duty to protect and the corporate responsibility to respect human rights in the UNGPs are 'not backed by a commitment by states or corporations to take any concrete steps to implement effective remedies: the [UNGPs] are phrased as soft law, not binding obligations, contain no enforcement mechanisms and rely heavily on voluntary procedures designed and implemented by corporations with no state supervision'. The UNGPs have 'perpetuated the gap between the promise of remedies and the reality of corporate impunity'.[55] In this context, a BHR Treaty 'should assist in

---

51   Surya Deva, 'Scope of the Proposed Business and Human Rights Treaty' in Surya Deva and David Bilchitz (eds), *Building a Treaty on Business and Human Rights: Context and Contours* (CUP 2017) 168.

52   Krajewski, 'Aligning Internal and External Policies on Business and Human Rights'.

53   Deva, 'Scope of the Proposed Business and Human Rights Treaty', 155.

54   See, for instance, European Parliament resolution of 4 October 2018, para 8. In this resolution, the EP regretted 'that the UNGPs are not embodied in enforceable instruments' and stated that 'the poor implementation of UNGPs, as in the case of other internationally recognised standards, has been largely attributed to their non-binding character'. For a discussion of the effectiveness of the OECD Guidelines on Multinational Enterprises, see Stéfanie Khoury and David Whyte, 'Sidelining Corporate Human Rights Violations: The Failure of the OECD's Regulatory Consensus' 18 (2019) Journal of Human Rights 363.

55   Stephens, 'Making Remedies Work', 408–409.

overcoming at least some of the obstacles in holding corporations accountable for human rights violations'.[56] In particular, the current negotiations offer 'an opportunity to envision a system that could actually offer effective remedies for corporate human rights violations'.[57]

Finally, the adoption of obligations for businesses under international human rights law would represent a philosophical shift in the international legal order vis-à-vis unchecked global capitalism and corporate power. Aragão and Roland suggest that the current treaty process is an opportunity to challenge neoliberal hegemony and corporate power in international governance.[58] They argue that, so far, 'the UN has mostly adhered to the neoliberal and global capitalist hegemonic project. Its recent initiatives on [human rights and business] served to legitimize [MNEs'] globalizing goals, instead of holding them accountable for human rights violations'. The current negotiations could represent 'an opportunity for the UN to effectively engage with and commit to counter-hegemonic demands grounded in the primacy of human rights'. Such demands require 'regulations and mechanisms that could constrain business privileged status of rule and authority in contemporary global politics'.[59] The active participation of global civil society in the treaty negotiations may contribute to overcoming corporate capture of the process. Ultimately, the negotiations represent an opportunity to put a people-centred approach to human rights back on track.[60]

Arguments against a BHR Treaty

Critics of the BHR Treaty initiative have argued that reopening the debate on the role of businesses in human rights abuse in treaty negotiations may weaken the consensus reached with the UNGPs and undermine their implementation.[61] For example, following the adoption of Resolution 26/9, concerns were raised that the resources of governments, CSOs, and businesses would be diverted

---

56   Deva, 'Scope of the Proposed Business and Human Rights Treaty', 156.

57   Stephens, 'Making Remedies Work', 409.

58   Daniel Aragão and Manoela Roland, 'The Need for a Treaty' in Surya Deva and David Bilchitz (eds), *Building a Treaty on Business and Human Rights: Context and Contours* (CUP 2017).

59   Ibid, 152.

60   Ibid.

61   Mark Taylor, *'A Business and Human Rights Treaty? Why Activists Should Be Worried'* (IHRB, 4 June 2014) <https://www.ihrb.org/other/treaty-on-business-human-rights/a-business-and-human-rights-treaty-why-activists-should-be-worried> accessed 1 May 2021; Sara Blackwell and Nicole Vander Meulen, 'Two Roads Converged: The Mutual Complementarity of a Binding Business and Human Rights Treaty and National Action Plans on Business and Human Rights' (2016) 6 Notre Dame Journal of International Comparative Law 51, 61; US Mission to International Organizations in Geneva 2018 and 2020.

from implementing the UNGPs at national level towards the treaty process.[62] Some stakeholders have also argued that the UNGPs are still new and growing in impact, and that more time is required to implement them.[63]

Furthermore, critics have raised questions about the form and substance of a potential BHR Treaty. With regard to the form of a future instrument, the International Chamber of Commerce stated that it is unconvincing that 'a treaty-based approach can be truly effective in dealing with the web of complex interrelationships between business and human rights'.[64] The US has also contended that the one-size-fits-all approach represented by the proposed treaty is not the best way to address all adverse effects of business activities on human rights.[65] Similarly, various scholars have expressed doubts about the feasibility and the practical added-value of an international legally binding instrument on BHR, particularly one that is comprehensive in scope.[66]

The content of the BHR Treaty is also the subject of a controversial debate among stakeholders. In particular, the scope of the future instrument raises a number of contentious questions.[67] The first question relates to its application to business actors. Should the treaty apply to all types of business enterprises (ie transnational and domestic ones) or should it be limited to transnational corporations only?[68] According to Resolution 26/9, the BHR Treaty should focus on 'the activities of transnational corporations and other business enterprises'. However, here the term 'business enterprises' refers to all business enterprises that have a transnational character in their operation activities, but not to local businesses registered in terms of relevant domestic law.[69] The EU and the US have criticized this exclusive emphasis on transnational corporations. For the EU, it 'neglects the fact than many abuses are committed by enterprises at domestic level, thus undermining a fundamental element of the UNGPs

---

62   Taylor, 'A Business and Human Rights Treaty'.

63   Cassel and Ramasastry, 'White Paper', 10; BIAC, ICC, IOR and WBCSD, 'UN Treaty Process on Business and Human Rights: Initial Observations by the International Business Community on a Way Forward' (29 June 2015) <https://www.ohchr.org/Documents/HRBodies/HRCouncil/WGTransCorp/Session1/IOE_contribution.pdf> accessed 17 July 2021.

64   International Chamber of Commerce, 'Briefing'.

65   US Mission to International Organizations in Geneva 2018 and 2020.

66   Jolyon Ford and Claire Methven O'Brien, 'Empty Rituals or Workable Models: Towards a Business and Human Rights Treaty' (2017) 40 UNSW Law Journal 1223; Pierre Thielborger and Tobias Ackermann, 'A Treaty on Enforcing Human Rights against Business: Closing the Loophole or Getting Stuck in a Loop' (2017) 24 Indiana Journal of Global Legal Studies 43; Lee McConnell, 'Assessing the Feasibility of a Business and Human Rights Treaty' (2017) 66 International and Comparative Law Quarterly 143.

67   For a discussion of the scope of the BHR treaty, see Deva, 'Scope of the Proposed Business and Human Rights Treaty'.

68   See ibid, 155; Bilchitz, 'The Necessity for a Business and Human Rights Treaty', 220.

69   See footnote to UNHRC Resolution 26/9.

that cover all businesses, regardless of whether firms are transnational'.[70] A second scope-related question refers to which human rights should be covered: all international human rights or only selected human rights, such as gross or serious human rights violations?[71] Here again, there are various opposing views.[72]

Another important issue regarding content relates to business obligations under international human rights law. Will the future instrument impose obligations on States only or will it also impose obligations on businesses?[73] It has been argued that imposing obligations on businesses under international human rights law would raise complex normative issues and would be difficult to enforce. Furthermore, it is unclear whether such an approach would provide a better avenue for victims than the traditional State-centric one.[74] States are already obliged to enact a regulatory framework that establishes obligations of third parties, including businesses, in relation to fundamental rights. Where the law provides a means of adequately addressing the problems caused by business impacts on human rights, it may be more effective to focus on ensuring enforcement of that law instead.[75]

Some stakeholders, including the US, the EU, and the business community, have criticized the way the negotiations have been conducted. The process has been decried for its lack of consensus building (in opposition to the UNGPs) and the exclusion of the business community from the negotiations. The US has contended that '[t]he process has become irreconcilably broken and dissenting voices are routinely silenced by those running the process, including by omitting dissenting views from the annual reports, ostensibly to project an appearance of greater consensus'.[76] Businesses have also criticized the public release of the various drafts while, at the same time, arguing that 'no real effort has been

---

70   EU, 'Inter-Governmental Working Group (IGWG) on the elaboration of an international legally-binding instrument on transnational corporations and other business enterprises with respect to human rights – Submission of the European Union'.

71   Deva, 'Scope of the Proposed Business and Human Rights Treaty', 154.

72   For a discussion of the options, see Cassel and Ramasastry, 'White Paper', 41–43.

73   For an overview of views in favour of companies' direct obligations under international human rights law, see Bilchitz, 'The Necessity for a Business and Human Rights Treaty', 208; Nicolás Carrillo-Santarelli, 'A Defence of Direct International Human Rights Obligations of (All) Corporations' in Jernej Letnar Černič and Nicolás Carrillo-Santarelli (eds), *The Future of Business and Human Rights: Theoretical and Practical Considerations for a UN Treaty* (Intersentia 2018); Andrés Felipe López Latorre, 'In Defence of Direct Obligations for Businesses under International Human Rights Law' (2020) 5 Business and Human Rights Journal 56.

74   Tara Van Ho, '"Band-Aids Don't Fix Bullet Holes": In Defence of a Traditional State-Centric Approach' in Jernej Letnar Černič and Nicolás Carrillo-Santarelli (eds), *The Future of Business and Human Rights: Theoretical and Practical Considerations for a UN Treaty* (Intersentia 2018).

75   Ibid, 138.

76   US Mission to International Organizations in Geneva 2018 and 2020.

made to ensure a robust, transparent and open process that fully draws on the expertise and experience of all stakeholders'.[77]

Finally, there have been concerns about the lack of political adherence to the BHR Treaty project. So far, many key stakeholders have been absent from the negotiations (eg the US) or have been present without participating in the negotiations (eg the EU). There are fears that the lack of political consensus in the negotiations may be felt when States have to adopt and/or ratify and implement the future instrument.

3 The added-value of an international treaty on BHR for access to justice

One aim of a future BHR Treaty must be to improve victims' access to justice. As discussed earlier, the persistent difficulties faced by victims in accessing justice, and discontent with how the UNGPs have dealt with corporate accountability and access to remedy, have largely contributed to calls for the adoption of a BHR Treaty. The future instrument must therefore include provisions to enable victims to obtain corporate accountability and redress. This section sets out provisions that should be included in a future instrument in order to guarantee access to justice in the context of litigation against MNEs in the home State. These provisions are suggested on the basis of the various normative, procedural, and practical obstacles identified in the previous chapters of this book. Although the issue of access to justice in the host State is important in the context of the more general debate on the necessary contribution of a BHR Treaty to access to justice, it remains outside the scope of this book. This section also briefly analyses whether the most recent BHR Treaty draft includes the suggested provisions. The negotiations were still ongoing at the time of writing, with no final version of the BHR Treaty in sight. It is therefore likely that the provisions analysed here will change in the future. However, an analysis of the drafts is valuable in assessing whether the OEIGWG is directly addressing the issues that have impacted access to justice in the home country in recent years.

The type of international instrument

The question of the type of instrument to be adopted has been the subject of debate. CSOs and academics have suggested a variety of hard law and soft law instruments, ranging from international treaties and framework conventions with optional protocols to declarations.[78]

---

77 IOE and others, 'Business Response to Zero Draft Legally Binding Instrument', 2.

78 For a non-exhaustive list of the potential instruments outlined so far, see Ford and Methven O'Brien, 'Empty Rituals or Workable Models?', 1232.

From an access to justice perspective, a legally binding instrument appears to be more appropriate than a soft law instrument. There are two main reasons for this argument. First, as discussed in Chapter 2, a number of legally binding international instruments already protect the right to an effective remedy where human rights are violated and/or provide for the necessary procedural safeguards to ensure the right to a fair trial. However, these instruments do not address the specific barriers that victims face when seeking redress for human rights abuse involving transnational business actors. Second, soft law instruments have failed to improve access to justice for victims of business-related human rights abuse. The UNGPs provide for the need for effective remedy through judicial and non-judicial grievance mechanisms. However, they are 'phrased as soft-law, not binding obligations, contain no enforcement mechanisms and rely heavily on voluntary procedures designed and implemented by corporations with no State supervision'.[79] As a result, the implementation by States of Pillar III of the UNGPs has been unsatisfactory to date, and victims of business-related abuse continue to struggle to seek redress. Having said this, it is important to keep in mind that a legally binding instrument is not a panacea. International human rights treaties have been criticized for being ineffective or even counterproductive, sometimes exacerbating, rather than attenuating, human rights abuses, especially in authoritarian countries.[80] Many of them lack strong enforcement mechanisms to ensure that States respect and protect human rights.[81] However, as Bilchitz argues, only legally binding instruments have the authoritative nature required to expand the scope of international law with regard to businesses, in particular to create corporate obligations under international human rights law.[82]

A number of scholars have advocated for the adoption of a framework convention.[83] A framework convention or agreement is a type of legally binding treaty that establishes general obligations for its States Parties and leaves the adoption of specific targets or more detailed obligations either to subsequent

79   Stephens, 'Making Remedies Work', 409.

80   For a discussion of the effectiveness of human rights treaties, see Oona Hathaway, 'Do Human Rights Treaties Make a Difference?' (2002) 111 Yale Law Journal 1935; Eric Neumayer, 'Do International Human Rights Treaties Improve Respect for Human Rights?' (2005) 49 Journal of Conflict Resolution 925; Emilie Hafner-Burton and Kiyoteru Tsutsui, 'Justice Lost! The Failure of International Human Rights Law to Matter where Needed Most' (2007) 44 Journal of Peace Research 407.

81   For a discussion of the role of enforcement mechanisms in international human rights law, see Yvonne Dutton, 'Commitment to International Human Rights Treaties: The Role of Enforcement Mechanisms' (2012) 34 University of Pennsylvania Journal of International Law 1.

82   Bilchitz, 'The Necessity for a Business and Human Rights Treaty'.

83   Claire Methven O'Brien, 'Transcending the Binary: Linking Hard and Soft Law through a UNGPs-Based Framework Convention' (2020) 114 AJIL Unbound 186; Simons, 'The Value-Added of a Treaty'.

protocols or to national legislation. Methven O'Brien suggests adopting a BHR Treaty modelled as a framework convention and centred initially on the UNGPs.[84] In a nutshell, the framework convention would define an overall purpose or common objectives that States must achieve. To attain this purpose or those objectives, States would use the UNGPs as guidance and NAPs as implementation tools. A Conference of the Parties could then adopt protocols in order to advance the objectives of the framework convention.[85]

The instrument suggested by Methven O'Brien undoubtedly presents a number of strengths. Framework conventions establish living treaty regimes. They contribute to a progressive development of international law in a manner that is flexible, sensitive to contemporary needs or circumstances, and based on continuous legislative activities.[86] Framework conventions also tend to secure State consensus more easily, which is useful in the context of controversial issues such as BHR. Moreover, a BHR framework convention centred on the UNGPs could capitalize on 'the widespread acceptance of the UN Framework and the UNGPs among governments, labour, business and other actors as well as substantial efforts since 2011 to implement them'.[87] An important characteristic of this approach is that 'if hardening the UNGPs would constitute a baseline, this approach would also offer scope to generate new soft and hard law standards on topics of global concern as they emerge, such as systematic human rights challenges posed by big tech, AI, and the platform economy'.[88] This approach could, in Methven O'Brien's words, 'bridg[e] the hard law-soft law divide and contribut[e] meaningfully to advancing respect for human rights in the global market sphere'.[89]

At the same time, a BHR Treaty modelled as a framework convention centred on the UNGPs presents a number of pitfalls. First, past and current examples of framework conventions, such as the United Nations Framework Convention on Climate Change (UNFCCC),[90] show they can be difficult to implement in the long term. Despite near-universal membership, the UNFCCC has failed to achieve its objective of stabilization of greenhouse gas concentration in the atmosphere since it came into force in 1994. One reason for this failure is the UNFCCC's excessive reliance on subsequent protocols that States are increasingly reluctant to adopt or that are devoid of meaningful commitments.

---

84 Methven O'Brien, 'Transcending the Binary', 186.

85 To support her proposal, Methven O'Brien released a Draft text for a BHR treaty in June 2020.

86 Rüdiger Wolfrum, 'Sources of International Law', MPEPIL (2011) <http://opil.ouplaw.com/view/10.1093/law:epil/9780199231690/law-9780199231690-e1471> accessed 1 May 2021.

87 Methven O'Brien, 'Transcending the Binary', 190.

88 Ibid.

89 Ibid, 189.

90 UNFCCC (adopted 9 May 1992, entered into force 21 March 1994) 1771 UNTS 107.

Furthermore, the flexibility offered by the nature of framework conventions in general has led to the creation of a complex and, at times, opaque institutional structure whose effectiveness is dubious.

Second, there is a risk that an excessive emphasis on the UNGPs, even initially, could limit the possibility of imposing corporate human rights obligations. Such a risk could materialize in two different ways. First of all, as discussed earlier, the UNGPs provide that business enterprises should respect human rights. A number of actors have been critical of the corporate responsibility to respect human rights under the UNGPs because it does not formulate an obligation on companies to respect human rights and fails to consider whether companies could have other human rights obligations, such as the protection and the fulfilment of human rights.[91] A BHR framework convention centred on the UNGPs is therefore more likely to require States to encourage corporate respect of human rights instead of requiring States to impose appropriate corporate human rights obligations.[92] In addition, there is a risk that any future attempts to adopt or implement innovative corporate human rights standards that go beyond those established under the UNGPs may fail due to reluctance on the part of States to accept these or to delays in adopting the necessary additional protocols. Although this risk is also possible in the context of a more 'classic' conventional instrument, the potential negative impact of the absence of new standards would nevertheless be minimized if the BHR Treaty established strong corporate human rights obligations from the outset. In addition, it could be argued that, in the context of a framework convention centred on the UNGPs, voluntary responsibility could become a binding duty of care over time. However, it would be left to the national courts to decide this. This approach would be uncertain and likely to take years without providing legal certainty to businesses as to what is expected of them and victims as to whether they can have access to remedies.

Finally, the State implementation of the UNGPs through NAPs has been rather disappointing to date.[93] As of May 2021, only 24 countries had produced a

---

91   David Bilchitz, 'The Ruggie Framework: An Adequate Rubric for Corporate Human Rights Obligations?' (2010) 12 SUR – International Journal on Human Rights 199.

92   The UNGPs remain ambiguous as to whether States must impose corporate human rights obligations. On the one hand, GP 1 states that States *must* protect against human rights abuse within their territory and/or jurisdiction by business enterprises by taking appropriate steps to prevent, investigate, punish, and redress such abuse through effective policies, legislation, regulations, and adjudication. On the other hand, GP 2 provides that States *should* set out clearly the expectation that all business enterprises respect human rights throughout their operations, while GP 3 states that States *should* enforce laws that aim or have the effect of requiring businesses to respect human rights.

93   ICAR, ECCJ and Dejusticia, 'Assessments of Existing National Action Plans (NAPs) on Business and Human Rights' (2017 Update); Humberto Cantú Rivera, 'National Action Plans on Business and Human Rights: Progress or Mirage?' (2019) 4 Business and Human Rights Journal 213.

NAP,[94] and 16 of them were EU Member States that were explicitly asked by the EC to develop a NAP by 2012.[95] Furthermore, the content of NAPs has been problematic. In particular, States have paid insufficient attention to the implementation of Pillar III in their NAPs.[96] Access to remedy has received little to no attention in a large number of NAPs,[97] although the most recent NAPs have begun to address this flaw. Observers have criticized States for their passive attitude towards developing NAPs and strengthening their national systems to improve corporate human rights accountability. There appears to be a clear contrast between this attitude and the consensus reached at the time the UNGPs were adopted.[98]

In this book, it is suggested that the BHR Treaty could be modelled as a convention that establishes the basic principles governing the relationship between business and human rights. At a minimum, the BHR Treaty should require States to: (1) impose human rights obligations on business actors; (2) hold business actors liable when they fail to comply with their human rights obligations; and (3) ensure access to justice and effective remedy for victims of business-related human rights abuse. The BHR Treaty should distinguish between main obligations, which should be formulated in a clear and concise manner directly within the body of the convention, and more detailed obligations, which seek to address specific issues. For example, ensuring access to justice and effective remedy is likely to require specific obligations in relation to aspects such as jurisdiction, cause of action, rules on evidence, costs of proceedings, and so on. These obligations may be too detailed or contentious to be included in the main body of the treaty.[99] In this event, it may be appropriate to have these detailed obligations in a separate document. They could be set out in an annex or could be developed over time in optional protocols adopted through procedures and mechanisms established by the convention (eg meeting of the Parties). Furthermore, the BHR Treaty need not be centred on the UNGPs to ensure consistency with them. Its provisions could incorporate the UNGPs as minimum standards. However, the BHR Treaty should probably go further than the UNGPs on

---

94   'State National Action Plans on Business and Human Rights' (OHCHR) <https://www.ohchr.org/EN/Issues/Business/Pages/NationalActionPlans.aspx> accessed 1 May 2021.

95   It should be noted that many Member States did not respect the 2012 target originally set.

96   UNWG, 'Report of the Working Group on the issue of human rights and transnational corporations and other business enterprises on the sixth session of the Forum on Business and Human Rights' (23 April 2018) UN Doc A/HRC/38/49, para 20. The Working Group, business associations and civil society speakers pointed out that existing national action plans were limited in terms of action to improve access to remedy.

97   Blackwell and Vander Meulen, 'Two Roads Converged', 57–58.

98   Jernej Letnar Černič, 'European Perspectives on the Business and Human Rights Treaty Initiative' in Jernej Letnar Černič and Nicolás Carrillo-Santarelli (eds), *The Future of Business and Human Rights: Theoretical and Practical Considerations for a UN Treaty* (Intersentia 2018) 231.

99   Methven O'Brien, 'Transcending the Binary'.

certain aspects, such as corporate human rights obligations and effective access to remedy, in order to fill current normative gaps.

Scope

The scope of the future instrument will have a significant impact on the ability of victims to seek redress when they have suffered human rights abuses committed by or involving business actors. To date, the scope of the BHR Treaty has been one of the most contentious issues in the negotiations.[100] In particular, there are two aspects that have proved to be problematic. First, should the BHR Treaty apply to all types of business enterprises or should it be limited to MNEs?[101] Second, should the BHR Treaty cover all international human rights or only selected ones, such as gross violations of human rights.

With regard to the first question, the OEIGWG was originally mandated to elaborate a BHR Treaty to regulate the activities of transnational corporations and other business enterprises. This mandate excluded domestic companies with no transnational character from the scope of the BHR Treaty. This approach attracted considerable criticism from various stakeholders, including governments, NGOs, and academics, who have argued that the BHR Treaty should apply to all business enterprises.[102] Deva suggests that in the situation where States cannot reach a consensus on whether the BHR Treaty should apply to all types of businesses, a 'hybrid option' should be considered. For example, the BHR Treaty could apply only to MNEs, and a subsequent or optional protocol could extend the BHR Treaty provisions to all other types of business enterprises.[103] However, the risk with this approach is that standards that apply to all companies will never be adopted.

At the time of writing, the scope of the 2020 Draft covered 'all business enterprises, including but not limited to transnational corporations and other business enterprises that undertake business activities of a transnational character'.[104] Importantly, States Parties had the possibility 'to differentiate how business enterprises discharge these obligations commensurate with their size, sector, operational context and the severity of impacts on human rights'.[105]

---

100 Deva, 'Scope of the Proposed Business and Human Rights Treaty', 154.

101 Ibid.

102 US Mission to International Organizations in Geneva 2018 and 2020; EEAS, 'HRC – Open-ended Intergovernmental Working Group'; Amnesty International, 'Amnesty International Position on the New UN Process to Elaborate a Legally Binding Instrument on Business and Human Rights' (4 July 2014) <https://www.amnesty.org/en/documents/ior40/005/2014/en/> accessed 17 July 2021; Deva, 'Scope of the Proposed Business and Human Rights Treaty', 155.

103 Deva, 'Scope of the Proposed Business and Human Rights Treaty', 155.

104 2020 Draft, Article 3(1).

105 Ibid, Article 3(2).

This approach had the advantage of avoiding either the unique regulatory challenges posed by MNEs or the limited capacity of small and medium-sized enterprises.[106]

With regard to the second question, from an access to justice perspective, the future instrument should cover a broad – rather than narrow – range of human rights. In accordance with the UNGPs, it should at least refer to internationally recognized human rights expressed, at a minimum, in the International Bill of Human Rights and the principles concerning fundamental rights set out in the International Labour Organization's Declaration on Fundamental Principles and Rights at Work. However, the BHR Treaty should go further and require respect for the human rights of individuals and communities belonging to vulnerable groups, such as women, children, indigenous peoples, migrant workers and their families, or persons with disabilities.[107] Furthermore, standards of international humanitarian law should be respected in situations of armed conflict.[108] The future instrument should also not be limited to gross human rights violations because, in Deva's words, 'such a narrow focus might not be able to capture how people are suffering in diverse ways, especially in the Global South, from human rights abuses linked to corporate activities aimed at profit-maximization'.[109] Focusing on gross human rights violations would de facto exclude economic, social, and cultural rights from the protection afforded by the BHR Treaty.

At the time of writing, the 2020 Draft provided that the BHR Treaty must 'cover all internationally recognised human rights and fundamental freedoms emanating from the Universal Declaration of Human Rights, any core international human rights treaty and fundamental ILO convention to which a state is a party, and customary international law'.[110] While this list provided an extensive coverage of human rights, it did not include the ILO Declaration on Fundamental Principles and Rights at Work.[111] Furthermore, Deva suggests that a reference to the Rio Declaration on Environment and Development would be desirable.[112]

---

106 Surya Deva, 'BHR Symposium: The Business and Human Rights Treaty in 2020 – The Draft Is "Negotiation-Ready", But Are States Ready?' (*OpinioJuris*, 8 September 2020) <http://opiniojuris.org/2020/09/08/bhr-symposium-the-business-and-human-rights-treaty-in-2020-the-draft-is-negotiation-ready-but-are-states-ready/> accessed 1 May 2021.

107 Corinne Lewis and Carl Söderbergh, 'The Revised Draft Treaty: Where Are the Minorities?' (BHRRC, 8 October 2019) <https://www.business-humanrights.org/en/blog/the-revised-draft-treaty-where-are-minorities/> accessed 1 May 2021.

108 GP 12 provides useful guidance on this.

109 Deva, 'Scope of the Proposed Business and Human Rights Treaty', 155.

110 2020 Draft, Article 3(3).

111 Deva, 'BHR Symposium: The Business and Human Rights Treaty in 2020'.

112 Ibid.

Content

A future BHR Treaty should include a general objective to ensure access to justice and effective remedies for victims of business-related human rights abuses. A positive aspect of the treaty negotiations at the time of writing was that the 2020 Draft already provided for such an objective in its statement of purpose.[113] In terms of content, a future instrument should contain provisions imposing general obligations on States to ensure access to justice and effective remedy for victims of business-related human rights abuses. To date, the various BHR Treaty drafts have included detailed provisions imposing different obligations on States with regard to key aspects of access to justice, such as business legal liability, jurisdiction, applicable law, victims' rights, procedural and practical barriers, and remedy.

Business liability for human rights abuse

From an access to justice perspective, a future instrument should recognize that all business enterprises have human rights obligations. As Bilchitz points out, there is a significant link between the recognition of binding obligations and the right to access remedies. 'Without an understanding of the legal obligations corporations bear with respect to fundamental rights, it will not be possible for victims of rights violations to claim access to a legal remedy against such a private corporation.'[114] Imposing legally binding human rights obligations on businesses is 'the crucial precondition for providing legal remedies to individuals against such entities'.[115] The BHR Treaty could recognize that businesses have obligations either under international human rights law or under national law.[116] Importantly, it should clarify the nature and extent of business human rights obligations (ie respect, protect, or fulfil human rights). However, if this approach is too controversial, the instrument could provide States Parties with discretion in defining the scope of such obligations. In any case, business human rights obligations should not mirror the obligations of States under international human rights law and should be tailored to the nature and capabilities of business actors.

A future instrument could use corporate responsibility to respect human rights under the UNGPs as a basis for the development of business human rights obligations. It could recognize that, at the very least, all business enterprises have an obligation to respect human rights. For example, it could mirror the language used in GP 11 by stating that business enterprises *shall* respect human

---

113 2020 Scope, Article 2.

114 Bilchitz, 'The Necessity for a Business and Human Rights Treaty', 209.

115 Ibid.

116 Bilchitz 'Corporate Obligations', 186.

rights (as opposed to *should* in the UNGPs) and that 'they *shall* avoid infringing on the human rights of others and *shall* address adverse human rights impacts with which they are involved'. If this proposal is too contentious, the future instrument could alternatively provide that States shall take the necessary or appropriate measures to require all business enterprises to respect human rights. This approach would guarantee consistency with the UNGPs and ensure that both instruments are mutually reinforcing. It should be noted that the business obligation to respect human rights might not be sufficient to protect human rights in some circumstances. Therefore, it may be appropriate for the future instrument to allow States Parties to consider the imposition of other human rights obligations on business enterprises in such situations.[117]

So far, the various BHR Treaty drafts have not explicitly provided that all business enterprises have human rights obligations. In its Article 2 on the statement of purpose, the 2020 Draft provides that one of the purposes of the BHR Treaty is 'to clarify and facilitate effective implementation of the obligation of States to respect, protect and promote human rights in the context of business activities, as well as the responsibilities of business enterprises in this regard', and 'to prevent the occurrence of human rights abuses in the context of business activities'. Nonetheless, in its Article 6(1) on prevention, the 2020 Draft provides that 'States shall take all necessary legal and policy measures to ensure that business enterprises, including but not limited to transnational corporations and other business enterprises that undertake business activities of a transnational character, within their territory or jurisdiction, or otherwise under their control, respect all internationally recognised human rights and prevent and mitigate human rights abuses throughout their operations'. Therefore, the 2020 Draft indirectly creates an obligation for business enterprises to respect human rights.

Given the recent momentum gained by the concept of HRDD introduced by the UNGPs, the BHR Treaty should require States to impose mandatory HRDD on business enterprises.[118] Every business enterprise should be obliged to carry out HRDD for its own human rights impacts as well as for those within its value chain, including subsidiaries, suppliers, and other third parties.[119] The UNGPs provide valuable inspiration in this regard. On the basis of HRDD under GP 17, the BHR Treaty could require States Parties to impose on business enterprises the obligation to: (1) identify and assess any actual or potential adverse human

---

117 On the need for different types of corporate human rights obligations, see Bilchitz, 'The Ruggie Framework'.

118 Robert McCorquodale and Lise Smit, 'Human Rights, Responsibilities and Due Diligence' in Surya Deva and David Bilchitz (eds), *Building a Treaty on Business and Human Rights: Context and Contours* (CUP 2017) 216.

119 Ibid, 236.

rights impacts with which they may be involved either through their own activities or those of their business relationships; (2) prevent and mitigate adverse human rights impacts; (3) verify whether adverse human rights impacts are being addressed; and (4) account for how they address their human rights impacts. Strong compliance mechanisms should be in place (eg liability mechanisms, a set of sanctions for non-compliance, and/or a supervisory body with monitoring and sanctioning powers), and business enterprises should be required to provide effective remedy where adverse human rights impacts occur. Furthermore, contrary to the UNGPs, a future instrument should require that failure to conduct reasonable HRDD be punishable by robust penalties.

In the 2020 Draft, Article 6(2) provides that 'State Parties shall require business enterprises, to undertake human rights due diligence proportionate to their size, risk of severe human rights impacts and the nature and context of their operations'. HRDD should be conducted in a manner similar to the four-step HRDD process outlined in the UNGPs.[120] The formulation of an HRDD obligation in the 2020 Draft is now more in line with the UNGPs (compared to previous drafts of the BHR Treaty).[121] The 2020 Draft also provides that HRDD measures should include various processes or display certain characteristics, such as the integration of a gender perspective, meaningful consultation with rightsholders, and consultation with indigenous peoples in accordance with free, prior, and informed consent standards. Importantly, according to Article 6(6), failure to comply with HRDD duties shall result in 'commensurate sanctions, including corrective action where applicable, without prejudice to the provisions on criminal, civil and administrative liability under Article 8'.

Finally, victims must be able to hold businesses liable for the harm they have suffered as a result of a human rights violation involving those businesses. The BHR Treaty should therefore require States Parties to take the necessary or appropriate measures to establish liability for legal persons that infringe human rights falling under its scope in the context of business activities. Importantly, in order to have meaningful home state remedies, the future instrument should recognize substantive legal norms that hold parent companies liable for their subsidiaries' unlawful actions and abuses in their supply chains. This means that the parent company should be held liable not only when it has been directly involved in human rights abuses, but also when it has conspired with, assisted, or otherwise furthered conduct that violates human rights.[122]

---

120 2020 Draft, Article 6(2).

121 Deva, 'BHR Symposium: The Business and Human Rights Treaty in 2020'; Carlos López, 'Symposium: The 2nd Revised Draft of a Treaty on Business and Human Rights – Moving (Slowly) in the Right Direction' (OpinioJuris, 7 September 2020) <http://opiniojuris.org/2020/09/07/symposium-the-2nd-revised-draft-of-a-treaty-on-business-and-human-rights-moving-slowly-in-the-right-direction/> accessed 1 May 2021.

122 Stephens, 'Making Remedies Work', 428.

In the event that the BHR Treaty provides for, or does not exclude, the possibility of criminal liability, its drafters should take into account certain aspects that may give rise to difficulty. First, it is unlikely that States can and should criminalize all human rights violations, especially those committed outside their territory. As Darcy argues, 'Not all violations of human rights are recognised in positive law as criminal acts, and corresponding offences for violations of socio-economic rights, for example, tend not be found in national criminal codes or in the statutes of the various international criminal courts.'[123] The future instrument should therefore define a set of crimes, most likely crimes under international law, that are subject to domestic criminal prosecution.[124] Second, as a result of the variance in domestic approaches to criminal liability, drafters should probably defer to States the decision as to whether they want to impose criminal liability on legal persons. The BHR Treaty should require States to impose liability on legal persons and let them choose whether such liability should be criminal, civil, or administrative.[125] Criminal liability could be imposed on natural persons within the company only, such as corporate directors. Nevertheless, where States impose criminal liability on legal persons, such liability should not prevent the criminal liability of the natural persons who have committed the offence. Third, the BHR Treaty should clarify modes of liability and complicity, as those play an important role on assertion of jurisdiction over crimes committed by or involving MNEs.[126]

In the 2020 Draft, Article 8 contains 11 provisions governing legal liability. Article 8(1) generally provides that:

> State Parties shall ensure that their domestic law provides for a comprehensive and adequate system of legal liability of legal and natural persons conducting business activities, domiciled or operating within their territory or jurisdiction, or otherwise under their control, for human rights abuses that may arise from their own business activities, including those of transnational character, or from their business relationships.

Therefore, Article 8(1) provides direct liability of the business for its own activities and indirect liability of the business for the activities of its business relationships. Article 8(7) also posits liability of a business for its failure to prevent another person with whom it has a business relationship from

---

123 Shane Darcy, 'The Potential Role of Criminal Law in a Business and Human Rights Treaty' in Surya Deva and David Bilchitz (eds), *Building a Treaty on Business and Human Rights: Context and Contours* (CUP 2017) 439.

124 Stephens, 'Making Remedies Work', 431.

125 Darcy, 'The Potential Role of Criminal Law', 470.

126 Stephens, 'Making Remedies Work', 431; Darcy, 'The Potential Role of Criminal Law', 450.

causing or contributing to human rights abuses. This liability should apply when the former controls or supervises the person or the activity that caused or contributed to the human rights abuse, or should have foreseen risks of human rights abuses in the conduct of its business activities, including those of transnational character, or in their business relationships, but failed to put in place adequate measures to prevent the abuse. The introduction of 'business relationship' and a broader notion of control is a useful advance.[127] An important aspect is that the transnational nature of business activities cannot prevent corporate liability. Other provisions of Article 8 also govern various important aspects, such as reparation and the financial security obligations to cover potential claims of compensation.

Article 8(9), (10), and (11) deal with criminal liability. 'States Parties shall ensure that their domestic law provides for the criminal or functionally equivalent liability of legal persons for human rights abuses that amount to criminal offences under international human rights law binding on the State Party, customary international law, or their domestic law.'[128] In this context, States Parties must provide for the application of penalties that 'are commensurate with the gravity of the offence'. Furthermore, the liability of legal persons shall be without prejudice to the criminal liability of natural persons who have committed the offences under the applicable domestic law.[129] Finally, 'State Parties shall provide measures under domestic law to establish the criminal or functionally equivalent legal liability for legal or natural persons conducting business activities, including those of a transnational character, for acts or omissions that constitute attempt, participation or complicity in a criminal offence in accordance with this Article and criminal offences as defined by their domestic law.'[130]

The 2020 Draft aims to cover a number of long-standing issues related to business liability for human rights abuse. However, while the drafters' intentions are good, the manner in which they address certain issues is problematic. Currently, there are a number of structural and substantive issues with how liability is addressed in the 2020 Draft. First, Articles 6 and 8 appear to be catch-all provisions, which are excessively long and complex. They provide a disproportionate level of detail which is inappropriate in the context of an international instrument that should impose general obligations on States. Such an approach could create more resistance to future adherence to the BHR

---

127 Justine Nolan, 'BHR Symposium: Global Supply Chains – Where Art Thou in the BHR Treaty?' (OpinioJuris, 7 September 2020) <http://opiniojuris.org/2020/09/07/bhr-symposium-global-supply-chains-where-art-thou-in-the-bhr-treaty/> accessed 1 May 2021.

128 2020 Draft, Article 8(9).

129 Ibid, Article 8(10).

130 Ibid, Article 8(11).

Treaty. Second, while various observers have suggested that the 2020 Draft has improved in comparison with previous versions of the BHR Treaty, a number of substantive issues remain. For instance, the use of HRDD as a defence to potential liability under Article 8(7) is unclear.[131] Furthermore, Article 8(9) on liability for international crimes removes the list of widely accepted criminal offences under international law found in the 2019 Draft, which would have provided States, businesses, and victims with welcome guidance and legal certainty.[132] Finally, the 2020 Draft neglects to clarify important concepts, such as complicity in criminal law.

Jurisdiction

As discussed earlier in this book, establishing jurisdiction in the home country remains a significant obstacle for victims of business-related abuse seeking redress. It is therefore crucial that the BHR Treaty clearly addresses the question of jurisdiction, particularly procedural issues in transnational litigation against MNEs, in both civil and criminal proceedings.[133]

Jurisdiction in civil cases

It is important to note from the outset the difficulty of clarifying jurisdiction in transnational civil cases in the context of an international human rights instrument. The question of which court is competent to hear a case involving natural and/or legal persons from different countries normally falls within the scope of private international law, which operates under different rules and conditions from public international law. Therefore, in drawing up provisions on jurisdiction in transnational civil cases, the OEIGWG should ensure that such provisions remain consistent with private international law rules applicable to jurisdiction.[134]

In general, the BHR Treaty should clarify that victims of human rights abuse involving MNEs may choose to bring a civil claim before the courts of either the host or home State. Therefore, it should impose obligations on both host and home countries to allow victims to bring civil claims before their courts. Any requirements for establishing jurisdiction, such as nationality or domicile of parties, should be carefully weighed in order to avoid unduly restricting the ability of victims to access the courts of the home State.

---

131 López, 'Symposium: The 2nd Revised Draft'.

132 Deva, 'BHR Symposium: The Business and Human Rights Treaty in 2020'.

133 Stephens, 'Making Remedies Work', 429–430.

134 This comment also applies to the question of the law applicable to a transnational civil case, which is dealt with below.

The BHR Treaty should also address other jurisdiction-related issues. One issue relates to claims made against multiple defendants domiciled in different countries (eg parent companies and their subsidiaries). The BHR Treaty should provide for rules that allow the joining of subsidiaries in claims against their parent company (ie joining of co-defendants).[135] Allowing the joining of co-defendants would provide for faster dispute resolution and, importantly, limit the risk of conflicting judgments if claims against the parent company and the subsidiary are litigated in separate tribunals.[136] Furthermore, in order to avoid situations where victims are denied justice on the grounds of jurisdictional issues, NGOs, lawyers, and academics have also called for the BHR Treaty to address the doctrine of *forum non conveniens*,[137] and allow for the application of the doctrine of *forum necessitatis*.[138]

In the 2020 Draft, Article 9 governs adjudicative jurisdiction. Article 9(1) provides that jurisdiction with respect to claims made by victims shall vest in the courts of the State where: (1) the human rights abuse occurred; or (2) an act or omission contributing to the human rights abuse occurred; or (3) the legal or natural persons alleged to have committed an act or omission causing or contributing to such human rights abuse in the context of business activities, including those of a transnational character, are domiciled. Importantly, Article 9(2) establishes a broad definition of domicile,[139] and the nationality or place of domicile of the victim is irrelevant when establishing jurisdiction.

The scope of Article 9(1) seems at first sight to be sufficiently broad to allow victims to bring claims against parent companies in the home State. Indeed, the courts of the State where the parent company is domiciled may hear claims against the company. However, the wording of Article 9(1) has raised concerns by NGOs that victims may be obliged to prove that the acts or omissions that resulted in the human right abuse are those of the parent company in order to be

---

135 Daniel Blackburn, 'Removing Barriers to Justice: How a Treaty on Business and Human Rights Could Improve Access to Remedy for Victims' (ICTUR, August 2017) 71.

136 Ibid.

137 Richard Meeran, 'The Revised Draft: Access to Judicial Remedy for Victims of Multinationals' Abuse' (BHRRC, 8 October 2019) <https://www.business-humanrights.org/en/the-revised-draft-access-to-judicial-remedy-for-victims-of-multinationals-abuse> accessed 1 May 2021; Stephens, 'Making Remedies Work', 429.

138 Sandra Cossart and Lucie Chatelain, 'Key Legal Obstacles around Jurisdiction for Victims Seeking Justice Remain in the Revised Draft Treaty' (BHRRC, October 2019) <https://www.business-humanrights.org/en/key-legal-obstacles-around-jurisdiction-for-victims-seeking-justice-remain-in-the-revised-draft-treaty> accessed 1 May 2021.

139 Article 9(2) 2020 Draft provides that 'a legal person conducting business activities of a transnational character, including through their business relationships, is considered domiciled at the place where it has its: a. place of incorporation; or b. statutory seat; or c. central administration; or d. principal place of business'.

heard by the court of the home State.[140] As Sherpa has pointed out, attributing those acts and omissions to the parent company is precisely the difficulty in many cases. 'Conversely, if the victim is not able to link the violations to acts or omissions of the parent company, then it will only be able to rely on acts or omissions of the local subsidiary, supplier or subcontractor, and the local court will have jurisdiction.'[141] Furthermore, with regard to domicile, some commentators have suggested that the BHR Treaty should adopt a broader definition of domicile, which could include the place where the company has, or 'recently had', its main corporate governance office, its registered office, or, interestingly, its main stock market listing.[142]

The 2020 Draft takes a significant step forward with the introduction of provisions addressing *forum non conveniens* and *forum necessitatis*, and the joining of co-defendants.[143] Article 9(3) provides that where the victim chooses to bring a claim in a court in accordance with Article 9(1), jurisdiction shall be obligatory and, therefore, that court shall not decline it on the basis of *forum non conveniens*. Article 7(5) on access to remedy also provides that States Parties shall ensure that their courts do not use the doctrine of *forum non conveniens* to dismiss legitimate judicial proceedings brought by victims. Furthermore, courts shall have jurisdiction over claims against persons not domiciled in the territory of the forum State where the claim is closely connected with a claim against a person domiciled in the territory of the forum State (Article 9(4)), or where no other effective forum guaranteeing a fair trial is available and there is a sufficiently close connection to the State Party concerned (Article 9(5)).[144] In practice, Article 9(4) and (5) would allow victims to sue the foreign subsidiary of a parent company in the home State on the grounds of the joining of co-defendants and *forum necessitatis*. However, commentators have warned that limiting the scope of application of Article 9(3) to claims brought in accordance with Article 9(1) 'preserves room for courtroom battles' over the application of *forum non conveniens* where jurisdiction arises under Article 9(4) or (5).[145] This means that, in practice, courts could still invoke *forum non conveniens* in cases where a foreign subsidiary of a parent company is sued in the home

---

140 These concerns were formulated for Article 7 of the 2019 Draft on adjudicative jurisdiction. However, they remain applicable here.

141 Cossart and Chatelain, 'Key Legal Obstacles'.

142 Blackburn, 'Removing Barriers to Justice', 71.

143 The previous drafts of the BHR treaty did not address co-defendants, and the doctrines of *forum non conveniens* and *forum necessitatis*.

144 2020 Draft, Article 9(5).

145 Sarah Joseph and Mary Keyes, 'BHR Symposium: The Business and Human Rights Treaty and Private International Law' (OpinioJuris, 9 September 2020) <http://opiniojuris.org/2020/09/09/bhr-symposium-the-business-and-human-rights-treaty-and-private-international-law/> accessed 1 May 2021.

State on the grounds of the joining of co-defendants and *forum necessitatis*. As a result, the true scope of the rule excluding *forum non conveniens* should be clarified.

Jurisdiction in criminal cases

As discussed in Chapter 5, criminal prosecution of corporations is possible in many States. Furthermore, in some countries victims of crimes can seek redress for the harm they have suffered in criminal courts (eg France). In practice, however, prosecutors rarely decide to prosecute corporations, and many hurdles prevent victims from seeking redress through criminal proceedings. This situation is exacerbated when MNEs are involved in crimes that relate to human rights violations occurring in a foreign country. One reason is that prosecuting companies, especially MNEs, is expensive and complex. Moreover, corporate criminal liability standards may not be adapted to hold MNEs liable for their involvement in human rights violations occurring in a foreign country.[146] As a result, prosecutors are generally reluctant to investigate corporate crimes involving human rights abuse committed in a transnational context.

In order to ensure that MNEs can be held criminally liable when they are involved in human rights abuse, the BHR Treaty should ensure that prosecutorial authorities are independent and capable of investigating allegations of transnational crimes involving business offenders, and of prosecuting them. The BHR Treaty could encourage States to engage in legal reforms to permit criminal prosecution of businesses and commit sufficient resources to fund prosecutions.[147] Furthermore, the future instrument should require States to establish the criminal liability of business actors (either natural or legal persons) for their involvement in transnational or extraterritorial human rights-related crimes. In this context, a State Party could establish its jurisdiction over human rights-related crimes when the offence is committed in whole or in part within its territory, or when the offence involves business actors under its jurisdiction. As previously indicated in Chapter 5, the application of criminal law and the exercise of criminal jurisdiction are intertwined. A court's exercise of jurisdiction usually follows from the application of its State's criminal law. It is therefore necessary that a State provides adequate criminal offences applicable to companies before it can establish jurisdiction to prosecute companies. The question of corporate liability for criminal offences is addressed earlier in this book.

The 2020 Draft does not directly address the question of jurisdiction in the context of transnational or extraterritorial crimes. However, in the context of

146 Stephens, 'Making Remedies Work', 430.
147 Ibid, 431.

protection of victims, its Article 5(3) provides that 'State Parties shall investigate all human rights abuses covered under this [BHR Treaty] effectively, promptly, thoroughly and impartially, and where appropriate, take action against those natural or legal persons found responsible, in accordance with domestic and international law'. Nonetheless, this provision does not seem to apply to the investigation and prosecution of transnational crimes.

Importantly, all the successive drafts have contained a specific article on mutual legal assistance (MLA).[148] MLA generally refers to a form of cooperation in civil or criminal matters between the authorities of different States for various purposes, such as the exchange of information or the collection of evidence. Provisions on MLA could solve the difficulties faced by prosecutors in collecting evidence located in the territory of a foreign State. In the 2020 Draft, Article 12 is long and covers MLA in criminal, civil, or administrative proceedings. In general, it provides that:

> States Parties shall make available to one another the widest measure of [MLA] and international judicial cooperation in initiating and carrying out effective, prompt, thorough and impartial investigations, prosecutions, judicial and other criminal, civil or administrative proceedings in relation to all claims covered by this (Legally Binding Instrument), including access to information and supply of all evidence at their disposal that is relevant for the proceedings.[149]

Several provisions of Article 12 are relevant in the context of criminal proceedings. Pursuant to Article 12(3), MLA should include evidence-gathering,[150] facilitating the voluntary appearance of persons in the requesting State Party, facilitating the freezing and recovery of assets, assisting and protecting victims, their families, representatives, and witnesses, and assisting in regard to the application of domestic law. MLA could also include any other type of assistance not contrary to the domestic law of the requested State Party. Furthermore, Article 12(4)(a) provides that with respect to the criminal offences covered under this BHR Treaty, MLA 'shall be provided to the fullest extent possible, in a manner consistent with the law of the requested Party and

---

148 Zero Draft, Article 11; 2019 Draft, Article 10; 2020 Draft, Article 12.

149 2020 Draft, Article 12(1).

150 Evidence-gathering activities under Article 12(3) include taking evidence or statements from persons; executing searches and seizures; examining objects and sites; providing information, evidentiary items and expert evaluations; providing originals or certified copies of relevant documents and records, including government, bank, financial, corporate, or business records; and identifying or tracing proceeds of crime, property, instrumentalities, or other things for evidentiary purposes.

its commitments under treaties on mutual assistance in criminal matters to which it is Party'.

The inclusion of MLA requirements is welcome in order to remedy the practical difficulties arising from the exercise of extraterritorial jurisdiction.[151] Article 12 has the potential to significantly enhance the ability of prosecutorial authorities to access critical evidence in order to demonstrate corporate liability. Currently, however, it lacks in clarity and precision, and presents certain shortcomings that could ultimately affect the ability of victims to have access to justice. Article 12(10) is particularly problematic. It provides that MLA or international legal cooperation may be refused by a State Party if the human rights abuse is not covered by the BHR Treaty or if it is contrary to the legal system of the requested State Party. Ultimately, the vagueness of this provision could allow States to justify refusals to cooperate with other State authorities.

Applicable law

As noted in this book, the issue of the law applicable to a transnational civil case is a significant barrier to victims seeking redress. It is therefore recommended that this issue be addressed by the future BHR Treaty.[152] Bright has called for the introduction of a choice-of-law provision allowing victims to make a choice between various options for the law governing disputes on business-related human rights or environmental damage.[153] At the very least, the BHR Treaty could provide that, in the context of claims directed at parent companies, victims should be able to request the application of the law where the parent company is domiciled or has its main place of business. This approach would not contradict the principle of legal certainty. Furthermore, where the home country is a State Party to the BHR Treaty, such a provision would be essential to ensure that the standards of the BHR Treaty on business liability for human rights apply to transnational civil cases.[154]

---

151 De Schutter, 'Towards a New Treaty on Business and Human Rights', 63–66; Bilchitz, 'The Necessity for a Business and Human Rights Treaty', 219. For a general discussion of the role of cross-border legal cooperation in achieving access to remedy in business and human rights cases, see Jennifer Zerk, 'Justice Without Borders: Models of Cross-Border Legal Cooperation and What They Can Teach Us' in Liesbeth Enneking and others (eds), *Accountability, International Business Operations and the Law: Providing Justice for Corporate Human Rights Violations in Global Value Chains* (Routledge 2019).

152 As mentioned earlier, in drawing up provisions on the law applicable to transnational civil cases, the OEIGWG should ensure that such provisions remain consistent with standard private international law rules.

153 Claire Bright, 'Comment on Article 9 (Applicable Law) of the Revised Draft of the Proposed Business and Human Rights Treaty' (NOVA and BIICL, 3 July 2020).

154 This is even more important if the future BHR Treaty sets standards that are sufficiently progressive to ensure corporate accountability.

In the 2020 Draft, Article 11 governs the law applicable to civil cases. In particular, Article 11(2) provides that the victim of a business-related human rights abuse, or its representatives, may request that all matters of substance regarding human rights law relevant to claims before the competent court be governed by the law of another State. However, this possibility is limited to two situations: (1) the law of the place where the acts or omissions that result in the human rights violation have occurred; or (2) the law of the place where the natural or legal person alleged to have committed the acts or omissions that result in the human rights violation is domiciled. Article 11(2) introduces a welcome choice-of-law provision allowing victims to choose the law of the home State. However, it is unclear what the expression 'all matters of substance regarding human rights law' refers to.[155] In addition, the 2020 Draft excludes the law of the place where the victim is domiciled, which was a potential option under the 2019 Draft.

Participation of victims in proceedings

The BHR Treaty should ensure that States adopt procedural rules to facilitate the ability of victims to bring a claim against business actors and to participate actively in the proceedings. In particular, it should address the issue of standing. The BHR Treaty should require States to grant standing, at the very least, to persons who have suffered direct harm as a result of business action or omission. Ideally, standing should also be granted to individuals who have suffered indirect harm as a result of human rights violations (eg family members). Secondarily, the BHR Treaty could require, or encourage, States to grant standing to other actors, such as NGOs defending victims interests.

The BHR Treaty should also require States to allow group claims and remove any barriers that prevent groups from seeking redress. This is important, for example, when a community has suffered harm from the same human rights abuse (eg employees of the same company who suffered labour rights violations or rural communities who suffered from environmental pollution). Furthermore, the BHR Treaty should require States to ensure that plaintiffs enjoy a number of guarantees during the proceedings, such as the right to receive information on their case without undue delay, the right to a review of a decision not to prosecute, the right to be protected from reprisal, or the right to be protected from revictimization.[156] Finally, the BHR Treaty should pay attention to the participation of vulnerable groups, such as women, minorities, or persons with disabilities, in proceedings.

---

155 Bright, 'Comment on Article 9'.

156 International and regional instruments, such as the Basic Principles on Remedy or the Victims' Rights Directive, may provide valuable guidance.

The successive drafts of the BHR Treaty have addressed victims of business-related human rights abuse. In the 2020 Draft, Article 1(1) defines victims as:

> any person or group of persons who individually or collectively have suffered harm, including physical or mental injury, emotional suffering, or economic loss, or substantial impairment of their human rights, through acts or omissions in the context of business activities, that constitute human rights abuse. The term 'victim' shall also include the immediate family members or dependents of the direct victim, and persons who have suffered harm in intervening to assist victims in distress or to prevent victimization. A person shall be considered a victim regardless of whether the perpetrator of the human rights abuse is identified, apprehended, prosecuted, or convicted.

The definition of victims in the 2020 Draft is in line with that of the Basic Principles on the Right to a Remedy. Nonetheless, the 2020 Draft also contains welcome additions. For example, it recognizes that victims can be persons and *groups of persons*. In addition, it refers to acts or omissions in the context of business activities that constitute human rights abuse, as opposed to gross violations of international human rights law, or serious violations of international humanitarian law under the Basic Principles on the Right to a Remedy.[157]

Each draft of the BHR Treaty has contained an article dedicated to the rights of victims.[158] This could undoubtedly represent an important contribution of the BHR Treaty towards rebalancing the asymmetry that exists between business actors and victims of business-related human rights abuse. The 2020 Draft lists a number of rights that are relevant for ensuring the participation of victims in proceedings. It provides that victims shall be 'guaranteed the right to fair, adequate, effective, prompt and non-discriminatory access to justice and effective remedy in accordance with this BHR Treaty and international law'.[159] Furthermore, victims must 'be guaranteed the right to submit claims, including by a representative or through class action in appropriate cases, to courts and non-judicial grievance mechanisms of the State Parties'.[160] They must also 'be protected from any unlawful interference against their privacy, and from intimidation, and retaliation, before, during and after any proceedings have been instituted, as well as from revictimization in the course of proceedings

---

157 This modification was necessary as the human rights scope of the BHR Treaty is different to that of the Basic Principles on the Right to a Remedy.

158 Zero Draft, Article 8; 2019 Draft, Article 4; 2020 Draft, Article 4.

159 2020 Draft, Article 4(2)(c).

160 Ibid, Article 4(2)(d).

for access to effective remedy, including through appropriate protective and support services that are gender responsive'.[161] The 2020 Draft also requires that victims have 'access to information and legal aid relevant to pursue effective remedy'.[162]

Other articles of the 2020 Draft contain welcome provisions to ensure victims' participation in the proceedings. Article 5(1) on the protection of victims provides that the State must protect victims, their representatives, families, and witnesses from any unlawful interference with their human rights and fundamental freedoms, including during proceedings and before and after they have instituted any proceedings to obtain an effective remedy. In addition, Article 7(3) on access to remedy provides that States must offer adequate and effective legal assistance to victims throughout the legal process. In particular, they should make information available to victims on their rights and the status of their claims, guarantee the rights of victims to be heard in all stages of proceedings, and provide assistance to initiate proceedings in the courts of another State Party in appropriate cases of human rights abuses resulting from business activities of a transnational character. Unfortunately, the 2020 Draft does not refer to the participation of vulnerable persons in proceedings. It makes only passing reference to vulnerable rightsholders in the preamble.

Regarding the role of NGOs in legal proceedings, the 2020 Draft adds very little value. While the preamble emphasizes that civil society actors, including human rights defenders, have an important and legitimate role in seeking effective remedy for business-related human rights abuses, the 2020 Draft does not contain legally binding provisions on the role of NGOs in legal proceedings. Article 5(2) requires States to take adequate and effective measures to guarantee a safe and enabling environment for persons, groups, and organizations that promote and defend human rights and the environment, so that they are able to exercise their human rights free from any threat, intimidation, violence, or insecurity. However, this provision is vague and does not impose any obligations on States or encourage them to guarantee that NGOs can participate in legal proceedings.

Procedural and practical barriers

The BHR Treaty should address the most important procedural and practical barriers that victims face in proceedings. Here, two types of obstacles seem to be the most relevant. The first obstacle relates to gaining access to evidence held by businesses, the existence of procedures for disclosure and/or discovery, and burden of proof.[163] The practical question of the costs of the proceedings should also be addressed in the BHR Treaty.

161 Ibid, Article 4(2)(e).
162 Ibid, Article 4(2)(f).
163 Stephens, 'Making Remedies Work', 415–416.

The various drafts of the BHR Treaty have dealt with burden of proof.[164] In the 2020 Draft, Article 7(6) provides that 'State Parties may, consistent with the rule of law requirements, enact or amend laws to reverse the burden of proof in appropriate cases to fulfil the victims' right to access to remedy'. While the inclusion of a provision on burden of proof should be welcomed, the wording of Article 7(6) is problematic. First, it gives States the discretion to take the necessary steps to give effect to that provision. Second, this provision is too vague and open-ended.[165] For instance, what is a rule of law requirement? Similarly, what situations fall within the category of 'appropriate cases'? It is also unclear if the reversal of the burden of proof should apply in both civil and criminal cases. However, as Cassel points out, the reversal of the burden of proof should not be taken lightly in criminal matters where it could negatively impact the presumption of innocence and the right to a fair trial.[166] Furthermore, the expression 'to fulfil the victim's access to remedy' is ambiguous. Third, the 2020 Draft remains silent regarding the conditions for reversing the burden of proof. For instance, should the victims play an active role in demonstrating the need to reverse the burden of proof? Would the reversal of proof be left to the discretion of courts? Article 7(6)'s lack of clarity could jeopardize its application at national level and contribute to legal uncertainty for parties that want to use it.

In addition, the various BHR Treaty drafts have left out procedures that would allow victims to access information held by companies, such as discovery and/or disclosure. Overall, the various drafts have not adequately addressed issues related to the production of evidence in trials against businesses. From an access to justice perspective, this absence is one of the most serious flaws in the drafts produced so far, especially when one considers that the lack of fair rules on evidence exacerbates the severe asymmetry between victims and businesses.

The successive drafts of the BHR Treaty have addressed the issue of costs.[167] In the 2020 Draft, Article 7(3) requires States to provide adequate and effective legal assistance to victims throughout the legal process. They must avoid unnecessary costs or delays for bringing a claim, during the cases and the execution of rulings, and ensure that rules concerning allocation of legal costs do not place an unfair and unreasonable burden on victims. Furthermore,

---

164 2019 Draft, Article 4(16); Zero Draft, Article 10(4).

165 This critique was made in respect of the 2019 Draft, but it remains applicable here. Doug Cassel, 'Five Ways the New Draft Treaty on Business and Human Rights Can Be Strengthened' (BHRRC, 9 September 2019) <https://www.business-humanrights.org/en/five-ways-the-new-draft-treaty-on-business-and-human-rights-can-be-strengthened?mc_cid=8bd5647dfc&mc_eid=%5bUNIQID%5d> accessed 1 May 2021.

166 Ibid.

167 Zero Draft, Article 8; 2019 Draft, Article 4.

States Parties shall ensure that court fees and other related costs do not become a barrier to commencing proceedings and that they allow waiving of certain costs in suitable cases.

Drafters have also included two important provisions that could contribute to reducing litigation costs. First, States Parties may require natural or legal persons conducting business activities in their territory or jurisdiction, including those of a transnational character, to establish and maintain financial security, such as insurance bonds or other financial guarantees to cover potential claims of compensation.[168] Litigators for victims in transnational litigation against MNEs have generally welcomed the inclusion of such a provision.[169] Second, all the BHR Treaty drafts have included the establishment of an international fund to provide legal and financial aid to victims.[170] However, the Conference of Parties will define and establish the relevant provisions for the functioning of the Fund. This provision has been criticized as 'far too vague to give any confidence that this would translate into a legal fund sufficient for complex and protracted litigation against well-resourced multinationals'.[171] Furthermore, it is unclear how such a fund could realistically finance all cases brought against businesses for human rights abuse and remedy inequality of arms between parties, especially when States already allocate little, if any, resources towards legal aid.[172]

Remedies

In line with the UNGPs, the BHR Treaty should require States to provide effective access to an adequate remedy through judicial and non-judicial mechanisms. It should also encourage effective access to remedy through 'operational-level grievance mechanisms' established by businesses. However, victims should be in a position to choose which mechanism to use to seek redress. The BHR Treaty may require both State and non-State non-judicial grievance mechanisms to comply with the effectiveness criteria set out in GP 31. In particular, they should be legitimate, accessible, predictable, equitable, transparent, rights-compatible, a source of continuous learning, and, for business operational-level mechanisms, based on engagement and dialogue.

The BHR Treaty should also specify that persons injured by business-related human rights abuse must have access to a full range of remedies, as appropriate to the specific harm they have suffered.[173] Remedies should include: interim or

---

168 2020 Draft, Article 8(6). See also Zero Draft, Article 9(2)(h); 2019 Draft, Article 6(5).
169 Meeran, 'The Revised Draft'.
170 Zero Draft, Article 8(7); 2019 Draft, Article 13(7); 2020 Draft, Article 15(7).
171 Meeran, 'The Revised Draft'.
172 Ibid.
173 Stephens, 'Making Remedies Work', 416.

provisional measures to halt abusive activities or prevent further violations; measures to restore the situation that would have existed prior to the wrongful act (eg restitution, compensation, rehabilitation, satisfaction and guarantees of non-repetition); and sanctions against those responsible for human rights abuses.[174] Stephens points out that monetary compensation may often be insufficient, especially when communities have been forced off their land or have lost access to fields, water, or other essential resources. In such cases, a full remedy includes restoring access to the resources upon which these communities depend.[175]

References to remedy can be found throughout the 2020 Draft. First, Article 7 is dedicated to access to remedy. States must provide their courts and State-based non-judicial mechanisms with the necessary jurisdiction to enable victims to have access to adequate, timely, and effective remedy.[176] Furthermore, States shall provide effective mechanisms for the enforcement of remedies for human rights abuses, including through prompt execution of national or foreign judgments or awards.[177] Second, Article 8 on legal liability contains a provision on reparation. It provides that States must adopt necessary measures to ensure that their domestic law provides for adequate, prompt, effective, and gender-responsive reparations to the victims of human rights abuses in the context of business activities, including those of a transnational character, in line with applicable international standards for reparations to the victims of human rights violations.[178] Third, Article 4(2)(c) on the rights of victims provides that victims shall be guaranteed effective remedy in accordance with the BHR Treaty and international law, such as 'restitution, compensation, rehabilitation, satisfaction, guarantees of non-repetition, injunction, environmental remediation, and ecological restoration'.

4 Conclusions

This chapter has discussed the current UN initiative to elaborate an international BHR Treaty to regulate the activities of businesses in international human rights law, and its potential contribution to improving access to justice for victims of business-related human rights abuse.

Prevalent substantive, procedural, and practical barriers faced by victims in accessing justice and discontent with the UNGPs, together with the recurrent

174 Ibid, 416.

175 Ibid.

176 2020 Draft, Article 7(1).

177 Ibid, Article 7(7).

178 Ibid, Article 8(5).

regulatory preference for soft law or CSR initiatives more generally, have led some States, CSOs, and academics to advocate for the adoption of binding international standards on BHR. There is a strong expectation that the future BHR Treaty must aim to improve victims' access to justice. To do so, the future instrument should therefore include provisions to enable victims to obtain corporate accountability and redress. In particular, it should recognize that all business enterprises have human rights obligations and that failure to comply with those obligations may lead to liability of business actors. The BHR Treaty should also ensure that States take measures to facilitate the ability of victims to bring a claim against business actors when human rights abuses have occurred, and to participate actively in the proceedings. In particular, it should address procedural issues arising from the transnational nature of home State litigation against MNEs, such as jurisdiction in both civil and criminal proceedings or the law applicable to civil proceedings. In addition, the BHR Treaty should address access to evidence and costs of proceedings. Finally, it should require States to ensure that those injured by business-related human rights abuses have access to a full range of remedies appropriate to the specific harm they have suffered through various State and non-State judicial mechanisms.

To date, the various drafts of the BHR Treaty have contained a strong focus on victims and access to remedy. However, they have included provisions on the other issues mentioned above to varying degrees. The 2020 Draft does not explicitly provide that business enterprises have human rights obligations, but it indirectly imposes an obligation on companies to respect human rights by requiring States to take measures to ensure that business enterprises respect all internationally recognized human rights and prevent and mitigate human rights abuses throughout their operations. Furthermore, the 2020 Draft provides for the direct liability of businesses for human rights abuse arising from their own activities and for indirect liability for human rights abuse arising from the activities of their business relationships. These two aspects represent important milestones towards legally binding corporate accountability.

That said, the 2020 Draft contains a number of weaknesses that may limit the added-value of a BHR Treaty in order to ensure access to justice. In general, it addresses most of the procedural and practical issues that victims face when seeking redress in transnational litigation against MNEs. However, it fails to address in concrete terms legal rules or principles that contribute to the maintenance of asymmetry between victims and MNEs, such as the application of *forum non conveniens* and access to evidence. In addition, the structure and wording of the 2020 Draft, as well as the legal coherence between its various provisions, are generally still in need of improvement. It is crucial that these weaknesses be addressed in the next draft. Hopefully, this chapter has helped to provide guidance on how the future draft could be improved to ensure that a BHR Treaty fulfils the long-awaited wish of victims, CSOs, and academics for effective achievement of justice.

Even if the future BHR Treaty contains provisions that could, in theory, contribute to more effective access to justice for victims, it is crucial that these provisions do not turn into dead letters. Such a result is possible if the BHR Treaty fails to garner universal acceptance by a large majority of States, and if the drafters do not envisage proper enforcement mechanisms.[179] To date, the creation of the OEIGWG and the negotiations of the BHR Treaty have created controversy. A significant number of actors are opposed to or are hindering negotiations. Future negotiators and NGOs must therefore temper expectations as a result of the risk of a lack of adherence to the BHR Treaty project and weak enforcement of the treaty, as they could undermine effective access to justice on the ground otherwise achieved through a robust and comprehensive international legal framework.

---

179 Khalil Hamdani and Lorraine Ruffing, 'Lessons from the UN Centre on Transnational Corporations for the Current Treaty Initiative' in Surya Deva and David Bilchitz (eds), *Building a Treaty on Business and Human Rights: Context and Contours* (CUP 2017), 43.

Chapter 9

Conclusions

1 Main findings

This book has questioned whether transnational litigation, and ongoing legal and policy reforms at international, European, and national level, can achieve access to justice and corporate accountability where MNEs cause or contribute to human rights abuses and environmental pollution in host countries. In order to answer this question, a three-stage analysis was carried out.

First, this book set out the legal and social backdrop against which transnational litigation against MNEs emerged. It started by discussing how international and European legal frameworks regulate the activities of business actors in the fields of human rights and environmental protection and ensure access to justice for victims of corporate harm. Given the transnational nature of MNE activities, an internationally coordinated approach appears to be an appropriate way to provide an effective normative framework for the regulation of MNEs and ensure that victims of corporate abuse obtain redress. However, public international law is currently lacunary in addressing transnational corporate human rights abuse and environmental damage. Under the traditional State-centric approach to international law, non-State actors, such as MNEs, do not have international legal personality. Therefore, they have neither rights nor obligations, and they cannot be held liable for violating international human rights or environmental standards. This view has been increasingly challenged by scholars, lawyers, and CSOs over time, and along the way international bodies have occasionally accepted that non-State actors should have international obligations under specific circumstances. However, the dominant legal reality remains that MNEs fall outside the scope of international human rights and environmental regimes. Moreover, under the main international and European human rights instruments, victims of human rights abuse and environmental damage theoretically enjoy a number of rights and guarantees related to access to justice. However, these instruments do not take into account the specific needs required to ensure access to justice in the context of transnational business-related abuse. While the adoption of the UN Framework and the UNGPs represented a breakthrough in the BHR field, both instruments insufficiently fill existing gaps in international law on corporate accountability and access to justice for victims of business-related abuses. Ultimately, at the moment public international law does not offer clear or adapted solutions for addressing the negative consequences of MNE activities, or for securing effective remediation to victims of human rights abuse and environmental pollution caused by MNEs.

This book also provided a historical account of transnational litigation against MNEs by describing the origins of this type of litigation in common law jurisdictions and its progressive rise in European civil law countries. It described how the first transnational claims against MNEs began to emerge in common law jurisdictions in the 1980s–1990s in an effort to hold companies perceived to be directly responsible for abuses occurring in host countries accountable in jurisdictional forums deemed more conducive to the achievement of justice for victims of abuse. In the US, ATS-based litigation held promise for holding corporations accountable for their involvement in human rights abuses abroad. However, since 2010 the US Supreme Court has gradually, and significantly, limited the possibility of using the ATS as a tool for corporate accountability. More generally, tort claims against parent companies of MNEs have been predominant in common law countries. However, jurisdictional issues and application of the *forum non conveniens* doctrine have limited the prospect that tort claims could lead to corporate accountability. Moreover, at present, the contours of liability in corporate groups remain uncertain. At the same time, recent case law developments in England and Canada have raised some interesting prospects for the development of substantive standards recognizing the liability of parent companies in the context of the activities of MNEs.

Transnational litigation against MNEs is not solely a tort law phenomenon limited to common law countries. On the contrary, it has spread to civil law countries, particularly in Europe, where litigators have creatively used the opportunities offered by and/or worked around the constraints of their legal systems to bring claims against MNEs. In these countries, plaintiffs have initiated civil and criminal proceedings to hold MNEs accountable and seek redress. Litigation culture, legal tradition, and procedural rules that allow plaintiffs to engage and participate in proceedings are significant factors that help explain the different legal strategies used in civil law countries to seek corporate accountability. If tort proceedings appear to be the favoured way to seek remedies and encourage reform in common law countries, criminal and specialized civil proceedings can be viable alternatives to achieve similar goals in civil law countries.

The book also explored the socio-legal dimension of transnational litigation against MNEs by examining its links with social movements and cause-lawyers, and how activists of the corporate accountability movement have used legal mobilization as a political strategy to hold MNEs accountable in the public sphere and to trigger legal and policy reform. It showed that, in both common law and civil law jurisdictions, efforts to litigate against MNEs and hold them accountable have strong ties with the broader corporate accountability movement that developed at the beginning of the 21st century as a result of perceived increased corporate power, as well as limited results of CSR initiatives to effectively prevent MNE human rights and environmental abuse. The corporate accountability movement is characterized by various national, regional, and international coalitions specifically dedicated to the pursuit of corporate accountability through legal and policy reform, awareness-raising, and advocacy. The existence of law firms and legal NGOs dedicated to ensuring corporate accountability has provided the main impetus for the development of transnational litigation against MNEs. These actors have used legal mobilization not only to gain access to remedy for victims and hold MNEs liable for human rights abuse and environmental damage, but also to raise awareness and initiate legal and policy reform. While legal victories in courts have so far been rare, litigation has produced other legal and non-legal benefits. Litigators have obtained successful judicial clarification on a range of legal and procedural issues, such as court jurisdiction to hear transnational claims raising liability within MNEs. Legal mobilization has also contributed to improving the visibility of the corporate accountability movement, especially in the context of campaigns against specific MNEs. Moreover, the difficulties faced by victims in relation to access to justice have provided a legitimate justification for calls for legal and policy reform by CSOs. However, the conclusion of confidential out-of-court settlements between complainants and corporate defendants has occasionally been a source of tension within the corporate accountability movement that can be detrimental to the cohesion of activist networks. Furthermore, such settlements may prevent the development of binding corporate accountability standards.

Second, this book identified how French and Dutch procedural and substantive laws affect the opportunities for access to civil and criminal justice for business-related abuse in these particular jurisdictions. The study of transnational claims against MNEs in France and the Netherlands has shown that victims face a number of procedural and practical hurdles that prevent them from seeking redress for the damage they have suffered as a result of harmful corporate group activities. There is an asymmetry between victims and MNEs in terms of financial and human resources or access to the information needed to support their arguments when entering into litigation. However, in civil litigation, rules relating to the production of evidence and legal costs are inadequate to remedy this asymmetry in court proceedings. Similarly, there is insufficient development of collective redress mechanisms to facilitate claims from communities or employees that have suffered the same damage. Other obstacles may result from EU harmonization, particularly in the field of private international law. While EU law makes it easier for the French and Dutch courts to exercise jurisdiction over parent companies established in their territories, the Rome II Regulation prevents French and Dutch law from applying to key substantive and procedural aspects of litigation, such as corporate liability, evidence, or financial compensation. In criminal litigation, the traditional criminal law jurisdictional principles appear to be inadequate for ensuring the prosecution of MNEs when they commit crimes in an extraterritorial or transnational context. Furthermore, public prosecutors in France and the Netherlands have generally been reluctant to sue MNEs for human rights abuse or environmental pollution taking place in host countries. However, French law allows victims and NGOs to play a significant role in criminal proceedings. At EU level, the Victims' Rights Directive has, to some extent, reinforced the role and ability of victims to participate in criminal proceedings. Ultimately, French and Dutch civil and criminal law and procedure are unfit to confront the challenges posed by human rights abuses caused by powerful economic actors in a transnational context.

The existence of standards of liability to punish abuses in the context of corporate group activities is crucial to the success of transnational claims against MNEs. However, under French and Dutch law, the lack of legal personality of the corporate group, and the application of a separate legal personality and limited liability to entities of the corporate group make it almost impossible for victims to hold the parent or controlling company liable for human rights abuses and environmental pollution resulting from group activities. This situation effectively shields the actual perpetrator from liability and encourages companies to carry out hazardous or imprudent activities through complex and opaque group structures. Nonetheless, a study of liability regimes in various areas showed that statutory rules and court doctrines may, in certain circumstances, allow the parent company to be held liable for the harm caused by its subsidiaries. In particular, opportunities arise where the parent company has committed a fault. Courts are also willing to punish fraud and abusive arrangements where the parent company seeks to avoid liability by subsidiarizing an activity. However, there are still no clear standards for parent company liability for human rights abuse and environmental pollution. Judging from the few transnational claims against MNEs that have reached the merits stage, courts remain reluctant to hold a parent company liable for harm arising in an MNE context. In the absence of hard legal standards, plaintiffs have had to rely on soft instruments, such as voluntary codes of conduct. French and Dutch courts have rarely accepted that the breach of voluntary commitments of companies could lead or contribute to the liability of parent companies in the context of group activities. The courts' anecdotic and cautious use of these soft law norms as a basis for corporate liability has impeded the 'legalization' of such norms. Ultimately, there is a pressing need for the adoption of binding standards that impose clear human rights and environmental obligations on MNEs, in particular parent companies, and that allow victims to hold them liable for infringing such obligations.

Third, this book assessed ongoing legal initiatives at national, European, and international level to create corporate obligations towards human rights and the environment and their contribution to improving access to justice. The first set of initiatives revolves around the adoption of mandatory HRDD standards requiring companies to identify potential human rights and environmental risks in their activities and prevent those risks from materializing. Although HRDD legal regimes are not generally intended to address obstacles faced by victims seeking redress, they can nonetheless have a significant impact on access to justice. In particular, they can make it easier or harder to establish corporate liability or obtain adequate remedies where human rights abuses occur. In Europe, a growing number of countries have adopted, or are considering adopting, mandatory HRDD standards. The French Act on the Duty of Vigilance is the most notable example of HRDD legislation adopted so far. It requires certain large companies to identify human rights and environmental risks and prevent those risks from occurring in the context of their group activities. Importantly, it provides that failure to comply with due diligence obligations can engage the company's liability where this failure results in damage. The inclusion of this provision is important progress from an access to justice perspective, as it provides a clear cause of action for victims of MNE misconduct. However, in practice it is unclear which improvements this provision will bring, as victims still have to face many of the same procedural obstacles that have plagued transnational litigation against MNEs, such as the burden of proof and access to evidence. Furthermore, the Act does not provide remedies appropriate to the nature of the damage caused by companies to human rights and the environment. More generally, the effective implementation of the French Act on the Duty of Vigilance has proved to be problematic as a result of its lack of effective monitoring and enforcement mechanisms. The shortcomings of the French experience should be taken into account in the context of other mandatory HRDD legislation initiatives. In the EU, the EC will soon propose a piece of legislation imposing mandatory HRDD on companies that is supposed to include provisions on access to justice.[1] Given that a large number of MNEs are headquartered in the EU, such an instrument could have a major impact on corporate respect for human rights and the environment, both in and outside the EU. Therefore, the future EU HRDD instrument must require Member States to ensure that companies can be held liable for their failure to respect and/or protect human rights as part of their HRDD obligations. Having said that, while the inclusion of provisions on liability or access to justice in mandatory HRDD instruments is laudable, it is important to bear in mind that these instruments are insufficient to address all procedural and substantive issues that may arise when victims seek redress for human rights abuses in the home country.

---

1   The EC pledged to propose an EU-wide human rights due diligence law some time in the latter half of 2021.

This brings us to the role that a future international BHR Treaty could play in addressing procedural and substantive barriers in transnational litigation against MNEs and, more generally, in triggering necessary domestic legal reforms to provide corporate accountability and access to justice. The ongoing negotiations on a BHR Treaty at the UN are partly the result of the recurrent dissatisfaction of many actors, including CSOs and States from the Global South, with the UNGPs, the lack of robust international corporate accountability standards for human rights and the difficulties for victims to obtain redress in both home and host States, as well as at international level. However, there has been a lot of resistance from home countries to the BHR Treaty project. To date, the drafters of the BHR Treaty have placed a strong emphasis on access to justice. This has been demonstrated by the development of provisions on aspects such as victims' rights, jurisdiction, and applicable law. Various drafts of the BHR Treaty have also addressed, to some extent, the sensitive question of corporate human rights obligations, and have included provisions on liability of business actors both in general terms and in the context of HRDD. However, the 2020 Draft still needs improvement. In particular, it fails to consider several aspects that exacerbate asymmetry between victims and MNEs (eg *forum non conveniens*; access to evidence; burden of proof). Furthermore, the looming threat of lack of buy-in from States, either through refusing to ratify the future BHR Treaty or by simply failing to properly enforce it, could turn the Treaty into a sword of Damocles. As it stands, there is a great deal of uncertainty whether the future BHR Treaty will be capable of effectively improving corporate accountability and access to justice.

2 Looking forward

To date, transnational litigation against MNEs has yielded few direct results for plaintiffs. As a result of the various procedural and substantive barriers outlined in this book, most of the claimants were unable to obtain redress for the harm they suffered. Having said that, this type of litigation has indirectly contributed to increasing corporate accountability by exposing harmful business practices and the limits of legal and judicial systems to ensure access to justice. This exposure has, in turn, reinforced and legitimized the arguments put forward by corporate accountability advocates for binding standards and justice reforms.

During the research for this book, despite existing obstacles, the number of transnational claims against MNEs has increased in a growing number of home countries. These claims are unlikely to run out of steam; in fact, they appear to be evolving in order to shed light on the need to protect a variety of interests from corporate harm. In particular, climate change litigation against MNEs, which is emerging in various home and host countries around the world, is a major development that should influence the development of corporate accountability norms in the next decade.[2] Furthermore, the transnational nature of climate litigation against MNEs, due to the global threat of climate change, poses legal and procedural challenges that are similar to those encountered in the litigation at stake in this book. For example, one challenge for plaintiffs is to prove causation between current and/or future human and environmental damage resulting from climate change and MNEs' acts or omissions. Another difficulty arises in having access to evidence to show the misconduct of companies in the production of the damage. Such obstacles are likely to give rise to calls for climate justice reforms that take into account the needs of a new generation of plaintiffs. Moreover, the digital revolution currently under way is creating new human rights issues relating to the protection of freedom of expression, privacy and personal data, or labour rights in the context of increasing robotization and use of artificial intelligence.[3] Given the global nature of these issues and the role of the private sector in promoting and developing digital technology, transnational claims could also emerge as a tool for holding businesses accountable in the absence of adequate standards to prevent business interference with human rights.

This leads us to question potential future regulatory developments. Since the adoption of the UNGPs almost a decade ago, legal and policy initiatives within the BHR field, both private and public, have developed at an astonishing pace. At present, we are at a decisive turning point in the normative development of BHR-related standards. The keen interest in the adoption of mandatory HRDD standards at national and supranational level and the current BHR Treaty negotiations offer unparalleled opportunities to fill the gaps in the current regulatory framework governing corporate accountability and access to justice in BHR. It is crucial that these initiatives do not exist in a vacuum and that they complement each other to create a more coherent legal framework to reduce the occurrence of corporate abuse and improve access to remedies for victims. Furthermore, the enforcement of new binding BHR norms and instruments is likely to be an important challenge for the coming years. The effective

---

2   BHRRC, 'Turning Up the Heat: Corporate Legal Accountability for Climate Change' (2018)   <https://www.business-humanrights.org/en/from-us/briefings/turning-up-the-heat-corporate-legal-accountability-for-climate-change/> accessed 17 July 2021; Samvel Varvastian and Felicity Kalunga, 'Transnational Corporate Liability for Environmental Damage and Climate Change: Reassessing Access to Justice after Vedanta v. Lungowe' [2020] Transnational Environmental Law 1. See also DC The Hague 26 May 2021, C/09/571932/HAZA19-379 (*Milieudefensie v RDS*).

3   See Open Global Rights, BHRRC and University of Washington Rule of Law Initiative, 'Technology and Human Rights: How Can Technology Be a Powerful Force in Support of Human Rights?' (Open Global Rights) <https://www.openglobalrights.org/technology/> accessed 1 May 2021.

implementation of rules through adequate monitoring and sanctions in the event of non-compliance is often overlooked in many pieces of legislation, however progressive they may be. In order to ensure that mandatory HRDD instruments and a future BHR Treaty do not become dead letters, they should provide for robust enforcement mechanisms designed to induce compliance and monitoring mechanisms to check the progress and effectiveness of these instruments. Reflection on this issue is particularly needed among BHR practitioners and scholars.

Having said that, mandatory HRDD instruments and the future BHR Treaty are unlikely to be sufficient to address all the issues that have generally hindered access to justice and corporate accountability over the last two decades. Mandatory HRDD instruments are not intended to create a general obligation for all companies to respect and prevent human rights abuses. They could potentially frustrate long-standing efforts to improve corporate accountability by providing companies with a defence when they comply with weak HRDD obligations, even though harm still occurs. Furthermore, they are also not envisioned as tools for the advancement of access to justice in general and cannot address the procedural and substantive issues affecting access to courts, equality of arms, and a fair trial. Similarly, it would be overly-ambitious to assume that a single international instrument such as a BHR Treaty can fix all the procedural and substantive issues affecting domestic access to justice in the BHR context. It is therefore crucial that legal reform efforts do not focus solely on the adoption of due diligence norms and on an international BHR Treaty. Equally important is the need for domestic reforms of justice systems – reform of company laws that were originally designed to shield companies from liability and of liability regimes that neglect impacts on humans and the environment. Such reforms are needed in order to protect and empower those individuals, workers, and communities most vulnerable to the damaging impacts of globalization.

However, the recent economic and social turmoil caused by the global COVID-19 pandemic risks diverting attention from corporate accountability and access to justice concerns. The pandemic has already posed serious threats to the progress made in embedding respect for human rights throughout business activities.[4] Every day brings its share of business-related human rights abuses that directly and indirectly result from the COVID-19 crisis: companies are using force majeure to withdraw from contracts in ways that contribute to serious human rights risks; workers, such as those in the clothing sector, are left without jobs or are due large amounts of unpaid salaries; infringements of health and safety standards have increased; human rights defenders, including union

---

4   UNWG, 'Summary Report: UN Working Group on Business and Human Rights Dialogue with European Civil Society Groups' (2020).

leaders, are increasingly being threatened.[5] There are also legitimate concerns that environmental commitments will be swept aside to revive the economic activity that has suffered from the successive lockdowns enforced to prevent the spread of COVID-19.[6] In such a context, there is a risk that governments and international institutions will not prioritize long-awaited reforms of justice systems and corporate accountability. It is therefore now more important than ever to close the regulatory gap that has led to corporate impunity over the last decades. Arundhati Roy recently wrote this in an essay on the COVID-19 pandemic:

> Our minds are still racing back and forth, longing for a return to 'normality', trying to stitch our future to our past and refusing to acknowledge the rupture. But the rupture exists. And in the midst of this terrible despair, it offers us a chance to rethink the doomsday machine we have built for ourselves. Nothing could be worse than a return to normality. Historically, pandemics have forced humans to break with the past and imagine their world anew. This one is no different. It is a portal, a gateway between one world and the next. We can choose to walk through it, dragging the carcasses of our prejudice and hatred, our avarice, our data banks and dead ideas, our dead rivers and smoky skies behind us. Or we can walk through lightly, with little luggage, ready to imagine another world. And ready to fight for it.[7]

The possibility of imagining a new world resonates with the desire of many stakeholders for a change in the way businesses, particularly MNEs, are regulated, and to move away from a 'business as usual' ideology which has placed supremacy on business interests over those of society and has led to the design of legal and policy tools that frustrate the protection of human rights and the environment. In this sense, the current context provides a historic opportunity to re-envision and adopt laws and justice systems that effectively put people and the environment at the heart of our societies.

---

5   Ibid.

6   Beth Gardiner, 'Why COVID-19 Will End Up Harming the Environment' (*National Geographic*, 18 June 2020) <https://www.nationalgeographic.com/science/2020/06/why-covid-19-will-end-up-harming-the-environment/> accessed 1 May 2021.

7   Arundhati Roy, 'The Pandemic Is a Portal' *Financial Times* (London, 3 April 2020) <https://www.ft.com/content/10d8f5e8-74eb-11ea-95fe-fcd274e920ca> accessed 1 May 2021.

Index

Lightning Source UK Ltd.
Milton Keynes UK
UKHW020625150222
398711UK00003B/141